ART
THE CRITICS' CHOICE

150 MASTERPIECES OF WESTERN ART

SELECTED AND DEFINED BY THE EXPERTS

INTRODUCED BY JOHN RUSSELL ∞ EDITED BY MARINA VAIZEY

WATSON-GUPTILL
PUBLICATIONS

New York

Design copyright © The Ivy Press Limited 1999
Text copyright © The Ivy Press Limited 1999

First published in the United States of America in 1999
by
Watson-Guptill Publications, a division of
BPI Communications, Inc.,
1515 Broadway, New York, NY 10036

The moral right of the authors have been asserted.

Library of Congress Catalog Card Number: 99-62741

ISBN: 0-8230-0620-8

This book was conceived, designed and produced by
THE IVY PRESS LIMITED
2/3 St. Andrews Place
Lewes, East Sussex
BN7 1UP

Creative Director: Peter Bridgewater
Editorial Director: Sophie Collins
Managing Editor: Anne Townley
Designer: Jane Lanaway
Editor: Sarah Polden
Senior Project Editor: Rowan Davies
Picture Researcher: Vanessa Fletcher

This book is set in 11.5/14 Perpetua

Printed and bound by Star Standard, Singapore

Front cover illustration: *St Jerome in his Study*, Antonello
da Messina, e.t. archive and National Gallery
Back cover illustration: *Waterlilies*, Claude Monet:
© DACS, 1999 and private collection
Frontispiece: *California*, David Hockney

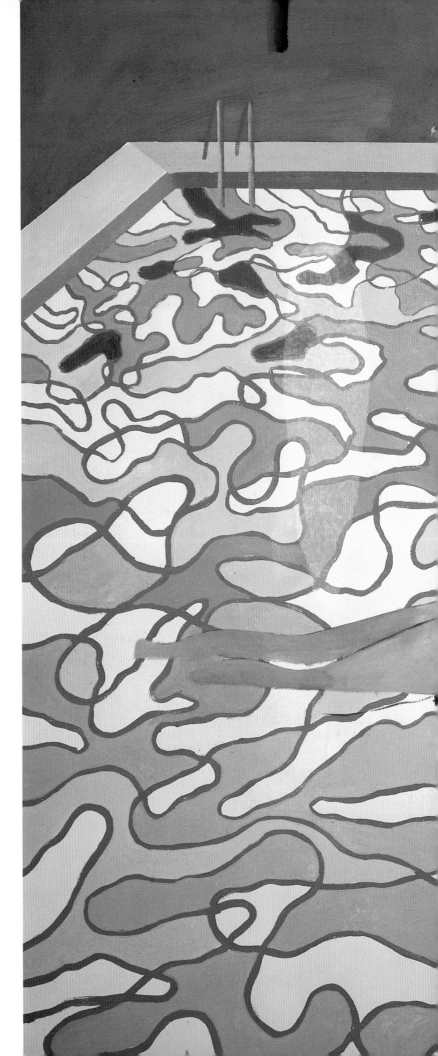

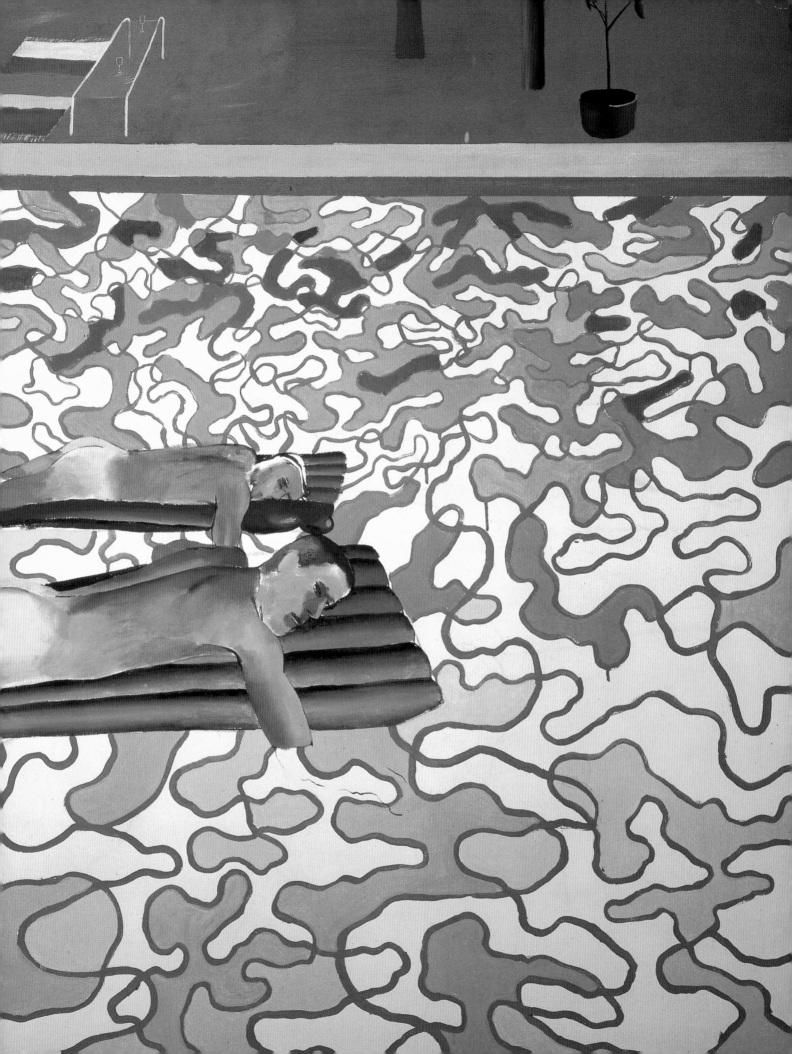

CONTENTS

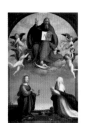
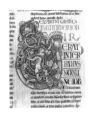
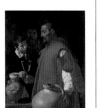

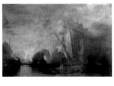
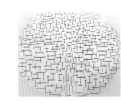
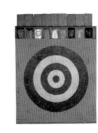

FOREWORD
John Russell

BIG FAT COMPREHENSIVE *histories of art are in every good bookstore. Some of them have been there forever. Like mammoth freight engines newly repainted every ten years, they are built for colossal loads and still render good service. Mammoths of more recent lineage do not always last as well.*

But none of them, old or new, has had the specific ambition of this one. Put briefly, Art: The Critics' Choice *moves fast and travels light. The intention from the first was that it should be a brief history of art, fired by the personal choices of proven authorities. It is aimed at an intelligent audience that likes to be led sentence by sentence, clearly and conversationally. Contributors were asked to write short, with everything said and never a word too many.*

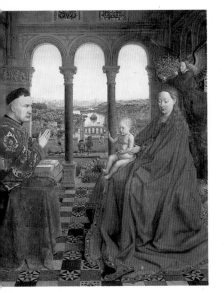

The Virgin and Child with Chancellor Rolin, *c. 1433–34, Jan van Eyck.*

All this is new. By their very nature, histories of art often run too thick. There is so much to say, and there are so many flanks to cover, and so many ifs and buts to be negotiated.

For that matter, history in general encourages historians to write long, and find comfort in doing so. Each feels energized by a personal Freedom of Information Act. As the pages pile up, hour by hour, they say to themselves, "Move over, Thucydides!" And by nightfall, they believe that their great forebear, Edward Gibbon, has a personal message for them: "Nice work today," he says, "keep going!"

But there can be none of that in this particular history. To write short is the very devil to bring off. Yet it can be done. Even John Ruskin, who generally took his time, was able to define "Greatness in Art" in just over two pages in his monumental, five-volume work Modern Painters.

Self-portrait, *1498, Albrecht Dürer.*

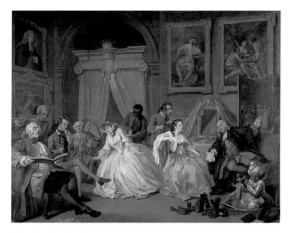

Marriage à la Mode,
IV The Countess's
Morning Levée,
1742–46,
William Hogarth.

So I, for one, welcome the notion of a history of art in which contributors pass the baton from one to another like an Olympic relay team. Decision, quick thinking, and a cool head are indispensable. Dawdling is outlawed.

In this context, mine has been a lifelong commitment. If I could take just one book into the next world, it might be John Aubrey's Brief Lives, *a 17th-century compendium of English oddities in which room is found, almost as an afterthought, for the personal appearance and conversational powers of William Shakespeare.*

When my Latin was less rusty, I delighted in the four-line improprieties in the epigrams of Martial. Many of my favorite British painters, from Nicholas Hilliard to Thomas Jones and beyond, worked small (and to marvelous effect). I stand in awe before the terrible concision of the great French aphorists, and I treasure the makers of music, Schubert and Hugo Wolf preeminent among them, who excelled with very short songs. In all these matters, "Much in little" is my motto, and it has rarely let me down.

*In 1934, Ezra Pound caused a stir with the title—*Make it New*—of his collected essays. Those three words still ring out like a call to arms. But so does the double motto of this book, which is "Make it short! And make it good!"*

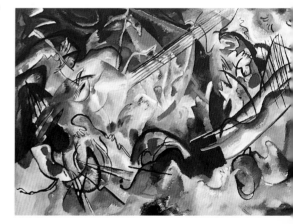

Composition VI,
1913,
Wassily Kandinsky.

John Russell

JOHN RUSSELL
New York, November 1998

7

PREFACE
Marina Vaizey

"THERE IS REALLY no such thing as Art. There are only artists." These are among the most famous phrases in art history, the opening sentences of Sir Ernst Gombrich's The Story of Art, which first appeared in 1950. They reflect a long-held Western belief that individuals matter and make a difference. By extension, it could be argued that there is no such thing as art history, only art historians.

Art history, as a conscious study of the qualities and importance of individual artists and artistic movements, is only a few centuries old. While there are certain undisputed masters, the spotlight shifts on other artists. And context is an essential part of the story. Different forms of art have wielded considerable influence at different times across the centuries; and so medieval altarpieces, imbued with religious fervor, served one type of society, while rich and imposing Renaissance portraits of kings, courtiers, and merchants served another.

The subject of art is as large as human history. Our critics' choice encompasses Western art, made over two millennia in Europe and, latterly, North America, from antiquity to the end of the 20th century. We have concentrated, moreover, on the art that seems most typically Western, the medium that fills our galleries—painting.

We asked experts from many different fields of art history—writers, critics, directors of art galleries, curators, and academics—to choose the fifteen works from their specialized period that have meant most to them, for reasons both subjective and objective. Familiar masterpieces are, of course, included; they are a crucial part of our common culture, our visual vocabulary. But artists usually known only to a specialist audience are also to be found in the selections, reflecting the broad spectrum and great diversity of Western art. And the reader will notice that, as there are different styles and idioms in art history, so there are in art historians, and *each contributor has his or her own distinctive voice. Issues are covered as they are appropriate to the period and subject and as they interest the writer. The relationship between artist and subject matter is explored, and works are examined in terms of notions such as beauty and symbolism. Paintings are looked at not only for themselves—an exercise in connoisseurship—but for the position they occupy in public esteem and for their significance in the development of Western art. Their history involves the ways in which they were commissioned, purchased, and displayed, and the actual materials and techniques of their making. The meanings of paintings in both their own time and now are explored. We ask both how and why.*

Indeed, individual works of art themselves can tell many different stories. Rubens, for example, was an integral part of the development of northern European art in the 17th century, as well as a shining example of what we mean by Baroque, so he appears twice in this book. In other cases, in the name of variety within a select band of artists, the editors had to arbitrate between contributors. There is often consensus but not unanimity, a true reflection of both art and art history.

Above all, we want to share the excitement and enjoyment that great works of art give. We all have our favorites, new and old. Here, for our informed delight, leading authorities have chosen what they see as the marvels of their periods.

The editors would like to thank the contributors for their fascinating insights and for revealing the absorbing debates within art history today, and to acknowledge the kind help and advice given by Tabitha Barber, Dr. John Golding, Michael Kauffmann, Sir Michael Levey, Christopher Lloyd, and Professor Robert Rosenblum.

Marina Vaizey

MARINA VAIZEY
London, February 1999

INTRODUCTION

GRECO-ROMAN AND EARLY CHRISTIAN ART

Jaś Elsner

THE NATURALISTIC FORMS of Classical art, in particular of the Greco-Roman sculpture made in Italy, have been of fundamental importance in the genesis of later European art. Not only were ancient originals actively collected by Renaissance humanists and connoisseurs, but the ancient styles—above all, those associated with naturalism—were consciously revived. In the visual arts specifically, the Renaissance was perceived as having inaugurated a rebirth of the illusionistic techniques that had been discovered and practiced by the Greeks and Romans, but which were believed to have been lost in the "decline" of the Middle Ages. This view of a Renaissance revival of Classical culture from the depths of medieval decadence—a view which was a formative influence on the writings of the major art historians, such as Johann Winckelmann (1717–1768), of the 18th and 19th centuries and is still influential—was formulated in a masterly way by the artist and biographer Giorgio Vasari (1511–1574) in the preface to his great book on the *Lives of the Artists*, published in its definitive edition in 1568. The passion for antiquity in European culture continued unabated through the Baroque and the Enlightenment periods, when the Grand Tour to Italy became the essential requirement of an elite education. This spawned an enthusiasm for collecting and connoisseurship among Europe's aristocracy and intellectuals and, in the late

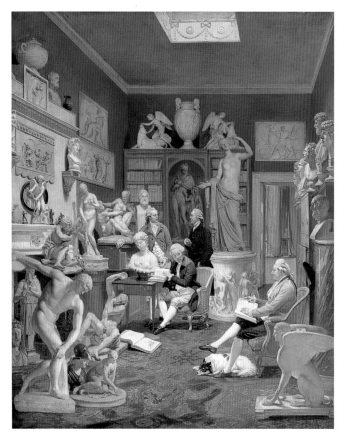

Charles Townley's Library, *1781–83, reworked in 1798, Johann Zoffany. Townley (seated right) is shown with fellow collectors and antiquarians and with the cream of his remarkable collection, which was bought after his death by the British Museum.*

18th and early 19th centuries, stimulated the prevalent, elegant Neoclassical style that drew inspiration from the grandeur of Roman imperial architecture as well as from the more mundane artefacts, decorative motifs, and wall paintings found at Pompeii and Herculaneum. The Grand Tour only met a serious challenge with the rise of modernism early in the 20th century.

But while antiquity was undoubtedly the cradle of the Renaissance, it is more often forgotten that it was also the mother of the Middle Ages. What the apologists of Renaissance naturalism could hardly bring themselves to accept was that most of the forms and techniques of medieval art, both Western and Byzantine, not to mention the uses of images, were themselves part of, and selected from, antiquity's rich heritage. Take the icon, the most archetypally "Byzantine" of medieval forms from which Vasari's Cimabue and Giotto are presented as rescuing art in the 13th century. The wax encaustic technique of the earliest surviving icons, such as the 6th-century *Virgin and Child with Angels and Saints* now in the Monastery of St. Catherine on Mount Sinai, was inherited from ancient panel painting (for example, the wonderful mummy portraits that were excavated late in the 19th century from Roman Egypt). Moreover, many of the forms used in these Early Christian images belonged to the repertoire of Classical illusionism; for instance, the niche behind the Virgin's throne that suggests a spatial setting for the scene, or the slight contrapposto of her stance with the eyes glancing in one direction, the feet pointing in another, and the knees clearly taking the weight of the Christ Child, who glances in yet another direction. But, above all, it is in the uses to which this kind of image was put that we can see antiquity's influence most profoundly. The Sinai Virgin—like countless other sacred panels in the East and the West—was worshipped, probably carried in processions, very likely kissed, and certainly adored as a visual container of the

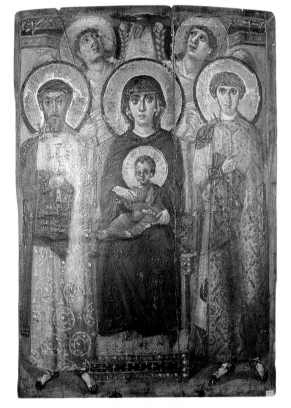

The Virgin and Child with Angels and Saints *(Theodore and George?), wax encaustic on wooden panel, 6th century A.D., in the Monastery of St. Catherine on Mount Sinai, but perhaps from Constantinople.*

living presence of the Incarnate Godhead as well as his divine mother and two of his principal saints. All these practices (though not, of course, the specifically Christian iconography of the Sinai image) go back to ancient pagan uses of sacred images that were carried in civic rituals, dressed, undressed, washed, kissed, and worshipped just like medieval icons.

Undoubtedly there are differences. A Christian icon like this one is a two-dimensional painted representation, whereas most of the icons of Greco-Roman polytheism were statues made in wood, metal, or stone. The Christian image is steeped in a detailed theology and set of scriptural narratives to guarantee its orthodoxy (which, in the case of early icons like this one, was rigorously tested by Iconoclast theologians in the course of the 8th and 9th centuries and vigorously defended by Iconophile thinkers). By contrast, pagan sacred images tended to be holy by local tradition, through ritual practice and according to oral versions and variations of popular myths. It is one of the cardinal differences between Christianity and the polytheistic religions of antiquity that the latter had no written scripture or canonical set of texts, while Christianity shared with Judaism the exclusive emphasis not only on a single God but on a single and orthodox set of scriptures revealed by God. Yet, a major iconic cult image from the ancient Greek East such as the famous statue of Artemis of the Ephesians (against which Saint Paul inveighed) was clearly no less sacred to its worshippers than was a Christian icon to its congregation. Moreover, the great cult deities of Greco-Roman paganism exhibited as complex a hierarchy of religious visual symbols—for example, the animal heads, zodiac, and so-called "breasts" displayed across the body of the Ephesian Artemis—as did the Sinai Virgin, seated in her divine hierarchy of saints, angels, the ray, and the hand of God. Both kinds of icon, pagan and Christian, served to bring their devotees closer to the divine presence that their respective religions worshipped.

The deep difference between the disparate interpretations of Classical art touched upon here—one might broadly call them the "Renaissance" and the "medieval"—makes it very difficult to answer the question: What was Greco-

Artemis of Ephesus, marble copy of the great lost cult statue from the Artemision at Ephesus, perhaps made in the second century A.D. This copy was found at Ephesus.

Roman art really like? It is as if, instead of having access to a dynamic reality, we are offered the particular viewpoints of several static cameras, each with a different colored lens. The actuality of Classical art is not easy to access through the melange of apparently conflicting and tinted views. In part, this is because of the inevitable unreliability of later interpretations, but it is also because so much has been lost. Not a single autograph work survives from the hands of the greatest Greek sculptors and painters mentioned in the history of art included in the *Natural History* of the Elder Pliny (A.D. 23–79). Of the veritable army of bronze statues erected by republican grandees and Roman emperors in the city of Rome, only one, the famous equestrian statue of Marcus Aurelius that Michelangelo used in the center of his Renaissance design for the Capitol, survived the depredations of the Middle Ages into the modern era. Ancient painting has fared very badly in the lottery of survivals, with only the "bourgeois" murals (high-class wallpaper at best rather than prestige panels) of the cities and villas around Vesuvius being preserved in anything like reasonable numbers. And these—the chance result of a volcanic eruption in A.D. 79 (the same natural catastrophe that killed the Elder Pliny) —can hardly be claimed to be representative of all painting at all times throughout the Roman empire.

Yet, much does survive. Some objects were buried for centuries and discovered by chance, like the artefacts of Pompeii and Herculaneum in the 18th century; some were preserved with special, even loving care throughout the Middle Ages into modernity, such as the imperial gems that later came to decorate Christian liturgical treasures and reliquaries, or the greatest monuments of the city of Rome, such as the Pantheon and Trajan's Column. From these material survivals, representing objects from a striking range of media and social levels, from ancient texts on art that have also survived into the modern world, and from the range of later interpretations and reworkings of Classical art in the medieval and modern eras, we can construct a picture which is—at least in some respects—not hopelessly far from the understandings and experiences of ancient Greeks and Romans in commissioning, buying, and viewing their art.

This chapter will address the arts of the Roman empire and of Early Christianity by looking specifically at themes that have proved influential in later European culture. The focus will be on the continuities of the Middle Ages with antiquity and also on some of the more significant ruptures between the Classical tradition and the medieval world view.

CONTINUITY

The Byzantine empire, which lasted until the fall of Constantinople to the Turks in 1453, always considered itself to be the direct and undisputed continuation of the Roman empire. Indeed, the Byzantines called themselves *Romaioi* ("Romans" in Greek). In the Early Christian period, the Byzantine empire included the territories of the eastern, mainly Greek-speaking half of the Roman empire, including the Balkans, Greece, Asia Minor, Palestine, and Egypt; and, after A.D. 330, it was centered on the great capital city that Constantine established on the Bosphorus (at a place previously known as "Byzantium") and named "Constantinople" after himself. In time, the territories and prestige of the Byzantine empire came to be eroded: by the Islamic conquest of Africa and the Levant in the 7th century, the Venetian sack of Constantinople in 1204, and by the constant pressure of the Turks on Asia Minor and Greece, which finally led to the empire's demise. But for much of the Middle Ages, Byzantium was Christendom's most powerful and most splendid kingdom, with an extraordinarily rich intellectual and artistic life and with a characteristic Orthodox form of Christian belief and ritual which—after about A.D. 800—was frequently in doctrinal disagreement with the Catholic Christianity of Western Europe.

Byzantine and Early Christian art were thus the products of a culture that saw itself as the direct inheritor of the Roman world. Although the religious realm was now defined in terms diametrically opposed to ancient polytheism, and although the imperial capital had been moved from Rome to Constantinople (the new Rome), in many other respects both urban and rural life from the 4th to the 7th century continued according to the patterns established under the Roman empire. Luxurious private villas continued to be built as the country retreats of the elite; cities maintained their grand array of public amenities (baths, arenas, amphitheaters, gymnasia); the educational curriculum—dependent on the ancient Greek and Latin canon such as the works of Homer and Virgil and on the mastery of the various skills of rhetoric—simply acquired a Christian veneer. Even in the arena of the visual arts, the development of Roman techniques of architecture continued unabated through the Early Christian period and culminated in a supreme building in the 6th century, the church of St. Sophia in Constantinople which surpassed such masterworks of Roman design as the Pantheon. Within the great cities such as Rome, Antioch, and Constantinople, the ancient statues, dedications, and relief sculptures, some depicting such "pagan abominations" as the cult practice of animal sacrifice, were preserved for posterity, valued for their fine

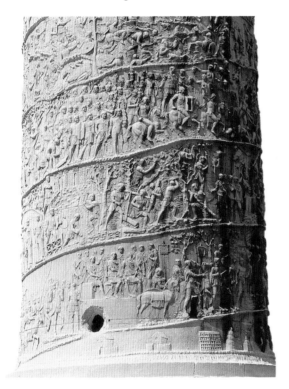

Trajan's Column, marble, c. A.D. 113, Rome. Highly influential, this spiraling sculptural narrative of Trajan's Dacian wars was originally topped by a gilded portrait statue of the emperor.

workmanship and their direct link to the imperial past, and even occasionally subjected to restoration.

At the level of state patronage, the Byzantine emperors in the East and to a lesser extent the popes in the West (who took on the old imperial title of *pontifex maximus*), continued the ancient traditions of public munificence for which the Roman emperors were paradigms. Imperial Rome had always prided itself on the grandeur of its state buildings and monuments as well as the extravagance of its public displays and festivals. Emperors competed with their predecessors in constructing ever more splendid fora or baths, ever more lavish temples or memorials. Trajan's Column, for example, erected in Rome in the grandiose setting of Trajan's Forum in about A.D. 113, might have been a fairly traditional pillar-base for a gilded bronze imperial statue (although it would always have been unusually grand—it has an internal staircase leading up to a viewing platform beneath the statue), but it was deliberately marked out as revolutionary by several unique features. First, Trajan's successor, Hadrian (ruled A.D. 117—38), had the ashes of his predecessor buried in a chamber beneath the column. This was a virtually unheard-of honor, since almost never was anyone buried within the confines of the city, even an emperor. Most mausolea, including those of the first Roman emperor, Augustus, his dynasty, and Hadrian himself and his successors, were outside the city walls. Second, the column itself became a remarkable work of art in its own right. Either Trajan or Hadrian had it carved with a dense frieze of twenty-three bands which wove up the shaft in a beetling narrative of the Dacian wars conducted by Trajan in 101–106. These had resulted in a series of mighty victories and in the extension of the empire by the addition of the province of Dacia across the Danube to the north (comprising much of modern Romania). As a result of the frieze, Trajan's Column turned into an extraordinary honorific celebration of Trajan's (and by extension Rome's) victories, as well as being a remarkable testimony to the inventive skill of Rome's official sculptors. The Column's seemingly endless narrative of battles, sacrifices, imperial audiences, and yet more battles tells a story of the endless burden and the virtually infinite glory of being emperor, which reflected no less on Trajan's successors than on Trajan himself. So great was the impact of the Column that at the end of the century, Commodus (ruled 180–92), the son of Marcus Aurelius (ruled 161–80), chose to commemorate his father's wars against the German tribes by erecting a second sculpted column in Rome.

In the 4th century, two emperors resident in Byzantium, Theodosius I (ruled 378–95) and his son Arcadius (ruled 395–408), emulated these two Roman monuments by having their own carved columns raised in Constantinople. It was as if an imperial city could not be conceived as adequate until it possessed sculpted columns to rival those of Trajan and Marcus. The same applied to other kinds of imperial adornments found in Rome: the great baths of Caracalla, Diocletian, and Constantine, to be rivaled by the baths of Zeuxippus in Constantinople; the grand arenas like the Circus Maximus, the Colosseum, or the Circus of Maxentius on the Via Appia, to be rivaled by the Hippodrome in Constantinople; the imperial fora of Caesar, Augustus, and Trajan, to be challenged by the Forum Tauri and the Forum of Constantine in Constantinople, and so on. In each case, emperors vied with their predecessors in providing amenities of beauty and grandeur by which their reigns would be remembered.

The effect of such monuments on later generations is vividly rendered in a striking passage by the mid-4th-century historian Ammianus Marcellinus, who described the first entry into Rome of one of Constantine's sons, the Emperor Constantius II, in A.D. 357:

> He stood amazed, and on every side on which his eyes rested he was dazzled by the array of marvelous sights … the sanctuaries of Tarpeian Jove [the Capitol], so far surpassing as things divine excel those of the earth; the baths built up in the manner of provinces; the huge bulk of the amphitheater [the Colosseum], strengthened by its framework of Tiburtine stone, to whose top human eyesight barely ascends; the Pantheon, like a rounded city district, vaulted over in lofty beauty; the exalted columns [of Trajan and Marcus Aurelius] which rise with platforms, to which one may mount, and bear the likenesses of former emperors; the Temple of the City, the Forum of Peace, the Theater of Pompey, the Odeum, the Stadium, and among these the other adornments of the Eternal City. But when he came to the Forum of Trajan, a construction unique under the heavens, as we believe, and admirable even in the unanimous opinion of all the gods, he stood fast in amazement, turning his attention to the gigantic complex about him, beggaring description and never again to be imitated by mortal men.
>
> AMMIANUS MARCELLINUS, RES GESTAE (16.10.13f.)

This piece of purple prose captures not only the cumulative effect of Rome's proud public buildings, but also the tremendous esteem in which they were held in late Antiquity. Interestingly, the bulk of the monuments listed here by Ammianus can still be seen in Rome—they were deliberately preserved for posterity through the Middle Ages and the early modern period.

While Trajan's Column celebrates victory over foreign foes, other monuments, such as the arch erected by the Senate in A.D. 312–15 to honor Constantine, who had conquered Rome from his rival Maxentius in 312, drew on the imagery of foreign conquest to justify civil war. The Arch of Constantine is remarkable not only for its traditional form (emulating, for example, the Arch of Septimius Severus in the Roman Forum, erected in 203), but for its extensive sculptural program, much more visible than the minuscule morass

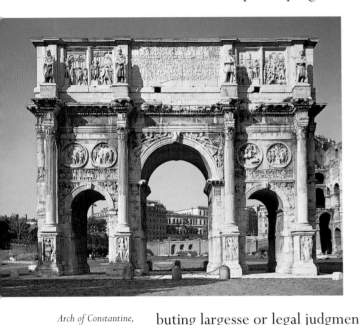

Arch of Constantine, Rome, A.D. 312–15, dedicated by the senate to the emperor who had wrested Rome from the grip of his co-emperor Maxentius in 312 at the Battle of the Milvian Bridge.

on Trajan's Column, and because it, too, provided an impressive testimony to the way late Antique Rome honored its great past. The designers of the arch incorporated into their 4th-century structure a series of carved relief panels from civic monuments dedicated to Trajan, Hadrian, and Marcus Aurelius (three "good" emperors of the 2nd century A.D.). These were carefully grouped to show the emperors in their most "iconic" or archetypal roles, such as hunting, giving audience, distributing largesse or legal judgments, and performing sacrifices. Into the faces of Constantine's illustrious predecessors the arch's sculptors cut Constantine's own likeness, replacing the heads of Trajan, Hadrian, and Marcus so that the new usurper was literally the embodiment of ancient imperial glory. Immediately above the two smaller arches on either side of the central bay was placed a small frieze that runs right around the arch (including the two shorter sides) and celebrates Constantine's campaign and conquest over Maxentius. There are rows of columns on both sides of the arch; these columns stand on pedestals carrying images of defeated barbarians and are crowned by statues of vanquished Dacians, as if to imply that Constantine's victory in civil war was parallel to Trajan's defeat of foreign foes. The rather dubious triumph of the present is cast against the backdrop of the glorious past—just as the arch was added, in a prominent position close to the Colosseum, to the great mass of earlier imperial monuments.

In parallel with these monuments, the emperors erected likenesses of themselves throughout the empire. In an age when few citizens ever saw their ruler and when news traveled slowly, these portraits were a way of establishing the imperial image in the minds of the empire's subjects (no less than were the coins stamped with the emperor's head). Of course, there is no guarantee that emperors looked as they were portrayed—Augustus' image changed remarkably little in a reign of well over forty years—but what mattered was not accuracy so much as defining a portrait-type that could be recognized from image to image. If an emperor fell from power, his images might be removed or destroyed, and when a new emperor ascended the throne, his images were ostentatiously added to the collection already in place in most cities of the empire. The range of these imperial portraits was large: from crude street-paintings to extraordinarily worked and very expensive cameo gems boasting complex allegories; from slick public statues in stone or bronze to virtuoso portrait studies by the most skillful hands. Some were intended for public display in prestige sites of the empire's urban environment, others as relatively simple affirmations of loyalty in taverns or shops, much like presidential or royal portraits are used in many countries today. From the artistic point of view, the finest images, whether gems or portrait statues, generally adorned elite private residences and were usually commissioned by the court.

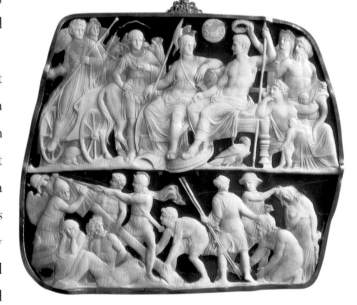

One notable aspect of many of the most elaborate surviving imperial images is an emphasis on religious meanings coupled with dynastic succession. This is seen to great effect in the exquisite Gemma Augustea, a sardonyx cameo probably cut for Augustus early in the 1st century A.D. (and now somewhat reduced in size from its original state). In the gem, Augustus is enthroned beside the goddess Roma, in heroic semi-nudity, in the pose of the cult statue of Jupiter from the Capitol. All heads turn toward him in the gem's upper zone, and he alone sits in strict profile, like the golden image on a coin. Augustus gazes toward Tiberius, his designated successor, who emerges from a chariot to the left. In front of Tiberius is the youthful Germanicus, Augustus' great-

Gemma Augustea, cameo, c. A.D. 10. The Augustan period was a golden age for the cutting of cameos, where gems with multicolored layers were carved in relief.

nephew, whom Tiberius had adopted as his heir in A.D. 4. The upper tier of the gem thus presents a complex portrait of succession through the language of hereditary monarchy, although in each case the heir is not the natural but the adoptive son of his father (in fact, Germanicus did not live to inherit the throne from Tiberius, who was succeeded by Germanicus' son, the infamous Caligula). In the lower register of the cameo is a scene of Roman soldiers erecting a trophy in honor of the imperial victories accomplished in the names of Augustus and Tiberius.

Equally beautiful as a masterpiece of Roman carving is a splendidly cut and polished marble bust of Emperor Commodus, son of Marcus Aurelius, probably made for the court in about A.D. 191–2. While the Commodus portrait does not boast the complexities of dynastic politics of the gem, his flamboyant beard and the style of his portrait clearly mark him out as the son and heir of Marcus. But what is remarkable about this portrait is the way the emperor is presented in the guise of the god Hercules, who was in fact regarded by Commodus as his particular patron. Commodus wears the lionskin and bears the club of Hercules, while in his left hand he carries the apples of the Hesperides, which formed the goal of one of Hercules' most difficult labors. Beneath the imperial bust are an orb and cornucopia, as well as a kneeling Amazon, who represents not just one of the defeated foes of Hercules, but also the vanquished barbarian enemies of the empire. It is as if the emperor is indistinguishable from the deity, and the viewer is no longer able to tell whether to revere the image as the statue of a divine ruler or as an Olympic god.

Polished marble bust of Emperor Commodus represented as the god Hercules, c. A.D. 191–92. It was found in Rome in 1874.

By the 5th and 6th centuries, although many of the types of honorific imagery changed with the advent of the Christian era, imperial images continued to be created with as much pomp and panache as in pagan times. From the beginning of the 5th century, although the great mass of earlier statues remained in position, very few new ones were made. Instead, the focus for imperial imagery moved into the interior spaces of palaces and churches;

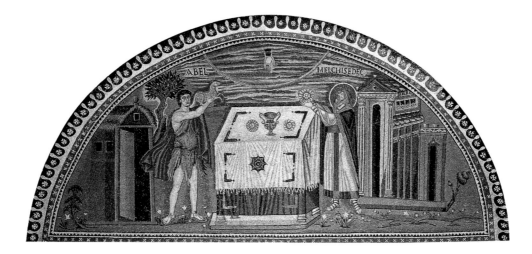

A mosaic showing the offerings of Abel and Melchisedec from the Presbytery Chapel, the church of San Vitale, Ravenna, c. A.D. 530–550.

out of the three-dimensional naturalism of sculpture and into the splendidly hierarchic and colorful two dimensions of mosaic and paint. Take the great panels made of stone, glass, and gold mosaics representing the Byzantine Emperor Justinian (ruled 527–65) and his wife, the Empress Theodora (died 548), which adorn the walls of the presbytery of the church of San Vitale in Ravenna. On the north wall of the presbytery, Justinian is shown in supreme splendor walking with his court officials and his bodyguard following Maximian, the Bishop of Ravenna (from 546). Theodora is shown on the opposite wall in the same liturgical procession, surrounded by the ladies and eunuchs of her court, walking into the church and carrying a jeweled golden goblet as her offering. The gift is paralleled by the image embroidered on the hem of her gown of the three Wise Men bringing their gifts to the newborn Christ. Together, in a church far from Constantinople whose decoration was altered to celebrate the reconquest of Italy and of Ravenna by Justinian's troops in 540, the emperor and his empress (neither of whom ever visited Ravenna) are depicted as pious, if spectacularly grand, worshippers.

Like the earlier portrait statues of the Roman emperors, this group of mosaics creates an official image of Ravenna's new rulers for the benefit of its population. There was no need for Justinian or his empress (who may well have been dead by the time this set of images was erected) to have really looked as they are depicted, but what is interesting is that they are no longer represented as deities. The Augustus of the Gemma Augustea is a kind of Jupiter *manqué*, enthroned side by side with the goddess Roma, while it is impossible to tell whether Commodus is masquerading as Hercules, or Hercules has taken on the features of Commodus. Here, however, despite their haloes, neither Theodora nor Justinian is a god. Rather, they are saintly rulers, model worshippers of Christ, and paradigms for the population both of piety and of generosity

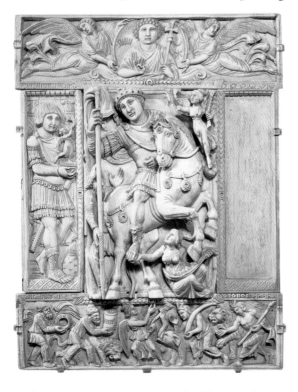

to the Church. Instead of being visualized as gods, they are presented as exemplary servants and devotees of the one God. The continuity between these mosaics and the earlier imperial images is significant: they are opulent, impressive, complex in the range of political messages implied, and unflagging in their single-minded advertisement of royal glory through religious connections. Where they differ is in the kinds of religious connotations the image-makers appropriated, calculating what would appeal most powerfully to the images' respective audiences.

On a small scale, in the world of elite imperial art an object like the so-called "Barberini ivory,"

The Barberini ivory, four panels from a five-part ivory wing of a diptych, 6th century A.D., probably from Constantinople. This remarkable object entered the collection of the Barberini family in Rome in 1625.

most probably cut for Emperor Justinian in 6th-century Constantinople, occupied a similar role in its time to the cameo-gems of Augustus. It is the spectacular private equivalent of the Ravenna panels—a splendid Classicizing evocation of imperial majesty, with the equestrian emperor rearing triumphant over a personification of the earth, a flying Victory to his upper-left-hand side and attendants offering small statuettes of Victory in the panels at the sides (if the lost right-hand panel resembled that on the left, as is probable). Beneath, again in emulation of much earlier Roman visual patterns, human and animal personifications of the various nations of the earth offer obeisance to the great emperor. The only gesture to Christianity in this elaborate piece of virtuoso ivory carving, with its deep undercutting of the imperial spear and the rearing horse's legs that enhance the prominence of the emperor, is the figure of Christ in the upper panel, who oversees the glory of Justinian much as Jupiter and Roma oversaw Augustus in the Gemma Augustea.

While the imperial and elite worlds have undoubtedly provided us with the majority of the most exquisite surviving images from antiquity—which is hardly surprising since the court could afford to monopolize the finest artists in any period—less elevated sections of the population also lived with a rich abundance of imagery. Townhouses and villas, even relatively low on the social scale, were decorated with wall paintings, floor mosaics, numerous sculptures, and other fitments such as decorated cloths. The objects used for dining, decoration, and self-adornment—from silver tableware to terracotta pottery, from blown-glass pitchers and vases to mirrors and perfume flasks—boasted a vast array of mythological, humorous, and erotic imagery and continued to do so well into the Christian era. In a culture where rates of literacy were relatively low and where education was the preserve of a select elite, the visual functioned as a key purveyor of traditional narratives and myths to which most people would have had only aural access.

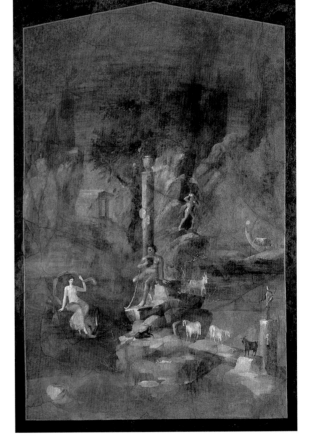

Landscape fresco with Polyphemus and Galatea from what might have been an imperial villa at Boscotrecase near Pompeii, last decade of the 1st century B.C.

In trying to understand the place of the arts in daily life and in the private sphere, we are fortunate that the eruption of Vesuvius caused such a catastrophe for the inhabitants of Pompeii, a city on the bay of Naples, and its port, Herculaneum, in A.D. 79. The excavation of these cities—complete with streets, shops, houses, gardens, bathhouses, and brothels, many containing furniture, countless artefacts, numerous wall paintings (some spectacular, many very unremarkable), central heating, and even plumbing—gives us a unique window into antiquity's social life. In the arena of painting and mosaics, it is clear that many Pompeian works cast a jokey light on the doings of Pompeii's citizens, from the mosaics at the entrances of houses depicting ferocious dogs with the inscription "beware of the dog," to the vignettes showing cupids engaged in the business of daily life, to mythological paintings that frequently contrive to reflect the activities that went on in the room they decorated. For example, a painting behind a dining couch placed over a pool in the house of Loreius Tiburtinus in Pompeii shows Narcissus entranced by his own image in a spring, and thus prods viewers into wondering about their own relationship with the pool beside which they recline during dinner.

One notable aspect of Pompeian painting is its tendency to elaborate the rural and landscape settings of myths and garden scenes, as if the paintings were being employed specifically to conjure a world of country leisure separate from the busy urban life. Often myths—like the scenes of Perseus and Andromeda or Polyphemus and Galatea from the impressive cycle found in a villa at Boscotrecase near Pompeii—were cast as grand landscapes with a few distant figures. Since these images were only discovered in the 18th century, it is striking how they appear to presage the great 17th-century tradition of landscape painting with mythological scenes associated with masters such as Poussin or Claude (*see pages 154–57*). In the Polyphemus panel (see previous page), which once adorned the west wall of a room lit from the south, Polyphemus, the giant one-eyed Cyclops, sits on a rocky crag beneath a tall column crowned with a bronze vase. He plays the pipes while the goats he is tending sit or wander on the rocks below. To the left, the nymph Galatea (with whom Polyphemus would fall hopelessly in love) rides the waves on a dolphin. In the background to the right is a second image of Polyphemus, this time flinging rocks at the ship of Odysseus, which sails away after its captain has hoodwinked and blinded the Cyclops. The elegant, impressionistic landscape is made to represent a kind of idyllic space, a pastoral as evoked in the bucolic poetry of Theocritus and Virgil, or the romantic novels of Longus and Achilles Tatius. This is a world where more than one event involving the same individual can appear in the same visual frame and landscape setting (a device still used in the Middle Ages and into the Early Renaissance). The world of mythical landscape is one of love and tragedy—a magical reality far from the more mundane concerns of Roman villa or town life that continued to appeal to urban dwellers in the Early Christian period.

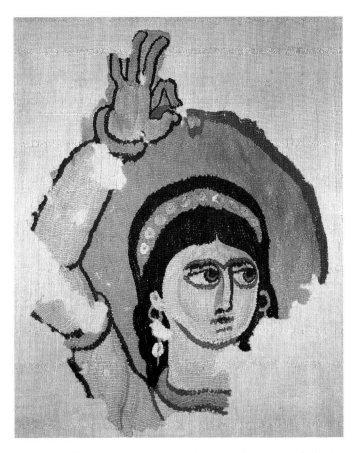

Fragment of textile, perhaps representing a dancer, late 4th or early 5th century A.D. From a group of late Roman tapestries from Egypt showing human and divine figures, often with Bacchic iconography after the Roman god of wine and fruitfulness.

Much rarer still than paintings are ancient textiles; very fragile, large numbers from antiquity have been preserved only in the dry climate of Egypt. The Egyptian examples—which range from highly elaborate mythological and pagan religious scenes to icons of the Virgin and saints, as well as secular and abstract images—may have particular qualities special to the Coptic culture of late Antique Egypt, from which they come. But in many respects—not least their breathtaking handling of color and form, their sheer mastery of the techniques of tapestry (which has rarely been rivaled at any time in the history of art), and their exquisite combination of abstraction with naturalism—they probably represent a small sample of the lost richness of ancient household decoration. Imagine such ravishing images as the fragment of a dancer, woven from wool in the late 4th or early 5th century and now in the Louvre, adorning the couches, bedcovers, or walls of private houses in Egypt and throughout the empire. One surprising feature, seen especially in the tapestries, is how late the traditions of mythological imagery appear to have been preserved in the "secular" sphere of social life within the household, despite the strongly Christian nature of society in Coptic Egypt. Some of the representations of pagan myth appear as late as the 7th century, just at the time when Byzantine Egypt fell to the great new invading force of Islam. Effectively, within the home, many of the most potent myths of ancient paganism—such as the adventures of Dionysus or Meleager—enjoyed a continued existence from archaic Greek times through the painted walls and mosaic floors of the Roman empire (for example, in the famous frescoes of the Villa of the Mysteries at Pompeii) to the early Byzantine period.

RUPTURE

Yet, for all the continuities between ancient and early medieval culture (at least until the Islamic conquests in the East), one arena of human experience met with cardinal change. When, in A.D. 312, the Emperor Constantine proclaimed the legalization of Christianity (after a period in the early 4th century known as the "Great Persecution"), he set in train an unstoppable flood sustained by the combination of voluntary conversions, imperial patronage, state legislation, and the promotion of Christians to posts of high power. By 391, the Emperor Theodosius I was able to promulgate an edict banning paganism and forbidding sacrifice—within less than a century turning the tables of persecution from the Christians to the polytheists. Within the span of a lifetime, from, say, 290 to 350, Christianity had moved from a tiny minority sect of almost no popular influence within the empire, to the dominant state-sponsored religion whose huge new churches—and Constantine himself was responsible for many of these in Rome, Antioch, Constantinople, and Jerusalem—were now the principal temples of the empire. From 361–63, the last pagan emperor (indeed the only pagan emperor after Constantine), Julian the Apostate, vainly tried to turn the clock back by reinventing a pagan church and theology that owed much to the Christianity he so detested. He failed.

It is impossible to measure precisely the huge impact of these changes, but certainly religion figured as one of the principal aspects of social life, with its influence felt not only in all the activities of living, but also in the commemoration of the dead. What the Christianization of the empire effected in the long term was not only the replacement of ancient traditions of ritual by new Christian ceremonies and liturgy, but also the radical uprooting of a culture of religious toleration and inclusiveness that had been built up over centuries. The one exclusive God of the Christians not only rejected all the other gods of the pagan pantheon, but wished them utterly eradicated and forgotten: He all but succeeded. As a result, a whole canon of Christian imagery was invented that came to predominate over all other kinds of iconography and subject matter in the Middle Ages. This imagery was tied to specific narratives that were described in scripture and explained in the commentaries of priests and theologians.

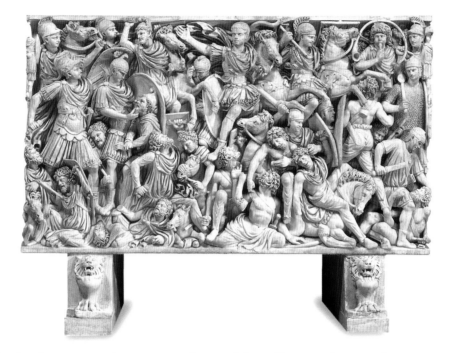

The huge and quite spectacular Ludovisi Sarcophagus, marble, c. A.D. 260, is carved in deep relief and may have been intended for a member of the imperial family. It was discovered in Rome in 1621.

In the funerary sphere, something of the effect can be seen by comparing one of the most spectacular burial monuments of the 3rd century, the Ludovisi Sarcophagus, with the most elaborate example from the 4th, the great sarcophagus of Junius Bassus. Already a throwback to the great military sarcophagi of the later 2nd century, the Ludovisi Sarcophagus was probably made in the third quarter of the 3rd century. The unidentified deceased man (an epitaph may have been painted on the empty plaque in the center of the lid, not shown) is shown in an act of military glory on behalf of the Roman state. His portrait is carved into the face of the rider who is leading the Romans in victorious battle over barbarians. The entire face of the sarcophagus is covered with the entwined bodies of battling soldiers, rendered in virtuoso style. On the lid, the deceased is shown as a general granting clemency to the defeated barbarians, and there is a portrait bust of a woman, presumably the man's mother or wife. The imagery of this spectacular tomb monument draws on the public art of the Roman state, not only for the wars against foreigners rendered in the great columns of Trajan and Marcus, but also for the scene of clemency that echoes reliefs of Marcus Aurelius inserted into the Arch of Constantine. In contrast with this Roman emphasis on the glorious achievements of a lifetime, on the detailed portrayal of the dead man and his family, and on the relationship of the sarcophagus' imagery with that of the public art of the city of Rome, stands the Junius Bassus Sarcophagus. Carved for the Christian prefect of the city of Rome (who in A.D. 359 "went, newly baptized, to God," as it says in the inscription on the much-damaged lid), this outstanding tomb monument presents nothing that can be termed personal (at least in the imagery of the parts that survive). The bravura sculpture on the face of the sarcophagus shows Christ in both the central panels: above, enthroned over a personification of the world and giving the Law to Peter and Paul, and below, entering Jerusalem on a donkey. These images of triumph during Christ's life and after his death are supported by scenes of martyrdom in the interview of Jesus with Pilate before the Crucifixion and the arrests of Peter and Paul. It is as if Christian triumph is inevitably implicated in the ideology of martyrdom, not only that of Jesus, but especially that of the two great Roman saints whose deaths in witness of their faith imitated his. Interspersed with these scenes are Old Testament images of the Fall (Adam and Eve and the Distress of Job), sacrifice (Abraham's Sacrifice of Isaac, which was seen as a foreshadowing of God's sacrifice of his only son), and triumph through tribulation (Daniel in the Lions' Den). This imagery takes Junius Bassus far away from anything to do with his lifetime's achievements or his family. Instead, his death is implicitly mirrored against the triumphant deaths of Christianity's founder and the most important Roman saints. The message is a *tour de force* of interpretative theology, reading the Old and New Testaments together with the narratives of the saints.

The complexity of such Christian typological imagery—combining Old and New Testament scenes so that the former anticipated the latter—and the use of images of the saints to bring the dynamic of the scriptural narrative closer

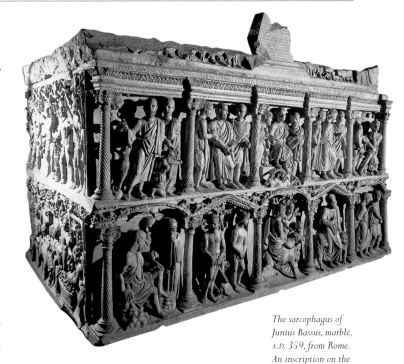

The sarcophagus of Junius Bassus, marble, A.D. 359, from Rome. An inscription on the upper edge reads: "Junius Bassus, a man of Senatorial rank, who lived 44 years and 2 months, when he was Prefect of the City, went, newly baptized, to God…."

to the viewer's own day, are fundamental to Early Christian art. The wall paintings of catacombs, no less than carvings on sarcophagi, provide wonderful examples of such instructive juxtapositions of Christian themes that formed a new narrative for viewers to interpret. For example, Cubiculum O of the Via Latina Catacomb in Rome, probably painted in the third quarter of the 4th century, includes Old Testament images of Noah, the Hebrews in the Fiery Furnace, Daniel and the Crossing of the Red Sea by the Israelites, as well as the New Testament Miracle of Loaves and Fishes and the Raising of Lazarus.

Occasionally, both on sarcophagi and in catacombs, Christian themes were combined with pagan ones, as in the Hercules cycle in Cubiculum N of the Via Latina Catacomb (probably painted by the same artists as Cubiculum O). Such license would have been seen as quite heretical under later orthodoxy.

One aspect of the great power of Christianity—and perhaps something that contributed significantly to its survival as a tiny set of related sects in the long years before Constantine's reign— was its emphasis on the written word. Out of the religious groups of antiquity,

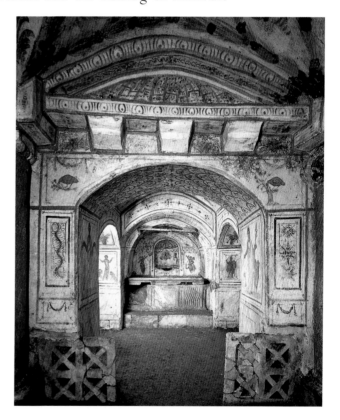

General view of Cubiculum O, Via Latina Catacomb, Rome, c. A.D. 360–70.

only the Jews (who provided, after all, the source of Christianity) shared with the Christians an obsession with scripture. The other religions—from the state's imperial cult, via the ancient cults of civic deities like Artemis of the Ephesians or Olympic Zeus, to the various new religions of the mystic fringe such as the cult of Mithras or that of Cybele and Attis—insisted on oral transmission of their mysteries (if at all) and preserved virtually no written texts. Christianity, on the other hand, was a religion run by intellectuals who could read, debate, and decide on orthodoxy; and the process of the development of the Church after Constantine is one of ecclesiastical councils in which the precise canon of scripture was established, the correct interpretations and commentaries were decided upon, and the panoply of heretics (who were soon regarded as much more dangerous than pagans) was excluded and anathematized.

On the art-historical side, this emphasis on writing gave rise to the production of books containing scripture which, as early as the 5th century, began to be illustrated with cycles of images. Such illuminations (which may have inspired or may have been imitated from a late Antique tradition of illustrating the texts of Homer and Virgil in deluxe manuscripts) are not only illustrations of the text; they may serve as scriptural commentaries in their own right. Take the story of the Good Samaritan (Luke 10: 30–37) in the great 6th-century Rossano Gospels, an exquisite codex written in Greek in silver capitals on purple parchment (and hence possibly for the imperial court). In the main image at the top, beneath the Greek inscription which reads "about the man who fell into the hands of thieves," the Good Samaritan finds the half-dead man on the road leading from Jerusalem (on the far left) to Jericho. The Samaritan

The Good Samaritan, the Rossano Gospels, 6th century A.D. This exquisite illuminated Bible gathers all its illustrations at the beginning of the book in a kind of visual commentary and frontispiece to the scriptural text.

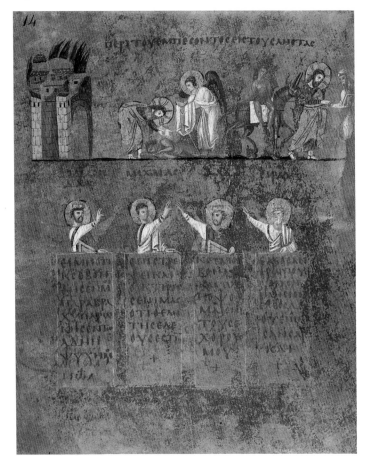

puts him on his donkey with the help of an angel and leads him to the innkeeper to whom he gives money for his care. What is unusual is that the image represents Christ himself, with the cruciform halo, in the guise of the Good Samaritan, thereby importing into the story something that is never made explicit in the biblical text. Instead, the artist or designer has borrowed from a theological tradition of exegetic interpretation (that is, the explanation of biblical texts) such as this passage from St. Gregory of Nyssa's late 4th-century commentary on the Song of Songs 13: 427–28:

The Word of God explained in a story the full dispensation of God's love for mankind. He told of man's descent from heaven, the ambush by robbers, the removal of the garment of incorruptibility, sin's wound and the progress of sin over half of man's nature while the soul remained immortal... However, Christ put on our full nature... With his body, that is, the ass, he hastened to the place where evil had befallen man, healed his wounds, put him on his own beast, and made for his loving providence a resting place in which all those who labor and are heavy-laden can find rest.

Following an allegorical interpretation like Gregory's, the Rossano painter turns what Luke's Gospel presents as just a parable told by Christ, into what Gregory describes as the "full dispensation of God's love for mankind," in which the whole drama of Christ's mission to save the world is represented in figural form. Beneath the main image, as on a number of other pages in the Rossano Gospels, are the busts of two pairs of Old Testament prophets, facing each other and sitting on top of columns inscribed with quotations from their works which embed the Good Samaritan story in the Old Testament tradition. From left to right, the prophets are David and Micah, and David and Sirach. Their quotations read: "Unless the Lord had been my help, my soul had almost dwelt in silence" (Psalm 94: 17); "Because he delighteth in mercy, he will turn again, he will have compassion upon us" (Micah 7: 18–19); "The Lord taketh my part with them that help me: therefore shall I see my desire upon them that hate me" (Psalm 118: 7); "The mercy of man is for his fellow men, but the mercy of the Lord is for every living being" (Sirach 18: 13). The kinds of typology we saw in the Via Latina Catacomb and the Bassus Sarcophagus are again marshalled into play, but instead of following a fairly standard line where specific and common image types like Jonah, Daniel, or the sacrifice of Isaac were repeatedly summoned to give a broad suggestion of Old Testament presagings of New Testament events, here very specific examples in chapter

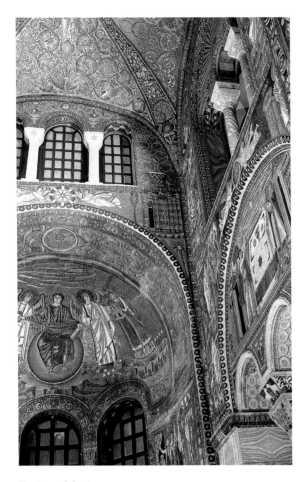

Mosaic panel showing the apse and walls of the presbytery chapel, the church of San Vitale, Ravenna, c. A.D. 544/45.

and verse are arranged to provide a scriptural support for a visual interpretation of the Good Samaritan that extends the meaning of the parable well beyond Saint Luke's original text into the complex area of exegetic theology.

Alongside the Christian emphasis on writing and on art as a means of illustrating the written—for the aid of the illiterate as well as to embellish and perhaps expand upon the bare words on the page—went the need to decorate sanctuaries in a splendor appropriate to the sacred rites that were performed there. This impulse was much the same as the desire to adorn pagan temples with marble revetments and gilded ceilings; the difference was that Christianity eliminated the extravagant cult statues, often made from ivory and gold, which had been the main focus of pagan shrines and replaced them with elaborate cycles of biblical and religious scenes, represented on walls and vaults in painted fresco or mosaic. The 6th-century church of San Vitale in Ravenna provides a spectacular example. The presbytery, the chapel at the eastern end of the church, is lavishly decorated in fine-cut marble veneer on the lower walls and in sumptuous mosaics on the arcades, upper walls, and ceiling. The apse itself contains the episcopal throne, with the panels of Justinian and Theodora on the north and south walls, and in the apse concha is an image of Christ enthroned on a blue globe as Lord of all the world (an iconography presaged in the central panel of the upper tier of the Bassus Sarcophagus). Jesus, holding a scroll with seven seals (according to Revelation 5: 1), receives the church from its original founder Ecclesius (on the far right) and hands a martyr's crown to its dedicatee, the late 3rd-century martyr Vitalis, whose relics had been exhumed by St. Ambrose in the 4th century and which were the church's main focus of devotion. In the vault of the main presbytery dome is the Lamb of

God, who appears out of a blue sky with stars and is contained in a wreath teeming with animals that is supported by four angels. The Lamb (Christian symbol of the ultimate sacrifice when God gave his only son to save the world) is the culmination of a program dedicated to the imagery of Christian sacrifice: that is, the Eucharistic rite of the Mass that took place in this space.

The liturgy of the Mass was the principal sacramental occasion where Christian worshippers might confront their God. But it would be through relics, like those of Vitalis at San Vitale, and icons such the Sinai Virgin that Christians would have their most direct contact with the holy. While the body of Christ was believed to enter the Eucharistic bread of the Mass, the very presence of a saint was deemed to inhabit his bones or his images. The hierarchy of mediation with the divine is particularly apparent in the Sinai panel, where the two saints—probably Theodore and George—gaze frontally at the viewer, representing a stage of contact before access to the Virgin and Christ (who both look away) and above them, via the immaterial white of the angels and ray, to the unseen hand of God himself. The theological implications of imagery such as this, suggesting direct access to divinity through the material forms of pigment and wood, were profound. The move away from the naturalism of Classical art toward the more abstract or symbolic styles of the Middle Ages had shown, in part, an attempt to distance image-making from the dangers of idolatry, yet were icons not a form of idolatry just like (perhaps even descended from) the pagan worship of cult images such as Artemis of Ephesus? Had the medieval denaturalism of the styles and forms of antiquity's art not sufficiently freed itself from the idolatrous uses to which the pagans had put their images?

Such considerations would ultimately result in a profound crisis within Byzantine image-making during the period of Iconoclasm (726–843). At this time, images were destroyed, and the very justifications for their existence were attacked theologically. In response to the Iconoclasts, a theological defense of icons was formulated that would transform Byzantine painting and change representational art in the West. The Iconoclastic Controversy shows that, even as late as the 8th and 9th centuries, the tensions arising from the tradition of Classical image-making within Christian art were deep and manifold.

THE MIDDLE AGES

700–1400 ❧ MICHAEL KAUFFMANN

The term "Middle Ages" can be defined in different ways. At its most extensive, it covers the whole period between the end of the Roman Empire and the Renaissance, around 500–1500. At the earlier end, terms like "Early Christian," "Migration period," or, more pejoratively, "Dark Ages" are usually inserted, and at the far end, the Italian Renaissance is often seen as beginning with Giotto in about 1300.

THE PERIOD under consideration has three parts; the first, very broadly, covers the years 700 to about c. 1050, the time of the later barbarian invasions and the first imperial revivals. "Barbarian" indicates "not Christian" rather than any other standard of civilization.

From the collapse of the Roman Empire, Europe had been like a sponge, squeezed from all sides while absorbing outside elements. By the 8th century, most of the barbarian tribes had settled and converted to Christianity, but then the threat of Islam from the south coincided with the invasions of the Vikings from the north and the Magyars from the east, and local cultures were devastated.

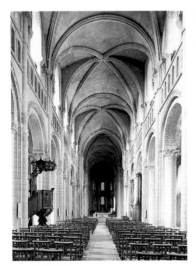

Church of the Trinity, Abbaye aux Dames, Caen; the apotheosis of 12th-century Gothic architecture.

From the time of Charlemagne (ruled 768–814), kings of what were to become France and Germany sought to revive the power and glory of the Roman empire, which had repercussions for the history of Europe and its culture. Yet, in spite of these imperial efforts, cultural fragmentation remained. The principal categories of art—Insular, Carolingian, Ottonian, Anglo-Saxon—are delineated not only by periods but by restricted geographical areas.

The middle period, c.1050–1200, is marked by relative peace and growing prosperity. The invasions of Western Europe by peoples on its frontiers came to an end. They were either repulsed or, like the Vikings, Christianized and assimilated. This was a time of land reclamation and forest clearance, of a settled feudal society and population increase. Church reform from the mid-11th century and the growing wealth of monasteries led to an increase in church patronage. New and splendid church buildings had the most striking impact. In about

1040, the chronicler Radulfus Glaber wrote of "the white mantle of churches" covering the world. The "12th-century Renaissance" lacked the self-conscious revivalism of 15th-century Italy but it did entail an intellectual revival centered on the great cathedral schools, particularly in France, and on the major monasteries.

There was much greater internationalism within Europe. Pilgrims, teachers, merchants, and, above all, senior clerics were constantly on the move. Anselm, Abbot of Bury St. Edmunds, for example, was born in Lombardy, educated at Canterbury, was Abbot of St. Saba in Rome, and Papal Legate in England and Normandy, all before he became Abbot of Bury in 1121. This internationalism profoundly affected the visual arts. Allowing for regional variations, Romanesque was the first international style in European art since the Roman period and it appears in architecture, sculpture, and painting.

The third period, c.1200–1400, is generally characterized by economic diversity and growth until the plague years, which began around 1350. Agricultural surplus led to a growth in trade and towns; a more complex society demanded literate administrators, which led to the foundation of universities and schools. The Church sought to enforce greater control of the laity, and emphasis on private devotion and lay participation in Church activities led to an increase in lay patronage of the

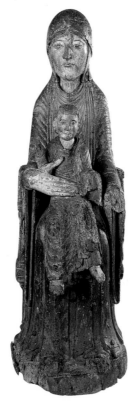

Painted wooden sculpture of the Virgin and Child, 12th century.

arts. In the 13th century, this was still largely the preserve of the aristocracy but by the 14th century, it had spread to the gentry and the trading classes, as individuals and in confraternities. Lay scriptoria also replaced those of monasteries in the production of illuminated manuscripts.

It seems likely that this growth in lay patronage was a major factor in the gradual change from the hieratic, spiritual art of the 12th century to the naturalism of later medieval art. The Virgin and Child ceases to be a stern and remote cult image and becomes a mother and child engaged in a human relationship. For the Passion of Christ, the faithful were urged in Franciscan writings of the 13th century to contemplate the agony and humiliation suffered by the Savior and saints, depicted in gory and inspiring detail.

The fifteen objects in this chapter represent a variety of categories in terms of chronology, country of origin, material, and subject matter. What they have in common is an imposing presence, an artistic mastery, for which they were chosen to convey the power and impact of medieval art.

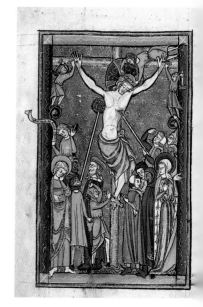

Christ Suffering from the Huth Psalter in the British Library.

The Man, Symbol of Saint Matthew

THIS FULL-PAGE MINIATURE immediately precedes the text of Matthew in the Book of Durrow, the earliest illuminated Gospels to survive complete in Western book illumination. The four symbols of the Evangelists—man (Matthew), lion (Mark), bull (Luke), and eagle (John)—were derived from beasts in the vision of Ezekiel (Ezekiel 1: 5–14) and in the Apocalypse of Saint John (Revelation 4: 4–8). Their link with the Evangelists was first expressed by Irenaeus, Bishop of Lyons, in the 2nd century, who also allied them to the four regions of the cosmos and four winds that symbolize the worldwide spread of the Gospels.

Apart from the evangelist symbols, all the miniatures in the Book of Durrow are entirely nonfigurative, consisting of carpet pages of plaited interlace, spirals, and geometric forms usually embodying one or several crosses. Here, too, the emphasis is on decoration. The spiral forms of the frame are Celtic in origin, whereas the checkerboard patterns on the dress are close to Anglo-Saxon metalwork, comparable with the finds of the 7th-century Sutton Hoo ship burial. The carpet pages demonstrate the artist's command of a large repository of decorative motifs and his outstanding esthetic sensibility in composing them, but this is balanced by his extreme reluctance to come to terms with the human figure. The man, while unforgettably monumental, is one of the least human of beings in post-Classical Western art. Only the geometrically constructed head and the feet protrude beyond the rigidly outlined, bell-shaped, checkered cape that covers the body. It may be that the hairstyle represents the tonsure of Irish monks, for which the front of the head was shaved, but this is speculation. The nearest parallels to this figure are in Irish and Pictish carvings.

The book was apparently in the monastery of Durrow in County Offaly, Ireland, in the late 11th century, but its place of origin has been a matter of considerable dispute and there is still no agreement as to whether it was produced in Ireland or Northumbria. Iona, a small island off the west coast of Scotland, where Saint Columba founded a monastery in about 563, has been suggested as a possible place of origin, but this is no more than a reasonable compromise solution.

THE BOOK OF DURROW

☙

IRELAND OR NORTHUMBRIA

C. 675

In considering the origin of the Book of Durrow and other manuscripts in this tradition, modern concepts of nationalism and national boundaries should be set aside. In the later 6th century, Aidan was king of the Dal Riada, a people whose lands covered northeastern Ulster and southwestern Scotland. The Northumbrian king Oswald and his brother Oswiu had lived among the Dal Riada, and Iona lay in the kingdom. It was above all from Iona that Irish monasticism exerted its profound influence on Northumbrian religious practice and culture. Irish monasticism was characterized by its asceticism, its fervor, and its learning. For the monks, the strict penal discipline and ascetic way of life followed the rules of Saint Columba and Saint Columbanus, and not the more widespread rule of Saint Benedict.

In a wider cultural perspective, Ireland differed fundamentally from Britain and Gaul in having never been colonized by the Romans, and its art remained resplendent in a non-Classical, nonfigurative tradition. In Northumbria, however, there had been a tradition of Roman figural sculpture. This classicism in architecture and the visual arts was reinforced in the 7th century when the Anglo-Saxon population was missionized from Rome and church leaders established links with Gaul and Italy.

At the Synod of Whitby in 664, King Oswiu of Northumbria decided to follow Roman rather than Irish church customs, but Irish Christianity and culture continued to play an important part in Northumbria. Indeed, it is precisely this dualism of the Celtic and the Classical traditions which marks the 7th and 8th centuries as the golden age of Northumbrian culture, encompassing the art of the Lindisfarne Gospels and the Classically inspired carvings of the Ruthwell cross.

The Book of Durrow is very much a work on the Irish side of this equation. Yet it is likely that, for his images of the evangelist symbols, the Durrow artist followed an exemplar from Italy or elsewhere in the Mediterranean area. It is probable that the Irish monasteries, renowned for their ascetic lifestyle, produced such luxurious Gospel books because of their liturgical importance, since they were carried in the procession of the Holy Gospel and, after the reading, were laid on the altar as a symbol of Christ.

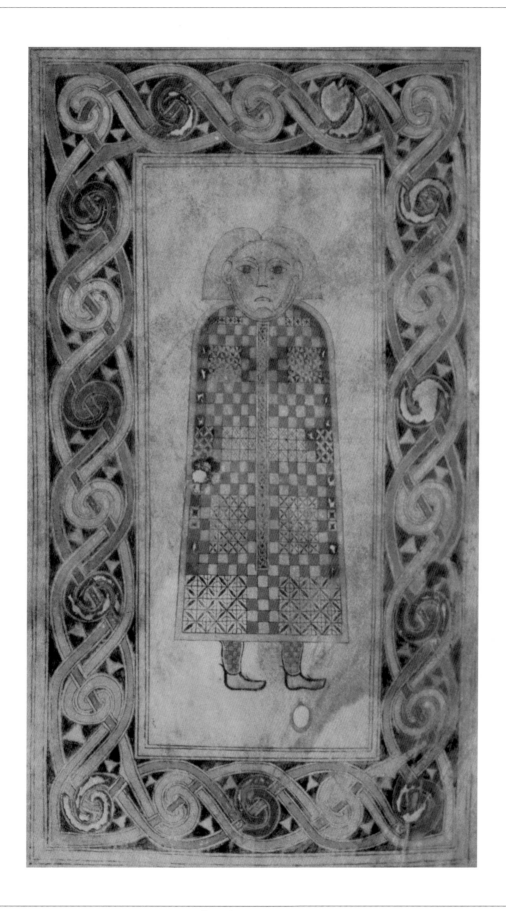

c. 675 | *manuscript illumination on parchment* | page size 9½ x 5½in (24.5 x 14.5cm) | Trinity College, Dublin (MS A.4.5)

The Four Evangelists with their Symbols

THIS REMARKABLE ILLUMINATED PAGE, which immediately precedes the Gospel text, shows the four Evangelists busily writing. The surprisingly free and painterly technique is probably directly based on models from late Antiquity; the figures are modeled in color and not in line, their solid, weighty bodies seated in an illusionistic landscape indicated by rapid, sketchy brushstrokes. These Evangelists, dressed in togas, look like Classical philosophers; and the impressionistic landscape, with its bluish-green hills and pink sky, is inspired by Roman painting. Such illusionistic landscape emerged in Roman wall painting in the 1st century B.C., and we know of it from survivals found in Rome, Pompeii, and Herculaneum, but the Carolingian artist who produced this miniature probably derived the technique from late Classical book illumination. The Evangelist symbols—as in all Gospels, a man for Matthew, lion for Mark, bull for Luke, and eagle for John—are embedded in the hills above the figures and are all holding scrolls. Underdrawing indicates that the artist originally intended to add architectural backgrounds behind the Evangelists. The frame, with its gilt scrollwork and precious stones, is similar to Carolingian goldsmiths' work.

THE AACHEN GOSPELS

&

AACHEN, COURT OF CHARLEMAGNE

C. 800–820

This is one of a small group of manuscripts, which includes the Coronation Gospels of c. 790–800 (Vienna, Hofburg) and the Xanten Gospels of c. 810 (Brussels, Bibliothèque Royale), produced at Charlemagne's court at Aachen in Germany and illuminated in this very Classical style. Most Carolingian painting is indebted to Classical art, in contrast to the non-Classical tradition exemplified by the Book of Durrow, yet these three manuscripts appear much closer to their late Roman source than most Carolingian illumination, including even the other works of the court school at Aachen, and it is conceivable that they are the work of Italian or Greek artists employed at Charlemagne's court. These artists would have had the best opportunity to work directly from Classical models. The Classical style was particularly influential on the Carolingian school at Rheims in France, and from there its influence spread to England. The Aachen Gospels never left the Palatine chapel at Aachen for which it was, in all likelihood, produced.

Charlemagne (c. 742–814) succeeded his father Pippin, King of the Franks, in 768, becoming sole ruler on the death of his brother in 771. For some two decades he fought bitter campaigns to extend his kingdom into Germany and Lombardy. In 794, his fighting days over, he began to build a grand residence at Aachen. Hitherto the court had been itinerant, with royal residences at Frankfurt, Forscheim, and Basle, but there was no proper palace before the one at Aachen. Charlemagne's status as successor to the Roman emperors was formally recognized when he was crowned Emperor in Rome on Christmas Day 800.

This proclamation of the restoration of the Roman Empire was accompanied by a drive to forge a degree of unity among the very different peoples of the new empire, some of whom were never colonized by the Romans and had only recently converted to Christianity. A central part of this drive was the establishment of conformity of religious practice, and Charlemagne sent for books from Rome and commissioned scholars to correct existing manuscripts. The English theologian Alcuin of York, one of the outstanding scholars called to Charlemagne's court, attempted to establish a uniform Sacramentary (the liturgical book of the Mass) based on the Roman model, while a collection of canon law was brought from Rome in 787.

The body of richly produced Carolingian manuscripts, finely illuminated in a Classical style, forms part of the project of *Renovatio imperii romanorum* (Restoration of the Roman Empire) of Charlemagne and his successors. These books were clearly and beautifully written in a reformed script, the Carolingian minuscule, which was based on late Classical cursive and which in turn was to be revived by Italian humanists during the Renaissance and remain standard to the present day. They were produced at major monasteries, particularly Tours and Rheims, as well as at the court. Nor was it only religious books that were copied from late Roman models. Many illustrated secular books, including, for example, astronomical texts, herbals, and the comedies of the Roman dramatist Terence (?190–159 B.C.), owe their survival to the policies of Charlemagne and the activity of Carolingian scribes and illuminators throughout the 9th century.

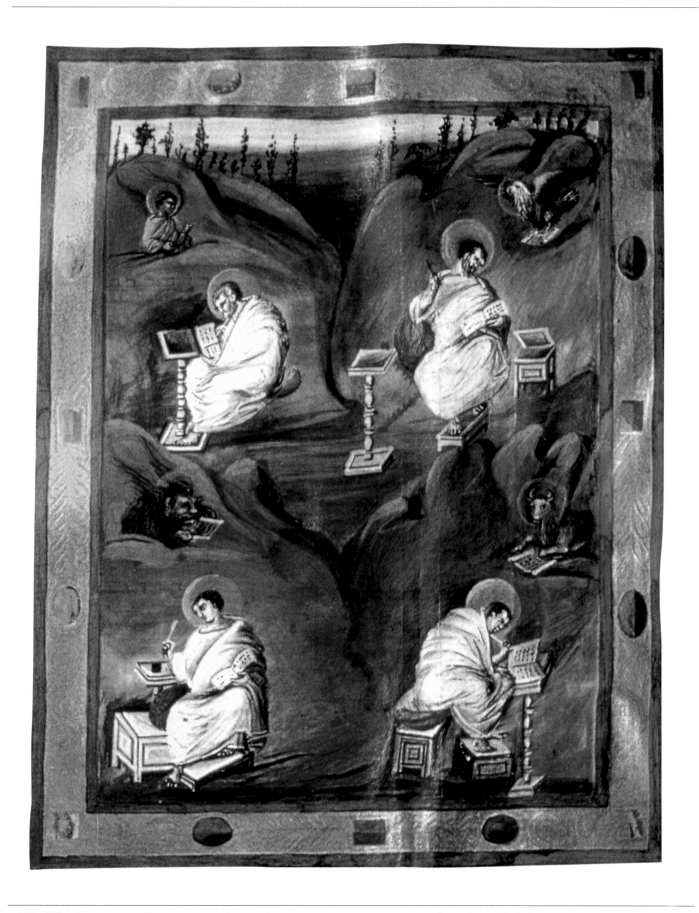

c. 800–820 | *manuscript illumination on parchment* | page size 12 x 9in (30.5 x 24cm) | Aachen Cathedral Treasury

Christ Washing the Apostles' Feet

WHEN, DURING THE LAST SUPPER, Jesus came to wash Peter's feet, Peter felt uncomfortable and said, " 'Thou shalt never wash my feet.' Jesus answered him, 'If I wash thee not, thou hast no part with me.' Simon Peter saith unto him, 'Lord, not only my feet but also my hands and my head.' " (John 13: 6–9.) It is the first part of this exchange that is illustrated here; Christ forcefully overcomes Peter's objection by explaining the importance of the foot-washing ceremony. It has remained a central part of the Maundy Thursday liturgy, and Christ's reply to Peter has been interpreted both as an example of his humility and as a symbolic reference to the sacrament of baptism.

This famous book has been assigned to the patronage of Otto III (983–1002), primarily because of its double-page miniature of the enthroned emperor receiving the homage of female figures representing the provinces of his empire: Roma, Gallia, Germania, and Sclavinia. Otto III was the fourth member of the Saxon (or Ottonian) dynasty that ruled the East Frankish or German kingdom from 919 to 1024. Otto I (reigned 936–73) had successfully extended his kingdom eastward across the Elbe and into Italy, and in 962 was crowned Holy Roman Emperor in Rome. Otto III, whose mother, Theophanu, was a Byzantine princess, was crowned emperor in Rome at the age of 13 in 996. Like Charlemagne, he laid great emphasis on the *Renovatio imperii romanorum* (see page 38) and built himself a palace on the Aventine Hill in Rome. He died at twenty-one, but his impact was considerable and his reign has been seen as a high-water mark of Ottonian rule and culture in Germany.

The flowering of manuscript illumination in the period 965–1030 was, to a considerable extent, centered on the school of Reichenau, though it is not clear whether all the manuscripts in this style were actually produced at the monastery on the island of Reichenau in Lake Constance. The Gospels of Otto III belong to a group of manuscripts associated with the scribe Liuthar, apparently working at Reichenau at the turn of the millennium. It contains twenty-nine full-page miniatures, some with two scenes per page, illustrating the Gospels. These run chronologically from the Infancy to the Resurrection and are

GOSPEL BOOK OF OTTO III

∾

REICHENAU

C. 998–1001

spread at intervals throughout the four Gospels, thus providing a coherent and continuous account of the life of Christ and unifying, in pictorial form, the separate texts of the Evangelists. In these paintings, the three-dimensional modeling and the atmospheric coloring of the sky in pastel shades of pink and blue demonstrate the survival of some of the classicism of Carolingian art, yet it is a classicism transformed into an essentially expressive, religious, and transcendental art. The emphasis is on the figure of Christ and the eye contact and gesture conveying his stern words to overcome Peter's reluctance. He points with two very extended fingers while securely holding the apron or towel with which he intends to wash Peter's feet.

The basic iconography had been standard since Early Christian times, and instructive comparisons can be made with late Roman sarcophagi as much as with Ottonian manuscripts. A sarcophagus dating from about 400 in the museum in Arles, France, shows Peter, with his left foot over the water basin, facing Christ, who stands before him. Yet the Ottonian illuminator and his immediate predecessors have transformed the scene. Where the two figures are shown on an equal plane with minimal gestures in the Roman relief, the central emphasis is now on Christ's prominence in the dramatic conversation with Peter. The earlier Ottonian version in the *Codex Egberti* of 977–93 (Stadtbibliothek, Trier, MS 24), which appears to have been copied from the same model, lacks the gold background which here highlights the central figure of Christ. This miniature brilliantly demonstrates both the tenacious continuity of traditional compositions and also the Ottonian artist's inventiveness. The basic scheme derives from Early Christian models, which were often filtered to the 10th century through Carolingian models, yet the very essence of the miniature, with its emphasis on the power of Christian teaching, is medieval.

This manuscript, which is resplendent in a golden cover studded with gems, appears to have been inherited by Otto's successor, Henry II, who gave it to the Cathedral of Bamberg which he founded in 1007. With the Napoleonic secularization of 1803, it passed to the Bavarian State Library in Munich.

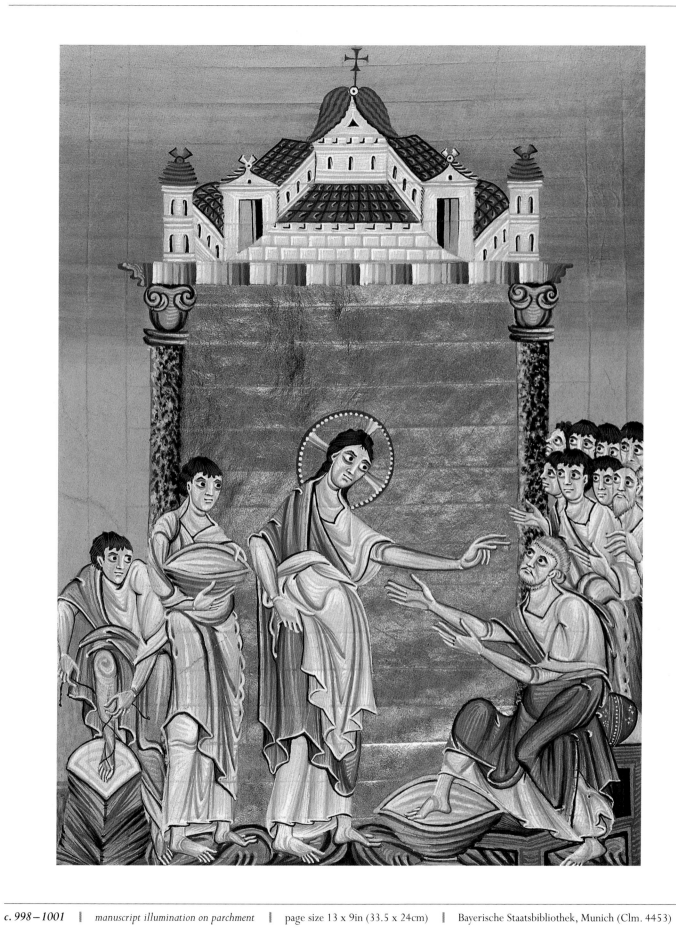

c. 998–1001 | *manuscript illumination on parchment* | page size 13 x 9in (33.5 x 24cm) | Bayerische Staatsbibliothek, Munich (Clm. 4453)

The Crucifixion with the Virgin Mary and Saint John

THE OLD TESTAMENT Book of Psalms played an important part in Jewish liturgy, and consequently the singing of psalms took on a similar role in Christian liturgy from the 4th century A.D. Indeed, in the Middle Ages the Psalter, which contained various prayers and hymns and a litany, or list of saints, as well as the psalms themselves, became the most important liturgical book, rivaled only by the Gospels. In the Western Church, psalms played a major part in the service of the Mass, in the daily Offices, and in private prayer. Theologians interpreted the psalms as prophetic of the life of Christ, and consequently it became the practice, particularly in England, to preface the Psalter with New Testament pictures. These are not strictly illustrations of the content of the Psalter; rather, they provide a visual amplification of the psalms as Christian prayers.

The Ramsey Psalter's depiction of the Crucifixion, which immediately precedes the Psalter text, is one of the earliest examples of this trend. It is drawn in fine brown outlines, firmer on the figure of Christ, more flickering and broken on the Virgin and Saint John, and the draperies are shaded in translucent washes of pale red and blue. For the violent agitation of the draperies, the artist was indebted to the Carolingian school of Rheims and in particular to the famous Utrecht Psalter which was in Canterbury at this period. Yet the method of tinted outline was, as far as we know, a new invention. It is found in four other late-10th-century manuscripts that have been attributed to the same artist; two of them were produced in continental monasteries, probably St. Bertin and Fleury, which suggests that the artist was a professional, perhaps a clerk in minor orders or a layman rather than a monk, who worked in England and on the Continent. The script, decoration, and textual features indicate that this Psalter was written at one of the monasteries in Winchester; however, there is evidence in the litany of saints that suggests it was prepared for the use of the Abbey of Ramsey in Huntingdonshire.

In the early Middle Ages, Christ on the cross was most often shown as Ruler and Judge, upright and with open eyes. This image, by contrast, shows an alternative perception that was to

THE RAMSEY PSALTER

☙

PROBABLY WRITTEN AT WINCHESTER

LATE TENTH CENTURY

become increasingly popular: the human, suffering Christ with whose agony the viewer can readily identify. He hangs on the cross, his head slumped on his shoulder and blood spurting from his wounds. The presence of Mary and John is only mentioned in the Gospel of Saint John, which describes how Jesus entrusted his mother to the care of his favorite disciple (John 19: 26–27). John is inscribing his scroll, and in translation the text reads: "This is the disciple who beareth witness of these things" (John 21: 24), stressing the importance of what was seen as an eyewitness account. Modern biblical scholarship distinguishes between the disciple John and the author of the fourth Gospel and the Apocalypse, but in Early Christian and medieval times, they were seen as the same person.

Whereas Saint John, bearing witness, looks up at Christ, the Virgin is shown in deep sorrow, her head sunk on to her veil. This posture was used for mourners in Classical and Early Christian art, but the figure here expresses intense grief. Like the human, suffering Christ, the sorrowing Virgin is in line with the affective piety of later Anglo-Saxon prayers. The drawing is intended for religious meditation as in the emotive prayers of Saint Anselm, written some decades later, in which the Virgin is described as sobbing beneath the cross with tears streaming down her face.

The monastic culture that had produced the Gospels of Durrow (see pages 36–37) and Lindisfarne, and equally magnificent books at Canterbury, did not survive the Viking invasions that devastated the country in the 9th and 10th centuries. King Alfred turned the tide in the wars of 892–96 and embarked on a program to raise the standard of education, especially of the clergy, but it was not until the monastic revival associated with St. Dunstan, Archbishop of Canterbury; St. Aethelwold, Bishop of Winchester; and St. Oswald, Bishop of Worcester, in the reign of King Edgar (959–75) that the ground was prepared for the artistic flowering of late Anglo-Saxon England. Most of the artefacts in metals, embroidery, and jewelry did not survive the Norman Conquest, but the tradition of outline drawing, of which the Ramsey Psalter is arguably the finest representative, marks a high point in the history of English art.

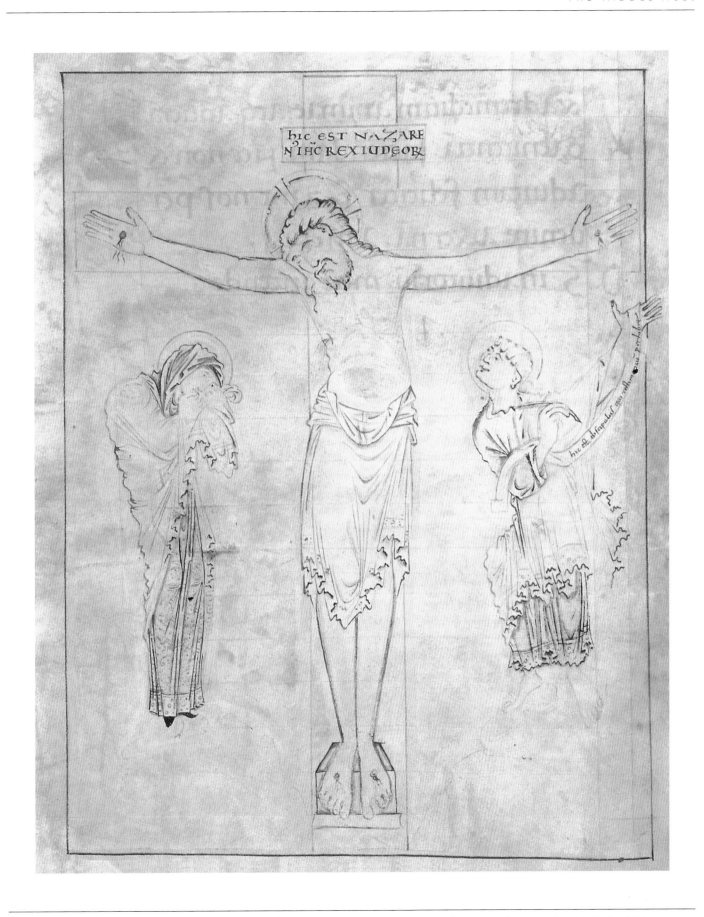

hic est NAZARE
N IHC REX IUDEOR

Late 10th century | *tinted line drawing on parchment* | page size 11 x 9in (28.5 x 24cm) | British Library, London (MS Harley 2904)

The Raising of Lazarus *(detail)*

ONLY JOHN'S GOSPEL (John 11: 1–45) describes the Raising of Lazarus, Christ's most stupendous miracle, demonstrating God's power over death itself. While performing the miracle, Christ explains its nature to Martha, Lazarus's sister, while Mary, the other sister, prostrates herself at his feet. Two helpers, untying Lazarus's bandages, ostentatiously hold their noses for "by this time he stinketh, he has been dead four days." The small buildings in the foreground are tombs, denoting the cemetery.

The composition, including a group of onlookers behind Christ, conforms closely both to the text and to the standard pictorial tradition. As a prefiguration of the Ascension, the scene had been commonly depicted since the 3rd century in catacomb paintings and on sarcophagi. In Roman images, Lazarus is raised from a sepulchral building, contrary to the biblical text which states that "it was a cave and a stone lay against it." The cave is depicted from the 6th century in Eastern Christian and Byzantine art, where the kneeling sisters and the attendants holding their noses also become standard. The mixture of East and West that characterizes south Italian art can be seen most effectively in this detail from Sant' Angelo in Formis, which combines the Roman building with the Byzantine cave.

Stylistically, the solidly modeled draperies, revealing the body beneath, owe much to Byzantine forms, but they are stylized in linear folds. The faces also are carefully modeled in ocher with shades of green, but the crudely applied red splodges on the cheeks suggest a local tradition. The emphasis is on expressive drama rather than refinement.

Nearly a hundred biblical scenes originally decorated the abbey church of Sant' Angelo in Formis. Only about sixty remain, but this is still one of the most complete medieval Italian fresco cycles to have survived. A large enthroned Christ dominates the apse, and the Last Judgment covers the western wall. The Old Testament scenes decorated the aisles; the New Testament in three registers covered the walls above the arcades in the nave. Again, following tradition, the narrative moves from left to right along each register, starting at the left (north) wall. These biblical compositions are essentially the same as those in

OLD AND NEW TESTAMENT FRESCO CYCLE

☙

SANT' ANGELO IN FORMIS

C. 1072–1087

books, but they occupy a public, rather than a private, space and were seen by a large audience of lay as well as monastic worshippers. Behind Sant' Angelo in Formis lies the immeasurably grander institution of its parent, the Abbey of Monte Cassino, founded in the 6th century by Saint Benedict himself, but sadly destroyed many times in its long history. Monte Cassino was rebuilt in the 1070s by Abbot Desiderius, who brought craftsmen from Byzantium, particularly for the mosaics and the marble floor. In 1072, the Norman Richard of Aversa, Prince of Capua, gave the monastery and church of Sant' Angelo to Monte Cassino, and Desiderius restored it and commissioned the extensive picture cycle. He is depicted in the apse offering the model of his church to Christ enthroned. He has a square halo, usually reserved for living holy figures, so the date of the paintings is given as 1072–87, the latter being the year of his death, although they may have been completed a few years later. To what extent the Sant' Angelo frescoes echo those that were once in the atrium at Monte Cassino remains uncertain. Certainly, their style is similar to that of the illuminated manuscripts produced at Monte Cassino, and the patronage of Desiderius indicates a close link between the monasteries. Yet Sant' Angelo in Formis is part of the wider history of south Italian wall painting as well as being an important monument.

Indeed, no simplistic explanation of "Byzantine influence" can do justice to the complexity and variety of south Italian culture in the Middle Ages. The Lombards had been established there since the 6th century; the Byzantine reconquest under Justinian had been reinforced by the Macedonian dynasty (867–1025), particularly in Apulia; the Normans settled from the 1030s and subordinated the Greek administration and some of the Lombard principalities. In addition, both the pope and the emperor laid claim to the overlordship of the area and contributed to the shifting alliances. The Norman nobles never became a centralized force as they did in England under William the Conqueror, and Richard of Aversa seized the Lombard principality of Capua in 1058. His gift of Sant' Angelo in Formis was due to his desire to ally himself with the powerful Abbot of Monte Cassino.

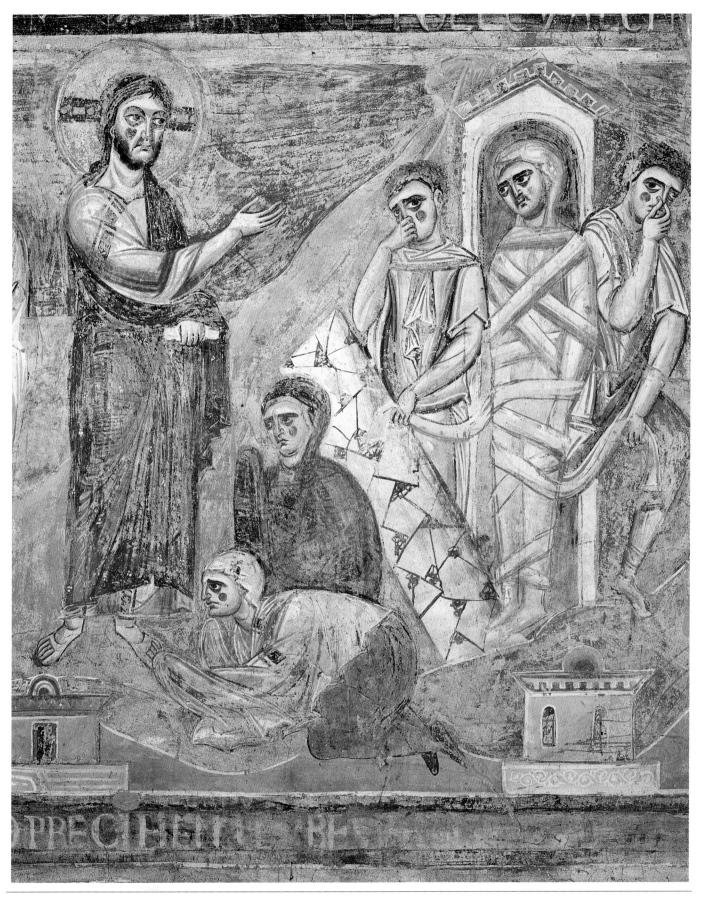

c. 1072–87 | *wall painting* | Sant' Angelo in Formis, near Capua

Saint Matthew and the Nativity

SAINT MATTHEW, whose portrait faces the opening of his Gospel, is shown in the Byzantine tradition as an older man with gray hair and beard. He is copying from the scroll on the lectern on to a sheet on his lap. On the desk there are two knives and an inkwell; the Evangelist is dipping his pen into red ink. Within the arch above are the Nativity and the Annunciation to the Shepherds. Grouping these scenes with Saint Matthew is based on liturgical grounds: the opening part of his Gospel was read on the Feast of Christmas.

The Greek *Codex Ebnerianus*—named after the 18th-century owner, H.W. Ebner von Eschenbach of Nürnberg—which contains eleven such miniatures of Evangelists and authors of the Epistles, marks one of the high points of Byzantine illumination in the period of the Comnene dynasty (1057–1180). The solidly modeled bodies enveloped in voluminous draperies demonstrate a close understanding of Classical form. This was developed from the revival of Classical and Early Christian art inaugurated by the emperors of the Macedonian dynasty (867–1056) in the period after Iconoclasm when icons and religious images were destroyed. The enthusiasm for works of antiquity was subsequently modified by more hieratic, spiritual concerns, but Classical norms of modeling the human face and body were never completely abandoned in Byzantine art. Typical of Comnene illumination are the tiny figures, meticulously painted in brilliant colors on a unifying gold background. The artist, whose style is recognized in several other manuscripts, worked for members of the imperial family, yet it is not known whether this book was written in a monastery or in the court scriptorium. This period of Byzantine art, which had been so influential in the West, came to an abrupt end with the sacking of Constantinople by western crusaders in 1204.

Portraits of Evangelists in Gospel Books, derived from Classical Roman author portraits, became standard from the 6th century and, indeed, formed the most prevalent type of figure illustration in Byzantine manuscripts. The composition here, varying only in details, was absolutely standard in Byzantine art of the high Middle Ages.

GREEK NEW TESTAMENT

☙

CONSTANTINOPLE

C. 1120–1140

The Nativity has been one of the most popular scenes in Christian art, but it is only briefly reported in the Gospels (Luke 2: 6–14), and interest in it only arose in the 4th century on the introduction of the Feast of Christmas. The earliest images contained the ox and the ass, even though they are not mentioned in the Gospels. Their origin lies in Isaiah's text: "The ox knoweth his owner and the ass his master's crib; but Israel does not know..." (Isaiah 1: 3). Origen, one of the earliest Fathers of the Christian Church, connected this passage with the manger at Bethlehem, and the point was taken up in subsequent biblical commentaries. They identified the ox with the Jews and the ass with the heathens; the Son of God lies between them, freeing the world from Jewish law and heathen idolatry. Their presence in every depiction of the Nativity, down to the present day, shows the power of the ideas of commentators over and above the biblical text itself.

In most respects, the medieval Byzantine iconography of the Nativity derives from imagery developed by the 6th century, possibly in Palestine or Syria. It was set in a cave, which was again derived from biblical commentary—as opposed to the wooden stable that remained standard in the West—with Mary resting and Joseph seated, pensive, to one side. The Child lies in an altarlike structure, a reference to the Eucharist. The legendary motif of the midwife bathing the Child, mentioned in the *Protoevangelium* of James (A.D. 200), is an allusion to the humanity of Christ and looks forward to the baptism. Finally, the angel announcing the holy birth to the shepherds was added to the scene in the late 9th century and remained a regular feature from that time. Indeed, the iconography of the Nativity, like that of all the main scenes from the life of Christ, remained standard throughout medieval Byzantium. This was due to centralized Church control; in 787, the Council of Nicea, which ruled that images were lawful after the period of iconoclasm, decreed that strict control should be exercised over the subject and form of religious art. The *Codex Ebnerianus* was still prized in 1391 when the scribe Joasaph glossed and extended the text for liturgical use in the Hodegon Monastery in Constantinople.

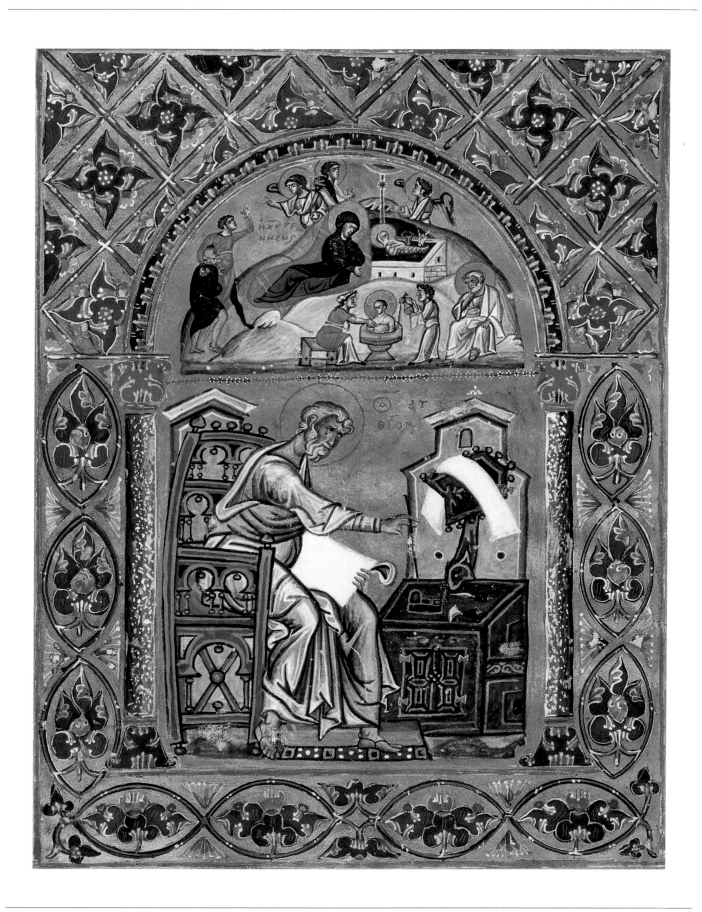

c. 1120–40 | *manuscript illumination on parchment* | page size 8 x 6in (20.5 x 15.5cm) | Bodleian Library, Oxford (MS Auct. T inf.1.10)

The Adoration of the Magi

THE THREE MAGI, crowned, offer their gifts of gold, frankincense, and myrrh to the Child, while the star that guided them is shown above their heads (Matthew 2: 9–12). The Virgin and Child are on a much larger scale, and the Virgin's imposing presence is enhanced by her severe stare and her melancholy expression. She wears a jeweled crown over a pleated linen headdress and holds a lily (used as a symbol of her purity from the time of the theologian Bede in the early 8th century) in her right hand, while the Child blesses the approaching Magi. The scene is set within a substantial architectural framework. Below on the right, the palm tree is an ancient symbol of Paradise and of the Church, but the sagittarius (the archer on the far left) and the biting animals below the main scene are, in all likelihood, purely decorative, as in a number of English Bibles from the mid-12th century (see pages 54–55).

Epiphany was one of the great feasts of the Church from the earliest times, and the Adoration of the Magi was therefore one of the most popular subjects of Early Christian and medieval art. At first, the Magi were shown wearing Phrygian caps, denoting their Eastern origin and adopted from late Antique scenes of barbarians paying homage to Roman emperors, but from the 10th century onwards they wear crowns and are thought of as kings. The architectural framing arch occurs in Ottonian art, indeed, in the Gospels of Otto III (see pages 40–41); what is new here is the lovingly depicted building, and the owl and the male figure on the roof. The figure originally blew a horn, but this has broken off. Such horn-blowing figures, representing the watchmen on town towers and bringing the secular world into a religious image, occur particularly in French art in the early 12th century. Like the elaborate and prominent church building above the Virgin's head, such figures convey an urban setting that is not indicated in the biblical text.

Ivories, carved by professional lay sculptors, had been used to convey Christian imagery on all manner of artefacts from the 4th century; indeed, these provide some of the earliest surviving depictions of biblical scenes. However, unlike illuminated manuscripts, which contain the evidence of their text, and wall paintings, which are usually still *in situ*, most surviving ivories are dismembered masterpieces, providing us with no concrete evidence of their origin. Consequently, they are often subject to widely different interpretations as to date and place of origin, and this unusual piece provides a good example of such a dispute.

This remarkable carving was long catalogued as English or Anglo-Norman on the basis of stylistic similarities—for example, the pleated draperies fanning out at the hem—with Anglo-Norman illumination of the late 11th century. Equally, the geometric ornament on the building was compared with the actual decoration on Norman and English churches of the period around 1100. However, in 1960, a Spanish scholar, Carmen Bernis, attributed the piece to northern Spain on the grounds of close similarities she had identified with Spanish works. In particular, the Virgin's cap is paralleled only in Spain, for example, on the late 11th-century tomb of Doña Sancha in Jaca. More generally, a comparison was made with a Spanish whalebone plaque of the Virgin and Child that is now in the Louvre and with the tympanum above the doorway of the church of Santa Maria at Uncastillo. Although, when compared to the Adoration of the Magi panel, these are much inferior in workmanship and in their power of expression, the similarities were felt to be significant enough to suggest a Spanish provenance for the carving.

Unfortunately, the material provides no help in this controversy. Whalebone, like walrus (or morse) ivory, was a northern substitute for elephant tusks for such carvings. Yet the whale was equally at home in the North Sea and the Atlantic, and whalebone was carved in northern France and England as much as in northern Spain. Spain is now thought to be the likeliest place of origin, but the piece remains unique and will probably continue to defy more precise placing. The same applies to its purpose and function. Carved ivory panels were most frequently used individually on book covers and reliquaries or in groups on altar frontals. Yet the bulk and irregular shape of this whalebone panel makes it difficult to visualize it in such settings, and it has been suggested that it was perhaps used as a portable devotional image, easily transported and ever inspiring.

DEVOTIONAL CARVED PANEL

∽

PROBABLY SPANISH

EARLY TWELFTH CENTURY

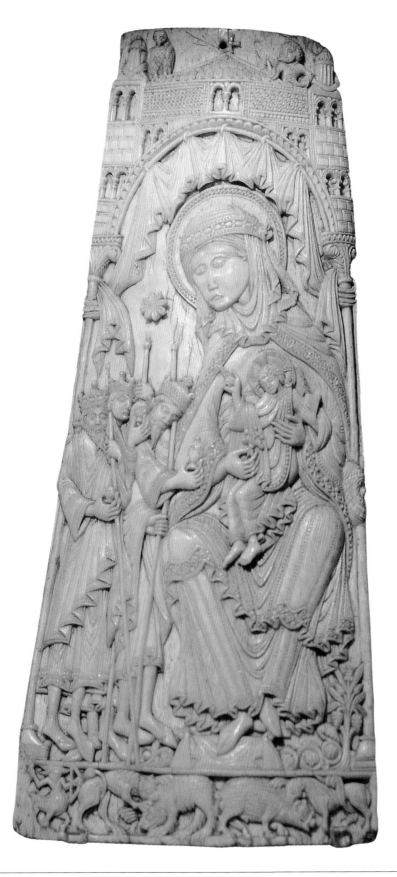

Early 12th century | *whalebone* | height 14in (36.5cm), width (at the base) 6in (16cm) | Victoria & Albert Museum, London

Christ Adored by the Twenty-four Elders of the Apocalypse

THE ABBEY OF MOISSAC, north of Toulouse, was a 7th-century foundation. It was at a low ebb in the 1040s: the collapse of the abbey church in 1042 was followed by the disappearance of the abbot some three years later. The revival of its fortunes dates from 1053 with its submission to the great Burgundian Abbey of Cluny. It benefited from Cluny's prestige and from the monastic reforms and partial freeing from lay control which submission to Cluny entailed. The cloister and church were largely rebuilt under Abbot Hunauld (1072–85) and Abbot Ansquitil (1085–1115), and the south porch was apparently completed under the next abbot, Roger (1115–31).

The south porch is now lower than street level, but within the porch the carved tympanum above the church doorway retains a remarkable visual impact. A dominant figure of Christ, crowned and holding a book in his left hand and blessing with his right, is accompanied by the four living creatures of Saint John's vision and two seraphim, and is adored by the Twenty-four Elders. The Elders, seated, crowned, and holding viols and cups (Revelation 5: 8), are similar figures but differ remarkably in posture and attitude. They all look up at Christ, and their twisting movements contrast with the massive immobility of this central figure. A sophisticated composition, in which a multitude of figures is squeezed into the curving frame, is achieved by a sculptural technique of deep undercutting; the limbs and heads of the smaller figures are almost completely detached from the background. As a further demonstration of technical mastery, this composition was carved on twenty-three stone slabs, not necessarily corresponding with individual figures.

The solid forms, the expressive, spiritual faces, and the linear pattern of the draperies are typical of Romanesque sculpture in general, and of Toulouse and northern Spain in particular. More unusually, the rosettes below the tympanum can be compared with Islamic ornament current in Moslem Spain.

In essence, the central group consists of the traditional composition of Christ in Majesty with the four Evangelist symbols, which are derived from the four living creatures of Revelation Four. The beasts hold books, except for the eagle

SOUTH PORCH TYMPANUM

ↄ

MOISSAC ABBEY CHURCH

C. 1125

which is differentiated in holding a scroll, a symbol of St. John's priority. The adoration of the Twenty-four Elders illustrates Revelation Four: "and upon the thrones I saw four and twenty elders sitting arrayed in white garments; and on their heads crowns of gold." Only the two six-winged angels to the left and right of Christ are not part of this scene, and they have been interpreted as the two seraphim of Isaiah's vision (Isaiah 6), but it has proved difficult to explain why the one on Christ's right holds a closed scroll and the other one an open scroll. Indeed, the interpretation of the precise theological content of the tympanum has been controversial, and it is now often called the Second Coming, prior to the Last Judgment, although for the lay viewer the essential message was the adoration of the triumphant Christ.

Below the tympanum, representing the Old and New Testaments, are reliefs of Jeremiah and Saint Paul on the central pillar and Isaiah and Saint Peter on the right and left door jambs. On the walls of the porch there are further carvings representing the Infancy of Christ and the Last Judgment, which were doubtless intended to be viewed in conjunction with the tympanum.

The early Middle Ages was rich in freestanding sculpture, particularly crosses and crucifixes, but examples of monumental architectural sculpture are rare before the 11th century. Such large-scale works blossomed in the period around 1100, particularly in the economically advanced regions of Burgundy, the Rhineland, and Lombardy, and along the pilgrimage routes, notably to Santiago de Compostela, on which Moissac was a staging post. The theological complexity, compositional sophistication, and technical mastery of the Moissac tympanum give it an important place in this development, a generation before the sculpture of Saint-Denis and Chartres.

Images of the triumphant Christ, hitherto depicted within churches in the apse or dome, were now taken to the façades and doorways, entering the public space of the lay viewer. At Moissac, the tympanum is within the porch, but the intention to proclaim its triumphal theme beyond its walls is confirmed by the triumphal archway—very like a Roman triumphal arch—which encloses the porch and faces the secular world outside.

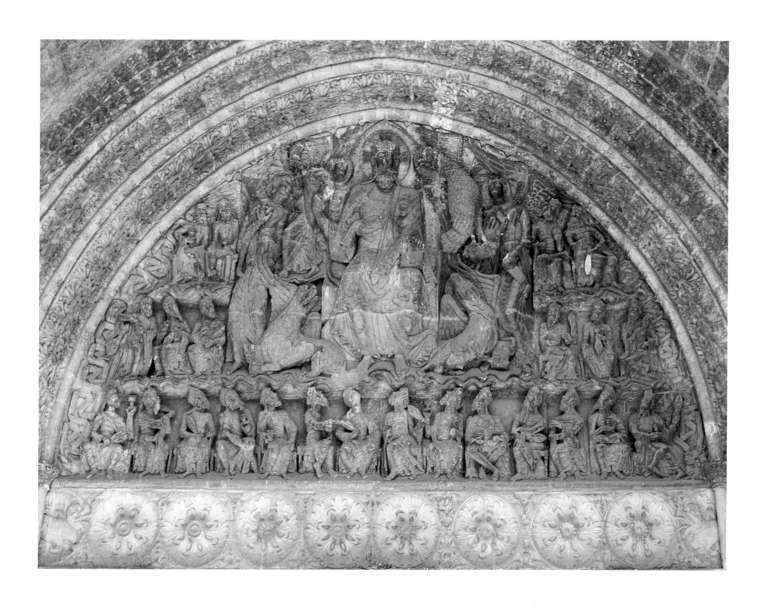

c. 1125 | *stone* | diameter 224in (568cm) | Moissac Abbey Church, near Toulouse

Scenes of Moses Teaching

MOSES EXPOUNDING THE LAW after his descent from Mount Sinai is the principal event at the beginning of the book of Deuteronomy, to which this miniature is the frontispiece. Aaron is identified by his rod and Moses by his horns. The latter first occurred in English art in the early 11th century, apparently as a visual rendering of the Anglo-Saxon "he was gehyrned," which misinterpreted the Latin *cornuta*, here meaning "with rays" but also translatable as "horned." Aaron is depicted as the younger brother; this is contrary to the biblical text but follows a tradition of showing the more venerable status of Moses.

Moses expounding the Law of the Unclean Beasts (the lower panel) occurs in the middle of Deuteronomy (Deut. 14: 3–21) and may have been selected for its symbolic content. In medieval biblical commentary, God's commands to the Israelites on unclean animals had much wider meaning, referring not merely to the dietary laws but to all the customs and actions of man.

This miniature epitomizes the expressive drama and high seriousness of 12th-century religious art. Moses and Aaron, respectively Patriarch and Priest, are larger, better-looking, and more imposing in appearance than their followers. Their powerful presence and natural authority is conveyed, above all, by the severity of their gaze, which is reinforced by the dark shading around their eyes in the Byzantine manner. Equally important as a vehicle of expression are the gestures, here, as most often, of pointing with an elegant and enormously extended index finger. The sense of movement created by eye contact and gesture is reinforced by the dominant drapery folds whose rhythmical, clinging curves serve both to indicate the human body beneath and to provide a surface pattern for the composition. It is these drapery patterns which, above all, differentiate Romanesque forms from the similar ones of Ottonian painting, as in the Gospel Book of Otto III (pages 40–41). Another difference is the way that space is limited to the square background panels in green and blue, whereas the Ottonians had retained something of the pink and blue sky of Roman painting. In the Bury Bible miniature, nothing is allowed to compete with the principal figures.

THE BURY BIBLE

℅

BURY ST. EDMUNDS

C. 1135

We are better informed about the origin of this Bible than about most manuscripts of the time, thanks to its prominence in various monastic chronicles of the Abbey of Bury St. Edmunds in Suffolk, England. We are told that Hervey the sacrist, who was the brother of Prior Talbot, "bore all the expenses … for the writing of a large Bible and for having it incomparably illuminated by Master Hugo," and set aside certain rents to cover the considerable costs of such a venture. The period in office of the brothers suggests a date of about 1135 for the Bible. Originally, there were two volumes; the surviving volume has 714 pages, indicating a total of about 1,400 pages for the complete work. Given the size of the book, the cost of parchment alone must have been considerable. For the paintings, special materials were acquired: "as Hugo was unable to find any suitable calf hide in these parts, he bought some parchment in Ireland."

Bury was one of the richest monasteries in England and could afford the best. The writing may have been done by monks, but there were originally up to two dozen miniatures and numerous illuminated initials in the two volumes, and Master Hugo was a layman, a professional artist, who had to be paid for his work. He is mentioned four times in the monastic records: he cast the bronze doors of the abbey church and also the great bell, and carved a cross and statues of the Virgin and Saint John for the choir stall of the church. Nothing survives of all this, but it is clear that Master Hugo was a painter, sculptor, and worker of metals—an all-round medieval man of great renown in his time.

The Bury Bible is a particularly splendid example of Romanesque Giant Bibles which emerged at the period of Church reform initiated by Gregory VII (pope 1073–85) and his immediate predecessors. Old monasteries were brought back to stricter observance and many new ones founded. A good Bible text was an essential part of this reform, since monastic constitutions of the time describe the practice of reading the whole Bible in both church and refectory in the course of a year. These stately volumes, beautifully written and illuminated, contained the word of God, fulfilled an important liturgical function, and reflected upon the status of their monastic owners.

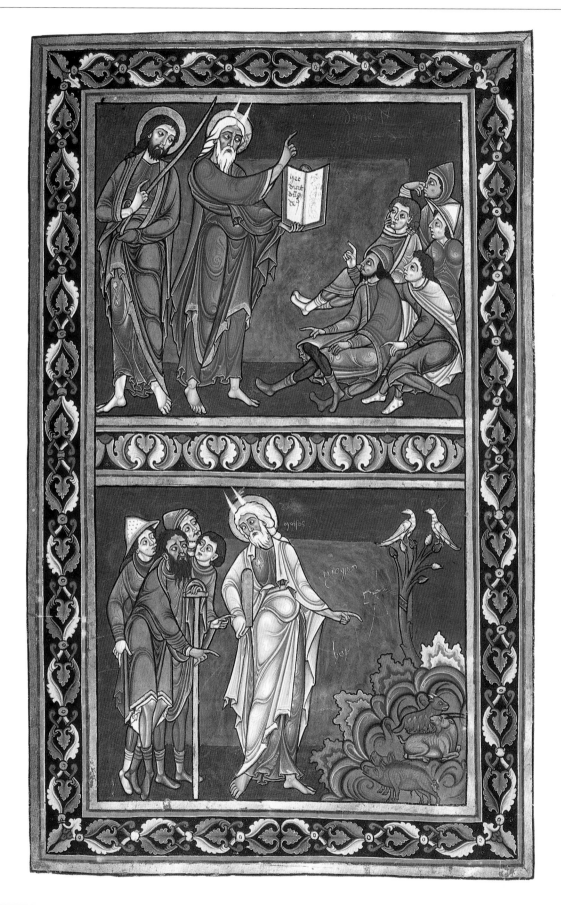

c. 1135 | *manuscript illumination on parchment* | page size 20 x 14in (51.5 x 35.5cm) | Corpus Christi College, Cambridge (MS 2)

Decorated Initial V to the Book of Job

"WHAT SIGNIFIES *these ridiculous monsters, those amazing things, horrible in their beauty and beautiful in their horror? To what purpose are these filthy monkeys, these savage lions, these monstrous centaurs ... these half- human creatures?"*
SAINT BERNARD OF CLAIRVAUX, *An Apologia for Abbot William,* 1125

Saint Bernard of Clairvaux, founder of the Cistercian Order and one of the greatest theologians of the 12th century, was writing about the carvings on the capitals of cloisters "where the brothers do their reading." But such "ridiculous monsters" appear on all manner of artefacts—goldsmiths' work, ivories, textiles, and wall paintings—as well as on stone sculpture and in manuscript illumination. This example is from an English manuscript of about 1160, but it represents a whole aspect of Romanesque art. Typically, as here, human figures, animals, and monsters are caught up in spirals of fleshy stems, sprouting leaves and blossoms. Students of 20th-century Surrealism will admire the endless transformation of these creatures: a foliage stem gradually emerges from the spiral to become the tail of a monster whose claws grasp a head, which may be its own, which in turn becomes the extended neck of another creature (or is it the same one?), which terminates in the profile of a large human head, bearded and capped with a crown of foliage. Elsewhere there are biting animals and blossoms that turn into human profiles. The man in the middle struggles in vain to escape from the tangles of vegetation in which he is enmeshed.

"What signifies?"—St. Bernard's question has remained unanswered. It has often been suggested that these images of man's battles against beasts symbolize the daily struggle against Satan. There may well be occasions when such an interpretation is justified, particularly if there is some indication in the adjoining text, but otherwise it seems too uniform an explanation for such a wide variety of images. The common characteristic shared by them all is the strict order imposed on this wholly chaotic world. At no point in this example does the decoration extend beyond the confines of the initial, however agitated the activity within these confines, and this control is typical of such decoration.

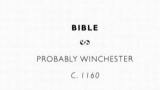

BIBLE
♋
PROBABLY WINCHESTER
C. 1160

Philosophical writings of the 12th century are replete with examples of man's search for order in a chaotic world: Alan of Lille (d. 1202) for example, describes a situation in which Nature approaches Divine Providence to plead for the creation of order in the chaos of the universe. It is precisely this imposition of order that seems to be reflected in such decorative inventions. Inventions, however, are what they remain. At a time when the principal religious themes were bound by rules and convention, these "ridiculous monsters" provided artists in all media with the chance to demonstrate their powers of invention, and it was an opportunity that was avidly taken.

The artist of this initial, who is known for obvious reasons as the Master of the Entangled Figures, worked on several manuscripts at different centers in England from the 1130s to the 1160s and was clearly an itinerant lay professional. This detail is taken from an English Romanesque Giant Bible (see page 52), although, unlike most of the others, its illumination is largely decorative, as with this splendid initial, and not illustrative. It was probably produced at Winchester, or at least it was there in the 1170s when the great Winchester Bible was corrected from this Bible's text. It is recorded as having been used for reading at meals in the refectory.

An unusual story is told of this manuscript, which serves to demonstrate the importance of these Bibles to monastic houses in the 12th century. Not long after 1180, Hugh, Prior of the Carthusian Priory of Witham in Somerset (he was later Bishop of Lincoln and canonized in 1220), asked his patron, Henry II, for help in building up a library for his new foundation. The king gave him ten silver marks to buy parchment and hire professional scribes, and also presented Witham with a complete Bible that had recently been completed for Winchester Cathedral Priory and which he had obtained from the Prior. The monks at Witham were delighted with the gift, particularly for the correctness of the text and also for the general beauty of the manuscript. However, when Saint Hugh discovered that the Bible had been acquired in this irregular way, he insisted that it should be returned to its rightful owner.

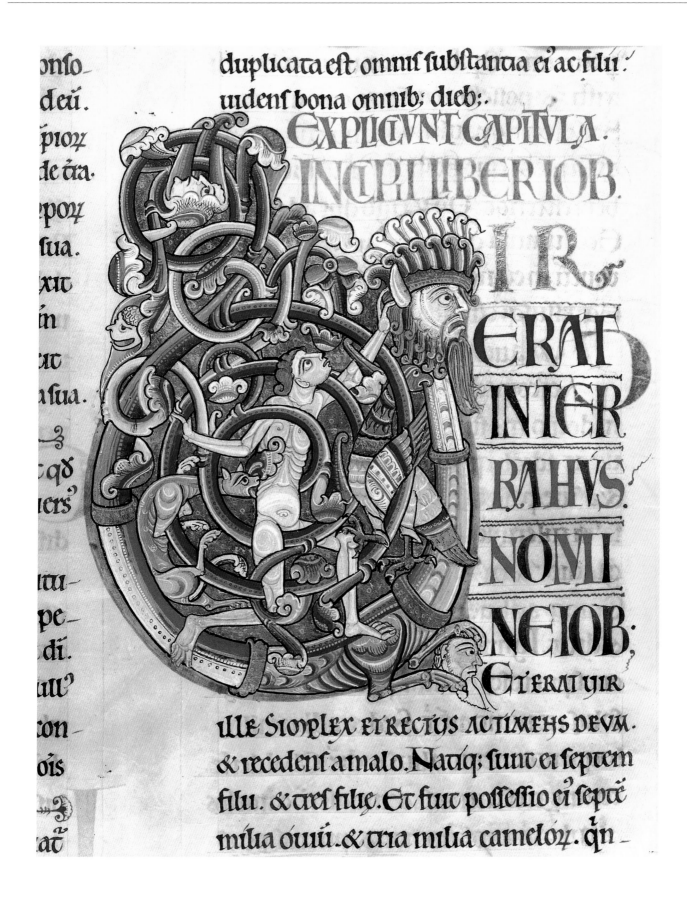

duplicata est omnis substantia ei ac filii.
uidens bona omnib; dieb;.

EXPLICVNT CAPITVLA.

INCIPT LIBER IOB.

IR
ERAT
INTER
RAHVS.
NOMI
NE IOB:
ET ERAT VIR

ILLE SIMPLEX ET RECTVS AC TIMEHS DEVM.
& recedens a malo. Natiq; sunt ei septem
filii. & tres filiç. Et fuit possessio ei septē
milia ouiū. & tria milia cameloꝝ. qn

c. 1160 | *manuscript illumination on parchment* | page size 20½ x 14in (52.5 x 36cm) | Bodleian Library, Oxford (MS Auct. E inf.1)

Typological Scenes

THE SAINT-OMER CROSS, which has lost the upper portion, was long in the Abbey of Saint-Bertin at Saint-Omer in northern France, for which it may have been made. The four Evangelists, seated in a variety of postures, support the base, which has enameled panels illustrating four Old Testament scenes prefiguring the Crucifixion: Moses and the brazen serpent (Numbers 21: 8–9), Jacob blessing the sons of Joseph (Genesis 48: 14), the mark "T" on Israelite houses at the Exodus (Exodus 12: 17), and Moses striking water from the rock (Exodus 17: 6).

The four Evangelist symbols lead to four more Old Testament prefigurations on the column: Joshua and Caleb carrying grapes from the Promised Land (Numbers 13: 23), Elijah and the widow of Sarepta (I Kings 17: 10), the marking of the "T" on the forehead of the righteous (Ezekiel 9: 4), and Isaac carrying the wood of the sacrifice (Genesis 22: 6). At the top of the pedestal are four busts, two inscribed "*Terra*" and "*Mare*" (Earth and Sea); the other two may be Air and Fire to make up the four elements, but they have also been identified as Moses, representing the Old Testament, and the centurion who witnessed the Crucifixion.

Typology, the textual interpretation of the Old Testament as the supposed forerunner of the New Testament—so that the ancient Hebrew Scriptures may be seen as witness to the salvation through Jesus Christ—is as old as Christianity itself. In the 12th century, typological picture cycles became quite commonplace, doubtless because these religious parallels were of particular and abiding interest to the leading biblical theologians of the time. According to Saint Luke's Gospel in the New Testament, Christ told the Apostles that "all things must needs be fulfilled which are written in the Laws of Moses and in the prophets and in the psalms concerning me" (Luke 24: 44). The Church Fathers followed these age-old exhortations by selecting particular passages in the Old Testament as prefiguring particular events in the New Testament.

A good example of this prefiguration is provided by the biblical story of Jacob blessing the sons of Joseph, the detail on the base of the cross shown here. Genesis 48:14 relates how Jacob blessed Ephraim, the younger son, with his right hand, an

BASE OF A CROSS

☙

REGION OF THE MEUSE

C. 1160–1170

honor which should have been accorded to the elder son, Manasseh. For the Church Fathers the meaning was clear; Jesus gave preference to the younger son just as God had given preference to the New Testament over the Old. The incident became an Old Testament type of Crucifixion, as Joseph's arms form a cross when he transposes his hands to accord the right hand to his younger son, a point which is clearly made in this image.

There are many examples of Mosan enameled crosses and portable altars with Old Testament scenes, often coupled with cosmological symbols and other allegorical figures that render complex theological ideas in visual terms. The Saint-Omer pedestal was taken to be a much reduced version of one of the most famous of all medieval artefacts, the huge cross made by goldsmiths from the Meuse region and erected by Abbot Suger in his abbey church at Saint-Denis, near Paris, in c. 1147. Unfortunately, this great cross—it was 20ft (6m) high—no longer exists, and it is probable that the Saint-Omer base is only loosely related to the Saint-Denis cross, rather than being a reduced replica. But, in itself, the Saint-Omer cross is a remarkable work.

Apart from the complexity of its imagery and its esthetic appeal, this work demonstrates the technical mastery of the medieval goldsmith. The Evangelist figures, with their individualized expressions and physical contortions, are masterpieces of bronze casting. The narrative panels around the base and the column are of champlevé enamel, an ancient technique reintroduced into Western art at this period. With this technique, the areas to be colored are gouged out of the copper plate and filled with a mixture containing powdered glass and pigment, which is then fired at high temperatures.

Once the enamel has successfully hardened, the uncolored areas are then gilded and the whole surface has to be polished. Champlevé enameling of this kind reached a peak of technical and artistic perfection in the region of the Meuse—an area rich in the mining and production of metals—in the period c. 1140–80. Indeed, for the subtle fusion of colors combined with a striking boldness of contours, as may be seen opposite, it has never been equaled.

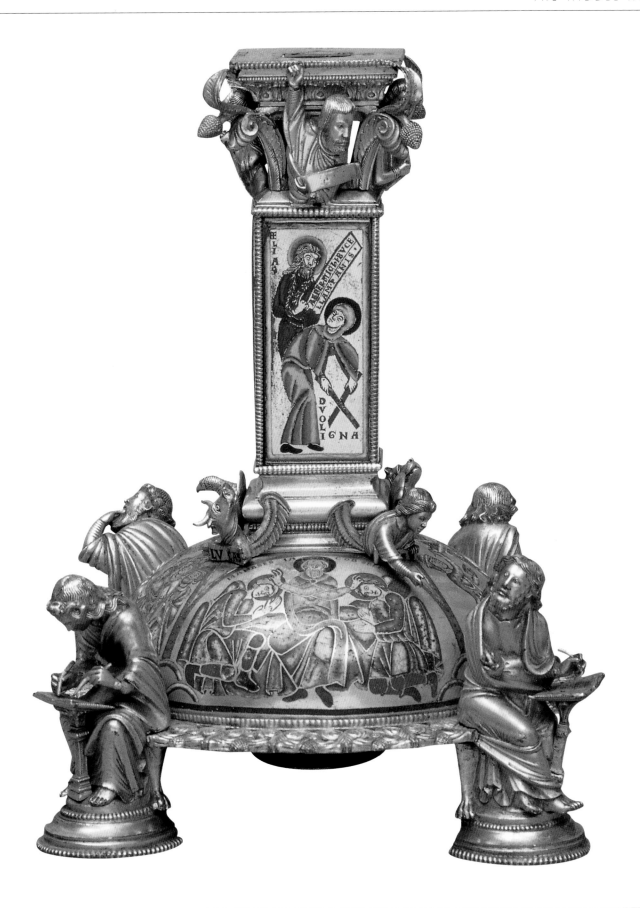

c. 1160 – 70 | *cast bronze, gilt, and champlevé enamel* | height 12in (31.5cm) | Musée de la Ville, Saint-Omer

Frogs Come Out of the Mouths of the Dragon, the Beast, and the False Prophet

"AND I SAW *from the mouth of the dragon, and from the mouth of the beast, and from the mouth of the false prophet, three unclean spirits like frogs. For they are the spirits of devils working signs, and they go forth unto the kings of the whole earth ...*"

(Revelation 16: 13–14)

Saint John, the supposed author of the Apocalypse, stands on the left of this miniature, expounding his fifth vision to the viewer. We have been told that the dragon has seven heads and ten horns (Revelation 12: 3), as does the beast, which is like a leopard with the feet of a bear and the mouth of a lion (Revelation 13: 1–2), and the false prophet has two horns like a lamb (Revelation 13: 11). Between them, they represent all the evil of the Devil and Antichrist, against which the forces of good battle daily.

The Book of Revelation is a unique feature of the New Testament, but it also forms the culmination of Judeo-Christian apocalyptic writing which first appeared in the Book of Daniel. Typically, such writings originated in times of persecution, promising God's vengeance upon the peoples' enemies at the end of time. Like the rest of the apocalyptic tradition, the Revelation of Saint John is written in a fairly obscure way, unfolding in a structure of numbers, mainly sequences of seven. Successive seals are opened, trumpets blown, and vials poured to present a series of visions, culminating in the Last Judgment and the emergence of the heavenly Jerusalem.

This marvelously inventive text proved to be a gift and a challenge to literary and visual interpretation. Commentaries were written in considerable numbers from the time of Saint Jerome in the late 4th century to the 12th century, and there are illustrated Apocalypse manuscripts from the early Middle Ages at a time when few books of either the Old or New Testament were so fully illustrated. By the 12th century, themes from the Apocalypse, detached from their text, had permeated Christian iconography: Christ with the symbols of the Evangelists, the vision of the Twenty-four Elders (see pages 50–51), and the Last Judgment appear frequently on Romanesque tympana, beneath which worshippers passed as they entered the church.

THE LAMBETH APOCALYPSE

ℰ

ENGLISH (? LONDON)

C. 1260–1275

Yet, with the exception of some Spanish works, illustrated manuscripts are rare in the 11th and 12th centuries, and there is nothing to prepare us for the sudden flowering of luxuriously illuminated Apocalypse manuscripts in England from the middle of the 13th century. More than twenty such manuscripts survive from the period 1250–80, with texts in Latin or Anglo-Norman French. The Lambeth Apocalypse, its text and commentary in Latin, contains seventy-eight miniatures followed by twenty-eight tinted drawings of the life of St. John and of devotional images. It was produced for a female owner who is shown kneeling before the Virgin in one of the devotional images. She has been identified, from the heraldry, as Lady Eleanor de Quincy, Countess of Winchester (c. 1230–74).

The sudden burgeoning of these splendid works has been linked with prophecies of the approaching end of the world that were current at the time. In particular, the year 1260 had been predicted as the last, and the excommunication of Emperor Frederick II in 1239 was taken as proof of the beginning of the reign of Antichrist described in the Apocalypse. Yet these manuscripts were, above all, devotional texts, often produced for upper-class laity.

Both for its readership and its method of production, the Lambeth Apocalypse represents a fundamental change when compared with the monastic manuscripts of the 12th century such as the Bury Bible (pages 52–53). From around 1200 and led by Paris, lay workshops, often family concerns, replaced monastic scriptoria as the principal centers of book production. The growth of literacy and the effort of the Church to extend its influence over the laity led to the increased production of devotional texts and images for lay patrons, and it was upper-class women who played a central role in art patronage from that time. We do not know whether Lady Eleanor could read Latin, but in any case, she would have had the help of the pictures and of her chaplain to elucidate the complexities of the text.

Several of the Apocalypse manuscripts were produced in the same workshop, and it is clear that the illuminators copied from one to the other. Even so, each picture demonstrates the artist's enjoyment in depicting these extraordinary visionary events.

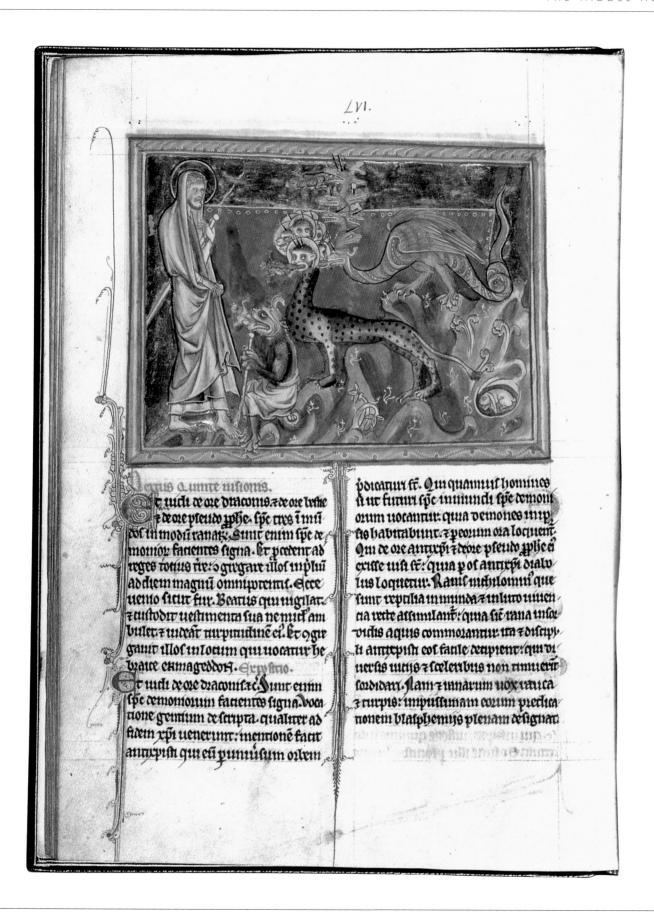

c. 1260–75 | *manuscript illumination on parchment* | size of page 10½ x 7½in (27 x19.5cm) | Lambeth Palace Library, London (MS 209)

The Four Cardinal Virtues

IN THIS MINIATURE from a manuscript of the *Somme le Roi*, the four cardinal Virtues, inscribed *prudence, attrempance, force,* and *justice*, are shown in individual compartments within a framework of Gothic architecture. They are all female, as is usual with allegorical figures, and all are crowned. Prudence is teaching three seated young women; Temperance instructs a girl to decline a cup being offered to her; Fortitude holds a medallion featuring a lion and stands on the River Tigris—one of the rivers of Paradise and, according to St. Ambrose, representing fortitude—and Justice is enthroned holding aloft the traditional sword and scales.

These figures epitomize the elegance, grace, and refinement attained by French Gothic art in the late 13th century. It is expressed in the finely drawn features and curling hair, the slightly swaying postures, and the polite gestures with which the figures are endowed. The colors are subtly shaded and the forms softly modeled in the Italian manner, giving solid substance to the draperies and the body beneath. This is, therefore, an elegance balanced by the growing naturalism of later medieval art. The artist, who also illuminated the Breviary of Philippe le Bel, King of France (Bibliothèque Nationale, Paris), was clearly one of the leading illuminators of the time, and he has traditionally been identified with a Maître Honoré whose name appears in a manuscript dated 1288 and who is recorded in the tax registers and the royal accounts in the period 1292–1300. The evidence is by no means as clear as was once held, but the name of Honoré remains attached to these manuscripts. In any case, this is a royal commission; the appearance of the fleur-de-lis and the arms of Navarre in the book refer to the marriage of Philippe le Bel and Jeanne de Navarre, which took place in 1284.

The *Somme le Roi*, a devotional treatise built around the Virtues and Vices, was compiled by the Dominican Frère Laurent for Philippe III le Hardi, King of France (ruled 1270–85), to whom he was confessor. It is a French version of the Latin *Summae*, systematic collections of religious instruction compiled for the laity in the 13th century. It discusses the Ten Commandments, the Creed, the Seven Deadly Sins, the Art of Living

SOMME LE ROI

PARIS, POSSIBLY BY THE MINIATURIST MAÎTRE HONORÉ

C. 1290–1295

and Dying, the Seven Gifts of the Holy Spirit, and the Seven Cardinal and Theological Virtues. Fifteen pictures were designed for this treatise, of which eight are of the Virtues and Vices. They illustrate the text in general terms but are independent of it in detail; for example, the attributes of the Virtues and the scenes associated with them are not described in the text. The popularity of the *Somme le Roi* is demonstrated by the fact that there are four surviving illustrated manuscripts of the work from the decade 1290–1300 alone.

The Cardinal Virtues were known in Classical times. Socrates had defined them as forces of the soul that work together to perfect the human being, but it was from Cicero and Macrobius that they were known to Christian theologians. St. Ambrose Christianized them in defining them as gifts of divine grace praised by Jesus Christ.

In medieval art, the Virtues were often shown fighting their opposed Vices, but from the Carolingian, period there were also images of Virtues identified solely by their attributes: Prudence holding a book; Justice with a balance; Temperance with a torch and a jug of water; and Fortitude with a sword and a shield. They were widely used in manuscripts and on altars and reliquaries, often in combination with other fours such as rivers of Paradise, Evangelists and major prophets, or linked with the three Theological Virtues, Faith, Hope, and Charity. The lion medallion, seen here, was substituted for Fortitude's sword and shield with the growing use of heraldic coats of arms in the 13th century, and she appears with it in the north portal of Chartres Cathedral. Increasingly, the illustrations were expanded to include scenes of daily life demonstrating the Virtues' nature. In this case, Prudence's book has become a scene of teaching while Temperance is shown at table warning a young woman of the dangers of drink.

Although most books continued to be written in Latin, a growing number were now written in vernacular languages. It was in the reign of Philippe le Bel (ruled 1285–1314) that a complete French translation of the Bible was produced for the first time, and, increasingly, devotional texts were written in the vernacular for the benefit of a growing class of literate laity.

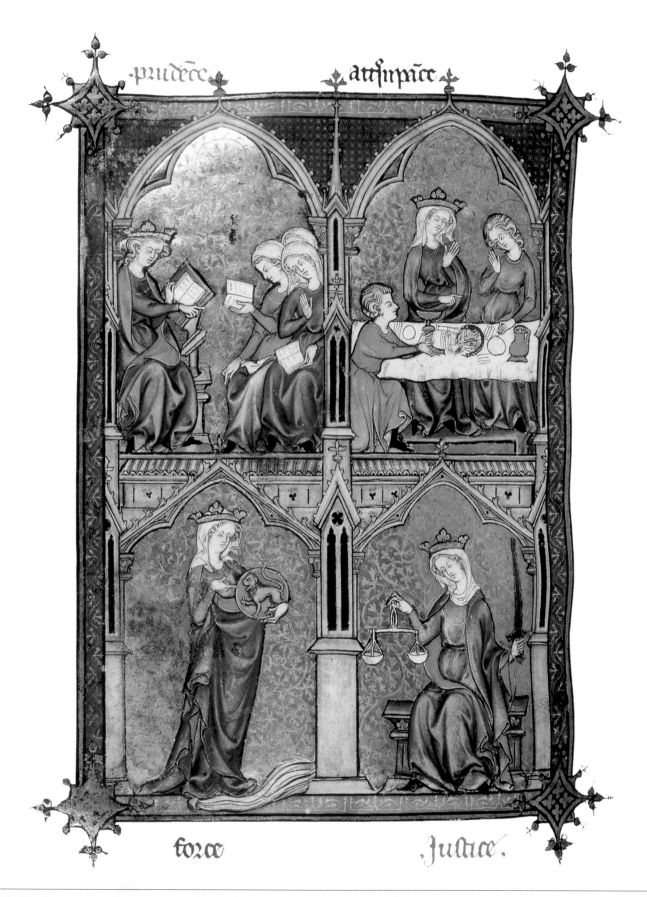

c. 1290–95 | *manuscript illumination on parchment* | page size 7 x 5in (18 x 12cm) | British Library, London (MS Add. 54180)

Harrowing *(with the Luttrell Arms in the Margin)*

IN THE LOWER MARGIN of this page from the Luttrell Psalter is a scene of harrowing. A peasant leads a single horse, which is pulling the harrow to cover the seed; the sowing of the seed has been shown on the previous page. The horse wears a leather bridle and a collar, at this date probably made of plaited straw, while the traces, the side straps, are of rope. The harrow is a rectangular wooden construction set with iron or wooden teeth. Behind the harrow, a man slings stones to scare away the birds. In the margin, a man seated on a monstrous bird supports a shield bearing the Luttrell arms.

More precise information concerning the ownership of the Psalter is given in the dedication miniature, which shows a mounted knight attended by his wife and daughter-in-law and bears the inscription (in Latin, as is the whole work): "The Lord Geoffrey Luttrell caused me to be made." This was Sir Geoffrey Luttrell (1276–1345) of Irnham, near Stamford, Lincolnshire, an English landowner of considerable local importance who also owned estates in South Yorkshire, Leicestershire, and Nottinghamshire. In another miniature, Sir Geoffrey and his family are shown seated at table with their two Dominican confessors, and it is possible that this large and luxuriously illuminated Psalter was linked with a family crisis. Soon after 1320, Sir Geoffrey and his wife Agnes discovered that they were related by third and fourth degrees of consanguinity (that is, related by blood) which would make their marriage contrary to ecclesiastical law and their children illegitimate. In 1331 they sought a mandate from the Pope that would allow them to "remain in the marriage which they had contracted in ignorance." Dispensation was granted in 1334, and it may be that this Psalter was not only a prayer book and a status symbol in general terms, but one that was linked with these particular events.

In style, the Luttrell Psalter is comparable with East Anglian manuscripts of the 1320s, though it is not known whether it was produced in an East Anglian center or by itinerant scribes and artists. Both the illustrations and the marginal decoration demonstrate the growing naturalism of later medieval art. The leaves that sprout from the marginal foliage stems, while not observed from nature, are quite close in appearance to real trilobed leaves, such as ivy, and the horse and its equipment and the birds appear to be quite accurately depicted.

In contrast to its Romanesque predecessor which was confined to initial letters (*see pages 54–55*), Gothic decoration has spread to the margins, and the Luttrell Psalter contains many splendidly monstrous hybrid creatures within its spiky foliage. It has been suggested that they represent the sins of the flesh, but equally, they may be purely decorative. However, in several instances there is a connection between the Psalter text and the marginal illumination. On this particular page, the text of Psalm 94.4, "The furthest places of the earth are in his hands and the folds of the hills are his," appears exactly alongside the arms of Sir Geoffrey Luttrell. It is likely that there is an intentional parallel between the lands of the heavenly lord and those of this earthly landowner that are depicted below.

The agricultural scenes in the lower margins of this section of the Luttrell Psalter represent the basic annual cycle of the 14th-century estate: plowing, sowing, harrowing, breaking clods, weeding, and harvesting. On the lord's demesne, the land retained for his own use, this work was done both by laborers on the permanent staff and by tenant farmers owing labor service to the lord. These pictures have often been reproduced in history books to illustrate medieval agriculture, but this raises problems. Here, the scene of harrowing appears to be accurately shown (except for the decorative color and pattern on the wooden harrow) since there is documentary evidence to support the use of the one-horse harrowing team and the rectangular wooden harrow. However, such illuminations cannot be taken too literally as accurate illustrations. They are too dependent on the pictorial tradition of earlier farming scenes that illustrated the calendars of liturgical manuscripts, and it should be borne in mind that they were produced for the delectation of the landlord and his family, so the elegance of the two figures, their lavender and orange and peach costumes, were more geared to the artist's palette and the patron's taste than to the actual dress of the peasantry in the 14th century.

THE LUTTRELL PSALTER

∞

EAST ANGLIA

C. 1330

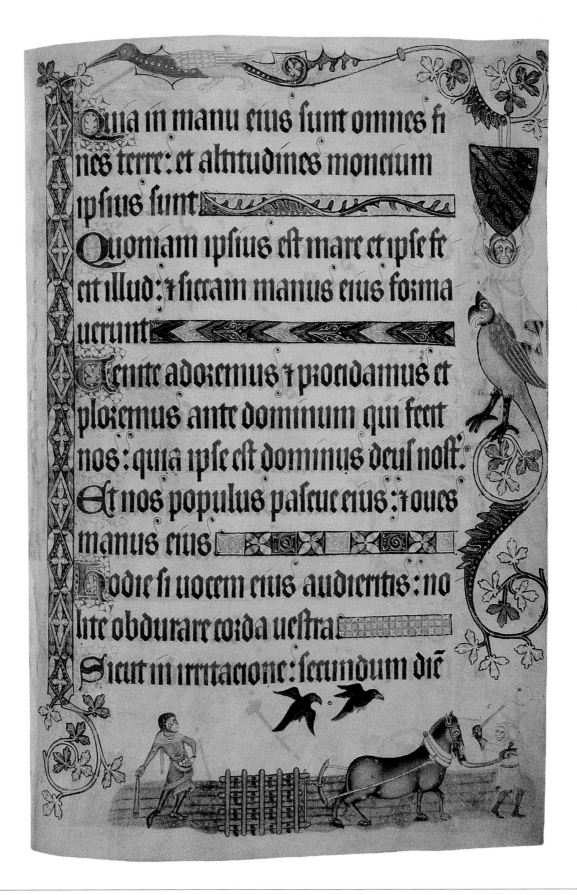

c. 1330 | *manuscript illumination on parchment* | page size 14 x 9^{1}/2in (36 x 24.5cm) | British Library, London (MS Add. 42130)

63

God Creating the Animals

THE HALF LIFE-SIZE figure of God the Father is sharply silhouetted against a patterned gold ground. His robes are massively bulky, a sculpturesque effect achieved by soft highlighting and subtle gradations of tone; his large head and somewhat rustic features differentiate this style from the elegance and refinement of Gothic art in France and Italy. His gesture shows him in the act of creating the animals (Genesis 1: 24–25); the birds and fishes had been created on the previous day. All the figures are naturalistically depicted. On the left are an ox, bear, horse, and boar, a donkey, stag, and deer, a lamb and wolf, a fox and rabbits, and an owl and a bat flying above. On the right there are two crabs, a monstrous fish, a garfish with its long nose, a sturgeon, and carp; then a swan, a rooster, peacock, and two goldfinches.

This is one of twenty-four painted panels from an altarpiece that would only have been opened on Sundays; on High Holy Days this surface, in turn, was opened to reveal a carved screen. The twenty-four scenes divide into sections of six depicting, in turn, the Creation; the story of Adam and Eve; Cain and Abel; Abraham, Isaac, and Jacob; the Nativity; and the Infancy of Christ. The Creation cycle has considerable symbolic content over and above the narrative of the six days. For example, the first scene shows the Fall of the Rebel Angels, a subject not in Genesis but widely known from biblical commentaries explaining the origin of evil in the world. The Creation of the animals appears to be an idyllic genre scene, but appearances can be deceptive. In fact, the wolf is savaging the sheep and the sea monster is aggressively baring its teeth, confirmation that there was evil in the world before the Fall of Adam and Eve, and that even the Paradise of Genesis required salvation through Jesus Christ.

The altarpiece bears the date 1379, and we know from documents that it was erected in St. Peter's Church in Hamburg in 1383 and was the work of Master Bertram, native of Minden in Westphalia. He is recorded in Hamburg from 1367, by which date he appears to have been the leading painter in the city, until his death in 1414/15. Hamburg belonged to the Baltic trading federation, the Hanseatic League, and by the late 14th century, was recovering from the disastrous plague of the 1350s. It was a prosperous city but not at this time a major artistic center, being better known for its five hundred breweries and its export of beer to Flanders, England, and Denmark. Nothing is known of Master Bertram's origins as a painter. The soft modeling of bulky figures derives ultimately from the Italian painting style of the period of Giotto (c. 1267–1337), but how and where Bertram learned his art remains in dispute. Stylistically, his figures are closest to those of Master Theodoric and the Bohemian school of 1370, but Italianate modeling was also current in Paris at the time. Both the solidly presented humanity of the figure and the naturalism of the landscape and animals are typical of the International Gothic style of around 1400 that heralded the Early Renaissance in northern Europe.

The altarpiece, or retable, was to become the dominant form of religious painting in Europe, but it was a relative newcomer at this time. Compared to the altar frontal, which covers the area from the ground to the top of the altar (there are many surviving examples in textile, ivory, and metalwork, as well as painted panels, from the 11th to the 13th centuries), the retable stands behind and above the altar. Its universal popularity from the mid-13th century appears to have been linked with increasing lay participation in the Mass. Altarpieces like this one, with a complex theological program, must have been devised by a member of the clergy, but they were mainly donated by laymen and women, either individually or in groups such as confraternities.

Master Bertram's altarpiece survived the iconoclasm of the early Reformation, but in 1596, it was partially dismantled at the behest of the vicar; the wings were taken down and disappeared from view. In 1731 it was given to the parish church at Grabow in Mecklenburg—hence it has been known as the Grabow altarpiece—where it was rediscovered and identified by the art historian Friedrich Schlie in 1900. At about the same time, the wings were also rediscovered. They had been reused by the Flemish painter Aegidius Coignet in about 1600, and when his paint layer was removed, Master Bertram's painting came to light once more. The whole altarpiece was reunited in the Hamburg Kunsthalle in 1904.

MASTER BERTRAM

BORN MINDEN c. 1340,
DIED HAMBURG 1414/15

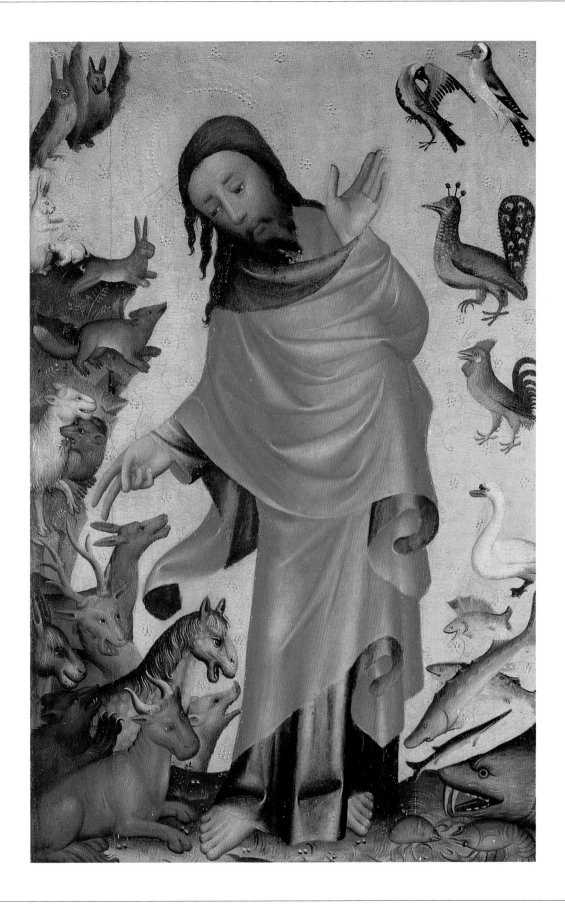

1379–83 | *tempera and gold on oak panel* | 33 x 22in (85 x 56cm) | Kunsthalle, Hamburg

THE EARLY RENAISSANCE

1400–1500 ❧ PAUL HILLS

In the Early Renaissance, style emerges as a critical concept governing visual art. When, in 1424, Leonardo Bruni advised Ghiberti (c. 1378–1455) that his bronze doors for the Florentine Baptistery should be distinguished and significant, he was borrowing his terms from Classical rhetoric. Disregarding subject or symbolism, the humanist chancellor was urging the sculptor to exemplify grace of style and variety of design. The manner as much as the content of art would be the focus of judgment.

THE SUBJECT MATTER of art in the 15th century remained overwhelmingly religious and many of the functions—devotional, civic, dynastic—

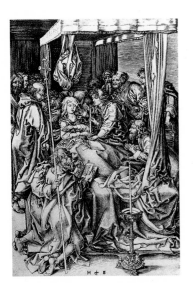

Martin Schongauer was the finest German engraver before Dürer. Death of the Virgin *(c. 1475) was widely imitated.*

remained unchanged from previous centuries, but the relationship between the material and the spiritual was renegotiated. A ducal administrator could be shown almost on a par with the Virgin Mary, while Saint Francis was exalted by immersion within the natural world. In Florence and Bruges, dominated by a numerate and literate class of bankers and traders, a market developed for new kinds of realism, which in turn was fueled by a group of highly competitive sculptors and painters whose works provoked new habits of attending to, writing about, displaying, and eventually trading in artworks.

This did not happen suddenly. In Italy already at the beginning of the 14th century, Giotto in his fresco cycles had heightened empathy between viewer and narrative. His example of modeling figures by light within measurable space was crucial for Masaccio. Giotto's *Mocking of Christ* (c. 1305–6, Arena Chapel, Padua) is played out like a drama upon the stage. In basing his setting—the praetorium of Pontius Pilate—on the columnar peristyle of the Roman house, Giotto anticipated Donatello in looking to antique models for historically appropriate architecture. In signaling difference and distinction—being other than the Gothic and recent past—antique style sharpened messages about the taste of patrons and the imagination of their artists.

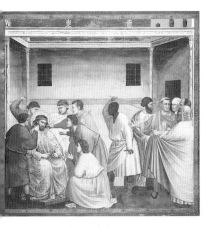

Giotto's Mocking of Christ *(c. 1305–6) shows the grasp of dramatic essentials that laid the foundations for the Renaissance style.*

The revival of the antique would not have gathered pace without political motivation. For the councillors of Borgo San Sepolcro, the Roman connotations of Piero della Francesca's figures conferred the dignity of antique foundations upon their town; for the Marquis Lodovico Gonzaga, the imperial imagery of the Caesars offered an image of authority; for Etienne Chevalier in France, an antique hall gave the cachet of being a leader in international fashion. For female patrons—a notable minority, the wives or widows of rulers or nuns—the antique had less to offer in terms of self-image. In Italy, female fashions remained in thrall to the luxurious dress of the courts of France and Burgundy.

Contrast between Italy and northern Europe is most marked in representations of the body. Humanists elevated the body as the quintessence of order and discovered in the nudes of antiquity models of strength and grace, whereas northern artists, such as Bouts, conceived the body as vulnerable, painstakingly recording skin, tears, and hair. For Italians, attuned to form rather than matter, the body was an emblem of proportion and—in the case of the male nude—of energy. This was not represented as the working body of the laborer but as the socially acceptable body of the hero.

Portraiture was an expanding field throughout Europe, and no artist was of service without the ability to dignify and animate the appearance and status of his patrons. Following medieval precedent, portraits were inserted within religious scenes, while secular portraiture flourished, due in part to the prestige of ancient Roman busts and coins. Commemoration of lineage and marriage were high on the agenda of any family with aspirations to power, and as the palace came to supplement the chapel as a commemorative space, so scope for portraiture expanded. In Mantegna's *Camera Picta* it embraced the whole Gonzaga family and court.

In the 15th century, techniques were refined and ideas circulated rapidly. Van Eyck's use of oils in thin glazes was being taken up in Italy by the 1460s. Art aiming at descriptive realism or perspectival virtuosity required gestation; examination of early Netherlandish panels and canvases frequently indicates complex underdrawings, while in Italy, drawings on paper became ever more essential to planning perspective and design. By the last third of the century, the circulation throughout Europe of high-quality prints, whether secular or religious, enabled the artistic inventions, and the demonstrations of style valued by Bruni, to be exchanged both between workshops and patrons.

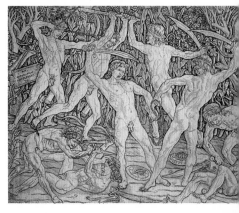

Antonio Pollaiuolo's Battle of Nude Men *(c. 1472) provided a repertoire of nudes in action.*

The Banquet of Herod

IN EARLY 15TH-CENTURY FLORENCE, in the ambience of the scholars of grammar and rhetoric known as humanists, the goal of returning to Classical models spread from literature to art. In their eyes, the Gothic came to be seen as a foreign, almost barbarian import. Filippo Brunelleschi (1377–1446), by study of the local Tuscan Romanesque and by the revival of the measure and proportions of the Classical orders, led the way in purging architecture of the Gothic. But before any of his buildings had been completed, he proved his command of geometry in a pair of panels demonstrating the laws of single-point perspective. His fellow Florentine, Donatello, was among the first to see the compelling importance of this illusionistic technique, for the contemporary biographer who describes the panels records that Brunelleschi visited Rome in the company of the young sculptor and that together they measured and even excavated antique buildings. In his first relief in bronze, Donatello conceived the palace of Herod as an uncompromisingly Roman building, organized to display the dramatic power of linear perspective.

The story of how Saint John the Baptist came to be beheaded is one of the most horrific in the Gospels. Salome agrees to dance at the birthday feast of her stepfather Herod on the condition that he grants her any request; prompted by her mother, Herodias, she asks for the head of John the Baptist, and Herod reluctantly fulfills his promise.

In a relief that is no more than 3in (7.5cm) deep, Donatello forces the terrible climax upon the eye, marshaling perspective to rivet the viewer's attention. Between the presentation of the head to Herod and the dancing Salome, the vanishing point impacts like a blast at the center. In fact, there are slightly different vanishing points for the floor and for the hall above, but what is more obvious is how details within the composition, such as projecting beams or knives on the table, accent the rhythms. In the shallow relief of the upper half, the architecture separates scenes—a musician in the middle ground, a procession with the head of the Baptist at the rear—in the manner of the narratives on Trajan's Column in Rome. Baptisteries in Italy were the focus of communal pride, for at baptism a child was enrolled in civic as well as Christian society. At Siena the *Operaio,* or committee of works, which maintained the cathedral and its baptistery, was dominated by laity. In 1416, this committee initiated a plan for a hexagonal font inset with reliefs in bronze of the life of the Baptist. In 1423, Donatello took over *The Banquet of Herod,* origically commissioned from the Sienese sculptor Jacopo della Quercia (c. 1374–1438): four years later it was ready for collection from Florence. In the same period, Lorenzo Ghiberti, author of two bronze doors of the Florentine baptistery and Donatello's early teacher, was also commissioned; thus, like many costly sculptural projects of the Early Renais-sance, the Siena font brought the major sculptors of the time into competition, a rivalry that fueled personal ambition and stimulated what a discerning public would increasingly judge as artistic progress.

DONATELLO (DONATO DI NICCOLÒ DI BETTO BARDI)

∽

BORN FLORENCE c. 1386, DIED ? FLORENCE 1466

No artist contributed more to this Early Renaissance dynamic than Donatello.

Guided by Classical masters, the politics of Aristotle, and the rhetoric of Cicero, humanists believed in the will or "virtue" of the individual as agent in civic life, and Donatello gave this resolve potent expression. Just as oratory was composed to persuade the audience, so Donatello's art, like the staging of theater, was designed to affect the viewer. To this end he exploited contrasts of body and drapery, the ecstatic movement of dance, and pictorial effects of texture, both rugged and smooth. Seen in the twilight of the Baptistery, ideally by the light of candles, the gilding and chasing of the surface of *The Banquet of Herod* provokes a shifting and pictorial chiaroscuro. Donatello's sculptures taught artists from Masaccio to Michelangelo how gesture should be carried right through the body from hands, through the torsion of shoulders and neck, to tensed brows. It was an art, owing little to Christian symbolism, which spoke to a society dominated by a largely mercantile, lay culture, and one concerned with finding political solutions to violence and tyranny. In the context of civic humanism, Donatello's sculpture proposed a more forthright engagement with the body as seeing and seen; the body as affective instrument, the site of power, grace, and pain. He was the most widely influential artist of the Early Renaissance in Italy.

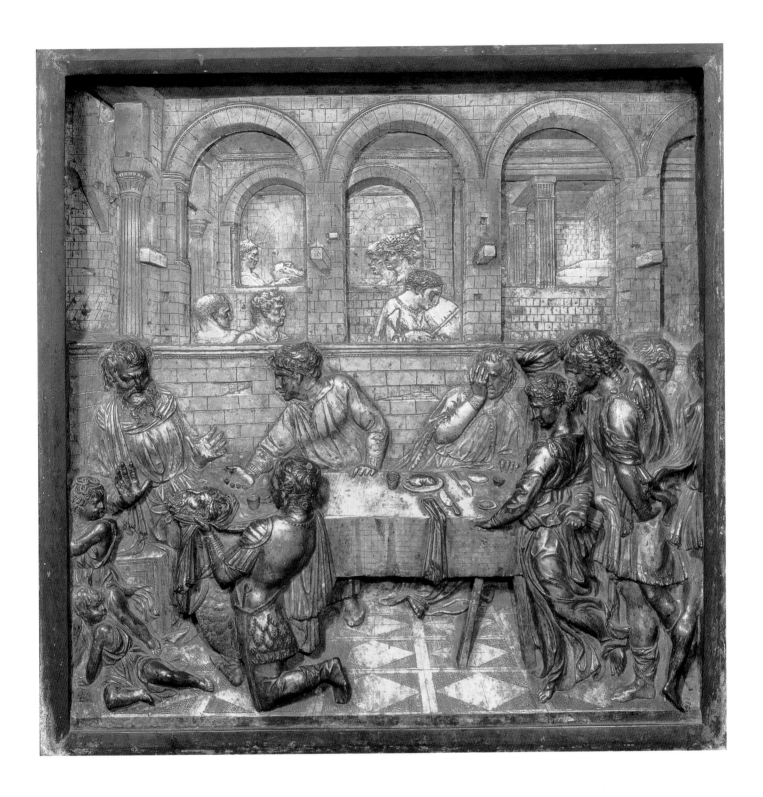

1423–27 | *gilt bronze* | 24 x 24in (60 x 60cm) | Cathedral Baptistery, Siena

Saint Peter Baptizing the Neophytes

LIGHT IN MEDIEVAL ART, as manifested by glow within color or as surface splendor, signified the precious and the divine. Light in Renaissance art would come to intimate daylight—something more mundane yet clarifying and invigorating. "We all," declared Alberti (1404–1472), humanist, art theorist, and champion of Florentine artists of the early 15th century, "love things that are open and bright." Masaccio's figures in the Brancacci Chapel, whether biblical or contemporary, step out to share the light of day. In one scene, he successfully tackled the story of Saint Peter healing with his shadow. In *St. Peter Baptizing the Neophytes* (that is, the newly converted), the light is interrupted by bodies; as it falls on faces, it becomes an agent in the story, recalling that the Greek for baptism is *photismos*, meaning "enlightenment."

The Brancacci Chapel is painted in fresco, a technique of working on wet lime plaster that was perfected in Italy around 1300. In fresco, the first step was to cover the masonry with a layer of plaster, on to which the painter sketched his composition in a red-earth pigment; then, working from the top down, he laid a layer of fine plaster, the *intonaco*, in patches large enough for one day's work. Since the painter had to work on wet plaster, the size of the day-patch, or *giornate*, depended upon what was to be painted. Masaccio, who was famously fast with the brush, needed only ten *giornate* for *St. Peter Baptizing the Neophytes*, completing most of the sky and mountains in one session, then reserving a single *giornate* for the head of Peter. Once paint and plaster had bonded in drying, radical changes could only be made by chipping off the plaster. In the great tradition of central Italian fresco, in which Masaccio excelled, the painter had to think ahead, plan on site, taking into account the space, lighting, and viewpoints in the chapel, and then execute without hesitation.

Teamwork was the norm at this time. The life of Saint Peter was most likely begun in 1424 by the painter Masolino (c. 1383–? 1447) who soon brought in his friend Masaccio as co-worker. Masaccio must have devised the classisizing framework of architraves and corner pilasters that divide the tiered narratives, and the same designing mind can be discerned in the pairing of scenes. On the upper level, *St. Peter Baptizing* is

MASACCIO (TOMMASO DI SER
GIOVANNI DI MONE)

✧

BORN CASTEL SAN GIOVANNI
DI VALDARNO 1401,
DIED ROME 1428

pendant to Masolino's *St. Peter Preaching*, the repetition of steep mountains linking the backgrounds of the two across the altar wall. It was probably Felice Brancacci, a moderately wealthy silk merchant, who commissioned the Petrine cycle. Felice adhered to the pro-papal party in Florentine politics, which goes far to explain the choice of a life of Peter, the first pope. Additionally, the Carmelites, to whom the Carmine belonged, were supporters of the papacy. They traced the origins of their order to the earliest days of the Church when they claimed to have witnessed the preaching of Saint Peter himself. If Brancacci paid the painters, the Carmelites surely advised them on the exact subjects to represent and their significance.

What neither the Brancacci nor the Carmelites could have foreseen, however, was that over the next century and more the chapel would, as Vasari records, become the classroom where Leonardo, Michelangelo, and Raphael would come to learn. What so impressed later artists was the manner in which realism was combined with moral grandeur. In *St. Peter Baptizing* they admired the nude who waits his turn for baptism, shivering with cold—note how a shift from green to purple in the drapery behind sets up an optical vibration. But Masaccio restricts such realistic details to essentials and builds his narrative from contrasts that speak of human destiny. If the shivering man vividly suggests trembling—human frailty even in a healthy body—the man who kneels is as heroic and confident as an antique nude. Such antitheses are never mechanical; they are articulated in a spatial sequence, ordered in depth, and kinetic in effect.

While Masaccio undoubtedly studied the sculpture of his friend Donatello as well as antique gems, sarcophagi, and figurines, the sources testify that he also studied from life, portraying his artist friends, patricians, and porters. He had the knack of mixing lofty formality with tender informality, and delighted in painting a Christian society open to talent and one that accommodated all conditions of men. The two figures in contemporary garb who stand behind Peter may well be portraits of members of the Brancacci family, their detached decorum a foil to the awe of the neophytes.

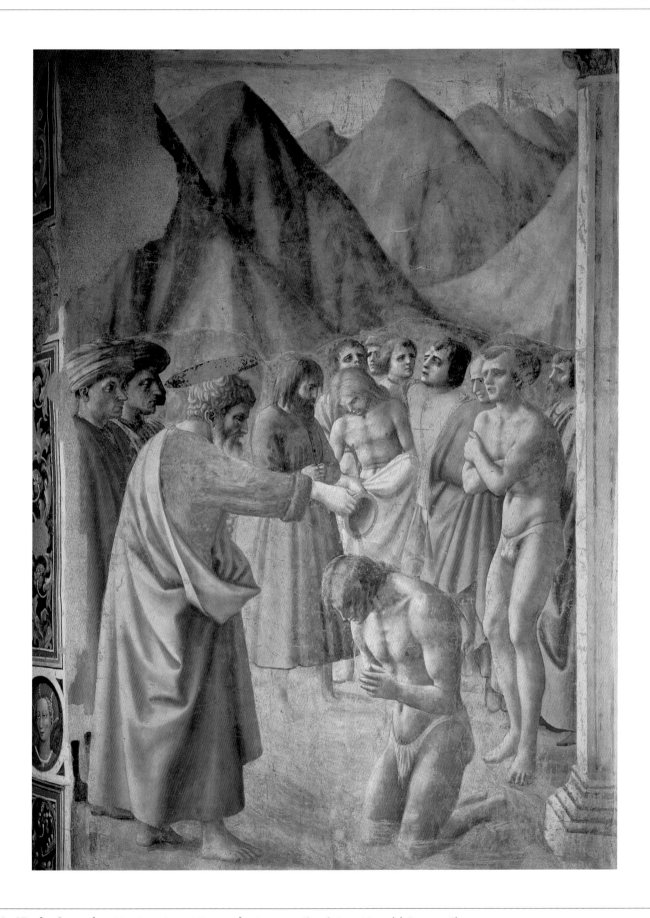

1426–27 | *fresco* | 100 x 64in (255 x 162cm) | Brancacci Chapel, Santa Maria del Carmine, Florence

The Deposition of Christ from the Cross

SOON AFTER MASACCIO painted his frescoes in the Brancacci Chapel, a young Dominican monk known to posterity as Fra Angelico completed an altarpiece in which we can trace the turn in Florentine art from Gothic to Renaissance. The three finials, depicting the Resurrection, Maries at the Tomb, and *Noli me tangere* ("Touch me not," the words spoken by Christ to Mary Magdalene after the Resurrection), had been painted by an older artist, Lorenzo Monaco, just before his death in 1425. Lorenzo's figures and rocks, silhouetted against the traditional gold background, sway with the rhythm of the Gothic pointed arches of the frame. By contrast, in Fra Angelico's main panel, a new, more stable order is manifest.

At the center of the painting is the body of Christ, as entirely visible as its Eucharistic equivalent, the Host, at its elevation in the Mass. In medieval piety the ladder was a common image of the stages of ascent from the material to the spiritual, and here Christ's body has an immaterial lightness that intimates ascension. Christ's face is bathed in light, recalling the words inscribed on the halo, "Crown of Glory." His body is marked by the bruises of his flagellation; these are painted not with the brutal realism seen in paintings north of the Alps, but with tender slashes of green on pale flesh.

Angelico's painting is executed with loving care in a matchless tempera technique (where an emulsion is used). Egg tempera is an inherently clean, fast-drying medium in which the paint must be patiently applied with tiny strokes of soft minever brushes. The luminosity of Angelico's painting depends upon the underlying whiteness of the smooth gesso (chalk) ground and the high quality of the pigments, applied without complex mixture, only the addition of white to lighten them. Most beautiful of all are the contrasts of warm and cool colors, such as rose tints on greenish flesh, a chromatic sign of the pulse of life.

In accord with a period when men and women were segregated in church or when listening to preachers in town squares, Angelico segregates the genders. The task of the women is to prepare Christ's body for entombment. Mary Magdalene bathes his feet with her tears, other women prepare the shroud and napkin, while Mary kneels before the shroud. The task of the men is more intellectual; they meditate on the body of Christ and the instruments of the Passion. On the right, one holds up the three nails and the Crown of Thorns, and in doing so encircles the sepulcher. By this cunning placement of the crown, Angelico converts a symbol into a spatial device and, like Donatello in his relief of *The Banquet of Herod* (see page 69), invites the eye to traverse from foreground to distance.

The gold background has been replaced by sky. Even here, in a work that tends toward an iconic stillness, the art of the Early Renaissance incorporates signs of narrative passage, of before and after. On the left, the dark clouds that bought darkness at noon when Christ died on the cross are receding behind the city of Jerusalem. On the right, as we have noted, the sepulcher, the destination of Christ's body, is indicated.

The *Deposition* comes from the Strozzi Chapel in the Florentine church of Santa Trinità, in all probability commissioned by the head of the family, Palla Strozzi. The richest member of the Florentine oligarchy, and like his political rivals the Medici, a banker, Palla had already commissioned an altarpiece for this same family chapel in 1423. Painted by Gentile da Fabriano (c. 1370–1427), its subject was the *Adoration of the Magi* (Uffizi, Florence) and its style combined lavish use of gold with exquisite detail. Angelico's *Deposition* is an equally high-quality production. Whereas Gentile conveyed luxury by the textures of fabrics, the descriptive realism of surface, Angelico chose to emphasize less material qualities of refined outline, balanced interval, and unsullied color. But the legend of Angelico's piety, established already in the 15th century, has obscured how these and other qualities appealed to the Strozzi and his future patrons, the Medici. For all its spirituality, perhaps even *because* of its equation of purity with refinement, there is no place in this *Deposition* for the laboring poor. Instead, Angelico has accommodated on the right a group without haloes in idealized versions of contemporary dress, with hats that indicate high social status. It is possible that they include portraits of males of the Strozzi clan, privileged to share the space and light with the sacred figures.

FRA ANGELICO

☙

BORN NEAR FLORENCE c. 1397,
DIED ROME 1455

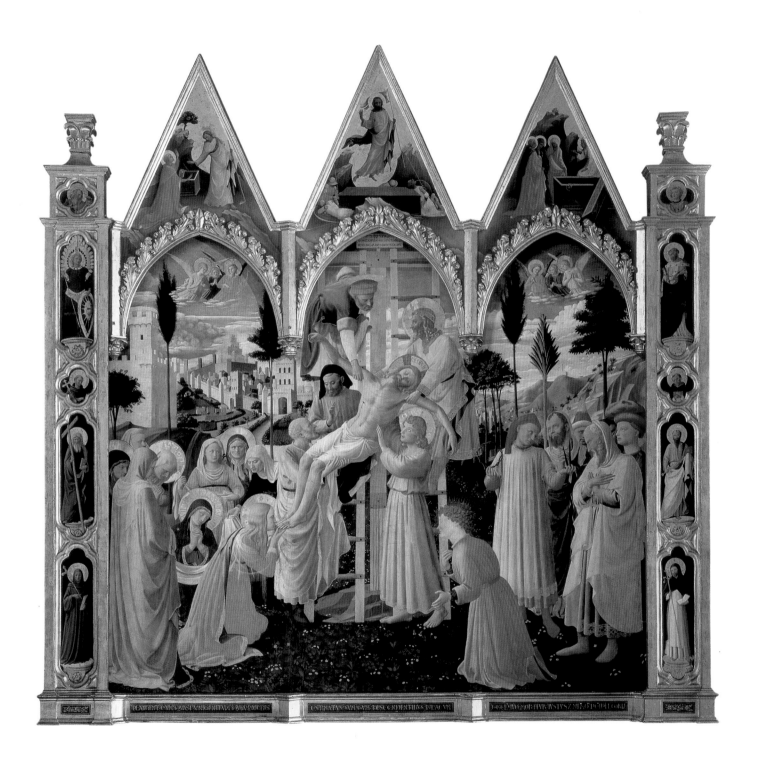

c. 1430 | *tempera on panel* | 69 x 73in (176 x 185cm) | Museum of San Marco, Florence

The Virgin and Child with Chancellor Rolin

ART IN THE 15TH CENTURY was dominated by two schools, one based on Tuscany and northern Italy, the other on Burgundy and the Netherlands. Linked by trade, these were the most heavily urbanized regions of Europe. In Tuscany, sculptural projects and frescoes manifested the new style; in the Netherlands, painting on panel in oil challenged manuscript illumination as the medium setting new standards of realism.

Oil as a binder had been used piecemeal since 1300, but it was not until about 1420 that it started to be used throughout a painting and applied, for some colors, in as many as six layers or glazes. The man credited with perfecting oil in translucent glazes was Jan van Eyck. For much of his maturity and until his death he was the salaried painter of the Duke of Burgundy, Philip the Good. Apart from Philip, van Eyck's patrons were predominantly Italian merchants resident in Bruges, or lawyers and financiers employed in the service of the duke—men who were neither clerics nor vastly wealthy compared to the landed aristocracy. Nobles spent fortunes on liveries for their households, fine cloth, tapestries, metalwork, jewels, and sumptuous manuscripts; the merchants and professional class of administrators paid a fraction of the price to buy painted panels. In doing so they acquired representations of luxuries, such as cloth-of-gold (silk or wool fabric interwoven with gold thread), marbles, pearls, and rubies that few could have afforded, and they commanded pictorial prospects over town and countryside more extensive than any estates they could have owned.

Yet to explain Early Netherlandish painting simply in terms of new-money buying virtual reality would be to miss the delicate negotiation between lay patrons, traditional Christian piety, and the new possibilities of oil painting. It is apparent from the many Latin inscriptions in van Eyck's panels that the painter and his clients learned to find their way among complex liturgical texts and commentaries. In the late Middle Ages, lay piety focused increasingly on the Virgin, sometimes in her domestic role as mother, sometimes in her regal aspect as Queen of Heaven. The combination of the domestic and the spiritually exalted seems to have appealed to well-to-do townsfolk, and van

JAN VAN EYCK

BORN NEAR MAASTRICHT c. 1390, DIED BRUGES 1441

Eyck became adept at celebrating both. In *The Virgin and Child with Chancellor Rolin,* the regal predominates. No doubt this suited the aspirations of Nicholas Rolin (1376–1462), chancellor to Philip the Good and wealthiest member of the administration. Rolin could actually afford the latest fashion in cloth-of-gold in which he appears in the painting, commissioned for his family chapel in the church of Notre Dame du Chastel in Autun. Rolin also lavished gifts on the church, including a crown for the Virgin. But if the golden crown held above the Virgin by an angel in van Eyck's painting alludes to a real object, and the portrait of Rolin is remarkable for verisimilitude; the palace—implausibly open to the elements—was surely unlike any in Burgundy. Van Eyck's reality is an effect. The city so minutely described beyond the high terrace incorporates buildings observed in Utrecht or Liège, but the combination is new, and the mountains are a fiction.

What van Eyck offered to Rolin was, in more senses than one, the answer to a prayer. The chancellor's meditation on a Book of Hours has summoned the vision of the Virgin in the Heavenly Jerusalem, that is, the richly robed Virgin sitting in glory with the Christ Child. Scenes from Genesis carved on the capitals of the columns recall the Fall of Man and the need to seek salvation; the Christ Child, bearing the orb of the Savior of the World, raises his hand to bless Rolin. Unescorted by any saint and slightly larger than the Queen of Heaven, Rolin is united with his vision by the space and light of the palace. Donor and vision are also yoked by color. Normally, the Virgin is dressed in red and blue whereas here, van Eyck has "borrowed" the blue to drape Rolin's prie-dieu. Red and blue were also the colors that dominated the stained glass in the windows of northern cathedrals, as we are reminded by the colored glass in the two windows cut off above the arcade. Just as stained glass required a dark setting in which to glow, so van Eyck manipulated his setting to make sure that jewels and deep colors are foiled by comparative darkness so they, too, should glow. But the new cathedral or shrine of Eyckian art is opened to the urban world, so the towers and spires of the distant city furnish a filigree crown for Christ.

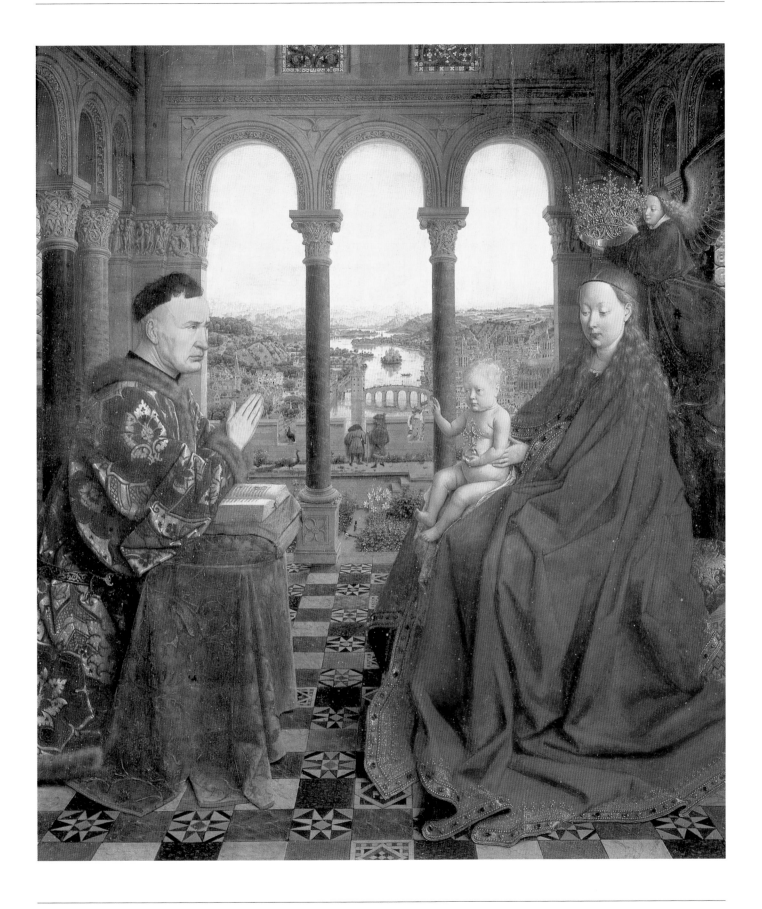

c. 1433–34 | *oil on panel* | 26 x 24in (66 x 62cm) | Louvre, Paris

Princess of the d'Este Family

PISANELLO BUILT HIS CAREER around service to the princes of the Italian peninsula, the d'Este in Ferrara, the Gonzaga in Mantua, and Alfonso I of Aragon in Naples. A larger body of drawings survives by him than by any artist before Leonardo, and it shows how he looked beyond the pattern-books that were the stock-in-trade of late Gothic painters and illuminators, honing his powers of observation by drawing animals, birds, people, and figures in costumes. He recorded the muzzles of horses, fur of hounds, feathers of herons, and the ears of humans with equally sharp and dispassionate attention. Unlike Donatello, Masaccio, or Piero della Francesca, he did not picture people in terms of a dominating intelligence addressing the spectator in a theatrical manner; rather, he depicted them as detached, totally independent of an observer, and for his sharpness of eye he was lauded by poets and eulogized by Guarino of Verona, Greek scholar and tutor of Leonello d'Este. Recording animals and humans stimulated his imagination. Wittily, he gave a strutting courtier a costume modeled on a peacock's tail.

In addition to being a painter, Pisanello perfected the form of the Renaissance medal, with a portrait head on the front and pictorial device on the reverse. His skill as a medalist recommended him to princes avid to revive the antique custom of distributing likenesses of themselves, and it guaranteed his fame both as a designer who could place a profile perfectly in a circle, and as an inventor of pictorial devices. These witty personal emblems tickled the powers of interpretation of the sophisticated viewer, and they grew in popularity in courtly circles as supplements to the devalued—because overextended—system of coats of arms.

In this painted portrait, Pisanello commemorates a princess in her prime. The panel appears to be designed to stand on its own. No inscription records the sitter's name, but the jug with roots growing from its bowl embroidered on the back of her sleeve is one of the devices of Leonello d'Este (1407–1450), Marquis of Ferrara. If, as is likely, the sprig of juniper (*ginepro*) pinned to her shoulder alludes to the woman's name, she may be Leonello's sister Ginevra (1419–1440) who in 1434 married Sigismondo Malatesta, the Lord of Rimini. The red, white, and

PISANELLO (ANTONIO PISANO)

BORN PROBABLY PISA 1395,
DIED PROBABLY ROME 1455

green trim to her gown bear the colors of the d'Este livery. Sometimes portraits such as this were sent to prospective husbands; occasionally they commemorated recently deceased brides. The profile format was standard in Italy for both male and female portraits in the earlier 15th century. Gradually, the three-quarter or full-face view, pioneered by Netherlandish painters, was adopted for males because it allowed a more assertive rendering of identity and a frank meeting of the gaze between sitter and viewer. But the profile endured for females because it accorded with the contemporary decorum that decreed that ladies should keep their eyes lowered in modesty. Some recent critics have interpreted such profile portraits as women trapped under the male gaze, spread out for view like an impaled butterfly. Certainly the princess seems quite passive; yet, alert and dignified, she differs little in presentation from Pisanello's profile portrait of the powerful Leonello (1441, Accademia Carrara, Bergamo).

The *Princess* is at least one-third larger than most portraits of the early 15th century, and Pisanello used this extra space to extend the figure to below the bust and to include a floral background, artfully bringing together what on a medal would be divided between obverse and reverse. The head itself—incisive in outline, shallow in relief—is as beautifully designed as the medallic profiles. The princess's hairline, high above the brow, corresponds to contemporary ideals; the ear has been raised by the artist to accentuate a fashionably long neck. Growing in the floral hedge are carnations, columbines, and roses, flowers associated with marriage, love, and passion; the butterflies they attract—red admirals, a clouded yellow, and a rare swallowtail—are commonly symbols of resurrection. The flowers and butterflies together allude to that favorite theme of Renaissance poetry, the beauty and brevity of youth. One red admiral appears to be too large to be *behind* the Princess. Could it be that Pisanello wished his courtly viewers to think that it has landed on the surface of the panel itself, as though the butterfly, like the birds that pecked the painted grapes of the ancient Greek painter Zeuxis, had been deceived by art? If so, it is a conceit worthy of a painter praised by poets.

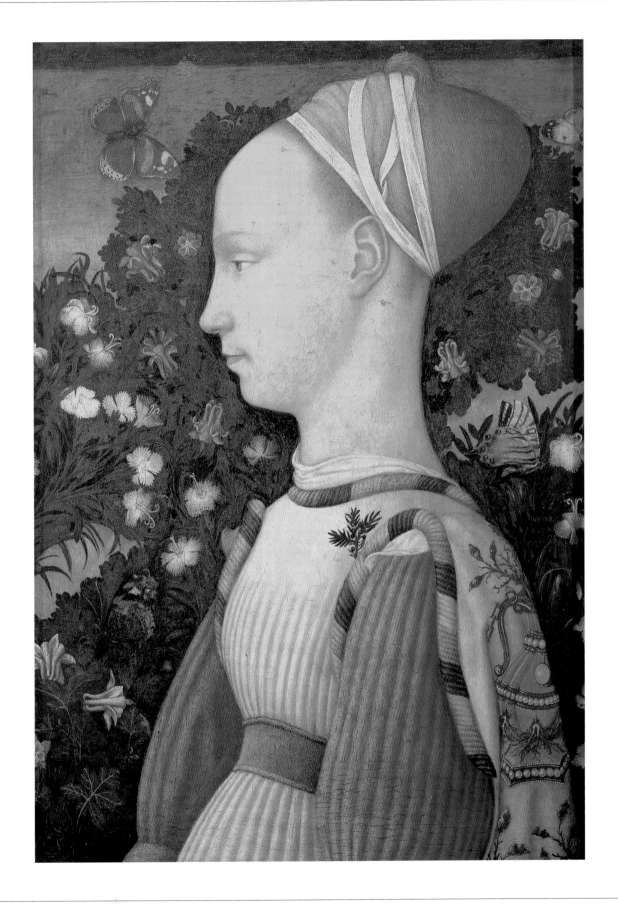

c. 1440 | *panel* | 17 x 12in (42 x 30cm) | Louvre, Paris

The Miraculous Draft of Fishes

CENNINO CENNINI, writing in Italy in the 1390s, advised painters that a landscape setting could be invented from a few rough stones brought into the workshop; by the mid-15th century, painters were increasingly motivated by local pride to record topography and terrain. Fra Angelico included a view of Lake Trasimene in an altarpiece for nearby Cortona (scene of *The Visitation* in the predella to *The Annunciation*, c. 1435, Diocesan Museum, Cortona), while Piero della Francesca depicted his birthplace, Borgo San Sepolcro, several times. The advance of landscape painting within Christian art is linked to the influence of lay patrons and to a desire to make religious subjects more accessible and *local* in reference. Even the Heavenly Jerusalem in *The Virgin and Child with Chancellor Rolin* (see page 75) is built from credible elements of townscape and vista.

The setting of the so-called *Miraculous Draft of Fishes* is probably one of the most vivid depictions of topography in Early Renaissance painting. Konrad Witz set the biblical story on Lake Geneva, taking a vantage point looking south-east across the Savoy Alps toward the snow-capped massif of Mont Blanc. The panel formed the wing of an altarpiece in the church of St. Pierre in Geneva, therefore, the conviction with which Witz has translated Christ to the Swiss lake would have been recognized and appreciated by the Genevans.

Setting the miracle on Lake Geneva bore a message to be understood in the light of ecclesiastical politics. The commission for the St. Peter altarpiece came, in 1444, either from Cardinal François de Mez or from Amadeus VIII, Count of Savoy, who at the Council of Basle in 1439 had—with the Cardinal's support—been elected antipope. As antipope, the Count of Savoy took the name Felix V and pretended to the throne of Peter for just a decade. Konrad Witz, who worked in Basle, would have been broadly familiar with the politics of the Council. Doubtless he was advised by his ecclesiastical patron to set the story of Saint Peter within the dominion of the Counts of Savoy in order to affirm that this was the new patrimony of Peter. These new papal lands are shown in Witz's painting as enjoying peace. Beyond the lake a troop of horses, headed by the

KONRAD WITZ

*BORN ROTTWEIL? c. 1400,
DIED BASLE 1445/6*

banner of Savoy, proceed toward the right, the direction of Geneva. Women wash their laundry on the far bank, farmers safely tend the fields, and a shepherd watches his sheep.

If topography and background incident are propagandist, so too is the hybrid story represented in the foreground. It is not precisely the *Miraculous Draft of Fishes,* because the account (Luke 5: 1–11) mentions two boats with Christ in one, as well as a broken net; neither does it conform precisely to Peter's attempt to emulate Christ walking on the water, for that took place (Matthew 14: 22–23) on a stormy night. The calm in Witz's painting—which surely underlines its message—is closer to the scene when the resurrected Christ appears to his disciples fishing on the Sea of Galilee (John 21: 1–19) and commands Peter to "feed my lambs." Clearly, the painting borrows elements from all three accounts: the miraculous draft, the walking on the water, and the pastoral injunction to Peter. In accord with the spirit of the conciliar debates at Basle, which emphasized that the pope needed the support and guidance of the cardinals, the painting illustrates that, unaided, Peter will ignominiously sink. On the other hand, the steady, solid boat behind him, which carries the other apostles, is emblematic of the true image of the Church, the vessel of salvation.

Konrad Witz turns propaganda into visual poetry. Working in egg tempera, he combines naive delight in realistic detail—the grasses fringing the shore, the pebbles seen through the water—with a sculptural grasp of shape. Triangles hold the composition in tension: Christ is framed between the prow of the boat and the wedge of wall on the bank to the right. The mountain above reiterates Christ's form, and its peak in cloud may refer to his forthcoming ascension into heaven. Compositionally, the mountain is linked to the rock that breaks the surface of the water near the shore. Placed below Peter, this rock may allude to the rock on which Christ built his Church. Witz's landscape of the miraculous is far from Cennini's studio stones and remarkably free from stereotype. It has a convincing feel for the outdoors and captures a moment when the discovery of landscape was novel and exciting.

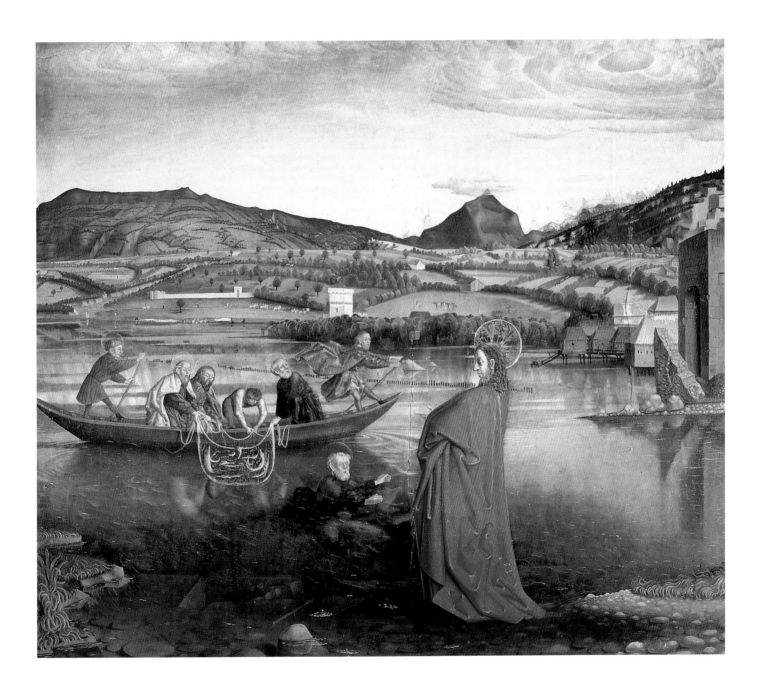

1444 | *tempera on panel* | 52 x 61in (132 x 154cm) | Musée d'Art et d'Histoire, Geneva

The Braque Triptych

THE ROUGH VIGOR of Konrad Witz was soon eclipsed by the style of the most influential artist of northern Europe in the mid-15th century, Rogier van der Weyden. Born in Tournai, Rogier served an apprenticeship with Robert Campin (active 1406–44) and in 1436, was appointed the official painter of Brussels where he pursued a highly successful career. Like Jan van Eyck, he worked for a prosperous urban clientele, for Philip the Good—though he was never the salaried painter of the duke—and for court functionaries such as Chancellor Rolin. The great demand for his panel paintings was fulfilled by a large and efficient workshop. The success of Rogier's enterprise can be attributed to his skill as a designer, his invention of new formats, and his ability to convey emotion. Realism tempered and slightly idealized was a quality that his refined patrons came to value in preference to the homey detail and sometimes brutal violence of his master Campin. Rogier's elegance of design owed something to the influence of Italian art from a trip he made to Rome, but, like most painters working north of the Alps, he used perspective in an approximate fashion. Albertian perspective treated pictorial space as a stage into which figures were inserted; Rogier conceived of figure and space together as mutually supporting.

The Braque triptych exemplifies the qualities of refinement and unity. Surviving in its original frame, the folding panels are smaller than an altarpiece, yet larger than most portable works on panel. Van der Weyden's new format of half-length figures against a landscape was widely imitated and was adapted to portraiture by Hans Memlinc (c. 1430/40–1494). In devotional works it brought Christ and the saints into close-up while it removed the need to delineate foreground. Landscape with a common horizon spreading across the background of the Braque triptych establishes continuity of space and mood. How words are inscribed on the panels distinguishes between speech and reportage. They curve when they are the words spoken by the Baptist, the Virgin, and John the Evangelist in reference to the Savior, but they are horizontal above the Magdalene to record what she did: "Then took Mary a pound of ointment of spikenard, very costly, and anointed the feet of Jesus."

ROGIER VAN DER WEYDEN

⁊

BORN TOURNAI c. 1399,
DIED BRUSSELS 1464

The Magdalene panel, in its tender relationship of the part to the whole, color to form, is one of the artistic peaks of the 15th century. No single element of the design could be moved without disturbing the unusually delicate interlocking or the articulate placement of the figure within the frame. Instinctively bringing the Magdalene into sympathy with the tones of the landscape, Rogier declines to dress her as "the scarlet women," but does accent her stylish allure by showing her in a low-cut, figure-revealing dress with luxurious detachable sleeves. The volume of the Magdalene's pale silk headdress is echoed in the cylinder of her white ointment jar. Whereas van Eyck used white selectively to create strong accents of luster, Rogier uses it more generously to create passages of cool pallor. These whites, distributed more broadly and repeated at various depths of space, prompt meaningful associations: the purity of the ointment jar against the limestone cliffs calls to mind that other container, quarried out of stone, the Holy Sepulcher. In contrast to the cool tones that bind the three panels, a brilliant, dramatic orb highlights the central figure of Christ.

In terms of subject matter, the Braque triptych modernizes the traditional Byzantine iconography known as the Deësis in which the Virgin and John the Baptist intercede with the Savior on behalf of Christians seeking salvation. The exterior of the triptych bears the arms of Jehan Braque and Catherine de Brabant, who were married in 1451. Jehan, who was one of Philip the Good's administrators, died in 1452, so the triptych may have been commissioned by his wife for the salvation of her husband's soul. The presence of two Johns—Baptist and Evangelist—is accounted for by Jehan's name. We can only speculate that perhaps Catherine de Brabant was prepared to forego representation of her name saint because she preferred to identify with the Magdalene's fervent act of sepulchral piety. What is certain is that the Braque triptych remained in the possession of Catherine and her heirs. When the family opened it for their private devotions, the gloom of the exterior, with skull and cross against a dark ground, was dispelled to reveal the Savior and saints, close and physically present, alive against the brightness of sky.

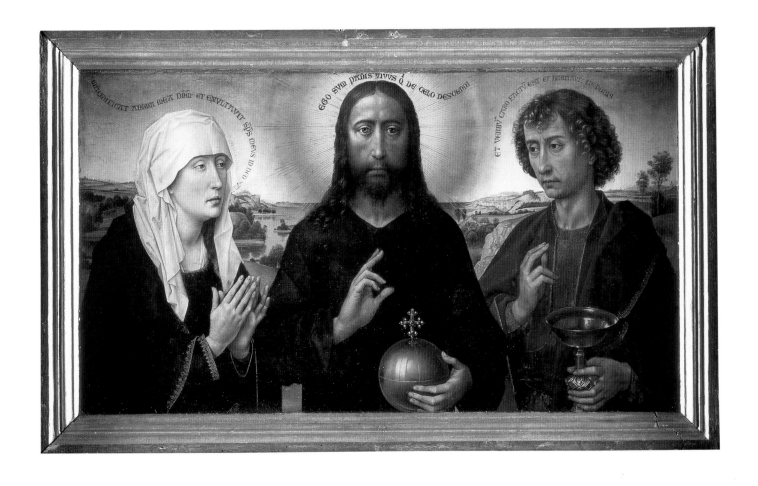

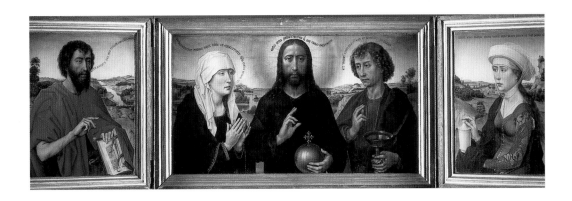

c. 1451–52 | *oil on panel* | 16 x 14in (41 x 35.5cm), 16 x 27in (41 x 68cm), 16 x 13$\frac{1}{2}$in (41 x 34.5cm) | Louvre, Paris

The Melun Diptych

FRANCE UNDER THE VALOIS MONARCHY was dominated by an aristocratic taste for the chivalric and fabulous. Between the Battle of Agincourt in 1415 and the conclusion of the Hundred Years' War in 1453, frequent military campaigns discouraged grand commissions. Only by the middle of the 15th century did opportunities for patronage expand and painters take note of recent developments in Italy.

The painter who introduced a new spirit into French art was Jean Fouquet. Born in the Loire valley, he lived and worked in the heartland of royal France and duly attracted commissions from members of the court. Yet, little is known of his life. An early portrait of a jester reveals an eye for character and familiarity with the realism of Campin and van Eyck. By the mid-1440s, he was in Italy, already with a reputation sufficient for him to be invited to paint Pope Eugenius IV. While he was in Italy, the Frenchman probably came into contact with the work of Fra Angelico and Jacopo Bellini, and like Angelico, he was fascinated by the buildings of Rome.

On his return to Tours, the knowledge Fouquet acquired in Italy was put to use in the Book of Hours illuminated around 1452 for Etienne Chevalier, treasurer to King Charles VII. In several miniatures he included references to monuments in Rome, such as Trajan's Column, Castel S. Angelo, and Old St. Peter's—references no doubt recognized by the widely traveled Chevalier, who frequently acted as ambassador for the king. In the miniature depicting the donor's presentation to the Virgin, Chevalier kneels in a Classically-inspired hall articulated by pilasters with slabs of colored marble inset between them. Clearly, the Treasurer relished the gleaming modernity of this architecture—at once ahead of its time in France, yet redolent of the civilization of antiquity—for it is the setting in which he appears again in the diptych also commissioned from Fouquet.

Whereas Rogier van der Weyden's Braque Triptych (see page 81) is intimate and intense, Fouquet's diptych for Chevalier is grandiose and public, its panels more than twice as tall. Now divided between museums in Antwerp and Berlin, the diptych was originally framed in sumptuous blue velvet and placed above

JEAN FOUQUET

BORN TOURS c. 1420,
DIED TOURS 1481

the tomb of Chevalier's wife in Notre Dame in Melun, where the force of its colors—predominantly red, white, and blue—and the grandeur of its forms, must have made an impact from a distance within the church. Chevalier, dressed in a robe of deep red (a most expensive dye reserved for high-ranking magistrates), is supported by his name-saint Stephen. The donor's name is inscribed in gold letters on the base of the pilaster. By cutting off the architecture, Fouquet gave the setting unprecedented magnificence, and by deploying a plunging perspective, he lent commanding presence to the figures.

Several miniatures in the Book of Hours borrowed devices from contemporary theater, and the diptych, too, is dramatized with panache and deadpan wit. Saint Stephen has a Gallic physiognomy and almost surreal haughtiness; he bears the stone of his martyrdom like some exquisite meteor, while the blood drips from the wound it made in the crown of his head. In contrast to Nicholas Rolin's vision, where the Virgin shares his space (see page 75), Chevalier's vision is abstracted from any setting, at once other-worldly and strangely carnal. The Virgin and Child are seated on a jeweled throne and supported by cherubim and seraphim in red and blue. Unlaced and slender-waisted, the Virgin offers a perfectly spherical breast to the Child, a presentation which appears to be a frank celebration of female beauty, for the Christ is not about to feed at the maternal breast, but calmly points across to Chevalier. Never before had the allure of the youthful Virgin been so flaunted; like Pisanello's *Princess of the d'Este Family* (see page 77), she belongs to a world of court fashion, her skin ivory-pale, her ears placed far up her head to accentuate the sweep of bare neck visible through an absolutely transparent veil. All this lends credence to the tradition that the Virgin was modeled on Agnès Sorel, mistress to the king and friend of Chevalier, whom she had appointed her executor. Agnès died in 1450, and her memorialization in the features of the Virgin Mary must have been painted shortly after. In Fouquet's diptych it is more than usually obvious that representations of the Heavenly Court consciously reflected the ideology of the earthly court that commissioned them.

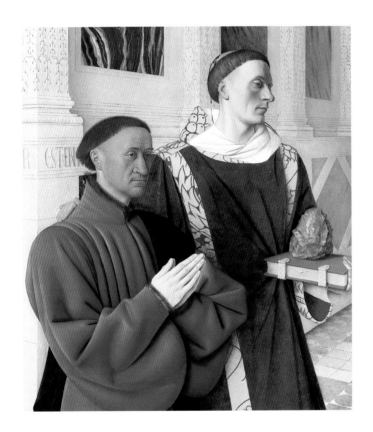

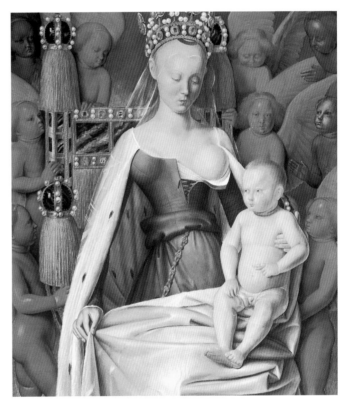

c. 1452 | *panel* | each panel 37 x 34in (94 x 86cm) | Gemäldegalerie, Berlin (left) | Museum of Fine Arts, Antwerp (right)

The Resurrection

IN THE 15TH CENTURY, an artisan's entitlement to make and sell his artefacts was regulated by the guilds. The guild in which he enrolled depended upon the materials he used, and within the painters' guild there were further divisions among those who painted on panel, leather, or other supports. Painting on gessoed panels (that is, coated with a smooth, white plaster) was the most expensive and highly esteemed work; decorating furniture, leather shields, or playing cards was the most lowly. Painting on cloth was deemed inferior to panel painting because fabric supports took less time and less skill to prepare, and their lightness made them convenient for relatively humble works such as ephemeral festival decorations or processional banners. According to Netherlandish guild statutes, the cloth-painters were not qualified to paint on panel, whereas panel-painters like Bouts could, if required, try their skills on cloth.

Works on cloth were painted in large numbers on both sides of the Alps, but especially in the Netherlands where, as the center of the European linen trade, linen cloth was readily available. The loss of most of these works too easily distorts our historical perception of the range of function and quality in 15th-century painting.

DIERIC BOUTS

∾

*BORN HAARLEM c. 1415,
DIED LEUVEN 1475*

The *Resurrection* by Dieric Bouts is exceptional. It belonged—together with the *Annunciation* (Getty Collection, Los Angeles), the *Adoration of the Magi* (private collection), and the *Entombment* (National Gallery, London)—to the wings of a folding altarpiece, with *Crucifixion* (Musées Royaux des Beaux-Arts, Brussels) in the center. All five scenes were painted on fine linen. In its frame the altarpiece would have stood over 6ft (1.8m) high. Since the canvases were recorded together in an Italian collection in the 19th century, it is quite plausible that they were painted for export to Italy, the linen support being chosen for ease of transport. In quality, they are a match for any altarpiece on panel, therefore untypical of the vast mass of cloth-paintings.

The linen support of the *Resurrection* was lightly sized with animal glue and then painted in thin layers of pigment suspended in the same water-based medium. In the absence of any gesso, the plain-weave canvas tells as a delicately unifying grain in the painting, an underlying microtexture and buff tone; it has become more apparent with the abrasion of the paint, yet Bouts's handling of tone and texture must have always served to sustain pictorial unity of surface. Whereas van Eyck's oil medium enhanced translucency, the glue medium lent pigments, especially chalk-whites, a degree of opacity. Bouts responded to this by modulating tones of white, shading them into gray or oatmeal, and setting them off with garments and ribbons in vermilion. In all the canvases of the altarpiece this finely tuned chromatic restraint creates an intense meditative calm. In the *Resurrection,* it also evokes the aura of dawn.

Christ, victorious over death, rises from the tomb like the sun at dawn breaking through the horizon. Around this Resurrection Bouts stages an intimate drama, contrasting the sleep of the prone soldier, the oblivion of the guard in profile, and the astonishment of the soldier on the right. The angel, dressed in a white alb (a long white vestment worn by priests), repeats the blessing of the angel in the *Annunciation*, so that the salutation which initiated the altarpiece's narrative of salvation here concludes it with acknowledgement of Christ's rebirth.

Working in Leuven in the Dutch Netherlands, Bouts ran a large, successful workshop and was appointed city painter in 1468. His style is more down-to-earth than that of his contemporary Rogier van der Weyden; its humble realism has come to be seen as characteristic of a Dutch tradition. Bouts painted for confraternities, for townsfolk rather than nobles. Renouncing grand gestures or heroic physiognomies, as well as caricature or crude brutality, he painted human beings from whatever station in life with equal dignity and searching regard for emotional truth. This sympathy, prophetic of Rembrandt, is evident in the Dutch face of the startled soldier.

Molanus remarked in the 16th century that Bouts "excelled in painting the countryside," and this, too, contributed to the accessibility of his art. Contemporary viewers of his *Resurrection* did not need to be versed in theology to identify Christ with the sun. The twilit landscape invites exploration and extends the time frame. Figures are absorbed within the narrative, and the three Maries still have a long walk from the city to reach the tomb.

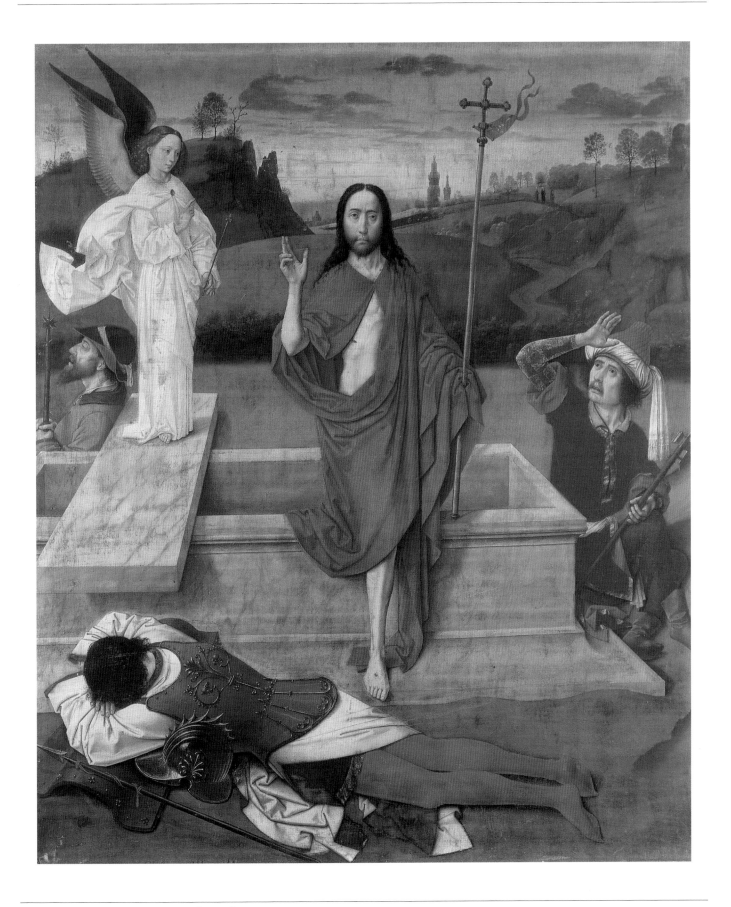

c. 1455 | *glue size on linen* | 35¹⁄₂ x 29¹⁄₂in (90 x 74.5cm) | The Norton Simon Foundation, Pasadena

The Resurrection

DIERIC BOUTS conceived the *Resurrection* as an unfolding drama, the Italian painter Piero della Francesca staged it as a tableau. Piero's was painted in fresco in the town hall of his birthplace, Borgo San Sepolcro, a name that means "Town of the Holy Sepulcher." Therefore, this public image of Christ, reigning from his sepulcher, is an emblem of civic pride. The citizens of Sansepolcro are left in no doubt that, strong and watchful, their Risen Lord is here to stay and that the soldiers are less his adversaries than their surrogates, sleeping safe beneath his protection.

Sansepolcro is a small town in the upper Tiber valley, lying to the southwest of Florence and separated by mountains from the major artistic centers. Starting from this relatively remote base, Piero della Francesca became one of the most intellectual painters of the mid-15th century. Early on he was exposed to the Sienese coloristic tradition, notably in the paintings of the Lorenzetti (active 1319–48) and of Sassetta (c. 1390–1450), then a sojourn in Florence in 1439 brought him into contact with Masaccio's frescoes in the Brancacci Chapel (see pages 70–71), the Classicism of the sculpture of Luca della Robbia (1400–1482), and the theoretical expositions of Alberti's recent treatise, *On Painting* (1436). Piero himself became a formidable mathematician and expert in Euclidean geometry, writing treatises on the five regular solids and on perspective, in which he adapted Alberti's division of the art of painting into design, composition, and coloring. Piero defined design as the "profiles and contours that enclose objects"; for Alberti's "composition" he substituted *commensuratio*, a Latin word implying both symmetry and proportion. Coloring he defined as (in Michael Baxandall's translation) "how colours show themselves on objects—lights and darks as the lighting changes them."

For Piero, the shape and arrangement of forms had to work in unison with perspective to create a visual order that was itself a manifestation of the immutable laws of mathematics. Construction preceded and governed observation. As noted in the essay on Masaccio, fresco demanded forethought and precluded changes of mind; working out the "profiles and contours that enclose objects" and fitting them together in the wall space was

**PIERO DELLA FRANCESCA
(PIERO DEI FRANCESCHI)**

*BORN BORGO SAN SEPOLCRO c. 1420,
DIED BORGO SAN SEPOLCRO 1492*

an essential part of planning. In Piero's *Resurrection,* this involved coordinating the foreshortening of individual shapes with the overall geometry. The sleeping soldiers are drawn according to a viewpoint below the top of the tomb. The virtuoso foreshortening of the head of the soldier leaning back was plotted on paper and then the lines were transferred on to the wet plaster by rubbing fine black powder through perforations in the design. This plotting included the demarcations between light and dark that vividly inform about the tilt of the head relative to the light. How lighting changes colors is integral to design, while alternations between green and red—in shield, helmets, boots, and cloak—here accent surface geometry. The beauty of Piero's color depends upon the lucidity with which modeling is coordinated with clear-cut design.

The soldiers are seen from the eye-level of a spectator standing in the town hall, whereas Christ is viewed frontally. In releasing the divine figure from the subjective viewpoint of the spectator, Piero has taken his cue from Masaccio's fresco of the *Trinity* (c. 1426, Santa Maria Novella, Florence) in which Christ on the cross and God the Father were not foreshortened in accord with the low vanishing-point that governed the rest of the illusion. Looking straight out and aligned on the central axis of the painting, Piero's Christ is the linchpin of the pictorial order and its symbolic meaning. This geometric order has historic as well as sacral connotations. The scene is framed by antique architecture, the soldiers are dressed as Romans, and Christ is draped like a statue of the god Apollo. In addition to the attempt at archeological accuracy in placing the Resurrection in the time of the Roman occupation of Judaea, this realization of an antique world in the town hall conferred the dignity of ancient origins upon Sansepolcro itself—a highly desirable attribute in mid-15th-century Italy. In Piero's tableau of Apollonian clarity, landscape has an explicit grandeur. The columnar trees on the left are bare in token of winter and the death of Christ, while on the right the younger trees have burst into leaf, a sign of Easter and the spring. This landscape has none of Bouts's twilit mystery; rather it includes vegetation symbolism as ancient as the gods themselves.

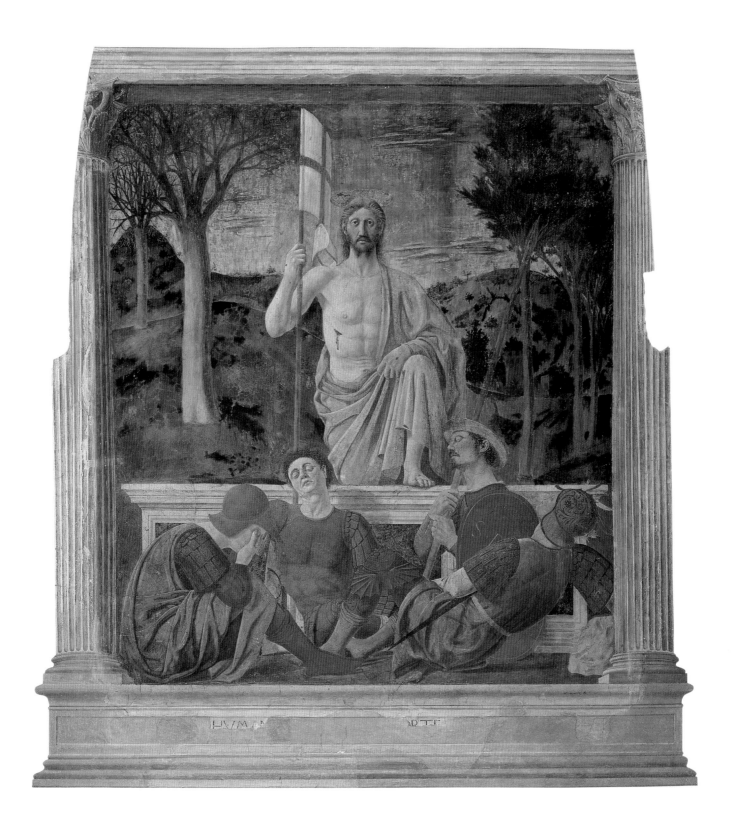

c. 1460 | *fresco* | 89 x 79in (225 x 200cm) | Museo Civico, Sansepolcro

Camera Picta

I F THE LOSS of paintings on cloth can skew assessment of art production in northern Europe, the loss of frescoes in secular settings in Italy might be equally misleading. Descriptions of rooms painted for princes such as the Sforza and the d'Este indicate the importance of murals with portraits of the rulers, their families, courtiers, horses, and dogs. By the standards of Burgundy or France, north Italian courts were small and therefore dependent upon marriage alliances and diplomatic maneuvering. In these principalities, patronage played a role in statecraft and the maintenance of political prestige. Artists were called upon to fashion the image, portray the dynasty, and display the magnificence of the prince.

Lodovico Gonzaga, Marquis of Mantua from 1444 until his death in 1478, understood the presentational value of art. He had been educated in Roman history and ethics, poetry and oratory, mathematics and music, astronomy and the martial arts, in the school of the humanist Vittorino da Feltre. He consulted closely with Alberti, who designed two churches for him that incorporated the Roman triumphal arch and temple pediment into Christian architecture. In 1460, shortly after Alberti arrived in Mantua, Lodovico finally secured as his salaried court painter Andrea Mantegna, an artist who would also appropriate the antique for the glorification of the Christian prince.

Mantegna had trained in Padua, an ancient university city and meeting place of artists, scribes, scholars, and antiquarians. In his early works, he already responded to the spirit of antique sculpture, to the proportions of Classical inscriptions, and to the dramatic possibilities of linear perspective demonstrated in the paintings and sculptures recently executed in Padua by Paolo Uccello (1397–1475) and Donatello. Mantegna's intellect and skill were put to many uses by Lodovico and his successors. As a court artist he was not constricted by guild membership as to the materials in which he might work. He advised on a monument to the Roman poet Virgil, supplied drawings for vases and tapestries, refined the art of engraving as a demonstration of skill and imagination (greatly influencing Dürer), painted small devotional works and the large-scale canvases, *The Triumphs of*

ANDREA MANTEGNA

BORN NEAR PADUA 1430/31,
DIED MANTUA 1506

Caesar (c. 1486, Hampton Court Palace, London). But his masterpiece was the decoration of a painted chamber in the Castello San Giorgio. When distinguished visitors were ushered into the Camera Picta, they entered a work of art mirroring and elevating the Gonzaga court. Mantegna created a theater which allowed living persons and painted representations to interact. On the three bays of each wall he devised the fiction of a loggia with curtains drawn back. On the vault he painted *trompe l'oeil* monochrome bas-reliefs imitating the form of mosaic, of eight Roman Caesars against a field of gold, pierced at its center by an oculus, a circular opening. Here the visitor's gaze, directed through the virtuoso perspective of the aperture, is answered by the gazes, imaginary and matter-of-fact, of putti, a peacock, and servants; their playfulness contrasts with the solemnity of the Caesars. On the right-hand wall, Mantegna accommodated the fireplace. Courtiers and pages ascend steps, then cross in front of a painted pilaster as if in the space of the room itself, an illusion enhanced by the pictorial lighting that corresponds to the actual fall of light from a window to the right.

The walls carry portraits of the Gonzaga family, their retainers, and allies. Mantegna animated these groups with implications of narrative, but it is unlikely that they record specific events. In keeping with the dedication to Lodovico and to his "illustrious wife Barbara, incomparable glory of womanhood," Barbara of Brandenburg is prominent on the fireplace wall, attentive to her husband as befits a consort who took over business of state when the marquis was absent. She is also shown as mother of the dynasty, surrounded by five of her children.

Mantegna blends Netherlandish realism, courtly decorum, and antique stylization. He describes the precise cut and livery colors of the costumes. His portraits, unlike Pisanello's before him (see page 77), do not flatter his sitters but endow them with resolve. He learned from the antique, as well as from Donatello, that the angle from which a head is seen, the rhythm in the foreshortening, is the key to form and expression. To his patron the marquis, represented on both walls, he gave a dignity comparable to that of the imperial Caesars overhead.

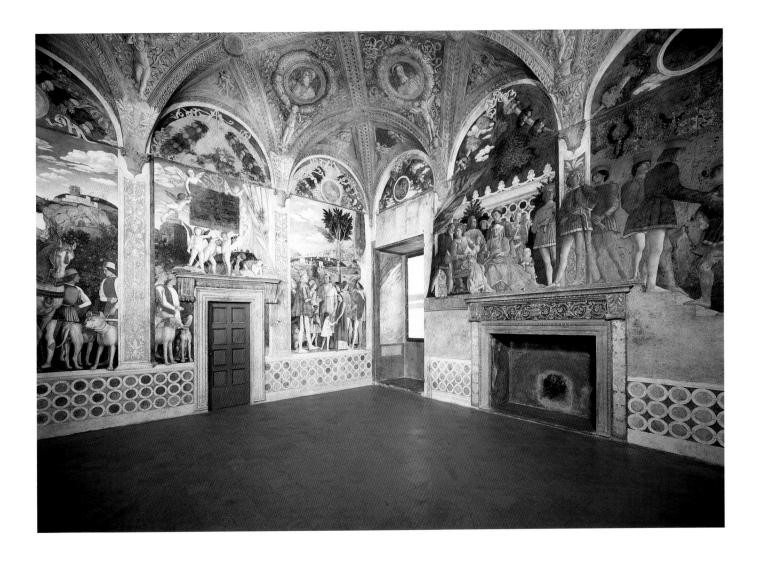

1465–74 | *fresco* | vault 23ft (7m) high, walls 26ft 6in (8.1m) wide | Castello San Giorgio (Palazzo Ducale), Mantua

Saint Jerome in his Study

By THE 1450s, Eyckian panel paintings were highly prized in Italy. Bartolomeo Fazio describes a triptych by Jan van Eyck in the apartments of Alfonso, King of Naples, admiring on one wing "Jerome like a living being in a library," on the outside portraits of the donor Battista Lomellini and his wife, and between them a ray of sunlight falling through a chink in the wall. A saint in his library, portraits, and sunlight penetrating an interior, are all features of Netherlandish art that made an impact on Antonello da Messina, a Sicilian-born painter working in Naples. Antonello was also precocious in learning the subtleties of Eyckian oil technique, applying glazes in translucent layers and also counterfeiting hard surfaces with opaque and textured paint. In portraiture he excelled. Starting from Netherlandish formats for close-up presentation of the head in three-quarter view behind a parapet, he intensified the contrast between light and dark, slightly regularized the volumes, and projected the sitter more assertively toward the viewer.

Some historians have argued that the exquisite panel of *St. Jerome in his Study* might be a portrait of a contemporary learned cardinal in the guise of Saint Jerome. More plausibly, it may be interpreted as a showpiece made to advertise the range of Antonello's skills, including the rendering of architectural space, interior and exterior light, still life, birds, animals, and possibly portraiture. The panel is first mentioned in 1529 in a Venetian collection, yet since there is nothing remotely Venetian about the architecture, it is likely that Antonello painted it in Naples and brought it with him when he came to work in Venice in 1475–6 to display his credentials to strangers.

If so, Jerome was a canny choice. As a scholar educated in Classical rhetoric and grammar, famed for his library, whose Latin translation of the Bible, the Vulgate, was the authorized text of the Western Church, Saint Jerome appealed to the learned elite of the 15th century as they strove to square their Christian faith with their enthusiasm for the philosophy and style of ancient Greek and Roman authors. To men seeking to balance an active life in politics or the Church with a contemplative life of study, discovery of the letters of Jerome brought a breath of

ANTONELLO DA MESSINA

*BORN MESSINA 1430,
DIED MESSINA 1479*

fresh air into the world of scholastic theology. Jerome's penitence in the wilderness and his friendship with the lion offered a pattern for how scholars should be in sympathy with nature and with other living creatures.

Van Eyck, it appears from derivatives of his lost original, depicted Jerome hemmed in by his library, whereas Antonello—with a Mediterranean feel for clear light and proportioned space as a tonic to the intellect—imagined the Church Father in a setting open to the sunlight and the swallows. The threshold, framed by a depressed Gothic arch, calls to mind in its fine-jointed finish that Antonello was the son of a stonemason; he has flecked the stones and incised the wet paint with a pointed instrument in a painterly rendering of veining and chisel marks. This threshold admits to a structure, bare and high-vaulted like a church, into which he has inserted the finely carpentered carol or study of the saint. As the Church Father identified with *Ecclesia*, Jerome was often shown holding a model church illuminated by rays to symbolize how his teaching dispelled the darkness of error and heresy. Antonello expanded the attribute into the overarching setting and naturalized the golden rays into a wonderfully modulated spatial interplay of light and darkness—in the midst of which, in the shadows of the aisle, the saint's lion pauses. Facing Jerome, lit only by reflected light in the darkness above the carol, a tiny crucifix signals the source of salvation.

Many of the objects and creatures positioned around the saint may bear symbolic meaning—the apothecary's jars may refer to the salving of man's ills by the death of Christ, and the peacock could allude to immortality and the garden of Paradise. The shoes that Jerome has taken off at the bottom of the steps to his study intimate that, like Moses before the Burning Bush, he is in the presence of divine inspiration. But it was not by coded meanings that Antonello impressed prospective clients. The grace by which Jerome's intellect was illuminated is given a self-evident visual form by the proportioned combination and lighting of the pictorial elements. Such lucidity and poise was not lost on the Venetians, both patrons and artists, including the great Giovanni Bellini.

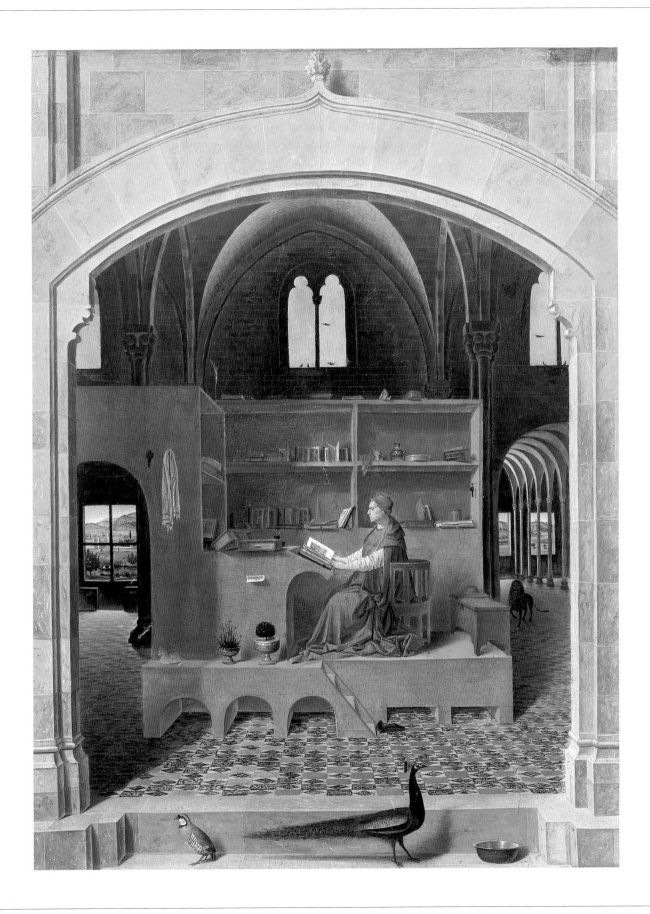

c. 1465 | *oil on panel* | 18 x 14in (46 x 36cm) | National Gallery, London

Saint Francis

DURING HIS VISIT to Venice in 1475–76, Antonello da Messina painted portraits, small-scale devotional images, and an altarpiece. These must have been admired for their realism, their spatial lucidity, and their oil-based technique by the man establishing himself as the most accomplished painter in *la Serenissima*, "the most serene Republic" of Venice, Giovanni Bellini. Giovanni had learned from Netherlandish paintings how to naturalize the rocky landscapes drawn by his father, Jacopo, in his two remarkable drawing-books (British Museum; Louvre). The twilit landscape of Bouts's *Resurrection* (see page 85) may have inspired his rendering of dawn in the *Agony in the Garden* (National Gallery, London) in the mid-1460s, and Bellini returned to the theme of light, setting the mood of a religious painting in the following decade in his *St. Francis*.

Apparently a private commission for a domestic setting, this painting conforms neither to an altarpiece format nor—at well over 3ft (1m) high—to the kind of small-scale devotional panel that was usually hung in a bedroom. The identity of the patron is uncertain; however, the identity of the saint is not in doubt, but the subject is ambiguous. The picture is recorded by Marcantonio Michiel, in 1525, in a house in Venice, as *San Francesco nel deserto*. In Italian, *deserto* suggests a wilderness, a place that is not necessarily barren but one that is lonely, beyond the civilization of the city and the cultivated fields, a place for spiritual retreat, prayer, and penitence. Like Christ, who withdrew into the wilderness for forty days in preparation for his Passion, Saint Francis withdrew to the mountain of La Verna, where he received on his body the marks of Christ's wounds, the stigmata. The rocks behind Francis in Bellini's painting refer unmistakably to the celebrated rocks of La Verna; their strata is recorded in a small panel by van Eyck, *St. Francis Receiving the Stigmata* (c. 1430, Museum of Art, Philadelphia), which was in Venice for a few months in 1471.

Bellini transformed his Eyckian model from the subject of the Stigmatization into one that is more generalized, potentially more appealing to a secular patron and one that gives freer scope to a painter's skills. Later Bellini declared that he liked to "wander at will in his paintings," and we may suppose that

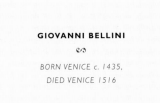

GIOVANNI BELLINI

☙

BORN VENICE c. 1435,
DIED VENICE 1516

already in his *St. Francis* he adapted iconography according to the prompting of his poetic imagination. Playing down the stigmata themselves, Bellini imagined the saint in prayerful ecstasy.

Saint Francis is small in relation to the format, absorbed within God's creation which he praised in his *Canticle to the Sun*. Since about 8in (20cm) have been trimmed from the top of the panel, this immersion in nature must originally have seemed even more complete. Bellini employs light to signal the reception of grace. The foreground, the place of penitence and meditation on the Passion, is dominated by a cool bluish-gray, while the saint and distant landscape are warmed by the rays of the sun. Meaning is not preordained but emerges from the play of difference—cool and warm, barren and cultivated, bare and leafy. Behind Francis is his humble but lovingly pleached and joinered cell where, reading in the Gospels of Christ's death, he kept before his eyes on his desk a simple cross above the skull of Golgotha. Together with the Eucharistic vine above and the sepulcherlike cave behind, this side of the painting evokes the death of Christ on Good Friday. The left side, by contrast, evokes Christ's rising from the dead at Easter: the sunlight, as it emerges from the clouds at the top right, inclines the laurel tree—token of Christ's victory over death—toward Francis, as if in acknowledgment that the saint was "another Christ."

Giovanni Bellini was reluctant to take on the complex allegories or Classical subjects mastered by his brother-in-law Andrea Mantegna. Instead, he was a shrewd operator in the market for devotional art that was particularly strong in the conservative society of Venice. With top-quality works, he fed the developing taste of the patriciate, in their lagoon city, for landscapes, at first introducing a glimpse of a view behind sacred figures, later, as in the *St. Francis*, immersing them in it. For a slightly lower level of the market, he trained his large workshop to produce variations, sometimes with the help of tracings from cartoons, of his serene compositions of the Madonna and Child.

Bellini initiated the greatest period of Venetian painting, and his paintings influenced the finest masters of the next generation, including Giorgione, Sebastiano del Piombo, and Titian.

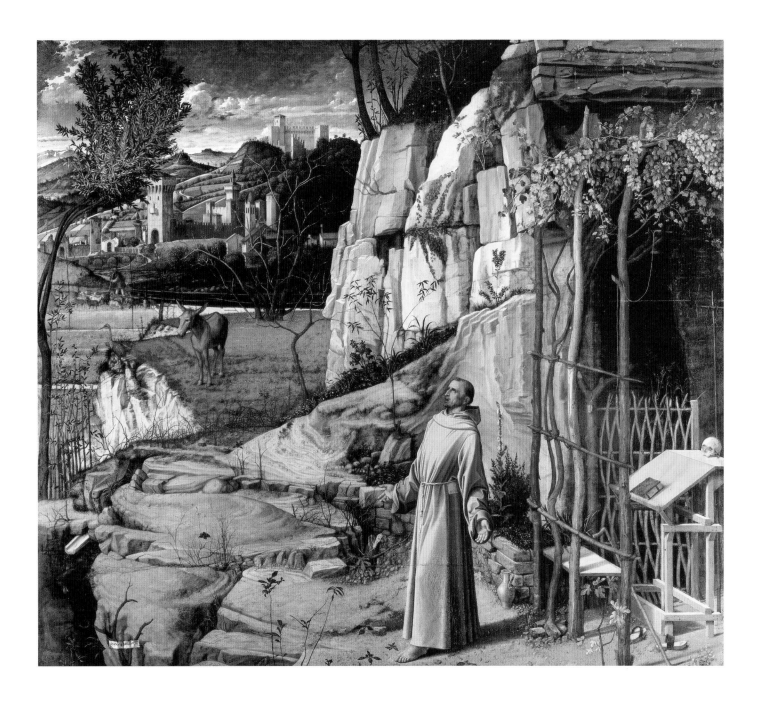

Late 1470s | *tempera and oil on panel* | 49 x 56in (124 x 142cm) | Frick Collection, New York

Primavera

GIOVANNI BELLINI was a master of stillness, Sandro Botticelli of movement. Both Venice and Florence were republics, but whereas Venice was dominated by a patrician ethos that stressed corporate values, Florence offered more opportunities for professional advancement. Venetians valued the glow of color that captured life as a continuum; in Florence, no artist could hope for critical acclaim during the quattrocento unless he answered Alberti's call to animate the narrative or *historia* through movement. In sculpture, Donatello (see page 69) energized his compositions by the action of figures and the movement of draperies; for Leonardo da Vinci (see pages 100–101), born just seven years after Botticelli, the movement of the body was the outward sign of the movement of the mind.

The *Primavera,* or '*Spring,*' by Sandro Botticelli is a fable about the power of love, told through interlinked movement of figures. In creating his own poetic invention, Botticelli blended images drawn from Classical and contemporary poetry, notably Ovid's *Fasti* and the *Stanze* of Poliziano. The picture is first recorded in the house of a young cousin of Lorenzo the Magnificent, Lorenzo di Pierfrancesco de' Medici, and bears the hallmarks of the tastes of the young Medicean circle that was the ruling faction in Florence. It is set in a grove of oranges, the tree known in Latin as *arbor medicus* and whose fruit resembles the golden balls that were the emblem of the Medici bank. The young Lorenzo de' Medici wrote love poems invoking Venus as the figure for the beloved, and organized jousts and festivals in which rustic nymphs and goddesses mingled with the trappings of chivalry. Botticelli's panel would probably have been mounted above shoulder height as part of the furnishings of a palace room.

The narrative—exceptionally—reads from right to left. The west wind, Zephyr, blue and chill, bends the trees as he rapes the bare winter earth, personified by Chloris, an insemination that-transforms her from a shy nymph into the confident figure of Flora. This blossoming is realized by flowers issuing from the mouth of Chloris and entwining with the blooms that cover Flora, and by the dozens of varieties of spring flowers, drawn with botanical accuracy, that cover the earth. Flora, abandoning

**SANDRO BOTTICELLI
(ALESSANDRO DI
MARIANO FILIPEPI)**

*BORN FLORENCE 1445,
DIED FLORENCE 1510*

maidenly modesty, looks straight out as she scatters blooms from her lap. The fertility and passion of this opening trio is tempered by Venus, who stands framed by myrtle, symbol of marriage. April is dedicated to her as ruler of the spring. Unlike the Classical goddess of love, this Madonnalike Venus appears fully clothed; her head inclined, she gently welcomes the spectator to approach her court. In this guise she represents the power of the beautiful woman, an idealized beloved—a secular version of Dante's Beatrice—who guides the heart from carnal to spiritual things. Above her is her son, blind Cupid, shooting his arrow tipped with a golden flame. Their influence is celestial, governing the dance of the Three Graces who, by their circling union, restore harmony to the garden. The central Grace gazes toward Mercury. In the Roman rustic calendar Mercury is associated with May, the month that marks the end of spring. In Classical mythology, as messenger of the gods, he is intermediary between the human and the divine, conductor of souls and god of sleep and dreams. As the god associated with the power to illuminate mysteries, he was much revered by philosophers in the Medicean circle, such as Ficino, who were attracted to the wisdom of Neo-Platonism, which contended that man could reach a higher spiritual plane by the contemplation of beauty and love. Mercury is recognizable from his winged helmet and boots; tongues of golden flame blazon his crimson cloak. He gazes heavenward and with his staff parts the clouds. In contrast to Zephyr, who set the fable in motion with a violent descent, Mercury brings it full circle with ascent to a higher realm of spirit and truth.

Botticelli's gods are not modeled on archeological evidence of their antique form. Mercury's stance is derived from that of Donatello's bronze *David* (c. 1440, Bargello, Florence); the females are still slightly elongated according to Gothic ideals of beauty. The costumes, rendered with sure rhythm by Botticelli's brush, are based on contemporary festival costumes for nymphs and goddesses. Unlike the stony Classical world of Mantegna's Caesars, the world of the *Primavera* is a wistful allegory. The young elite of Florence appreciated how, with lightness and grace, Botticelli distanced the body from the common and base.

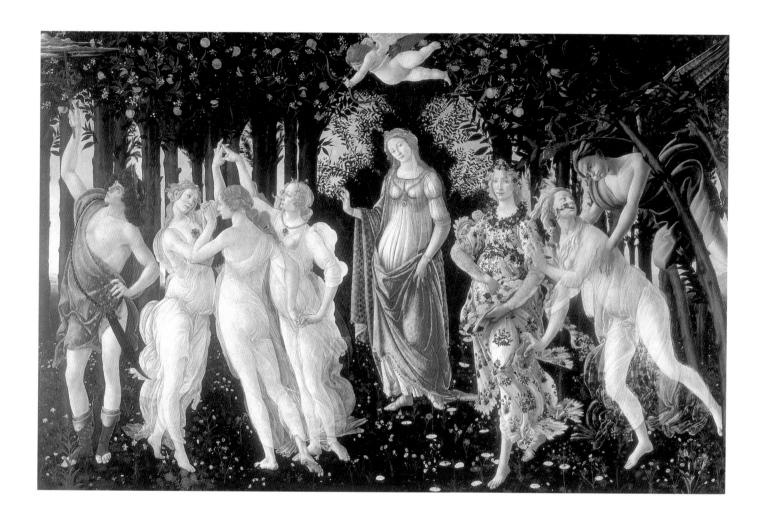

c. 1478 | *tempera on panel* | 80 x 124in (203 x 315cm) | Uffizi, Florence

The Four Church Fathers

IT IS FITTING to end this selection of 15th-century paintings with one that challenges any rubicon between northern and Italian art, or between Gothic and Renaissance. Michael Pacher worked near Bruneck (Brunico) in the southern Tyrol in what is today northern Italy. His winged altarpiece was commissioned, around 1483, by Dean Leonhard Pacher—possibly a relative—for the Collegiate Church at Neustift. Closed, it shows stories of Saint Wolfgang; open, it reveals the four Church Fathers, the most revered early writers on Christian doctrine. Originally it would have been completed by a predella (a row of small paintings beneath the altarpiece) and a carved frame which doubtless Pacher—as head of a sculptor's workshop as well as a painter—would have designed to echo the canopied stalls in which he placed the Fathers.

From the Rhineland to the Tyrol, many carved and polychromed altarpieces, extended by elaborate latticework and finials, presented the most compelling and three-dimensional images of the saints. They set the agenda—the standards of realism and complexity—with which paintings had to compete. Moving between carving and painting on panel, no artist was more aware of this than Michael Pacher. As a painter he relished counterfeiting a range of materials more varied and valuable than those available in the Tyrol. The canopies are in limestone ornamented with golden leaves, the interior facing of the stalls is in rectangles of porphyry, serpentine, and gray-veined marble. Pacher must have traveled in northern Italy to Padua and perhaps to Ferrara, where he saw the work of such masters of the marmoreal as Mantegna and Cosimo Tura (c. 1430–1495). In Italy he evidently studied perspective and light, noting how these could be coordinated to dramatize the presentation of subject.

Raised above the predella, *in situ* the Church Fathers would have been viewed from below. Pacher plotted a sharply foreshortened floor with a central vanishing point shared by all four panels; its level is well below the knees of the Fathers so that we look up to their heads and under their canopies. Contrasting with this low viewpoint, the light falls steeply from the top right-hand side. Sharp and strong, it emphasizes the carving out of

MICHAEL PACHER

~

BORN BRIXEN c. 1432,
DIED SALZBURG 1498

figures and architectural moldings as three-dimensional and faceted shapes. Pacher has followed the dramatic consequences of this directional light as it falls on the monochrome statuettes of saints in niches: John the Baptist, bearing the Lamb of God, initiates the series at the top left above Saint Jerome and, as befits the prophet of the light of Christ preaching to those who still dwelt in darkness, he is largely cast in shadow. By contrast, the Church Fathers, Jerome, Augustine, Gregory, and Ambrose, whose preaching and patristic writings illuminated the Catholic Church, are fully in the spotlight. Above or beside each hovers a dove, its whiteness an epitomy of light, symbol of the inspiring presence of the Holy Spirit. Pacher has enjoyed transcending the possibilities of sculpture by suspending his doves in mid-air, varying their flight paths and even introducing touches of humor—Jerome's dove peers nervously down at the approaching lion.

Four theologians in their stalls might not seem the most promising subject for the *corpus* or interior of an altarpiece. Pacher abandons the iconic presentation of saints in preference for condensed narratives that allow him—almost like a Florentine or Ferrarese painter—to animate his figures with movement. Within the overarching tempo of the traceries, the Fathers are like conductors articulating the rhythm; the outer pair, Jerome and Ambrose, turn inward, their masses of red and green robes bracketing the composition. The presentations rely on the Collegiate congregation being familiar with the stories connected with the saints. Cardinal Jerome gestures with open palm to encourage the lion to raise its paw and with the other hand holds the knife that will cut out the thorn. Augustine has a vision of the Christ Child on the seashore, who shows him that it is as hard to define the doctrine of the Trinity as it is to drain the sea with a spoon. Pope Gregory comforts the Emperor Trajan. Ambrose examines his quill, while below he is represented in his cradle in an allusion to a miracle in his infancy.

This is an art that is monumental, direct, and a shade naive. For the Protestant reformers of the next century, such vividness—such literal realization of theological mysteries—could be dangerously misleading to the faithful.

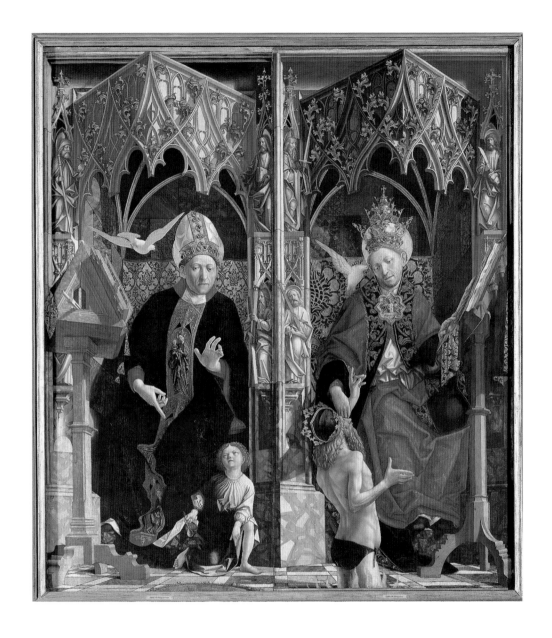

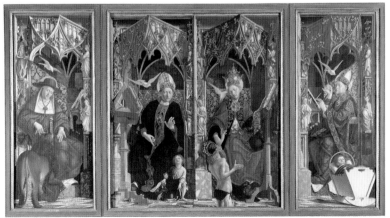

c. 1483 | *panel* | *central panels* 85 x 77in (216 x 196cm) each, wings 81 x 36in (206 x 91cm) each | Alte Pinakothek, Munich

THE HIGH RENAISSANCE AND MANNERISM

1500—1600 ❧ SHARON FERMOR

The early 16th-century High Renaissance is so called because it has traditionally been seen as the culmination of ideals and developments current in the previous century. This view has a certain validity, and there are some concerns common to the artists of the Early and the High Renaissance that were explored in different ways and to different degrees.

THE MAIN preoccupations shared by the Renaissance artists were the convincing representation of the human figure; the perfection of the dramatic narrative, or *istoria*; the mastery of space through a combination of perspective and light and shade; the emulation of the antique; and the refinement of color. However, to look at the High Renaissance in terms of the perfection of these ideas should not lead us to view the period in terms of a narrow uniformity. On the contrary, it was a time of tremendous innovation, seen at its best in the work of Italian artists. For example, we see Leonardo da Vinci, Fra Bartolommeo, Sebastiano del Piombo, and

Jacopo Sansovino's
Bacchus *(1506).*

Titian all experimenting with the form of the altarpiece and with the ways in which an artist could convey a religious theme or message. The same freshness of approach was true of private devotional works.

The narrative, or *istoria,* is explored most dramatically by Raphael, but the importance of the genre is also apparent in the work of Sebastiano, Tintoretto, and Veronese. Portraits also became increasingly popular, representing the middle classes, intellectuals, and collectors, as well as kings and courtiers. The importance of the antique is visible in the work of Michelangelo, but also in the architecture of Donato Bramante (1444–1514), seen in his richly classical Tempietto. The innovative *Bacchus* of Jacopo Sansovino (1486–1570) shows a variation on the antique in its sculptural exploration of the male nude, using a daring pose that displays his virtuosity.

The dynamism of High Renaissance art was partly a product of enlightened and increasingly ambitious patronage. The artistic schemes of Julius II (pope 1503–13) gave Raphael, Michelangelo, and Bramante the opportunity to develop their work in new ways while setting them formidable

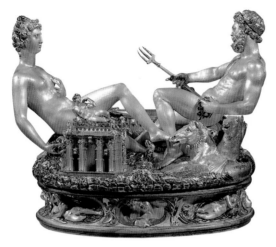

Cellini's Saltcellar of Francis I *(1539–43).*

artistic challenges. The example of the pope fostered a new appetite for art among members of the papal court in Rome, which stimulated the patronage of enlightened members of the merchant class in Florence. In Venice, the government of the Republic and the Scuole (charitable lay confraternities), as well as private individuals, also created new markets for art. Competition among the Italian city states was a remarkable stimulus for artistic expression.

Ever since the 16th century, it has been a commonplace that Florentine and Roman artists excelled in drawing, or *disegno*, especially of the human figure, whereas the strength of the Venetian artists lay in their handling of color, *colore*. The images reproduced here bear this out to a large extent. No one looking at Titian's *Pesaro Madonna*, for example, can fail to be struck by the brilliance of the palette and the vibrancy of the application of color, made possible by the use of oil. But we should not underestimate the refinement of color achieved by Florentine artists, such as Michelangelo (in the Sistine Ceiling) and Raphael.

Mannerism, in its most specific sense, describes Italian art of the post-High Renaissance, particularly of Rome, c. 1530–90. Art historians are divided over the question of whether Mannerism, with its stylized, overtly emotional qualities, was a rebellion against, or an extension of, the High Renaissance. Neither viewpoint is particularly useful, but the early period of Mannerism, as represented by Parmigianino, for example, shows an awareness of High Renaissance ideals. This is perhaps less true of Bronzino, whose work was very largely the product of an autocratic court that sought stimulation in an antinaturalistic type of art, and of artistry taken to its highest and most obvious degree by the sculptor and goldsmith Benvenuto Cellini (1500–1571).

Ultimately, perhaps, it is helpful not to separate the two phases of 16th-century art too rigorously, but to be sensitive to both their similarities and differences. As a whole, 16th-century art showed remarkable ambition and creativity, if somewhat restrained by the traditions of earlier years, in a climate that fostered artistic competition.

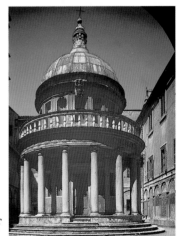

The Tempietto, *designed by Bramante and built in 1502.*

The Virgin of the Rocks

THE SUBJECT of Leonardo's painting, the Virgin and Child with Saint John the Baptist, was a popular one for private devotional images in Florence from the early 15th century on. This is partly explained by the fact that John the Baptist was the patron saint of the city, but the subject also offered considerable pictorial and emotional possibilities, posing the challenge of uniting three figures in a meaningful relationship in three-dimensional space. Experiments with the subject reached a high point in the first decade of the 16th century with a long series of Madonnas executed by Raphael and, to a lesser extent, Michelangelo. In this respect, although Leonardo left Florence in 1483 to work for the Duke of Milan, his work reflects the Florentine art to which he was exposed early in his career.

In other ways, Leonardo's interpretation of this popular theme is utterly unconventional and very much reflects his own interests. The painting was part of a commission for an altarpiece from the Confraternity of the Immaculate Conception of San Francesco Grande in Milan, but Leonardo completely broke with the conventions of the subject of the Immaculate Conception, which would usually require the Virgin to be shown standing, surrounded by prophets holding scrolls that proclaimed the miracle and the Virgin's exemption from Original Sin. This break with tradition, together with the fact that another, earlier version of the painting exists (Louvre, Paris), suggests that Leonardo had been developing an idea that he decided to explore here, based on a theme that was familiar to him from his time in Florence.

Leonardo's interpretation of the relationship between the Virgin, Christ, and Saint John is one of the most intensely moving of the Renaissance, despite the strangeness of the setting. The warmth of this relationship has been strengthened by the inclusion of an exquisite angel whose identity has never been satisfactorily explained. Unusually, the Virgin is shown kneeling, stretching her arms protectively around the figures. On the left, the young John the Baptist kneels in homage to his cousin, under Mary's sheltering arm and cloak. The Christ Child raises his hand in blessing, the other hand steadying himself on the ground. While earlier painters had generally shown Christ as a miniature adult or at least as self-possessed, Leonardo stresses the vulnerability of the child as the angel gently supports his back with his hand. Mary raises a brilliantly foreshortened hand in a gesture of blessing, but also of protection, over Christ's head.

The setting of the painting is certainly extraordinary and is peculiar to Leonardo. There is no biblical text that can adequately explain the placing of the figures within this rocky grotto. On the other hand, Leonardo had a fascination for geological formations and drew them endlessly in his notebooks. A rocky panorama similarly forms the background to the *Mona Lisa* (1503–6, Louvre). Here, the dark, watery grotto seems to be inhospitable, yet there are signs of luxuriant growth among the rocks, exquisite plants and leaf formations based on Leonardo's studies from life which presage fertility and hope.

The rocky cavern also allowed Leonardo to explore what he saw as one of the most important aspects of painting—chiaroscuro, or light and shade. The figures emerge like pale specters from the darkness around them, the shadows both giving them form and lending them an enigmatic air. Chiaroscuro is used to mold and define the figures, imbuing them with a powerful three-dimensional presence. The setting also displays Leonardo's intense study of atmospheric phenomena. Instead of the more conventional treatment of distance as a sudden jump from brown to blue, Leonardo subtly modulates the colors from brown through blue-green, to azure, to misty blue-white in the farthest reaches. These and the blue of Mary's robe are the only colors in the painting—in stark contrast to the work of Leonardo's Florentine contemporaries who tended to use a wide palette— apart from the brilliant flash of gold drapery across the Virgin's stomach, which marks the highest point of illumination in the painting and indicates the subject of the commission.

Leonardo's genius and versatility as artist, scientist, engineer, and thinker were acknowledged in his day. Through him, the artist was elevated far above craftsman status. The monumentality and balance of his works, his mastery of oils, and his dynamism as a draftsman had an enormous impact from the High Renaissance onward.

LEONARDO DA VINCI

*BORN VINCI 1452,
DIED CLOUX 1519*

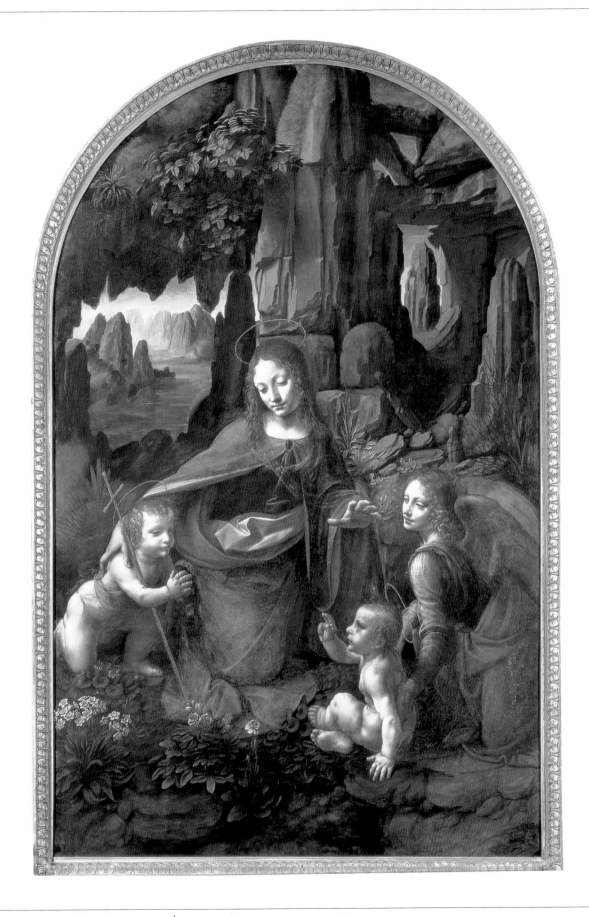

c. 1508 | *oil on panel* | 189 x 119cm (74$\frac{1}{2}$ x 47in) | National Gallery, London

Disputà

ONE OF RAPHAEL'S most remarkable gifts as a painter was his ability to communicate complex ideas in an apparently simple way. The subject of this painting is the dispute, or discussion, over the real presence of Christ in the Eucharist; that is, whether the Host consumed during the Mass actually transforms into the body of Christ. It does not show one historical debate, but emphasizes the importance of this doctrinal issue to the Church across the centuries. Raphael structures this complex theme by building the painting around three golden circles that diminish in size. At the top, against a large gold dome, stands God the Father, one hand raised in blessing and the other holding the orb that symbolizes his dominion over the world. In the center circle sits Christ, on a tier of clouds with a dais resembling that of the altar below, his hands raised to display his wounds. Directly below Christ is a small gold disk where the Holy Spirit is represented by the traditional symbol, the dove. Below is the Host itself, placed on the altar in a circular monstrance; the perspective of the tiled pavement—and so the viewer's eye—focuses on this tiny object. All these elements are on the same vertical axis, explaining almost diagrammatically how, by the authority of God the Father and the agency of the Holy Spirit, the wounded body of Christ is turned into the wafer of the Host: a clear visual expression of the complex notion of transubstantiation. Witness to this momentous fact is an assembly of saints, the Virgin, martyrs, evangelists, and prophets.

But what is also striking about this image is the way in which Raphael has turned it into a narrative, as if something immediate and urgent was happening at that moment. This may reflect the fact that *istoria*—narrative, or history painting—was coming to be seen as the greatest subject for a painter's skill. All Raphael's figures move, gesticulate, consult books, and interact with one another in a way that suggests something portentous is taking place at that very instant. People from the past and present are brought together in a vigorous debate that is entirely fictional but which gives the painting a large part of its interest and visual beauty. Raphael was known by his contemporaries for his skill as a narrative painter, and the *Disputà* in particular shows the

RAPHAEL (RAFFAELLO SANZIO)

*BORN URBINO 1483,
DIED ROME 1520*

influence of Leonardo's work in Florence, especially the latter's unfinished *Adoration of the Magi* (1481–82, Uffizi, Florence). The gestures are extremely expressive and varied, and are full of grace and beauty. Their eloquence is accented by the single raised arm of the figure to the right of the altar who points up to the heavens, unifying the two parts of the composition. Raphael has peopled the scenes with monks, cardinals, bishops, the Church Fathers, and particularly Sixtus IV (pope 1471–1484), who had written a treatise on the blood of Christ, on the right. Dante is also included, as is the then-living architect Bramante.

The fresco was commissioned by Pope Julius II in 1508 as part of the decoration of the Stanza della Segnatura in the Vatican, which he almost certainly used as his private library and study. This may explain the large number of books shown in the frescoes. The decoration of the room was divided into the four faculties of knowledge—theology, philosophy, poetry, and jurisprudence—along the lines of the organization of ancient libraries. The *Disputà* represented theology, and a figure of Theology is included in a roundel in the ceiling above the fresco. On the opposite wall is the equally dynamic *School of Athens* (representing philosophy) which, in contrast to the open space of the *Disputà*, groups ancient philosophers within an imposing architectural setting of perspectival brilliance. Both paintings have been enormously influential on contemporary and later artists.

Like all work undertaken for Julius II, the *Disputà* had an element of propaganda, not just in the prominent inclusion of his uncle, Sixtus IV, and the inscription of his own name on the altar, but in the references to his building works, on the right, to the new St. Peter's, and in the left background probably to work on the Vatican Palace, both being carried out by Bramante.

Raphael's work is characterized by dignity and refinement, seen repeatedly in his numerous Madonna and Child scenes, remarkable portraits, and tapestry designs. Also an architect and decorative designer, he was rich, famous, and revered on his premature death, regarded all but unanimously as the greatest painter ever well into the 19th century, and was held up as the ideal of academic art.

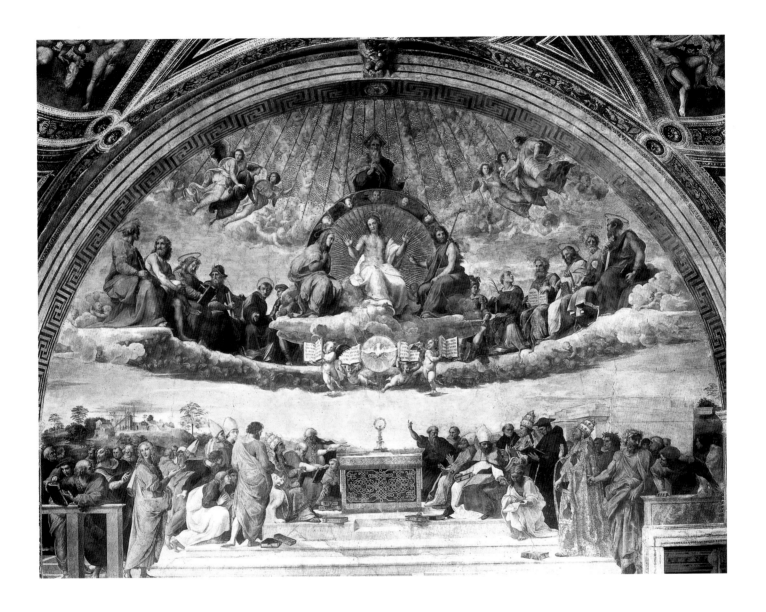

c. 1509–11 | *fresco* | Stanza della Segnatura, Vatican Palace, Rome

Sistine Ceiling

MICHELANGELO WAS THE most gifted artist of the High Renaissance and worked with equal brilliance in painting, sculpture, and architecture. His preferred medium was sculpture, and he initially resisted Pope Julius II's commission to paint the Sistine Ceiling on the grounds that he was not a painter. It is therefore no coincidence that the figures are extremely sculptural and are set within a complex architectural framework that is purely illusionistic. Unwilling to take on the commission, Michelangelo eventually painted the enormous work almost singlehanded. Although the content of the ceiling is clearly religious, it was conceived partly as a monument to Julius II, whose family emblem, the acorns and oak leaves of the della Rovere ("of the oak"), is interwoven throughout.

The basic subject matter of the ceiling are the Old Testament stories of the Creation of the world and of Adam and Eve, the Fall, and the story of Noah. Reading from the altar backward, each rectangular compartment contains a story or pair of stories flanked by pairs of nudes (ignudi) which support gold medallions containing further Old Testament stories. In the spandrels are the prophets and their pagan counterparts the sibyls, who both foretold the coming of a savior in human form. The ancestors of Christ are painted above the windows. The overarching theme that binds all these elements together is probably that of the Incarnation, making flesh of the divine. While the newly created Adam is a model of physical perfection, the sinful Noah, shown in a similar pose but drunk, is crumpled and sagging, a reflection of his fallen state. Also present is the theme of Salvation, as Christ was seen as a second Adam who came to redeem the latter's sins and those of his successors. This complex theme was designed, with the guidance of advisers, for the theologically learned audience of the Sistine Chapel, made up mainly of the pope and his immediate entourage. It also reflects the subjects of sermons preached there as well as continuing the subject matter of the walls, the Lives of Moses and Christ, painted in 1481–82.

One of the great strengths of the ceiling is Michelangelo's use of a fictive architectural structure that seems to spring from the upper part of the walls. This allowed him to create a complex interweaving of the levels of the ceiling, while maintaining the clarity of the narrative elements. In addition, recent cleaning has revealed the brilliance of Michelangelo's color in the prophets, sibyls, and ancestors of Christ, which relieves the somberness of the architecture, the nudes, and the central narrative scenes.

The nudes have long been one of the most controversial aspects of the ceiling. It seems most likely that they are part of an overall celebration by Michelangelo of the beauty of the male nude, captured in their Mannerist twisting movements. While this was a subject dear to the artist's heart and a central preoccupation of High Renaissance art, the beauty and dignity of man as a sign of God's greatness was the subject of sermons in the chapel, so the nudes are appropriate to the scheme.

The most famous of the images on the ceiling is God's Creation of Adam. Lying on his side, Adam is turned slightly toward the viewer to display the full beauty of his torso, modeled on an antique fragment known as the Belvedere Torso that was in Julius II's own collection. Unlike earlier depictions, which show Adam being physically raised by God, Michelangelo's Adam is fully formed and awake. He lacks only the will to live that God is about to transmit through his fingertips. In contrast to the languid Adam, God is a powerful and dynamic force, sheltering under his arm the soon-to-be-created Eve and surrounded by clusters of angels. The rudimentary nature of the background accentuates the figures and reveals Michelangelo's roots in the tradition of Early Renaissance narrative painting in Florence. This focus on the very essence of the scene contributes much to the greatness of the ceiling as a work of narrative art.

Exactly twenty-nine years after the Sistine Ceiling had been completed, Michelangelo's Last Judgment was finally unveiled on the front wall of the chapel. A brooding menace hangs over this work, which reflects the militancy of the Catholic Counter-Reformation. It expresses emotional turmoil, where above in the ceiling there is clarity and confidence. Michelangelo inspired great awe in his contemporaries and, from Raphael through the centuries to Reynolds and Rodin, has had an enormous influence on Western art.

MICHELANGELO BUONARROTI

☙

BORN CAPRESE 1475,
DIED ROME 1564

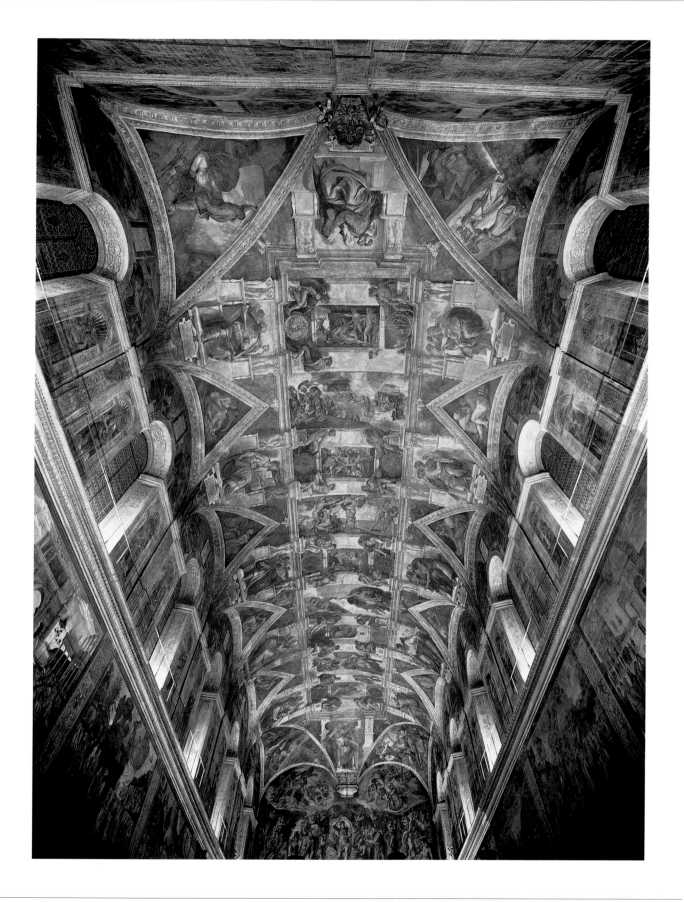

1508–12 | *fresco* | 133 x 43ft (40 x 13m) | Sistine Chapel, Vatican Palace, Rome

God the Father with the Magdalene and Saint Catherine of Siena

BACCIO DELLA PORTA was known as Fra Bartolommeo after he became a Dominican friar in 1500 under the influence of Savonarola (1452–1498), the religious and political reformer who dominated a severely puritanical republic in the city in the late 1490s. He entered the monastery of San Marco in Florence in 1504 and took control of the workshop. Fra Bartolommeo was one of the first painters to work in the High Renaissance style in Florence and bridged the gap between the late 15th-century manner of painting, exemplified by the often cluttered works of his master Cosimo Rosselli (1439–1507), and the simple, restrained classicism of the early 16th century. His early work influenced the young Raphael, but he in turn was influenced by the gravity and complexity of the mature Raphael. His work also shows the influence of Leonardo's chiaroscuro, and, in some cases, the color harmonies of the Venetians. Most of his paintings are religious, in keeping with his vocation, but he also had a passionate interest in landscape and left behind him several hundred exquisite landscape drawings.

This painting shows the friar's art at its purest and most direct. The space is airy and open and is constructed within an architectural surround which dissolves into the clouds at the top of the painting and creates the impression that we are looking at the scene through a window. Within this limpid space the figures dominate, and they are monumental, dignified, and restrained. Although the two saints are shown kneeling in pronounced contrapposto, or twisting poses, they are simply constructed, with large, unfussy folds of drapery and a direct, eloquent use of gesture. In the foreground, the lily and the book of Saint Catherine have an almost hallucinatory realism that makes the two saints seem tangible.

Behind the powerful presence of the saints, Fra Bartolommeo presents the viewer with a strange and dramatic leap to an equally vivid landscape, filled with signs of human activity. In its very ordinariness—the rustic buildings, the peasants, and the unremarkable features of the land—this scene is quite remote from the idealized landscape backgrounds of 15th- and 16th-century Florentine or Roman painting and shows the influence of early 16th-century Venetian works. Fra Bartolommeo visited Venice in 1508 and was much impressed by Giovanni Bellini's altarpieces. At the same time, the influence of Leonardo's chiaroscuro is apparent in the robust and shadowy figure of God the Father and in the delicate sfumato of the rest of the painting. The influence of Raphael is evident in the strong contrapposto of the saints and in the positions of the angels. These are disposed in two pairs, within which the figures mirror each other's poses, creating both symmetry and variety. This device is best known from the work of Raphael and developed from the 15th-century convention of showing single figures as mirror images on each side of a painting.

FRA BARTOLOMMEO (BACCIO DELLA PORTA)

∾

BORN FLORENCE 1472/5, DIED FLORENCE 1517

The commission for the altarpiece came in fact from a Venetian patron, the Dominican foundation of San Pietro Martire on the island of Murano. While the painting exemplifies the artist's restrained classicism, from an iconographic point of view it is very unusual. It was rare, for example, to include a full-length figure of God the Father in a painting, while it is unusual in postmedieval art to see saints levitating on banks of cloud. Interestingly, none of the figures looks at the spectator. Saint Catherine looks up at God, who seems to direct his gaze and his blessing toward her, while the Magdalene seems to be unaware of the figure of God and casts her eyes slightly downward.

The most likely explanation for the composition is that the altarpiece represents a vision of Saint Catherine, whose unworldliness is suggested by the fact that she is borne on the cloud. God is her vision and so is the Magdalene, to whom Saint Catherine had a particular devotion. The Magdalene herself does not share the vision, but nor does she engage the spectator, preserving the idea of a private revelation of which the privileged viewer is allowed a glimpse. The mystical aspect of the scene, which must have been at least partly Fra Bartolommeo's invention, is reinforced by the stark contrast with the homey, inhabited landscape behind the foreground stage. And the sanctity of the scene is enhanced by the sheer beauty of the image, with the dominant red of the Magdalene's gown contrasting with the sober black and white of Saint Catherine's garments and being picked up in the delicate jeweled chain held by the angels.

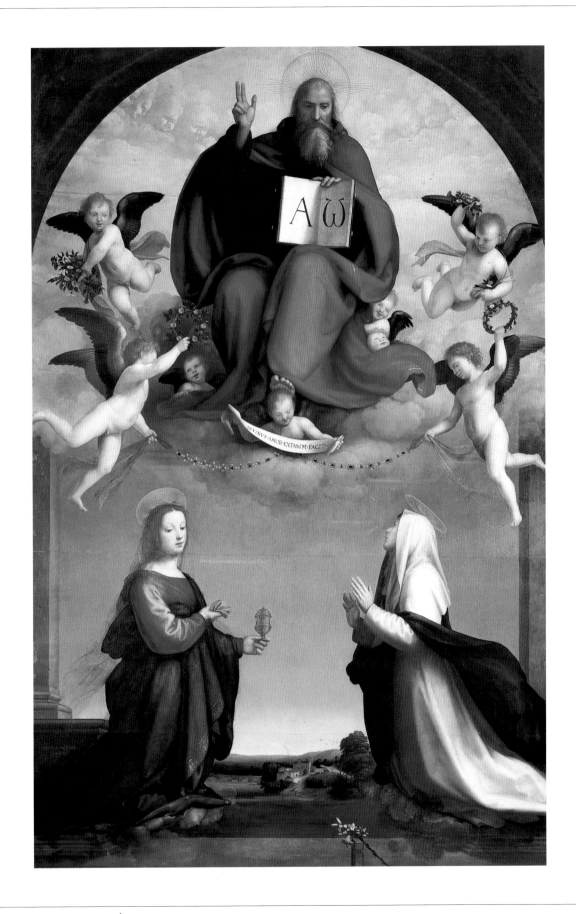

Concert Champêtre

SOME AUTHORITIES attribute this painting to Titian, but the subject matter links it most closely with Giorgione. Giorgione was recognized by his contemporaries as he is today, as an artist of singular talent and imagination whose works, which have often been confused with those of Titian (who completed some paintings after Giorgione's death), were very much in demand. Yet almost nothing is known of his life except that he was born in Castelfranco and was active in Venice from c. 1506 until he died, probably from the plague. He may have been a pupil of Giovanni Bellini, and he was greatly influenced by the chiaroscuro of Leonardo. Only a few securely attributable paintings survive, including religious works, portraits, and a handful of secular works for private patrons. He also painted frescoes on the façades of buildings in Venice, but most of these have disappeared. Writing of such a work on the Fondaco dei Tedeschi (the German warehouse), Vasari noted, "there are no scenes to be found there with any order, representing the deeds of any distinguished person … And I for my part have never been able to understand his figures."

This comment highlights a key aspect of Giorgione's works, which also tells us about the character of Venetian patronage. In addition to public and ecclesiastical patrons, private collectors, who often valued esthetic qualities over the clarity of the message, were becoming important to Venetian artists. Giorgione was one of the first to specialize in "cabinet pictures," small works for domestic settings, for such connoisseurs. So the artist's secular paintings, such as *Concert Champêtre*, are hard to interpret. This is true of a number of Venetian works from the early 16th century, whose mysterious qualities must have allowed for endless debate, in contrast to most secular works from Rome and Florence which were usually based on clearly identifiable texts.

That is not to say that Venetian paintings were never based on texts but that they were often drawn from evocative rather than narrative writings, such as pastoral poetry. In the case of this work, Giorgione was almost certainly influenced by the arcadian visions of contemporary poets who praised the charms of rural life over those of the town or the court. A well-dressed man

GIORGIONE (GIORGIO DA CASTELFRANCO)

BORN CASTELFRANCO, c. 1477, DIED VENICE 1510

plays the lute while conversing with a shabbily dressed companion. The musician, with his rich clothing, hat, and fine stockings, must surely be a courtier who has fled the civilized life for the charms of communing with a shepherd. The suggestion of music adds to the air of ease and rustic charm. In front of them are two naked women who are probably nymphs. They seem to belong to the world of the shepherd, for one plays a rustic pipe and the other draws water from a well which, intriguingly, is in the shape of a sarcophagus, and both have only plain white drapes. This scene has all the delights conventionally associated with the pastoral life. The figures sit on a grassy knoll in peaceful isolation, apart from another shepherd who goes about his daily work; they are away from the bustle of the city and enjoy the shade of verdant trees, with water readily available.

Yet, questions remain, mostly concerning the nymphs. The men do not appear to acknowledge their presence, so are these spirits of the countryside invisible to them? Many scholars continue to debate the meaning of this picture, assuming that the disjunction between the figures might well have some deeper allegorical significance.

Regardless of its meaning, the painting has an aura of tranquility, enhanced by the glowing colors of the courtier's clothes and the golden light that bathes the whole scene. The landscape background is characteristic of Giorgione's work as it is not idealized or improved upon, although it is remarkably green and fertile, in keeping with the pastoral vision. The unidentified buildings, together with the tower on the horizon, evoke the city life from which the young man has escaped. A taste for landscape was a feature of Venetian patronage long before it developed in other centers, so the landscape was almost certainly part of the painting's appeal. Ultimately, perhaps, the painting is not so complex but is simply an arcadian vision, set in familiar pastures and inspired by pastoral poetry.

The seductive appeal of Giorgione's paintings led to many imitations. Among later artists, Watteau was a great admirer of his compositions and style, and the 19th-century enthusiasm for Giorgionesque works led to many misattributions.

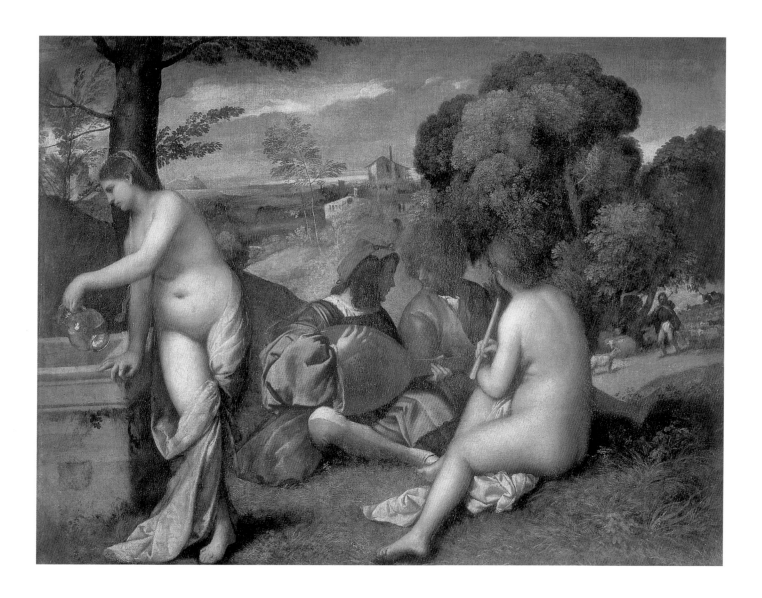

c. 1508 | *oil on canvas* | 43 x 54in (109 x 137cm) | Louvre, Paris

Madonna with Members of the Pesaro Family

TITIAN'S *Pesaro Madonna*, as this painting has been called, caused a revolution in the format of the altarpiece in Venice by elevating the Virgin and Child on a flight of steps and, most significantly, moving them from their traditional central and frontal position to one side. Titian created a type of dynamic, asymmetrical, diagonal composition which set a pattern for Venetian painting that lasted until the late 16th century. It has been suggested that he presented an oblique view so that the holy figures would be visible from the aisle of the church, but it seems equally likely that this was Titian's response to a complex commission that demanded the inclusion of numerous figures of varying status.

The altarpiece was a votive offering to the Virgin from the crusader Jacopo Pesaro in thanks for the victory of Saint Maurice in 1502, when Venice defeated the Turks. Jacopo, shown kneeling on the left, commissioned the painting in 1519 for the church where it still hangs. It was also intended to commemorate the male members of the family, several generations of whom are shown on the right. Saint Peter, possibly representing the papacy, acts as a mediator between Jacopo and the Virgin. She is both accessible, in the direction of her gaze, and remote, because of her elevated position and the backdrop of soaring columns. Above the members of the Pesaro family stand Saint Francis and Saint Anthony of Padua, the most important saints of the Franciscan order, to which the church belonged. Finally, Titian included the figure of Saint Maurice, bringing in a bound Turk and an African slave, under the dominant form of a billowing flag that bears both the Pesaro and the Borgia emblems, the latter denoting the family of Alexander VI (pope 1492–1503), pope at the time of the victory. On top of the flagpole is the olive branch of peace.

Titian solved the problem of joining this disparate group by the unusual device of showing the Virgin and the Christ Child facing in different directions. The playful Child faces the front of the picture, looking down at the adoring Saint Francis who in turn, by his gesture, recommends to Christ the members of the Pesaro family. The Virgin, through Saint Peter, focuses her attention on Jacopo, who is also linked to Saint Maurice by the rich, gleaming black of his clothes.

TITIAN VECELLIO

*BORN PIEVE DI CADORE c. 1485,
DIED VENICE 1576*

By displacing the center of the picture and showing most of the figures in motion, Titian brought to a traditionally static form a tremendous sense of energy and movement, further enlivened by the use of light and color. The columns, originally intended to be part of a basilica that Titian chose not to complete, contribute to the sense of an ambiguous and dramatic setting, neither clearly interior nor exterior, lit by the limpid light of the Venetian lagoon. Yet the light also comes from the front and picks up particularly the Virgin and Saint Peter, and the armor of Saint Maurice. The light has a joyous, festive air overall, yet above the Virgin there is a small cloud, carrying two putti with symbols of the Crucifixion, which casts a shadow on the column and over Christ and his mother. These remind us that the Virgin and Child should remain the focus of devotion.

Titian further unifies the composition by the brilliant use of color, especially the red triangle formed by the Virgin, the kneeling figure, and the flag, and the blue connecting the Virgin and Saint Peter. The yellow robe and green cloth of honor of the saint form accents in the very center of the painting. The richness and fluidity of the color and the many subtle reflections of light in the garments amply demonstrate Titian's mastery of the oil medium and the breadth of effects he was able to achieve. The finely characterized members of the Pesaro family also make clear why Titian was the most sought-after portraitist of the age.

Titian is regarded as the greatest painter of the Venetian school, superseding his teacher, Giovanni Bellini. His style continued to evolve throughout his career; Giorgione was an early influence, and Florentine monumentality. The 1530s saw a more meditative style, the 1540s the influence of Michelangelo and Mannerism, and a growing interest in the antique. By the 1560s, Titian's colors had become more muted and his method looser and almost Impressionistic, revolutionizing oil technique.

He painted magnificent mythologies and court portraits that set the pattern for generations to come. He served both Emperor Charles V and King Philip II of Spain as a highly honored court painter and, through his varied works, influenced Poussin, Rubens, Van Dyck, and Velázquez among many others.

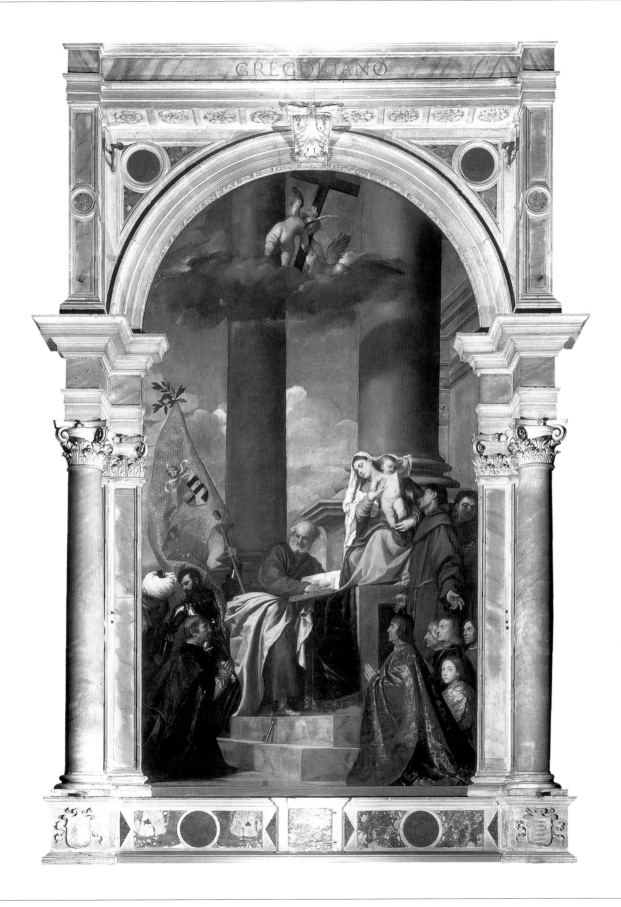

1519–26 | *oil on canvas* | 188 x 106in (478 x 268cm) | Santa Maria Gloriosa de' Frari, Venice

The Raising of Lazarus

AROUND 1510, following the death of his master Giorgione and while Titian was working in Padua, Sebastiano was the leading painter in Venice. In 1511, he was summoned to Rome by Agostino Chigi, the pope's banker, to participate in the mythological decorations of his villa, the Farnesina. He remained in Rome for the rest of his career, becoming the leading painter after Raphael's death in 1520 and during Michelangelo's absence in Florence. In 1531, he was appointed keeper of the papal seals, earning his nickname (*piombo* means "lead," from which the seals were made). Of particular importance to his career was his friendship with Michelangelo, who presented him with compositional drawings on several occasions, and Sebastiano certainly became a player in Michelangelo's rivalry with Raphael.

The Raising of Lazarus was commissioned in 1516 by Cardinal Giulio de'Medici for Narbonne Cathedral. Earlier that year he had commissioned the *Transfiguration* (1517–20, Vatican, Rome) from Raphael for the same church, and it seems almost certain that an unspoken competition was being set up between these two outstanding painters. *The Raising of Lazarus* shows more clearly than virtually any other contemporary work the extent to which, in the High Renaissance, altarpieces and their traditional biblical stories became vehicles for subject and history paintings rather than simply the focus of devotion. The subject depicted here had particular relevance to the commission, because the relics of Lazarus were venerated at Narbonne.

Lazarus, the brother of Martha and Mary Magdalene, had been dead for four days by the time Jesus arrived at Bethany. The sisters met Jesus on the road, Mary prostrating herself at his feet. At the grave, Jesus ordered the covering stone to be removed. Martha was afraid that the corpse would smell and is shown here averting her face, but she was told to have faith and she would see a miracle. Jesus ordered Lazarus to come forward, and the dead man appeared, wrapped in linen bands.

This huge work is full of life and movement, created through the varied interplay of hand gestures and arm movements. Only the center is still, where an imperious Christ summons forth the elegantly seated Lazarus. Three preparatory drawings by Michelangelo survive of Lazarus and his helpers, and he must also have assisted with the figure of Christ. The counterpoised Lazarus recalls the *ignudi* on the Sistine ceiling (see pages 104–5), while his muscular aides remind us of Michelangelo's famous mastery of the male nude. As in the Creation of Adam from the Sistine Ceiling, no touch is exchanged, life being transmitted simply by a pointing finger and a commandingly raised hand. Between the male figures, beautiful but ignored, is the imploring figure of Mary; the connection is simply between Christ and the resurrected man. This concept would have had particular significance for the cardinal whose family name was often used as a punning metaphor for doctor or healer (*medicus*).

While Sebastiano brought to the painting a certain Roman grandeur and the Romano-Florentine quality of *disegno* ("drawing," the notion of "line"), he combined this with his Venetian training in color (*colore*) and light. (Vasari was an early exponent of these two concepts and pronounced on the superiority of drawing and so, while greatly admiring certain Venetian masters, the overall inferiority of Venetian art.) This combination may have been intended by Sebastiano to outshine his Romano-Florentine rival Raphael, by showing himself to be a more "universal" painter. The scene is set in a landscape that takes up almost half the painting, emphasizing the Venetian love for the genre. And although it is full of ruins in the antique style, which recall the baths of Caracalla in Rome, the construction, light, and color are entirely Venetian. The representation of the scene at dusk demonstrated Sebastiano's skill with light and added a further element of drama to the scene. The brilliance and jewel-like range of the colors is remarkable. Central is Christ's ultramarine cloak, set off against a red gown that would originally have been much more vibrant, picking up the tone of the garments of Lazarus's sisters. The scattered repetitions of bright blues, acid greens, and golden yellows help to pull together a painting which, for all its splendor, has something of a fragmented, experimental air. When the two paintings were exhibited together, the cardinal preferred Raphael's *Transfiguration* and kept it in Rome, sending Sebastiano's altarpiece to Narbonne.

**SEBASTIANO DEL PIOMBO
(SEBASTIANO LUCIANI)**

☙

BORN VENICE c. 1485,
DIED ROME 1547

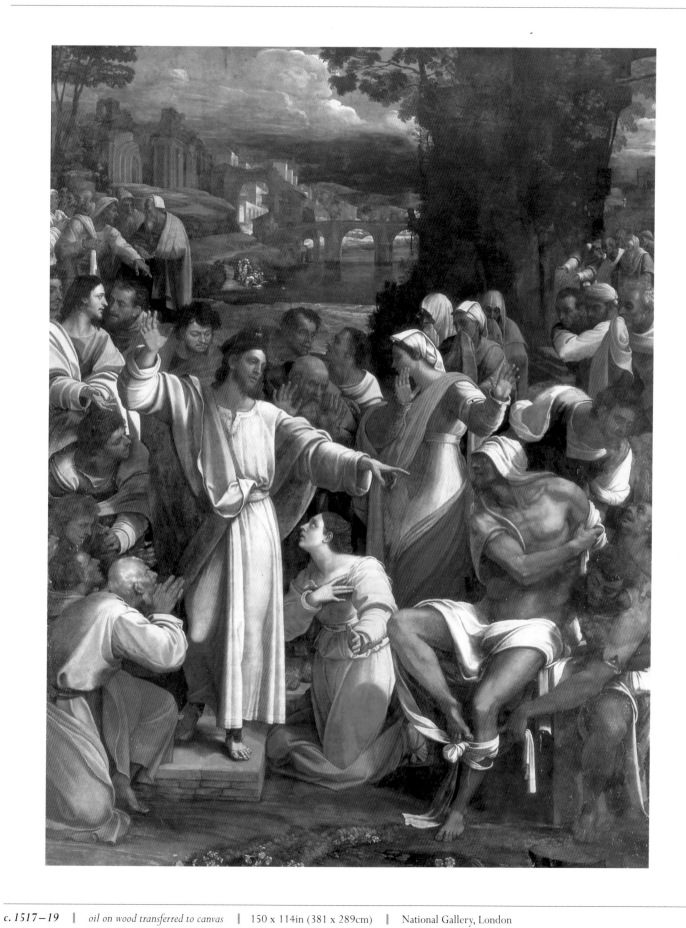

c. 1517–19 | *oil on wood transferred to canvas* | 150 x 114in (381 x 289cm) | National Gallery, London

Portrait of Andrea Odoni

LORENZO LOTTO was born in Venice but spent relatively little time in the city, working instead in towns in the Marches and in the city of Bergamo, where many of his altarpieces still remain. The origins of his artistic style are hard to determine. Although he shares with Titian and Giorgione a concern with light and color and a love of landscape, and is known to have been influenced by north European artists such as Dürer, he often had an idiosyncratic and highly individual approach to the figure and to composition. In his *Dialogue on Painting* (1557), the Venetian art critic Ludovico Dolce did not include Lotto in his list of notable Venetian artists of the 16th century, clearly finding it difficult to accommodate Lotto's style. He also criticized his use of light. Lotto was, nonetheless, one of the most gifted and distinctive artists of his time, whose work moves between High Renaissance and Mannerist traits.

This portrait is one of his most conventional works. It illustrates a trend among connoisseurs to have themselves portrayed as collectors, surrounded by their treasures—in Odoni's case, mainly antiquities. The collecting of antiquities had begun in the early 15th century when it was mostly confined to coins, gems, and small bronzes. It was only gradually that collectors sought and acquired large-scale fragments of antique sculpture. Odoni, a Venetian merchant, was a renowned collector and is shown surrounded by substantial pieces as well as coins and a precious book. The inclusion of such objects in a portrait imbued the sitter with considerable social and cultural status, and a collection also implied wealth.

Most of the pieces in the portrait can be identified and would actually have formed part of Odoni's collection. In his outstretched hand, which demonstrates Lotto's skill at foreshortening, he shows to the viewer a statuette of Diana of Ephesus in the Egyptian style. The fragment on the left is a reproduction of the Hercules and Antaeus, then in the Belvedere courtyard in the Vatican, which Lotto would have seen on his visit to Rome in 1509. In the right background there is a small statue of Hercules, a female nude, and a small putto. In the foreground is a Venus, missing its arms and head, and a giant male head in a late Roman style.

LORENZO LOTTO

♔

BORN VENICE c. 1480,
DIED LORETO 1556

The dramatic yet restrained presentation of the sitter, thrown into relief, and his direct engagement with the viewer, are characteristic of much early 16th-century portraiture, and this work shows the strong influence of Titian. In addition to his collected artefacts, Odoni's status can be read in the painting in a number of ways. His confidence and ease are emphasized but also his modesty, as the ostentatious action of his right arm is tempered by the placing of his left hand on his chest, a common gesture of humility. He is a model of the greatest virtue described by the Italian diplomat and writer Baldassare Castiglione in his influential work, *The Book of the Courtier* (1528); *sprezzatura*, or unselfconscious ease, was considered to be the main source of grace in an ideal courtier, essential for winning social favor. Odoni confronts the spectator with assurance but without bravura. The light gives him solidity and presence while allowing him to blend into the surrounding shade so that he does not appear too dominant. It also defines his broad forehead and nose and throws his cheeks into slight shadow, giving character to his face. The plain background offers no distractions.

At the same time, Odoni's clothes proclaim his wealth and status, from his impeccable white shirt to the gold chain around his neck, which he handles casually, suggesting a certain distractedness or absorption in his collection. His sober black undergarment reinforces this impression of discreet riches, as does his luxuriously textured fur-lined cloak, skillfully arranged to display the many-colored lining. The rich, opulent folds of thick fabric recall, for example, Titian's *Portrait of a Man with a Blue Sleeve* (c. 1512, National Gallery, London) as well as Raphael's *Portrait of Baldassare Castiglione* (c. 1515, Louvre, Paris) and illustrates how, even in Venetian art, known for its abundant use of detail and vibrant color, the suggestion of wealth could be subtly drawn out of apparent sobriety.

Lotto is now known chiefly for his portraits, but he actually worked mainly on religious subjects. His *Annunciation* altarpiece (1520s, Pinacoteca, Recanati) is full of originality and vigor, from the exuberance of the angel to Mary's surprise and her cat's terror, all couched in brilliant colors and lighting effects.

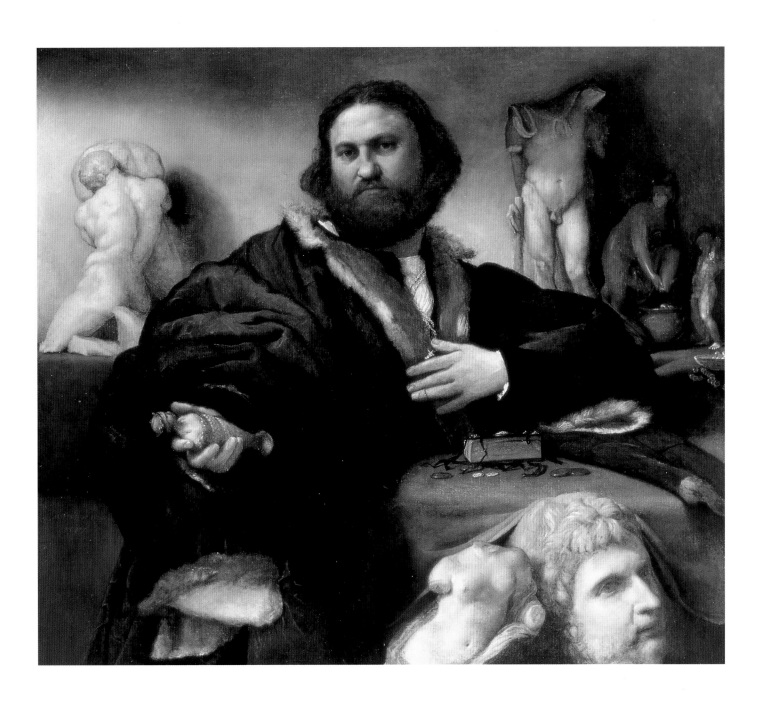

1527 | *oil on canvas* | 41 x 46in (104 x 117cm) | The Royal Collection, Hampton Court Palace

Portrait of a Woman with a Volume of Petrarch

ANDREA DEL SARTO was the most gifted, original, and prolific artist working in Florence in the 1510s and 1520s after Michelangelo and Raphael had left the city for Rome. Although he had a brief apprenticeship with the eccentric and influential Piero di Cosimo, the greater influence on Andrea's style was the work of Raphael and Leonardo, especially the latter's use of sfumato where colors or tones are blended so subtly that they melt into each other (Vasari saw this blurring of precise outlines as a defining difference between Early Renaissance and "modern," that is High Renaissance, art). At the same time, Andrea's figures often have an element of tension in them which, coupled with unusual and asymmetric compositions, look forward to early Mannerism. Both the young Pontormo (1494–1556) and Rosso Fiorentino (1495–1540), Mannerist pioneers, are thought to have worked on the predellas of Andrea's altarpieces, and Andrea is often credited with sowing the seeds of Mannerism in Florence. Vasari considered Andrea to be a fine colorist but with a slight timidity in his drawing that was apparent in his delineation of figures, particularly when compared with those of Raphael and Michelangelo, although the biographer did praise the exceptional softness of his figures and the sweetness of their expressions.

ANDREA DEL SARTO (ANDREA D'AGNOLO DI FRANCESCO)

❧

BORN FLORENCE 1486, DIED FLORENCE 1530

This portrait of an unidentified woman is one of the most interesting to emerge from the early 16th century because it represents the confluence of two trends: the realism of the High Renaissance and the idealization of Mannerism.

Portraiture, particularly of members of the middle classes, flourished as a genre from the early 15th century. In female portraiture, it was most usual to show the sitter in profile (see pages 76–77); her eyes would thereby be averted from the viewer, who would most usually be male, thus preserving the woman's modesty. By the end of the 15th century, however, artists began to show women in three-quarter or full face, to enable them to capture the full beauty of their subject's features. The eyes of the sitter would generally still be turned away or lowered to preserve the necessary modesty and decorum. In Andrea's portrait, however, the sitter confronts the viewer with a direct, almost complicitous gaze, with both eyes visible and a slight smile playing around her lips. These features are accentuated by the use of a plain dark background, a device that had been made popular for portraits by Leonardo. Thus, the sitter's features become both more evident and enigmatic. Yet, in spite of her direct gaze, Andrea's subject is a model of propriety. She is seated, as befits a woman of status, and her clothing is both plain and demure. While many female sitters were represented in opulent clothing to show off their husbands' wealth, this sitter's clothes are modest and sober in color. She wears a chaste, high-necked blouse and a blue overgarment that serves to conceal rather than reveal her body. The only sign of embellishment are her fashionably slashed sleeves. Her hair is very simply dressed, almost unkempt, and held with a modest clasp, and she has a small bunch of flowers as an adornment around her neck.

Most interesting in this portrait is its lack of idealization. Generally speaking, by this point in the 16th century, artists tended to idealize their female sitters, emulating the model of female beauty encapsulated in the writings of the 14th-century poet Petrarch and the 16th-century writer Agnolo Firenzuola, who published a treatise on the beauty of women in 1541. These writings identified fair hair, white skin, bright eyes, an oval face, regular features, and a long neck as the components of beauty. Yet, Andrea does not appear to have idealized his sitter at all, with her olive skin, plump face, and brown eyes. The only trace of the idealization of Mannerism is in the artificial elegance of her hands, her fingers long and slender and parted to emphasize their gracefulness. Most interesting of all, she herself holds a volume of Petrarch's poetry, probably designed to indicate that she is well-read—one of the few distinctions that could be expected of a well-bred woman. Thus, while hinting at the ideals of Mannerist painting and literature, Andrea's portrait retains an engaging realism and directness, showing an enigmatic sitter whose gaze continually draws us in. In addition to being an excellent oil and fresco painter, Andrea was also one of the finest draftsmen of the Renaissance. The best collection of his drawings is in the Uffizi in Florence.

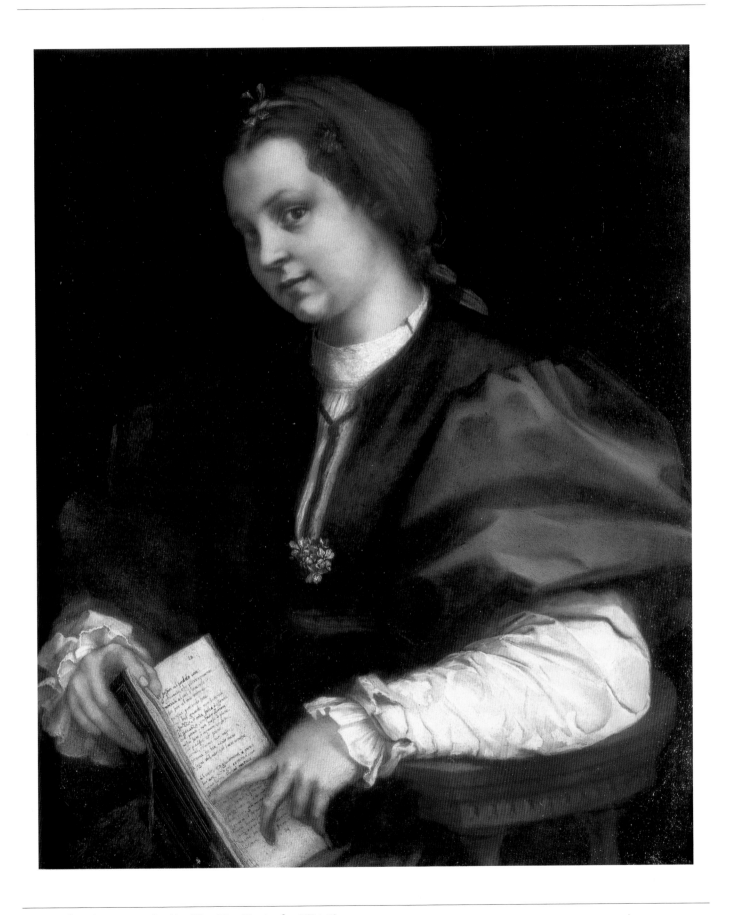

c. 1528 | *oil on canvas* | 33 x 27in (84 x 69cm) | Uffizi, Florence

Jupiter and Io

Jove had seen Io coming
From the river of her father, and had spoken:
"O Maiden, worthy of the love of Jove,
And sure to make some lover happy in bed,
Come to the shade of these deep woods …
Come to the shade, the sun is hot and burning,
No beasts will hurt you there, I will go with you,
If god is at your side, you will walk safely
In the vast, deepest woods. I am a god.
And no plebeian godling, either, but the holder
Of Heaven's scepter, hurler of the thunder.
Oh, do not flee me!" She had fled already…
When the god hid the lands in murk and darkness
And stayed her flight and took her.

OVID (43 B.C.–A.D.17), *Metamorphoses*, C. A.D. 10

Correggio took his name from his birthplace, a small town between Mantua and Parma in the north of Italy. Most of his works—altarpieces and illusionistic dome paintings (the latter very influential in the Baroque period)—remain in Parma, so he is one of the least-known painters of the High Renaissance, despite being one of the most original. In the development of his style, Correggio drew on different influences from cities in the north, particularly Venice and Milan. His works show the clear influence of Leonardo and Giorgione, but he was little influenced by Raphael or Michelangelo; and although he certainly had a knowledge of antique sculpture, he avoided the overt Classicism of the more prominent artists of the day. Partly in response to this, Vasari wrote that Correggio's art would have been perfect had he studied in depth the antiquities of Rome to develop his skill in drawing the human figure. Nonetheless, the biographer acknowledged that no artist of the day was better at handling colors or at depicting the softness of flesh and of hair.

Correggio executed a number of canvases on themes from classical mythology for Federico II Gonzaga, Duke of Mantua, and this is one of four based on the loves of Jupiter, possibly intended to be a gift for the Emperor Charles V. While some patrons in the 16th century commissioned scenes from classical

CORREGGIO (ANTONIO ALLEGRI)

BORN CORREGGIO c. 1494,
DIED CORREGGIO 1534

myth or legend to display their own erudition or for allegorical purposes, others, like Federico, chose them primarily for their erotic potential through the depiction of naked figures. Particularly popular as a source for such paintings were the *Metamorphoses* by the Roman poet Ovid, which contained many descriptions of the loves of the gods. Jupiter often transformed himself into another shape to seduce women he desired; *Jupiter and Io* formed a pair with *Jupiter and Ganymede* (Kunsthistorisches Museum, Vienna), when Jupiter assumed the form of an eagle to ravish the beautiful youth, who then became cupbearer to the gods. The other canvases show *Leda* (Stäatliche Museum, Berlin) and *Danaë* (Borghese Gallery, Rome), who Jupiter seduced in the form of a swan and a shower of gold respectively.

Ovid relates how Jupiter had approached Io in his own guise and asked her to come into the woods with him, but when she fled, he turned himself into a cloud and took her. He then turned Io into a white heifer to protect her from the jealous wrath of Juno, his wife.

Correggio's inventive painting fully exploits the erotic nature of Ovid's story while staying true to his text. The scene is set in a woodland grove, with Io sitting on a tree trunk with a deer drinking at her feet. Sprays of leaves emerge from the "murk and darkness" which ranges in color from deep blue to smoky gray. Io's slightly unbalanced position suggests that she has been caught by surprise; as she grasps Jupiter with her left hand, her right indicates physical weakness and abandon. Her body is extremely sensual, showing the influence of Giorgione in depicting the quality of soft flesh, particularly around the buttocks and in the melting effect of her whole form. Correggio has also solved the pictorial problem of painting a cloud by hinting at the presence of Jupiter within the mist, as the god gives Io a shadowy kiss and clasps her with his right hand. The elusiveness of his presence within the cloud adds to the mystery of the encounter, while the softness that Correggio achieves in the cloud accentuates its sensuality. Correggio's reputation was at its highest during the 18th century, the sensuousness and sophistication of his mythologies foreshadowing works by artists such as Boucher.

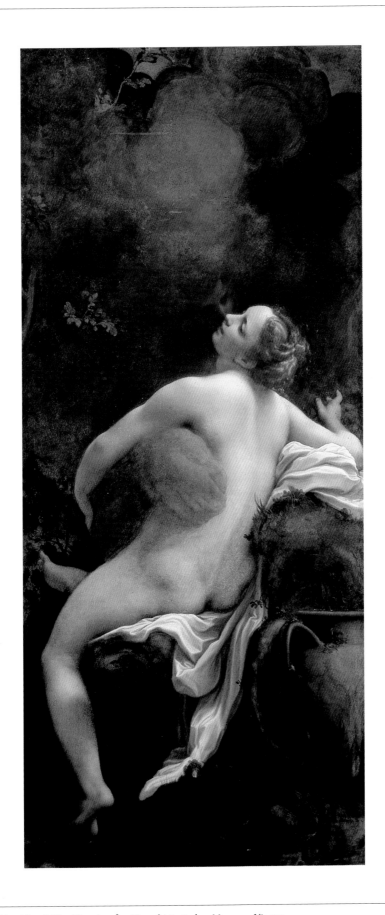

c. 1532 | *oil on canvas* | 64 x 28in (163 x 71cm) | Kunsthistorisches Museum, Vienna

The Virgin and Child with Angels
(The Madonna of the Long Neck)

VASARI USED *maniera*, meaning "style" or "grace," to describe the beauty and elegance of 16th-century Italian art, following the supreme examples of Raphael and Michelangelo. From the 17th century, much painting after 1530 was viewed by many as decadent, superficial, artificial, and distorted; and the term Mannerism was used in a pejorative sense. Characteristic features of the art were heightened emotion, elongated, often muscular, figures, stylized poses, strange effects of scale, lighting or perspective, and vivid colors. At its best, Mannerism is powerful and very moving.

This painting is often seen by art historians as the epitome of Mannerist art, partly because of the artificiality of its forms and partly because its obvious quest for grace and beauty appear at first glance to have been pursued at the expense of its subject. Yet, a search for such qualities was also a characteristic of High Renaissance painting and sculpture, which, while rooted in the observation of the real world, was often idealized. The exploration of Mannerist ideals by Parmigianino, who was influenced by Correggio as well as Raphael and Michelangelo, was in fact very much part of his understanding of his subject, despite the many seemingly bizarre aspects of the painting.

The subject matter is largely conventional, showing the Virgin and Child with angels. The Christ Child is asleep in the Virgin's lap—a presaging of his death and of the moment when she will hold his body at the foot of the cross. This reference is emphasized by the large size and adult proportions of the Child, who lies right across the Virgin's ample lap while she looks down at him in adoration. The wingless angels also pay homage to the Christ Child and his mother.

The Mannerist quality of the painting is probably most evident in the figure of the Virgin, which is very literally and self-consciously the epitome of female beauty as detailed by Petrarch and his later followers, especially Agnolo Firenzuola (see page 116). Firenzuola compared the figure of the perfect woman to the shape of a vase, with a small head, long neck, and rounded torso, and this may be the significance of the vase carried by one of the angels. Here, the Virgin has a small and perfectly formed head with elaborately dressed fair hair, a symmetrical face with delicate chiseled features, and an elongated, swanlike neck. Her body is disposed along the lines of the favorite Mannerist device, the *figura serpentina* or serpentine form, as she forms an S-shaped curve. The shape of her breasts and her stomach are disconcertingly clear beneath her drapery and her elongated hand with its parted fingers and arched foot are the epitome of Mannerist elegance. Unusually, the angels are all individually characterized, bringing a rare variety to the group. Two of them look directly out to engage our attention.

Yet this emphasis on beauty and refinement, and the overt reference to secular texts on female perfection, do not mean that the painting should be seen as secularizing or irreligious in its intention. As indicated, the subject matter is relatively orthodox, and the painting was meant to be a functioning altarpiece as much as any of the High Renaissance. Rather, the search for ultimate grace and beauty were a tribute to the importance and sanctity of the Virgin. With the rich drapery behind her and her opulent footstool, she appears as the Queen of Heaven, regal and beautiful. Even the obvious physicality of the Virgin and the naked legs of the angels were probably seen as part of a legitimate exploration of the human body, perfected in its rounded forms, not irreconcilable with the religious content of the work.

More difficult to explain is the role of the man with the scroll and the line of columns in the background, although this part of the painting is actually unfinished. He may be a prophet, and it is possible that the first column was intended to emphasize the size and slenderness of the Virgin. However, it is characteristic of Mannerism as a whole to introduce elements of enigma or ambiguity into a work, such as would invite learned comment or discussion, and these details may be an example. Whatever the case, and despite the seeming strangeness of this picture, there is no doubt that it is as much a tribute to the Virgin and Child as any of Raphael's clearer and more familiar works.

Parmigianino's work had considerable influence on the elegant decorative schemes of the first school of Fontainebleau, c. 1530–60, and, through it, on French art.

PARMIGIANINO (GIROLAMO FRANCESCO MAZZOLA)

&

BORN PARMA 1503,
DIED CASALMAGGIORE 1540

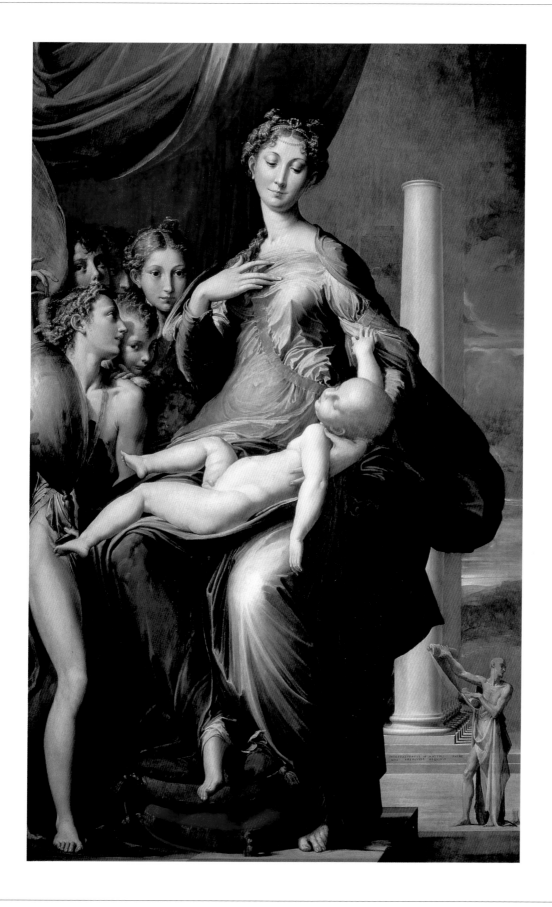

c. 1534–36 | *oil on canvas* | 84 x 52in (214 x 133cm) | Uffizi, Florence

Allegory of Love with Venus and Cupid

BRONZINO WAS THE MOST IMPORTANT of the second generation of Mannerists working in Florence. A pupil of Pontormo, he worked extensively at the court of Duke Cosimo I de' Medici, the city's autocratic ruler, and is best known for his portraits of the duke, his family, and the court. The aristocratic, cool detachment of these portraits, which influenced European court portraiture for a century, has become almost synonymous with Mannerism in its later years and contrasts markedly with the flesh-and-blood quality of Pontormo's portraits. Bronzino also painted altarpieces and religious cycles, that display the same cool beauty and air of unreality.

This allegory was painted for the French King Francis I as a gift from Cosimo de' Medici. The king was known for his taste for the erotic and his liking of Italian art and, as with many Mannerist paintings, the unraveling of the image's complex symbolism would have given him and his courtiers the opportunity to engage in intellectual games and debates. While many of the symbols and attributes would have been quite familiar to Bronzino's viewers, others, such as the figures of Folly and Deceit, were probably invented by the artist with the help of emblem books or a learned adviser, and would have warranted closer scrutiny.

The painting's overall theme is that of illicit or impure love. In the center is Venus, her body in a serpentine curve, arranged to display her beauty to the full. In one hand she holds the golden apple presented to her by Paris as the most beautiful goddess, while with the other she plucks a golden arrow from the quiver of Cupid, her son. Cupid embraces her in a manner that is both tender and lascivious, one hand cradling her bejeweled head while the other firmly grasps her breast, giving her at the same time a probing kiss. His right foot rests on one of the doves of Venus. The way in which he is posed, with his lithe limbs and protruding buttocks, also has homoerotic overtones. The voluptuousness of the embrace is accentuated by the luxurious cushion between Cupid's knees and the rich blue drapery behind the pair. Ultramarine was the most expensive pigment at the time, and its extensive use makes clear the costliness of the painting; no expense was spared by Cosimo for the French king.

**AGNOLO BRONZINO
(AGNOLO DI COSIMO)**

~

*BORN MONTICELLI 1503,
DIED FLORENCE 1572*

Around the two main figures are personifications of vices attendant upon unchaste love. On the right a little boy, with a dancer's anklet of bells, prepares to shower the embracing couple with the roses of Venus. He laughs, despite the fact that his foot is being pierced by a thorn, and can be identified as Folly or Foolish Pleasure. Behind him is Deceit, who has the face of a pretty child but the body of a monster. With one hand she proffers the honeycomb of pleasure, while in the other, she conceals the deadly sting of a scorpion's tail. On the far left, in the center, is a figure which for many years was identified as Envy, but which may in fact represent the symptoms of syphilis, as he displays many of the features identified in contemporary treatises as characteristic of the disease: severe headaches, discolored skin, thinning hair, and swollen joints.

At the top is Father Time, with his wings and his hourglass, who pulls back a curtain to reveal this tableau. His strong, muscular arms and dark skin provide a powerful contrast with the body of Venus. On the left is a figure who might represent Oblivion, since she has the eyes to see what is before her, but not the head to form memories and regrets, and she tries in vain to stop Father Time from displaying the scene.

Allegory of Love with Venus and Cupid is a picture of exquisite beauty and stylishness, one that could be best appreciated within the context of the court, with its love of artifice, refined culture, and intellectual aspirations. The painting is quite striking in its obvious artificiality, with the porcelain whiteness of the two main figures standing out against the vibrant colors of the rest. The composition is compressed, so it is not clear how the figures relate to each other spatially, and the poses are contrived. These features add to the hypnotic quality of the erotic allegory and help to explain why Bronzino was so valued as a court artist by Cosimo I de' Medici.

Rejected by subsequent centuries for being overblown and excessive, with the 20th century, particularly in the interwar period, Mannerism came to be judged as exciting and original. The sophisticated work of the best artists, such as Parmigianino and Bronzino, found a new and appreciative audience.

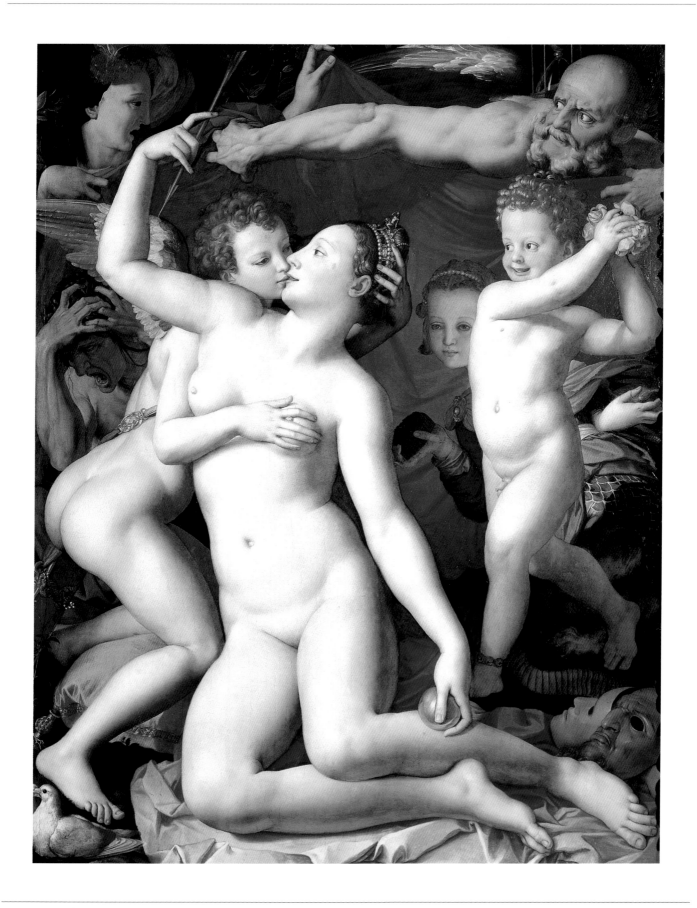

c. 1540–60 | *oil on wood* | 58 x 46in (146 x 116cm) | National Gallery, London

The Crucifixion

TINTORETTO WAS THE MOST ORIGINAL PAINTER working in Venice in the later 16th century. Although Mannerism is a difficult term to apply to Venetian painting, which never underwent the same transformations in the latter part of the century as it did in Florence and Rome, Tintoretto's extraordinary and dynamic compositions, raking perspectives, shifts in scale, and Michelangelesque figures provide a point of contact with the movement. It was said of Tintoretto that his ideal in painting was to combine the drawing of Michelangelo with the color of Titian—an ambition that is particularly well expressed in the painting shown here.

Tintoretto was a deeply devout man and spent much of his life painting altarpieces and religious cycles for the Venetian scuole, the lay confraternities devoted to charitable works, which were also significant patrons of the arts (most of his works are still *in situ*). His greatest work is probably the huge and complex series of more than fifty canvases painted in 1565–87 for the meeting rooms of the Scuola Grande di San Rocco, depicting scenes from the life of Christ and the Virgin in the upper and lower halls respectively, and scenes from the Passion, dominated by this huge *Crucifixion*, in the Sala dell'Albergo. The *Crucifixion* illustrates a number of key characteristics of Tintoretto's art. The teeming canvas, full of incident, also recalls certain of Veronese's works, although it should be borne in mind that the sheer scale of the canvases sometimes used by these artists necessitated a wealth of activity to fill the large area. This canvas took up a whole wall. To help him perfect his intricate poses and compositions, Tintoretto used small wax models which he moved around and lit from different angles.

This is one of the most unusual and dramatic images of the Crucifixion to have been painted in the 16th century. Rather than concentrating on the people directly involved in the event, Tintoretto provides us with a panorama of bustling activity and explores every aspect of the scene. One very rare feature for the Renaissance is the inclusion of the two thieves in the composition, one being nailed to a cross, the other being raised. All four Gospels relate that two thieves were crucified with Christ.

**TINTORETTO
(JACOPO ROBUSTI)**

❧

BORN VENICE 1518,
DIED VENICE 1594

According to Luke, the one on his right rebuked the other, saying that their punishment was deserved whereas Christ was innocent. Christ said to him, "Today you shall be with me in Paradise." The role of the thieves clearly gave Tintoretto a means of filling the vast canvas. At the same time, all his paintings for the Scuola stressed the humility and mercy of Christ and his links with ordinary sinners, the poor, and the destitute, and the story of the thieves fits into this theme well.

The raising of the crosses gave Tintoretto the opportunity to depict numerous muscular individuals in vigorous motion, testifying to his interest in the figures of Michelangelo, while it also enabled him to introduce two strong diagonals that bring dynamism to the scene and create a strong underlying structure. Most important, the diagonals focus on the figure of Christ, who is still and calm on his cross—a figure of repose looking down on the turmoil below. His body is parallel to the picture-plane, reinforcing the impression of stillness, and he looks with particular compassion upon the group of the swooning Virgin surrounded by his friends at the foot of the cross.

One feature of the scene that is distinctly Venetian is the introduction of huge numbers of people, mostly richly dressed, who have come to witness the event. Men in armor and in luxurious clothes and exotic headgear crowd around from all directions, turning the episode into a spectacle. The horseman on the left, pointing to Christ, may be Longinus, the Roman soldier who pierced Christ's side and was converted at that moment to Christianity. There are also the two men who offered Christ a sponge soaked in vinegar, pretending to help slake his thirst. It is a painting that involves the spectator in the highest degree, especially as details such as the ladder on the left are so close to the picture-plane and to the viewer's space.

Although the palette is limited, the dusky setting, out of which emerges a pattern of brilliant reds and whites, is reminiscent of some of Titian's early works and is almost certainly designed to take account of the lighting of the room. After Tintoretto's death, Venice had to wait for Tiepolo before it had a master of such stature again.

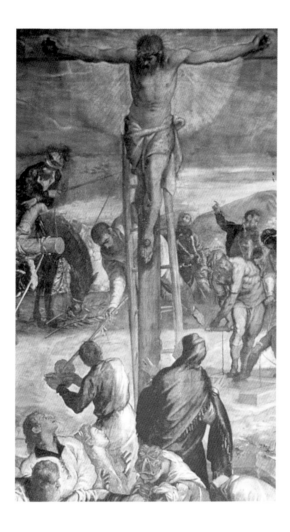

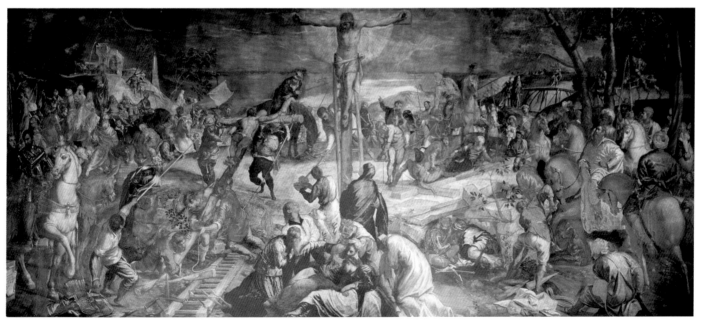

1565 | *oil on canvas* | 17ft 9in x 40ft (5.4 x 12.25m) | Scuola Grande di San Rocco, Venice

The Family of Darius before Alexander

VERONESE, TOGETHER WITH TINTORETTO, dominated painting in Venice after the death of Titian. He painted altarpieces for churches, large-scale religious canvases for convents and for the meeting rooms of religious confraternities, allegories and history paintings for civic buildings, and a range of secular works for villas in the Venetian territories. All are perfectly suited to the thriving city-state in its Golden Age.

In many ways, Veronese's painting had more in common with that of Venetian artists of the late 15th and early 16th centuries, such as Vittore Carpaccio (c. 1450/60–1525/6) and Gentile Bellini (c. 1429–1507), than it did with Titian's. His works are characterized by a love of pageantry and processions, a taste for the exotic and for luxurious materials, and a tendency to compose the images close to the picture-plane. Veronese combined these features with a mastery of daylight color, an extraordinary luminosity, and a great sensuality, especially in his painting of the nude. He had a favorite, delicate palette— pale blue, silver-white, orange, and lemon yellow—and his style developed little during his career (few works are dated, so a chronology is problematic, and the high quality of his studio's large output can make it difficult to identify the master's hand).

By the end of the 15th century, it had become common for patrons to decorate their private apartments and residences with paintings. The damp climate of Venice did not suit fresco, the preferred medium for such works in the rest of Italy, so artists used vast canvases and oil paint which enabled them to create subtler effects of color, light, and shade, as well as more detailed compositions—all of which Veronese exploited to the full.

This work is a history painting—or narrative—based on a classical legend, and it was painted for the private villa of the Pisani family. The historical story revolves around the magnanimity of Alexander the Great. After he defeated the Persian King Darius at Issus, Alexander spared his enemy's family, sending them a message to say that Darius was alive and that they would be protected. The next day he went to visit them with his general, Hephaestion. As they entered, the Queen Mother knelt before Hephaestion, thinking that he was Alexander.

PAOLO VERONESE (PAOLO CALIARI)

❧

BORN VERONA c. 1528, DIED VENICE 1588

Hephaestion stepped back in confusion, but Alexander saved Sisygambis from her embarrassment by saying that it was indeed no error for Hephaestion, too, "was an Alexander."

This may have been a theme with which the Pisani family identified, or it may simply have been chosen for the opportunity it offered to display a knowledge of ancient history. Some of the figures, particularly of the family of Darius, are almost certainly portraits of members of the commissioning family.

Veronese clearly reveled in the challenge of the subject and characteristically depicted the scene as the meeting of two great retinues. He took care to include an element of drama in the painting and to involve the spectator, for we have to wonder which figure is Alexander. Is the man with arms outstretched the discomfited Hephaestion, trying to fend off the Queen Mother's greeting, or is it Alexander, stepping forward to reveal himself and resolve her dilemma?

The meeting of the two parties is linked by the background architecture and the standing male figure in blue. The feeling of a procession is accentuated by the linear presentation of the figures at the front of the canvas and by the onlookers in the distance, craning over the balustrade. As is customary with Veronese, the figures wear a mixture of contemporary and fantasy clothing, displaying a wonderful richness of color and detail. The women's furs and brocades impart an air of luxury; the fantastical armor and the dress of Alexander's retinue add a touch of the exotic. The monumental backdrop is largely imaginary, although it shows an awareness of the harmonious, classicizing architectural ideas of Andrea Palladio (1508–1580) and Sebastiano Serlio (1475–1554). Its neutral tones allow the foreground colors to sparkle like jewels.

Veronese's taste for pageantry brought him up against the Inquisition in 1573. He had filled a vast *Last Supper* with accessory figures such as "a buffoon with a parrot on his wrist … a servant whose nose was bleeding … dwarfs and similar vulgarities," considered highly irreverent by the Counter-Reformation Church. Veronese vigorously defended the artist's right to poetic license, but the case was resolved only by changing the name of the work to *The Feast in the House of Levi* (Accademia, Venice).

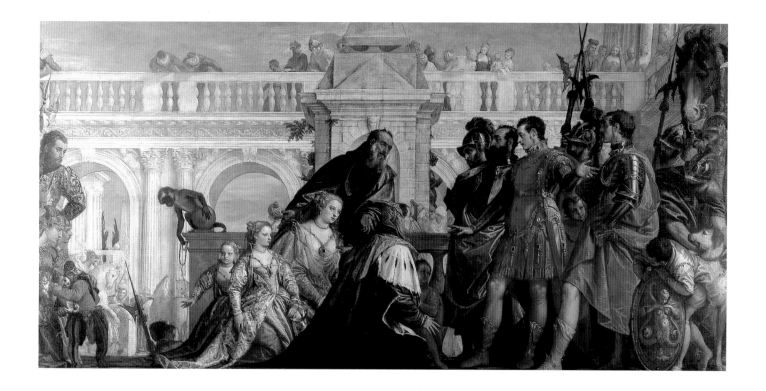

c. 1565–70 | *oil on canvas* | 93 x 187in (236 x 475cm) | National Gallery, London

The Burial of the Count Orgaz

EL GRECO was born in Crete. The island had been a Venetian possession for centuries, so like many Greek artists, he left for Venice, in 1567, in search of the patronage and artistic opportunities that were lacking in his homeland. Little is known of his early life in Crete except that he had been trained as a painter of icons in the Byzantine style. Once in Venice, El Greco became a pupil of Titian and was also influenced by the Mannerism of Tintoretto and of Jacopo Bassano (c. 1510/1592). He then spent some years in Rome, where he developed a great admiration for Michelangelo and mixed with an influential group of scholars in the circle of Cardinal Farnese. El Greco was a sophisticated and intellectual man who was well read in a range of philosophical and Christian treatises, a background which becomes evident in much of his later work. By 1577, he had moved to Spain and settled in Toledo, where he acquired the pseudonym by which he is known. He painted numerous major works for the Spanish Church.

This altarpiece was commissioned in 1586 by the parish church of Santo Tomé in Toledo, and shows the lasting influence on the artist both of Titian and of Venetian Mannerism. Count Orgaz, a benefactor of the church who died in 1323, had donated land and money to the Augustinian order, helped with the reconstruction of the church, and left it an annual endowment. A few years before the commission, a parish priest of Santo Tomé had won a battle with the count's home town of Orgaz, which had stopped the annual payments, and this victory may have been the occasion of the commission. The painting was to be placed above the count's tomb in his burial chapel in the church.

El Greco chose to depict the moment when, during the funeral service, Saint Stephen and Saint Augustine were said to have miraculously intervened to place the body in its tomb with their own hands. Although he had lived three centuries earlier, the count is shown in contemporary 16th-century armor with Saint Stephen at his feet and Saint Augustine supporting his head, creating the impression for the viewer that the body is being lowered into the actual tomb below (the direction of the saints' gaze enhances this idea). An angel transports the count's soul, in the form of a baby, into the celestial realm. At the top of the painting, Christ sits in judgment; the Virgin and Saint John the Baptist intercede with him on the count's behalf, while Saint Peter, with his prominent keys to heaven, awaits Christ's decision before admitting the count's soul into Paradise.

In the lower half of the painting, the influence of Titian is apparent in the brilliantly colored and painted vestments, the count's gleaming armor, and the wonderful array of robust portraits of contemporary Toledan dignitaries. Saint Stephen's vestment includes at the bottom a scene representing his own martyrdom by stoning, which stands out almost as a separate image and highlights the continued importance of martyrdom. Behind the burial party, El Greco included the portraits of contemporary figures to emphasize the continued relevance of the count's good works as an example to the pious of his day, and also as a means of satisfying their vanity by including them in such a prestigious work. In the straight, uniform arrangement of their heads and bodies, with little regard for spatial depth, we may perhaps see something of El Greco's origins as an icon painter. The simple but eloquent hand gestures in this more restrained half of the painting, however, point to the influence of the Italian High Renaissance.

In the upper half of the painting, El Greco employed elongated and slightly distorted ghostly figures, characteristic of his style, that evoke Tintoretto in his later work at the Scuola Grande di San Rocco in Venice (see page 124), as do the broken highlights on the draperies. Indeed, the whole construction of this arbitrary space, with its fitfully illuminated figures and eerie nocturnal light, recalls Tintoretto, while the predominantly acid colors show the influence of Jacopo Bassano.

In *The Burial of Count Orgaz*, as so often in the paintings of El Greco, the unworldliness of much of Mannerist painting provides the perfect vehicle with which to express a mystical event, while the human aspects, the lower part of the painting, remain more rooted in the earthiness of Titian. El Greco's unique style, which gave expression to deep emotions, was ideally suited to the religious fervor of Spain.

EL GRECO (DOMENIKOS THEOTOKOPOULOS)

*BORN CANDIA 1541,
DIED TOLEDO 1614*

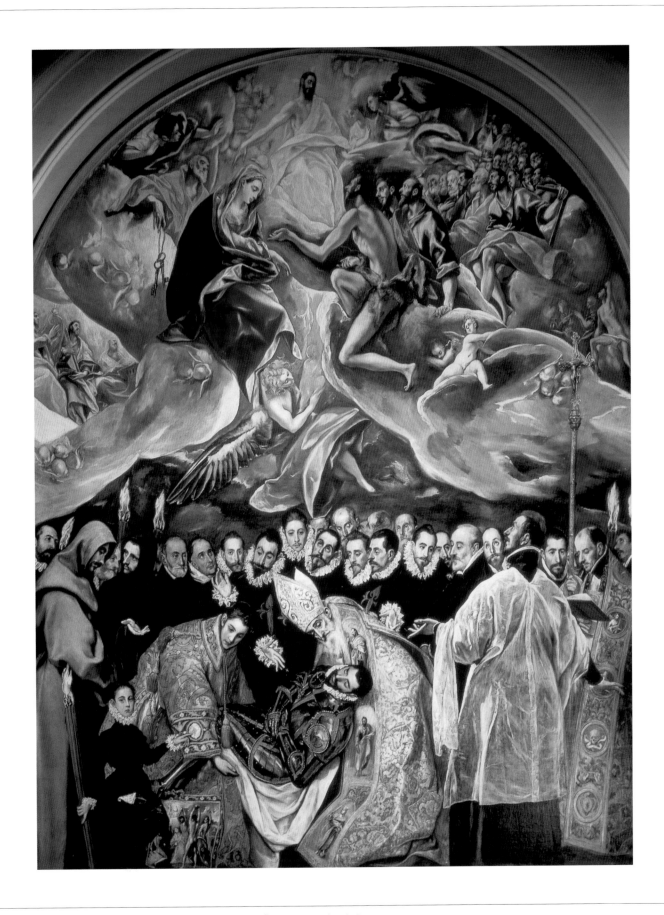

1586 | *oil on canvas* | 179 x 141in (455 x 358cm) | Santo Tomé, Toledo

THE BAROQUE

1600–1700 ❧ J. DOUGLAS STEWART

I became a convert to the excitement of the "Baroque" in 1959 at London's Courtauld Institute of Art, which refused to define the term closely. It was just the style that had developed in the 1590s in Italy in the works of Annibale Carracci and Caravaggio, in reaction to Mannerism; it had spread throughout Europe, mutating into the lighter, more decorative "Rococo" about 1720, and then around 1750 it was succeeded by "Neoclassicism."

There was virtue in the Courtauld's vagueness. It avoided setting up categories and a canon that exclude artists who have been undervalued or virtually forgotten.

"Baroque" originally meant bizarre or misshapen, as it still does for pearls. The term became one of abuse for neoclassical and later critics who saw 17th-century art, especially that of Bernini, as over-dramatic, oversensual, and insincere. Baroque illusionism especially outraged 19th-century believers in the doctrine of "truth to materials."

From the mid-16th century, soon after the Protestant Reformation in Europe, the Catholic Church embarked on a century of reforms and missionary activity. Art and architecture were seen as powerful propagandist weapons for the cause, and dynamic, awe-inspiring works from the period bear the stamp of Counter-Reformation confidence and religious militancy. As a result, with the Vatican at its center, Rome became the artistic capital of Europe in the 17th century, and the exuberance of baroque art spread from the religious to the secular sphere.

The Baroque fervently wished to persuade the spectator. Heavenly figures—both religious and mythological—had to be "brought down to earth" and made almost palpably "real." The period was renowned for illusionistic ceiling decorations, the first great project being Annibale Carracci's *Farnese Gallery*. It shows the loves of the ancient gods, and has a great cornice supported by nudes. It is all paint, but in 1601, a visitor commented that this ceiling "was so skillfully decorated with paintings that on first entering it you would have said they were sculptures."

Baroque art is meaningful in ways which today we reject or find difficult to

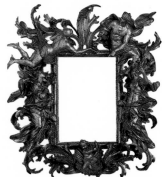

Filippo Parodi's gilded carving, c. 1675, is Baroque in its blend of art and reality.

130

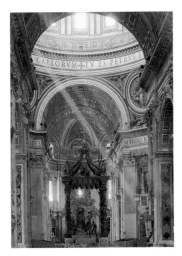

St. Peter's, Rome. The breathtaking vista through Bernini's Baldacchino to his Cathedra Petra.

comprehend. Counter-Reformation fervor was in full swing, and allegory was still a natural means of expression. When Bernini was temporarily out of favor with the papacy, he worked out his frustrations on a life-size group of Time unveiling Truth and left it to his heirs, in perpetuity, as a permanent moral lesson (*Truth Unveiled*, c. 1646–52, Galleria Borghese, Rome).

The Baroque looks back to the High Renaissance. Next to antiquity, Raphael was god for the 17th century, assuming the position Michelangelo had held for the Mannerists. The Baroque was not excited by Raphael's gentle early Madonnas (which the Victorians loved and which still appear on Christmas cards), but rather by massive, vigorous later figures like the *Sibyls* (1514) in Santa Maria della Pace in Rome.

At the head of the Baroque stand Caravaggio and Annibale Carracci. Caravaggio, with his dramatic light and shade, his "realistic," "plebeian" figures, and his apparently antiestablishment lifestyle, is now the most popular Italian Baroque painter. In the late 17th century, the art historian Bellori considered Caravaggio too close to nature; by contrast, he felt Annibale Carracci's style was based on the proper study of antique sculpture and of Raphael. Yet,

Caravaggio used these sources, too. Discerning contemporary collectors recognized differences between the two artists, but acquired works by both.

Radiating out from Rome, the baroque style influenced religious and secular art across Europe and beyond. It became more passionate in the ardent religious atmosphere of Spain and Latin America, and in Catholic Flanders found one of its greatest exponents in Rubens, while in Protestant Holland and England, its influence was tempered by cooler tastes and traditions.

The High Baroque (c. 1625–75) was dominated by the all-embracing talent of Bernini. In his work, all the visual arts were forged together to create an overwhelmingly impressive whole. In the secular world, this approach was epitomized by Louis XIV's Palace of Versailles, where grandiose architecture, sculpture, painting, decoration, and even landscape gardening proclaimed the king's glory.

Taking the lead from Annibale Carracci, the period also saw the development of ideal landscapes, a tradition that was to continue for two hundred years. The most memorable were by Poussin and Claude, heroic visions of ancient Rome by one, and pastoral depictions of a Golden Age by the other.

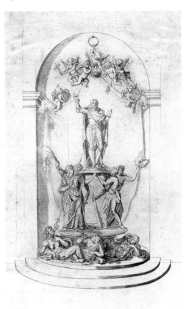

Part of a Mausoleum Chapel (1678) for Charles I. Flamboyant and expensive, it was never executed.

Pietà

THIS PICTURE has rightly been called "one of the great masterpieces of European art around 1600." The *Pietà* was commissioned by Annibale's Roman patron Cardinal Odoardo Farnese for his family palace in Rome. The picture was sent to Naples after 1734, following the union of the Farnese with the Bourbons of Naples through marriage.

Annibale's first master is not known. In the early 1580s, together with his brother Agostino and their cousin Ludovico, he founded the Accademia degli Incamminati (Academy of "those on the go," or "the Progressives") in Bologna, which emphasized study from nature. They wanted to replace the *maniera statuina* (the dry, "statuelike manner") of the Mannerists with a style that was of *viva carne* ("living flesh," red meat!). In 1594 Annibale was called to Rome to decorate rooms in the Palazzo Farnese. After first frescoing the ceiling of Cardinal Odoardo's study, Annibale and his team set to work on the ceiling of the large *Galleria* (Gallery), which was completed by 1600. This quickly became renowned as a modern masterpiece and until the 19th century was revered on the same level as Raphael's *Stanze* and Michelangelo's Sistine Ceiling (see pages 102–105).

The *Pietà* was praised by Giovanni Pietro Bellori (1613–1696) in his *Lives of the Modern Painters, Sculptors, and Architects* (1672). As a Classicist, Bellori appreciated the ideal beauty of the figures and the rigorous, geometrical structure of the composition. He also drew attention to a poignant detail: "[Annibale] made there with great expressiveness a little angel who touches a thorn of the crown with his finger and is pained by the wound."

The *Pietà* (literally "pity," or "compassion"), which is used in art to refer to a representation of the Virgin Mary with the dead Christ, is not a biblical subject, and, despite its Italian name, it developed first in medieval Germany as an *Andachtsbild* ("image of devotion"), showing the seated Virgin holding her dead son across her lap. The most famous example of the theme is Michelangelo's marble group in St. Peter's, Rome (1498–99). In his painted version, Annibale uses the gesture of Michelangelo's Virgin, but makes it more urgent by bold foreshortening. Michelangelo followed tradition by placing Christ in the Virgin's

ANNIBALE CARRACCI

*BORN BOLOGNA 1560,
DIED ROME 1609*

lap, but in the Annibale, she cradles only her son's head and the upper part of his body. Annibale was doubtless partly responding to baroque realism, since it is impossible for a seated woman to hold a dead thirty-year-old man comfortably. In a preparatory drawing, now at Windsor, the Virgin kneels beside her son, the upper part of whose body is propped against the open tomb. In another drawing, now lost (known from a photograph), the artist approximated the final composition.

Annibale's Virgin is more active than Michelangelo's slight, pensive figure. Here, her mouth partly open, she looks directly down at her son and cradles his head in her right hand. She is full-breasted, and her leaning pose and the upward twist of Christ's torso brings their chests close together. This, along with the baby angels (who are reminiscent of the infants Christ and Saint John the Baptist), evokes Christ's childhood, another tender note, like the angel touching the thorn. The gesture of that angel also recalls Annibale's beautiful *Silenzio* (now in the British Royal Collection), a half-length picture, also of 1599–1600, in which the Virgin enjoins the infant Baptist to silence as he touches the foot of the sleeping Christ Child. That last motif was understood as prefiguring Christ's death.

The allusion to the infant Christ and Saint John the Baptist with the Virgin Mary reminds us of the many versions of that theme by Raphael, as does the arched top of the composition. Indeed, it is to Raphael far more than Michelangelo that Annibale's *Pietà* is indebted for notions of ideal form and especially of *grazia* ("grace"). For Bellori, Italian art had reached perfection with Raphael and then fallen from that peak with the Mannerists, and was only revived by Annibale. Yet, there is also a sensuousness in the Naples *Pietà*, especially in the lines of the Christ, which recalls neither Michelangelo nor Raphael, but rather Correggio, while expressive chiaroscuro and color (like the Titianesque pink loincloth) show Annibale's deep debt to Venice. But the synthesis of these different elements is entirely Annibale's, and unlike 16th-century painters, Annibale pushes his figures right up to the picture plane, creating that baroque immediacy and urgency he shares with his contemporary, Caravaggio.

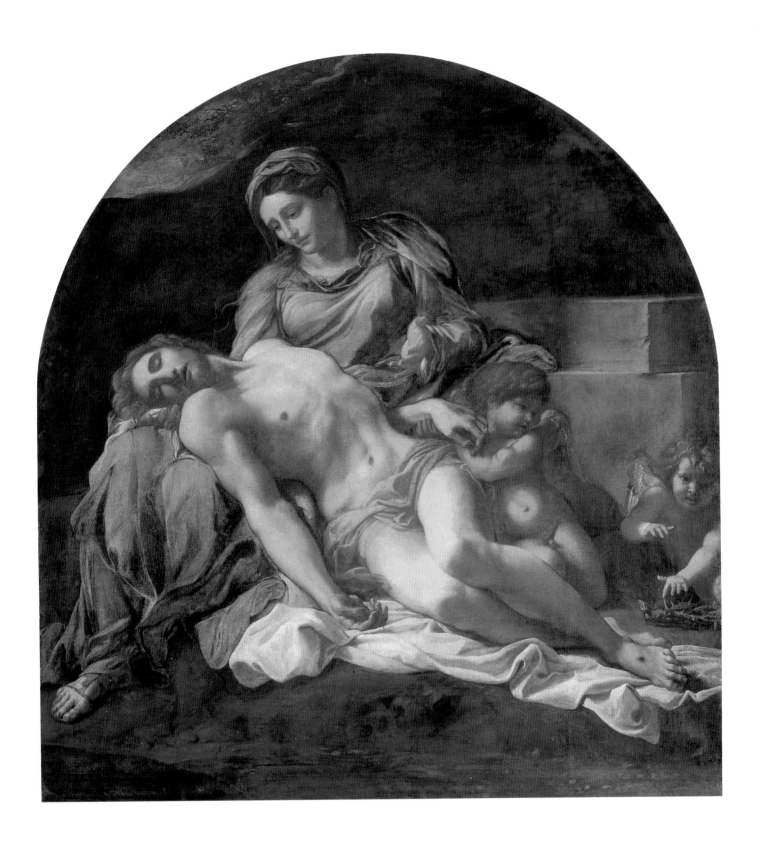

1599–1600 | *oil on canvas* | 61¹⁄₂ x 59in (156 x 149cm) | Museo e Gallerie Nazionali di Capodimonte, Naples

The Martyrdom of Saint Ursula

THIS IS PERHAPS CARAVAGGIO'S last completed work, finished just two months before his death. It arrived at Genoa from Naples on June 18, 1610, for Marcantonio Doria, Prince of Angri, whose Neapolitan agent had written on May 11 saying that Caravaggio had delivered the picture while it was still wet. The agent had tried to dry it in the sun but the "varnish was … rather thick." Angri was Caravaggio's friend, having sheltered the painter during his first flight from Rome in 1605. He had offered Caravaggio 6,000 scudi (a huge sum) to fresco a loggia, an offer that was refused, doubtless because he disliked the medium, which he is not definitely known to have employed. For this later picture, Angri chose the subject because his stepdaughter, Anna Grimaldi (who, according to his will, Angri "loved as his very dear daughter"), had entered a convent as Sister Ursula.

Saint Ursula was a legendary Early Christian Breton princess who had agreed to marry Condon, the son of the pagan King of England, on condition that her future husband accompanied her and 11,000 virgins on a pilgrimage to Rome, where he had to become a Christian. Condon was baptized by the pope as Etherius. The pilgrims returned to the north via Cologne, where they encountered Hunnish hordes. The virgins were massacred, as were Etherius and his attendants. Ursula, refusing to marry the barbarian leader, was shot with an arrow at point-blank range.

Whole cycles of paintings as well as single works were devoted to the legend of Saint Ursula; most frequently represented was the mass martyrdom. Rubens made one oil sketch in c. 1602 and two in c. 1618–20, but apparently never followed through with a finished picture. Occasionally, Saint Ursula's execution was represented, as by Carpaccio in 1493 as part of his St. Ursula cycle (Accademia, Venice), and Caravaggio could have seen this on a visit to Venice before he went to Rome.

Caravaggio's earliest works are lost. He was in Rome by 1592, where his secular half-length figures, painted from the model with strong chiaroscuro, attracted the attention of Cardinal del Monte, who obtained for Caravaggio a commission for large pictures for Santa Luigi dei Francesi. Their success gained Caravaggio fame and further commissions for religious

**MICHELANGELO MERISI
DA CARAVAGGIO**

◊⁄◊

*BORN CARAVAGGIO 1571,
DIED PORTO ERCOLE 1610*

works, which became increasingly grand and austere. Yet a quarrelsome disposition (he never took pupils, so that his widespread influence, ultimately including Rembrandt, was indirect) led to exile from Rome in 1605, and final flight in 1606 to escape a manslaughter charge. In his last years, Caravaggio traveled to Naples and Malta (where he was made a knight), finally dying while trying to return to Rome.

What is astonishing about Caravaggio's treatment is his reduction of the theme to five half-length figures, placed perilously close to the viewer. The naturalism, brutality, blood reds, and dramatic contrasts of light and shade all appear in Caravaggio's mature Roman works (1600–6). But here, as is characteristic of his last works (1606–10), the darks have absorbed almost all of the lights, which fall only on the most salient features, and the brushwork has become a sort of ghostly shorthand. The result is an almost claustrophobic intensification of the drama. Yet, the relieflike composition and quiet gestures are also "classical." The Hun has just shot the arrow, but his expression shows sorrowful repentance; Ursula, in profile, looks down with pained acceptance. The furrow-browed figure in the center, whose features and position recall the central figure in Caravaggio's early *Cardsharps* (c. 1595, Kimbell Art Museum, Fort Worth), has no narrative function but is like a chorus figure from Greek tragedy. The painter himself appears behind the armored soldier, in a pose he had occupied in the early *Capture of Christ* (c. 1600, National Gallery of Ireland, Dublin). Such recollections of his own earlier works are also typical of Caravaggio's latest period, when he was often on the move from place to place and doubtless had less opportunity to paint directly from the model as had been his earlier practice.

The story of the loss of the identity of this picture, and its reinstatement, is almost as dramatic as the work itself. As late as 1845 it was cited in the possession of the Angri family; then it vanished, reappearing only in a 1963 exhibition as an allegory by Mattia Preti (1613–1699), an artist with a strongly Caravaggesque style. But the discovery of documents, published in 1980, convinced experts that this was indeed a great lost Caravaggio.

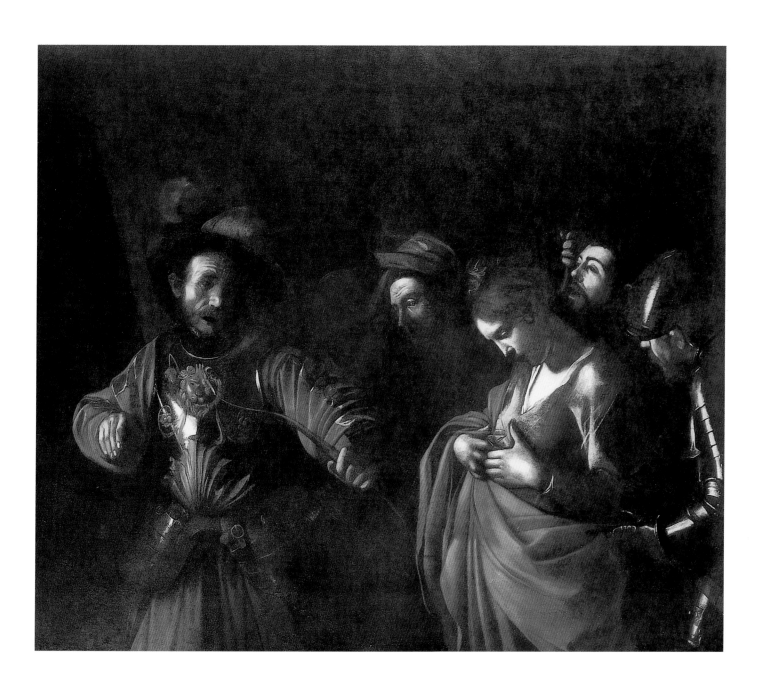

1610 | *oil on canvas* | 61 x 70in (154 x 178cm) | Banca Commerciale Italiana, Naples

The Water Seller

VELÁZQUEZ IS THE first great Spanish painter and is also among the greatest painters of the Baroque era. This is the finest of a series of *bodegones* which he painted in the southern city of Seville between the ages of sixteen and twenty-four. The Spanish term *bodegón* (meaning literally "tavern" or "public eating place") had recently come to be applied to paintings depicting the preparation or eating of food. This type of painting had been developed in the mid-16th century by Flemish artists like Pieter Aertsen (1508/9–1575) and was later practiced by northern Italian painters like Vincenzo Campi (c. 1530–1591). Works by both men and other similar artists were imported into Spain.

These earlier works are large, with life-sized figures, and are bright in color. Velázquez's picture includes substantial figures but is entirely different in mood and is restricted to earth tones. This may reflect a passage from the ancient Roman writer Pliny, that "Four colors only … were used by Apelles, Aetion, Melanthios and Nikomachos [famous early Greek painters] in their immortal works." Pacheco (1564–1644), Velázquez's first teacher and father-in-law, cited Pliny's high praise for ancient painters of "humble things like barber-shops, stalls, meals and similar things" in defense of Velázquez's *bodegones* which, he argued, were "deserving of the highest esteem. From these beginnings and in his portraits … he hit upon the true imitation of nature."

Baroque naturalism or realism must not be confused with 19th-century "Realism," nor the Impressionist "slice of life." Nor is the term "genre" (referring to scenes from daily life) helpful since it dates from the late 18th century. As Pacheco's citation from Pliny shows, baroque naturalism, like baroque classicism, was imbued with the idea of "true," that is, highly selective, "imitation of nature." Far from depicting an actual street scene, here the painter has arranged three carefully chosen models in his studio. The boy and the water seller are strikingly noble in feature; the profile head of the latter might easily have been found depicted as a general on an ancient coin or medal. The closely viewed water jar in the foreground (whose roundness is emphasized by the adjacent jar with indentations) has the simple sculptural grandeur of an ancient Greek amphora; and the water seller's cloak, despite its tear,

DIEGO VELÁZQUEZ
☙
BORN SEVILLE 1599,
DIED MADRID 1660

recalls the dalmatic, a priestly vestment. The water glass is being presented to, and received by, the boy with the solemnity of a sacramental ritual. Water was sold in the streets of Seville, but not in such costly, fragile vessels as the exquisite glass shown here, whose tapering lines echo the sides of the water jar. Is there a "hidden" meaning in the *Water Seller*? Such an idea is perfectly in keeping with the usual 17th-century approach to art. However, so far, there is no consensus among art historians on what cryptic meaning the picture might have.

The origins of Velázquez's style seem equally mysterious. For a long time it was thought to show the influence of Caravaggio. But apart from strong contrasts of light and shade and naturalism (neither of which was Caravaggio's invention), the Spaniard and the Italian are not close. Also, it is doubtful if Velázquez had seen any of Caravaggio's work at this date.

The *Water Seller*, with its realism and vigorous brushwork combined with immense gravity, foreshadows the style that Velázquez was to develop as a court portraitist. The supreme expression of this was to be *Las Meninas* ("The Maids of Honour") (c. 1656, Prado, Madrid), painted in 1656 for Philip IV for the king's summer office in the Alcázar. This arresting composition shows the artist at his easel in the company of the Infanta Margarita and her attendants, with the king and queen reflected in a mirror. In his role as court painter, Velázquez traveled to Rome to acquire works of art for the king. There he also painted memorable portraits of Pope Innocent X (1650, Galleria Doria, Rome) and Cardinal Camillo Massimi (1649–50, Kingston Lacy, Dorset), the pupil, patron, and friend of the French painter Nicholas Poussin.

In 1623, Velázquez moved from the provincial town of Seville to the capital city of Madrid. He took the *Water Seller* with him and gave it to Juan de Fonseca, an amateur painter and the writer of a treatise on ancient painting, now lost. The painting was then bought by Gaspar de Bracamonte, passed to the Cardinal Infante don Fernando, and then entered the Spanish royal collection. It was part of Joseph Bonaparte's loot captured by the Duke of Wellington at Vitoria in 1813; three years later, it was presented to the duke by the grateful King of Spain, Ferdinand VII.

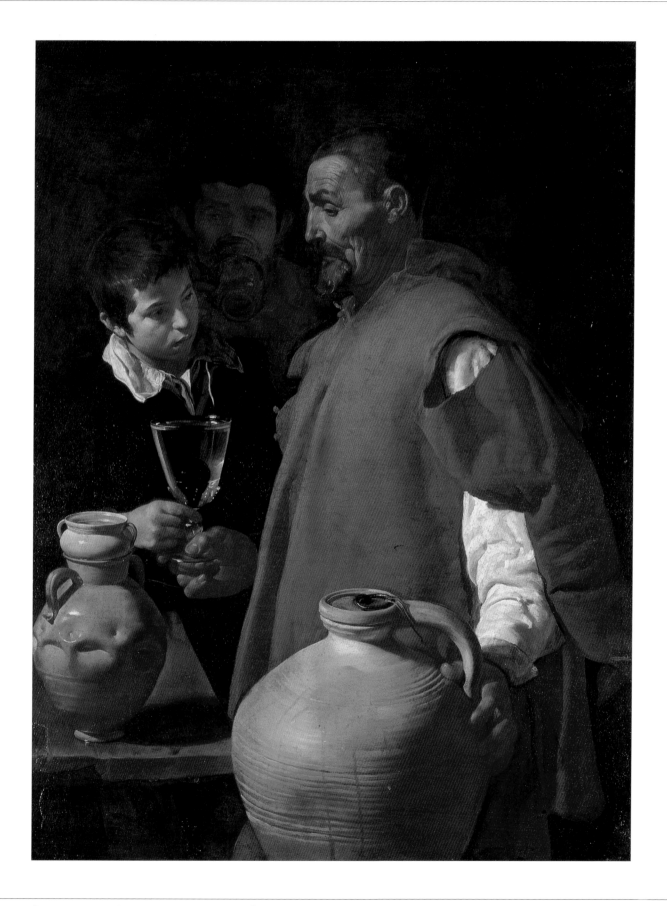

c. 1620 | *oil on canvas* | 42 x 32in (107 x 81cm) | Apsley House, The Wellington Museum, London

The Countess of Arundel and Her Train

RUBENS WAS TRAINED IN ANTWERP, but in 1600, he went to Italy. In Genoa, drawing on his experience of Venetian and Roman art, he painted a series of portraits of Genoese ladies in which elegant costumes and accessories such as curtains and architecture, hitherto reserved for state portraiture, together created a new vision of beauty and informal grandeur. He also painted a boldly dramatic portrait of the Marchese Giovanni Carlo Doria (1606, Palazzo Spinola, Genoa), the brother of Marcantonio Doria, Caravaggio's Genoese patron. In Rome, Rubens gained the greatest available public commission, the high altar of the Chiesa Nuova (1606–8). In 1608, he returned to Antwerp and became court painter to the Governors of the Spanish Netherlands, the Archduke Albert and Archduchess Isabella. In the next year a truce ended hostilities with the northern Netherlands and brought renewed prosperity to the city of Antwerp, including lavish commissions for Rubens and his large studio.

This painting is the most elaborate group portrait by Rubens. It is documented by a letter from the Earl of Arundel's servant Vercellini, who was acting as the countess's major-domo. She and her husband had planned to travel together on the Continent, but the illness of King James I had forced the earl to remain in England. Vercellini reported that he had presented the earl's letter to Rubens who, although he had refused to paint the portraits of many princes, would not refuse Arundel's request because he was *"uno delli quattro evangelisti e soportator del nostro arte"* ("one of the four evangelists and a supporter of our art"), a flamboyant way of praising the earl, who was indeed an enthusiastic collector of antiquities as well as contemporary paintings.

The earl must have written the program for the painting which, despite its genrelike character, is highly symbolic. The Countess and Sir Dudley Carleton (British ambassador to the Hague, friend of the Arundels, and also a patron of Rubens) are shown beneath a portico of Solomonic columns, inspired by the spiral columns in St. Peter's at Rome, which were thought to have come from the Temple of Solomon in Jerusalem (Bernini was also to base his St. Peter's *Baldacchino* on them). Rubens' columns have been interpreted as an allusion to the countess's

PETER PAUL RUBENS

&

*BORN SIEGEN 1577,
DIED ANTWERP 1640*

Roman Catholicism, but this cannot be so because the earl had converted to Anglicanism in 1616 and Carleton was a firm Protestant. Solomon's Temple was believed to be modeled on the Heavenly Temple. It was considered to be a type (prefiguration) of the Christian Church, and King Solomon was the type for the wise, just monarch. Here, the Solomonic columns seem to be a proclamation of the Arundels' loyalty and service to the British crown—to James I, the "British Solomon" as he was often called. Later, on the *Whitehall Ceiling* (1629–35), Rubens was to portray James enthroned between Solomonic columns. Queen Elizabeth I had been godmother to the Countess of Arundel and gave the countess her name—Aletheia (Greek for "truth")—because her family, the Talbots, "was ever true to the State." In front of the countess is a Talbot hound, her heraldic supporter.

The banner is emblazoned with the arms and motto (*Sola Virtus Invicta*: "Only Virtue is Unconquerable") of the dukedom of Norfolk, which had been lost by Arundel's grandfather, who had been executed for supposedly plotting to put Mary Queen of Scots on the English throne. Arundel's greatest ambition was to restore his family's honor, including the dukedom. His 1641 will contained a plea to James I's son, Charles, "for the memory of his Grand Mother Queene Mary ... to have a tender and Princely care of the great losses of my Family, and of the helping it to subsist in honour ... just Monarchy never had a more faithfull Servant."

The reduced status of the Arundel family in 1620, together with their hopes for the future, are alluded to by the hooded falcon held by the dwarf. In 1559, Bruegel used a hooded falcon for "Hope" in engravings of the seven Virtues. The hooded falcon and the motto *Post tenebras spero lucem* ("After shadows I hope for light") became a common emblem among printers, French, Flemish, and Spanish. Cervantes used it in *Don Quixote* (1605).

Here, we see a great artist further develop conventions that he had invented for the Genoese while also using "disguised symbolism," a tradition with northern artists since van Eyck's *Giovanni Arnolfini and his Wife* (1434, National Gallery, London). Also, Rubens was painting for a most discerning patron. The result is a picture that is unique in the artist's oeuvre.

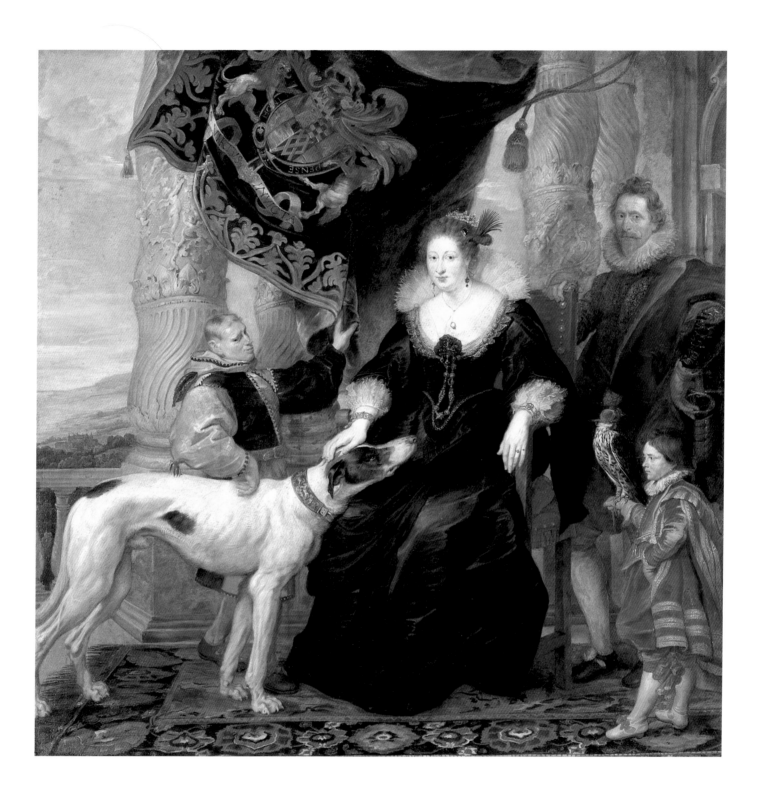

1620 | *oil on canvas* | 105 x 105in (267 x 267cm) | Alte Pinakothek, Munich

Self-portrait as the Allegory of Painting

ARTEMISIA WAS BORN in Rome and was trained by her father, Orazio (1563–1639), a Tuscan who went to Rome where his style was greatly influenced by Caravaggio, yet remained lighter and more decorative. Artemisia's earliest dated work, the 1610 *Susannah and the Elders* (Schloss, Pommersfelden), is influenced by her father but displays a powerful, individual sense of design, characterization, and dramatic gesture. It has been claimed that Susannah's vulnerability relates to Artemisia's rape by the painter Agostino Tassi (1581/2–1644). However, the Tassi trial took place in 1612, and Susannah's gesture (used by Michelangelo in his *Expulsion of Adam and Eve* on the Sistine Ceiling, see page 105) derives from the nurse on the 2nd-century A.D. Roman *Orestes Sarcophagus* (Palazzo Giustiniani, Rome) which had been found in the 15th century and was well known through drawings.

Artemisia painted the subject of Judith and Holofernes several times, her finest rendition being the huge picture (with over-life-sized figures) of c. 1625 (Institute of Arts, Detroit), where she depicts Judith pausing, boldly, sword in hand, beside a lighted candle while her kneeling maid puts Holofernes's severed head into a bag. It has been claimed that Artemisia was attracted to this story for motives of revenge, but it was a common subject during this period in Italy, painted by artists like Caravaggio, Elsheimer (1578–1610), and many others. No doubt the dramatic theme appealed to the times. It was also an Old Testament type (prefiguration) of the Virgin Mary destroying the Devil by giving birth to Christ. Protestants had condemned Marianism (the worship of the Virgin), so Judith naturally had special appeal for Counter-Reformation countries.

Artemisia was in Florence from 1614 to 1620 and then returned to Rome. Her *Susannah and the Elders* (1622, Burghley House, Northamptonshire) is influenced by the early "dark manner" of Guercino (1591–1666), which he was still practicing at the beginning of his stay in Rome (1621–23). The picture was bought from the Barberini in the late 17th century by the fifth Earl of Exeter as an Artemisia, but was attributed to Caravaggio in the 19th century. In 1968, Artemisia was proposed as the painter, which was accepted by some authorities but rejected by a feminist critic "because its expressive character is incommensurate with Artemisia's work." Recent cleaning revealed the Burghley picture to be signed and dated; thus, ideology can be counterproductive in trying to understand Artemisia. Yet, it is very clear that she was a *femme forte* ("strong woman"), the term her century used. Her letters to Don Antonio Ruffo of Sicily, one of her last great patrons (and of Guercino and Rembrandt), show this: "I will show … what a woman can do … You will find the spirit of a Caesar in this soul of a woman."

By 1630, Artemisia had moved to Naples which, apart from a period in England (1638–c. 1641), remained her home until her death. She was famous in her day and obtained high patronage, including that of the Medici in Florence, the King of Spain in Naples, and King Charles I of England. But her peripatetic existence meant that she did not become attached to any one city, so her achievements tended to be forgotten. For Naples (where she and her daughter, also a painter, were visited by the English tourist and diarist Bullen Reymes in 1634), there was a special reason for neglect. There was no 17th-century history of Neapolitan art, unlike Roman, Bolognese, or Florentine. The region had to wait until De Dominici's history, published in 1742–43, by which time much 17th-century art history had been forgotten.

Artemisia's *Self-portrait* (which may have been presented to Charles I) is unique, in a century whose artists' self-portraits include masterpieces by Van Dyck and Rembrandt. She based her image on the female personification of *Pittura* ("Painting") described in Cesare Ripa's famous 1593 handbook on iconography, which was dedicated to Cardinal Del Monte, Caravaggio's first great Roman patron. From this source come the medallion with a mask (representing "Imitation"), the disheveled hair (for the "fury of creation"), and the green sleeves of her dress. But the power of this work derives from the difficulties which the artist has brilliantly overcome, because to portray herself in this manner she must have worked with two mirrors. Through the simplicity and boldness of her design, Artemisia has created an image that conveys her strong, fiery, artistic personality and is equally compelling as a portrait of her profession.

ARTEMISIA GENTILESCHI

ↂ

*BORN ROME 1593,
DIED NAPLES 1652*

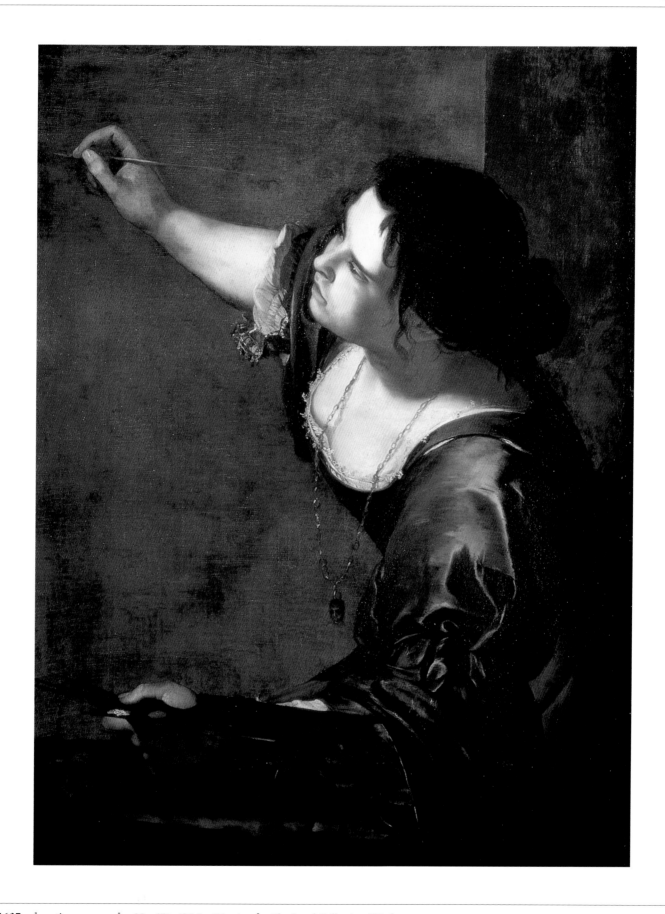

c. 1637 | *oil on canvas* | 38 x 29in (96.5 x 74cm) | The Royal Collection, Windsor

Jupiter and Europa

RENI WAS THE child prodigy of a musician who wanted his son to follow his profession but eventually gave in to the boy's wishes to be a painter. After studying with Denys Calvaert (c. 1540–1619), a Flemish Mannerist living in Bologna, Reni switched to the Carracci Academy in 1593. He then worked in Rome from 1601 to 1614, where his masterpiece is *Aurora* (1613–14), a ceiling fresco in the Casino Rospigliosi painted for Cardinal Scipione Borghese. Its friezelike composition is indebted to Annibale Carracci's Farnese Ceiling, *The Triumph of Bacchus*, but also to Raphael's graceful manner, and it is framed with real stucco figures. Remarkably for a fresco, it glows with light and color. Guido returned to Bologna in 1614 and remained there. His fame enabled him to operate a mail-order business for his paintings, selling to the aristocracy and crowned heads of Europe for the rest of his life.

As late as 1855, Jacob Burckhardt (author of the influential book *The Civilization of the Renaissance in Italy*, 1860) wrote of Guido, "Of all modern painters it is he who most approaches high and true Beauty, and his *Aurora* … is certainly the most perfect painting of the last two centuries." About his *Massacre of the Innocents* (c. 1616, Pinacoteca, Bologna), Burck-hardt further enthused: "He did not represent the massacre … In the executioners he personified cruelty but no bestial savagery … [he] elevated something tragic by means of a handsomely con-structed composition and nobly conceived forms. He achieved this result without adding a vision of glory in the sky … this work is also the most passionately moving composition of the [17th] century." Yet, just forty years later, Bernard Berenson could write that "we turn away from Guido Reni with disgust unspeakable."

For much of the 20th century, Guido Reni, like the Baroque generally, remained under a critical cloud. A special problem with Reni is his apparent lack of drama. In his *Lot and his Daughters* (c. 1615–16, National Gallery, London), a handsome old man and two Raphaelesque young women come toward us. Only the wine jar embossed with *amorini* ("little loves") gives the clue to the sordid Old Testament story that these beauties will seduce their father with wine so he will sleep with them and

GUIDO RENI

BORN BOLOGNA 1575,
DIED BOLOGNA 1642

continue their race. Reni's oblique, delicate approach is novel. Normally, painters showed the figures carousing, as in a brothel, or reclining exhausted outside a cave. Reni's concerns for classical beauty and abstraction are partly legacies of his Mannerist training, but his use of large, half-length figures close to the picture-plane (a device popularized by Caravaggio) and rich color are thoroughly Baroque.

The Ottawa *Jupiter and Europa* depicts one of the many loves of the king of the gods. In this case, Jupiter was smitten by a daughter of the King of Tyre and approached her in the form of a bull when she was playing with her companions by the sea. Europa was attracted by the creature ("So wondrous beautiful, so void of ire"), placed a floral wreath around his neck, and mounted his back. He swam out into the sea, and Europa shrieked to her friends. Titian shows the fear of that moment in his painting of the subject for Philip II of Spain (1562, Gardner Museum, Boston). Characteristically, Reni avoids drama, showing Europa fondly embracing the bull with her right hand and looking upward as though seeing a vision of heaven. Europa realizes her incredible good fortune. She has been chosen by the king of the gods; she will be taken to Crete where she will bear Jupiter three royal sons.

Europa's gaze resembles that of a Christian martyr, about to enter heaven. Reni knew the medieval allegory of the same story—Christ, incarnate as a bull, carrying off the human soul to Paradise, through the sea of Purgatory (Annibale Carracci had shown the theme in this way on the Farnese Ceiling). Europa's exquisite pink, orange, and lilac coloring had appeared in Reni's early *Martyrdom of St. Catherine* (c. 1606, Museo Diocesano, Albegna). In this late work, the tone is silvery.

The painting was commissioned by the Duke of Guastalla for 700 scudi (a large sum) as a gift for Don Diego Felipe de Guzman, Marqués of Leganés, the imperial governor of Milan, who had patronized Rubens and Van Dyck in Flanders (it carries Leganés's inventory number, 817). Eventually, the painting was looted by Napoleonic troops, returned to Spain, then sold to England in the early 19th century. Now in Canada, it is arguably the greatest Italian Baroque work in the country.

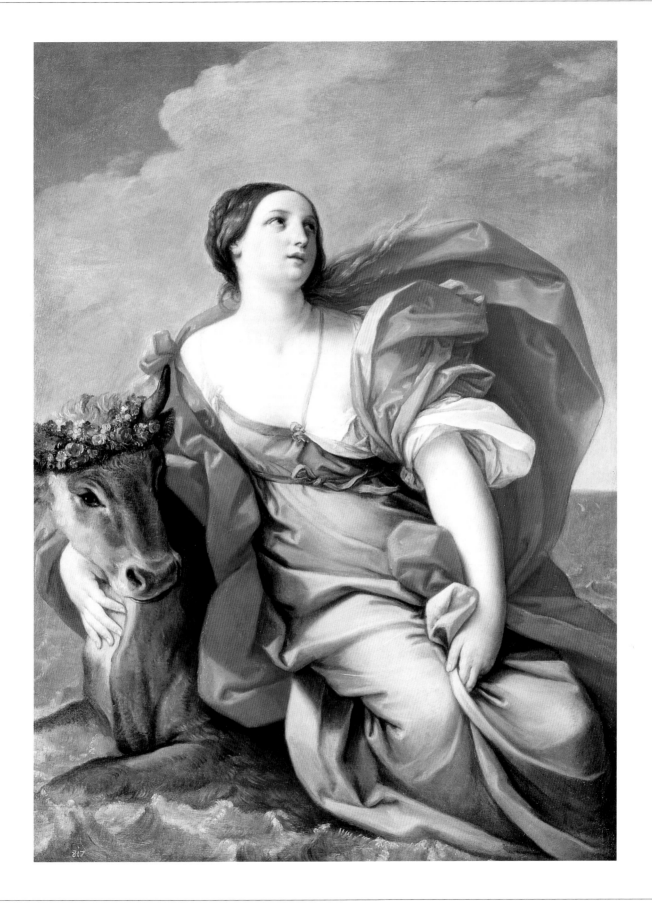

c. 1636 ❘ *oil on canvas* ❘ 62 x 45in (157.5 x 115cm) ❘ National Gallery of Canada, Ottawa

Divine Providence

THIS FRESCO IS THE GRANDEST secular decoration of the Roman High Baroque, ordered by the greatest pope of the age, Urban VIII (pope 1623–44). Cortona's scheme marks the apogee of papal power and display. During the Thirty Years' War (1618–48), the papacy was able to maintain the appearance of a great power by exploiting the divisions in Europe, but the end of the war saw the emergence of France as the dominant European force. It is indicative of that great change that Louis XIV (reigned 1643–1715) could call Bernini, the papal architect and sculptor, to Paris in 1665–66. Alexander VII (pope 1655–67) had to acquiesce in something his predecessor would have forbidden.

Pietro da Cortona was apprenticed to an undistinguished Florentine painter with whom he traveled to Rome in about 1612. Cortona's great chance came when he attracted the attention of Marcello and Giulio Sacchetti, rich Florentine brothers who had also moved to Rome. The Sacchetti were friends of Urban VIII, formerly Cardinal Maffeo Barberini (a fellow Tuscan) and it was through them that the artist gained the patronage of the pope.

Cortona's ceiling decorates the guardroom (*Sala dei palafrenieri*), or Gran Salon, which was the central public reception room of the Barberini Palace, designed by Carlo Maderno (1556–1629) with the assistance of Bernini, and Borromini (1599–1667). Each family elected to the papacy took advantage of its good fortune to erect a palace for its secular heirs. (In 1672, Cardinal Altieri was elected Clement X. He was in his eighties so work on the new Palazzo Altieri went on night and day in case the pope died before its completion!)

Popes are elected, thus God could intervene to fulfil his plans, and hence the papal signature: *Divina Providentia Pontifex Maximus* ("Supreme Pontiff by Divine Providence"). Cardinal Barberini enjoyed a "heavenly sign" foretelling his election—a swarm of bees (the family coat of arms) from Tuscany (the family's home) alighted on the wall of his conclave cell. A reference to this forms part of the central section of the decoration where Divine Providence, seated on clouds (with Time and the Fates beneath her), commands a personification of Rome to crown the Barberini arms. At the bottom is Minerva, goddess of Wisdom, as the 1640

PIETRO BERRETTINI DA CORTONA

ɕɔ

*BORN CORTONA 1596,
DIED ROME 1669*

guidebook explained, "overthrowing the Giants who are seen hurled down by those mountains they had amassed in order to challenge Heaven. Here is expressed the defence of ecclesiastical things." The virtues of Barberini rule were emphasized through other mythologies and personifications in the rest of the ceiling.

Cortona's ceiling is coved, as is the Palazzo Farnese Gallery which Annibale Carracci had frescoed in the 1590s. Like both Annibale's scheme and Michelangelo's Sistine Ceiling (see page 105), Cortona's masterpiece has a great painted cornice. This allowed him to compartmentalize various scenes. It also formed a backdrop in front of which many of Cortona's figures (including Minerva and the Giants) were represented in dynamic poses on a large scale at the front of the picture-plane. However, Divine Providence is more remotely shown high above, foreshortened in the central sky. The Barberini Gran Salone, unlike Annibale's Galleria, is two stories in height. This enabled Cortona to give his ceiling an "ideal" station point from which to be viewed. This, together with the rich, Venetian color and the weighty, powerful figures, gives the ceiling an epic grandeur and immediacy of impact, despite its episodic character.

The ceiling is incredibly rich in details, especially at the corners, where there are simulated bronze reliefs of scenes representing the Cardinal Virtues (flanking the Minerva scene are Mucius Scaevola putting his hand in the fire, for Fortitude; and Scipio "sending back untarnished to her Saguntine spouse the young maid he had captured as his booty," for Temperance; Prudence and Justice are opposite) and a profusion of mermen, nymphs, garlands, and bucrania (ox skulls), usually executed in stucco but here shown illusionistically. Cortona had assiduously studied ancient Roman antique sculpture and architecture, and had a large library for reference. He even paid tribute to Raphael in the central figure of Divine Providence, as her pose is taken directly from one of Raphael's *Sibyls*, a fresco of 1514 in the Chigi Chapel in Santa Maria della Pace in Rome. In 1656–7, Cortona, who was also an architect of great distinction, at the command of Pope Alexander VII, Fabio Chigi, restored the church and gave it a brilliant new façade.

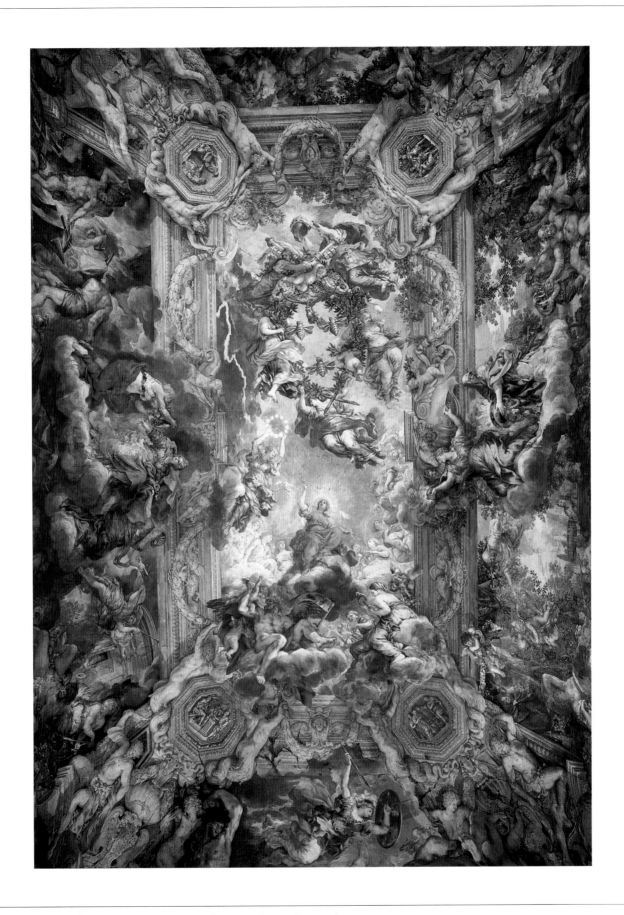

1632–39 | *fresco* | 82 x 49ft (25 x 15m) | Gran Salone, Palazzo Barberini, Rome

As the Old Sang, the Young Pipe

JORDAENS'S ARTISTIC REPUTATION has fluctuated enormously. He kept a flourishing practice in Antwerp from the 1620s to the 1640s, painting altarpieces, mythologies, and portraits, despite the competition of Rubens, the founder of the Flemish Baroque school, Van Dyck, and others. With the deaths of Rubens and Van Dyck, Jordaens became the acknowledged leader of the school, a position he held until his death. He was courted for commissions by the Dutch House of Orange and Charles I of England.

Yet, when I attended the Courtauld Institute of Art in London in the early 1960s, there were tutorials on Rubens and a lecture on Van Dyck, but Jordaens was not even mentioned. Although it was never actually stated, I think that Jordaens was regarded as an embarrassment—he was just far too vulgar to be taken seriously. It was not until 1968 that I had my eyes opened to Jordaens, by the great exhibition organized for the National Gallery of Canada in Ottawa by the late Michael Jaffé.

I still remember vividly the excitement of seeing religious masterpieces like *The Adoration of the Shepherds* (1657, North Carolina Museum of Art, Raleigh), *The Four Doctors of the Latin Church* (c. 1640, Stonyhurst College, Blackburn, England), and the incredible *Holy Family Embarked* (1652, Skokloster, Sweden). All of these are very large in size and rich in color and in the handling of the paint. They are also extremely powerful compositions, especially the latter, with the great curving forms of a ferryboat under sail, seen head-on. In the Skokloster picture, the Virgin wears a straw hat woven in the form of a halo. To anyone with more than a slight knowledge of the 15th-century Flemish school (Jordaens's artistic ancestors), the straw halo recalls the earlier use of another everyday domestic item for a halo, the *Madonna of the Firescreen* by Robert Campin (active 1406–44) (c. 1430, National Gallery, London), where the curve of a wicker screen frames the Virgin's head.

Jordaens, like Pieter Bruegel the Elder before him, painted Flemish proverbs with great vigor and ingenuity. He took the proverb "As the old bird sang, so the young one twitters" but substituted for *piepen* ("twitter") the word *pijpen* ("pipe" or "play the flute"). This allowed him to portray people instead of birds,

JACOB JORDAENS

☙

BORN ANTWERP 1593, DIED ANTWERP 1678

with the old singing and the young playing on pipes. He depicted his figures seated around a table at a feast, recalling a theme he also painted frequently, The King Drinks. The latter is based on a Flemish custom of electing a king of the feast that was held at Epiphany (January 6, marking the arrival of the Three Kings to visit the Christ Child).

In the Ottawa proverb picture, there is a topical reference. The old lady holds a song sheet which is identifiable as the *Nieu Liedeken van Calloo* ("New Song of Calloo"), celebrating the victory of the Spanish forces led by the Cardinal Infante over Prince Frederick Henry of Orange at Calloo near Antwerp in 1638 (the Spanish, at this time, were rulers of the southern Netherlands). Jordaens had worked under Rubens on the designs for the pageant for the Cardinal Infante's 1635 ceremonial entry into Antwerp. It is a nicely ironic touch that in this work the old are singing a new song.

Yet, it would be wrong to think that Jordaens was depicting real events or painting in praise of excessive consumption of food and drink. In one version of *The King Drinks* (1656, Kunsthistorisches Museum, Vienna) where he used, as he often did, his father-in-law, the painter Adam van Noort as a model for the king (painted for the Archduke Leopold Wilhelm, Governor of the Spanish Netherlands), Jordaens included a motto in a cartouche above the scene: *Nil similius insano quam ebrius* ("Nothing is more like a madman than a drunkard"). The Ottawa painting shows in the niche at the upper left symbols of the transience of human life—a snuffed candle and flowers that will fade and die—while in a version of the same subject in Berlin (c. 1640, Schloss Charlottenburg), Jordaens included the motto *Cogita mori* ("Think on death").

However, both the Ottawa and Berlin paintings are essentially optimistic, as is shown by the opulence of the still life and the good humor of the people. Both pictures have prominent parrots, "disguised symbols" of Christian salvation since van Eyck's *Madonna of the Canon van der Paele* (1436, Groeningemuseum, Bruges) and Dürer's *Adam and Eve* (1507, Prado, Madrid). The Ottawa parrot perches beside the Eucharistic symbols of bread and wine.

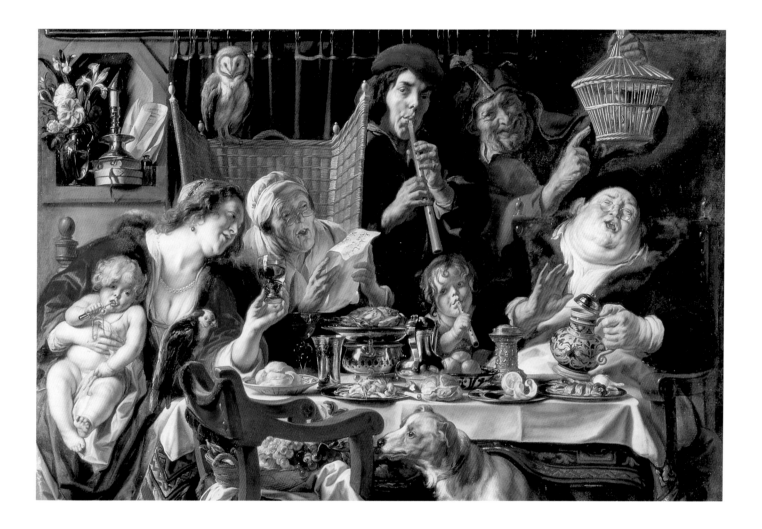

Early 1640s | *oil on canvas* | 57 x 86in (145 x 218cm) | National Gallery of Canada, Ottawa

The Encounter of Saint Leo the Great and Attila

ALGARDI WAS TRAINED by a minor sculptor, Conventi, in the modeling of stucco figures; his native Bologna has no natural stone. Algardi's early works are mediocre; he was a late developer. In 1625, he arrived in Rome, where the sculptural scene was dominated by the towering figure of Gianlorenzo Bernini, the favorite of Pope Urban VIII. During Urban's pontificate (which continued until 1644), papal commissions went almost entirely to Bernini. For some time, Algardi had to be content with sculptural bread-and-butter activities like the restoration of antique sculpture. Fortunately for him, he had come to Rome with an introductory letter to Cardinal Ludovisi, the nephew of the former Pope Gregory XV and a member of a leading Bolognese family, who possessed a great collection of antique sculpture on which Algardi worked.

Ludovisi introduced the sculptor to the Bolognese painter Domenichino (1581–1641), then working in Rome, who secured for Algardi his first public commissions, stucco figures of *St. Mary Magdalene* and *St. John the Evangelist* for the Bandini Chapel in San Silvestro al Quirinale, which he completed in 1629.

In the following decades, Algardi received important commissions in Rome and Bologna. These included an over-life-sized marble statue of *St. Philip Neri* for the sacristy of the Oratorian Fathers in the Chiesa Nuova, Rome (1636–38). The saint stands in a niche looking upward, open-mouthed, with his head tilted; he gestures open-palmed with his right hand while his left is placed firmly on an open book held by a kneeling angel. It is a very structured, weighty composition, set in an arched-topped niche. The curving lines of the saint's vestments contrast with the straight sides of the niche. The figures are on a plinth that projects beyond the niche; Algardi allowed the angel's robe to fall over the plinth's edge and his wing to overlap the right-hand boundary. *St. Philip Neri* has the character of a restrained classical work of art along with Baroque qualities of chiaroscuro, texture, weight, movement, and proximity to the spectator. Algardi's great opportunity came during the pontificate of Innocent X (pope 1644–55), the successor to Urban VIII, who dismissed his predecessor's artists. Plans to decorate the altar of Pope Leo I in

ALESSANDRO ALGARDI

⚭

BORN BOLOGNA 1598,
DIED ROME 1654

St. Peter's had existed since 1626. Guido Reni had been asked for a painting to represent the encounter in A.D. 452 between the pope and the Hunnish King Attila, when, according to tradition, Saint Peter and Saint Paul appeared in the sky, an apparition that so terrified Attila he gave up his designs on Rome.

Reni (who died in 1642) never took up the commission which, although it involved a large work, also had drawbacks; the space was tall, narrow, and poorly lit. Also, it was discovered that pictures in St. Peter's were being damaged by the excessive humidity, which led Innocent X to suggest in 1646 that the St. Leo altar should be a marble relief, and the commission was given to Algardi. That still left the other physical problems of the altar, compounded by the traditional iconography of the story, which called for the encounter to be on horseback. Algardi, realizing the impossibility of this in the narrow space, made the revolutionary suggestion that the protagonists should be shown dismounted, which was duly accepted.

No marble relief of this size had been carved before, yet Algardi completed the task of designing and carving it triumphantly, and his work became a model for the next century. Especially brilliant is the range in the depth of his carved figures, from those of the pope and his attendant and Attila, which are almost fully in the round, to Saint Peter and Saint Paul, who are perhaps in three-quarter relief, to the half-relief page holding the helmet, and ultimately to the almost flattened relief of the soldiers behind Attila. Many heads show great nobility, including Saint Paul's (apparently taken from an *Abraham* by Pietro da Cortona) and the head of the pope's attendant (which is based on the antique Ludovisi *Gaul,* which Algardi would have known well). As in the *Saint Philip Neri,* there is a wonderful balance between moving, weighty, tangible figures coming very close to us and the containing character of their gestures and the frame. Along with plenty of drama and countless textures, there are also classical restraint, dignity, and grace, even in the figure of the hated Attila. Algardi was also a prolific sculptor of penetrating portrait busts. Rather less well known are his small-scale bronzes, a medium that he exploited superbly.

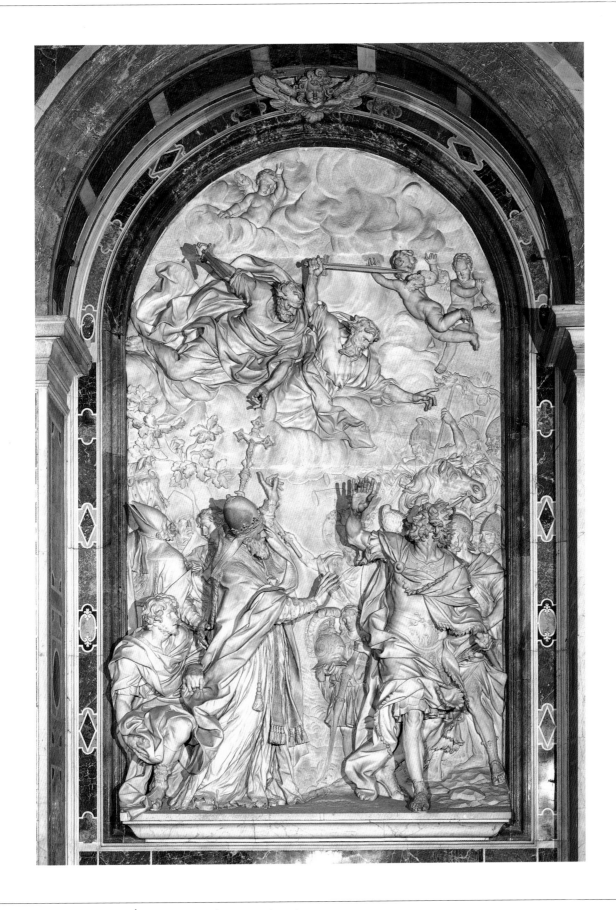

1646–53 | *marble* | 28 x 16½ft (8.5 x 5m) | St. Peter's Basilica, Rome

Daedalus and Icarus

DURING HIS LIFE, Thys enjoyed the patronage of the Archducal and Orange courts at Brussels and The Hague. As late as 1754, the French critic Descamps enthused that he was "one of the greatest artists … it is only just to put him with the first of his nation. He was a great designer; his color and his manner are vigorous." But in later centuries, his reputation plummeted.

From recent research it is clear that Thys was a major Flemish painter, with a distinctive voice. His signed *Toilet of Bathsheba* (c. 1650, Shipley Art Gallery, Gateshead, England) shows, like most depictions of this Old Testament theme, a female nude (here modest) with King David spying from his balcony. But the story is one of tragedy as well as lust. Bathsheba was married to Uriah, and to conceal Uriah's adultery, David ordered him into battle to be killed. God, angered by David's actions, caused his and Bathsheba's child to die. Thys, using the classical rhetorical device of prolepsis (anticipation) suggests the outcome by placing in the foreground, between Cupid (shooting at David) and the king's messenger, an old woman dressed in black. Above are cypresses, an ancient symbol of death and grief. This work shows Thys's mastery at incorporating symbols into his paintings.

Daedalus and Icarus first appeared in Earl Spencer's 1742 Althorp inventory as by Van Dyck. In 1831, the critic Smith called it "one of the artist's most natural productions … the body of Icarus, both in drawing and colour, is a model of perfection in art." The attribution continued well into the 20th century (the picture meanwhile having been sold to Frank Wood, a Toronto collector, who bequeathed it to the present gallery). Yet, while there are distinct periods in Van Dyck's work, with well-defined characteristics, scholars do not agree on the picture's date.

In 1981, the *Daedalus and Icarus* was in the Ottawa "Young Van Dyck" exhibition. In a review, I rejected the Van Dyck attribution: "the surface is silky and smooth … There is no hint of that dry impasto, or the worked surfaces so characteristic of early Van Dyck." I noted that the same model as the Icarus had been employed by Thys for an angel in a *Madonna and Child with Donors* (c. 1655–60, St. Benigne, Arc-et-Senans, France), attributed to the artist because of a similar angel in Thys's signed Antwerp altarpiece, the *Virgin appearing to St. William of Aquitaine* (c. 1655–60, Koninklijk Museum voor Schone Kunsten, Antwerp). The head of Daedalus is also used by Thys for the executioner in his Brussels *Martyrdom of St. Benedict* (c. 1652, Musées Royaux des Beaux-Arts, Paris), and the proportions and modeling of Saint Benedict are strikingly reminiscent of Icarus.

Despite the strong surface pattern, the Toronto picture shows an un-Vandyckian interest in volume and depth. It is very "vigorous" (also uncharacteristic of Van Dyck), the adjective Descamps used to describe the manner of Pieter Thys. Although there are formal parallels between the Toronto picture and Thys's *Martyrdom of St. Benedict*, the former shows a tendency toward the paler color and tonality of Thys's later works, hence the Toronto picture probably dates from c. 1655–60.

Daedalus was an inventor, imprisoned by Minos (son of Jupiter and Europa), King of Crete. To escape, Daedalus constructed wings for his son Icarus and himself. Despite his father's warning not to fly too close to the sun, nor to fly too near to the earth or water, Icarus soared toward the sun and then fell to his death. The moral of Daedalus and Icarus, as recounted by Ovid, is the golden mean, keep to a middle course. In the 17th century, a new twist appeared. Georges Sandys wrote: "Icarus falls in aspiring. Yet more commendable than those, who creepe on the earth like contemptible wormes … whereas this hath something of magnanimity … So that of two vices, the one is braver, and the other safer." The Toronto picture incorporates this new interpretation. Icarus gestures with his right arm parallel to the earth, but his "fine surly expression" (as Horace Walpole put it so well) suggests that he is telling his father, "I wouldn't dream of flying too low! I am no worm!"

Again, Thys takes an ancient story and says something different about it. Recovering the Toronto *Daedalus and Icarus* for Pieter Thys—a very satisfying result of art-historical detective work—restores the reputation of a painter whose work has fallen into undeserved neglect. Despite its removal from Van Dyck's oeuvre, psychologically and formally, *Daedalus and Icarus* remains a masterpiece.

PIETER THYS

BORN ANTWERP 1624,
DIED ANTWERP 1677

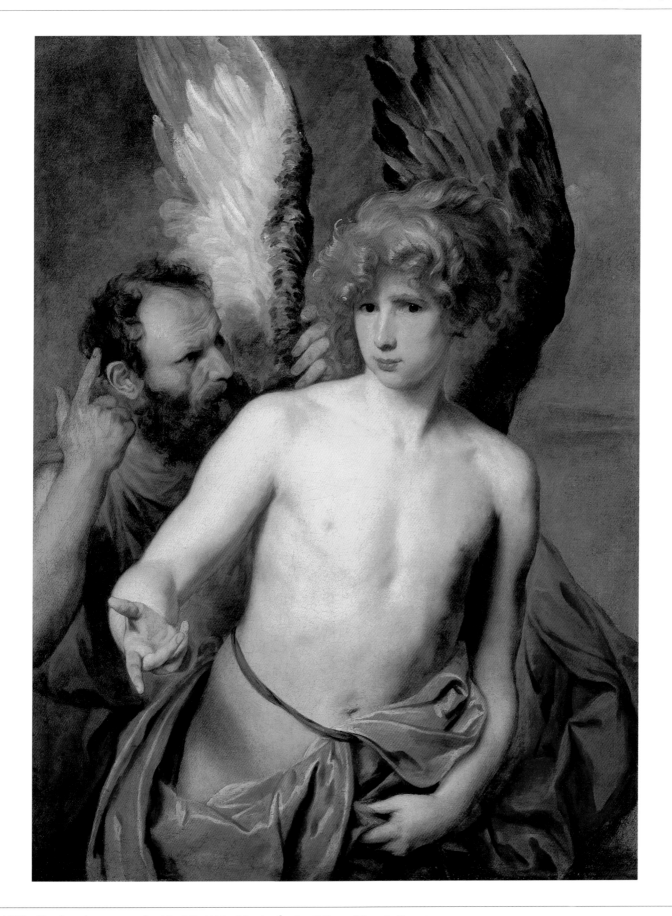

c. 1655–60 | *oil on canvas* | 45 x 34in (115 x 86cm) | Art Gallery of Ontario, Toronto

Cathedra Petri

A MASTERFUL SCULPTOR, architect, painter, and designer, Bernini was the supreme artist of the Italian Baroque. He was a child prodigy, the son of a Florentine sculptor and a Neapolitan mother. When the family moved to Rome, the young sculptor's work attracted the attention of the pope's nephew, Cardinal Scipione Borghese, for whom Bernini created a series of religious and mythological works of dazzling virtuosity, like the *Apollo and Daphne* (1622–25) and the famous *David* (1623, both Borghese Gallery, Rome), poised to sling his stone at Goliath who stands, invisible, behind the viewer. With these Baroque works, sculpture caught up with painting. Indeed, David's pose was partly inspired by the figure of Polyphemus throwing a rock at Galatea in the fresco in Annibale Carracci's Farnese Gallery.

Carracci may have been an even greater inspiration to the young sculptor. Filippo Baldinucci wrote in his biography of Bernini in 1682 that, in 1608, Annibale, together with some other artists and Bernini, was in St. Peter's Basilica, the church that had replaced the old Constantinian basilica. Bramante had designed the new building in 1506; its altar end, crossing, and dome had been modified by Michelangelo from 1546, and Carlo Maderno had begun to add a long nave in 1605. Annibale reportedly said, "the day will come … that a prodigious genius will make two great monuments in the middle and at the end of this temple on a scale in keeping with the vastness of this building." The ten-year-old Bernini exclaimed, "Oh, if only I could be the one!"

In 1623, Maffeo Barberini became Pope Urban VIII. He set Bernini to work on the interior of St. Peter's, where the nave had been finished in 1614. The first challenge was the decoration of the altar in the crossing under Michelangelo's great dome, a hallowed spot beneath which rest the remains of Saint Peter, apostle and first pope. Above the altar Bernini erected the *Baldacchino* (canopy) (1624–33), whose giant, twisted, dark-bronze columns contrast in form and color with the straight pilasters in the adjacent dome piers. Bernini's work is both illusionistic and symbolic. The lappets joining the columns echo those on canopies carried in procession over living popes; the columns derive from the twisted columns that had been given to

GIANLORENZO BERNINI

⟨⟩

BORN NAPLES 1598,
DIED ROME 1680

the Old Basilica by the Emperor Constantine and which were believed to have come from the Temple of Solomon, itself said to have been modeled on the Heavenly Temple. The Constantinian columns themselves were deployed by Bernini in the dome piers.

The second "great monument" is the *Cathedra Petri* (Chair of Peter) against the western wall (St. Peter's does not face east) above the apse altar, which Bernini executed in 1657–66 for Pope Alexander (Chigi) VII. Essentially, this is a huge reliquary. The great gilt-bronze chair, which is held aloft by giant statues of the Latin Church Fathers, encases a wooden chair believed to have been St. Peter's (right up to the 18th century, only important people, such as the pope or cardinals, sat in chairs during public ceremonials; others stood or sat on stools). On the back of the bronze chair is a relief with Christ's charge to Saint Peter, "Feed my sheep," echoing the relief over the central door of the portico.

Above the chair is a glory of angels and cherubs in clouds, all in gilded stucco, and shafts of light in gilded bronze, radiating from an oval, golden, stained-glass window, in the center of which is painted the dove of the Holy Spirit. Traditionally, sculptors had created figures in the round or in high or low relief, and sculpture had remained quite separate from architecture and painting. Here, Bernini created a work that defies these classifications, since it is "*un bel composto*" —"a beautiful mixture" of all, as he said of his aims.

Such a fusion could well have been chaotic, but Bernini's ecstatic, agitated figures are held together visually by the horizontals of the altar and the chair and by the verticals of the outer bronze Fathers, but above all by the verticals of the giant pilaster flutings that rise behind to support Michelangelo's great entablature. Yet the most powerful unifying agent—and also, artistically, the most brilliant stroke of all—is the golden light from the stained-glass window that is seen streaming through as soon as you enter the nave of St. Peter's: a bright, visionary glow beckoning through the dark *Baldacchino* columns. As always, Bernini unites the real and the symbolic: the light emanates from the dove of the Holy Spirit under whose guidance St. Peter and his successor popes act.

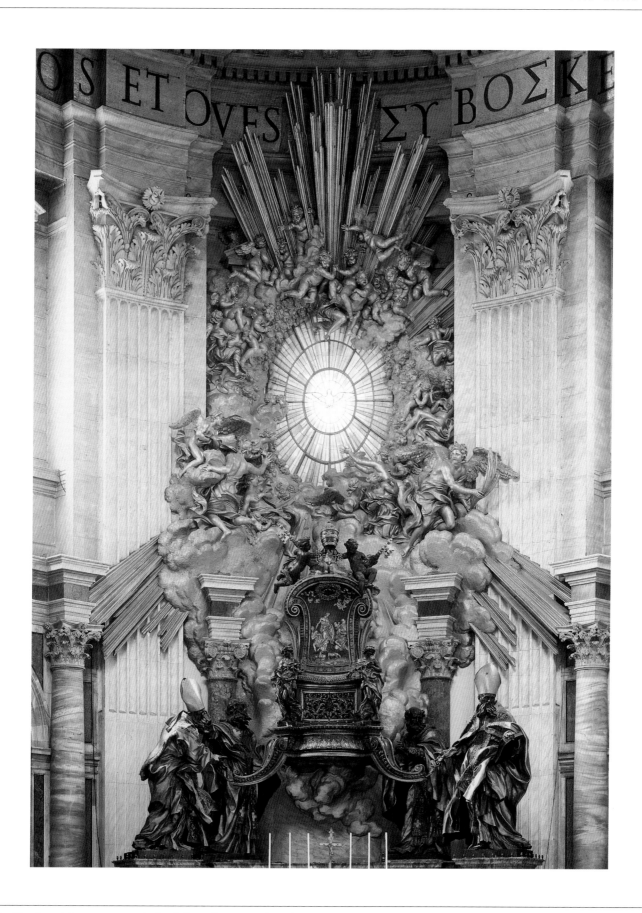

1657–66 | *gilt bronze, stucco, and colored glass* | St. Peter's Basilica, Rome

Spring *(Adam and Eve in Paradise)*

WE KNOW MUCH ABOUT POUSSIN from his fifties on but far less about his youth, and there has been a scholarly tendency to denigrate aspects of his early life and to project back into it some of the older artist's classicizing aims and ideas.

Poussin's earliest training was in Normandy in a late-Mannerist style, but early in his career he moved to Paris, where he obtained large commissions for decorations at Notre Dame Cathedral. He also produced drawings of mythological subjects from Ovid's *Metamorphoses* (c. 1623, Royal Library, Windsor) for the Italian poet Giovanni Battista Marino; they are Poussin's only surviving pre-Italian works. In one drawing, the enraged giant Polyphemus discovers his lover Galatea betraying him with Acis, and the use of dramatic perspective to portray impending violence (the giant killed Acis with a rock) is masterly.

Poussin went to Rome in 1624 and gained the patronage of Pope Urban VIII's nephew, Cardinal Francesco Barberini, who, in 1628, obtained a coveted St. Peter's commission for him. *The Martyrdom of St. Erasmus* (1628, Vatican Pinacoteca) is not a favorite with modern critics, probably because of the gruesome subject matter (martyrdom by disembowelment), yet in this work, which he signed prominently, Poussin demonstrated that he had absorbed the Roman Baroque trends toward bold drama, light, color, and sensuality. Contemporaries responded well: Poussin was given an extra payment on the picture's completion, many copies were made, and the Barberini displayed the *modello* (a small version to be shown to the patron) (National Gallery, Ottawa) in the state rooms of their palazzo. Poussin followed up with other large-scale works, both religious and secular.

However, around 1630 Poussin gave up competing for public works to concentrate on smaller studies of mythological, Old Testament, and historical subjects for private patrons. His best client was Cassiano dal Pozzo, Barberini's secretary and an antiquarian for whom Poussin painted more than fifty works and who encouraged him to study classical sculpture. Persuaded to return to Paris in 1640–42, Poussin, who was no courtier, had an unhappy time, yet he completed a superb ceiling painting for Cardinal Richelieu (Louvre, Paris) and a grand altarpiece for the

Jesuits (Louvre), demonstrating that he had not lost his ability to create large works of Baroque grandeur. He also met the intellectual bourgeoisie of Paris, who remained his patrons.

His compositions became more structured and solemn, and in the late 1640s, he turned increasingly to small landscapes with figures, often with subjects taken from Stoic philosophy (where submission to destiny was the driving force), like the 1648 pair (National Museum of Wales, Cardiff, and Walker Art Gallery, Liverpool) devoted to the story of the Athenian general Phocion. Descended from Annibale Carracci's "ideal" landscapes, these works were also a considerable departure as "heroic" landscapes in which ordered grandeur complements the narrative themes. In the early 1650s, Poussin's style changed again, and he created timeless, motionless allegories to express eternal truths. It is in this spirit that he painted his last completed works, *The Four Seasons*, which were bought by Louis XIV of France in 1665. They are landscapes with biblical themes—*Spring* (*Adam and Eve in Paradise*), *Summer* (*Ruth and Boaz*), *Autumn* (*The Grapes of Canaan*), and *Winter* (*The Deluge*)—and fully reveal how the artist had finally replaced cold rationalism with a poetic, mystical quality.

NICOLAS POUSSIN

BORN LES ANDELYS 1594,
DIED ROME 1665

In *Spring*, Poussin shows the lushness of nature in morning light, with a powerful sense of structure in the framing rocks and trees and the orderly recession of space. Adam and Eve are interlocked in profile like a classical relief. At the upper right is God. He is said to be "blessing his creation" but as he is raising his left not his right hand as Baroque decorum would require for a blessing, God's action is, rather, a horrified reaction to Eve. She points to the Tree of Knowledge; her gesture marks the beginning of Original Sin and the prelude to the Expulsion from Paradise. It is striking that God's recoiling movement derives from Polyphemus's in the Marino drawing—but it was entirely logical that Poussin should have recalled his earlier work (he must have kept preparatory sketches) and reused this pose. God, like the giant, was reacting to betrayal.

Ironically, it was in France, where Poussin had barely worked, that his influence was felt most profoundly, lying at the heart of Academic art, and he continued to inspire into the 19th century.

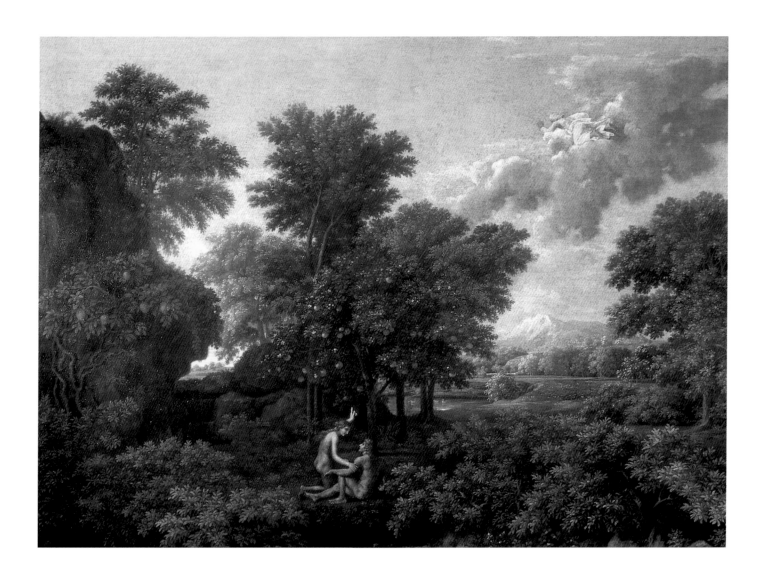

1660–64 ┃ *oil on canvas* ┃ 46¹/₂ x 63in (118 x 160cm) ┃ Louvre, Paris

Coast View with the Embarkation of Carlo and Ubaldo

CLAUDE'S PAINTINGS are, as Kenneth Clark put it, "the true heir of the poetry of Giorgione." They have never lacked champions; Joshua Reynolds is reported to have said that there would be another Raphael before there would be another Claude.

Claude came to Rome at the age of thirteen. After working as a pastry cook, he studied with Agostino Tassi, the Roman architectural painter who in 1612 had been tried for the rape of Artemisia Gentileschi, and later he may have studied in Naples with the German-born landscapist Goffredo Wals. From 1625–26 Claude was back in Lorraine, at Nancy, but by 1627 he had returned to Rome and remained there until his death.

Aside from his seaports, which derived from his experience of the Italian coast, most of Claude's paintings are based on sketches made in the Campagna, the countryside around Rome. The Campagna was dotted with medieval and Roman ruins (even the Forum in Rome was a cow pasture at the time and, along with other famous monuments like the Arch of Constantine, remained partially buried until the 19th century), but Claude, as Reynolds wrote, "was convinced that nature as he found it seldom produced beauty." Consequently, his pictures, although full of effects based on drawings from nature, are thoroughly "composed" affairs, painted in the studio. They are part of the "ideal" landscape tradition initiated by Annibale Carracci in *The Flight into Egypt* (c. 1605, Galleria Doria-Pamphili, Rome). Claude's pictures inevitably show sunrises or sunsets with the light flooding from the background, unifying the canvas.

Yet, Claude's paintings are not just formal constructions. Classical literature was a major source of inspiration for him, especially the arcadian tradition of the Greek and Roman poets Theocritus and Virgil. Claude also frequently took themes from Virgil's *Aeneid*, the story of the Trojan Prince Aeneas who was forced to flee his burning city to wander from place to place in the Mediterranean with his band of followers (including a sojourn in Queen Dido's Carthage and a descent to Hades). Aeneas and his retinue finally settled in Latium, Italy, where, according to the legend, their colony in time gave rise to the great empire of Rome.

**CLAUDE LORRAINE
(CLAUDE GELLÉE)**

*BORN CHAMAGNE 1600,
DIED ROME 1682*

Today, this epic poem is read as a dramatic narrative, but from antiquity until the 18th century it was also read morally and allegorically. In 1480, in his *Camaldulensian Dialogues*, the Florentine neo-Platonist Cristoforo Landino had interpreted Aeneas' journey and trials as a progress to virtue, and these ideas were incorporated into later Italian editions of the *Aeneid*. Claude's paintings of *Aeneid* episodes, like the *View of Carthage with Dido and Aeneas* (1675, Kunsthalle, Hamburg) and *Ascanius and the Stag* (1682, Ashmolean Museum, Oxford), show that Claude was well aware of these interpretations and aspired to be a "history" painter, the highest category of painting in the 17th century.

Claude also drew inspiration from the Italian poet Tasso's 16th-century *Gerusalemme Deliverata* ("Jerusalem Delivered"), an epic that remained popular until Victorian times (Sir Walter Scott was a devotee). It is a story about the first crusade, told in highly romantic terms, with magicians, dragons, and enchanted woods. In *Coast View with the Embarkation of Carlo and Ubaldo* (which was painted for Prince Falconieri together with another subject from the tale), Claude depicts the episode from Tasso's poem, where the hero Rinaldo has been lured from his Christian duty by an enchantress, Armida, who has spirited him away to the Fortunate Isles. Rinaldo's friends Carlo and Ubaldo are about to board a boat to rescue him, having just talked to the magician Ascalone, who is shown leaving on the right. Claude chose a moment from the poem that gave him the opportunity to paint his favorite coastal scenery, with a sunrise in the background (his compatriot and friend Poussin also painted Carlo and Ubaldo, but showed them after they had arrived at the Fortunate Isles, fighting a dragon). Typical of Claude's late works, this picture shows an airy, diaphanous approach to the forms of trees, matched by the elongated, elegant figures which are tiny but stand out sharply against a grand spacious view. It is one of Claude's most enchanting creations.

Claude's work was particularly admired in England. He inspired the English Picturesque tradition in the mid-to-late 18th century, seen in verse, landscape gardening, and painting, including artists like Wilson and Turner.

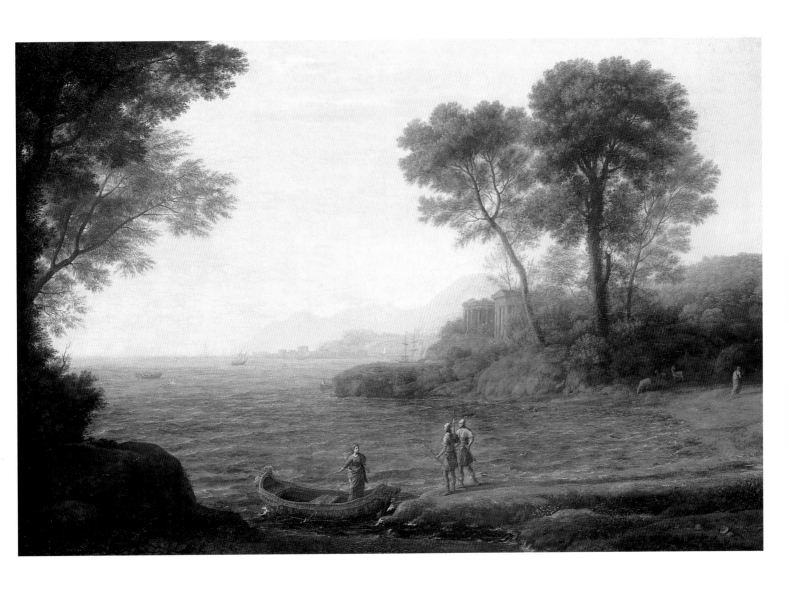

c. 1667 | *oil on canvas* | 37 x 54in (93 x 138cm) | Art Gallery of Ontario, Toronto

Portrait of Lady Charlotte Fitzroy with her Indian Page

LELY WAS BORN in Germany, the son of Captain Van der Faes, a Dutch officer on foreign service. Early in his career he took his nickname from a family house, "*In de Lelye*" ("In the Lily"). He studied painting in Haarlem with Frans Peters de Grebber (1573–1649) but, during the English Civil War (1642–48), emigrated to London, drawn by the gap left by Van Dyck's death.

Lely at first "pursu'd the natural bent of his Genius in *Landtschapes* with *small Figures*, and *Historical Compositions.*" However, there was little demand for such works in England, so he turned to portraiture, in which he was greatly influenced by Van Dyck. His subjects included both Charles I and Oliver Cromwell. His portrait style of the 1650s is often fresh, innocent, and charming, notably in works like *Henry Sidney, Earl of Romney* (c. 1650, Penshurst Place, Kent), the finest of his child portraits, where the sitter is shown in arcadian costume.

From 1660 and the Restoration of Charles II, Lely became England's most fashionable artist, producing a huge quantity of portraits with a team of assistants, and, like Van Dyck before him, he became court painter. From this influential position he consolidated the tradition of the English society portrait, which held good until the time of Sir Thomas Lawrence (1769–1830). His Restoration style, epitomized by the ten *Windsor Beauties*, which were commissioned by Anne Hyde, Duchess of York, and originally hung in Whitehall Palace (c. 1662–65, Windsor Castle), was lush and sensuous with a strong sense of volume, in contrast to Van Dyck's more restrained and linear style. However, in his last decade, Lely sometimes resorted to artificialities such as exaggerated contrapposto, perhaps under the influence of immigrant French artists. His colors could also be darker and his characterization morose.

But none of these criticisms apply to this portrait of Lady Charlotte Fitzroy, which is as enchanting as any of Lely's child portraits of the 1650s. The color is ravishing, with the girl's cool, bright-pink drapery set against the warm browns of the background and the subdued gold-brown of the boy's gown.

The picture was a royal commission, painted in 1672 when the eight-year-old sitter, the fourth child of the famous courtesan Barbara Villiers, Duchess of Cleveland, and Charles II,

PETER LELY

☙

BORN SOEST 1618,
DIED LONDON 1680

was betrothed to ten-year-old Sir Edward Henry Lee. They were married in 1677 when the groom was created Earl of Lichfield and Lady Charlotte became a countess.

Lady Charlotte is shown seated, looking outward. At the left is a kneeling servant, not a black page (usual during this period to add exoticism to a painting), but an Indian. He presents Lady Charlotte with a bunch of grapes, a Bacchic reference. According to mythology, Bacchus, the god of wine, conquered India. He then returned to Greece, soon afterward encountering and marrying Ariadne, upon whom he bestowed immortality. So Bacchic symbolism is associated with betrothal and marriage. Annibale Carracci's Farnese Ceiling, which culminates in *The Triumph of Bacchus and Ariadne*, was commissioned in part to commemorate the marriage of Duke Ranuccio Farnese to Margherita Aldobrandini, niece of Pope Clement VIII, while in 1674, Louis Grabu's opera *Ariane, ou le Mariage de Bacchus* was performed at the London wedding celebrations of the Duke of York and Princess Mary of Modena.

Above Lady Charlotte is a relief panel with a goat held by putti, one carrying a flagon, presumably of wine. The goat is the symbol of lust or earthly love, held in check by the putti, agents of divine love. The Bacchus-Ariadne myth was allegorized as the story of the soul's ascent to divine grace. In his handbook on iconography (1593), Cesare Ripa illustrated Divine Grace holding a wineglass and stated that, "Whoever is in God's grace is continually intoxicated with the sweetness of his love, for this intoxication is so strong and potent that it drives away the thirst for worldly things."

The story of Bacchus and Ariadne explains the composition of Lely's picture. Lady Charlotte, while taking grapes from the Indian boy, looks out to Sir Edward Lee, her betrothed. His unseen involvement, in the role of Bacchus, completes the story. This brilliant and witty combination of pictorial and real space is entirely characteristic of baroque illusionism.

For the relief, Lely used an early-16th-century drawing after Antonio Correggio (Devonshire Collection, Chatsworth, England). Lely was the greatest collector of Old Master drawings of his age and may actually have owned this work.

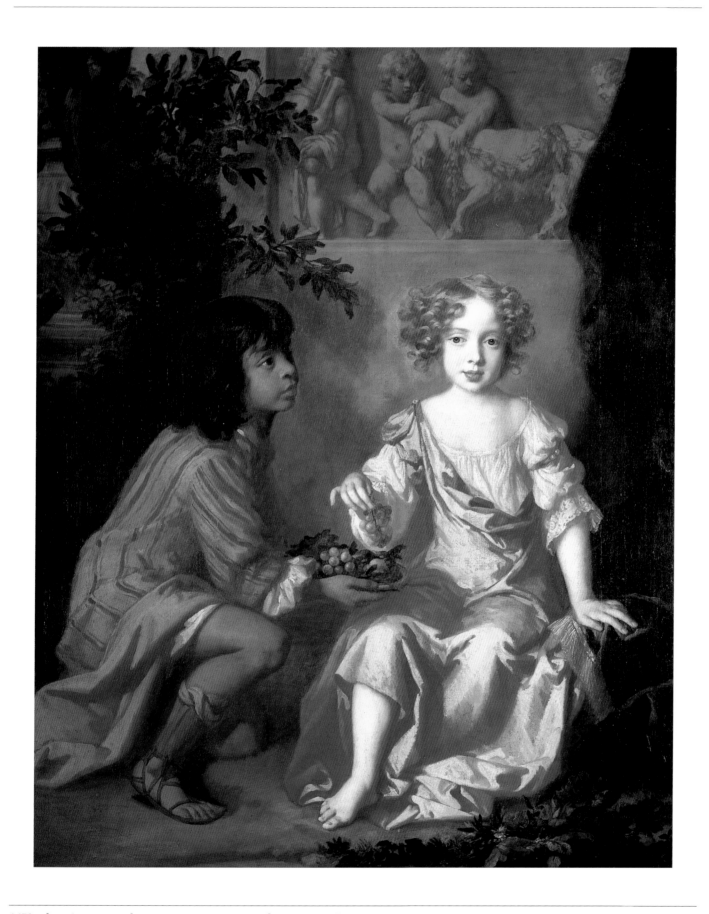

1672 | *oil on canvas* | 50 x 40in (127 x 102cm) | City Art Gallery, York

King William III on Horseback

KNELLER WAS SENT to Leyden University but turned to painting and moved to Amsterdam in the 1660s where he was apprenticed first to Ferdinand Bol (1616–80), a pupil of Rembrandt, and then to Rembrandt himself. In 1666, because of Kneller's German birth and the close ties between Amsterdam and the German Electors (the city's guarantors of freedom), he obtained the patronage of Johann Philipp von Schönborn, Prince-Bishop of Würzburg and Elector of Mainz, painting his portrait (1666, Kunsthistorischesmuseum, Vienna) and a large biblical "history," *The Dismissal of Hagar* (c. 1670, Alte Pinakothek, Munich).

In 1672, Kneller traveled to Rome where he studied with Bernini and Carlo Maratta (1625–1713). He then went to Venice, where he painted members of the leading families, and by 1676 had moved to London, the most cosmopolitan and experienced artist to arrive there since Van Dyck. Kneller would become the last foreign-born artist to dominate English painting.

He faced much competition from Peter Lely, Van Dyck's successor as Principal Painter to the King, as well as from other European immigrants, and native-born artists. Yet, in less than a decade, Kneller had outstripped or outlived his rivals and become the most fashionable painter in London. After the Revolution of 1688 (when James II effectively abdicated the English throne), William III and Mary II became his chief patrons. In 1691, Kneller was made sole Principal Painter and was knighted the next year. In 1699, the king gave him a large medal bearing the royal image and a gold chain. Kneller thus reached the level of honor that Van Dyck had attained under Charles I. In 1715, George I made Kneller a baronet.

Kneller created at least nine designs for large-scale equestrian portraits, more perhaps than any earlier artist. The Het Loo picture is a *modello* for his largest painting (this has suffered from repainting and has been cut down) which hangs in the Presence Chamber (Guard Room) at Hampton Court Palace.

As in a Roman *Adventus* (the ceremonial welcoming of an emperor), whose imagery reached back to descriptions of a divine arrival in Homeric hymns and forward to the coming of Christ, William is greeted by Ceres, with her cornucopia, and

GODFREY KNELLER

☙

*BORN LÜBECK 1646,
DIED WHITTON 1723*

Flora, with flowers. He tramples on the emblems of war. Above, with putti and Mercury, is winged Astraea, with a star on her breast. In the finished picture one of the putti holds a scroll with a quotation from Virgil's "messianic" *Eclogue*: "And he reigns over the pacified world with the virtues of his ancestors." That poem foretells the end of the Age of Iron under the reign of Saturn and the return of Astraea, a virgin personifying Justice. A child shall be born, says Virgil, who will rule a reconciled world with peace and justice and inaugurate a new Age of Gold. Later ages identified the child (on the basis of a prophecy told to Aeneas) as "Augustus Caesar of deified Caesar's race who shall establish in Latium a second time the golden age throughout the fields where Saturn once was king; beyond the Garamantae [a North African tribe] and beyond the Indians he shall extend his empire." As a British king, William, too, was a descendant of Aeneas, according to medieval and later English writers. William brings peace, prosperity, and justice by destroying James II's absolute rule, restoring parliamentary government and Protestantism, and ending the long wars with France by the 1697 Treaty of Ryswick. Also, like Caesar, the implication is that his empire shall be far-reaching.

The king rides on the seashore, alluding to his 1688 landing at Torbay and British naval power. Behind are Neptune (in mythology, the inventor of the horse), a Triton (in the finished picture), and distant hilltops, which evoke the passage in Ovid's *Metamorphoses* describing the rebirth of the world after the flood.

Kneller's *modello* and the finished picture (1701) are not only portraits but "histories." For Rembrandt and his school, "history" (that is, a narrative with a moral purpose) remained, as it had been since the 15th century in Italy, the highest form of painting. The Het Loo painting shows Kneller at his most inventive, taking elements from ancient literature, myth, allegory, pictorial tradition, and modern themes, and casting them into something original and vibrant. His style is a departure from that of the 1690s, the lively handling of the paint and the pale colors showing the impact of Rubens, whose late work Kneller had studied in Flanders in 1697. These Rubensian features, together with the lightness of the figures, foreshadow the Rococo.

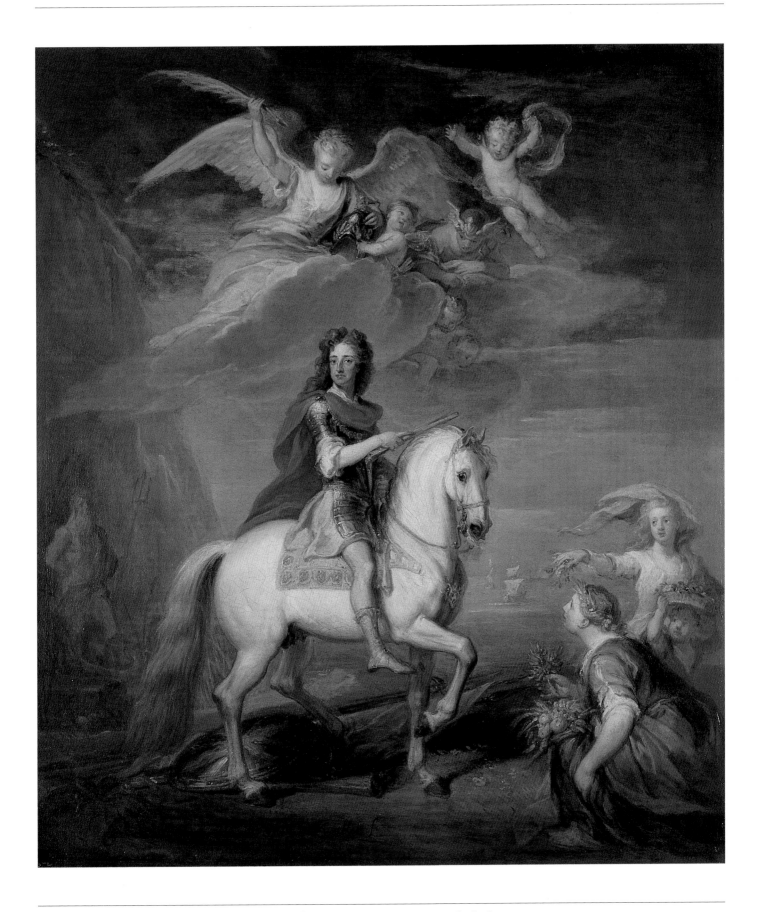

c. 1700 | *oil on canvas* | 41 x 36in (103 x 91cm) | Het Loo Palace, Apeldoorn, Netherlands

NORTHERN EUROPE

1500–1700 ❧ PAUL TAYLOR

Nowadays, we look back on North European painting of the 15th century,

the age of Jan van Eyck, Rogier van der Weyden, and Martin Schongauer (died 1491),

as one of the great periods of Western art. But in the years after 1500,

it was not so clear to the artists of Germany and the Low Countries

that their predecessors had made works worth emulating.

A FEW PAINTERS, like Gerard David (died 1523), were content to carry on with the elegant style of northern tradition, but others like Albrecht Dürer and Jan Gossaert were dissatisfied with what they saw as a provincial manner. They turned for inspiration to Italy where, they felt, the most impressive art of recent times had been created, founded on the beauty of Roman sculpture. At this time Roman prose was the model of learned writing, so it was understandable that artists should also try to catch the spirit of antiquity.

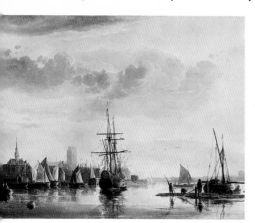

Aelbert Cuyp's View of Dordrecht, *c. 1655–60, is the realist landscape at its best*

Classical subjects poured into northern art, which had previously been mainly religious; and the figures in these new narratives were no longer the spindly creatures so loved by the "Flemish primitives." It was not easy for Northerners to emulate the muscular style of the south; and almost a hundred years of Flemish effort went into technically brilliant but strangely clumsy experiments. The works of Gossaert, Frans Floris, and others show how hard it is for artists to adopt a foreign manner when they have a strong indigenous style.

The Flemish tradition of fine detail and immaculate surfaces made it hard to adapt to looser Italian ways. It was only at the start of the 17th century

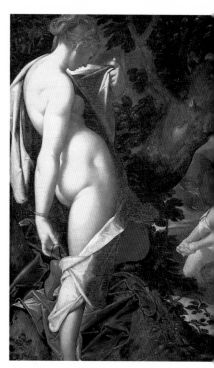

Bartholomeus Spranger's Salmacis and Hermaphrodite *(1582); mythological subjects gave more scope for the depiction of nudes.*

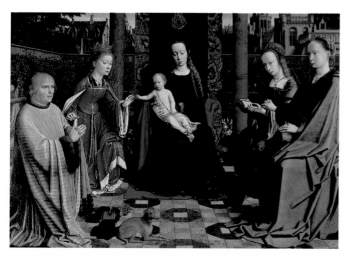

Virgin and Child with Saints and Donor,
c. 1510, by Gerard David, the last of the
Early Netherlandish painters.

that artists like Rubens, Van Dyck, and Jordaens were able to capture the red-blooded fullness of the southern manner. No sooner had the northerners mastered the style than they began to edge away from it; though Rubens and his contemporaries were the first northern artists to ape the Italians successfully, they were also the last. New forms of painting like landscape, genre, and still life began to gain popularity and to push history painting to one side. Traditionalists found this regrettable, and well into the 18th century, art writers lamented the fact that the public had little taste for classically inspired figure painting. But since the public did not read the art theorists' writings, the new forms of art slowly conquered the market.

It has often been suggested that these "minor genres" took root in the Netherlands because the Catholic Church had been expelled by Protestantism, which meant that there was no longer any call for churches to be decorated with images of the saints. This may have been a contributory factor, but it cannot have been the whole story, since landscape, genre, and still life were also popular, from the beginning of the 17th century on, in Catholic countries like Flanders, France, Italy, and Spain, where the Church was still busy commissioning religious art. We do not have a clear enough picture of the origins of the minor genres to say exactly where they were invented. Still life may first have emerged in Catholic Brabant (now Netherlands/Belgium), or Calvinist Holland, or Lutheran Germany, or in all three independently.

Between 1500 and 1700, art moved out of the shadow of the Church and became an independent source of pleasure to the classes of society that could afford it. In its own way, this was as momentous a change as the developments in the science of the times. The crumbling of the medieval worldview is apparent not only in new theories that placed the sun at the center of the solar system, but also in a simple contrast between Gerard David's *Virgin and Child* and Pieter de Hooch's secular variation on the same theme.

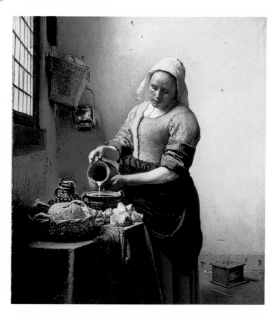

The Milkmaid (c. 1658–60),
by Jan Vermeer, is an example
of "genre painting."

Saint Barbara

TILMAN RIEMENSCHNEIDER is the only artist featured in this chapter who can be said to have learned nothing from the Italian Renaissance. Rather, his art is a continuation of North European traditions that go as far back as the 12th century.

From the emphasis that Italy and antiquity are given in discussions of "the Renaissance," it would be easy to think that the central artistic event of the period was the rediscovery of naturalism in antique sculpture by Italian artists, who then gave this new manner wholesale to an astonished and admiring Europe. But naturalism first returned to European art in the North, not in Italy. At the end of the 12th century, sculptors working on the great Gothic cathedrals of France and Germany began to produce figures that are sometimes strikingly realistic, albeit made in a sinuous and elegant style far removed from the burly equilibrium of Hellenistic sculpture. This Gothic realism was then picked up by Italian sculptors of the 13th century, who fused it with the more robust manner of the antique sculptures that still surrounded them. But the northerners continued to work with the Gothic style right up to the Reformation. It was only in the early decades of the 16th century that they developed a trade deficit of artistic ideas with Italy.

Riemenschneider represents the last and one of the loveliest periods of the Gothic tradition. Saint Barbara here seems to push out her hip while standing on tiptoe, a very uncomfortable posture, but a very beautiful one if the strain is disguised with enough elegant draperies. The irregularities of Gothic drapery folds, with their convoluted creases set off by large, smooth planes, make them very different from the regular fall of classical sculpted textiles, which, so the late 16th-century Dutch writer Karel van Mander complained, "look like wet linen and hang like cords." It is notable that, in this aspect of art, even Italian sculptors and painters followed gothic sculpture more closely than antiquity.

Riemenschneider was much the most prolific and sought-after sculptor in the town of Würzburg (of which he was burgomaster for a year), and he ran a large and efficient workshop. His art is somewhat formulaic, and it may be that this was both a cause and an effect of his success at mass production. His faces, for example, fit into a number of stock types. Eyes taper and droop with clearly cut bottom lids, noses are long and slender, mouths (on women) are grave and small with full bottom lips, faces are long with firm chins. The passions are almost always entirely absent; if he needs to show that people are crying, he will make them bend their heads and touch their eyes with draperies, but he does not twist up their eyes in anguish or carve their cheeks and mouths into sobs, as many of his contemporaries did. An ecstatically happy Riemenschneider figure looks much the same as a profoundly miserable one. This may be a limitation—but in many ways it is at the root of his success. Riemenschneider's art is always solemn and restrained, with a slow, majestic sway to it. His inability to depict human emotions, when coupled with his skill at carving clothes and his eye for a becoming posture, gives his sculptures an air of having transcended weak mortality. As in the best Byzantine art, Riemenschneider's figures have a deeply serious gravity and dignity.

TILMAN RIEMENSCHNEIDER

BORN HEILIGENSTADT c. 1460,
DIED WÜRZBURG 1531

This sculpture almost certainly formed part of an altarpiece and would have stood in a row with other sculpted saints, each in a tracery niche. It was probably commissioned by a secular donor who wanted an image of his or her favorite saint to grace the altar. Since Barbara was the patron saint of artillerymen, it is possible that the donor was a gunner; but then again, maybe she was a woman called Barbara. Saints inspired devotion for many reasons.

Before the Reformation, images of Christ, the Virgin, and the saints formed the stock-in-trade of almost all European sculptors, so the iconoclastic tendencies of the Reformers were to prove a disaster for sculpture in the North. Ecclesiastical commissions fell away sharply, and—since a statue is too bulky for most private homes—there was little in the way of a home market to turn to. At the same time, German and Netherlandish sculptors began to assimilate Italian ideas, and like their colleagues in painting, they found it tough going. As a result of these sizeable challenges to traditional ways, both the quantity and quality of sculpture declined, and after about 1530, it ceased to be a major art form in the North.

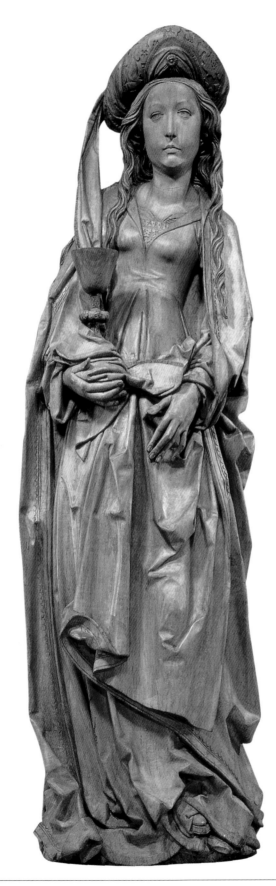

c. 1510–20 | *limewood* | height 52in (132cm) | Bayerisches Nationalmuseum, Munich

Self-portrait

ALBRECHT DÜRER was the most famous artist in Germany during his lifetime, and he has not lost that celebrity in the centuries since his death. Most of his fame and success rested on his abilities at engraving, an art form of which he had so complete a technical mastery that no one has equaled his almost super-human precision. His paintings have never won as many admirers, but some of them, especially this early self-portrait, have all the clarity and accuracy of his best work as an engraver.

This painting has been called "perhaps the first independent self-portrait ever produced." This is not quite as clearcut a statement as it sounds, since Dürer himself had made several before this one, and so had other artists, like Alberti and Jean Fouquet. But the art historian who penned that line (Erwin Panofsky) wanted to point to this work's apparently egotistical air. Dürer has dressed himself up in a striking outfit, combed his golden tresses fastidiously, put himself on the top floor of what must be an enormous castle, and looks out at the viewer with slightly too much nonchalance. Here, one might easily think, we have a new artistic manifesto: the artist, a spiritual aristocrat, who deserves to be treated as a gentleman.

Some writers have gone so far as to see in this self-portrait the beginning of a new era in history—medieval religiosity giving way to Renaissance humanism. No one has put it quite that crudely, but historians have seen the painting as a symptom of wider changes in European thought, toward individualism, a new self-awareness, and related attitudes.

However, it seems to me that we should be sceptical about ideas like these. Dürer was not the first young man in Europe to be interested very deeply in himself, to worry what others thought of him, and to wish to cut a dash in society. Nor was he the first person to think himself a snappy dresser and to admire his own hair in reflection. Medieval Europe was awash with dandies and vain young men, and there must have been many who would have enjoyed making a self-portrait, if they had thought of it and had the talent. It is also not at all clear that Dürer wanted to proclaim his high status to the world. His dress is not, as it happens, very aristocratic. German art of the early

ALBRECHT DÜRER

*BORN NUREMBERG 1471,
DIED NUREMBERG 1528*

16th century is full of low-life soldiers, the notorious *landsknechten*, who are depicted in clothes of the most outrageous cut and hue, which make Dürer's outfit seem quite staid in comparison. Urs Graf (see pages 174–175) was particularly fond of portraying these lethal dandies. The years around 1500 were some of the weirdest in the whole history of fashion, and Dürer is not out on a limb here.

We do not know for whom Dürer painted this self-portrait. He is unlikely to have made it for the benefit of anyone who knew him personally—they did not need to be told that it was a self-portrait (the inscription reads: "I painted that from my own form. I was twenty-six years old. Albrecht Dürer"). Almost all scholars seem to think that the painting was made purely for the artist's own pleasure, and this may be true, but it is also possible that his motives were more prosaic. It could have been painted for some rich aristocrat in an effort to drum up business, or perhaps it was meant to be kept in his studio, as a model portrait, to show prospective customers what he was capable of.

If this portrait was meant to display Dürer's talents, clearly part of his aim was to show off his novel style. Three years earlier, he had returned from a visit to Italy, and the color and fullness of form of Venetian art had a permanent impact on his manner; he particularly admired Giovanni Bellini (see pages 92–93). Unlike other northern artists of the time who headed south, Dürer succeeded in blending Italian elements into his work rather than adding Italianate bits onto an essentially Netherlandish underlayer (like Gossaert, see pages 170–71) or attempting to copy what he saw wholesale and failing (like Floris, see pages 178–79). The result, something like a tanned, well-built version of Rogier van der Weyden, made him one of the most convincingly naturalistic painters who has ever lived. Much of the appeal of this work lies in the perfection of the skin tones. You can almost put your hand to Dürer's neck and feel his arteries pulse. The tresses, too, are springy and silky; each lock has its own lithe bounce. But these achievements of naturalism are are held together by an overall design, built from the zebra rhythm of black and white, which gives the picture a rare élan.

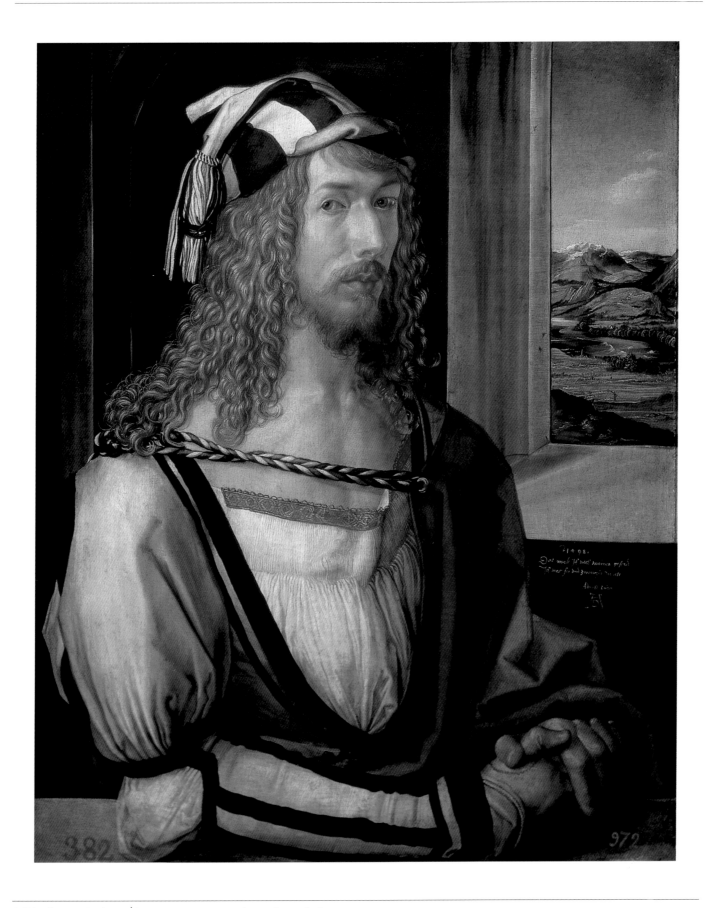

1498 | *panel* | 20¹/₂ x 16in (52 x 41cm) | Prado, Madrid

Saint Anthony Abbot Assaulted by Demons

WE KNOW very little about the painter of this picture except that his surname was probably not "Grünewald." Modern research has suggested that he used two surnames, Gothardt and Nithart, sometimes interchangeably and sometimes together. However, since "Gothardt-Nithart" is cumbersome, "Grünewald" has stuck in the literature.

Just as the artist's name sank into oblivion, so too did his artistic reputation. It was only in the 19th and early 20th centuries that the great Isenheim Altarpiece, of which *St. Anthony* is a part, came to be recognized as one of the masterpieces of 16th-century religious art.

The construction of the Isenheim Altarpiece is complex. It is an old sculpted altar (by Niklaus Hagenauer) which has had six painted wings by Grünewald attached to it, three on each side. Four of these wings are painted on both sides and move on hinges; the remaining two are painted on one side and are stationary. Thus, it is possible to change the image depending on the day. If you close all the movable wings, you see a Crucifixion, with Saints Anthony Abbot and Sebastian at the sides; if you open up one pair of wings you see an Annunciation, a Nativity, and a Resurrection; if you open another pair, you see Hagenauer's polychrome sculptures of Saint Anthony, Saint Jerome, and Saint Augustine, a painting of Saint Anthony with Saint Paul the Hermit, and the painting illustrated here. In all likelihood, the Crucifixion was only shown in the approach to Good Friday, and the colorful Nativity on important feast days of the Church. Most of the time it was the sculptures and the scenes of Anthony that were on display.

Anthony Abbot figures large on the altarpiece because it was commissioned for a church of the Hospital Order of St. Anthony. Of all the stories connected with the saint, the assault of the demons is the most famous and the most often depicted, so it is not surprising that Grünewald decided, or perhaps was asked, to paint this scene.

The story runs as follows: Anthony was so badly beaten by demons that his servant thought he was dead, and carried him off to be buried. His friends arrived and began weeping over his

MATTHIAS GRÜNEWALD

*BORN ? WÜRZBURG c. 1475/80,
DIED HALLE 1528*

body, but the saint regained consciousness and demanded to be taken back to the devils for another round of punishment. Lying in pain from his wounds, he nevertheless egged on the demons, who tore his flesh with their teeth, horns, and claws, until a wonderful light shone around him, as the Lord arrived to dispel the devils and ease his suffering.

In Grünewald's painting we can see an angel in the clouds winging down from God. Anthony's tribulations will soon end.

If the saint seems, oddly, to be enjoying himself, it is because he knows his faith will overcome these incarnations of evil.

The most striking thing about the picture, of course, is the monstrous appearance of the demons. In painting them, Grünewald was drawing on a long tradition of devil imagery, which had turned very bizarre in the works of artists of the previous generation, such as Martin Schongauer and Hieronymus Bosch (c. 1450–1516). By Grünewald's time, there seems to have been something of a competition among North European artists to see who could be the most inventively horrific in their devilries, which became, so to speak, the special effects of the 16th century. This may sound like a rather superficial way of thinking about evil beings that Grünewald may well have believed in, but it is hard to think that he is being completely, uniformly serious here. The demon on the right, with the goofy expression and the runny nose, is surely meant as a light touch. What Grünewald is doing is showing us how vividly he can invent a world, and how effectively he can impress it on our memories. He is being a self-conscious virtuoso.

Perhaps the fact that he could allow his art to triumph over a pious story tells us that he was growing sceptical of saints' romances. When he died, Grünewald was in possession of Lutheran texts, and Catholic art of the preceding centuries was beginning to collapse. European churches before the sixteenth century were filled with images of the Virgin and the saints, before which the pious murmured their hopes and their gratitude. During the Reformation, many of these works were smashed as graven images. Perhaps the monks of Isenheim saw Grünewald's devils as iconoclasts threatening their saint.

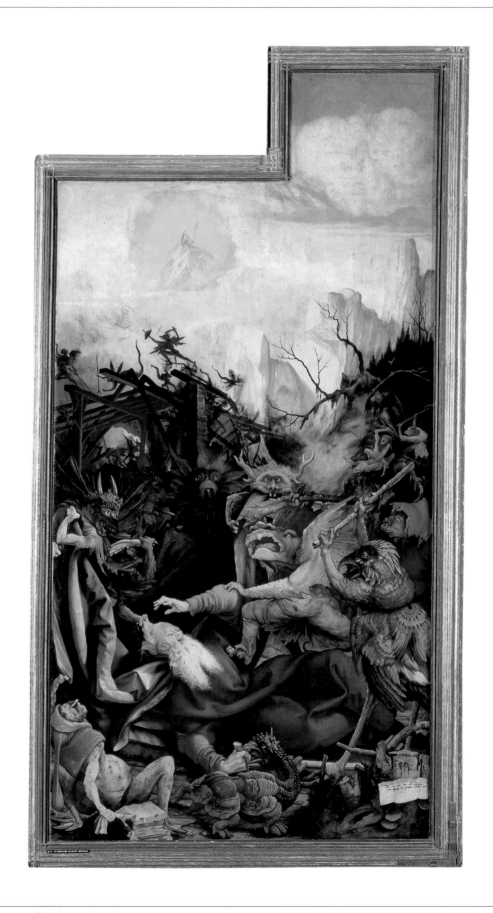

c. 1515 | panel | 104½ x 56in (265 x 141cm) | Musée d'Unterlinden, Colmar, France

Saint Luke Drawing the Virgin

JAN GOSSAERT, often called "Mabuse" because he came from the small town of Maubeuge, was in a sense the Netherlandish version of Albrecht Dürer. Like Dürer, he traveled to Italy and brought back with him many new ideas that were to change his own art, as well as those of his immediate successors. He also resembled the German master in that, while he admired the Italians, he remained true to his northern training; the Early Netherlandish style is still visible in Gossaert's minutely rendered interiors and textiles. But where Gossaert differs from Dürer is that the latter managed to forge a coherent style from north and south. With Gossaert, although many of his works are beautiful things, there is often the sense that Flanders and Italy, like oil and vinegar, have not really blended to form a new manner. His nudes, for example, have neither the slim delicacy of Early Netherlandish art, nor the full grace of Italian. They make a knobbly, gawky, half-and-half mix. Gossaert was one of the finest artists of his generation in Northern Europe, but his style shortcircuited when he tried to overload it with artistic novelty.

Nevertheless, he had a considerable number of admirers and followers in 16th-century Antwerp, where he settled. Probably no other painter did more to introduce Italian concepts into Flemish art. Unfortunately, few of his disciples managed to see Italian paintings through completely fresh eyes: Gossaert's manner is always in the background in the work of men like Jan van Scorel (1495–1562) and Maerten van Heemskerck (1498–1574).

This painting, which is one of Gossaert's most Italianate, shows his charm and his clumsiness side by side. The subject, of Saint Luke drawing the Virgin, was very popular in the Netherlands in the 15th and 16th centuries. The story is entirely apocryphal and probably was not thought up until after the 6th century, but over time, it became one of the most common ways of depicting Saint Luke, and a particular favorite for altarpieces commissioned by painters' guilds. However, we do not know for what or for whom this particular image was made. Gossaert's painting marks a departure from earlier Netherlandish images of Luke and the Virgin, in two respects. The scene was usually depicted in a very realistic manner, as if Luke was just sitting in a room with the Virgin, drawing or painting her. Gossaert, however, has made the Virgin appear to Luke in a vision rather than in the flesh. Quite why he decided to break with convention is not clear. It may be that his patron asked him to include the Christ Child and, because Luke was not an adult when Christ was an infant, Gossaert decided, from sheer historical logic, to make the Virgin and Child arrive for their portrait in visionary form. The other respect in which this picture differs from its predecessors is its architectural background, which is so obviously and jarringly ancient Roman. It seems, however, as if Gossaert may have picked up his antiquities at second hand. Some of the grotesque decoration is based closely on a painting by Filippino Lippi (c. 1457–1504) in Rome.

And yet in front of this stridently classical backdrop, we can see a Netherlandish artist, dressed in a fur-lined coat and wearing a standard Burgundian hat. The folds of his coat crinkle up in a way typical in Northern printmaking of the previous century. Only in the faintly suggested fullness of his form is he at all different from an Early Netherlandish Saint Luke; he could have stepped out of a painting by Rogier van der Weyden.

The Virgin is more obviously Italianate; she is far plumper than the Madonnas of Jan van Eyck or Petrus Christus (died 1472/3). But here, too, the tightness of the painting in the hair and draperies reveals the hand of a northern master, accustomed to the laser precision of 15th-century Flemish art. The combination of the styles becomes unsettling. A large expanse of luxuriant and unblemished flesh is placed right next to a tricksy little piece of detailed painting. Looking at the picture, one's eyesight constantly has to change gear.

Nevertheless, there is much to enjoy in this work: the wonderful luminous puff of cloud slicing through the intricate decor, and the way the whole room is lit by the radiance of the Madonna and Child. Luke cannot bring himself to look the Virgin in the face and entrusts his hand to the angel; the touch of her hand on his back steadies him, close to swooning perhaps from the impact of his vision.

JAN GOSSAERT

❧

BORN MAUBEUGE c. 1478,
DIED ANTWERP? 1532

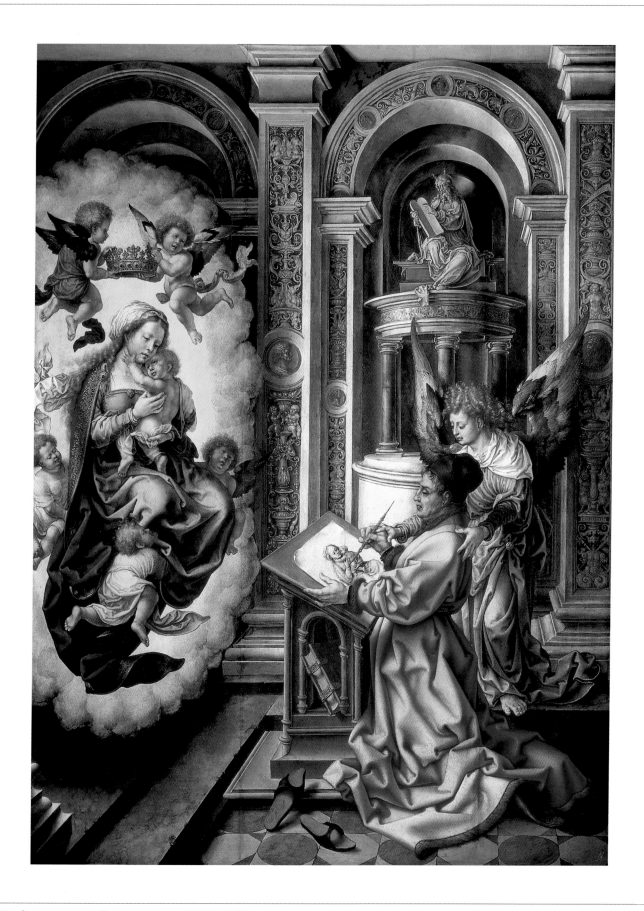

c. 1520 | *oil on panel* | 43 x 32in (109 x 82cm) | Kunsthistorisches Museum, Vienna

Landscape with Bridge

UNLIKE HIS namesake, Dürer, Albrecht Altdorfer entirely escaped the notice of the writers of his time. What we know about him, we know from archival research. This line of investigation, however, gives the impression that he led a pleasantly prosperous life. When he died, he was the owner of several vineyards and was a city councillor in the Bavarian town of Regensburg. It seems unlikely that he bought the vineyards purely from the proceeds of his art—very few artists can afford to become landowners—so we must assume that he either married a wealthy woman or came into an inheritance. In the last sixteen years of his life he painted, etched, and drew relatively little, presumably because he no longer needed to.

Although Altdorfer did not have a European reputation in his day, he has earned himself an important niche in the history of art. He is credited with being the first person to have made independent landscape paintings in postclassical Europe. Before this honor is granted, however, it needs much qualification. The word "independent" is very important; it means that the paintings were made with the exclusive intention of displaying a landscape for the esthetic satisfaction of the beholder. Paintings that contain any narrative element at all are not counted as "independent landscapes;" so the Netherlandish artist Joachim Patinir (died 1524), who, before 1515 was painting rocky landscapes containing tiny religious figures, is not allowed to enter the contest against Altdorfer. The slightest suggestion that a painting could have been intended as practice, or as a study for another work of art, also removes it from consideration. Thus, landscape watercolors made by Dürer in the mid-1490s are disqualified.

Once restrictions such as these have been established, it becomes possible to see Altdorfer as the first independent landscape painter, at around 1516. However, people had nevertheless been enjoying landscapes in works of art for at least fifty years before this. Consider, for example, paintings like Giorgione's *Tempest* (c. 1505, Accademia, Venice) or Giovanni Bellini's *Agony in the Garden* (c. 1460, National Gallery, London). At the same time, we should remember that no one is claiming that Altdorfer was the first independent landscape painter in art history. There were probably independent landscapes in existence in classical antiquity, and landscape had been an important genre in China since the 8th century A.D.

ALBRECHT ALTDORFER

ℰ⅊

BORN c. 1480,
DIED REGENSBURG 1538

Why did landscape painting re-emerge in Europe around the beginning of the 16th century? The art historian E.H. Gombrich once argued that the idea may have occurred to renaissance artists after they had read about ancient landscape painting in the writings of the Roman author Pliny. However, this is no more than reasonable speculation; we do not know if Altdorfer had ever read Pliny. It is not impossible that he could have had the idea of landscape without reading any Latin literature at all. The landscape element was growing more important in the work of numerous artists around 1500; works were being bought avidly because they contained beautiful landscapes, and it was only going to be a matter of time before someone decided to leave the figures out and sell the landscape on its own. Altdorfer's new pictures may seem momentous, but they do not seem particularly surprising.

For some reason, artists with new ideas often tend to be extremely gifted as well. Altdorfer certainly belongs in this class. Besides being the first landscape painter in modern European history, he is also one of the very best. Whatever he turned his hand to, he imbued with some unsettling wizardry. In his landscapes one senses a silence for miles around, broken only by the sound of the wind and random bird calls. In this painting, the absence of humanity seems total, despite the bridge and building. It will be a long time before anyone crosses that footbridge; perhaps the building is deserted. And the absolute emptiness of the sky, just blue in all directions, mirrors the desolation of the land over which it hangs.

Altdorfer was not only a landscape painter. Most of his surviving work is devoted to religious and mythological scenes, although he usually set such narratives in a lush and prominent landscape. His drawings were often made in light inks on dark-colored papers, setting up a gloomy, ghostly stage for the sufferings and raptures of his actors. He could be awkward as a figure painter, as his human figures are often elongated and ungainly; landscape was certainly the best outlet for his talents.

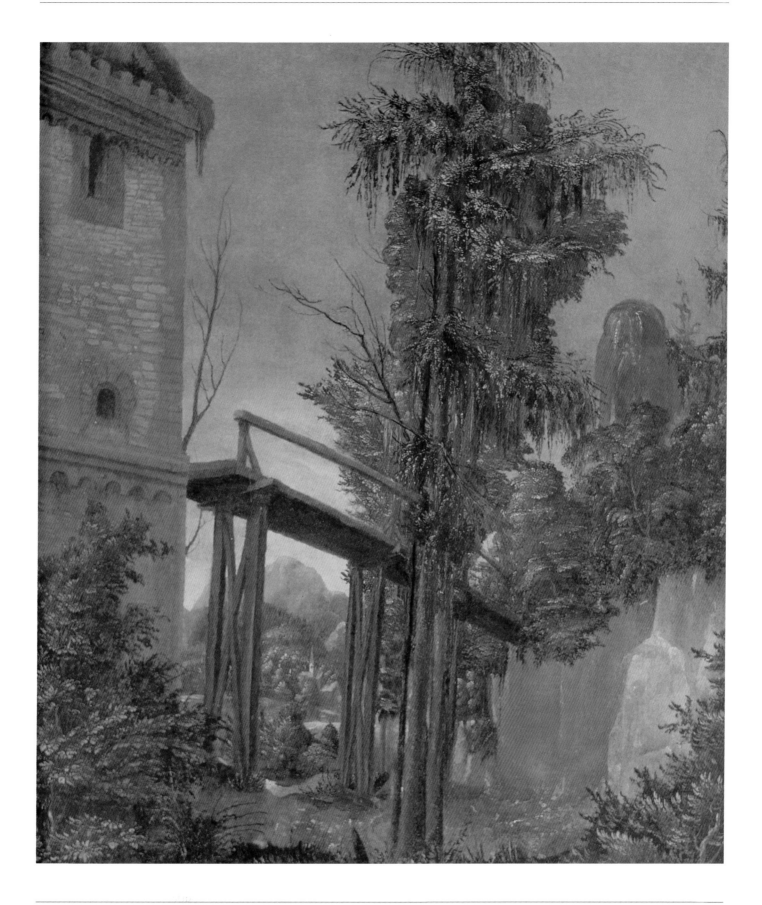

1516 or later | *oil on parchment attached to panel* | 16$^{1}/_{2}$ x 14in (42 x 35cm) | National Gallery, London

Young Woman and Hanged Man

THE VISUAL ARTS, like other walks of life, have attracted some violent and antisocial exponents, Caravaggio being the most famous example. But few artists of any time or place have been quite so vile as the Swiss goldsmith, etcher, and draftsman Urs Graf. Foul-mouthed, contemptuous, fond of cruel practical jokes, he was a soldier of fortune who slaughtered his way across Europe with the notorious Swiss mercenaries. He did this for pleasure. He was perfectly capable of earning a good enough income from his peacetime trade, but he was addicted to fighting and to the rape and pillage that came to the victors when towns were sacked. In between campaigns, he brought his taste for violence home. He had to flee the city of Basle for stabbing and crippling a stranger who had not exchanged a single word with him before the attack. He also regularly beat his wife and was openly unfaithful to her with prostitutes as often as he could afford it. He was imprisoned several times for riotous behavior, but it was impossible to frighten a man like Graf into the path of virtue.

This repulsive person, however, was also one of the most brilliant northern draftsmen of the 16th century. The fact that he was both so repellent and so gifted is what makes his art extraordinary. Graf earned his living as a goldsmith, but much of his finest work was done with the pen, in a series of drawings which he bequeathed to his long-suffering wife after his death. With no patron to worry about and no fear at all of any authorities, Graf set down an image of the world as he saw it and left us an absolutely unique record of alternative values in Reformation Europe. Anyone who thinks that Europe at that time was peopled entirely by pious Christians worried about the Day of Judgment need look no further than Graf's art to be disabused. His world is full of simpering prostitutes, preening dandies, debauchees lounging drunk in brothels, and soldiers laughing with joy as they kill. There is no doubt at all that Graf thoroughly identified with the values of the life he depicted. Piety and religion were the mental crutches of the foolish and the weak; morality was the arbitrary imposition of social power by hypocrites. The pleasures worth having were sex, drink, and murder.

URS GRAF

BORN SOLOTHURN c. 1485,
DIED 1527/9

Graf also found glamour in the complex trappings of dress and military pomp. In his drawings he returned time and again to the depiction of soldiers dressed in tight breeches and slashed doublets, and he liked to show them marching with a confident swagger to war, wielding their vast two-handed swords and carrying colossal billowing banners. Perhaps the ultimate statement of his credo is a drawing of a battlefield, covered with naked bodies that have been hacked to death. To one side a mercenary, with skin-tight leggings that cling between his buttocks, languidly throws his head back to take a deep, leisurely drink from his flask before returning to the fray. This kind of bravery, or nonchalance, or callousness—depending on your point of view—was the state of mind Graf most admired.

The drawing shown here is one of the most disturbing in a disturbing oeuvre. A camp follower, who is showily dressed and very pregnant, comes down to the lakeside to fetch water. The whole drawing would just be a pleasant image of a vain young woman, were it not for the corpse hanging from the tree, being pecked at by crows. The camp follower, however, has seen this kind of thing before, and she ignores the body, smiling in a winning way for the artist instead.

What is going on? It could be an angry retort from the ranks. Perhaps the soldier has been hanged for some minor misdemeanor, and Graf shows the heartlessness of an officer's woman, so he can point out oppression and injustice. However, this reading goes against what we know of the artist's character. Graf does not seem to have cared a great deal about oppression; he was too much of an individualist. It is more likely that what we see in the drawing is a cynic's worldly-wise acceptance of human indifference to suffering.

The subject matter is shocking, but nevertheless riveting, and the execution is simply imperious. One need only look at the artist's crosshatchings, so precisely parallel; here was a man in complete control of his pen. It seems entirely in character that he was also considered the best shot in Basle, whether drawing a line or aiming a crossbow. Urs Graf must have been proud indeed of his steady hand.

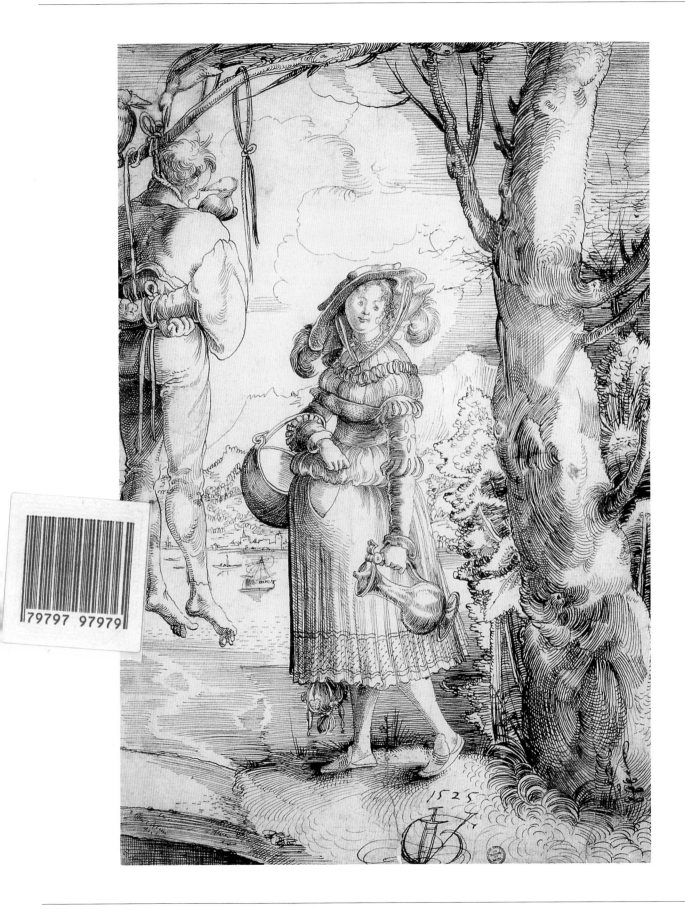

1525 | *pen drawing* | 13 x 9in (32.5 x 22cm) | Öffentliche Kunstsammlung, Basle

Portrait of Anne of Cleves

HANS HOLBEIN the Younger was the son of Hans Holbein the Elder (c. 1465–1524), a painter from Augsburg in Bavaria. Hans the Elder was an artist of middling abilities, but he was fully abreast of all the latest developments in German art. He painted for a while in the monastery at Isenheim, for which Grünewald had just made his great altarpiece (from page 168–69), and he probably met his contemporary Dürer when the latter visited Augsburg in 1505. The younger Hans, then, was decidedly a second-generation German Renaissance artist, who could look up to his pioneering elders and profit from their experience.

It is generally believed that Holbein must also have been aware of the work of Italian painters; Mantegna and Leonardo in particular are thought to have left stylistic traces in his art. There is no doubt that Holbein could have seen works by these men without straying too far, since he spent much of his adult life in Switzerland and could easily have made trips over the mountains. However, the artist from whom he learned the most was undoubtedly Dürer. The crisp exact line, the clear color, the love of detail, and the ability to stop that detail from getting fussy and intrusive, all these features of Holbein's art surely come from his great German predecessor. If Holbein did see much Italian art—and there is no direct evidence that he did—then he must have seen it through eyes that had already been well prepared.

Most of Holbein's career was spent in two cities, Basle and London. In both places, he divided his time between portraiture and painting large-scale allegories and histories. The great bulk of his history paintings have been destroyed over the years, but those that are left show that he was fond of learned allusions, fittingly enough for a man acquainted with scholars like Erasmus and Thomas More.

It is to his portraits, however, that Holbein owes his fame. He has—and had in his lifetime—a reputation for meticulous accuracy in these productions, but on one occasion his vaunted precision failed, with catastrophic results, when he painted this portrait of Anne of Cleves. The story behind the painting involves one of Europe's most repulsive egotists, his unscrupulous adviser, and a pious unworldly young woman.

HANS HOLBEIN THE YOUNGER

☙

BORN AUGSBURG 1497/8,
DIED LONDON 1543

Henry VIII wanted a new wife. Thomas Cromwell, his trusted secretary, had decided that an alliance with the sister of the Protestant Duke of Cleves would fit in nicely with England's foreign policy. Henry liked the political argument, but wanted to make sure his future queen would be attractive, too. So Holbein was sent off to Cleves to paint Anne's portrait.

On the basis of Holbein's picture, Henry agreed to the marriage. However, when Anne arrived in England, Henry was outraged at her plainness. The marriage went ahead in January 1540, but the king refused to consummate it, referring to poor Anne as his "Flanders mare;" and it was annulled after six months. In the wake of this disaster, Cromwell was beheaded. Holbein, however, seems to have been unharmed by the episode. The king continued to employ him until 1543, when the artist died of the plague. It is popularly believed that, of Henry's wives, only Catherine Parr survived him, but in fact, she was not alone; Anne of Cleves lived on for ten years after the king's death, dying at Chelsea in 1557.

So was Holbein's portrait just inaccurate? The answer, probably, is that it was not, but that it was economical with the truth. Holbein was a portraitist who put his shadows in very lightly, giving relatively little information about the contours of a face. This is an old portrait-painters' trick. Viewers who know the sitter will read her or his features into the painting, even though the artist has not given them enough information to do so. In this work, we are told almost nothing about the length or shape of the nose or chin. The frontal pose probably suggests that both were long and irregular, but Holbein knew he would get into trouble with Cromwell (the artist's most important patron) if he revealed this. By choosing his viewpoint very carefully and painting as little of what he saw as possible, he could fulfill his commission honorably without offending his patron.

Since Henry did not punish Holbein, we must assume that he was satisfied with the portrait. Once he had met Anne, he could see that she was the woman in the painting—just uglier than he had expected. His mistake was in failing to realize that images can lie while telling the truth.

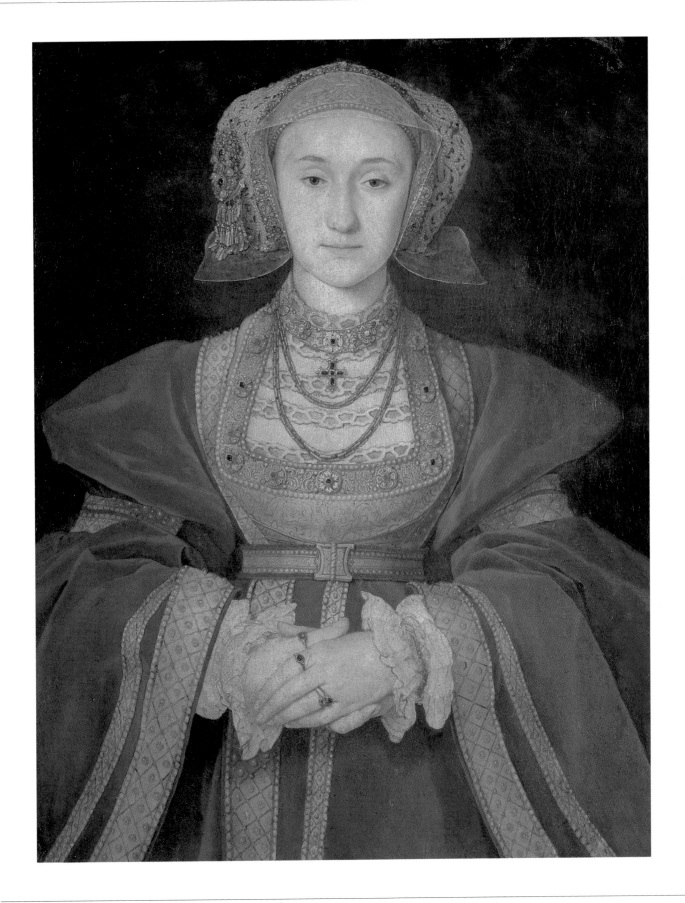

1539 | *tempera on parchment attached to panel* | 26 x 19in (65 x 48cm) | Louvre, Paris

Fall of the Rebel Angels

HISTORY IS LITTERED with painters who were thought by their contemporaries to be very great artists, but who have not benefited from hindsight. Il Cavaliere d'Arpino, Gerard de Lairesse, Anton Raffael Mengs, and George Frederick Watts are just some of the men who, after enjoying huge reputations in their day, have few admirers now.

To their number can be added Frans Floris, known during his lifetime as "the Flemish Raphael." Floris had more than one hundred pupils and was so successful that he could buy himself a palatial house in the middle of Antwerp and get drunk in the company of the noblest aristocrats of Flanders. No Flemish artist before him—not even Jan van Eyck—had known such extraordinary success, and only Rubens and Van Dyck were to surpass his wealth and fame in the years that followed. And yet today, Floris's name is little known among the gallery-going public, outside Antwerp at least. I would not want to argue that he deserves a massive revival, but his art is important historically, and his best work (this being an example) can be exciting to look at, even if it is cluttered, confused, and strangely wooden.

Around 1541, Floris traveled to Rome, just as Michelangelo was completing his *Last Judgment* in the Sistine Chapel (see pages 104–105). The young Frans was certainly not alone in being deeply impressed by the new work, and he sat down to make numerous drawings from its heroic nudes, in the midst of a crush of other artists doing the same thing. When he returned to Antwerp after six years studying Italian art, both ancient and modern, he settled down to become a figure painter in the grand manner and immediately won adulation as the leading northern exponent of Italian ideas. Indeed, his reputation crossed back over the Alps, thanks to engravings made after his work by Cornelis Cort, although these engravings were not as well received in the south as in the north. Giorgio Vasari wrote that "the engraver—skilled though he may be—comes nowhere close to the works, the design, and the execution of he who made the design." This may sound like an insult to Cort, but since Vasari had never seen any paintings by Floris, it was clearly a rather double-edged remark about Frans himself. It was certainly

FRANS FLORIS

∞

BORN ANTWERP 1519/20,
DIED ANTWERP 1570

taken as a wounding comment in the Low Countries; Floris's admirer, the painter and writer Karel van Mander (1548–1606), accused the Italian biographer of envy toward foreigners. While it is true that few writers about art at any time have been as patriotic as Vasari, his implied view that Floris was a rather weak follower of the Italian manner has tended to win the day.

Van Mander tells us that some people, especially Italians, thought that Floris's style was somewhat "dry." Looking at this picture, we can see what they meant. It is clear that Floris was most impressed by the chunky musculature of Michelangelo's figures, and went away with the maxim that muscles mattered. After studying anatomy with too much energy, he got to the point where he could tell when a pectoral stopped and a deltoid started, and he spent the rest of his career painting nudes that resemble flayed anatomical figures covered in flesh color. Michelangelo himself never painted muscles with this much definition; his figures are heavily muscled, but they do not look like body-builders straining for the photographer. Floris apparently failed to notice the organic softness of Michelangelo's nudes.

Perhaps a more significant problem in Floris's art is that he was never very good at constructing a readable pictorial space. His paintings are usually full to overflowing with bodies, and the spectator has to spend a lot of time actually visually disentangling limb from limb and working out who owns what. Floris seems to have felt that empty space was just a waste, so he failed to include those intervals of visual quiet that let us make sense of the action in an image.

All of which cannot detract from the fact that this picture is very enjoyable. A *Fall of the Rebel Angels* should be a sublime mess, and for Floris it was clearly the perfect subject. The way the demons seem to flow like lava away and down from the angels' assault is really superb, and the expressions on the angels' faces are beautiful, mingling fear, bravery, and righteousness. The steroid tension of the devils' muscles underlines their evil, contrasting as it does with the smooth, gracile limbs of the angels. Floris's perennial inability to make a lucid space here results in a seething chaos.

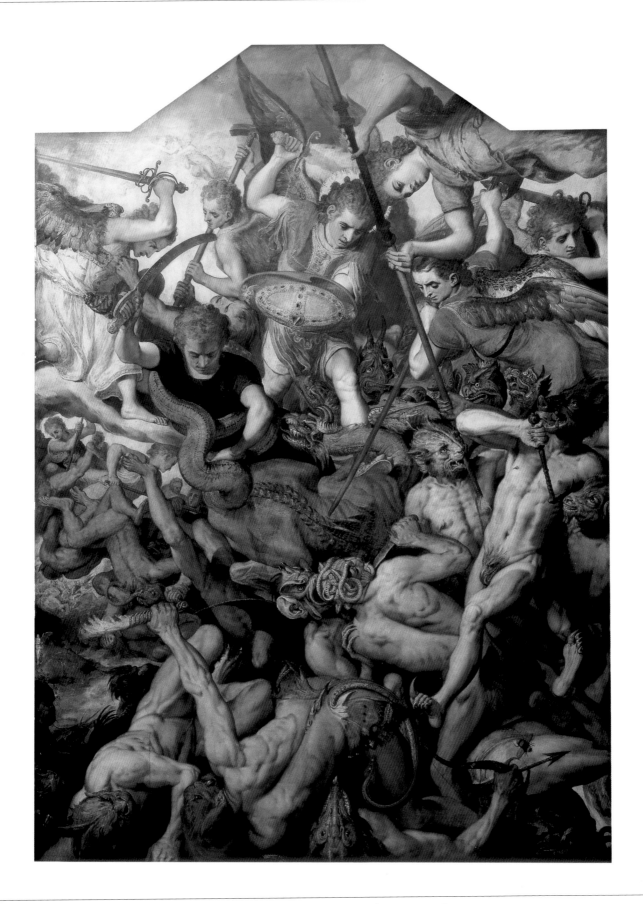

1554 ┃ *oil on panel* ┃ 119 x 87in (303 x 220cm) ┃ Koninklijk Museum voor Schone Kunsten, Antwerp

A Country Wedding

PIETER BRUEGEL is often called "Peasant Bruegel," and it was long thought that he was born among the peasants he painted. Modern scholars have become sceptical of this idea, although there is very little evidence to settle the matter either way. We do not know if he was born in a town or in the country, to rich or to poor parents. Whatever his origins, he spent most of his life in the cities of Antwerp and Brussels, and was feted there by the great and the learned; so his acquaintance with country life in his adult years must have had an element of distance to it.

A more important controversy surrounding his art grows out of the question of his background. What was Bruegel's attitude toward the peasantry? Some historians have seen him as a fond recorder of rustic life, while others see him as a satirist, sneering at the drunkenness and ignorance of coarse yokels. It is certainly true that prints made after his work during his lifetime sometimes include moralistic inscriptions that are far from flattering about peasant morals. Nevertheless, it seems likely that Bruegel's attitude fell somewhere between the two extremes. We know that his depictions of country people huffing and puffing in drunken dances amused his urban contemporaries, but it is surely possible to laugh at others without being utterly dismissive. Rustic clowns in Shakespeare's comedies often express shrewd insights that show their social superiors to be the real fools, and there is no reason to think that Bruegel was any the less able to see that societies are complex things, and that the urban rich do not have a monopoly on wit or virtue.

Bruegel, like Frans Floris, traveled to Italy, but he seems to have remained relatively immune to the southern style. It has been argued that he was led to paint fuller figures under the influence of Raphael, but if so, he clearly took very little else from the great Italian. The deepest visual impact made on him during his trip seems to have been the sight of the Alps; he made a number of drawings of the mountainous region which were later published as prints. Rocky mountains continued to enliven his landscapes for years after his return to the Low Countries. Bruegel's landscapes were very popular, and the success of his prints did much to inspire enthusiasm for the genre in Flanders and elsewhere. But his most important contributions to the history of art are paintings of everyday life, a genre which he more or less invented. Artists before Bruegel had painted scenes of weddings, or of people carousing, but only in the form of a story—Christ at the wedding feast of Cana, for example, or the prodigal son in the tavern. Bruegel, however, just painted people eating and drinking. This may seem a very obvious thing to do, but it was also one of the greatest breaks with tradition in art history. No man played a more important role in the secularization of European painting than Pieter Bruegel.

The picture illustrated here is often called *A Peasant Wedding*, but the proud father of the bride (sitting on the high-backed chair) is clearly more a prosperous landowner than a peasant. The barn in which the event takes place is stacked to the rafters with straw, which must have been harvested from a fair-sized farm. The father can also boast some social connections. The man sitting on the far right, who seems rather bored by the friar's conversation, is wearing a sword, a right reserved to the nobility. The furniture may not be very grand, and the food may not look very appetizing, but a lot of beer has been drunk, and the expense of musicians has not been spared; by 16th-century standards, this is conspicuous consumption.

There are certainly some comic touches. The man with the spoon in his mouth on the far side of the table, who is presumably the groom, looks glazed with drink or terror or both, while his bride, in front of the green awning, seems to be hatching plots to guarantee his future submission. But many of the other figures, like the barman in the foreground to the left or the large waiter in the center, seem to have little of satire to them. Perhaps Bruegel wants to draw our attention to the dangers of gluttony and excess, but he also wants to please our eyes with the bustle and color of a boisterous occasion. And it is the colors here that really make the picture, from the tomato reds of caps and jerkins to the striking sky blue of the central figure's jacket, which contrasts so richly with the glow of wheat that transfuses the whole painting. Wheat is the leitmotif here; the food and beer are made from it, the bills are paid with it.

PIETER BRUEGEL THE ELDER

❧

*BORN 1526?,
DIED BRUSSELS 1569*

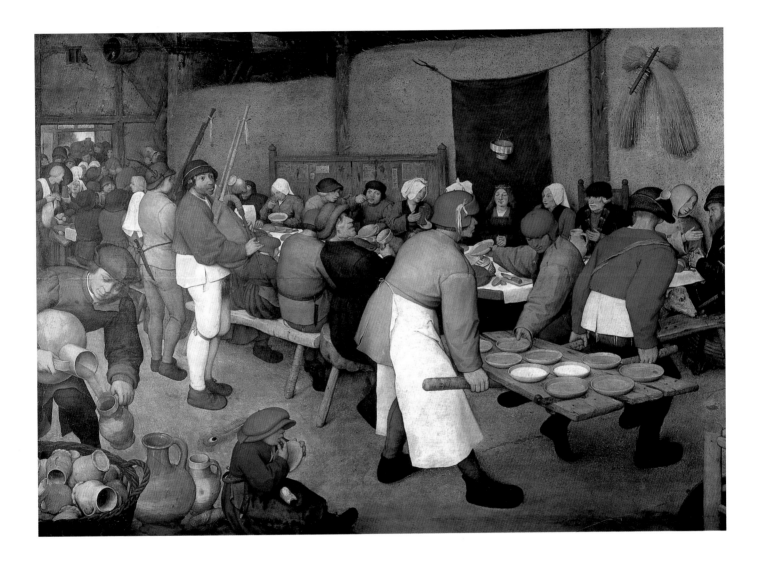

c. 1566 | *oil on panel* | 46½ x 65in (118 x 164cm) | Kunsthistorisches Museum, Vienna

The Horrors of War

FEW PEOPLE have known quite as much success as Peter Paul Rubens. He was the most famous painter in Europe in his day, courted by kings and cardinals, and revered by fellow artists from Madrid to Rome. He ran a massive studio that financed his huge and beautiful Italianate house in the center of Antwerp; he worked as a court painter both in Italy and Flanders, a rare double; he was on friendly terms with many distinguished scholars, who respected his profound command of Latin and Greek; he was employed as a diplomat by the king of Spain, and was knighted by the kings of Spain and England; and, on a personal level, he was happily married twice, his second wife being just sixteen when he married her in his early fifties. And the great respect he enjoyed in his lifetime has not diminished since. He is one of just three painters—the others being Raphael and Titian—who have always been thought princes of their profession, and who have never suffered even a temporary decline in their reputations. As far as the art establishment is concerned, Rubens is and always has been one of the greats.

However, it must be added that today's general public are not particularly drawn to him. Publishers find it hard to sell books about Rubens, and exhibitions of his work attract only middling crowds. In part this is a matter of body fashion, a common reason for disliking him is that his art is full of "all those fat women." Once the 20th-century love of abnormally thin hips has waned, we can expect this objection to fade. But people may still find it difficult to appreciate the conventions of his highly theatrical manner. Rubens often used huge doses of artifice to get his ideas across, and we have to develop a feel for his particular brand of artistic license before we can enjoy his work to the full. It is not too hard, if we let his color and his compositional brilliance sway our eyes with their visual oratory; Rubens' art is no more unreal than that of his contemporary Shakespeare, and no less moving.

This painting shows him at his most artificial, and also at his most brilliant. In a letter to the painter Justus Sustermans (1597–1681), he explained the allegory in detail. On the left we see a building with open doors—this is a reference to the Temple of Janus in ancient Rome, the doors of which were opened whenever the city was at war. In the center of the painting the god of war, Mars, is dragged forward by the Fury Alecto, a spirit of "never-ceasing" vengeance. On the ground before Mars lie a woman and child (to signify that Fecundity and Charity are destroyed by War), a woman with a broken lute (Harmony broken by War), and an architect (the Arts ravaged by War). Venus, the consort of Mars, together with their son Cupid, tries in vain to draw him back toward Love and Peace; behind her stands Europe who, as Rubens put it, "for so many years now has suffered plunder, outrage, and misery."

Many artists who later followed in the wake of Rubens painted densely allegorical pictures like this one, but almost none had the same ability to transform the personifications of such abstract ideas into a comparably moving expression of real emotions. The key here is surely the vivid nature of the flesh; Venus is so soft and pink and living against the ghastly greenish hues of Alecto and the victims of Mars. The contrast between life and death, peace and violence could hardly be made more stark in paint. The lighting underscores the point. Fractured glimmers of flame and smoke at the right contrast starkly with the even warmth of daylight on Venus's body. Then, in one of Rubens's most brilliant arrangements, a huge rent seems to tear the canvas, with the line of fire-lit cloud at the right cowing the victims, then moving beneath Alecto's feet to the bloody sword of Mars; the hilt in the god's hand makes an obvious sexual contrast with Venus's girded loins, especially since their son's head is so close. The sense of movement given by this gash and by the line coursing through the arms of Venus and Alecto hurls the painting's balance to the right and to war. The beautiful figure of weeping Europe with her upraised arms makes the underlying despair of the message inescapable.

At the time Rubens was working on this picture, Germany was being devastated by the Thirty Years' War, and this is a painting made by an old man with a profound love of peaceful family life. Entirely artificial though its conventions may be, they convey with passionate force a deep sense of moral anger.

PETER PAUL RUBENS

BORN SIEGEN 1577,
DIED ANTWERP 1640

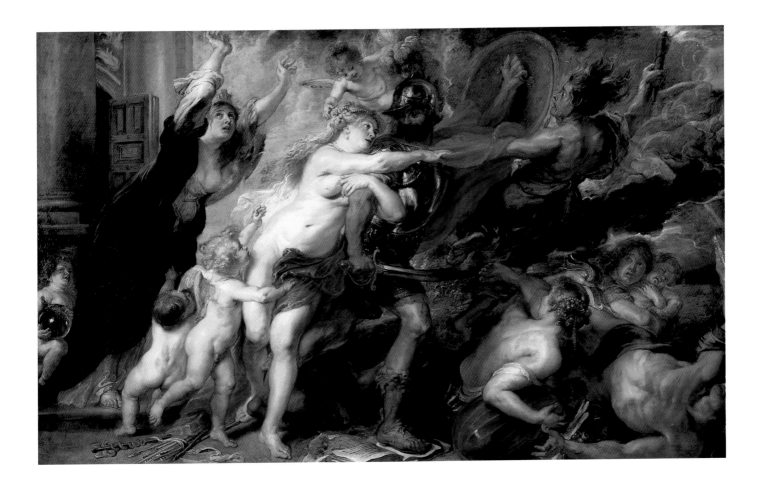

c. 1637 | *oil on canvas* | 81 x 135in (206 x 342cm) | Pitti Palace, Florence

The Tomb of the Horatii and Curatii

HERCULES SEGHERS has a rather strange place in the history of art. Those who know his work agree that he was probably the most original Dutch artist of the 17th century, as well as being one of the most brilliant etchers who has ever lived. But outside the world of museums and university art-history departments, hardly anyone has heard of him.

This does not happen very often; by and large, art historians do not try to hide great artists from the public. Perhaps the main reason for his obscurity is that people who write general books on 17th-century Dutch art find it all too easy to leave him out of their histories. Seghers is an entirely untypical artist, who does not fit into any of the neatly carpentered narratives art historians like to construct. Although he took some ideas from artists who came before him, especially from the German painter Adam Elsheimer, he transformed everything he used into something weirdly personal; and while one or two artists who came after were inspired by his work (among them Rembrandt) no one tried to follow his manner closely. His work is a beautiful ox-bow lake cut off from the river of Dutch art, and the historical vessels slip past it.

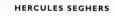

HERCULES SEGHERS

BORN HAARLEM 1589/90,
DIED AMSTERDAM BEFORE 1638?

In his own day, Seghers seems to have enjoyed some success, but not enough to keep him from financial hardship. In 1621, one of his paintings was given to the King of Denmark, and in 1632, two of his landscapes were bought for the Prince of Orange. After his death, discerning buyers owned his works; in the inventory of Rembrandt's bankruptcy there are no less than eight paintings by Seghers. Rembrandt also studied the etchings closely, and went so far as to rework one of Seghers's copper plates to make a kind of etched print duet. However, Seghers did not find it easy to make ends meet; in 1631 he was forced to sell his house in Amsterdam, making a loss. In a book published in 1678, the artist Samuel van Hoogstraeten (1627–1678) claimed that Seghers tried to blot out his despair with drink, and died after a drunken fall. Whether van Hoogstraeten knew this for a fact or made it up as a moralizing tale is impossible to say.

One or two of Seghers's paintings have erroneously been attributed to Rembrandt in the past; they are usually somber panoramic landscapes, often filled with the menace of rocky cliffs and brooding, gathering storms. His painted work undoubtedly had an impact on Rembrandt and the latter's follower, Philips de Koninck (1619–1688), but it seems that Seghers's etchings proved too idiosyncratic for imitation.

Most etchers use the technique of etching to produce multiple prints—it is, after all, in their financial interest to do so. From what we can gather about Seghers, however, he seems to have reworked his copper plates constantly, taking just a few impressions from each stage of the process. He would cut down large plates into small ones, extracting the particular detail that interested him; he would grind down old plates in order to reuse them, occasionally leaving details from previous compositions clearly visible (there is a bizarre sequence of landscapes draped with a ship's rigging from an earlier phase of etching); he would happily print off landscapes which contained random marks etched into the sky, apparently the result of test cuts that he chose not to conceal; and he would usually paint each individual sheet after he had printed it, turning it into a combined painting and etching. He also sometimes printed on linen, the grain of the fabric forming an integral part of the finished work, and he also began to experiment with colored papers in many different hues, often swapping them round between paintings to achieve different effects. Like Picasso, Seghers seems to have enjoyed the process of experiment as much as completion, but he was living in an era when experimentation did not have an artistic (or an economic) appeal of its own.

This etching is a scene of ruins in the Roman Campagna, but Seghers never traveled to Italy. He appears to have been inspired by the background of a print attributed to Adam Elsheimer, although there is little of Elsheimer left after Seghers's visionary changes. In the speckled gloom, stone succumbs to vegetation; the tree on the right is like a wave of decay that rises to crush the monument to the Roman heroes. The light is ghostly and unreal, made the stranger by a weighty blue sky that seems to crush the scene beneath it. Dutch art of the 17th century is famous for its realism, but here we have a brooding imaginary world not to be seen again in European art for a century and a half.

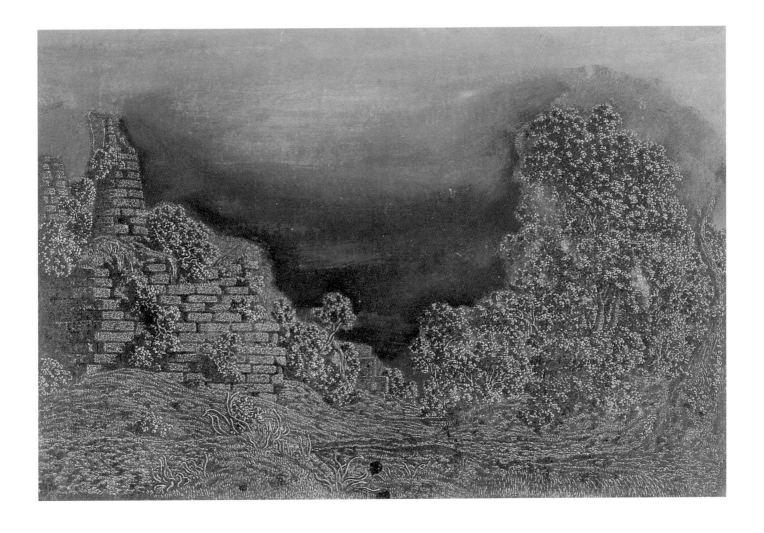

c. 1630–1635 | *etching, printed in black on paper and partly overpainted with blue oils* | 5 x 8in (13 x 19.5cm) | Rijksmuseum, Amsterdam

Still Life with Flowers and Shells

WE KNOW, thanks to a few comments made by Karel van Mander, that by the middle of the 16th century, there were one or two people in the Low Countries selling images of flowers in vases. If times had been more peaceful, then their new idea, the still life, would probably have caught on immediately. But with the disruptions caused by the revolt of the Netherlands against Spain in the decades after 1568, the genre had to lie low for a while and wait for good times to re-emerge. When the economies of the Low Countries began to recover in the 1590s, more and more still-life painters began to appear across Northern Europe, and soon they had colleagues as far south as Spain and Italy. They painted not just flowers, but fruit, vegetables, meat, cheeses, cakes, candy, glasses, skulls, silverware, and jewelry. In fact, almost the only thing these pictures had in common was that the objects themselves formed the main theme.

Many theories have been put forward as to why still life should have emerged so suddenly. The idea that it was connected with the rise of Protestantism has already been questioned in the introduction to this chapter, and still life was a Catholic phenomenon, too. It has also been suggested that accounts of still-life painting in Pliny may have inspired 16th-century artists, although, as with landscape (see page 172), there is no firm evidence for this. It seems to me that we should simply say that the idea of still life occurred to someone, and it then took off. There are plenty of similar phenomena in history, from the invention of the wheel to the invention of the Internet bookstore. That it should have come to mind when it did is not too surprising, given the effort expended on still-life elements in the work of painters like Jan van Eyck and Hugo van der Goes (c. 1440–1482). Still life, like landscape, was an invention just waiting to happen.

Balthasar van der Ast was a Dutch painter who began to produce works around 1620, so he was not one of the innovators of the genre. He was orphaned as a child and was brought up in the home of his brother-in-law, the great flower and fruit painter Ambrosius Bosschaert the Elder (1573–1621). Bosschaert was one of the very first still-life specialists in Northern Europe, since other early artists like Roelandt Savery

BALTHASAR VAN DER AST

∽

*BORN MIDDELBURG 1593/4,
DIED DELFT 1657*

(1576–1639) and Jan Brueghel (1568–1625, son of Pieter Bruegel the Elder) were predominantly landscape painters. Van der Ast followed Bosschaert's example, painting nothing but still lifes throughout his career. The latter half of his life was spent in Delft, where he became acquainted with Jan Vermeer's father. It is permissible to speculate that he gave some lessons in art to the young Vermeer; they share a tendency to render colors in a soft-edged, slightly underfocused way.

Van der Ast dated his paintings for only a few years, and his style remained extremely constant, so it is hard to say for sure that this painting was made in the 1630s. What makes it not unlikely is that tulips play such an important role in the work. The 1630s marked the peak of the Dutch frenzy for tulips, the "Tulipomania," and saw the prices of bulbs rise to absurd heights—some were worth as much as an expensive townhouse. The unusual tulip in the center left, with its two extra petals, must have appealed very strongly to some tulip fancier.

The shells on the table were also expensive objects that were popular with rich collectors, and when combined with the tulips must have exuded an odor of luxury that they have since lost.

It has been argued by some modern scholars that still lifes were full to the brim with hidden symbolism. In this picture, the flowers might be meant as a warning of life's brevity and the inevitability of death, picking up on lines in the Bible, such as: "Man … cometh forth like a flower and is cut down" (Job 14: 2). Then the extravagant shells could be seen as a moral warning: A life wasted on expensive fripperies like these will receive its due punishment after death.

It is hard to disprove arguments like this, and it is perfectly possible that a Dutchman with a moral turn of mind might have read the painting in this way. But we should remember that there were many thousands of shell and tulip buyers in the Netherlands, and they cannot all have thought they were destined for hell as a result of their hobby. And, surely, it is much more likely that van der Ast managed to sell this very beautiful painting to a tulip collector with a taste for art, than to a fire-and-brimstone preacher with no time for vain luxuries.

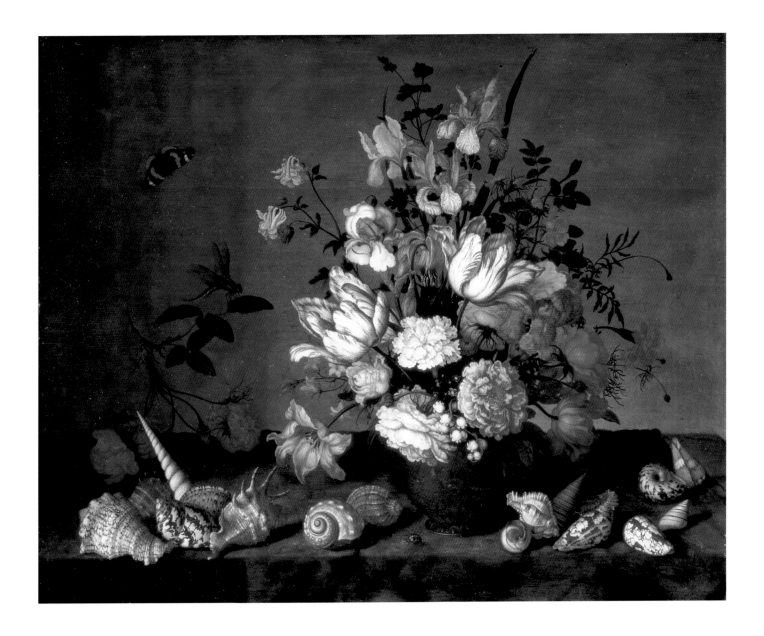

1630s | *oil on panel* | 24 x 30in (61 x 76cm) | Fitzwilliam Museum, Cambridge, England

Portrait of Maria Louisa de Tassis

SOME ARTISTS starve in garrets, but there have always been a select few who seem to enjoy a charmed life. One of these was Anthony Van Dyck. Unlike most artists of his time, he came from a wealthy merchant family. By his early teens, he was painting precociously brilliant portraits. He had the chance to work alongside the greatest European artist of the preceding generation, Peter Paul Rubens, who also lived in Antwerp; and at the age of twenty-one, he was being feted by King James I of England. This was just the start. Over the next twenty years, he traveled around Italy, France, Flanders, and England, painting elegant portraits of aristocrats, cardinals, kings, and queens, and became one of the most famous painters in Europe. Nor was this just empty success; his artistic colleagues were happy to acknowledge his extraordinary talents. When he was thirty-five, he was made Honorary Dean of the painters' guild in Antwerp, an honor that had previously only been bestowed on Rubens.

There was, perhaps, one artistic shadow that fell across his career. He was recognized as the most brilliant portrait painter in Northern Europe, but portrait painting, although lucrative, was considered esthetically inferior to the painting of histories and allegories, genres at which Rubens excelled (see pages 182–83). Van Dyck's own histories have never been praised as fulsomely as his portraits; they always seem a little embarrassed, like adolescents with stage fright. For all the brilliance of his technique, Van Dyck was never able to equal the passionate conviction of Rubens's compositions.

We do not know if Van Dyck worried about this shortcoming, or even if he noticed it. Perhaps he was content simply to be the master of one genre. He certainly dominated the art of the portrait, not just in his own time but for a century and more after his death. Gainsborough's last words are reported to have been a frail but rapturous, "We are all going to Heaven, and Vandyke is of the party!"—which says quite a bit about Van Dyck's near divine status in 18th-century England.

During his time as court painter to Charles I, Van Dyck was the acknowledged colossus of art in England, and he produced a long series of portraits that made Charles and his group look as elegant as any group of oligarchs in history. Van Dyck specialized in conveying a kind of nonchalant swagger which made his aristocrats seem righteous owners of the earth. The dashing couriers of later myth were in part Van Dyck's creations.

Maria Louisa de Tassis, the sitter in this painting, may look like a stylish Italian aristocrat, but she was in fact the daughter of a Flemish priest, one of the canons of Antwerp Cathedral. The two crucifixes on her chest were doubtless sincerely worn as emblems of her faith, and we should not suppose that, just because she dressed so lavishly, she did not take Christian teachings seriously. In any case, we cannot be sure that she really owned a dress as lovely as this one. It is possible that Van Dyck might have embellished her Sunday best.

This is one of Van Dyck's simpler portraits, with a plain background rather than the columns, drapes, and landscapes for which he was well known. Even so, it has incredible impact. One of Van Dyck's great skills was to be able to make a costume almost shimmer with life. The slashes in the sleeves ripple and tremble, the gold brocade is painted with countless brushstrokes to make it flicker, and the feather fan has all the instantaneous energy of a small dog jumping for a bone. None of this precisely captures the look of ordinary life, but it is all the more lively for being mannered. Note the cunning way Van Dyck has tied useless pink ribbons around Maria Louisa's waist and arms. Take them away, and the dress looks puffy and relatively somber.

It is easy to imagine from this painting that Maria Louisa must have been extremely beautiful, but we should not underestimate Van Dyck's talents as a portraitist. Perhaps she had an ungainly slouch, and gray teeth, and a twitchy way of talking; alternatively, perhaps her skin was not this clear, or her face not quite this shape. Paintings are ambiguous things, and it is possible that this *could* be the portrait of someone plain. Not that it matters, as far as the art goes. It is an enchanting picture, which conveys so much warmth and optimism and excitement about life. Maria Louisa de Tassis, unfortunately, did not live long; she died shortly before her twenty-seventh birthday, just nine years after this painting was made.

ANTHONY VAN DYCK

*BORN ANTWERP 1599,
DIED LONDON 1641*

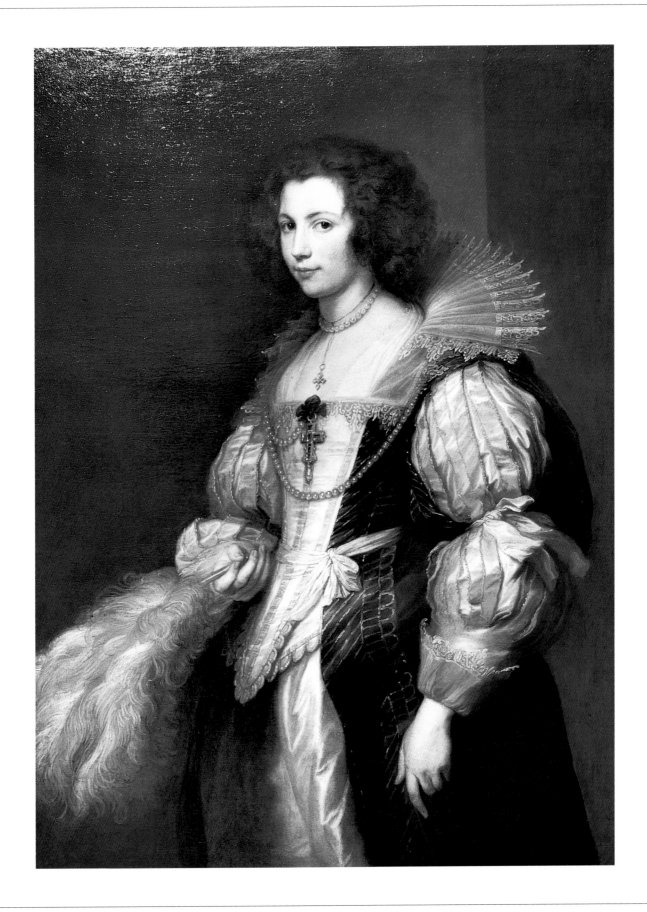

1629 | *oil on canvas* | 51 x 37in (129 x 93cm) | Collections of the Prince of Liechtenstein, Vaduz Castle

The Jewish Bride

WESTERN SOCIETY today seems obsessed with material success, but it says something about the ambivalence which underlies our attitude that material failures can also become heroes. For all our cult of wealth, there is something in the life of the impoverished genius that we find moving and inspiring.

Rembrandt van Rijn's life has been seen for almost two centuries as one of the classic examples of this myth. Inevitably, perhaps, there has been a move in recent years to debunk the romantic excess that clings to his story. Yes, he went bankrupt in his fifties—but he arranged his finances so that things could have been far worse; yes, his son and his mistress died in the last years of his life, leaving him to a lonely death—but he was not entirely destitute, as is often thought. And his bankruptcy was not due to his art being too radical for his fellow Dutchmen, as people like to think; rather, it was a result of his financial incompetence and his rather difficult, arrogant personality, which repelled buyers.

However, it seems to me that this revisionism misses most of the point. Whatever the reasons for his bankruptcy, Rembrandt really did have to move from an airy house to a cramped apartment; he really did become isolated artistically and personally in his last years, and must have suffered from his bereavements; and, most significant, we can see this encircling darkness in the intensely serious compassion with which he painted his fellow humans in his final years.

In retrospect, Rembrandt's life seems a perfect parable of hubris. His bankruptcy and final misery came after a youth in which he had been dazzlingly successful, and very aware of his artistic powers. It is telling that he is the only Dutch artist known by his first name—a self-conscious effort to emulate Tiziano, Rafaello, and Michelangelo.

And yet, unlike his Flemish contemporaries Rubens and Van Dyck, Rembrandt never traveled south to Italy. He saw Italian paintings that went through the Amsterdam art market, was aware of Italian etchings and engravings, and knew the work of Dutch painters who had picked up caravaggist ideas in Rome, but he never felt the need to cross the Alps himself. In fact, there is no evidence that he left the Netherlands at all. In the 18th century, it was common to lambast him for his lack of curiosity, and to claim that his art was both provincial and limited. But with more hindsight, it seems instead that his self-imposed isolation contributed both to the originality and to the contemplative intensity of his work.

A somber shadowed manner was the one stylistic constant in Rembrandt's art, everything else changed. He painted smoothly and roughly, thinly and thickly, with small figures and large figures in complex and simple compositions. Toward the end of his career, he painted for the most part on fairly large canvases, which contained one or two figures depicted in thick, loose brushwork, and this painting is one of the great glories of his late manner. The paint, which is almost half an inch thick in places, is honeyed over with glazes and varnishes until it has all the rich timbre of an old cello. This work is one of Rembrandt's great psychological studies, but perhaps its main fascination is the abstract succulence of its myriad visual textures.

REMBRANDT VAN RIJN

&

BORN LEIDEN 1606,
DIED AMSTERDAM 1669

The title of the picture, which dates from the 19th century, is almost certainly a misnomer. The costumes are not those normally worn by Jew or Gentile in Holland in Rembrandt's time; they seem to be meant as "ancient" in a rather vague way. It has therefore been suggested that the painting may represent an Old Testament scene, of Isaac and Rebekah being spied on by Abimelech (Genesis 26: 6–11). A preparatory drawing shows a man looking down on the couple, which supports the theory.

This may be right, but it does not get us very far in understanding what we see. What are the protagonists thinking? The book of Genesis does not help us appreciate the complexities of this ambivalent emotional situation. The man, with his hand on the woman's heart, and his look, which perhaps expresses longing, may be telling her of his love; but what is going through her mind? She seems to be lost in thought or memory, and yet the incredible delicacy of her touch on his hand shows him and us that she is still aware of his presence. What has just been said, and what will be said next? It is easy to come up with theories, and that is precisely the problem and the joy of the picture; it contains so many human possibilities.

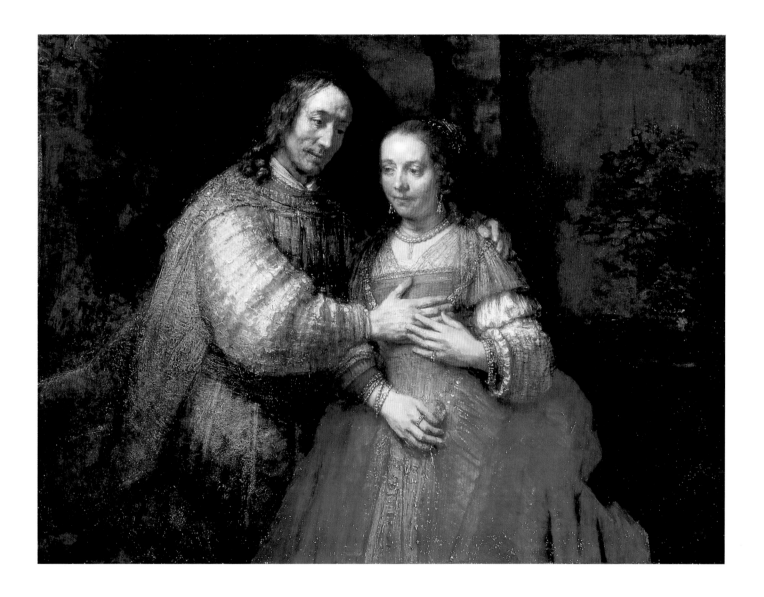

c. 1665 | *oil on canvas* | 48 x 66in (122 x 167cm) | Rijksmuseum, Amsterdam

Woman and Child

PIETER DE HOOCH has long been considered to be an inferior version of Jan Vermeer (1632–1675), but recent exhibitions devoted to the two artists seemed to me to reveal the weaknesses of the latter and the strengths of the former. Vermeer's technique may be immaculate, but he is a rather frigid painter, whereas de Hooch at his best gives us a wonderfully warm and moving image of Dutch domestic life.

Unfortunately, de Hooch was only at his best for a period of roughly six years. In the late 1650s he was living in Delft, where he began to paint light-filled interiors containing one or two figures, a genre Vermeer seems to have adopted under his influence. Around 1663 he moved to Amsterdam, where his art went steadily downhill. By the 1680s, he was painting gloomy works of sometimes startling technical ineptitude.

There seem to have been a number of reasons for his professional decline. He may have been unlucky in his choice of pigments; some of his late works are so dark that one cannot help thinking the chemicals in his paints have gone awry. Then, too, he changed his subject matter, turning away from the paintings of women and children that form the bulk of his best work. Perhaps the fact that he buried two of his own children in the early 1660s made the subject too painful. He also began to paint much more quickly, presumably in an effort to fend off creditors. The Dutch art market underwent a severe contraction after 1660, in part because paintings by dead artists were competing with those by the living, and de Hooch must have seen the value of his work decline sharply.

But private troubles seem also to have been important; de Hooch died in the madhouse in his mid-fifties. Ordinarily, madness does not kill its sufferers except in cases of suicide. Almost the only form of madness that might reveal itself late and lead to a premature death is delirium tremens. Therefore, it seems quite possible that de Hooch drank himself into the grave, and that the terrible and painfully obvious decline in his art was caused by excesses of the bottle. But for a few years at least, he created some of the finest paintings ever made in Holland, and these remain as his true legacy.

PIETER DE HOOCH

*BORN ROTTERDAM 1629,
DIED AMSTERDAM 1684*

De Hooch is often praised as a great realist, and analyses of his paintings tend to draw attention to the fidelity with which he rendered the fall of light on people and things. But, like any first-rate artist, de Hooch achieved his ends not by painting what he saw, but by distorting it in subtle ways. After all, we rarely take great pleasure in looking at the corner of a room as light bounces off the walls, whereas we can gaze in rapture at a de Hooch for a long while. As Pablo Picasso put it, "Art is not life; art is a lie which helps us appreciate life."

The whole relationship between beholder and beheld in a de Hooch painting is artificial. This is true of all paintings, of course, but a realist like de Hooch can easily make us forget the fact. You are sitting in a room looking at a stranger and her child; neither seems aware of your presence or, if they are, they seem untroubled that you are watching them. In real life, you will never get the chance to gaze in so leisurely a fashion at people you do not know.

Another artificiality is seen in de Hooch's pqrticular treatment of light. Everything is much softer in one of his paintings than it is in the real world. Each color in this work, even the white neckerchief and the red blouse of the mother, is dampened down with brown or gray. If you look up from the page you are reading and inspect the objects around you, you will see that things in nature have clear edges and that their colors are sharply distinguished. There is none of this in de Hooch, where each color is a sibling of the next, like the graining in a piece of polished walnut. In this painting, the ceramic tiles on the wall to the right of the door are a brilliant glossy white, but de Hooch has tamed them, until they have no more luster than the earth-fired tiles of the floor. And the sunlight on the wall at the left is muted; no sunset of the weakest sort could create a patch of light so delicate in hue. All these things produce a subdued harmony so soft that the world seen through this lens is drenched in calm, and the viewer is soothed into a reverie that gives the scene an almost religious sense of unity and peace. The woman in this painting has the features of de Hooch's wife, so the child is probably their own and may be one of those they buried a few years later.

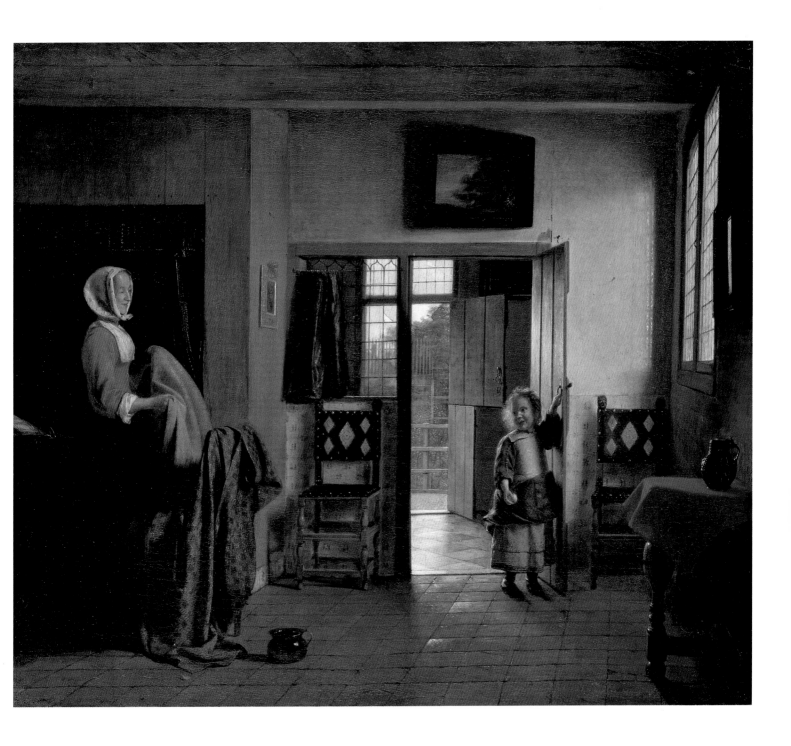

c. 1658–60 | *oil on canvas* | 20 x 24in (51 x 60cm) | National Gallery of Art, Washington, D.C.

THE 18TH CENTURY

1700–1800 ❧ ADELHEID GEALT

Heir to the separation of faith from reason and to a strict social hierarchy,

the 18th century emphasized the rational, pursued knowledge, advanced science

and technology, championed the individual, promoted democracy,

and launched our modern era. It also stressed education, public welfare,

and established the first public museums.

THIS AGE of Enlightenment was sexually tolerant and dedicated to comfort and pleasure. It popularized the Grand Tour of Europe as the finishing touch to a liberal education, the highlight being a visit to Italy and the newly discovered classical remains at the sites of Pompeii and of Herculaneum. Antiquities stimulated the neoclassical style and provided ample booty for aristocratic connoisseurs.

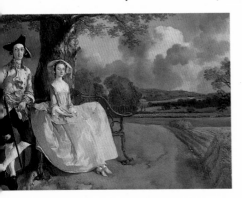

Status expressed through property, fashion, and the society portrait: Gainsborough's Mr and Mrs Andrews *(1748–49).*

Thanks to King Louis XIV of France (1638–1715) and his fabled court at Versailles, 18th-century culture was essentially French. Polite society spoke French, wore French fashions, and adopted French manners. Louis XIV's much-emulated Royal Academy institutionalized artistic education, affirmed the value of Italian art, and established an artistic hierarchy wherein history painting ranked above portraits and genre subjects, which ranked above merely imitative landscapes and still lifes.

Gifted artists practiced everywhere. In Venice, Tiepolo produced grand decorations; Canaletto, Bellotto, and Guardi supplied urban views; and Rosalba Carriera (1675–1757) started the rage for pastel portraits. In Rome, tourists sat for Pompeo Batoni (1708–1787) and bought etchings by Piranesi (1720–1778) of ancient ruins. In Holland, Jan van Huysum (1682–1749) and Rachel Ruysch (1664–1750) grew wealthy from their lavish floral paintings, while in Britain, Hogarth made his fortune. America showed promise with Benjamin West (1738–1820) and the Peale family, and France outdid herself with Watteau, Chardin, Boucher, and David. Framed by a delicate rococo style at the beginning and a robust classicism at the end, the 18th century found uses for realism along the way.

The century began with an art about love and fun, safe in the belief that human reason could master emotions, regulate society, and ultimately control nature. Optimism reigned. Fashionable salons were ruled by brilliant ladies, poets, philosophers, artists, and playwrights mixed with aristocrats and bankers. Wit was prized, conversation flowed, and new ideas were shared. The first encyclopedia was assembled, record numbers of diaries written, letters exchanged, and novels circulated. Dilettantes dabbled seriously in esthetics, theater, music, literature, philosophy, and science. People thronged to exhibitions.

David's Oath of the Horatii *(1785): the most famous history painting of its day, an inspiration to revolutionaries.*

By the mid-century, reaction had begun to set in. Diderot carped about the moral laxity of Boucher's work; Rousseau called for changes in the family and education; people wanted tax reform. An earthquake leveled Lisbon in 1755, a brutal reminder of nature's power. Within decades, the social and political fabric of Europe began to fray. America battled for independence from England in 1776, and by 1789, revolution had erupted in France. Louis XVI was beheaded, and ultimately, Napoleon took power. The century ended, steeped in the emotion and rhetoric of war.

Portraits, more abundant, varied, and brilliant than at any other time in history, recorded the faces of this century. Rigaud flattered the aristocracy and bourgeoisie of Regency France while David presented her revolutionary and postrevolutionary citizens. Thomas Gainsborough (1727–88) immortalized England's landed gentry, while Hogarth celebrated her sturdy, self-made men.

Largely ignored until mid-century, pure landscape was rediscovered by George Stubbs, Richard Wilson, and Joseph Wright of Derby. Despite the premium placed on the Grand Manner, which advocated generalization and idealization to represent universal qualities and truths, few history paintings succeeded on the scale of David's *Oath of the Horatii*. With its bold, ancient characters swearing a bloody oath, the picture gained instant notoriety, timed as it was on the eve of the Revolution. David's composition became the chief paradigm for history painting in the new pared-down, restrained, neoclassical style. A cooler note was struck by the Italian sculptor Antonio Canova (1757–1822), whose chaste marbles made a whole new esthetic out of white.

Spawning the Romantic era, 18th-century art left a prodigious legacy that cannot be matched for its urbanity, wit, and virtuosity.

Canova's Cupid and Psyche, *c. 1792, with its controlled grace and elegance, epitomizes the neoclassical style.*

Louis XIV in His Coronation Robes

IF GREATNESS can be measured by an artist's ability to alter reality, then Hyacinthe Rigaud's *Louis XIV* is a truly great picture. Rigaud transformed a shriveled, bald, crippled old man into the embodiment of potent majesty and bequeathed to posterity the portrait by which Louis is best known. In so doing, Rigaud contributed to the vitality of portraiture and set a standard for royal portraits that none of Louis's descendants could equal.

Crowned in 1654, Louis XIV had, by 1701, ruled for nearly half a century and had left his mark throughout his realm. His etiquette governed social behavior; his games of power managed the aristocrats at his court of Versailles; and his academies regulated learning. His Royal Academy of Art, established in 1648, elevated guildsmen into academicians and placed their talents at his disposal. Through diplomacy, stratagem, and will, Louis made France Europe's cultural if not political leader and himself its embodiment. But when he sat for Rigaud, the sixty-three-year-old Sun King was in decline, his powers waning, and his aging court was growing rigid.

A product of Louis' system, Hyacinthe Rigaud was the ideal painter to polish the king's image once more. Rigaud came to Paris in 1681 and entered the king's Royal Academy, winning the coveted Prix de Rome in 1682. Taking the advice of the director, Charles Le Brun, Rigaud passed up the award and a career in history painting to concentrate on portraits, a lesser category of painting but a lucrative one. Like Rubens, whom he admired, Rigaud combined instincts for art and business. He set up a workshop, hiring the best talents for specialized tasks: Charles Parrocel for battle scenes, Jean-Baptiste Monnoyer for flowers, and François Desportes for landscapes and still lifes. Reserving the handling of faces and drapery for himself, Rigaud made friends at court, and by 1688, painted his first portrait of the Duc d'Orléans.

Thus, when Louis XIV's grandson, Philip V, who had gained the Spanish throne in 1700, came to Rigaud for a portrait of his grandfather, Rigaud was ready. Acting as an impresario as well as a painter, he deftly used props to hide his subject's infirmities, to underscore his regal position, and to stage his presentation. Swathing Louis in his ermine-lined blue velvet coronation robes,

HYACINTHE RIGAUD

BORN PERPIGNAN 1659, DIED PARIS 1743

Rigaud set the king's sword of office at a jaunty angle and pointed his scepter to the crown with the informality of a walking stick. He was to be seen as "first gentleman" as well as "*Louis le grand.*" A luxurious wig crowned the head. A dainty pair of red-heeled shoes set off the royal legs, of which Louis was especially proud, and added height. A red curtain has just been lifted, and the king is presented in regal splendor.

Like all great artists, Rigaud reconciled opposites: the momentary with permanence, formality with informality, motion with stability, and reality with fantasy. Adapting Van Dyck's *Charles I as Hunter* of 1635 (Louvre, Paris) and quoting from the classical Apollo Belvedere, he created a new image of majesty. Despite its reliance on some familiar baroque models and trappings—swirling drapery, half-hidden columns, precise realism—this picture anticipates the 18th century. Its animation and luxury, its theatricality, and the emphatic enlargement of the figure within the picture are themes that were to evolve during the century. Moreover, this picture is *willfully* superficial. It celebrates the surface and chooses not to probe the psyche, preferring to dazzle the eye and converse with the intellect. The allusions to the past, the symbolic references, the virtuoso technique are meant to impress and communicate.

Known for working directly on canvas, Rigaud relied on his technical skills and direct observation to achieve astonishing verisimilitude. He probably had a dummy dressed in the king's regalia in a studio set up at Versailles, and the king's face, crown, and scepter were likely painted from oil sketches. Given his subject's status, Rigaud did most of the painting himself, letting assistants help with required copies.

Louis liked the results so much he kept the painting. Exhibited at the Salon of 1704 and then placed in the Throne Room of Versailles, his portrait gave a suitably magnificent preamble to an audience with the increasingly feeble king. A masterful performance by a great artist thoroughly in tune with his time and his patron, *Louis XIV* is the ultimate expression of elitism and facility. That modern eyes might view such values with suspicion is, ironically, a product of the very century this great icon launched.

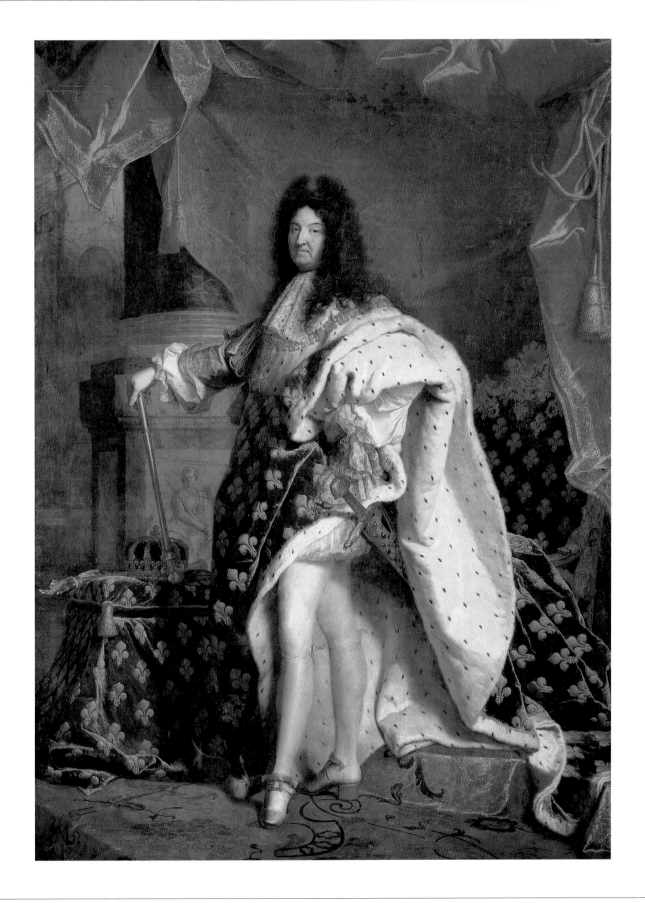

1701 | *oil on canvas* | 109 x 76¹⁄₂in (277 x 194cm) | Louvre, Paris

Embarkation to (or from) the Island of Cythera

RIGAUD GAVE a dying regime a final burst of glory while Antoine Watteau evoked the society that flourished in its wake. In the only official painting of his career, Watteau had the genius to weave the dross of ordinary life into the gossamer web of dreams, while endowing nature with the intimacy of a boudoir. His virtuosity differed from Rigaud. In laying out his fantasy, Watteau produced the most enchanting meditation on the nature of love that has ever been painted.

Only thirty-five when he died, Watteau, that student of society, was himself an outsider, solitary, unattached, and tubercular, protected by a few dedicated friends. Much imitated by Nicolas Lancret and others, he could never be equaled. Watteau came to Paris in 1702 and, working as a copyist on the Pont Notre-Dame, he could soon paint *Woman with Spectacles* (1660, St. Petersburg Hermitage) by Gerrit Dou (1613–1675) from memory. He trained with Claude Gillot, who gave him a love of theater subjects, and Claude Audran III, with whom he studied Rubens's great Medici Cycle (1622–25), a series of twenty-four canvases crammed with contemporary history and classical allegory that celebrates the Dowager Queen of France, Marie de' Medici. The cycle was an inspiration to Watteau.

In 1712, he was accepted to full membership in the Royal Academy. Permitted to choose his own subject, it took Watteau five years to submit his reception piece. By then he was in such demand he had little use for the Academy, his clients coming from outside the court. The art dealers Sirois and his son-in-law Gersaint had become patrons, as had the bourgeois collector Jean de Jullienne and the rich banking brothers Pierre and Antoine Crozat. Yet, Watteau respected the Academy and took considerable pains over his reception piece. The result was this work, which was accepted as a new category of painting, a *fête galante* or "scene of gallantry." Neither history painting, genre scene, landscape, portrait, or theatrical subject, it is a little of them all. Using a mythical landscape of Cythera (a Greek island devoted in classical times to the worship of Aphrodite, goddess of love), he drew an indelible portrait of his age, not as it was, but as it wished to be: young, well mannered, and tender.

ANTOINE WATTEAU

BORN VALENCIENNES 1684,
DIED NOGENT-SUR-MARNE 1721

With a nod to Rubens's cycle, Watteau staged a grand journey, not by a queen but by eight young couples, who, like Marie de' Medici, are transported by love, she to marriage with Henry IV of France, they to the island of love, a magical place with a Venetian air. Equally dainty regardless of gender, these charming young lovers are absorbed yet discreet. Nature resonates with passions that they hold in check. Vague about time, which is both evoked and suspended, Watteau, like Rigaud in his portrait of Louis XIV (see page 197), maintains a psychological and physical distance that, paradoxically, draws us into this intimate sphere.

Having adorned Aphrodite's statue with votives of roses, her special flower, these couples have been transported to paradise on dreams of happiness from which, alas, they must awake. Casting wistful glances back to her sacred grove, they make their way back—to where? The distant shores are even more hazy and fabulous than their present location. Are they in Cythera or preparing to go? Both answers are possible. Perhaps love is a perpetual dream state that renders every destination magical, and which suspends all reality until love has ended.

After years of thought, the picture was rapidly executed over eight months. Working without an overall preliminary sketch in oil or pencil, Watteau, like Rigaud, painted directly on canvas. But Watteau depended on hundreds of chalk drawings he had made from life to stage his romance. Sketchbooks filled with details of faces, expressions, and movements were his sources. From these he selected poses, scale, and position to give his picture the rhythm and pacing of a minuet. With instinct and intelligence he applied tones and washes, glazing here, scumbling there, adding details and nuance to every area of the canvas.

Thus Watteau held up a mirror, however stylized, to the youthful and fashionable society that emerged after Louis XIV's death in 1715. Pleasure seeking at times to the point of frivolity, this was a period that valued entertainment and, above all, conversation. Life was to be treated lightly, with good manners. "Trifle with life," Voltaire said, "that is all it is good for." In Watteau's hands, life was indeed a trifle, a celebration of surface that plumbs the depths of the soul.

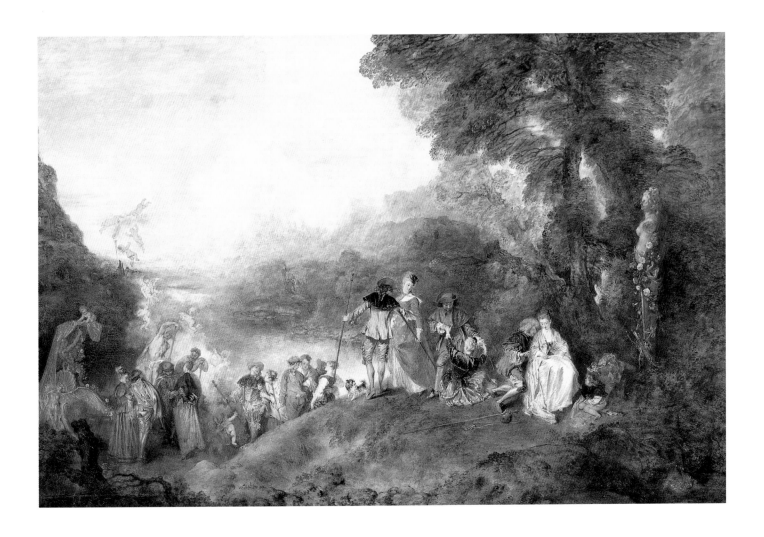

1717 | *oil on canvas* | 51 x 76¹/₂in (129.5 x 194cm) | Louvre, Paris

The Stonemason's Yard

WHILE WATTEAU probed the human heart, Canaletto examined physical reality. Around 1726, before unceasing demands for views of the Grand Canal, the church of San Marco, and other popular Venetian sights distracted him, Canaletto painted his most informal portrait of Venice and created his masterpiece. Selecting the square by the church of San Vitale, he concentrated on the jumble of stone and the temporary shed being used for the church's repair and opened a window into the laborer's world. A mason chisels his quota of stone, a woman attends her fallen child, another quietly spins on her loggia while a servant empties her basin out of the window. Santa Maria della Carità (now the Accademia) is seen across the canal, partially obscured by a house. Eclipsed in both scale and focus, the church is not the subject; the life in the city squares is. Working with the eye of a reporter and the heart of a poet, Canaletto knitted the whole together effortlessly and yet brilliantly. As lights and shadows trace their paths across surfaces and clouds are tossed across the sky, Canaletto guides the viewer through this quiet corner of Venice. Reconciling stability with change, balancing dark with light, formality with informality, near with far, this exceptional work is acknowledged as Canaletto's greatest achievement.

The son of a theatrical designer (and descended from minor nobility), Canaletto trained with his father, worked briefly in Rome, and was back in Venice by 1720. He enrolled in the painter's guild in order to ply his trade legally. His Venice was a declining maritime and economic power but, after a thousand years of building, eagerly catered to tourists. These included scores of English gentlemen who completed their education with the Grand Tour. Eager to obtain mementos of their experiences, more than any other foreigners, English travelers purchased pictures. Through Owen McSwinny, a British picture dealer, and Joseph Smith the British Consul in Venice who collected and acted as a picture agent, Canaletto's career was launched.

Like the Dutch merchants of the previous century, Canaletto's clients had a taste for clarity and precision. Essentially, his paintings continued the tradition of town views produced by such 17th-century Dutch specialists as Saenredam, the van der

**CANALETTO
(ANTONIO DA CANAL)**

BORN VENICE 1697,
DIED VENICE 1768

Heydens, and Caspar van Wittel. Canaletto was familiar with their work, especially that of van Wittel (who painted in Venice in around 1695) and used some of their techniques, perhaps including the use of a camera obscura through which outlines of buildings could be projected and traced against a flat surface.

But exactly how Canaletto worked remains uncertain. We know he made scores of rapid pen-and-ink sketches of views along the canals of Venice that can be connected to finished oils. Did he follow standard practice and draw at the site and then paint in his studio? Alessandro Marchesini, agent for one of Canaletto's early patrons the Venetian nobleman Stefano Conti, raised the startling claim that early in his career Canaletto painted his pictures on the spot—a dramatic departure from the conventional practice. Often dismissed as salesman's hyperbole, the assertion deserves consideration.

The impression that he worked on the spot is never more compelling than in *The Stonemason's Yard*. Using a subtle palette and different viscosities of paint, Canaletto crisply delineated architectural elements, only occasionally guided by the ruler and drawing compass that later became a favorite tool. The shadows cast by buildings are convincingly described and the textures of brick, stone, water, and sky marvelously achieved through modulations of color and brushstrokes. No underdrawing guided him, and no detailed sketches survive to explain how reality gained such a faithful yet esthetically satisfying translation into art. Either Canaletto *did* paint directly at the site, or he created such a convincing illusion of reality in his studio that it appears to be taken from nature. In either case, the results are staggering.

Its relatively large size and unusual subject matter suggest that *The Stonemason's Yard* was either painted for a local patron or to please himself. Given Canaletto's popularity in England and his trips there (1746–50; 1751–53; 1754–55), it is not surprising that it had entered a British collection by 1808 and the National Gallery by 1828, and forms part of the visual tradition upon which painters like Constable would build. It prompted Whistler (1834–1903) to observe that "Canaletto could paint a white house against a white cloud and to do that you have to be great."

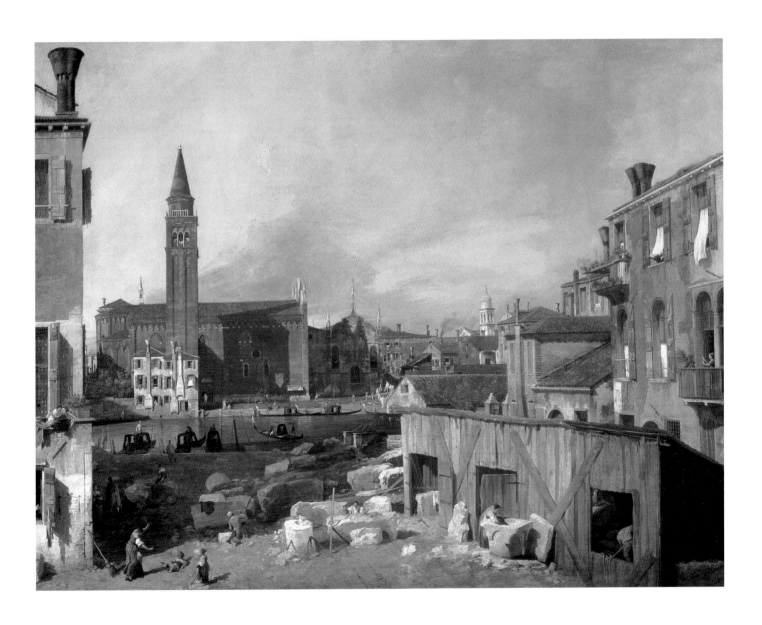

1725 | *oil on canvas* | 49 x 64in (124.5 x 162.5cm) | National Gallery, London

The Ray Fish

THE FRENCH PAINTER Chardin was a contemporary of Canaletto. One found greatness in a humble corner of Venice; the other found it in the kitchen. Against a masonry wall, a ray fish hangs on a hook, its entrails glistening in shades of silver, reds, and browns. The table has been casually laid with the pots, pitchers, fish, and oysters used in cooking. As a cat prepares to steal a fish, the scene gains excitement. Here is visual brilliance, with a mastery of texture, composition, and narrative. Building on Dutch as well as Italian still-life traditions, Chardin's *Ray Fish* is one of his earliest and most extravagant masterpieces in an oeuvre that, over time, discovered monumentality in much simpler forms: a pile of strawberries, a large pitcher, and a spoon. *The Ray Fish* demonstrates Chardin's youthful virtuosity and represents the work that gained him admission into the all-powerful Academy, thereby launching his career.

The son of a cabinetmaker who specialized in billiard tables, Chardin was, to some extent, self-taught, although he did spend time in the studio of two history painters, Pierre-Jacques Cazes and Noël-Nicolas Coypel. Aware of the high status of history painting, Chardin found he had no talent for it, and in 1724, he entered the lesser Academy of St. Luke instead of the Royal Academy. According to his biographers, the chance gift of a dead rabbit set him on the course of still-life painting. Conscious of the need to translate life into art, Chardin was never satisfied with mere verisimilitude but used a profound study of nature and prolonged meditation on composition to achieve images that are simultaneously natural and seemingly effortlessly composed.

"I must forget everything I have seen … I must place [the object] at a distance where I no longer see the details … I must strive for proper imitation of the general masses, the color tones, and the effects of light and shadows," he noted early in his career. In other words, Chardin was thinking like an artist in the most modern terms. His stated goals and many others were achieved in his *Ray Fish*. Far enough away to avoid detail, the essentials have been captured: the general forms, their colors, and their placement in light. Despite the apparently casual assembly of leeks, oysters, carp, sting ray, kitchen utensils, and

JEAN-BAPTISTE-SIMÉON CHARDIN

❧

BORN PARIS 1699,
DIED PARIS 1779

the agitated cat, thoughtful study of this picture reveals a carefully planned composition, with parallel alignments of diagonals moving downward from upper left to lower right and upper right to lower left, leaving the ray fish a diamond-shaped centerpiece. Moreover, Chardin moves the viewer across the picture and in and out of the space as well. If Whistler admired Canaletto for his sophisticated use of white, what would he have said of Chardin, who used it so brilliantly in this work.

Chardin displayed his *Ray Fish* in the annual exhibition that afforded young painters exposure, the Exposition de la Jeunesse held at the Place Dauphin in Paris on Corpus Christi day. The response was immediate. In a few months the Royal Academy received him, and the *Ray Fish*, together with another large still life, were accepted as his reception pieces. Thereafter Chardin exhibited regularly at the Salon and even gained royal patronage. In 1755, he was unanimously elected treasurer of the Academy and put in charge of hanging the Salon, a post he held until 1774. In 1757, the king granted Chardin living quarters in the Louvre; all this for a lowly painter of still lifes and genre pieces.

A survey of his patrons indicates that he was widely appreciated. Besides the royal connoisseurs Louis XV, Frederick the Great of Prussia, and Catherine the Great of Russia, Chardin was also eagerly collected both by the Scottish physician William Hunter and the Italian violinist and composer Francesco Geminiani, who lived in Paris between 1749 and 1755. Contemporary artists including the painter Joseph Aved, the sculptor Jean-Baptiste Lemoyne, the architect Pierre Boscry, and the jeweler Philippe Caffieri also collected Chardin's pictures. His visual intelligence and his ability to lift the ordinary into the extraordinary had great and lasting appeal.

Today, Chardin is one of the few painters of the 18th century who is universally acknowledged to have been a genius. Since he embraced common experience instead of, to modern eyes, the artificial rhetoric of history painting, he can be better appreciated. His impact was felt on a host of future painters, particularly of still life. One cannot imagine the work of Manet, Cézanne, or even Giorgio Morandi (1890–1964) without him.

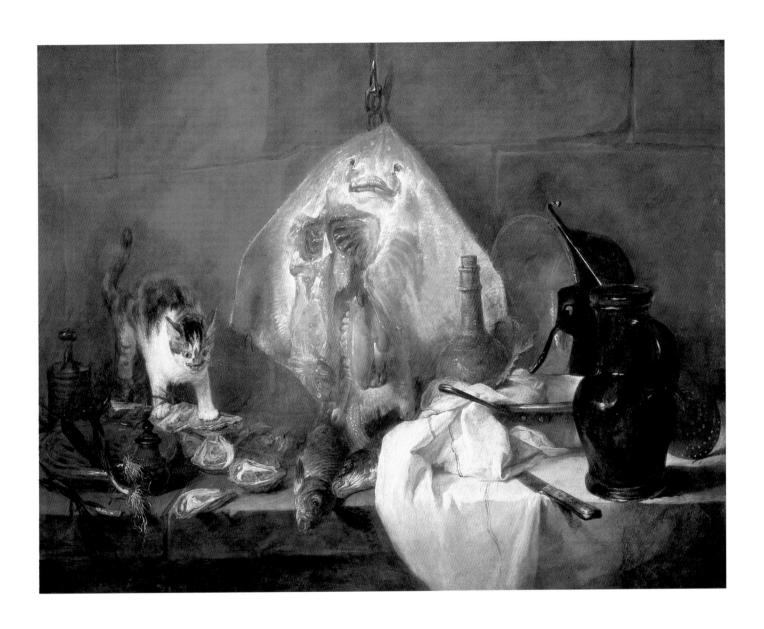

1728 | *oil on canvas* | 45 x 57½in (114 x 146cm) | Louvre, Paris

Marriage à la Mode, IV
The Countess's Morning Levée

By INVENTING A NEW kind of picture, the modern morality subject of which *Marriage à la Mode* is his greatest example, William Hogarth became the first English painter to place his country on the world's artistic stage. Deftly combining satire, comedy, and melodrama, Hogarth unfolded a story about marriage for money and social advancement that captivated his audience and remains relevant even today. He understood that his "readers" needed to laugh at, feel superior to, and yet connect with his characters. Hogarth fulfilled that need by choosing subjects close to home, built around some universally appealing topic. His characters reflected weaknesses of every class and type: vanity, cruelty, greed, pride, debauchery and lechery, dishonesty and selfishness. Hogarth used pictures the way satirists and novelists used words, to tell a rich and engaging story. Readers of Pope, Swift, and Fielding eagerly responded to Hogarth's depictions of human frailty with their abundant anecdotal details, their complex visual clues, and their devastating characterizations.

Hogarth began as an engraver and had little formal training as a painter. Despite some experience of life-drawing classes and familiarity with grand decorative painting through Sir James Thornhill, with whose daughter he eloped, Hogarth developed an unconventional working method and viewpoint as a painter. Instead of drawings and sketches, he relied upon his prodigious visual memory for faces and settings to recreate the world in paint. Established as a portrait painter, Hogarth painted his friend Captain Coram in 1740, an early masterpiece of English portraiture, but in his social subjects he found his métier. After treating the lower classes in his *Harlot's Progress* of 1732 and the middle classes in his *Rake's Progress* of 1733, Hogarth ridiculed both the aristocracy and the socially ambitious middle classes in the tale that unfolds in his *Marriage à la Mode* of 1742–46. Aspiring to a social history of his age that "may be Instructive and amusing in future times when the customs maners fasheons Characters and Humours of the present age in this country may possibly be changed or lost to Posterity," Hogarth's blend of sympathy, satire, and humor was hugely popular.

WILLIAM HOGARTH

ℰ◞

BORN LONDON 1697,
DIED LONDON 1764

In the fourth of six scenes in *Marriage à la Mode*, a rich alderman's daughter has become a countess by marrying the son of Earl Squanderfield. Idle and dissipated, the couple now lead separate lives. Seated in her boudoir, the countess apes the French custom of receiving visitors as her toilette is completed. Ten people crowd in, including a castrato (a satire on the current idols, Francesco Bernardi and Farinelli) and a flautist. Attended by her hairdresser, the countess ignores the performance, absorbed by her lawyer Silvertongue's invitation to a masquerade, which is, in fact, an assignation. Crébillon's sexually frank book *Sopha* (translated into English in 1741) is beside him, while their "naked" passion is underscored by Correggio's *Jupiter and Io* (see pages 118–19) just above. In a parody of overwrought sensibility, a lady swoons over the singer while a fop in curlers is quite unmoved. This marriage of convenience is clearly doomed. The husband is murdered by Silvertongue in part five, and Silvertongue is executed, whereupon the countess takes an overdose of laudanum in part six.

Blending tragedy with humor and showing how two foolish people become victims of their own shortcomings, Hogarth created an indelible picture of Georgian London and also a timeless comedy. How he did it is remarkable. Walking around London, he memorized all kinds of places and people: thieves, prostitutes, beggars, and lords. Adept at strong characterization, using both gesture and expression, Hogarth gave meaning to each detail. He considered his pictures to be dramas: "My picture was my Stage and men and women my actors who were by Mean[s] of certain actions and express[ions] to Exhibit a dumb shew." Assured of a broad middle-class audience through the sale of prints of his paintings (for which he wisely retained copyright), Hogarth's fame spread into Europe. His originality was acknowledged particularly in France.

Hogarth died four years before the English Royal Academy was founded. Even Sir Joshua Reynolds, *the* exponent of the Academy and the Grand Manner that Hogarth so detested, acknowledged his genius, which gave a distinctly English dimension to narrative painting and launched an outpouring of English social subjects that continued well into the 19th century.

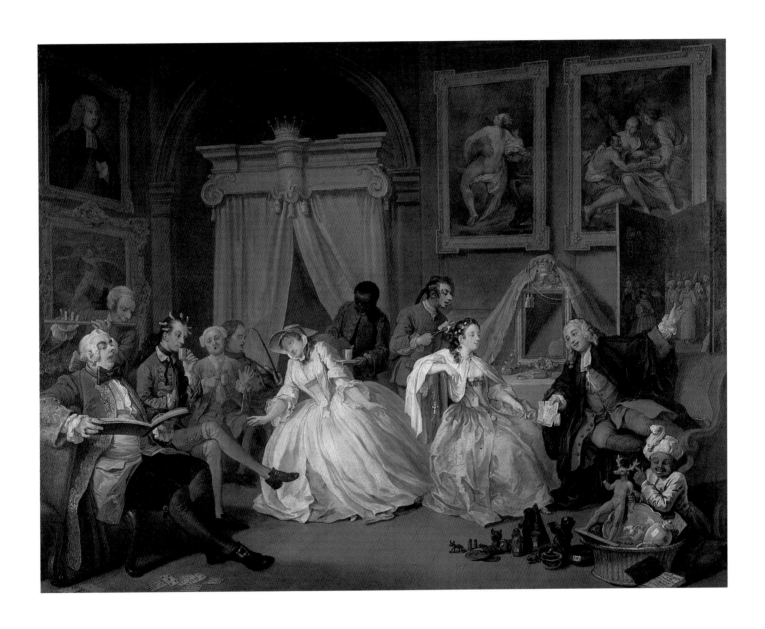

1742–46 | *oil on canvas* | 28 x 36in (71 x 91.5cm) | National Gallery, London

Würzburg Residenz, The Marriage of Friedrich Barbarossa *(detail)*

DURING THE 18th century, many European painters still aspired to paint large historical dramas. Only a few were good at this, while the Venetian virtuoso, Giambattista Tiepolo, was universally acknowledged as great. Genuinely precocious, Tiepolo briefly trained with the minor painter Gregorio Lazzarini and then studied the works of Sebastiano Ricci, Piazzetta, and, most of all, Veronese. He developed an urbane, sophisticated, and elegant style suitable for any kind of subject, including religious works, histories, and genre scenes as well as allegories and poetic themes. Unlike Canaletto, who made art out of life, Tiepolo had the genius to breathe life into art and thereby revitalize the grand but rather stuffy old classics. He also worked fast and could cover acres of walls and ceilings with graceful figures, lush colors, and dazzling compositions in relatively short periods.

Thus, when Prince-Bishop Carl Phillipp von Grieffenklau of Würzburg was looking for an artist to decorate his new palace, designed by Balthasar Neumann, the famous Venetian was a natural choice. The Prince-Bishop's scheme called for suitable historical and allegorical references, including the solemnization of the marriage between Kaiser Friedrich Barbarossa and Beatrice of Burgundy by an earlier Prince-Bishop of Würzburg in 1156. By 1750, Tiepolo was a veteran of numerous successful large-scale projects including frescoing the walls of the Archbishop's palace in Udine with Old Testament subjects (1728) and decorating the walls of the Palazzo Labia in Venice on the theme of *Antony and Cleopatra* (1745). Tiepolo readily saw the visual potential of the Prince-Bishop's program and accepted the 12,000 florins offered as partial payment. With his sons Domenico and Lorenzo, he set off for Würzburg in 1750 and was home again three years later, having covered the vast ceilings and walls of the Grand Staircase and the Kaisersaal with his masterpiece.

Using imagination and poetic license, he frescoed the Kaisersaal ceiling with the image of Beatrice being transported to her wedding in Apollo's horse-drawn chariot. At one end of the room he created the magnificent wedding scene. With a gesture reminiscent of Rigaud, using illusion worthy of a magician, Tiepolo had sculpted putti pull back his painted gilded

GIAMBATTISTA TIEPOLO

BORN VENICE 1696,
DIED MADRID 1770

and brocaded curtain—the transition from flat to three dimensions perfectly seamless—to reveal the historic union. A haughty, perfect Beatrice, dressed in the height of 16th-century Venetian fashion, kneels beside her red-haired consort, whose handsome face reflects his solemn attention to the Prince-Bishop's blessing. Displaying a profile reminiscent of his 18th-century successor, the Prince-Bishop's size, placement, and general splendor give him an appropriately starring role. A retinue of nobles attends, bearing the double eagle banners proclaiming Barbarossa Holy Roman Emperor. To the side of the altar, a series of stairs accommodates the royal dwarf, who offers a pillow to Beatrice, and another group of nobles. These stairs lead down to meet the entablature of the columns that mark the upper wall of the Kaisersaal—yet another deft transition from the fictional space of the fresco to the reality of the room. A superb fusion of architecture, sculpture, and painting, the whole work, with its rich colors, sinuous forms, and dynamic composition, is an inspired example of rococo decoration.

Besides the gorgeous array of costumes and the frankly Venetian-Renaissance architectural setting for this medieval episode, this sumptuous visual feast sparkles with anecdotal details. Its casual, unselfconscious actors balance solemnity with humor. Verging on sacrilege, Tiepolo shows Christ's disembodied legs dangling down from a crucifix behind the Prince-Bishop, while the pretty bridesmaid who holds the family lap dog is a study in gentle comedy. Copious and vulgar satire like Hogarth's is inappropriate here, but at least part of Tiepolo's genius was knowing how much levity and informality a situation needed. He was at his best when conjuring up pageants like this, juggling all the elements into a vibrant whole.

Debates still rage about how he created this masterpiece. Oil sketches and chalk drawings survive, but how they were used and how Domenico and Lorenzo assisted is still in question. The magnitude of Tiepolo's accomplishments obscures the mundane facts of process. Less controversial is his glorification of women in an age that reveled in female charms. His supremely flawless women and his decorative style had a deep impact on his younger contemporaries, such as François Boucher.

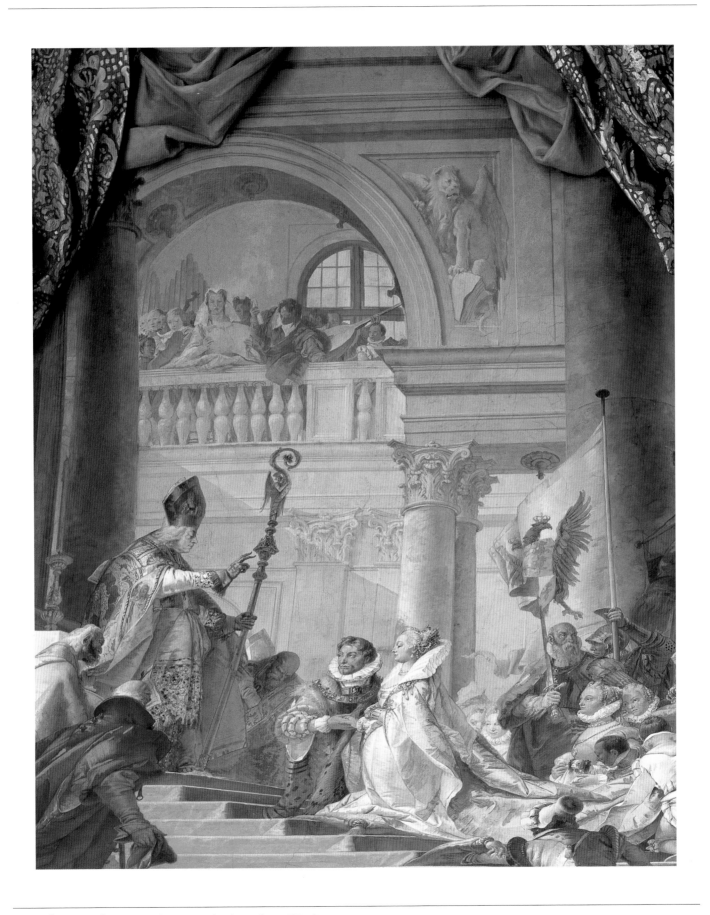

1752 | *fresco* | Kaisersaal, Prince-Bishop's Residence, Würzburg

Madame de Pompadour

TIEPOLO INVENTED the ideal woman, the French painter François Boucher worked for one. Madame de Pompadour (1721–1764), mistress to Louis XV, was the greatest patron of her day, and Boucher was her favorite artist. Through him developed the luxurious, fanciful, decorative style synonymous with the age of Louis XV. An indefatigable decorator, Boucher made his most impressive contributions to the art of the period with his portraits of his best patron, this being the supreme example.

Boucher won the Prix de Rome in 1723 and traveled to Italy in 1727. There, Tiepolo's paintings impressed him. Inspired also by Watteau and his fantastic *fêtes galantes* (see page 198), Boucher developed a robust decorative style that was endlessly adaptable. Versatile as well as prolific, he worked as a book illustrator (projects included the plays of Molière), a tapestry designer, decorator, and history painter. His fecund imagination was thoroughly in tune with the light and fanciful tastes of his clients and perfectly suited Madame de Pompadour.

Born Jean Poisson d' Etoiles, she caught the fancy of the king at a masked ball held at Versailles in 1745. She was beautiful and very intelligent, and by the autumn of that year, Louis had made her Marquise de Pompadour, installed her in her own apartments at Versailles, and granted her almost unlimited credit. She had also met Boucher, who became her advisor and drawing instructor. Their partnership yielded a breathtaking array of decorative ensembles, including overdoor, tapestry, and porcelain designs for her many homes, particularly Belleville, featuring charming pastoral or lightly erotic mythologies in which she herself was often the star. Usually transformed into Venus or a shepherdess, she was less often the subject of a straightforward portrait, but when Boucher painted her likeness, he outdid himself.

Boucher's largest, most elaborate, and formal portrait of Madame de Pompadour was painted in 1756. It coincides with her official appointment as a *dame du palais* to Queen Marie Leczinska, a post reserved for the highest-ranking ladies of society. A sensational event, marking a turn in La Pompadour's relationship to Louis to something strictly platonic, it might have occasioned this quasistate portrait. Here, Boucher faced a delicate problem: how to portray Madame to reflect her new dignity without overstating the case. Mingling disclosure with concealment, Boucher staged her presentation just as carefully as Rigaud had staged that of Louis XIV half a century before.

Boucher presented Madame in her boudoir, seated on a pillow-strewn divan and dressed in a magnificent flower-and-ribbon-bedecked satin gown. The model of physical perfection, Madame de Pompadour is also the ideal of style and cultivation. Her writing table nearby, her seal, pen, and paper recently in use, she looks up momentarily from her book, while the drawings, books, maps, manuscripts, and examples of her own etchings lie strewn about, alluding to her artistry, taste, literacy, and diverse interests. Louis's spaniel Mimi awaits her attentions with a bored mien that mimics that of her owner. Madame's perfectly powdered face is inscrutable while being highly animated and determined. Gazing at her books (visible to the viewer through their reflection in the mirror), she might be considering the encyclopedias which she persuaded the king to support, overcoming his resistance to the advanced thinkers of the day.

FRANÇOIS BOUCHER

❧

BORN PARIS 1703,
DIED PARIS 1770

Although few drawings survive for this work, Boucher, like Rigaud and Tiepolo, used drawings as well as studies from life to build up his painting. It is likely that Madame lent Boucher her dress. His many occasions to incorporate her likeness into his mythologies and their frequent contact indicates that familiarity as well as life studies contributed to the depiction of her face.

Always sensitive to fashion, Madame de Pompadour carried on a simultaneous love affair with the king and with art that lasted until her death. By then, she had accumulated enough treasures to fill several museums, and the sale of her belongings took eight months. Boucher went on to become Painter to the King and Director of the Royal Academy, but with her passing he had lost his favorite and most stimulating patron.

The perfect fusion of his art with his time yielded a reaction against Boucher that has yet to be overcome. The moralizing, sober art of the Neoclassicists was the antithesis of Boucher's art, which, in its cheerful superficiality and its unabashed sensuality, was destined, like all pleasures, to be short lived.

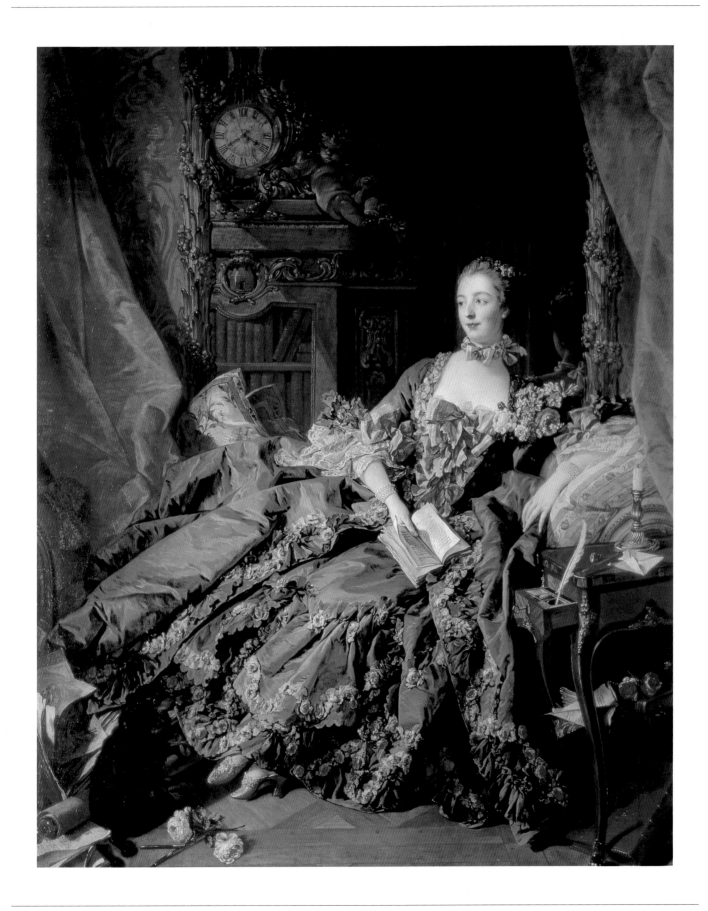

1756 | *oil on canvas* | 83 x 62in (211 x 157.5cm) | Alte Pinakothek, Munich

View of the Kreuzkirche in Ruins

BERNARDO BELLOTTO, the nephew and pupil of Canaletto, raised the chilling specter and drama of destruction with his scene of Dresden's Kreuzkirche. Here, he anticipated the appeal that ruins of all kinds, ancient, medieval, and modern, would have on 18th- and 19th-century audiences. Moreover, his dead-center approach, with the shattered bell tower confronting the viewer head on, leaps across the centuries and is essentially modern.

Chief assistant to his famous uncle, Bellotto broke with him in 1740, went to Rome, and then painted views of Italian towns until 1747. In an era when artists traveled widely, Bellotto was particularly peripatetic. From 1747 until 1758, he painted the graceful squares and fine buildings of Dresden for August III, King of Poland and Elector of Saxony. Between 1759 and 1761, he performed similar services for the courts of Maria Theresa in Vienna and the Elector of Bavaria in Munich before returning to Dresden from 1761–66, where he taught at the academy and continued to record this lovely baroque city. Bellotto's final years (1767–80) were spent at the court of Stanislaus Augustus in Warsaw, where his last urban views operate within established conventions and yet an increasingly eccentric realism.

Parts of Dresden had been damaged during the Seven Years' War (1756–63) during Bellotto's second stay in the city. The old Kreuzkirche burned down, and only her bell tower remained. The plan to incorporate the tower into the rebuilding project failed when a succession of heavy rains and poorly structured foundations led to its collapse on June 22, 1765. Attracted to the scene, Bellotto set about portraying the wreckage, which was being dismantled by hand rather than being blown up, the latter solution deemed too dangerous.

Bellotto was soon to leave Dresden for Poland, and in this, his last portrayal of the city, he produced the most compelling image of his career. Using the standard device of mathematical perspective, he draws the viewer into a new experience: a man-made construction, wrecked by the combined forces of war and nature, looms ominously before us. In an image reminiscent of his uncle's *The Stonemason's Yard* (see page 201), Bellotto shows the assembled supplies and materials for the reconstruction of the Kreuzkirche scattered about in the foreground. A small army of stonemasons is dwarfed by the towering wreckage, as is the crowd looking on at the right. But, despite the bustle, construction is not the theme here—*destruction* is. In a manner anticipating Caspar David Friedrich nearly half a century later, sightless windows frame the pale sky and the whole structure is reminiscent of a skeleton. Devoid of the religious overtones with which Friedrich's ruined churches echo, Bellotto's Kreuzkirche is described with all the dispassionate realism of a modern-day painter. Never sentimental, Bellotto here is downright grim. As a workman climbs a curiously long and perilous ladder and others stand precariously atop the tower's remaining wall, the scene hints at further danger. Perhaps Bellotto intended this image as a tragic pendant to his earlier view of the standing Kreuzkirche, also in Dresden. His unsparing concentration on the rubble makes this a striking contrast to his usual portrayals of life in the city's pretty, wide streets.

Working in a systematic manner not unlike the architects who planned the buildings that were his principal subjects, Bellotto combined free sketches from nature to compose his subject, used a camera obscura to work in motifs in detail and to set his perspective, and then refined the composition in the drawings that would transfer his design onto canvas. Always using a muted palette, he limited his colors more severely in this work, in response to this chance encounter with disaster, the tans and grays being only rarely interrupted by chaste touches of red and white.

Perhaps present-day knowledge of Dresden's fate in World War II has endowed this picture with a resonance it might not deserve. Nonetheless, it is the first of a host of real and imaginary ruins by other artists including Hubert Robert ("*Robert des Ruins*") (1733–1808), Constable, Friedrich, and Turner. Moreover, its insistent verticality, and the tension between distance and picture plane that pulls the scene up to the picture surface, is modern. The landscapes of Courbet and the Impressionists owe a debt to Bellotto who, working in the rather modest and traditional vein of city views, projected himself into a modern orbit with this strange, disturbing picture.

BERNARDO BELLOTTO

∽

BORN VENICE 1721,
DIED WARSAW 1780

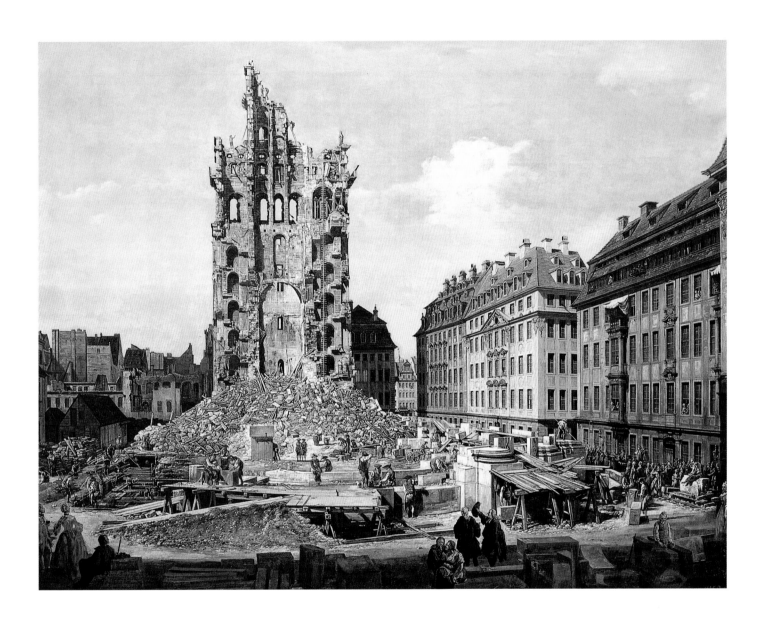

1765 | *oil on canvas* | 31¹/₂ x 43in (80 x 109cm) | Gemäldegalerie, Dresden

Cader Idris, Llyn-y-Cau

WHILE BELLOTTO made a stark record of the Kreuzkirche's destruction, his British contemporary Richard Wilson was in the wilds of North Wales painting, for the first time, its strange, inhospitable mountains. In doing so, Wilson changed the direction of landscape painting, toward the vast, overpowering expanses of nature. Largely ignored by painters during the first half of the 18th century, landscape would, a decade after Wilson's death, captivate artists throughout Europe. Thus, in a very real way, Richard Wilson's quiet excursion into his native countryside marked an artistic milestone.

Born in North Wales, the son of a clergyman, Wilson was educated in classical literature in London and was then apprenticed to a portrait painter. Independent by 1735, he was experimenting with landscapes by 1737. In 1750 he traveled to Italy, where, inspired by the classical visions of Claude, he abandoned portraiture for landscape. Imbued with moral value and dignity, Wilson's artificial landscapes appealed to the English nobles on the Grand Tour, intoxicated as they were by the classical grandeur of Rome. Yet, when he returned to England in 1756, Wilson struggled against the English bias toward foreign artists, particularly Italian ones, and their preference for frothy rococo confections. Committed to classicism, Wilson had something of an epiphany during his journey back to Wales in the 1760s.

What made him go? It was his native country, and he still had friends there. Current philosophical and social attitudes might have prompted him as well. With her natural fortifications of mountains, remote and isolated, Wales had become fixed in the popular British imagination as a pure world, uncontaminated by the artifice of urban life. This vision of untamed nature became for the British an icon of freedom.

Much written about in the 1760s, Wales was too remote for tourists and had actually been seen by few Englishmen. Perhaps hoping to exploit a potential market for Welsh views, Wilson made his difficult journey to the rugged mountains of North Wales in 1764, and there painted a series of remarkable landscapes. Blasted by icy winters, the barren glacial peaks he visited included Snowdon, the highest summit in England and Wales.

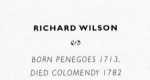

RICHARD WILSON

☙

BORN PENEGOES 1713,
DIED COLOMENDY 1782

There was also Cader Idris with its volcanic lake of Llyn-y-Cau, near the top. This lonely spot, devoid of habitation and softened by no vegetation, became Wilson's first Welsh subject and a real challenge. Instead of his pat classical formulas—foreground tree, lake in middleground, balancing forms toward the back—Wilson had to paint what he saw. From a spot on the slopes of Mynydd Moel, he looked down at the crater. Unable to resist inventing the scattered boulders (he needed a foreground), he described the icy lake just as it was. The crater's edge rises against the cloudless sky with an austerity reminiscent of Bellotto's haunting vision (see page 211). In the distance lie the cliffs of Craig Goch and beyond the Bay of Cardigan. The vistas are endless. Wilson has packed infinity into this small canvas.

While this picture does not yet embrace the enchantments of the sublime, the scene conveys subjective experience, a radical departure from Wilson's earlier intellectual inventions. And, though the picture is summary and economical in its description of this forbidding and fascinating place, the germs of a new reality, individually responsive to nature, are here. This is a new message about the scale and power of nature and her eccentric qualities. While Wilson himself has not succumbed to the overwhelming scale of the natural world, as a later generation of painters would, a character in his picture has. To underscore the site's advantageous vistas, Wilson shows a man scanning the horizon with a telescope. He seems to leap back, shocked perhaps by what he sees. Here is a proto-Romantic, experiencing the sublime.

Wilson sold the first version of Cader Idris to a Welsh nobleman friend, but his Welsh views did not find the audience he had hoped for. It is perhaps symbolic that Wilson's volcano is extinct, because a decade later, Volaire and Wright of Derby would find great success with pictures of Vesuvius erupting. The next generation, Turner and Friedrich, would capture the awesome scale of the Alps. Soon conflagrations, explosions, storms, and ruins would become the standard fare of Romantic art. Too deeply rooted in the 18th century, Wilson held back. Yet, the step he took makes his contribution both original and daring and certainly worthy of admiration.

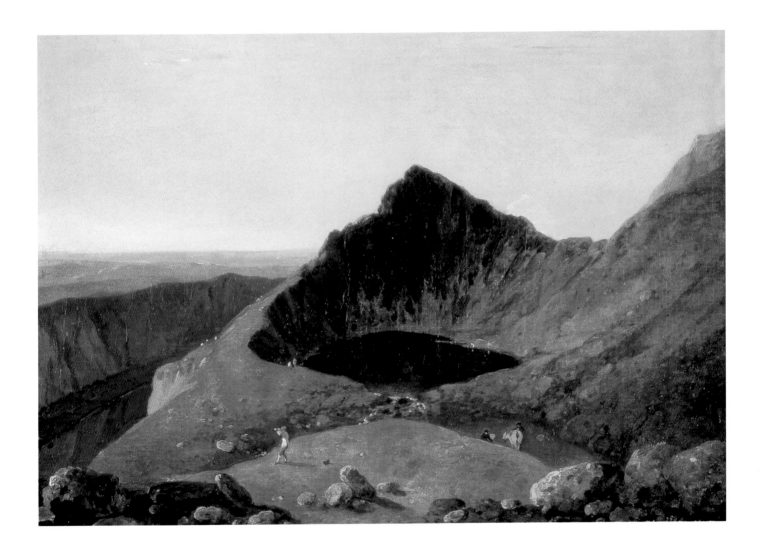

c. 1765–67 | *oil on canvas* | 19 x 28in (48 x 71cm) | Tate Gallery, London

An Experiment with a Bird in an Air Pump

RICHARD WILSON'S exploration of the Welsh mountains marked a new beginning for landscape painting. His younger contemporary, Joseph Wright of Derby, created a work that is an end in itself. *An Experiment with a Bird in an Air Pump* is a new invention, part genre, part portrait, part history painting. It remains unique and had no real imitators, yet it bears the stamp of genius. On a moonlit night in a darkened room, a company of amateurs and friends gather to witness a demonstration of a new device, an air pump. As air is pumped from a bell jar, a cockatoo collapses. Mingling direct reportage with high drama, Wright of Derby spins a timeless tale out of the prosaic reality of life around him.

After training with the portrait painter Thomas Hudson, Wright returned home to practice his trade in Derby, a manufacturing center that was actively engaged in current intellectual and scientific pursuits. Wright played his part in both spheres. In the mid-1760s he joined the group that, in the 1770s, came to be known as the Lunar Society. At monthly meetings on the Monday nearest to the full moon, members witnessed and discussed scientific experiments involving astronomy, chemistry, electricity, and medicine. The group included Josiah Wedgwood, the pottery manufacturer, James Watt, the engineer who made fundamental improvements to the steam engine, Dr. Erasmus Darwin, physician, poet, and Charles Darwin's grandfather, and Joseph Priestly, famous chemist, clergyman, and political theorist.

These gifted men were fascinated by the general availability of scientific instruments, including telescopes, orreries (which show planetary movements), and air pumps, which they added to their collections. They dabbled in geology, botany, medicine, archeology, and astronomy. Participants in the Enlightenment, when reason was emphasized and existing ideas and institutions were reappraised, the Lunar Society and others like it reshaped man's view of the world and his sense of his place within it.

The same curiosity that inspired Wright of Derby to join the Lunar Society probably assured his attendance at the scientific lectures given by the Scottish astronomer James Ferguson, who visited Derby in 1762 and demonstrated an air pump. What Wright created out of this experience makes the viewer *feel* like

JOSEPH WRIGHT OF DERBY

BORN DERBY 1734,
DIED DERBY 1797

a witness to this experiment, but this drama is the product of great artistic license coupled with careful observation of nature and a great respect for art history. From Caravaggio and his many followers Wright made this a candle- and moonlit scene, setting the whole event in dramatic chiaroscuro. From Rembrandt's Leiden followers, the so-called *fijnschilders* ("fine small-scale painters") of whom Gerrit Dou was the most famous, Wright developed his smoothly rendered, meticulous realism.

Using his friends and neighbors as models, the artist supplied a believable slice of life while creating archetypes of age, understanding, and gender. A young couple to the left are too involved in courtship to care much about the experiment, while the young girls on the right weep over the fate of their pet cockatoo (which is based on a bird Wright knew from a portrait commission). As their father tries to teach them about the harder realities of life, or comfort them with the news that not all the air will be removed—the picture is the ultimate cliffhanger—only the bewigged amateur and the young man beside him are completely absorbed in the experiment, and listen as the wild-haired old man expounds on his thesis as the experiment progresses. To the right, another gentleman is lost in thought, perhaps contemplating the larger meaning of this demonstration with respect to life, death, and mankind's place in the scheme of things.

Despite its enlightened approach to science, this picture's social attitudes are, to modern eyes, reactionary. Wright of Derby was one of the earliest artists to restore men and women (pictorially at least) to what society then believed was their proper spheres. Men think and reason, women feel. What a far cry from Watteau's androgynous couples rendered equal by mutual civility, or Tiepolo and Boucher's triumphant females! Here, women are marginalized and placed, so to speak, at the sidelines of human affairs. By expressing this shift in attitude, Wright anticipated by nearly twenty years the divided genders of David's *Oath of the Horatii* (1785, Louvre, Paris). However, in this work he accomplished far more than that. Wright's picture, so unique to his place and time, is an indelible snapshot of an era and one of the most memorable images ever painted.

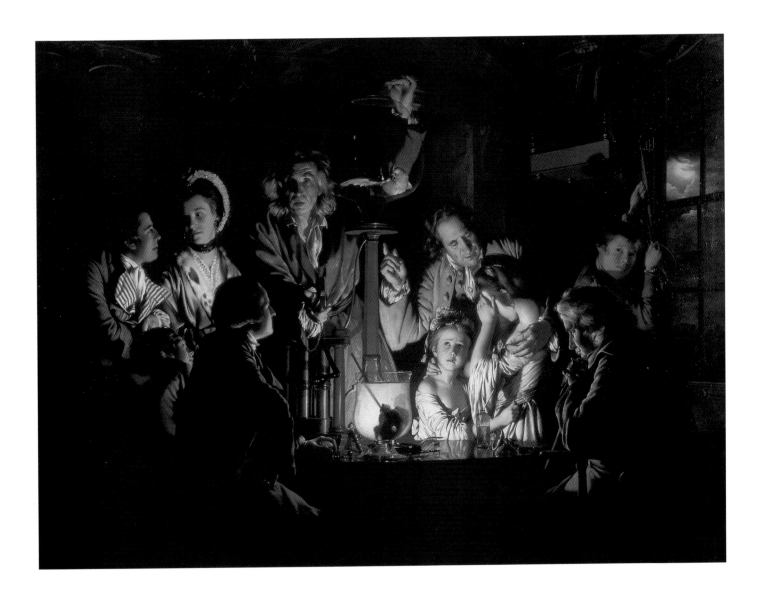

1767—68 | *oil on canvas* | 72 x 96in (183 x 244cm) | National Gallery, London

Horse Attacked by a Lion

GEORGE STUBBS was among the first artists to portray the untamed and brutal side of nature as the main subject of a painting, and he created one of the most famous icons of this theme with his *Horse Attacked by a Lion*. Chased to the edge of a cliff, a white stallion rears to a halt and turns to fend off the lion that has leapt on his back. His charged silhouette is an emblem of power, fear, and terrible beauty. Unlike the gentle dreams of Watteau, this is a nightmare, packed with furious emotion.

All this from an artist renowned for his scientific dispassion. Born in Liverpool, at fifteen Stubbs trained with a minor artist, briefly practiced as a copyist, and then struck out as a portrait painter. By 1750, he was in York producing anatomical illustrations and in 1754, went to Rome. Back in England, he spent four years (c.1756–60) dissecting horses in a barn in Lincolnshire to produce his famous *Anatomy of the Horse*, published in 1766. Supported by the horse-loving gentry and the aristocracy, Stubbs made a living painting sensitive and original portraits of brood mares, racehorses, and riders. Admitted to the Royal Academy in 1774, he resented his low status as an animal painter and the system that failed to recognize his genius.

GEORGE STUBBS

BORN LIVERPOOL 1724, DIED LONDON 1806

Like Wright of Derby, Stubbs *was* a genius and an original who stretched the boundaries of animal paintings far beyond conventional portraits. His *Horse Attacked by a Lion* is the most powerful of his portrayals of wild animals. One of his few paintings to be taken from an antique model (in this case the Roman sculpture based on a Hellenistic original that featured a lion attacking a horse, on view at the time in the courtyard of the Palazzo Senatorio), it might also be based on a real experience. On his return home from Rome, Stubbs stopped at Ceuta in Morocco where he reportedly saw a lion stalking and attacking a Barbary stallion by moonlight. Whether or not his inspiration was experience and/or ancient models, in this painting his *subject* was untamed nature at its most elemental: the hunter and the hunted engaged in a violent, mortal struggle.

By borrowing from ancient models, Stubbs allowed art for the first time to shape his vision more directly than nature. Certainly, the painted interpretation of the scene idealizes and exaggerates the situation. Not here the well-trained, domesticated horses who accept with docility the saddles, bridles, and harnesses applied by their grooms. Instead a fiery, magnificent beast is shown, starkly illuminated and simplified down to his most essential form, his body taut and whole energies concentrated on the terrible battle with his powerful adversary.

Six years earlier, the philosopher and political theorist Edmund Burke had anticipated such a change in Stubbs' style in his essay *A Philosophical Inquiry into the Origin of Our Ideas of the Sublime and the Beautiful*. Within the essay he stated, "What ever is fitted in any sort to excite the ideas of pain and danger, that is to say, whatever is in any sort terrible … is a source of the sublime." Quoting from the book of Job, he further observed that, in opposition to the draft animal which pulls a load and is not sublime, in the horse, "whose neck is clothed with thunder, the glory of whose nostrils is terrible, who swalloweth the ground with fierceness and rage … the terrible and sublime blaze out together."

Did reading Burke cause Stubbs to change his own vision? Perhaps, but more likely, like later artists, Stubbs was drawn independently to the wilder forces of nature. His general output remained dutifully clinical in its careful analysis and reconstruction of reality, but Stubbs remained captivated by the theme of the horse and lion, painting variations on it no fewer than five times between 1760 and 1772.

The example shown here comes closest to what may have been his experience in Morocco, with its nocturnal setting. Moreover, the landscape itself has become wild and restless with its dangerous jutting rockface and its swirling clouds. While Stubbs had abandoned his own treatment of this subject by 1772, his was one of the first sparks of a future explosion. Synthesizing in such summary form a primordial struggle, he linked the ancient past with a dreamlike present and anticipated the fascinations of generations to come. The sublime powers of the natural world increasingly captivated Europe's artists. Copley was entranced (see pages 222–23), and later painters such as Géricault, Delacroix, and Turner fulfilled their romantic visions with pictures rich in storms, cataclysms, and beautiful horses.

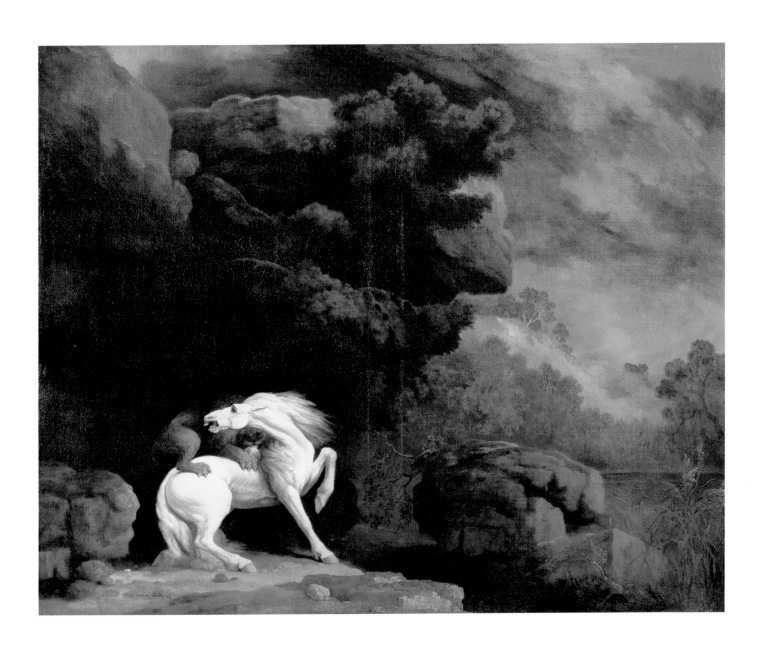

1770 | *oil on canvas* | 40 x 50in (102 x 127cm) | Yale University Art Gallery, New Haven

Mrs. Abington as "Miss Prue"

SOMETIMES ARTISTS achieve greatness when they are not even trying. Certainly Sir Joshua Reynolds was not striving for the grand historical style, which he held as the acme of painting, when he painted this intimate and casual likeness of his actress friend Mrs. Abington. Unfettered by the conventions that such grandiloquent portraits required, Reynolds created his freshest and most daring portrait of a society beauty. Sitting backward in a chair, Mrs. Abington has her thumb in her mouth as she stares distractedly, yet with bright, captivating eyes, out into space. Reynolds was the first artist to place a woman in such an unlady-like and sensually suggestive pose. No one dared try it again. Reynolds broke many rules; since he created many of them in the first place, he knew when and where to break them.

In the 1770s Reynolds was at the height of his powers. He had arrived in London from Devon in 1740 to study with Thomas Hudson (1701–1779), who would later train Joseph Wright of Derby. Already practicing as a painter in 1743, Reynolds had great ambition. He wanted to raise portraiture to the level of history painting, and went to Rome to learn how. Between 1750 and 1753, he studied Michelangelo, Titian, Raphael, and the Carracci, and learned the Grand Style, which was felt to be most appropriate for history painting and was based on generalities rather than the particular and on the ideal rather than the real. From Rembrandt he learned to read people. Like most geniuses, Reynolds was a great sponge, and his repertoire was inexhaustible. By 1755, he had already painted a hundred portraits. Everyone who mattered in society sat for him: men in uniform, grand ladies, mothers and children, writers, intellectuals, courtesans, actors, and actresses.

Reynolds promoted the need for a Royal Academy, and when it was established in 1768, he became its first president. In 1769, he was knighted. His famous *Discourses on Art*, delivered from 1769–90, laid out his artistic principles, which included the emulation of the great masters and the application of the Grand Style. The acknowledged leader of the English school, he was brilliant, profoundly learned, and inventive. In scores of portraits he achieved his hoped-for grandeur with his classical settings and mythological guises.

SIR JOSHUA REYNOLDS

☙

BORN PLYMPTON 1723,
DIED LONDON 1792

But he also knew when something else was needed, as with Mrs. Abington. At thirty-four, this former flowergirl and prostitute had become the leading actress in London, famed for her beauty and her highly fashionable style. In 1769–70, she was a success as the country ingénue Miss Prue in Congreve's 1695 play *Love for Love*, one of several restoration comedies that were revived in 1770. This was the role that Reynolds celebrated during the sittings recorded in March 1771.

Here, Reynolds faced the dual challenge of maintaining his sitter's identity while subsuming it within the character she is playing. Fresh from the country, lusty and direct, Miss Prue is both seduced and educated in the play, learning to lie as all well-bred people do. Still lovely enough for the part, Mrs. Abington plays her with style. No peasant dress for her Miss Prue; the piled-up hair, elaborate flounces, and black silk bracelets were the latest London fashion.

But Miss Prue was frankly sexual and quite ignorant of social refinements, so Mrs. Abington shows her sitting backward in her chair and distractedly sucking her thumb. Considered the height of vulgarity, the pose suited Reynolds exactly. How interesting it makes this painting. In this play within a play, Miss Prue is still learning her role. Juxtaposing horizontal and vertical elements, accented here and there by just the right diagonals, the picture is compact, direct, and unabashed. It has an alacrity, a dynamism, and a sense of fun that represents the best of what Reynolds could achieve. Mrs. Abington's tiny dog, partly obscured by the Chippendale chair, glowers ineffectually at intruders, while the role of Miss Prue gives Mrs. Abington the pretext to triumph in wanton sensuality.

One of the last and most playful expressions of female lust in 18th-century art, this portrait had no successors in English painting nor in European painting, for that matter. The second half of the century associated classical rigor with higher moral standards, renewed family values, and seriousness. This bias toward classicism blinded artists and patrons to the fun of rococo painting for more than a century. For Reynolds, it meant more grand and dignified portraits from which the only escape remained his endearing and fresh likenesses of children.

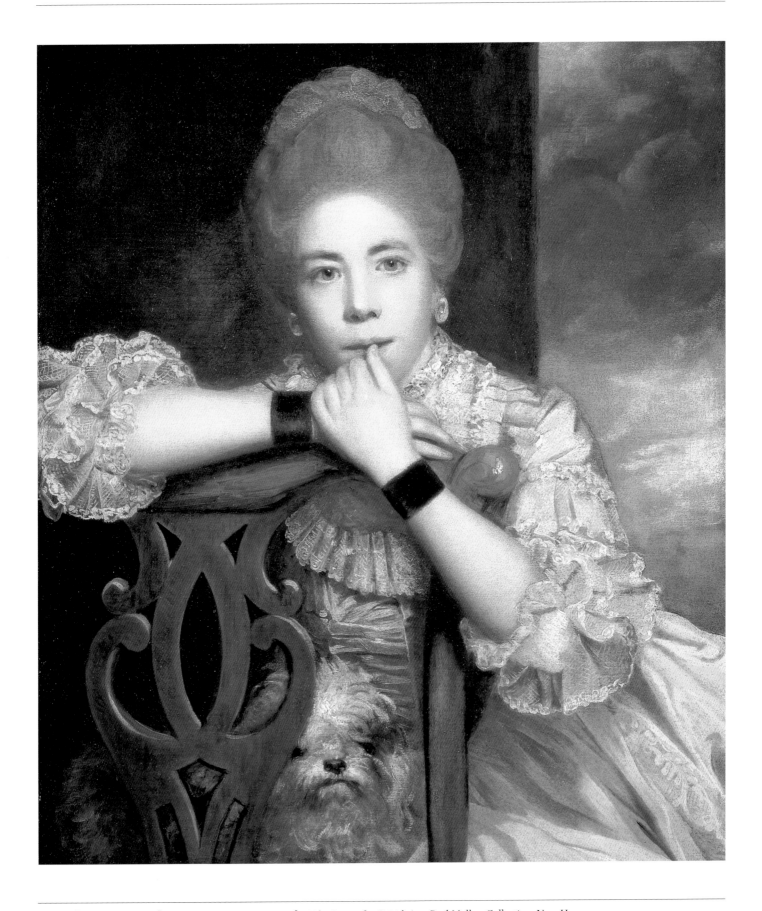

1771 | *oil on canvas* | 30 x 25in (76 x 63.5cm) | Yale Center for British Art, Paul Mellon Collection, New Haven

The Meeting, or Storming the Citadel, from Progress of Love

THE YEAR AFTER Reynolds produced his flirtatious portrait of Mrs. Abington, the French painter Jean-Honoré Fragonard completed a whole essay on flirtation, *The Progress of Love*, for King Louis XV's last mistress, Madame du Barry. Unlike her predecessor, Madame de Pompadour, whose name was synonymous with style and taste, Madame du Barry gained immortality for her bad judgment in rejecting what is now considered to be one of the greatest surviving decorative ensembles of the 18th century. She also had the misfortune to outlive her king, and was destined to fall victim to the Revolution.

Fragonard's career began well. After a brief period studying with Chardin and then Boucher, he won the Prix de Rome in 1752 and left for Italy in 1755. His *Coroseus Slays Himself to Save Callirhöe* (Louvre, Paris) was purchased in 1765 on behalf of the King and earned him membership of the Academy and the title "*peintre du roi*." Despite such official approval, Fragonard spent most of his career working for private clients. His technical mastery, fertile imagination, and deeply poetic sensibilities were applied to literary and classical subjects, and his many scenes of exuberant lovers made Fragonard the artist of choice to decorate fashionable Parisian drawing rooms.

For Louis XV, life had changed since Boucher's day (see page 208). Madame de Pompadour had died in 1764, and four years later his queen died. The sixty-eight-year-old monarch met Jeanne Bécu (1743–1793), an exquisite courtesan whose gifts at making love were legendary. She so pleased the king that he arranged for her swift marriage to the comte Guillaume du Barry in 1769 so that the new comtesse Jeanne du Barry could be presented at court. In 1770, she built a new chateau in the latest neoclassical style at Louveciennes. Fragonard was chosen to decorate it. For the apse-shaped gaming room he undertook a series of four large canvases illustrating the "four ages of love." By 1772, the pictures were reportedly in place. What could be more perfect for a gaming room than the game of love?

In his *Meeting*, also called *Storming the Citadel*, a charming doll-like creature with a creamy bosom and a gorgeous satin dress jumps in alarm at some sound in the distance. To the side, a young man has climbed up a ladder to join her. Using Boucher's device of implied portraiture, Fragonard cast Madame du Berry in the role of the beloved, and the king (remarkably rejuvenated) as the aspiring young lover. Set in a park festooned with buoyant rambling roses and light puffs of trees, the scene is presided over by a disdainful statue of Venus. It has the fantastic atmosphere of an opera stage, as the eager young lover and his beloved look out and away at some unseen distraction. Tense, beautiful, and highly charged, these lovers exhibit a passionate intensity never seen in Watteau or Boucher. Fragonard, like others of his generation, had invested a new degree of feeling into his subject.

Although his interpretation was original and the results visually ravishing, Fragonard's series was not appreciated. By 1772, Madame du Barry was severely limiting entry into "this sanctuary of pleasure." By 1773, for undeclared reasons, she returned Fragonard's pictures, although she paid him 18,000 livres. By 1774, she had replaced them with more fashionable but insipid neoclassical pictures with the same subject by Joseph-Marie Vien (1716–1809).

Fragonard's rococo style may have become dated, but he still had other clients, including Bergeret de Grancourt, a Minister of Finance who invited Fragonard to Italy in 1773. Eager to marry the king, Madame du Barry may have feared that his likeness in Fragonard's playful confections might offend him or members of his court. Regardless of her motives, her aspirations came to nothing. Louis died suddenly of smallpox in 1774. Madame du Berry was arrested and briefly confined in a convent. Some twenty years later, in December 1793, revolutionaries searched out the fifty-year-old woman and hanged her.

Had Fragonard's paintings remained at Louveciennes, they might not have survived such revolutionary passions. As it was, he took them home to his studio and later to Grasse, where he added panels of hollyhocks and a scene entitled *Reverie*, featuring a lonely figure which some believe was his revenge on Madame du Barry, who had lost her king. Fragonard himself survived the revolution under the protection of David. He lacked clients, however, and stopped painting in 1794. He was expelled from the Louvre in 1805 and died in obscurity in 1806.

JEAN-HONORÉ FRAGONARD

✥

*BORN GRASSE 1732,
DIED PARIS 1806*

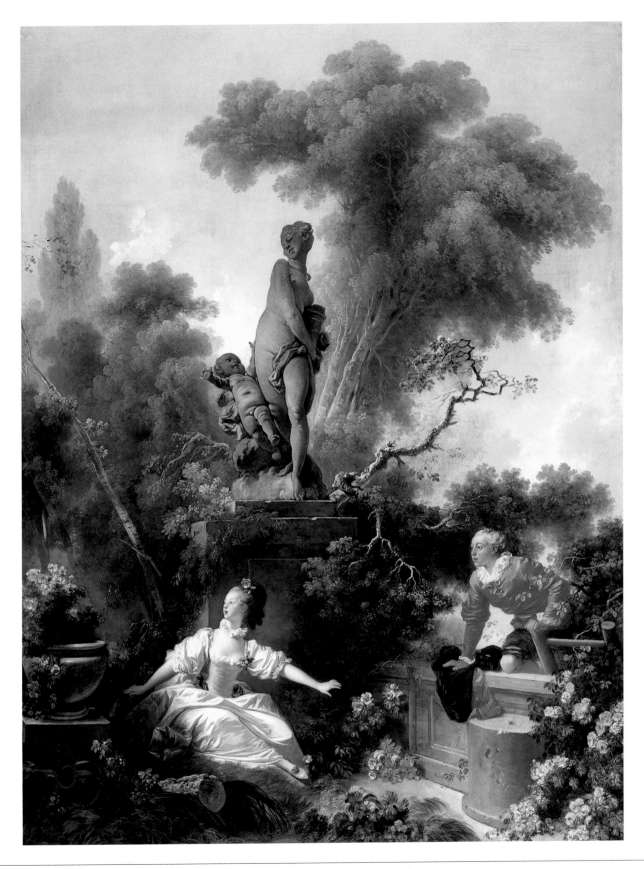

1770–72 | *oil on canvas* | 125 x 96in (317.5 x 244cm) | Frick Collection, New York

Watson and the Shark

DESPITE THEIR provincial status during the 18th century, American painters began to distinguish themselves at home and abroad. John Singleton Copley deserves special mention for producing a most unusual "history" painting. *Watson and the Shark* told the story of fourteen-year-old Brook Watson who, in 1749, lost his right leg to a shark in the harbor of Havana, Cuba, before being rescued. The boundaries of history painting were stretched to include ordinary people in extraordinary circumstances.

Having started as a portrait painter, with commissions from such notable Bostonians as John Hancock in 1765 and Paul Revere in 1768–70, Copley sent his portrait of Henry Pelham with a squirrel (1765, Museum of Fine Arts, Boston) to the Society of Artists in London in 1766. It won him praise from Joshua Reynolds, who advised a trip to Europe to improve his technique. Spending most of 1774 in Italy, Copley settled in London in 1775.

There he met Watson, by then a middle-aged merchant who made his way around London on a wooden leg. Having told Copley his story, Watson probably commissioned the picture, and the artist created a dramatic epic. On a vast canvas, the youthful Brook Watson became a blond Adonis while his rescuers gained a majesty of biblical proportions. Painted nearly thirty years after the rescue, the scene nevertheless retains the immediacy of an eyewitness account. Following on the heels of Benjamin West, whose *Death of General Wolfe* (1770, National Gallery of Canada, Ottawa) daringly portrayed a modern military scene in contemporary dress, Copley's subject, a rescue from a shark, was and is unique. Copley adapted the apparatus of history painting while retaining the veracity of experience. Exhibited at the Royal Academy in London in 1778, the painting entirely satisfied his audience. "Saved from the jaws of death," a letter published in a newspaper noted. The picture supplied drama, action, and life-and-death struggles, all from the safety of an exhibition space.

To give the scene the proper dignity, Copley borrowed from Rubens and Raphael, selecting appropriate biblical aquatic subjects. In Raphael's cartoon *The Miraculous Draft of Fishes* (1515/16, Victoria and Albert Museum, London), he found the

JOHN SINGLETON COPLEY

಄

BORN BOSTON 1738,
DIED LONDON 1815

poses for his rescuers, and from Rubens's *Jonah and the Whale* (1618/19, Musée de Nancy) he adapted the general layout of ship and fish. The shark, too, was probably based on prints of sea monsters rather than a life study. Copley worked out poses and expressions in scores of drawings, and then the whole composition was squared on a large sheet of paper for transfer to canvas.

Despite this methodical approach, the work did not lose excitement. Copley chose a compelling vantage point, placing the viewer alongside Watson and the shark. Is the viewer in another vessel or on the dock? Regardless of the answer, the onlooker has become the chief witness. The naked Watson is the epitome of vulnerability. His submerged hair seems to drag him toward the shark's open jaws, while his bloody partial leg is discreetly indicated. Part invention and partly borrowed from the antique, Watson is both individual and archetype, his body doubtless made up but his profile retaining traces of verisimilitude.

Locked into a series of parallel diagonals, the rescuers form several groups: first, the sailor with the whale hook preparing to stab the shark, the two men desperately straining to reach Watson before the shark closes in. Their own peril is emphasized by the man grasping one youth's shirt to keep him inside the boat (which is pathetically small compared to the monstrous shark). Behind them are the others, including the poignant black sailor, whose unguarded expression of helpless fear and pity parallel the reaction of the picture's viewers.

Combining under- with overstatement, Copley has modeled most of his characters from life drawings and oil sketches to give appropriate detail and credibility. Yet, the spear man and Watson possess profiles emblematic of fear (not unlike Stubbs's white stallion, see page 217). Exploiting the universal appeal of danger, Copley embraced several overarching themes, the sublime as well as redemption and salvation. Accepted into the Royal Academy in 1789, Copley prospered for some time in his adopted country, although eventually he fell out of favor and died in debt-ridden obscurity. But his remarkable *Watson and the Shark* remained in the minds of other artists; Géricault's *Raft of the Medusa* of 1819 (Louvre, Paris) cannot be imagined without it.

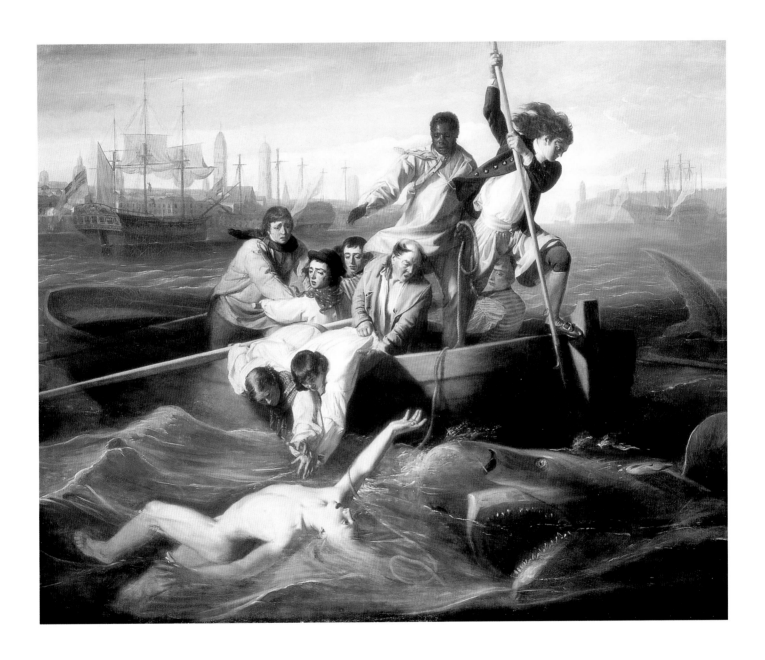

1778 | *oil on canvas* | 71½ x 90½in (182 x 230cm) | National Gallery of Art, Washington, D.C.

Death of Marat

COPLEY REINVIGORATED history painting, but the French master Jacques-Louis David made something new out of every subject he tackled. His dramatic versions of ancient moral tales enthralled salon audiences and fueled the fires of revolution. But his finest achievement is his memorial to his friend, the revolutionary Marat. A product of momentous historical events and personal intimacy, it fits no easy category but brilliantly combines political rhetoric, portraiture, an act of commemoration, and the construction of a myth.

By 1793, David had become the most potent artistic force in France, painting highly polished, didactic, neoclassical masterpieces. Encouraged by Boucher and a pupil of Vien (who had replaced Fragonard's pictures for Madame du Barry; see page 220), David won the Prix de Rome in 1774, after three failed attempts, and spent five years in Rome. He returned to Paris in triumph with his splendid *Portrait of Count Potocki* (Warsaw Museum), which was exhibited in 1781. His successes in portraiture and grand historical narratives continued and reached an apex with his *Oath of the Horatii* of 1785 (see page 195), a celebration of the antique, masculinity, and patriotism. In its wake, David joined the revolutionary forces and befriended Danton, Robespierre, and Jean Paul Marat. An unsuccessful candidate to the Royal Academy of Science, Marat was, by most accounts, an embittered, suspicious, and self-righteous journalist with a well-developed martyr complex. How he met David is not known, but by the storming of the Bastille in 1789 the two were fast friends.

Elected to the National Convention in 1792, David soon became the chief artist of the revolution. On July 12 he visited Marat who, because of a skin disease, was submerged in his bath. Charlotte Corday found him there the following day and stabbed him. Placed in charge of the funeral, David wanted Marat to lie in state in his bath. The summer heat so accelerated the body's decay that this proved impossible. David recreated the scene on canvas and produced his timeless memorial.

Moving close to his subject, David portrayed the nude Marat in his sheet-lined tub just after Charlotte Corday had struck. Still shrouded in toweling, Marat's head sinks back, and his face is bathed in light. With a sweet, beatific smile on his lips, his last breath escapes. A quill drops from his hand; the bloody knife lies nearby. Adapting his composition from traditional pietàs, David transformed a messy, chaotic assassination into an icon of peaceful martyrdom. Blending reportage with symbolism, he holds our attention. He has amended and edited the truth so carefully that nothing rings false. Although a withered invalid in life, Marat has been given long muscular arms in death. His oozing skin is now smooth and unblemished. Instead of listing candidates for the next round of executions (as was his habit), the paper on his makeshift table is inscribed in French with the words "you will give this assignation [a widow's pension] to the poor mother of five children whose husband has departed to defend the homeland." To heighten the emotional tone, David has added the simple, pathetic inscription and dedication to his friend, "À Marat, David."

First shown in the Louvre in October 1793, the painting was given to the republican National Convention the following month. David delivered a speech that was as verbose as his picture was simple, stating his belief that the image of this martyr for liberty would endure forever. While his speech is a footnote in history, David's *Marat* is one of its most memorable images. In assuring his audience that Marat really did look like the dead Christ, he deliberately deluded them about the nature and character of his subject. In that sense he adapted the tried-and-true methods of Rigaud (see pages 196–97) whose *Louis XIV* launched an era that Marat and his contemporaries had done so much to overthrow.

In 1795, Marat had fallen from favor, and David was given his picture back. David, whose revolutionary connections brought him into disrepute, gained a new role as an apologist for Napoleon. His fine images of Napoleon represent propaganda through grandeur, but none of them combine personal affection, direct experience, knowledge of art, and mastery of his medium with the deftness, conviction, and richness that underlie *Marat*. After Napoleon's fall and the restoration of the monarchy, David went into exile in Belgium, taking his *Marat* with him. Despite many invitations, the artist never returned to France.

JACQUES-LOUIS DAVID

❧

*BORN PARIS 1748,
DIED BRUSSELS 1825*

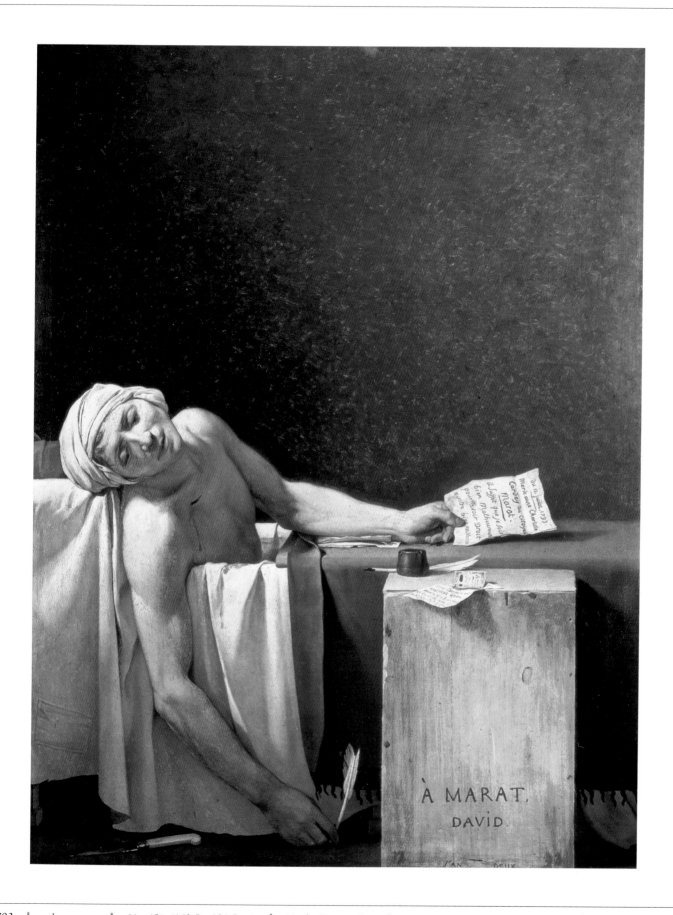

1793 | *oil on canvas* | 64 x 49in (162.5 x 124.5cm) | Musées Royaux, Brussels

THE EARLY 19TH CENTURY

1800–1850 ❧ CHRISTOPHER RIOPELLE

In 1808, the French artist Louis-Léopold Boilly (1761–1845) began to paint one of the most complex compositions of his career (private collection). It shows crowds of eager art lovers thronging the Grande Galerie of the Louvre to see the painting of the moment, Jacques-Louis David's monumental depiction of Napoleon's coronation as Emperor four years earlier (1805–7, Louvre, Paris).

I N THE PICTURE within Boilly's painting, Napoleon holds aloft a crown for his Empress, Josephine, while Pius VII raises his hand to bless the act; in reality, the Pope signally failed to do so. Napoleon's mother, a beatific Madame Mère, looks proudly on; in fact, she had been far away from Paris at the time. Not witnesses to the coronation itself, the crowd is enthralled by the (partially fictive) representation of the epic event.

Boilly's work highlights central themes of European art from the first half of the 19th century. More than ever before, art was public spectacle, viewed by increasing numbers of people who, anxious for novelty, flocked to museums and exhibitions. Rather than

Boilly's The Public Viewing the "Sacre" *(1808) captures the public zeal for art with a new "realism."*

ancient history or mythology, or the mysteries of religion, art took as its subject-matter the events of contemporary life, public or private, and rendered them in a realistic manner. Increasingly, art was about other art, and artists were ever more self-conscious in their borrowings (in this case, Boilly sought David's permission to use his painting). Art history, also an invention of the age, seemed to offer a groaning board of artistic possibilities, while new buildings, like Karl Friedrich Schinkel's Altes Museum of 1823 in Berlin, were purpose built to display art according to historical criteria. Just as David altered the events of the coronation ceremony, so too in the 19th century would artistic realism stand at a calculated remove from reality—but artifice had long been an essential component of art, and the modern world would be no different.

The century began in revolution—regularly repeated over the decades—and it frequently descended into war. Industrial expansion and economic speculation held sway. State control over art waned, and as it became mass entertainment, artists began to keep one eye on the market and the other on the press. Courbet was not alone in calculating which pictures to show where for maximum effect, and in knowing when to provoke a scandal. For the Dane Wilhelm Bendz (1804–1832), the artist's life was a subject of fascination, and he depicted his fellow artist Ditlev Blunck (1798–1854), in his studio, showing his art to his own reflection in the mirror, as if to a special friend (1826, Statens Museum for Kunst, Copenhagen). Others were equally self-conscious. Delacroix depicted the artist as a lonely, misunderstood exile; Constable and Corot drew distinctions between preparatory studies and the elaborate, highly finished works they wished the public to see; Turner turned varnishing day, when he added the final touches to his exhibition pictures, into a kind of theatrical performance, the great artist at work.

Neoclassicism and Romanticism, line and color, Delacroix and Ingres, the dichotomies battled for ascendancy in the early decades; but at the end, particularly in the art of Ingres, they became much the same thing. Naturalism, the depiction of the everyday world, was the dominant innovation. In portraiture, Géricault and Girodet explored psychological states. Landscape was newly important.

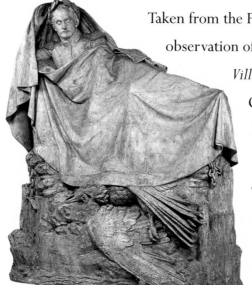

Supreme and bold propaganda: Rude, in Napoleon Awakening to Immortality *(1845–47), evokes the Risen Christ.*

Taken from the French countryside and close observation of light and atmospheric effects, *The Village at Becquigny* (1857–64, Frick Collection, New York) by Théodore Rousseau (1812–67) is deeply informed by the artist's knowledge of Dutch 17th-century landscape painting. Millet's depictions of peasant life share the grand rhythms of a Renaissance frieze.

Long after various new artistic currents had swept through France in the second half of the century, naturalism nevertheless remained a vital force in North America. The mere transcription of nature was not an end in itself, however. Artists sought to transcend the minute particularities, to probe historical and allegorical resonances.

At first sight, the famous sculpture of 1845–47 by François Rude (1784–1855) seems to depict Napoleon pulling back his cloak after a cold night sleeping on a windy battlefield. But that was not Rude's intention. What we see here is the Emperor, like Christ at the Resurrection, awakening to the glory of his immortality.

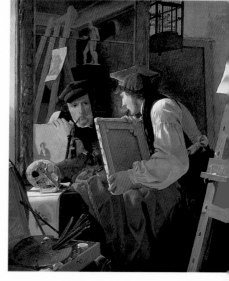

The very life of an artist was a worthy subject, as shown by Bendz's Young Artist Examining a Sketch in a Mirror, *1826.*

The Odalisque with the Slave

INGRES PAINTED little during his tenure as the director of the Académie de France in Rome from 1835 to 1841, devoting his time to teaching and administration. Only in his final years there did he take up commissions he had accepted years earlier from patrons in Paris. The first to be completed—in 1840, although it is signed 1839—was this long-promised work for Charles Marcotte d'Argenteuil. Ingres had met Marcotte in 1810 when the latter was a high French official in the Napoleonic occupation of Rome and Ingres was a struggling young artist. As he grew older, Ingres often felt more comfortable with solid, practical men like Marcotte, especially if they were connoisseurs, than he did with artists. After he painted Marcotte's portrait in 1810 (National Gallery of Art, Washington, DC), the two began a long friendship and correspondence that became a bedrock for Ingres. He could unburden himself to Marcotte, accepted criticism from him as from few others, and relied on his advice.

As Marcotte would have recognized, this strange and elegant painting harked back to those early years of their friendship in Rome; it evoked the formal experiments, the mining of eclectic sources, the deep strain of eroticism that had set Ingres's art apart from, and sometimes made it incomprehensible to, his contemporaries early in the century. Something in Rome—the heat and light? the passionate example of the Renaissance masters?—had unleashed a new sensuality in Ingres when he first arrived in 1806. In the next few years, he painted a series of single female nudes (including an astonishing image of his heavily pregnant wife, later destroyed by the artist and known only from a photograph) that are remarkable for their stylization of form, reticence, and sense of sensual self-possession. An 1808 painting of a reclining, sleeping nude became known as the *Sleeper of Naples* after it was acquired by the king of Naples. It was subsequently lost and is known only from a drawing. In 1839, Ingres recalled the abandoned pose of his lost and longed-for sleeper, arms raised, serpentine body curving toward the viewer, and used it as the central motif in his painting for Marcotte. This languorous odalisque in her seragliolike setting—one inspired by an 18th-century description of a harem—is a work of the

JEAN-AUGUSTE-DOMINIQUE INGRES

BORN MONTAUBAN 1780,
DIED PARIS 1867

most refined ostentation. The woman is tended by a musician; cool water splashes on glistening tiles. She has just laid aside her hookah before lapsing into a dream. In the background, a slave, framed between columns of jasper, guards not only the woman but the viewer from any interruption (painted by a man for another, that viewer is explicitly conceived as masculine). All the senses are evoked, and the eye traces the sleeper's swelling, marmoreal form in its polychrome setting. Given over to sensuality, the odalisque is both a prisoner in the stifling depths of a pleasure palace and of Ingres's meticulous painterly control.

The artist drew on his study of Islamic decorative motifs and objects to surround his nude with the accoutrements of oriental luxury. In keeping with the pedagogic tradition of his master Jacques-Louis David, he invited his students to help with the intensely worked architecture and ornament. Unusually, Ingres relied on earlier drawings rather than a live model to paint his nude, apparently a calculated decision as, working from drawings, he could achieve that sense of high artificiality that was his goal for the whole composition. She is an object of delectation, as unreal and provocative as an image in a fevered dream.

Such images of an exotic, sensual orient dated from the 18th century and were growing increasingly popular, especially in the light of French exploits in Egypt and Algeria. At the 1834 Salon, Ingres would have seen Delacroix's *Algerian Women* (Louvre, Paris), and his cool, enamellike creations are a Classical response to the painterly qualities of the leading Romantic artist's work. More than ever, Ingres was determined to maintain his role as the leader of the Classical school in French painting, and to pass on its lessons as the director of the Académie. Like *Antiochus and Stratonice* (1840, Musée Condé, Chantilly), the *néo-grec* masterpiece of the same period, *The Odalisque with the Slave* was meant not only for its patron but for the students who collaborated on it, as well as a wider audience of artists and critics. It was Ingres' statement of how the Classical artist should confront new and different themes in his art. At this phase of his career, every work Ingres made, even the most intimate and personal, was a public statement of his artistic purpose.

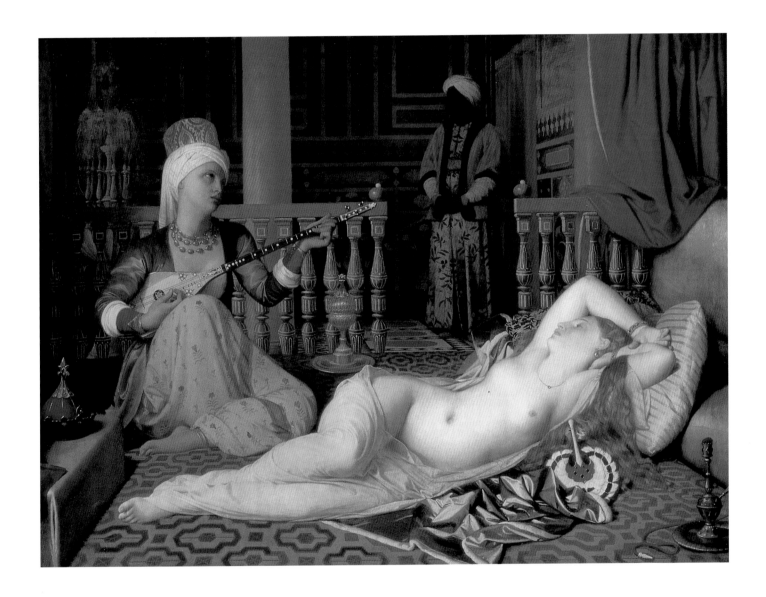

1840 ┃ *oil on canvas* ┃ 28$\frac{1}{2}$ x 39$\frac{1}{2}$in (72 x 100cm) ┃ Harvard University Art Museums, Fogg Art Museum, Cambridge, Massachusetts

Ovid Among the Scythians

EUGÈNE DELACROIX was a famous and celebrated artist, the widely recognized leader of the Romantic school of French painting, when he undertook this work in the final decade of his career. As successful as he was, Delacroix remained haunted by critical reverses of earlier years and by his meditations on the artist's role in an uncomprehending society. He had treated the theme of Ovid in exile in 1847 in the library of the Chamber of Deputies in the Palais Bourbon, Paris, although there the work was part of a large, public cycle and had been executed mainly by assistants. In 1856, as the result of a private commission, he returned to the subject. It took him almost three years of work, but in 1859, he finished and signed a large-scale although deeply personal painterly statement on the essential isolation that was, he believed, the artist's—or at least his own—inevitable lot.

For reasons that remain unclear, the Roman poet Ovid had been sent into exile by the Emperor Augustus in A.D. 8, ending up among the Scythian peoples on the Black Sea, where he would die. Delacroix depicts the poet "seated sadly on the cold, naked earth, in a barbarian land," awakening to find himself surrounded by curious natives. They are not threatening, but are uncomprehending of the stranger in their midst. They gather around to stare at and question him; shyly, a child approaches. One man milks a magnificent mare—as the Scythians were reputed to do—in order to offer the poet sustenance. For his part, Ovid rises on one elbow to study his surroundings. He is given over to melancholy as he remembers the brilliant civilization of Rome, now forever lost to him, and compares it to the open and empty landscape he will henceforth inhabit. He confronts a people whose language he does not know, on whose kindness he must rely, and with whom—his poetic gifts now all but useless to him—he must attempt to communicate. The isolation will deepen the sadness of his art.

Since the beginning of the 19th century, landscape had played an increasingly important role in French painting. Building on the innovations of Poussin and Claude in the 17th century, painters explored the potential for landscape to express and transmit moral values. Indeed, the Academy had initiated a prize for such historical landscapes. And here it is landscape as much as figures that communicates Delacroix's meaning. The small groups of men and animals, spread almost at random across a friezelike foreground, are dwarfed by the vast, mountainous world they inhabit. The upper half of the painting is landscape alone. At the center of the composition is a lake surrounded by hills, green and then blue as they rise. Clouds scud across the sky from the left. It is not clear where the Scythians have come from as few signs of habitation are to be seen. Rather, the panoramic sweep of the landscape—beautiful, varied, empty—is Delacroix's metaphor for the isolation that Ovid feels. His is the voice of civilization, and even surrounded by such beauty, he is alone and abandoned to his reflections.

Much of Delacroix's late work is made up of memory and literary reflections. The landscape here recalls the vistas of his beloved Morocco, visited decades earlier but always ready in his imagination to be poetically evoked. Or, indeed, it may relate to his readings of adventures in the South Seas. No artist of the 19th century was as deeply imbued with literary learning as Delacroix. He read widely in Classical and modern literature, drawing inspiration from both on a daily basis. If, as he grew older, his art relied less on the observation of nature—like the aged Titian, his long experience of paint and brush were now instinctual to him—more and more it served to provide Delacroix with visual equivalents for the emotions that literature suggested. In Ovid and his exile, Delacroix found the expression of his own feeling that worldly success was fleeting, loss and separation eternal. But with that realization he could reach a deeper level of sadness and personal truth in his art. Indeed, his greatest champion, Charles Baudelaire, immediately understood the equivalency that Delacroix proposed here between himself and the ancient Roman poet, writing of this painting: "All the delicacy and fertility of talent that Ovid possessed have passed into Delacroix's picture. And just as exile gave the brilliant poet that quality of sadness which he had hitherto lacked, so melancholy has clothed the painter's superabundant landscape with its own magical glaze."

EUGÈNE DELACROIX

✂

BORN CHARENTON 1798,
DIED PARIS 1863

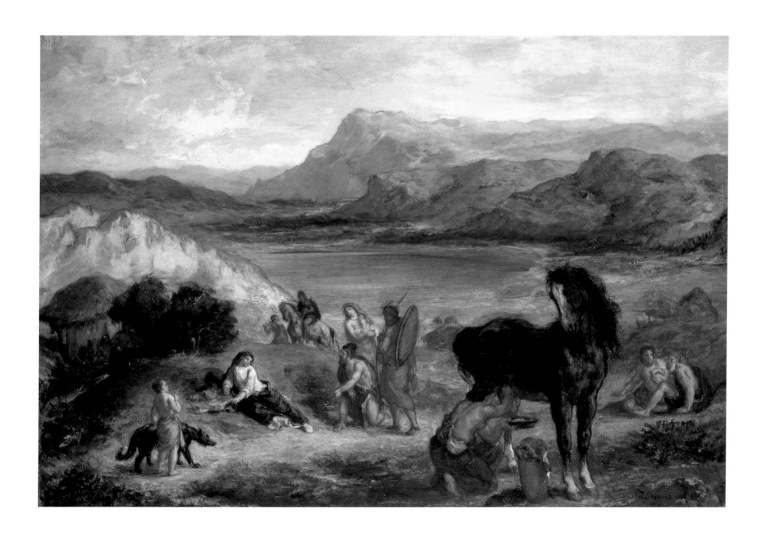

1859 | *oil on canvas* | 34½ x 51in (88 x 130cm) | National Gallery, London

The Meeting, or Bonjour, Monsieur Courbet!

Like Rembrandt, whose self-portraits chronicle every stage of his artistic life, Gustave Courbet discovered in himself one of the most compelling subjects for his art. Over and over, he depicted his own features, experimenting with multiple guises and the various ways in which he wanted to be known to the world. In some cases the results could be comic, as in one youthful, long-haired self-portrait where he contrasted himself with a floppy-eared, wet-nosed retriever (1842, Petit Palais, Paris). In others, the depictions were deeply melancholic and introspective, including one painting that showed him as a wounded man, his life ebbing away (1844, Louvre, Paris). In the early years of his career, his personality, his presence in the pictures, were intrinsic to Courbet's art; he offered himself for sale on the open market. He was vulnerable, but in control. In exposing, analyzing, and altering his personality so publicly, Courbet exploited what we would recognize today as a strikingly modern strain of self-consciousness. This was true, too, in the increasingly elaborate paintings in which he allegorized his life and artistic aspirations, culminating in the monumental *Studio* of 1855 (Louvre), where the artist at his easel—Courbet himself—stands at the very center of a vast social panoply, creating, instructing, inspiring.

GUSTAVE COURBET

BORN ORNANS 1819,
DIED LA TOUR DE PEILZ 1877

One of the numerous figures who appear in the *Studio* with Courbet is Alfred Bruyas. In Bruyas, two years younger than himself, the artist found a patron worthy of his own self-obsession. The son of a wealthy financier, he was highly sensitive and an assiduous collector of contemporary art. He bought works by leading painters like Delacroix, but until he began to collect Courbet, his taste did not necessarily run to the most advanced art of the day. What did concern him, however, was that collecting should not be a passive activity. Rather, he was determined to enter into a personal relationship with his artists, to participate in their lives, and they in his. And the collection he formed was to be, in an almost literal sense, the exact reflection of himself. Repeatedly, he commissioned his own portrait, finally owning some thirty-five depictions of himself, including four by Courbet. They were the instruments of his intense introspection. For Bruyas, acquisition and interrogation of the works

he acquired were inseparable activities. They represented as vital an engagement with art as did painting for Courbet. In 1853, Bruyas bought his first painting by Courbet, his much-maligned *Bathers* (Musée Fabre, Montpellier), and over the next two years bought a total of nine important works by the artist. For years he offered Courbet hospitality and friendship. The two men formed a strong bond: "Truth … will be God for us," they agreed, formulating plans for exhibitions and other entrepreneurial schemes. Courbet quickly recognized that Bruyas was that rare patron who could appreciate even his most audacious inventions and with whom he could collaborate to actively advance his career. For these two men, art, introspection, and entrepreneurship were intermingled, and both played all the roles. Courbet celebrated his relationship with his unusual patron in this monumental painting, undertaken in the summer of 1854 when, at Bruyas's invitation, he visited him in Montpellier.

Near Montpellier—and the depiction of the landscape is exact—Courbet has descended from the public carriage, which is about to disappear down the road on the right, and sets off on foot toward Bruyas's house. Along the way he meets his patron, accompanied by his servant Calas and a dog. They have graciously come out to greet him. Calas bows his head, Bruyas removes his hat, and Courbet, staff in hand, prophetlike beard jutting forward, receives their salutation. The imagery derives from a popular print of the time showing the Wandering Jew, a figure from medieval legend who was condemned to eternally roam the earth because he mocked Christ. Courbet presents himself as the outsider, the wanderer who makes his way alone through the world, who is also the keeper and seeker of wisdom. He is also a Christlike figure; there are echoes of Christ appearing to Saint Peter outside the walls of Rome, telling him that he is to be crucified again, and inspiring his disciple to return to his calling. For his part, Bruyas is a figure of immense dignity who greets the rough-hewn stranger in shirtsleeves as an equal. He is that rare man who is able to perceive and then freely acknowledge the genius of the artist. As he doffs his hat in greeting to Courbet, he accepts their almost sacramental alliance.

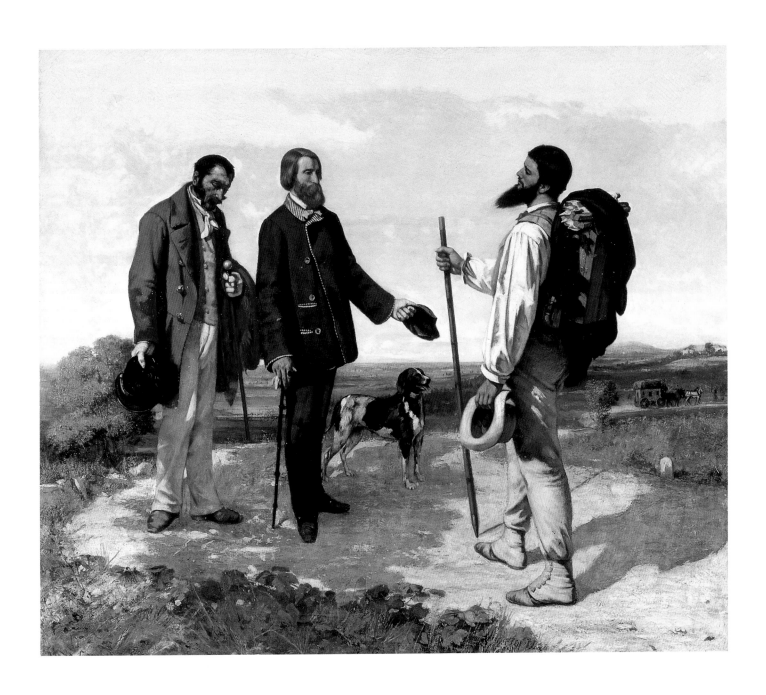

1854 | *oil on canvas* | 51 x 59in (129 x 149cm) | Musée Fabre, Montpellier

Man Grafting a Tree

RICHLY INFORMED by artistic and literary traditions, this is one of the grandest and gravest of Millet's depictions of peasant life. A young farmer bends over a humble farmyard task, the grafting of a branch onto the trunk of a tree. Simple implements are scattered around him, and the branches he has cut away lie in a pile. His placid, round-faced wife, babe in arms, has come from their thatched farmhouse to observe the age-old processes of husbandry that will provide continued fecundity. The infant also watches, recognizing its father, but as yet too young to understand that the act he performs will ensure its own future well-being. Their clothes are worn and old, but Millet animates them with subtle and muted touches of color that are unexpectedly elegant in their effect. The simplified and rounded forms of the figures, Giottolike in their gravity, suggest that an almost processional rhythm attends their modest actions. Nothing here evokes that numbing drudgery and abasement of the human spirit that Millet depicted in other scenes of peasant labor such as *The Man with a Hoe* of 1860–62 (J. Paul Getty Museum, Los Angeles). Rather, as his first biographer Alfred Sensier learned from the painter himself, Millet alludes in this painting to the bucolic verse of the ancient Roman poet Virgil: "Graft thy pear tree, Daphnis, and prosperity will pluck thy fruit." More than that, he also evokes the Holy Family, the hard-working Joseph and the Madonna and Child. The tree, fanning out above their heads, serves as a kind of baldachino, appropriate for the Queen of Heaven. And as commonplace as this motif may be, Millet's peasant family is nonetheless ennobled and timeless. They are frugal and hard-working, at one with the cycles of nature and, because of that, as prosperous as peasants need to be, as the neat farmhouse and sheaves of wheat attest. They participate in an eternal ritual of renewal, the coaxing forth of new life from the soil, and that, Millet implies, must itself be seen as a blessed act.

Having begun as a portraitist and painter of pastoral subjects, Millet came to artistic maturity with his naturalistic paintings of peasant life around the time of the Revolution of 1848. Such images quickly found favor with critics who saw radical political possibilities in the realistic depiction of the rural poor. Courbet,

JEAN-FRANÇOIS MILLET

∽

BORN GRUCHY 1814,
DIED BARBIZON 1875

too, who would go on to participate in radical politics, was also forging his career at this time by painting such scenes. It was also clear to many that the ancient traditions of peasant life were under siege, perhaps even coming to an end. Under the weight of industrialization, tens of thousands of peasants were leaving the land and flocking to the cities to work in factories and shops. Conversely, the railroad was beginning to cut through the countryside; henceforth, even travelers would have no need to attend to the realities of rural life as they hurried through the scenic fields. The peasant and his ways were quickly becoming the stuff of nostalgia. Millet's innovation—and the strategy was a conservative one—was to wed naturalism and the new appreciation of rural and peasant imagery with tradition in the form of Classical allusion and knowing references to earlier art. Piero della Francesca and Poussin were never far away.

Millet painted this work for the Exposition Universelle of 1855, where it enjoyed notable success. For the urban, middle-class viewer, sentimental about the rural life and vaguely hopeful that the elemental processes of the peasant existence—in which, thankfully, he need not participate—would endure, Millet's paintings were deeply reassuring. They helped defuse the fear, very real in the 1850s and 1860s, of peasant radicalism and the threat of political upheaval. While they were modern, in Millet's works the viewer could still perceive the roots and comforting lineaments of traditional art and traditional ways.

As resonant as Millet's imagery was for a contemporary French audience, it also struck a chord with American collectors. Indeed, two decades before the Impressionists, Millet may have been the first French artist to enjoy greater success during his lifetime in America than in France, with many of his most significant paintings quickly being sold here. Today, the Museum of Fine Arts in Boston is the greatest repository of Millet's works—despite the fact that folkways in the United States bore little resemblance to those in Europe—and no American wore wooden shoes. This painting, originally acquired by the Barbizon landscape painter Théodore Rousseau, had been sold into America by the mid 1880s and only returned to Europe in 1978.

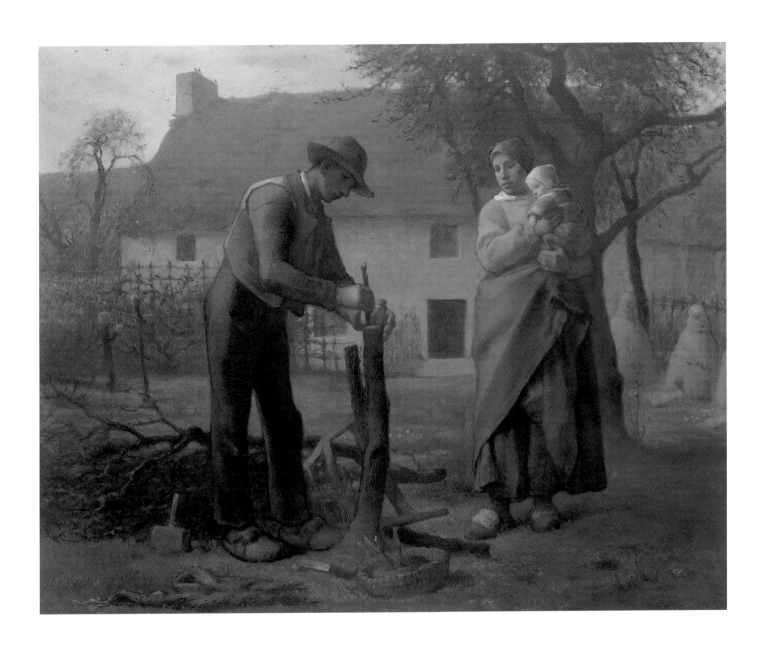

1855 | *oil on canvas* | 32 x 39½in (80.5 x 100cm) | Neue Pinakothek, Munich

Portrait of the Young Romainville Trioson

NOT AS WELL known today as many of the other artists discussed in these pages, Girodet was one of the most brilliant of Jacques-Louis David's pupils, and one of the most independent minded. Winner of the Prix de Rome in the year of revolution, 1789, in Rome he painted the strange and febrile moon-lit masterpiece *The Sleep of Endymion* (1792, Louvre, Paris), which quickly established his fame and identified him as a leading figure of the new generation. Returning to France in 1795—narrowly escaping a violent antirevolutionary Roman mob that sacked the Académie de France and wanted his head—he embarked on a career as a painter of ambitious, large-scale historical and allegorical compositions, and of portraits, and as one of the most original book illustrators of his age. Along with a few contemporaries like Baron François Gérard (1770–1837), Baron Antoine-Jean Gros (1771–1835), and Ingres, at the turn of the century he helped to renew and expand the expressive possibilities of the Neoclassical style that they had inherited from David, often in novel and ambiguous directions that the old master himself did not appreciate. Never keen on apostates, David would come to dismiss Girodet as "mad—what a pity!" He said worse of others.

ANNE-LOUIS GIRODET-TRIOSON
(ANNE-LOUIS GIRODET DE ROUCY)

∽

BORN MONTARGIS 1767,
DIED PARIS 1824

Nowhere is the difference between David and his rebellious pupil as obvious as in a comparison of his portraits and Girodet's. David's sitters, especially during the years of Revolution, were proud and confident men and women, frequently engaged in affairs of state, or at least well used to playing a role in the world. That is how David depicted them, turning to address the viewer with a clear, calm eye, a sense of purpose and control, sometimes, indeed, with a wry sense of humor. David's portraits are characterized by a remarkable directness, a mode that suited a milieu where quick, decisive actions were sanctioned and self-doubt was seen as an impediment to changing the world. Girodet, on the other hand, had always naturally preferred the shadows of night and moonlight, the enigmatic and elusive half-light to the glare of the sun. Returning to a France that, in some quarters, was itself beginning to experience doubt and to sense intimations of disaster, he introduced into his portraiture a different, more fleeting range of emotions and mental states. His sitters' thoughts are often hidden from the viewer, their eyes averted or somehow veiled, they themselves falteringly tentative as they confront the world. And who was more vulnerable than a child? The beautiful, sad boy here is Romainville, the young son of Girodet's patron, one Dr. Trioson. (Following the boy's death in 1804, Trioson adopted the painter and made him his heir, and Girodet added the doctor's name to his own.) His curly-haired head resting in his hand, the lad turns from both his schoolwork and his pleasures, represented by the crisply delineated still-life composition on the right. In his right hand, he loosely holds a Latin primer, decorated with graffiti and falling open, ironically, at the declension for "to be happy." A spinning top has been laid aside. The strings of his violin have snapped. One string leads to a beautiful blue butterfly impaled on the back of the chair on which Romainville leans. The boy gazes away distractedly. Brilliant light from the upper left falls on his face; it comes from a window or doorway, perhaps an escape route to the world beyond. But Romainville does not attend to that either, his eyes seeming to focus on nothing in particular. Rather, he is sunk in a deep and private reverie in which we are simply not asked to share. Trioson was worried about the direction of the boy's education, but Girodet, imbued with the spirit of the Romantic philosopher Jean-Jacques Rousseau's radical theories on education, expressed in his novel *Emile* (1762), advised the doctor to let his development take its natural course. In this elegant and minutely detailed portrait, in which an air of melancholy is so subtly evoked that we are not always clear in what it resides, Girodet introduced a new note to portraiture that would reverberate throughout the 19th century. His patron's young son, he observed, inhabited an essentially unknowable inner world of the mind and imagination. Through a combination of close description, the suggestion of atmosphere and the use of symbolic attributes tellingly arranged, he found the means to delineate that new truth. Exhibited at the Salon of 1800, this pivotal work in the history of modern portraiture descended in the artist's family and was rarely seen until it was acquired by the Louvre in the 1990s.

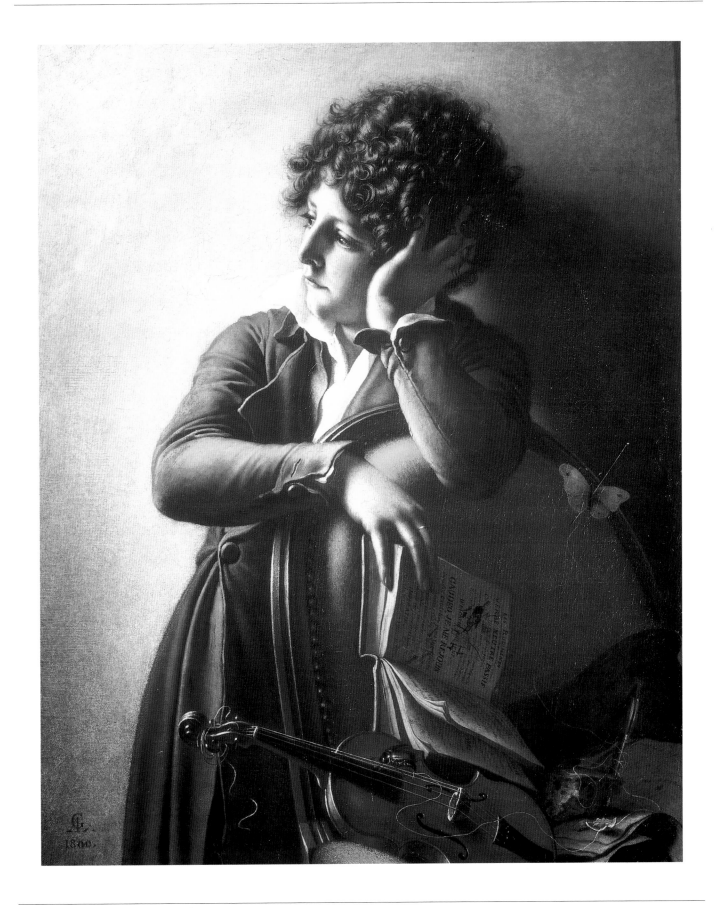

1800 | *oil on canvas* | 29 x 23½in (73 x 59.5cm) | Louvre, Paris

Portrait of a Woman Suffering from Obsessive Envy

For MORE THAN a century after his death, Géricault's portraits of the insane remained little known. While it is reported that he painted ten of them, only five have been identified. They were discovered in 1863 in an attic in the German spa town of Baden-Baden, unframed, rolled in a bundle, locked in a chest. The Louvre showed no interest in buying them (although one eventually made its way there), and they were scattered. It was only in 1927 that they received scholarly attention; since then, they have become among Géricault's best-known works. If their fame does not rival that of *The Raft of the Medusa* (1819, Louvre, Paris), they certainly are among the most widely recognized portraits of the 19th century, and still among the most unsettling.

They are conventional enough in format, not much different from the kinds of portraits that countless artists produced during the early 19th century. Bust length, the figures' heads emerge from the darkness of a largely undifferentiated background into the light. Indeed, one of the portraits, the *Kleptomaniac* (c. 1822–23, Musée des Beaux-Arts, Ghent), has something dashing, even romantic about it, perfectly in keeping with the spirit of the French Restoration era. Each of the five represents a different category of monomania, that is, an insanity that takes a particular form in each sufferer. In addition to the kleptomaniac, Géricault depicted a compulsive kidnapper, a man suffering from delusions of military command, a woman addicted to gambling, and, in this work, a woman suffering from obsessive envy. Without access to elaborate catalogs of symptoms, it is not at all clear that we would be able to identify the specific delusion that afflicted each victim. Instead, we must rely on Géricault's early biographer Charles Clément, who titled the portraits. However, even superficial observation reveals that we have entered an alien world. An odd detail such as a numbered metal identification tag around a neck, or red-rimmed eyes, or an averted gaze, soon establish that the people we observe inhabit a different realm.

The old woman driven mad by obsessive envy has strong features and a high, handsome forehead. One suspects that she was formerly a concierge, running her house with a firm, self-confident hand. But the anger and intense brooding that now eat

THÉODORE GÉRICAULT

BORN ROUEN 1791, DIED PARIS 1824

at her have altered her, and everywhere Géricault signals that alteration. The forehead is a dense plane of tortured brush-strokes. The bonnet she wears moves in an agitated pattern above her face, like the plumage of a fighting bird aroused to anger. The vigorous slashes of paint on her cloak and in the background suggest further turmoil. Her eyes, finally, are irregularly shaped, one wide and blank, seeming not to focus on anything, the other narrow, peering furiously at something unseen to her left. The man who has taken the time to paint her portrait, who stands in front of her, is of no interest whatsoever.

It is not clear why Géricault painted these somber images. He himself suffered a nervous breakdown in 1819, and the experience seems to have put him in contact with leading alienists of the day such as Dr. Etienne-Jean Georget and his master Dr. Jean-Etienne Esquirol of the Saltpêtrière Hospital in Paris. Both were at the forefront of attempts to observe and categorize the various manifestations of mental illness and to ameliorate the lot of the insane. Géricault may have made these uncompromisingly realistic portraits as records of patients whom the doctors were treating, clinically objective statements of how these people looked when caught in the throes of their dementia. Nor is it clear when Géricault painted them, in 1819 or, as stylistic criteria suggest, several years later; both arguments have been advanced.

What is clear is that the portraits reverse a long-established tradition in French art. From the 17th century of Poussin and Charles LeBrun (1619–1690), the attempt had been made to represent emotion and the movements of the human mind with such self-evident directness that any viewer, knowing how to read a painting, would be able to understand the action depicted and its moral import. This limpid, even transparent clarity represented the highest ideal of the Classical tradition in France. LeBrun himself published numerous prints of "expressive heads," codifying exactly how facial expressions were to be interpreted; one need only consult the source. By contrast, Géricault turns his eye on the insane with scrupulous objectivity, but rather than clarifying the workings of the mind, he throws into confusion and incomprehension our ability to read another human face.

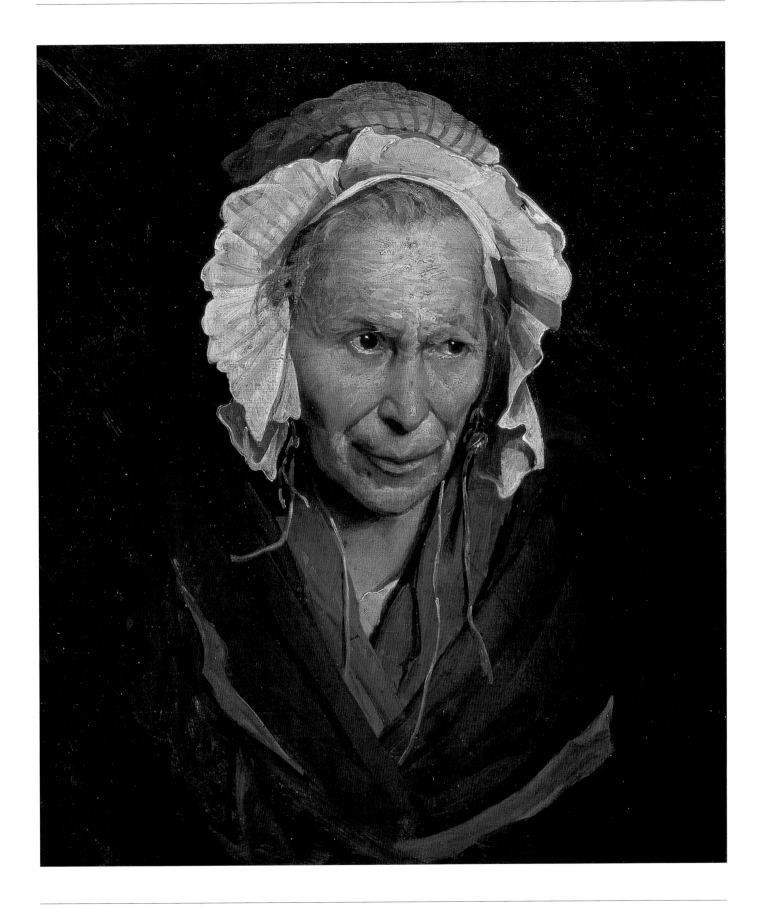

c. 1822 | *oil on canvas* | 28½ x 23in (72 x 58cm) | Musée des Beaux-Arts, Lyon

View at Narni

THE TRADITIONAL distinctions in French art between different categories of painting were strictly enforced throughout the first half of the 19th century. Even though, from the 18th century, landscape painters had been encouraged to paint outdoors, in front of the motif, the resulting oil sketches were in no way considered to be finished works of art. Rather, they were references, aides-mémoire that captured fleeting effects of light and atmosphere, from which, back in the studio, the artist could work up fully finished, Classically balanced compositions. Large in scale and elaborately framed, such completed works alone could adequately announce the painter's ambitions when exhibited at the Salon. The sketches themselves were filed away in a corner of the studio, forgotten or referred to from time to time as the artist worked on new compositions. Often, such works came to the attention of the public only decades later when the contents of an artist's studio were dispersed by the executors of his estate. If these *plein air* sketches are today highly valued and much sought as expressions of a painter's fresh, immediate, and unmediated perception, for a young landscapist of the 1820s like Corot, unknown and anxious to establish a name in the Paris art world, they were merely preliminary statements, one step in a complex painterly process, a means to a larger end.

In 1826, Corot was traveling in Italy, searching for motifs and painting brilliant, light-filled oil sketches throughout the Roman Campagna. In September, he reached the small hill town of Narni, on the Nera River. There, as many artists before him had, including his masters Achille-Etna Michallon (1796–1822) and Edouard Bertin (1797–1871), he painted and sketched the ancient Roman bridge (a hundred feet high by four hundred feet long), which, since the age of Augustus, had spanned the Nera as it flowed to join the Tiber. The oil sketch on paper that he made there (Louvre, Paris) is a masterpiece of concision and atmospheric observation. With wide, quick, open brushstrokes, Corot captured the crisp, dry light as it played across the valley floor, revealing the stark architectonic forms of the bridge and the soft fields and hills beyond. That the work is a sketch is immediately revealed by its vague foreground; the *plein air* painter did not observe what was immediately beneath his feet but concentrated on the middle distance. For generations, and especially in the light of later Impressionist innovations, Corot's sketch has been almost universally admired for its spontaneity and captivating breadth of vision.

In 1827, Corot introduced himself at the Paris Salon by presenting contrasting morning and evening landscape scenes. For the former, he chose to depict the bridge at Narni (the companion piece was *The Roman Campagna*, also called *La Carvara*, c. 1826–27, Kunsthaus, Zurich). The painting that Corot showed at the Salon is not merely a larger, more elaborate version of his oil sketch, but an artificial construct—in this context, the word *artificial* has no pejorative connotation—preceded by composition drawings, slowly elaborated in the studio, and altered and amended as work on the canvas continued. It refers to the earlier sketch almost in passing, but no more than that. This was perfectly in keeping with advanced landscape practice of the day. For the finished painting, the artist was expected to bring to bear not merely his observations of the motif—as essential as they were if truth was to be maintained—but his powers of composition, knowledge of landscape tradition, most notably the art of Claude Lorraine, and skills of invention. The esthetic worth of the painting lay not in the motif, but in the artist's ability to ennoble it. The Ottawa painting, which hung in Corot's bedroom until the day he died, brilliantly illustrates that process of elaboration. The viewpoint is more elevated, and therefore wider, than in the oil sketch. Carefully placed trees block the view on the left while allowing the eye to follow the river beyond the bridge to the open vista in the center. Light effects are subtly harmonized across the composition, but in addition to a general effect, the eye also finds interesting details, vivid touches, on which to pause. A path is introduced on the left, along which sheep and goats meander, while peasants animate the scene. Only in recent years have we again come to understand and appreciate the esthetic criteria that Corot himself brought to bear when, as here, he made the complicated, indirect, and self-conscious transition from oil sketch to exhibition picture.

JEAN-BAPTISTE-CAMILLE COROT

∽

BORN PARIS 1796,
DIED PARIS 1875

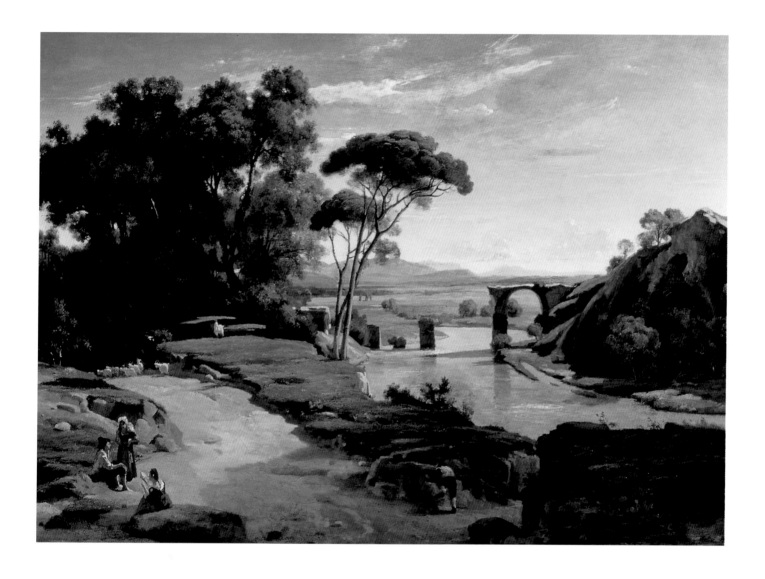

c. 1826–27 | *oil on canvas* | 27 x 37in (68 x 93cm) | National Gallery of Canada, Ottawa

The Cross in the Mountains
(Tetschen Altarpiece)

CASPAR DAVID FRIEDRICH stands at the vital heart of the German Romantic movement in painting. Born in Pomerania, trained in Copenhagen, and practicing as an artist in the innovative art center of Dresden, he devoted himself to the study of the local landscape. As minutely particularized as his depictions of landscape are, however, objective description was never his goal. Following the lead of German Romantic writers of the late 18th century, he strove to explore the spiritual dimension that for them was inherent in nature. The meticulous, austere canvases he painted in the latter part of his career—forest, seacoast, and clifftop scenes, sometimes in mist or under snow and often populated by solitary figures, silhouetted against the horizon in the strange light of dawn, dusk, or moonlight—expanded the expressive range of landscape painting. Most of Friedrich's earliest works, however, were sepia drawings. Only in 1807 did he turn to oil painting, perhaps upon accepting a commission to paint this work, an altarpiece for the private chapel of Count Thun und Hohenstein at his castle at Tetschen in Bohemia. The altarpiece was based on an earlier sepia design. The concept Friedrich proposed to the count, and the finished painting he displayed in his studio on Christmas Day 1808, could only prove controversial, so audaciously did the artist flout convention.

Whether painted or carved or combining many media, the Christian altarpiece had been a constant category of Western art since the Middle Ages. Depicting Christ or the Virgin and often peopled with saints and angels shown with precise attributes and accessories, it inspired believers to contemplate the mysteries of their faith. The representation of divine figures as if inhabiting a corporeal world was meant to lead the viewer to experience the presence of the divine. In the Tetschen Altarpiece, that divine presence is at a double remove. On a canvas rounded at the top and surrounded by a carved wooden frame filled with allegorical motifs and shaped like a pointed Gothic arch—made to Friedrich's own exuberant design—the artist depicted a mountain landscape filled with jutting fir trees. Emerging from the trees just off-center is a gilt crucifix that is angled away from the viewer. It is not a formal, iconographic representation of Christ crucified, but a homely devotional object depicting the crucified Christ, of a kind often found at the time in such mountain landscapes. It catches the rays of the setting sun sitting beyond and below the mountain top. Friedrich later said that the sun represented God the Father, but the canvas is pervaded by the melancholy sense of *failing* light, of impending darkness and oblivion. Further, Friedrich did not indicate to the viewer where we stand in relation to the mountain and the crucifix, nor do we have a firm sense of scale. That such an ambiguous landscape image, so far removed from the traditions of devotional painting, should present itself as a Christian altarpiece was seen by some critics as bizarre, deeply troubling, and even sacrilegious. This was mere nebulous mysticism without a grounding in faith. However, the critical hostility actually made Friedrich's name.

CASPAR DAVID FRIEDRICH

*BORN GREIFSWALD 1774,
DIED DRESDEN 1840*

In the 19th century, religious painting was a major artistic industry. Walls of church after church across Europe and America were filled with images depicting the lives of Christ and the saints. In the sheer scale of the collective undertaking, only the 15th century in Italy can compare. Nonetheless, very few, almost none, of those images are today seen to rank as major, canonical works of the time. In France, indeed, Baudelaire declared that only Delacroix's religious paintings carried any conviction whatsoever, while all the rest fell below the threshold of his critical attention. On the other hand, with the possible exception of Neoclassicism, landscape painting is seen as central to all the major artistic movements of the time, from Romanticism to Post-Impressionism. Earthly nature replaced the vaulted dome of heaven as a subject of artistic investigation and innovation, just as, inexorably, the sea of faith ebbed away. In retrospect, Friedrich's reconciliation of two traditions, religious painting and landscape, can be seen as one of the century's most convincing attempts to reanimate the representation of faith, and to resurrect a dying convention of vast significance to the Western tradition. It had limited effect outside Germany at the time, as Friedrich was little known beyond its borders until the 20th century. In Germany, however, his art has always been widely admired, indeed, seen as the linchpin of the national school.

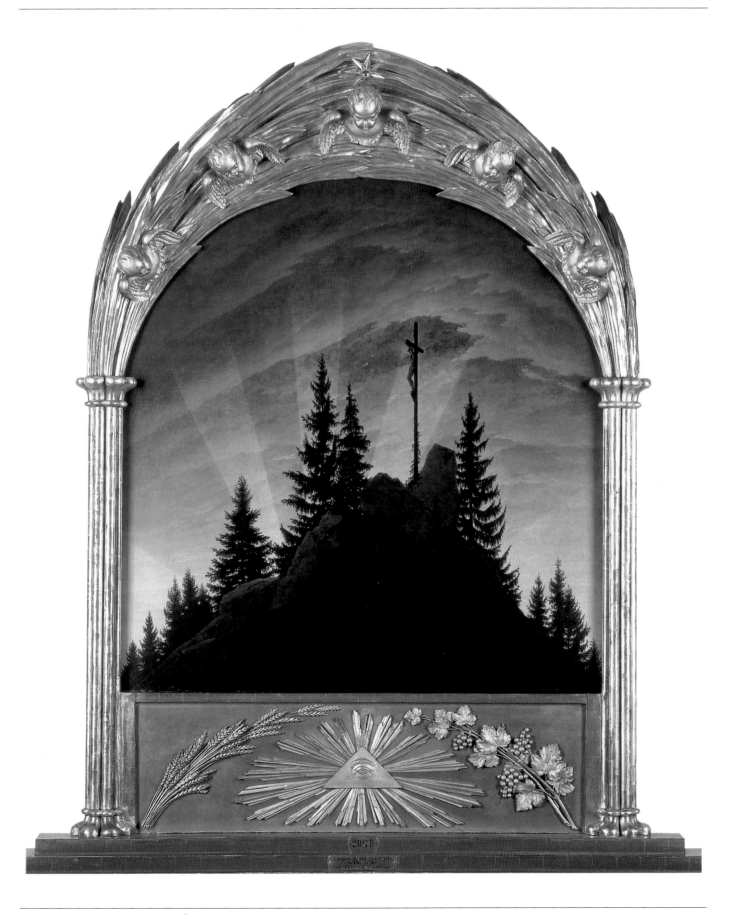

1807–8 | *oil on canvas* | 45½ x 44in (115 x 110.5cm) | Gemäldegalerie Neue Meister, Dresden

Living Room with the Artist's Sister

TODAY, EXHIBITIONS with eighty works of art in them are called "blockbusters." A century ago, art lovers had a longer attention span. When Adolph Menzel died in 1905, his memorial exhibition in Berlin included seven thousand items! That daunting figure was hardly adequate, however, to illustrate the artist's protean energy and encyclopedic accomplishments. During a career that spanned seven decades, Menzel was the indefatigable chronicler of Berlin, the city to which he moved in 1830. He turned up, it seems, for every ceremony of state, theatrical performance, construction project, and departing train and made rapid and dazzling pencil sketches of the passing scene, effortlessly capturing a fleeting gesture or random encounter. Often he turned his attention to the most unassuming aspects of daily life, an open grave with a few planks laid across it, a fur coat idly tossed onto a chair, a plate of Norwegian oysters. Suppurating corpses were a specialty. The countless details he recorded in his sketchbooks frequently found their way into Menzel's complex and crowded oil paintings of urban life. The emperor leaves to join his army, and the whole town—or at least the respectable half of it—turns out to say farewell. Revelers at a court ball sit down to a noisy supper. In the most ambitious painting he ever undertook, *The Iron Rolling Mill* of 1875 (Nationalgalerie, Berlin), Menzel meticulously recorded the efforts of dozens of sweating iron workers in a vast, gloomy factory, their actions eerily illuminated by the molten iron itself; a contemporary subtitled the painting *The Modern Cyclops*, and Menzel did not demur. The contemporary scene was not his only subject, however. Menzel was deeply nostalgic for the 18th-century Prussian past and the exemplary acts of his hero, Frederick the Great. Some of his happiest pictorial inventions are amusing evocations of court life amid the Rococo splendors of Frederick's palace of Sans Souci from a period decades before the artist was born.

With his ceaseless wandering across the face of Berlin in search of motifs, tireless travels through Europe to show his works and to see those of fellow artists, and the endless stream of paintings that emerged from his studio in Sigismundstrasse, it is a wonder that Menzel found time to spend at home. In fact,

ADOLPH MENZEL

BORN BRESLAU 1815,
DIED BERLIN 1905

although he never married, homelife—the intimate rituals of his family and the private and tranquil realm of the family apartment—was very important to him. Moreover, domesticity provided him with a compelling artistic theme, repeatedly explored. In 1847, following the death of his mother the year before, Menzel and the family moved to an apartment at 43 Ritterstrasse, where he painted this small oil sketch on paper. It is evening, lamps have been lit, and Menzel's twenty-four-year-old sister Emilie, her throat and cheek delicately illuminated by the candle in her hand, peers tentatively around the living room door. We do not know what she is looking at. Deep within the room, an older woman—her back to us, the silhouette of her shoulder outlined by the glow of a table lamp—sits reading. Loosely and quickly painted, the picture has the spontaneity of a chance encounter, a momentary conflation of flickering light and inconsequential domestic acts upon which Menzel had stumbled. Only slowly does the viewer realize how taut and architectural is the structure of this composition. The closed door around which Emilie peers and the open door on the left, seen obliquely, frame the interior space. Within, the lines where ceiling meets wall and wall intersects with tabletop create three rectangular pictorial areas, vertically stacked, while the framed pictures on the wall add two more. The women are crisply enframed by the space they inhabit. Everywhere, one form in the foreground echoes another further back. The white front of the girl's blouse repeats the white shade of the table lamp; her dark skirt mirrors the tablecloth and the dress of the other woman; candlelight glints off the edges of the doors and off the gilt picture frames on the far wall. Hanging from the ceiling, finally, is a lamp in the shape of a winged putto; it is as if a celestial being were bringing a blessing, an intimation of the divine, into the enclosed domestic realm.

Only at the turn of the 20th century would the Nabis painters in Paris, particularly Vuillard and Bonnard, and the Dane Vilhelm Hammershøi (1864–1916), who repeatedly painted his family apartment in Copenhagen, again explore what Menzel had so brilliantly captured here: that a spiritual dimension is indeed inherent to everyday life and quiet familial relations.

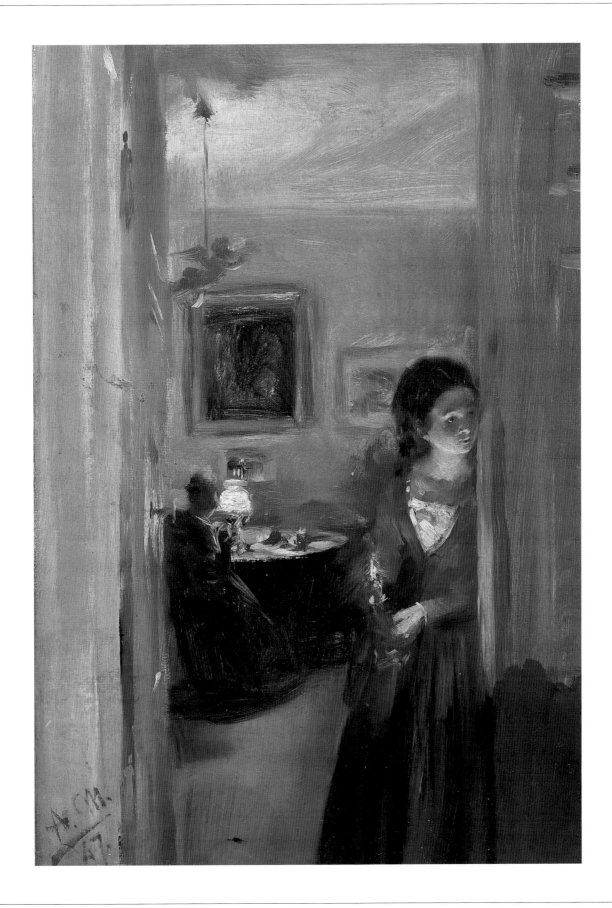

1847 | *oil on paper* | 18 x 13in (46 x 32cm) | Bayerische Staatsgemäldesammlungen, Neue Pinakothek, Munich

Work

By THE mid-19th century, artists across Europe were searching for ways to create an art that found its subject-matter in the modern world, addressed contemporary themes in a naturalistic manner, and aspired to the gravity, complexity, and monumental scale of traditional history painting. Living and working in the London suburb of Hampstead in the 1850s, Ford Madox Brown made one of the era's most novel and audacious attempts to achieve this ambitious synthesis. Poor and, as he confided to his diary, "a little mad," in 1852 he began to paint a complicated allegory of labor, grounded in the particulars of London life. Like contemporaries unknown to him—Courbet in Paris and Menzel in Berlin among others—he saw that the toil of working men—breaking stones, rolling iron or, as here, digging a water main—was an apt subject for an art that presumed to social and moral relevance. Slow, meticulous, full of doubt, it took Brown over ten years to complete his painting. At one point he put it aside until, in 1856, he received a firm commission for the work from a Manchester patron, and then another in 1859 from a Newcastle collector for a half-size replica (Birmingham [England] City Museum and Art Gallery). He finished them simultaneously in 1863.

Work shows Heath Street in Hampstead. Brown painted the background houses and twisting road on the spot as he began his project. He then filled the foreground with figures representing the various aspects of work. At the center of the composition are the manual workers; one is seen in noble profile while another bends to his task. They are surrounded by other manifestations of labor, including a pastry cook, who stands for superfluous work, a gatherer of botanical specimens, never trained to work, and a rich man and his daughter on horseback, who have no need of work. On the right, contemplating the social panoply, are the mental workers, or intellectuals, in this case the historian Thomas Carlyle and the Rev. F. D. Maurice, founder of the Working Man's College, both of whom Brown admired. Though seeming to be idle, the intellectuals regulate society and promote happiness in others. Many more figures, from urchins to merchants to fine ladies, swell the rumbustious scene. Dogs, pure-breeds and curs, scamper through the throng. Where the

FORD MADOX BROWN

*BORN CALAIS 1821,
DIED LONDON 1893*

vista opens and the street rises up the hill, Brown added several vivid vignettes of suburban life and topical details such as contemporary posters, all related in one way or another to the central group and controlling theme. We need be in no doubt as to the meaning of these figures and the incidents that Brown depicts. In the catalog of an 1865 exhibition, the artist provided a five-page description of every detail and its significance, and the frame, too, is inscribed with pertinent quotations.

Brown was not a member of the Pre-Raphaelite Brotherhood, founded in 1848, but a slightly older mentor to some of its members and an influence on the development of its high-minded art. He studied in Europe before settling in London in 1844. There, he soon left behind historical compositions in favor of many bright, vibrant paintings on modern themes. His most famous work, *The Last of England* (1852–55, Birmingham City Museum and Art Gallery), earnestly addressed a perceived social problem: middle-class emigration. If the English alone could take such a painting seriously, *Work* was a more provocative undertaking, with wider implications. It confronts a vast theme, and its pictorial space is full to bursting with anecdote and myriad detail. Its antecedents lie in part in the teeming, allegorical market scenes painted in the 16th century by Flemish artists like Pieter Aertsen and Joachim Beuckelaer (c. 1533–1573). Brown had studied in Belgium, and the sudden dive into deep space on the right of *Work* also reveals the artist's debt to such Flemish sources. Its true pictorial heirs were vanguard works such as Seurat's *Sunday on the Island of La Grande Jatte, 1884* (see page 272), Ensor's *The Entry of Christ into Brussels* (see pages 276–77), and *The Fourth Estate* (1898–1901, Civica Galleria d'Arte Moderna, Milan) by Giuseppe Pellizza da Volpedo (1868–1907). Like *Work*, these are monumental compositions, crowded with life, that dare to encompass a broad social spectrum and address social issues. Indeed, *Work* would have been more powerful still had Brown dared to execute it on a far grander scale. Its proportions, composition, and intellectual ambition owe a debt to Raphael's frescoes in the Vatican Stanze (see pages 102–3), but, small in size, *Work* unwittingly reveals its cramped, suburban origins.

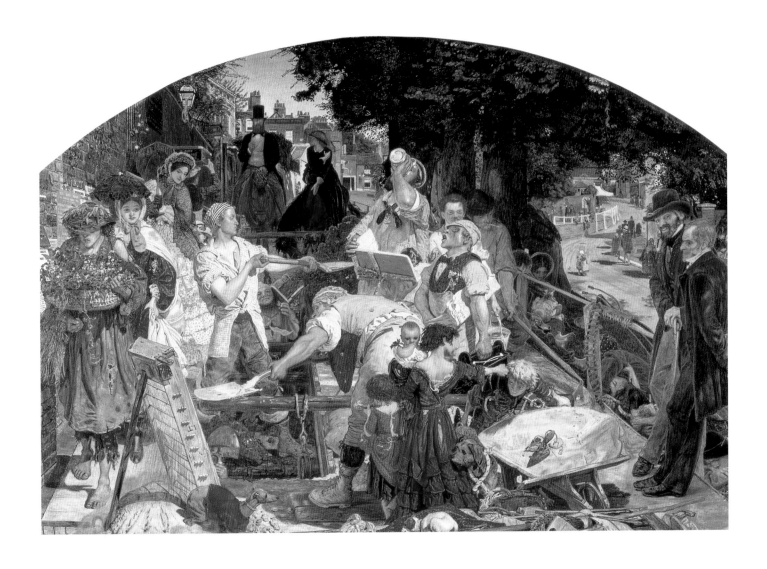

1852–63 | *oil on canvas* | 54 x 78in (137 x 197cm) | Manchester [England] City Art Galleries

The Opening of Waterloo Bridge

THIS IS THE largest painting Constable ever exhibited. It depicts the Prince Regent at the foot of Whitehall Stairs on June 18, 1817, as he embarked on a colorful royal barge, accompanied by other flag-bedecked barges, including that of the Lord Mayor on the right. He was about to make the short trip down the Thames to officiate at the ceremonial opening of the handsome, new, arched stone bridge seen in the distance, named in honor of Britain's decisive military victory over Napoleon two years earlier. This was one of the great public spectacles of the new peace and called vivid attention to the ceaseless expansion of London, the largest city in the world at the time, as yet another bridge was thrown across its principal thoroughfare, the River Thames. Constable was there that day and sketched the scene. He determined to make it the subject of a large-scale exhibition picture, but fifteen years passed before he displayed this painting at the Royal Academy. By then, his conception of the picture had been expanded and refined into a celebration of London itself.

Though the chronology is complicated, we can trace the evolution of Constable's vision almost step by step. In about 1819, he made two small oil sketches focusing on the embarkation of the Prince Regent and in the early 1820s, a very large study, again centering on the royal party. In about 1826, however, he returned to the site to make new drawings, but positioned himself farther up-river and on higher ground, on the terrace of Pembroke House. From this vantage point, the departure of the Prince Regent from Whitehall Stairs receded in importance, but the panorama of London opened up more fully before him. Two half-size versions of the final painting soon followed (Yale Center for British Art, New Haven; private collection). On the right, he incorporated into these studies and into the final work a tall shot tower (for making bullets) on the South Bank that was only constructed in 1826, a decade after the events depicted. Thus, for Constable, the specific historical moment was declining in importance. Instead, as he worked on the picture, he added more and more details of the city, and of the vast, cloud-filled sky that crowned it, as dramatic and full of interest as the watery pageant itself. As the opening of the Royal Academy's exhibition approached, Constable reported that he was "dashing away at the great London," as he had come to call the painting. It is indeed London that Constable lays before us, the great sweep of river-front from the bow-fronted house at 5 Whitehall Yard, left, past Somerset House—then the home of the Royal Academy, where the picture would first be seen—to the new bridge (demolished in 1937) and to the dome of St. Paul's beyond. The incomparable city shimmers in the sunlight, and the canvas itself, deeply encrusted with paint, is flecked with bright jewels of color that add to the sense of animation and swift, scudding movement. New to the finished work, to the foreground Constable added a parapet topped by urns; behind it the viewer stands to admire the panorama, while two boys, caught up in their own games, turn their backs on the festivities.

One early viewer said that the painting was the equal of Canaletto, and surely Constable was emulating the great Venetian master of cityscapes. In no other country had Canaletto found as many patrons as Britain; even today, no place is as rich in his works. Canaletto made extended visits to England in the 1740s and 1750s and painted some of the most compelling images of London, many of them representations of the Thames and the landmarks that line its banks. Conscious of English aspirations to monumental landscape painting, here Constable undertook a more ambitious representation of the capital than even Canaletto had attempted. When he saw it on varnishing day at the Royal Academy, Turner disapproved of the painting's bright colors. Fearing that they threw his own contribution into the shade, he added a last-minute note of red to his submission (*Helvoetsluys—the City of Utrecht, Going to Sea*, 1832, Indiana University Art Museum, Bloomington). And one wonders how well he remembered this dazzling, epic image of the city when, two years later, London offered another awesome spectacle as the Houses of Parliament blazed. Turner sketched the conflagration from across the river and produced two of his own most dramatic works of a London engulfed in flames (1834, Philadelphia Museum of Art; 1835, Cleveland Museum of Art) which, like Constable's vast panorama, reimagined the cityscape as history painting.

JOHN CONSTABLE

BORN EAST BERGHOLT 1776,
DIED LONDON 1837

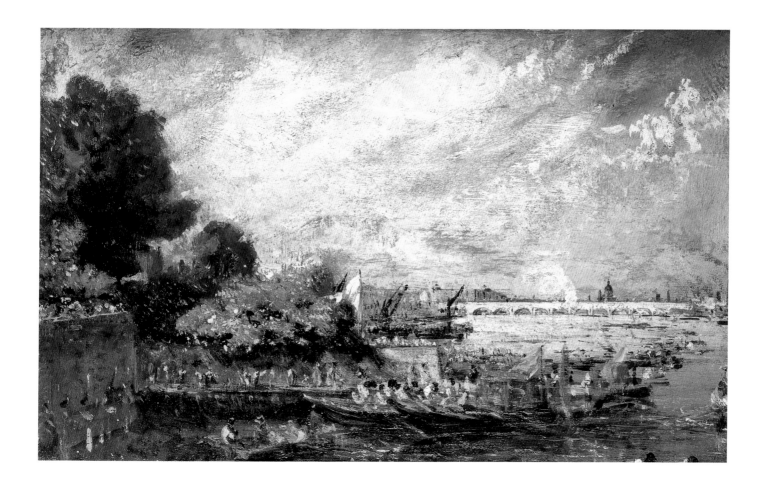

1832 | *oil on canvas* | 52 x 86in (131 x 218cm) | Tate Gallery, London

The Life Line

WINSLOW HOMER found one of the great themes of his art, the relentless power of the sea and the bravery of those who face it, when he spent time at Cullercoats on the northeastern coast of England in 1881. There, he witnessed the sinking off Tynemouth of the ship the *Iron Crown* and the daring rescue of its crew by the local lifesaving society. During the night of the disaster, Homer made sketches on the beach. Immediately after, he painted an austere and dramatic small canvas in oils, depicting sailors huddled against the sea wall as they waited to know the fate of their companions still on the water (private collection), then went on to paint a large watercolor showing a lifeboat making its way through the chopping waves to the listing ship where one man remained (*Wreck of the Iron Crown*, 1881, Collection of Carleton Mitchell, on extended loan to the Baltimore Museum of Art). Homer appreciated the quiet, steadfast nobility of the local fisherfolk whom he sketched and painted as they went about their daily rounds, working from life, in the manner of the French Impressionists. The dramatic and dangerous events surrounding the sinking of the *Iron Crown* and the rescue of its crew confirmed for him that, even *in extremis*, the strength and goodness of the people also manifested itself.

WINSLOW HOMER

BORN BOSTON 1836,
DIED PROUT'S NECK 1910

Early in the rescue of the *Iron Crown*, lifesavers used a breeches buoy to reach the sailors. This apparatus was relatively new. A rope would be tossed overboard from the sinking ship and carried to shore by the waves; it would then be secured on land and a lifeguard could make his way along it to the ship. With a victim supported in a breeches-shaped life-buoy, he could then be pulled back to shore and safety. Homer arrived on the scene too late to see the breeches buoy in operation that night, but he would have heard accounts of it. Two years later, in the summer of 1883, in Atlantic City on the New Jersey coast, he sought out the local lifesaving crew, questioned them about the device, and saw it demonstrated. Perhaps he sensed that, even more than a lifeboat tossed on the waves, the breeches buoy, with its rescuer and victim trapped in an elemental struggle with the overwhelming forces of nature, offered him a simple but powerfully immediate encapsulation of the entire drama of rescue at sea.

The following year, he exhibited this painting at the National Academy in New York, where it was rightly and enthusiastically acclaimed as one of the artist's masterpieces.

Shipwrecks remained a common aspect of sea travel throughout the 19th century, and lifesaving societies were a standard form of mutual aid in coastal communities. Homer's painting does not depict a specific rescue, but is a generalized representation of the distress and heroism that were inescapable aspects of life by and on the water. Indeed, having originally represented the lifesaver's face, Homer came to feel that even such a small detail drew too much attention away from the whole image, and so he covered the face with the woman's shawl. We are aware only of the physical strength and brute force of the rescuer as he clutches the woman and works his way back to shore. The woman herself is unconscious or partly so. Head thrown back, arm limp, clothing drenched and torn, she is held in the powerful arms of her faceless savior. He has carried her from the storm-tossed ship, its sails fluttering wildly and uselessly on the left. The two are suspended in a trough between two foaming waves, one soon to splash over them with possibly fatal force. Their fate at the riveting moment that Homer depicts remains, terrifyingly, unknown.

Locked in their frantic embrace, the couple resemble nothing so much as those figures of the damned clinging to one another in despair and sexual longing—*Paolo and Francesca, I am Beautiful*, and many others—that Auguste Rodin (1840–1917) was devising at the time in Paris to populate his monumental *Gates of Hell* (1880–1917, Musée Rodin, Paris, Philadelphia Museum of Art, and elsewhere). Eroticism is an essential component of Rodin's allegorical art, just as critics of Homer's painting have commented since it was first exhibited on its intense sensuality, as if, in different circumstances, the couple would be making love. Here they are each reduced to pure physicality, one body struggling against impenetrable natural forces, the other beyond comprehension. In its stark reduction of the drama to a single image of physical exertion in the face of annihilation, Homer's painting symbolizes the struggle of life itself.

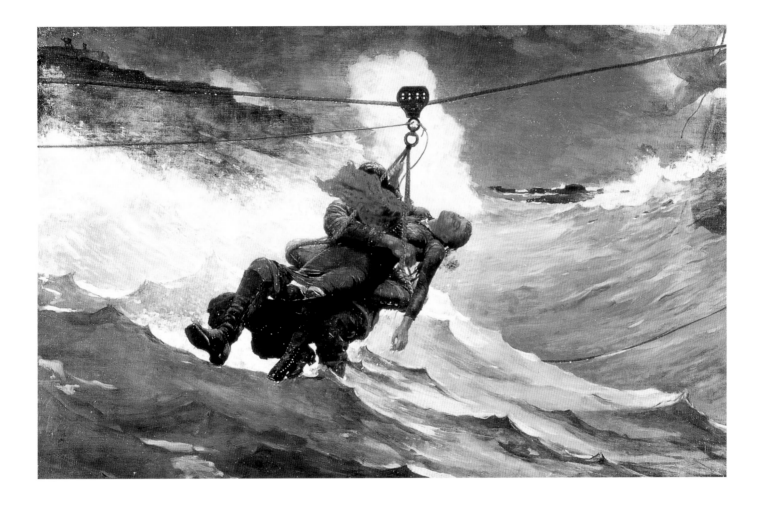

1884 | *oil on canvas* | 29 x 45in (73 x 114cm) | Philadelphia Museum of Art

Ulysses Deriding Polyphemus

IN AUTUMN 1828, Turner visited Italy for the first time in nine years. He made his way to Rome to paint finished exhibition pictures, some of which he exhibited there in the house of his friend, the painter and historian Sir Charles Lock Eastlake (1793–1865). Returning to London early in 1829, Turner awaited the arrival of his Italian paintings, which he had sent on separately, and he intended to show them at the annual exhibition of the Royal Academy, opening in May. The pictures were delayed at sea, however, and the artist set about preparing new works to show instead. Among them was this large, colorful, and richly detailed painting which, although it was executed in London, is full of dazzling Italian light, relates to ideas and themes the artist had explored in Italy, and triumphantly announces the coloristic brilliancy of his late works.

The painting depicts the story in Homer's *Odyssey* of the Ulysses escape from the one-eyed Cyclops, Polyphemus. Having blinded the giant as he fled, red-cloaked Ulysses loudly taunts him from the deck of his ship, while crewmen frantically take up their oars and scramble up the ship's masts to unfurl its sails. Free of the giant's clutches, Ulysses and his crew are not yet safe as, all but lost in shadows and smoke and hardly distinguishable from the mighty rocks on which he lies, Polyphemus hurls rocks down at the ship from the clifftop; blind, he uses the sound of his tormentor's voice to direct his missiles. On the right, the rest of the fleet awaits him. They will make their escape directly into the sunrise, but Polyphemus will ask his father, Poseidon, god of the sea, to harry Ulysses throughout his voyage home to Greece. Nonetheless, liberty is at hand, and the mood of the painting is exultant.

Turner had been thinking of the subject—one seemingly not represented in painting since ancient times—for some twenty years, since the time he had made a small pencil sketch. In Rome, in 1828 he painted an oil sketch that outlined the composition. This seems to have been one of the works whose return from Italy was delayed, and Turner was not able to refer to it as he executed the painting. He remembered it well, however, reproduced the composition, and then brilliantly, and with the improvisatory energy he often brought to his paintings as they

**JOSEPH MALLORD
WILLIAM TURNER**

*BORN LONDON 1775,
DIED LONDON 1851*

neared completion, embellished the canvas with countless inspired and subtle details. Thickly painted with unusually bright colors, especially in the area of the sunrise on the right, the picture is full of magical touches, including the enormous golden boat itself, riding high out of the water, the pennant that flies atop it inscribed "Odysseus" in Greek, and the phosphorescent sea nymphs and flying fish that gambol around the prow. On the left, the eye rises from the emerald water, past a mysterious burning sea cave, up hills of green and gold, to mighty snow-capped peaks and cloudy sky: all four elements, and the timeless cycle of nature, are implicated in that progression. To the right, the vista opens out beyond mighty rocks to sea, and salvation, and the rays of the morning sun, hallucinatory in their whiteness. That we are in the kingdom of myth is reinforced by the pale, wild horses—loosely based on sculpted horses from the eastern pediment of the Parthenon frieze—that pull aloft Apollo's chariot of the sun.

While one critic at the 1829 Royal Academy exhibition spoke of "colouring run mad," most others appreciated the mystery and breathtaking allure of Turner's painting, and some recognized that it represented an important new coloristic advance in the art of the greatest painter of the British school. John Ruskin would later describe it as "the central picture in Turner's career … as perfect and as great as human work can be." By 1829, Turner was a prosperous artist who sold his paintings only when he chose to, holding back more and more of them as he formulated his plans for a monumental bequest to the nation. *Ulysses Deriding Polyphemus* was included in that bequest, entering the National Gallery in 1856. A keystone of British painting, it exerted wide influence, not least in the United States. In the early 1860s, the young British-born American landscape painter Thomas Moran (1837–1926) returned to the land of his birth, determined to learn all that Turner's art could teach. He copied the painting and kept his version with him throughout his life. When he discovered the American far west, with its awesome cliffs, canyons, and natural wonders, and its mysterious effects of light, Turner's example of the sublime showed him how to paint it.

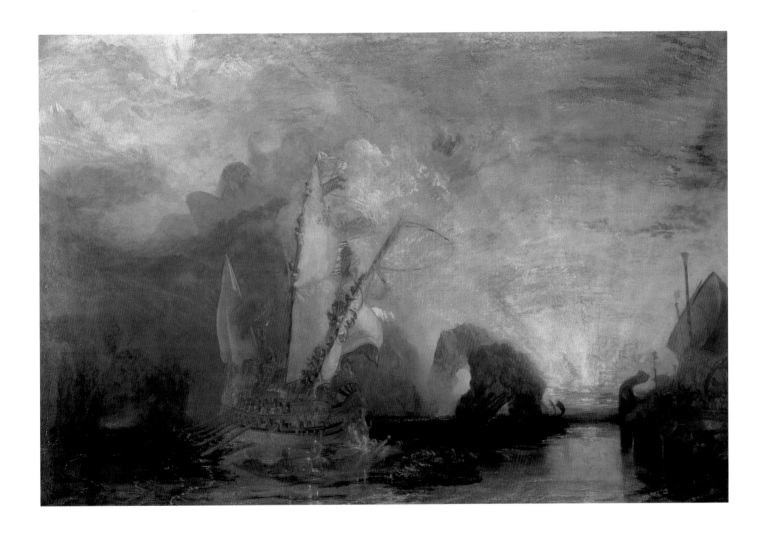

1829 | *oil on canvas* | 52 x 80in (132.5 x 203cm) | National Gallery, London

The Third of May, 1808

HISTORY PAINTING that took as its subject a more or less contemporary event can be said to have begun—and it was an influential innovation—with Benjamin West's *Death of General Wolfe* of 1770, depicting the demise of the victorious English general just as his troops took Quebec eleven years earlier, in 1759. Jacques-Louis David intended to paint the Tennis Court Oath of 1789 that launched the French Revolution but, under the impetus of events, never completed it; history was moving too fast. His pupil, Baron Gros, painted Napoleon in the propaganda image, the *Pest House of Jaffa* (1804, Louvre, Paris), the magnanimous future emperor laying a magical hand on the suitably grateful sick and dying in a newly conquered land. These depictions have in common a recognizable hero—in the case of the Tennis Court Oath, several of them—who performs a brave act, or nobly expires as a result of it. The viewer is meant to recognize the hero, appreciate his courage and wisdom, and learn a lesson about the aspirations and achievements of the nation as embodied in the exemplary acts of the leader.

Goya's painting is an altogether more ambiguous matter, but no less innovative. For perhaps the first time, a painter chose to depict on a monumental scale an essentially leaderless political event, a popular uprising, and its result. It is one of two paintings, equal in size, that in 1814 Goya devoted to the events in Madrid on May 2, and 3, 1808, during Spain's Peninsular War (1808–14). In March of that year, Napoleon's forces had entered Spain and, after complicated maneuvering, deprived both the recently abdicated Charles IV and his son, Ferdinand VII, of the throne, giving it to the emperor's own brother, Joseph Bonaparte. On May 2 rioting spontaneously broke out in Madrid as the people rose up against the French occupiers when members of the Spanish royal family attempted to leave the city. Goya's first painting, *The Second of May, 1808* (Prado, Madrid) shows that uprising, a maelstrom of frenzied activity as the people set on the French troops. The second canvas shows the results of the uprising, soon suppressed, when the next day the leader of the occupying army, Marshal Murat, ordered the rioters to be executed. Lined up against a stone wall, the simple peasants and laborers are shot to death by

FRANCISCO DE GOYA Y LUCIENTES

✧

*BORN FUENDETODOS 1746,
DIED BORDEAUX 1828*

a faceless firing squad that seems to stand only inches away from its victims. Blood runs thickly in the street, and as the bullets strike, one rioter raises his arms in a spasmodic gesture reminiscent of the crucified Christ. Their quixotic uprising had been futile; in the face of superior forces it was condemned to failure from the beginning. Here, the martyrs, common men without social or political position, are confronted by blind strength, the automatonlike soldiers who are the anonymous instruments of a cold, calculating power.

While there is little evidence that Goya had collaborated with the French occupiers—friends testified that he did not and he said that he had stayed at home working on prints—in 1808, artists and intellectuals with whom he associated had not been unambiguously anti-French; French rule briefly held out the hope of liberalization and enlightenment. When Goya undertook the paintings six years after the events they portrayed, the point was moot. By then the French had been driven from Spain, Ferdinand VII was safely on the throne, and commemorations were being planned for the martyrs of 1808. It was then that, pleading poverty, Goya appealed to the state for funds to allow him to carry out the project. In its unrhetorical directness and unflinching portrayal of brutality, *The Third of May* must have been all but incomprehensible, and certainly far from uplifting, to viewers used to the Baroque and Neoclassical conventions of history painting. Both works were quickly rolled away, forgotten until 1848 in the storerooms of the Prado. From c. 1810–14, Goya devoted a series of engravings to depicting the horrors of the Peninsular War, but the *Disasters of War* was published long after the artist's death, in 1863. Since then, however, *The Third of May* has had a tremendous impact on succeeding generations of painters, including Manet, Picasso and, today, Leon Golub (born 1922). It seems as modern as the long list of efficiently murderous wars and regimes that mark our times. Whenever artists have confronted and sought to condemn the brutality of the modern state, far more than the heroics depicted by a West, David, or Gros, it is Goya's abject depiction of murderous and anonymous state-mandated violence that stands powerfully before them.

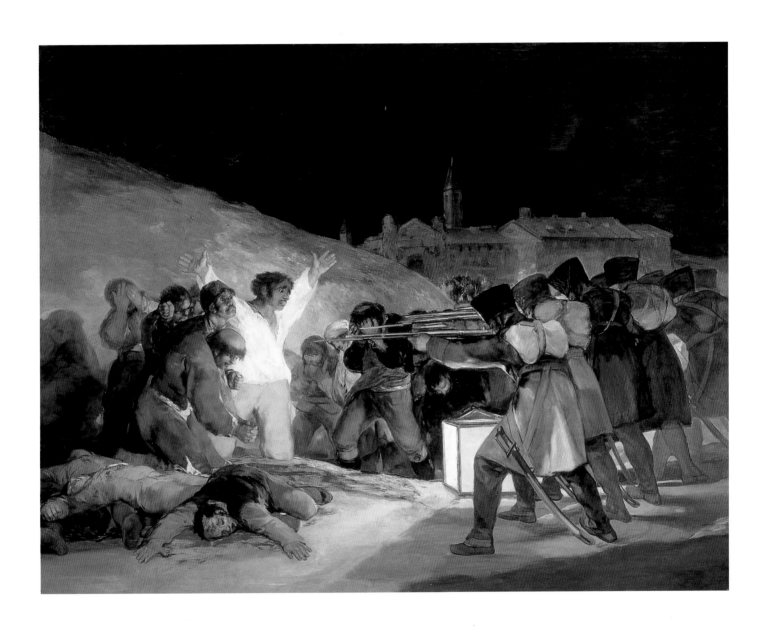

1814 | *oil on canvas* | 104 x 135in (264 x 342cm) | Prado, Madrid

The Champion Single Sculls

THE SCHUYLKILL RIVER that meanders through Philadelphia is an ideal location for rowing. As the sport grew in popularity in the mid-19th century, the city was acclaimed as America's rowing capital. This was fitting for the birthplace of American independence, and in the United States—unlike Europe, where it was a "gentleman's pursuit"—rowing was rigorously egalitarian and democratic, skill the only criterion. (As every Philadelphia schoolchild knows, in the 1920s, the king of England refused to shake the hand of the Olympic gold-medal-winning rower Jack Kelly of Philadelphia, because he was a working man; Kelly's daughter, Grace, married the prince of Monaco.) Today, the quaint old boat houses lining the Schuylkill, the vast Philadelphia Museum of Art towering over them on an adjacent hill, are one of the sights of the town, never more picturesque than when the river is filled with sleek, skittering sculls. The museum, where many of Eakins's greatest paintings now hang, had not been built—although the boat houses were already there—when the young artist returned to his hometown on July 4, 1870. He had been studying painting in Europe for more than three years—in Paris, Jean-Léon Gérôme (1824–1904) was his master—but had learned what he needed to know from the Old World and now intended to begin his career as a professional artist, painting the modern American scene. For the picture that would announce his return, Eakins chose an entirely novel, and quintessentially Philadelphian, theme.

Max Schmitt was the best oarsman in town. A lawyer, he won the first-ever single-sculls championship on the Schuylkill in 1867. His old friend Eakins, himself a rower, sent congratulations from Paris. On October 5, 1870, Schmitt won the race again, against stiff competition. This time, the young artist was there to cheer him on. Soon after, he began the painting that commemorated Schmitt's triumph, the first of several oil paintings and watercolors which he devoted to rowing and America's leading rowers over the next four years. Eakins did not depict the thrill of victory, that was for magazine illustrators; he had a more complex scheme. Instead, he showed the mustachioed Schmitt taking a moment of rest during practice,

THOMAS EAKINS

∾

*BORN PHILADELPHIA 1844,
DIED PHILADELPHIA 1916*

turning to scrutinize the viewer as his oars skim the still water in which he and his elegant scull are reflected, as in a mirror. His dominance of the sport is assumed. In the middle distance, Eakins introduced himself into the picture, pulling mightily on his oars—just as he struggled to perfect his art—his name and the date inscribed on his boat. Farther along the river, two rowers and a coxswain in Quaker dress toil away in a slow, old-fashioned boat. Philadelphia is the Quaker metropolis, and between themselves, the artist seems to say, Eakins and Schmitt will show the old town what it means to be modern. All the other details of the painting are relentlessly up-to-date. A steamboat chugs upstream while a train is about to cross one of the solid steel and stone bridges recently thrown across the Schuylkill. The scene is not, as might at first appear, set in the country. Rather, the river runs through Fair-mount Park, recently established as the largest urban park in the United States and the site a few years later of the 1876 Universal Exposition. Not half a mile away, in the direction Schmitt gazes, were the law offices, banks, row houses, and smoking factories of central Philadelphia.

Eakins was uncompromisingly committed to realism in his art, the foundation of which, as he had learned in Paris, was the study of the nude body. When he became a teacher at the Pennsylvania Academy of the Fine Arts, he insisted on the use of nude models in mixed classes. In that, he was too modern for Philadelphia, and it led to his expulsion. Indeed, he never enjoyed all the success that might have been predicted for him when he returned from Paris, and the recognition of his central role in American art is largely a posthumous one. When he painted this picture, Eakins seems to have sensed that struggles lay ahead. Max Schmitt's success derived from the strength, grace, and agility of his body. It is no accident that his muscular, bare arm is at the very center of the composition. In this image of athletic prowess, Eakins declared to Philadelphia the lesson Paris had taught him—that realism and modernity are inextricably linked. Like Walt Whitman, the local bard whose portrait he painted years later (1888, Pennsylvania Academy of the Fine Arts), the ambitious young artist elected to sing the body electric.

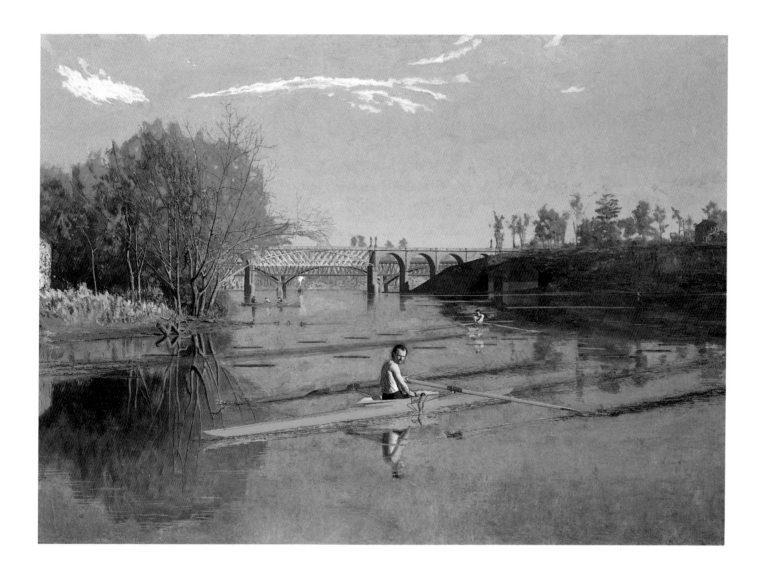

1871 | *oil on canvas* | 32¹⁄₂ x 46in (82 x 117.5cm) | Metropolitan Museum of Art, New York

MODERN ART

1860–1910 ❦ RICHARD R. BRETTELL

No previous period in the history of Western art—not even Florence in the second half of the 15th century or Rome a century later—was as inventive, productive, and important for painting as this short epoch. For the first time, Western art was truly international and reached a mass audience through the stimulus of photography, public art museums, and the private art market.

ARTISTS BECAME CELEBRITIES. Caricatures of contemporary paintings filled the mass print media, and virtually every great writer tried his hand at art criticism, from Baudelaire to Zola, Huysmans to Strindberg. At no time did advanced literature and painting relate more closely to each other.

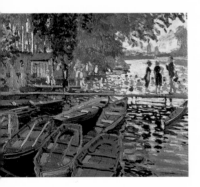

Monet's initial doubt turned to pride in La Grenouillère *(1869), recognized by artist and public as an early "impression."*

Artists had a clear sense of the cultural role and moral stature of their work and were at once liberated and burdened by this. With a boom in the number of galleries and reproductions and in art publishing, they felt the weight of the past more fully, and knew more about art history than earlier artists. Fortunately, they more often drew from rather than worshipped the past, trawling museums for details and chromatic solutions. And exhibitions—whether they were major "official"

events or smaller shows that attracted a more sophisticated audience—made it simple for artists to measure their achievements, and ease of travel and frequent shows of foreign art broke down regional schools and caused the rapid spread of artistic ideas.

The history of modern art is most often seen as a sequence of movements, each superseding the last: from Realism to Naturalism or Impressionism, to Post-Impressionism and/or Symbolism, to Cubism. The first trio were as concerned about museum art and complex pictorial strategies as the Symbolists or Post-Impressionists were about direct painting and formal clarity of expression, but, ultimately, all modern Western artists were responding to two fundamental forces: the unprecedented changes in their visual–social world through urban development, technology, and the breakdown of social divisions, and the shifting and burgeoning art world in which they were immersed. Art for art's sake and art for life's sake intertwined.

Perhaps because photography stole much of the merely representational function of painting and printmaking, artists in the second half of the 19th century were preoccupied with "style" and manners of representation. Each medium fought to establish its own character, and artists experimented more extensively with new materials and compositions. The independence of "the picture" from visual reality was asserted again and again by painters

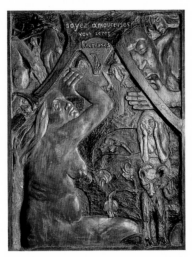

Gauguin exhibited the wood relief Soyez amoureuses et vous serez heureuses *(1889) with nine related works as a philosophical ensemble.*

Some of the works included here are not "typical" choices. Some are unfamiliar because of the circumstances of their ownership, but demand exposure, and all the artists are white and male. In the end, only Henry O. Tanner (1859–1937), among painters of African descent, and Mary Cassatt (1844–1926) and Berthe Morisot (1841–1895), as women, made works that have become canonical, and I chose a

and writers, who, like Degas, believed utterly in an artificial art rooted profoundly in the study of that reality. Thus, the paradox of modernism.

The city was the nexus of both the "art world" and the "real world." From Paris to Chicago, Melbourne to Moscow, the city changed totally between 1850 and 1900. This dizzying world produced all the anxieties of modernism as well as its many joys. Everyone—artists, art lovers, workers, entertainers, shop owners—had to be adaptable, open, and resilient to thrive in the modern city, and few artists were able to reinvent themselves often enough to succeed throughout their lives. Most of the greatest either worked in a fleeting burst of creativity—like van Gogh, Seurat, Munch, and Klimt—or retreated from the city—Monet, Cézanne, and Gauguin. Paris was the quintessential city of art, and Parisian art dominates this selection because it produced at least three-quarters of the writings on modernism, and its ideas were exported almost immediately.

Caillebotte in preference to a brilliant Morisot for the boldness of its conception. Sculpture is omitted, not only because Baudelaire, in his wonderfully sardonic review of the 1846 Salon wrote an essay called "Why Sculpture is Boring," but because, aside from Auguste Rodin and Medardo Rosso (1858–1928), the greatest sculptors of modern art were primarily painters. But I have mostly selected self-consciously constructed "masterpieces," intended by the artists for public display and as part of the public debate; and all had an effect on the subsequent history of art.

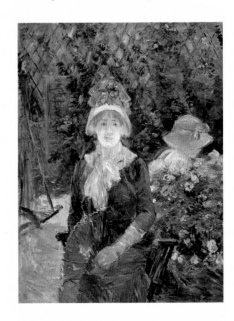

Greatly influenced by Manet, Berthe Morisot's Young Woman in a Garden *(1883) is her independent masterpiece.*

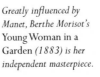

259

Déjeuner sur l'herbe

THE HISTORY of modern art begins in conflict between the "official taste" of the academy, with its historical or literary Classicism and its preoccupation with surface consistency, and the heroically independent artists who fought for an authentically modern urban art. And this beginning came in the spring of 1863 at the Salon des Refusés, an official exhibition ordered by the Emperor of France, Napoleon III, to show the many works of art rejected by the unusually harsh jury of the official Salon that year. The Emperor's aim was not to sanction the "refused" art but to allow the public a chance to "judge the jurors," and one work of art literally stole the show—Édouard Manet's *Déjeuner sur l'herbe* (Luncheon on the Grass). This was the first of many masterpieces of modern art defined by scandal and, finally, sanctioned by art history, entering the highest echelons of official taste.

Manet was forty and, although he had courted the attention of sophisticated Parisians, was known only to a small circle of friends, until he suddenly found fame with *Déjeuner sur l'herbe*. The painting scandalized Paris. Not since Géricault's *Raft of the Medusa* of 1819 had one work summarized the revolutionary tendencies of a generation. It was criticized for its crudity, amorality, and decadence.

Manet shows a naked (as opposed to nude) woman, whose clearly contemporary clothing is arranged with breads and fruit (and a large silver flask!) at the lower left. The two young men, wearing equally contemporary dress, have been identified as students. Clearly the nude is no goddess, but a modern woman—even a prostitute—who not only dares to cavort naked with men but brazenly acknowledges the viewer, making us accomplices in this amoral picnic. Another young woman, clad only in her chemise, washes herself in a stream. This is neither Susannah nor Bathsheba at the bath, and the fact that the picture was originally called simply *Le Bain* (The Bath) shows that Manet made no attempt to "clothe" his subject with allegory or history, choosing to represent what would have been in reality a private act in the completely public forum of a government sponsored exhibition.

Yet, the imagery would not, of itself, have ensured the painting's *succès du scandale*. Manet chose to paint the work

ÉDOUARD MANET

BORN PARIS 1832,
DIED PARIS 1883

rapidly, often with large brushes that summarily (some thought sloppily) described the landscape setting, and rendered the foreground figures and still-life elements with large, separate strokes of paint that, for many viewers, were as "crude" as the represented subject. Neither the elegant linear contrivances of Ingres nor the subtle color harmonies of Delacroix "offset" the subject. Instead, Manet wore the mantle of the ever-scandalous Gustave Courbet, who had painted nudes in his studio and used a palette knife in preference to a brush.

Manet was not a complete rebel. The work is full of allusions to the "museum" art of Giorgione, Raphael, and Titian and, closer still, to the gently amoral *fêtes galantes* of 18th-century French artists like Boucher and Fragonard (see pages 208–9, 220–21), both of whom occasionally painted with equally "crude" strokes of paint. It is, thus, as "academic" in its self-selected esthetic pedigree as any work by the ostensibly "academic" artists Alexandre Cabanel (1823–1889) or Jean-Léon Gérôme (1824–1904). Yet, even in his quotations, Manet teased the viewer into accepting the vulgar "reality" of his subject by treating it in terms set by "works of art" in museums. It was originally seen as a modern adaptation of Giorgione's *Concert Champêtre* (see pages 108–9), but the poses of all three central figures actually derive from subsidiary figures in the engraving by Marcantonio Raimondi (c. 1480–1534) after a lost drawing by Raphael of *The Judgment of Paris* (c. 1515–16). How more deliciously "postmodernist" (indirect, parodic, and ironic) could Manet have been than in ennobling ordinary models by posing them as unessential figures from a print after a great fresco that he had never seen!

It is, though, the forthright gaze of Manet's model, Victorine Meurent, that makes this self-conscious pastiche so compelling. The painting looks back at us and prods us into an act of esthetic and social judgment that we might otherwise avoid. Both the alert—and anti-erotic—pose of the model and the fact that her toe plays absentmindedly with the pants leg of the gesturing gentleman make it difficult for us to take this ambitious composition entirely seriously. How pompous Manet tried to be, and how delightfully he poked fun at his own pretensions.

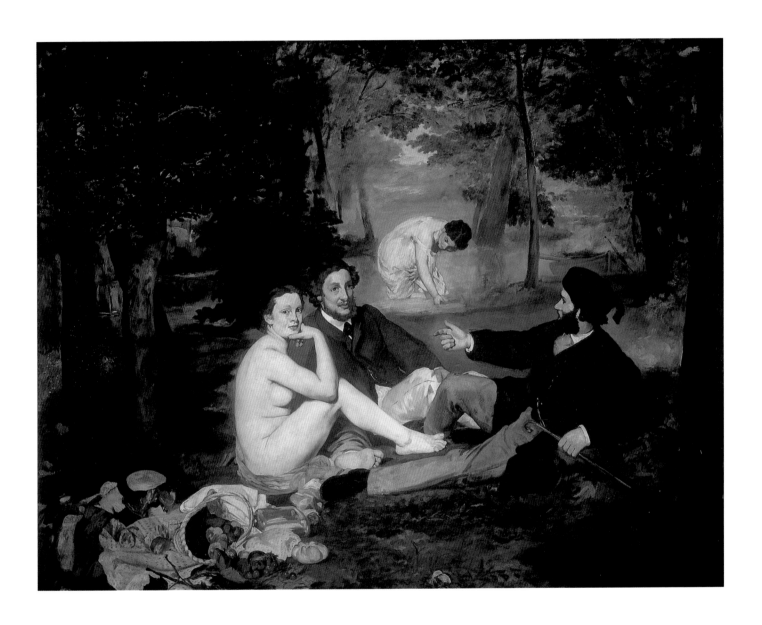

1863 | *oil on canvas* | 84 x 106in (213.4 x 269.2cm) | Musée d'Orsay, Paris

Ball at the Moulin de la Galette

I F THERE IS a self-conscious masterpiece of Impressionist figure painting, it is Renoir's *Ball at the Moulin de la Galette*. It occupied a wall of its own at the third Impressionist exhibition of 1877 and was the set-piece of the catalog produced by Renoir's friend, the critic Georges Rivière. In keeping with the ideology of *plein air,* or direct painting, espoused by these young artists, Rivière claimed that the painting was executed entirely outdoors while Renoir witnessed the daytime dancing scene at the famous Montmartre dance hall, but the fact that there is a painted sketch for the painting (Ordrupgaardsamlung, Copenhagen) and that Renoir executed a slightly smaller variant for a friendly collector (private collection), makes it clear that he worked on this large and beautifully painted picture mainly in his studio. Renoir's dealer, Vollard, even claimed later that the painting was executed from memory, hardly an admissible approach for a young "Impressionist" in 1876!

The painting is, in a way, an homage to the art of Watteau, Boucher, and Fragonard, which had been consciously revived and made relevant to modernism by the Goncourt brothers in their writings of the 1860s. The quality of feminized innocence that pervades this work was instantly recognized by critics, the most eloquent of whom used the pseudonym Ch. Flor O'Squarr (and may have been the Anglophile poet Stéphane Mallarmé, who had reviewed the Impressionist exhibition of 1876 in English): "The strong daylight is filtered through the greenery, setting the blonde hair and pink cheeks of the girls aglow and making their ribbons sparkle. The joyful light fills every corner of the canvas and even the shadows reflect it. In the centre we see a crowd of dancers caught up in frantic choreography. The whole painting shimmers like a rainbow and makes one think of the dainty Chinese princess described by Heinrich Heine: 'her greatest pleasure in life was to tear up satin and silk with polished, jade-like nails and watch the shreds of yellow, blue and pink drift away in the breeze like so many butterflies.'"

Renoir must have studied the drapery painting of Veronese, Rubens, Watteau, and Fragonard at the Louvre, but no single work, not even Watteau's *Embarkation to (or from) the Island of Cythera* (see pages 198–99), can serve as a viable prototype. The

PIERRE-AUGUSTE RENOIR

BORN LIMOGES 1841,
DIED CAGNES-SUR-MER 1919

Ball at the Moulin de la Galette has a unity of touch rare in Renoir's earlier large-scale paintings, suggesting that he was transcribing less forms in space than a "field of vision" in which figures, shadows, background elements, glasses, and fruit have equal visual status. The eye of the viewer darts across the form-filled and motion-filled surface, unable to dally on any one form. This esthetic "slippage" remains utterly modern to this day; a million individual observations are compressed onto a surface scarcely less active than a Jackson Pollock "drip" canvas of the late 1940s.

Many critics prefer the socially charged paintings of Degas and Manet to Renoir's optimistic and prosperous modernism. The people who crowd Renoir's dance hall cavort on a weekend (probably a Sunday), enjoying a "pay-as-you-drink-and-dance" capitalist urban entertainment. Most of them worked for a living—both men and women—and relished this moment of pleasure with a healthy abandon that sets them apart from the melancholy figures in the aristocratic painting of Watteau. Renoir's is, indeed, a modernist vision of an urban utopia of workers *freed* by their wages to dance and drink, in clothes acquired for public display. Yet, the pseudonymous critic was surely right in seeing a fair degree of nervousness, "frantic choreography," in this sun-filled canvas.

Rivière identified many of the figures in the painting as specific artists, writers, journalists, and even a civil servant; the women were models, milliners, and waitresses, and all of them gathered in Renoir's nearby garden studio on the Rue Cortot. Interestingly, none of Renoir's Impressionist colleagues are present, not even Gustave Caillebotte, the painting's first owner. Instead, the artists depicted were part of the academic or official world of painting, anathema to Impressionism. Thus, the painting represents not only a time in the history of France, after the horrors of the Franco-Prussian War and the Commune had begun to fade, but also a generational time, before the younger men and women of Renoir's circle began to marry and enter the "proper" realm of bourgeois civility that was to be the subject of the artist's later oeuvre. His Impressionist friends—Manet, Monet, Sisley, Morisot, and Pissarro—had already married and started families, and were no longer free to dance on Sundays.

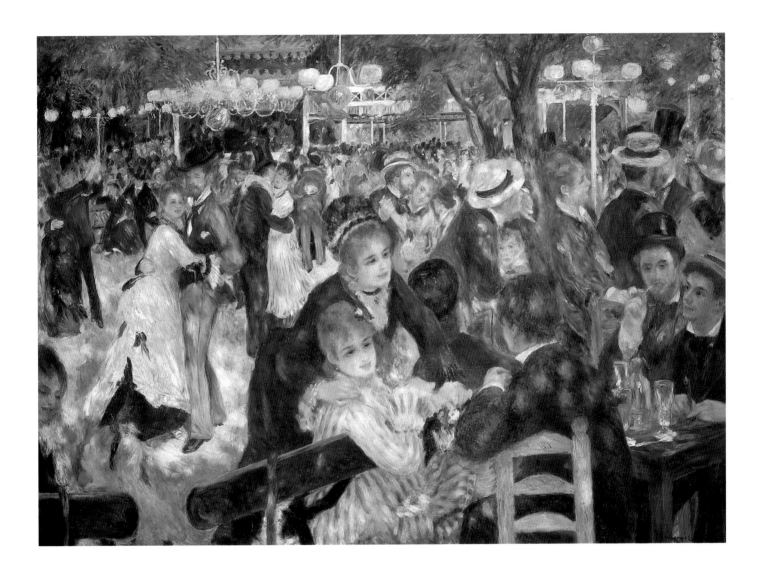

1876–77　│　*oil on canvas*　│　52 x 69in (131 x 175cm)　│　Musée d'Orsay, Paris

The Bar at the Folies Bergère

THERE IS NO more enigmatic—and ultimately frustrating—painting in 19th-century French modernism than Manet's last masterpiece, *The Bar at the Folies Bergère*, exhibited at the Salon the year before his death. Although smaller than Renoir's *Ball at the Moulin de la Galette* (see pages 262–63), its hieratic composition and single life-sized figure give it a monumentality that separates it from the consciously informal Impressionist practice of Renoir. Each element on Manet's bar-altar is deliberately placed, and the server, who looks through us into the space reflected in the mirror behind her, has the status of a priestess or even of the resurrected Christ at the moment of *Noli me tangere*. And, although filled with witty touches—like the feet of the female acrobat at the upper left and the opera glasses of the female spectator in the balcony opposite—these do little to undercut the somber, almost tragic aura of Manet's saddest painting.

Virtually every major historian and critic of urban modernism has weighed in against the work, calling it an "allegory of nostalgia" and the "Virgin and/or Whore at the Folies Bergère," and seeing in it Manet's "subversion of the natural." Most of this writing is fascinating, largely because the painting itself is a kind of perpetual conundrum whose "solution" can only be found in itself. Although there is one lost preparatory drawing and an oil study (private collection), Manet left no account about his intentions, forcing modern commentators to scour the literature for contemporary criticism, recorded visits to Manet's studio, or recollections of those who knew him in the early 1880s. Not even Berthe Morisot, Manet's closest female friend, uttered a word about the painting, and the critics of its first exhibition at the Salon wrote with as much ignorance as understanding. X-rays of the composition have even been used to tease out Manet's intentions by weighing the final appearance of the painting against the initial idea, in which the woman's head seems to turn slightly toward the viewer, as in the reflection.

Students of photography have made a neat dichotomy of representational art in two contrasting metaphors: representations are either mirrors or windows. Windows are easier to understand, because they are externally directed, controlling

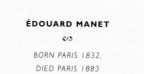

ÉDOUARD MANET

BORN PARIS 1832,
DIED PARIS 1883

"appearance" only through the agent of the framing edge. Mirrors, too, have frames, but when we look into them we see ourselves *in* the representation, making the "mirrored" metaphor inherently self-reflexive. Starting with the great writer-critic Huysmans, all students of *The Bar at the Folies Bergère* have recognized the intrinsic "impossibility" of the mirror in Manet's painting. The gilded molding on the mirror frame visible behind the barmaid is strictly parallel to the picture plane and is, hence, unable to "reflect" the back of the woman and her spectator-interlocutor as they appear in the painted reflection. And, should one want to list all the "inconsistencies"—the floating plane of the bar in the reflection, the misplaced reflections of the bottles at the left, the enormously greater space between the bottles and the figure in the reflection than in the "real" image, and so on—the discontinuities between "actual" and "reflected" realms are overwhelming. Clearly, Manet intended for us to puzzle over the painting, forcing us into a mode of looking that is analytical, time consuming, and ultimately ontological, dealing with the nature of being. What *is* a painted representation? Its freedom from the constraints of actuality seems to be one of Manet's subjects.

Or is the sheer discontinuity between two realms—actual and reflected—a metaphor for desire and its impossibilities? We have two "characters," a man and a woman. The man is the viewer-painter, whose presence we supply simply by looking at the painting. Yet, we see ourselves not in her—she *does* look through us—but in a reflection that cannot, in fact, be "real." This is the ultimate "solution" to Manet's painting—and its tragedy. The gulfs—between men and women, public and private, mirror and window, worker and bourgeois, life and death—can never be reconciled—not in life and not, in the end, in painting. We know that Manet was not well when he worked on this canvas, and, of all writers about *The Bar at the Folies Bergère*, only Françoise Cachin has highlighted its tragedy: "This was his last masterpiece, a final representation of sensuous objects, a wistful repository of the Parisian world that had been part of his life, between a smoke-tarnished mirror and a *regard regardé* whose unfathomable sadness is, as it were, a farewell to painting."

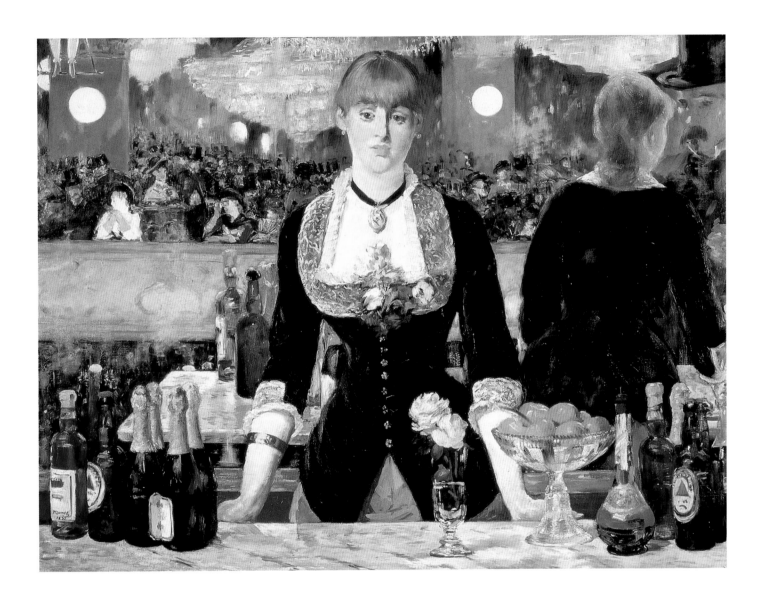

1881–82 | *oil on canvas* | 38 x 51in (96 x 130cm) | Courtauld Institute Galleries, London

The Daughters of Edward D. Boit

FOR A PICTORIAL study of modernist cosmopolitan culture, this great group portrait by the American painter John Singer Sargent cannot be surpassed. Although Sargent was an American citizen, he lived virtually all of his life in Europe. Born in Italy and raised there and in Germany, France, and England, he settled in the art capital of the 19th century, Paris, to learn his craft from Charles Carolus-Duran (1838–1917), among the most respected society portrait painters in the city. Sargent's early reputation was made in France. Like his fellow expatriate, Mary Cassatt, he clearly felt that American art and culture lacked the subtlety and polish of the European, and it was against the European masters that he measured his own achievements as an artist.

Mr. and Mrs. Boit were equally at home in Paris and London as in their native Boston. Sargent knew the family well enough to paint both this great exhibition work and a formal portrait of Mrs. Boit (Museum of Fine Arts, Boston), painted in 1887–88 when Sargent was staying at the Boit's Boston home. There is no record of payment for either work, and it seems likely that Sargent himself suggested that he paint the girls, to lure other wealthy American expatriates—and even the French bourgeoisie—into sitting for him. *The Boit Sisters*, as the painting is often called, was painted in Paris and shown at the Salon of 1883 where it was well received, eliciting positive comments from the novelist and critic Henry James who, like his friend Sargent, understood the world of American expatriates.

The many parallels between *The Boit Sisters* and Velázquez's monumental *Las Meninas* of c. 1656 have often been noted. In fact, Sargent had painted a fully resolved copy of the Velázquez (private collection) on his visit to the Prado in 1879, and this copy was in his Paris studio when he was working on *The Boit Sisters*. In both works, there is an implicit recognition on the part of the subjects that they are being portrayed. Yet, Sargent simplified the pictorial and ontological games of Velázquez, who asks viewers to "pose" for him and his royal entourage while, in the picture, he is actually painting the king and queen. How one yearns to find a ghost of Sargent himself lurking in the shadows of his work, behind the folding screen, engaged in painting *not*

JOHN SINGER SARGENT

☙

*BORN FLORENCE 1856,
DIED LONDON 1925*

the sisters but their unseen parents. The fact that the girls wear white pinafores to protect their clothing while they play in the house suggests that, indeed, they are not posing to be painted but have been captured at an informal, intimate moment. This is a very clever, esthetically layered work of art.

Typical for the public exhibition of society portraits, Sargent called the work simply *Portrait of Children* when it was shown, but its large scale and evident esthetic ambition separated it from the other works he exhibited in 1882–83. Many early critics recognized the affinities between Sargent's informal and rapidly painted style and that of Impressionist artists, but this similarity was always tempered by Sargent's "high art" training. Indeed, the full range of blacks and dark tones gives *The Boit Sisters* a quality of shadowy mystery completely at odds with the light-infused portraits of Sargent's only French rival as a painter of children, Renoir.

The most extraordinary achievement of the portrait is its composition. Rather than arranging the children, ages six to fourteen, in a pleasing group at the center of the picture, Sargent treated them separately. A reviewer of the 1883 Salon said the painting had been "composed from new rules; the rules of the game of four corners," and this must be correct. By locating the girls so that they either confront or avoid the light from a large unseen window, and by relating them to enormous—and decidedly vulgar—Chinese blue-and-white vases (witty stand-ins for the girls' parents?), Sargent seems to be giving us clues about their personalities and relationships. The youngest, Julia, sits comfortably on a great carpet and is, thus, isolated from her sisters both in pose and position. Her immediately older sister, Mary Louisa, stands at the very edge of the composition, fully accepting the light and acknowledging the fact of her representation. The oldest girls, Florence and Jane, inhabit the shadows, Florence leaning against the vast vase and avoiding the viewer, Jane looking shyly at us from the darkness. Curiously, Sargent seems to have understood the personalities of these girls, because it was precisely the older two who became increasingly disturbed and unstable, living their lives in the world of shadows in which Sargent set them in 1882.

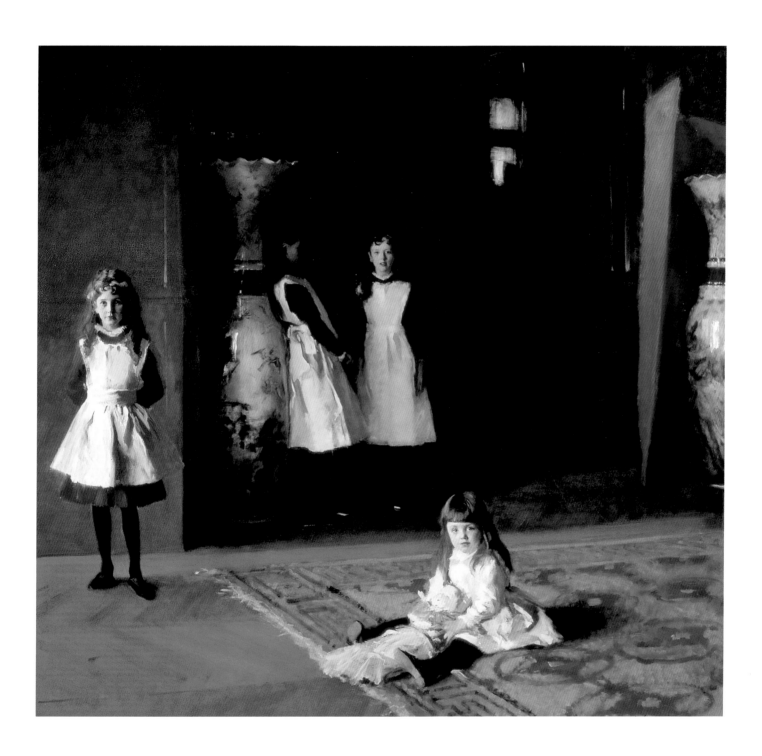

1882　｜　*oil on canvas*　｜　87¹/₂ x 87¹/₂in (222 x 222cm)　｜　Museum of Fine Arts, Boston

Man at His Bath

NO EARLIER 19th-century work of art can quite prepare us for this unusual—and powerfully physical—painting. It is a relatively late work by an artist who was seen as a wealthy amateur by many of his friends in the Impressionist movement and who became the first publicly recognized private patron of Impressionist painting when he bequeathed his important collection to the French nation at his death. The oeuvre of Gustave Caillebotte himself was almost unknown until after World War II.

Like most of Caillebotte's larger canvases, this one was surely made for exhibition. Many Impressionist artists made important works for an 1883 or 1884 exhibition, but infighting within the group prevented its organization, and in the event, the painting was not exhibited in France until 1994. However, Caillebotte sent it to a major exhibition of vanguard art held in Brussels in 1888 by Les XX (Les Vingt, "The Twenty"). There it fared badly; although it is listed in the catalog, there is evidence that it was removed from the exhibition because of its forthright— and esthetically offensive—male nudity and kept in a locked closet. Hence, it becomes the first male nude in the history of modern art to share the fate of so many female nudes from Courbet and Manet through Picasso to de Kooning and Jeff Koons (born 1955).

Caillebotte chose as his subject a middle-aged man seen from the back, drying himself after his bath. The lead tub sits in the corner of a Parisian interior, curtained from view, and the wooden floor retains the wet prints of his feet. His drying actions are vigorous, and there is an undeniable muscularity and, thus, an aura of athletic prowess in the body. Although we know nothing of the identity of the model, Caillebotte was an active swimmer and sailor throughout the 1870s and 1880s and often represented the physical contests among male athletes in his Impressionist paintings. None, however, deal so frankly with the body as this large canvas, and it is to the example of Cézanne and Degas that one must turn for the real esthetic impetus followed by Caillebotte in this bold and enigmatic painting.

Caillebotte bought Cézanne's monumental male *Bathers* (Barnes Foundation, Merion, Pennsylvania) from the artist after its inclusion in the 1877 Impressionist exhibition, and it is likely

GUSTAVE CAILLEBOTTE

∾

BORN PARIS 1848,
DIED PARIS 1894

that he acquired Degas' *Woman Leaving the Bath* (1876–77, Musée d'Orsay, Paris) at the same time. In *Man at His Bath*, Caillebotte has merged the "masculine" tradition of depicting group bathing outdoors, represented by Frédéric Bazille (1841–70) and Cézanne, with the modern and distinctly feminine tradition of interior bathing. The result was obviously so shocking that the painting was not even shown in a progressive exhibition for fear of inciting strongly adverse reactions. It is striking at so late a date in the history of vanguard art that a painting's subject matter retained the ability to shock and that, simply by clearly representing a male nude, Caillebotte broke an unspoken representational code analogous to that transgressed by Manet in 1863 with *Déjeuner sur l'herbe* (see pages 260–61). Bazille had already bowed to this prejudice in the late 1860s when he put bathing pants on his frontal male nudes so *Summer Scene, Bathers* (1869, Fogg Museum, Harvard University, Cambridge, Massachusetts) would be acceptable at the Salon, while Thomas Eakins lost his job at the Pennsylvania Academy the year before Caillebotte's painting was finished because he exhibited nude male bathers in *The Swimming Hole* (1883–85, Amon Carter Museum, Fort Worth).

Unfortunately, this memorable and significant painting has almost no place in the discourse of modernism. Its only exhibition in the 19th century—a partial one in Brussels—generated no public criticism, and the organizers of the 1894 Caillebotte retrospective in Paris were afraid to include it. It languished in the family's collection until the 1976–77 retrospective held in Brooklyn and Houston. Thus, ironically, it entered the history and criticism of art at a time when they were dominated by feminist critiques of male representations of the female nude.

The painting must have been admired by Edgar Degas, because the older artist started in earnest on his own quest to represent the "modern," but female, body in the act of bathing in 1884–85, just as Caillebotte signed and dated his most important late painting. Not until Cézanne returned to the male bather in the late 1880s and until Munch and Max Liebermann (1847–1935) liberated male nudity in painted representation around 1900 did Caillebotte's bather have worthy companions.

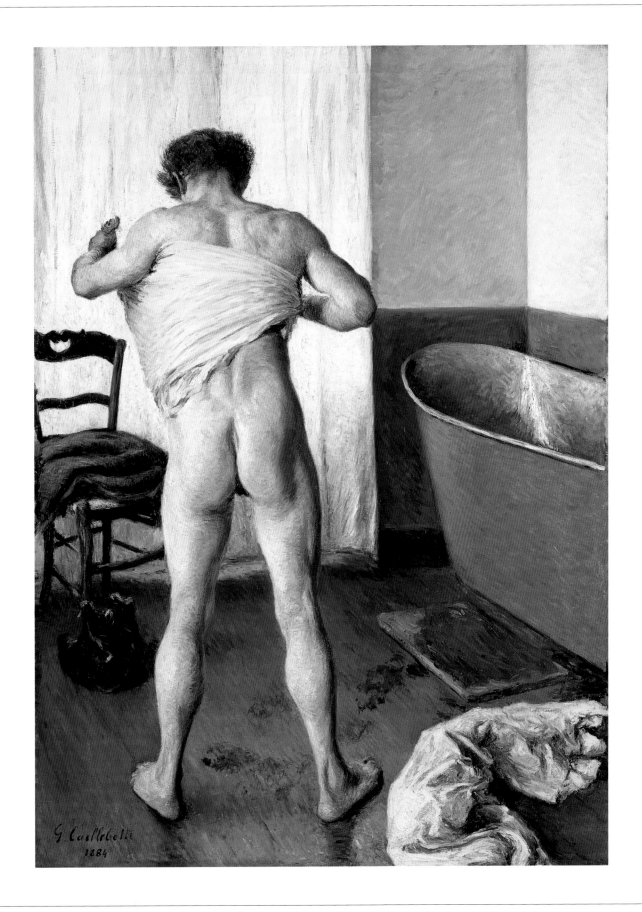

1884 | *oil on canvas* | 67 x 49in (170 x 125cm) | The Josefowitz Collection, on loan to the National Gallery, London

Woman Bathing in a Shallow Tub

IN 1886, the last Impressionist exhibition was dominated by the "Neo-Impressionists" led by the young Seurat, who stole the show with his vast painting, *Sunday on the Island of La Grande Jatte, 1884* (1884–86, Art Institute of Chicago). With its dotted surface and "Egyptian" composition of static, largely profile figures, this single painting denied all the central tenets of informal Impressionism and defined a new—and rigorously scientific—form of modernism. Of the stalwart Impressionists, Monet, Renoir, Caillebotte, and Sisley (1839–1899) abandoned the group in disgust, leaving only Pissarro (1830–1903) (who had "converted" to Neo-Impressionism), the ever-faithful Morisot, and the unpredictable Degas as Seurat's companions. Degas made the strongest impression on the critics, showing what he called a "Suite of Female Nudes," grouped together in their own room for maximum esthetic effect.

There were ten of these nudes in the 1886 exhibition, all pastels on paper, probably mostly mounted on pulp board. Various attempts to reconstruct this group have been made, all to no avail because they are so closely interrelated that even the most detailed descriptions can often apply to at least two surviving works. Surely, however, one of them was this bold pastel, later acquired through the advice of Degas's friend Mary Cassatt by the wealthy American collector Theodate Pope and her father. It has hung since the late 19th century in an important neocolonial house designed by Pope in Farmington, Connecticut, and is rarely exhibited outside this small private museum. Yet, it is among the pilgrimage objects of the Degas career, rightly taking its place in an art historical sequence of seminal "modern" indoor bathers that includes Caillebotte's *Man at his Bath* (see pages 268–69) and continues into the 20th century with Picasso's *Les Demoiselles d'Avignon* (see pages 292–93). Within the 1886 exhibition, it rhymed with one of the boldest paintings in the Neo-Impressionist manner, *Two Milliners* (1885–86, Buhrle Foundation, Zurich) by Paul Signac (1863–1935), in which a clothed woman, posed identically to the Degas bather, is shown at work in a city millinery shop. The working-class context of these figures has been discussed in recent literature; both

EDGAR DEGAS

BORN PARIS 1834,
DIED PARIS 1917

represent the working woman from the "superior" position of a male voyeur whose interest, it is argued, is exclusively prurient. Yet, there must be more to these "games" than is explained by such simple notions. In his "Suite of Female Nudes," Degas liberated the nude from allegory and history, allowing the female body to assume a variety of "anti-poses," as expressive and emotionally resonant as any in the history of art. That the figure is observed as if from an omniscient or unobserved (some say "keyhole") perspective is not necessarily sexist, and these works appealed to all the early women connoisseurs and collectors of Impressionism. Berthe Morisot and her daughter Julie Manet were enthralled by the Degas bathing bodies, never finding them vulgar or suggestive of low life as most modern critics assert.

The rhythmic contours of the body seem engaged in a formal dance with the tub that defies logical explanation. Is the woman balancing herself, cleaning the tub after her bath, or wiping up invisible water with her sponge? One thing is clear, that her bath, like that of Caillebotte's male nude of 1884, is being taken in the daytime, and we feel the powerful light of a sunny day as it washes across the bath sheet on the floor.

Many writers have related this pastel to the group of seven works that represent a single nude woman either kneeling or squatting in a large round tub, all of which were made in the years around 1886. When considered together, these works become almost a scientific analysis of a figure around which the artist seems to move until he "fixes" a point of view that suits his unspoken esthetic aims. The serial nature of this project can easily be related to motion photography, which was well known to Degas, but the comparison is certainly superficial. It was not the motion itself—either of the viewer or the model—that interested Degas (because he never exhibited these works together) but, rather, the successful images that could be wrested from that motion. Degas achieved an uneasy balance of figure and space, form and color in these pastels, which he pushed harder and harder to make the central theme of his work. The nude in *Woman Bathing in a Shallow Tub* from his first consciously exhibited "Suite" of nudes is complete on its own.

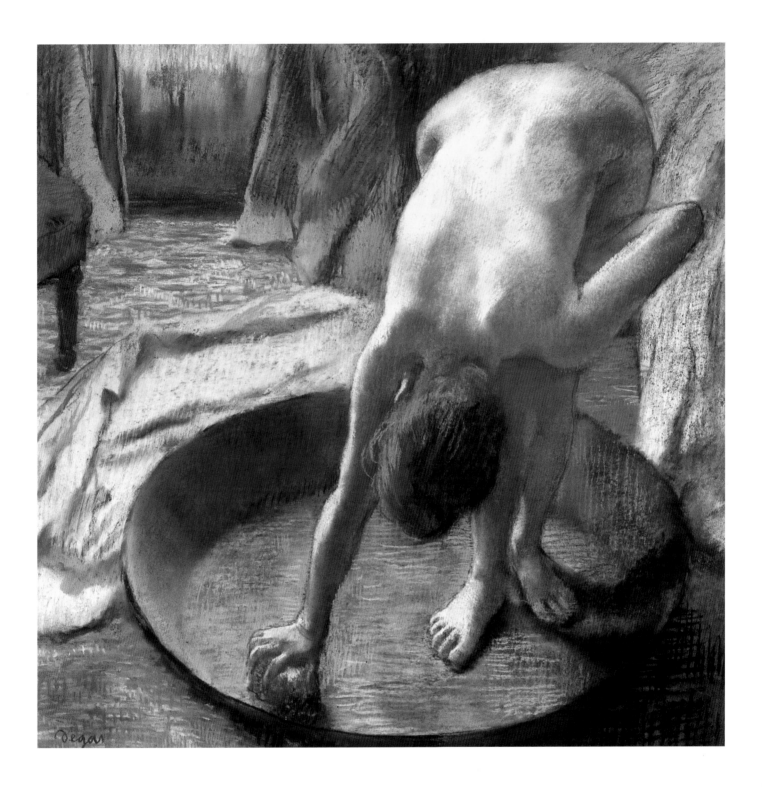

The Models *(Les Poseuses)*

THE *MODELS* IS the most perfect realization of Seurat's Neo-Impressionism. Although he had developed the dotted technique in 1884 when working on *Sunday on the Island of La Grande Jatte, 1884*, he had not been able to apply it consistently on a large scale until *The Models*, which complemented and commented upon *La Grande Jatte*, seen in the background, and which was the third and last of his immense exhibition pictures (the first was *Bathers at Asnières*, 1884, National Gallery, London). Seurat himself referred to these Neo-Impressionist works as *toiles de lutte* (canvases of struggle), and doubtless the struggle was his own.

He conceived and executed this very large canvas in a small studio on the Boulevard Clichy, working for more than a year, virtually daily and constantly, on a work that remained unsold at his death. His "struggle" was both with and against tradition, and the work abounds in quotations from Classical and Renaissance art, through to Ingres. The three models (clearly analogous to the Three Graces) pose—the title, in fact, is better translated as *The Poseurs* because the usual French word for models is *modèles*—in classic frontal, back, and profile poses, each firmly rooted in the history of Western figural art, but they do so in the artist's studio, which is treated as a kind of laboratory for the new art.

Seurat prepared his large canvas both carefully and also unconventionally by covering it with white gesso, or plaster, rather than with a traditional oil-based primer. This immediately connected the work to the long tradition of Classical wall painting, but, in choosing the thick, dry surface of plaster, Seurat presented himself with practical problems. The relatively porous nature of plaster turned his initial dots into "stains," the borders of which were not always easy to control. With its consistently dotted technique, the painting is literally a visual embodiment of Seurat's "struggle," each pictorial decision resulting in individual acts which, should a viewer have infinite time, can be literally counted and catalogued by size, color, and location. Each decision was at once a *color* decision, a *value* decision, and a *representational* decision, and, in order to better control the process, Seurat made several preparatory paintings (two for the whole composition and at least one each for the figures) and a group of

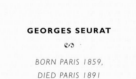

GEORGES SEURAT

BORN PARIS 1859,
DIED PARIS 1891

conté crayon drawings. These enabled him to think through chromatic, value (light and dark), and representational issues on a small scale as he worked on the large canvas.

Seurat adapted to painting the optical and physical theories of simultaneous color contrast in which reality is conceived as a field of vision decomposed into dots, comparable to the separate rods and cones of the human eye. As such, the painting is a chromatic reconstruction of colored reality. Each color perception is effectively reproduced by a dot, and each dot acts as part of a highly unstable and shifting series of color sensations, all of which respond quiveringly to every adjacent color sensation. When this complex series of notions, derived from optics, light theory, theories of perception, and philosophy were combined in Seurat's highly orderly mind with an equally complex and emotionally based theory of "composition," the theoretical claims of this painting almost overwhelm the viewer. Yet, Seurat's friends—and they were powerful and intelligent—were well prepared for the exhibition of *The Models* at the Salon des Indépendants in the spring of 1888 and for its triumphant trip to Brussels for the 1889 exhibition of Les XX (from which Ensor's masterpiece was rejected, see pages 276–77). The critics Félix Fénéon, Gustave Kahn, and Paul Adam wrote sympathetically about it, and only one anonymous reviewer allowed himself to fantasize that the models were "daubed in all colours of the rainbow … suffering, if would seem, from some horrible skin disease."

Although the painting is in pristine condition and has been on public display since the 1920s, its reputation suffered because no color reproductions of it were allowed by the Barnes Foundation until 1993, when it was first exhibited outside the collection and first published in color. This act restored the work to its proper place in what the art historian Griselda Pollock called the avant-garde "gambit" in which major male artists fight for supremacy in a battleground of painted female nudes. Manet fired the first shot in 1863, Renoir and Degas answered in the 1870s, and Seurat countered with *The Models* in 1888. Cézanne, Gauguin, Matisse, and Picasso entered the increasingly crowded field after Seurat's challenge with his "painting of struggle."

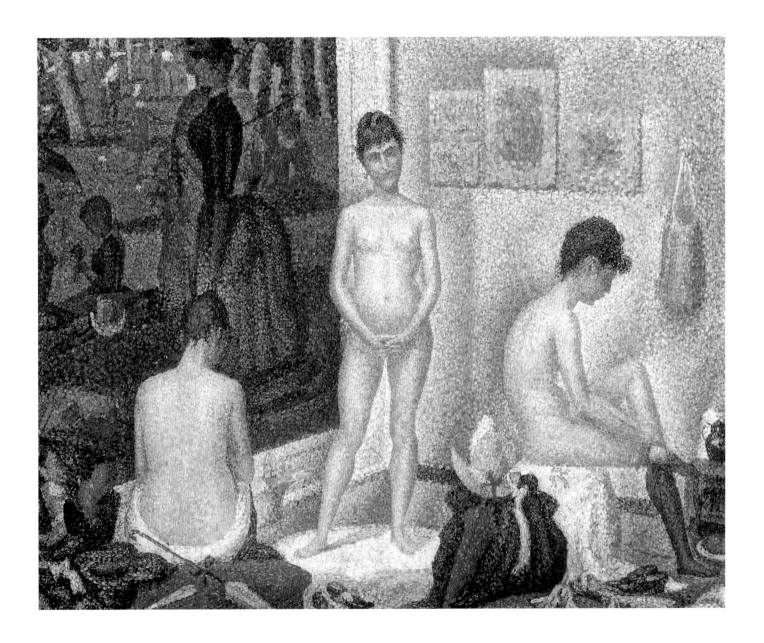

1886—88 | *oil on canvas* | 82 x 121in (208 x 308cm) | Barnes Foundation, Merion, Pennsylvania

The Night Café

VINCENT VAN GOGH lived such a short, powerfully intense, and productive life and wrote so many and such eloquent letters that both his life and his letters threaten to overwhelm his art. After serving as both a missionary and an art dealer and after an independent artistic apprenticeship in Holland, this son of a Dutch Protestant minister arrived in Paris in February 1886, saw the final Impressionist exhibition in May, and, in very short order, assimilated all the qualities of vanguard French painting from Monet, Pissarro, Seurat, and Gauguin. Indeed, no other non-French artist of the late 1880s had a better crash course in the esthetic aims of Post-Impressionism at the very moment of its creation. From Monet, van Gogh learned the independent expressive power of the heavily loaded brush worked with apparently free gestures of the wrist, elbow, and arm; from Pissarro and Seurat he learned of the advanced color theories developed for the newly doctrinal Neo-Impressionism; from Gauguin he learned the art theory of color exaggeration and compositional experimentation that the older artist had dubbed Synthetism. And, each of these lessons firmly assimilated, van Gogh struck out on his own in February 1888 to the ancient town of Arles in Provence to establish what he soon called the "Studio of the South."

His paintings poured forth as from a torrent. Before his breakdown on Christmas Eve 1888, van Gogh had produced hundreds of paintings and drawings, surpassing in sheer quantity the most prolific years of ever-prolific artists like Monet and Renoir. So it is difficult to identify a "masterpiece" or summary work from this crucial period in his oeuvre, and van Gogh himself might not have selected *The Night Café*, which he called in one letter "one of the ugliest I have done," and in another "atrociously ugly and bad." He seems to have created it as a form of esthetic payment for his rent, overdue to the owner of the so-called Café de Nuit, whom we see here as a virtual undertaker standing beside the coffinlike bulk of the billiard table at the center of the composition. Van Gogh called the work "the money I have paid to the landlord by my painting." Van Gogh's famous, vivid letter describing the painting at some length to his brother

VINCENT VAN GOGH

*BORN GROOT ZUNDER 1853,
DIED AUVERS-SUR-OISE 1890*

Theo and illustrated with a drawing made after it, deserves the long quotation that has become standard in the literature about this powerful—and depressing—work: "I have tried to express the terrible passions of humanity by means of red and green. The room is blood red and dark yellow with a green billiard table in the middle; there are four lemon-yellow lamps with a glow of orange and green. Everywhere there is a clash and contrast of the most alien reds and greens in the figures of the little sleeping hooligans, in the empty dreary room, in violet and blue. The blood red and the yellow-green of the billiard table, for instance, contrast with the soft tender Louis XV green of the counter on which there is a nosegay in rose color. The white coat of the patron, on vigil in a corner of this furnace, turns lemon yellow or pale luminous green … It is color not locally true…but color to suggest any emotion of an ardent temperament."

Here, van Gogh borrows the theory of color contrast developed to its highest form by the "optical" artists around Seurat (see page 272). But, rather than rooting his esthetic in that of human perception and the eye, van Gogh explicitly rejects the optical, preferring to locate the meaning of this painting in the emotional state of what he called "an ardent temperament." In this way, even the "atrociously ugly" quality of the painting is part of what he called in a later letter its "deep meaning." This painting is, in fact, part of a serious investigation of night, a subject all but unknown to the suburban and rural Impressionists, whose paintings seem to radiate the sunlight that van Gogh sought in the South. Here, night is coequal with hell, and the mirror on the wall behind the proprietor seems almost to reflect flames and congealed blood. The clock, set past midnight, floats in an inexplicable void, and the doorway on the left of the bar sets off a brilliant yellow inner room that might serve as a sun-yellow heaven to counter the hell of the mirror.

The fragility of this thickly—and quickly—painted work has prevented its inclusion in any of the important van Gogh exhibitions organized in the past generation, making a journey to New Haven—scarcely more than an hour by train from New York City—essential for a full appreciation of van Gogh's oeuvre.

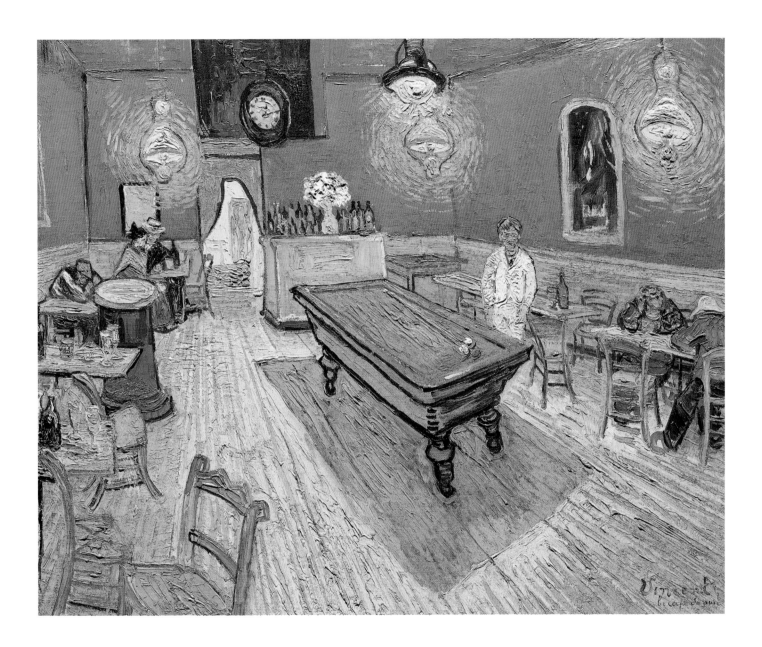

1888 | *oil on canvas* | 29 x 35in (74 x 89cm) | Yale University Art Gallery, New Haven

The Entry of Christ into Brussels

JAMES ENSOR was the greatest eccentric of European modernism and this extraordinary canvas is his masterpiece. Rejected by Les XX for their 1889 exhibition, it was never publicly exhibited in the 19th century and only received wide exposure after 1929 when Ensor's reputation was given a boost by the Surrealists.

James Ensor was a complex, difficult artist whose life can only be matched by those of William Blake (1757–1827) and Salvador Dalí (1904–89). The only son of a wealthy Anglo-Belgian couple, he lived almost all his life in the beach resort of Ostend, where he received an essentially private education before studying at the Royal Academy in Brussels for three years. Although independently wealthy, his parents ran a series of souvenir shops in Ostend, selling cheap trinkets like seashells, chinoiseries, gaudy Chinese porcelains, glass baubles, stuffed animals, ships-in-bottles, vases, puppets, and dolls, and, during the mid-Lent holidays, painted masks and brilliantly colored tinsel ornaments made to terrify and astonish. Prepared by this phantasmagoric mélange, Ensor was attracted to the highly charged works of artists like Hieronymus Bosch, Pieter Bruegel the Elder, Jacques Callot (1592/3–1635), Francisco de Goya, and J.M.W. Turner (he seems not to have known Blake) and to the fantastical texts of Cervantes, Rabelais, Poe, Baudelaire, Flaubert, and Heine. As a student, his associates included the Symbolist painters Willy Finch (1854–1930) and Fernand Khnopff (1858–1921), and his closest friends in Brussels collected insects and lived next to a natural history museum with its fossils, animals in formaldehyde, and other natural "curiosities." This background did not prepare Ensor to paint gentle landscapes and portraits!

When Ensor's supportive father died in 1887, his art took a decidedly apocalyptic turn, and he began to contemplate the creation of an independent masterpiece on the scale of the largest paintings of Rubens, Veronese, and Tintoretto. This became *The Entry of Christ into Brussels*, which he completed in his small attic studio in Ostend, working both with expensive oil paints and brilliantly colored house paints. The studio was so cramped that only the upper half of the painting could be tacked to the wall while the lower half was draped across the floor.

JAMES ENSOR

☙

BORN OSTEND 1860,
DIED OSTEND 1949

Thus, Ensor painted it both vertically and horizontally and was never able to see the entire composition while he worked on it; much of the lower portion was painted as he stood on the canvas.

The resulting image takes hours to scan. Its figures number in the thousands, and its setting is so architecturally complex and imprecise that it cannot be identified with Brussels. Even its central figure, Christ, with the face of Ensor himself, riding a donkey in an urban parade, is small enough to miss in the crowd of humans and masked figures. They rush toward the viewer in such tumultuous multitudes that we yearn to flee the painting. There is no more compelling representation of claustrophobia than Ensor's masterpiece, and given its genesis in a tiny attic room, this phobic mania becomes all the more intense.

Among the many remarkable aspects of the painting is its brilliantly vulgar palette. Only the Dutchman van Gogh and the French painters Paul Gauguin and Emile Bernard (1868–1941) could match the richness of Ensor's painting, and their works are so small by comparison that the Belgian wins through. And it is clear that Ensor had no interest in the complex optical and physiological theories of color perception espoused by Seurat and the Neo-Impressionists. It was the vivid colors of his parents' souvenirs that inspired him into an ecstasy of chromatic excess.

When *The Entry of Christ* first appeared in public in Antwerp in 1929, newly stretched and probably repainted, it entered an art world fully prepared for its eccentricities. At its moment of creation in 1888–89, it was unacceptable even to avant-garde artists who wanted to shock the bourgeoisie in their own narrow terms, not in those of James Ensor. In 1932, Ensor spoke evocatively of the work: "O the animal masks of the Ostend Carnival: bloated vicuña faces, misshapen birds with the tails of birds-of-paradise, cranes with sky-blue bills babbling nonsense, clay-footed architects, Obtuse socialists with moldy skulls, heartless vivisectionists, odd insects, hard shells giving shelter to soft beasts. Witness *The Entry of Christ into Brussels* which teams with all the hard and soft creatures spewed out by the sea. Won over by irony, touched by splendors, my vision becomes more refined, I purify my colors, they are whole and personal."

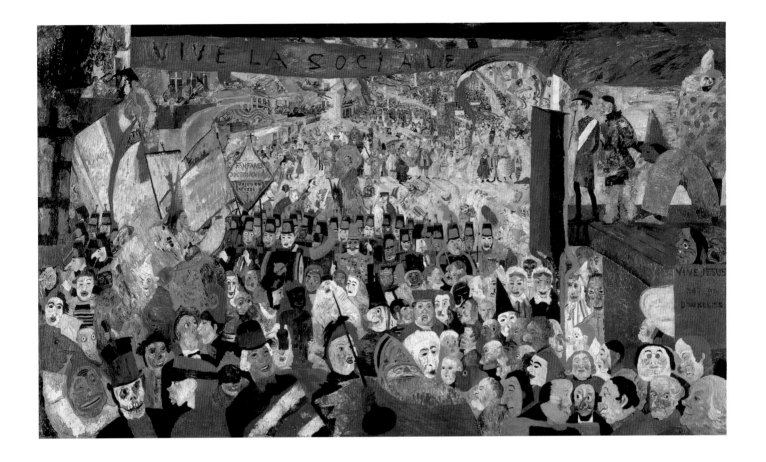

1888–89, reworked 1920 and possibly later | *oil on canvas* | 101¹⁄₂ x 169¹⁄₂in (258 x 431cm) | J. Paul Getty Museum, Los Angeles

Ashes

IN BERLIN in 1902, the painter Edvard Munch exhibited a series of large paintings and prints, arranged in bands as *Frieze: Cycle of Moments from Life*. It contained works from the past decade of Munch's career, many of which had previously been exhibited in a group called *The Love Series*. This cycle had consisted of four sections: on the left wall, *Seeds of Love*; in the center, *Flowering and Passion of Love*, which included *Ashes*, then called *After the Fall*; on the right wall, *Life Anxiety*; and on the rear wall, *Death*. Munch's display of grouped works was grounded in avant-garde practice; he explained his carefully planned arrangement for *Frieze*: "I have always worked best with my paintings around me. I placed them together and felt that some of the pictures related to each other through the subject-matter; when they were placed together a sound went through them right away and they became quite different from when they were separate: they became a symphony." However, Munch was unique among European painters in attempting to understand human life through an intensive examination of the bourgeois life cycle. Although *Frieze* looked closely at the subject of death, its main focus was on love and sexual relations between men and women, and in this it was a kind of visual embodiment of the contemporary experimental theater of Munch's friends August Strindberg and Henrik Ibsen.

Like these two playwrights, Munch was a Scandinavian and a true cosmopolitan. During the 1890s, he visited Paris several times but preferred to make his mark in the smaller and more intensely competitive art world of Berlin. By 1893, he had met and begun an affair in Berlin with Dagny Juel, who became the muse/vampire that the group of male artists and writers around Munch seemed to want and need. Her effect on the group, although catastrophic in personal terms—she had disastrous affairs with many of them—drove them to extraordinary artistic and literary productivity. *Ashes* is among the largest and most enigmatic of the paintings that Munch was to group in *Frieze: Cycle of Moments from Life*. It shows a man and woman in an unbearably intense moment in their relationship, and a damaged passage from Munch's diaries has often been related to it: "We walked out of the stifling, flower-filled woods into the light of

EDVARD MUNCH

*BORN LYTEN 1863,
DIED EKELY 1944*

the night—I looked at her in the face and I ... had committed adultery—a Gorgon's head—I bent over and sat down ... I felt as if our love ... was lying there on those hard rocks."

In *Ashes* we see a mythic visual translation of that experience. The left and lower border of the painting represent a stream of water, making its way around black rocks, and the wood itself becomes a place of unenterable, shadowy darkness. The male figure, a surrogate for Munch, crouches in the corner, turning away as much from the viewer as from the woman, who fully acknowledges our gaze and seems to draw us into this highly personal catastrophe. She is, in fact, a gorgon, whose hair separates in strands on her shoulders like snakes, rivers of blood, or stains. Her dress has been opened, revealing her flaming red undergarments (Munch was somewhat prudish throughout his career in his treatment of the female nude), and she faces us apparently with no shame or guilt. These emotions are projected onto the male figure who, for all his passivity, is at least morally conscious. Munch takes no prisoners in his quest for an unflinching revelatory honesty, but to many early viewers, and particularly to French critics who were less burdened by the effects of sexual indiscretions, his work seemed like visual melodrama.

Munch's most significant contribution to modernist art was in his adaptation of the synthetist theory of Gauguin—which laid emphasis on color exaggeration and artifical composition—and his followers to a proto-psychoanalytical representation of bourgeois life. No French artists of the 1890s produced such haunting and disturbing works; they preferred to use art to comment on other works of art rather than on life. Munch, the northerner, descended into depths of the human psyche explored most powerfully by northern writers like Ibsen and Strindberg and the Russians Dostoyevsky and Gogol. Unfortunately, for the history of modernism, the majority of Munch's greatest paintings—most of which were shown in Germany, Austria, and France during the painter's lifetime—remain in Norwegian institutions, ensuring that Munch's work is not as powerfully integrated into modern European cosmopolitan art history as are those of Gauguin, van Gogh, and Seurat.

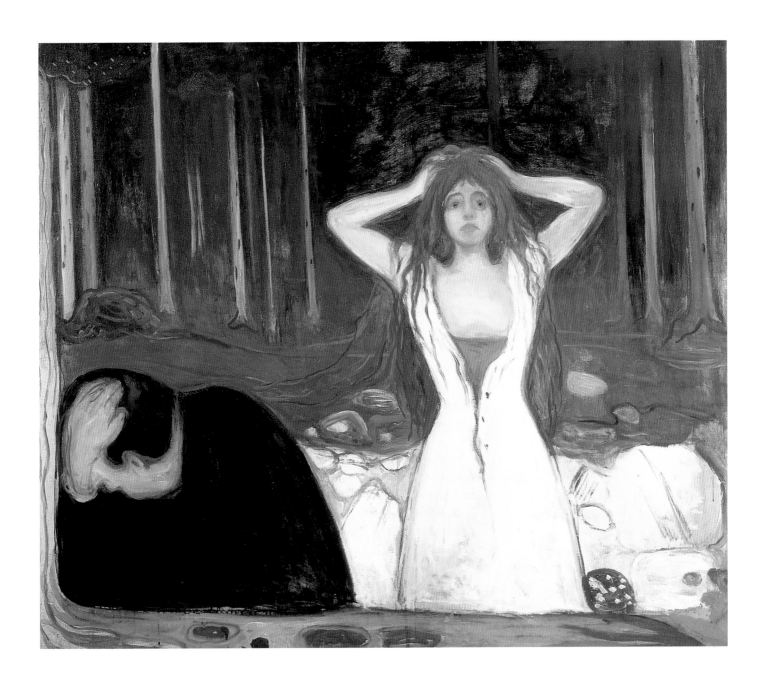

1894 | *oil on canvas* | 47$^{1}/_{2}$ x 56in (120.5 x 141cm) | National Gallery, Oslo

Large Interior with Six Figures

IF MUNCH laid bare human passions, exposing their brutality and harnessing the power of self-loathing, his French contemporary Edouard Vuillard was a master of subtle inference, discretion, and, occasionally, disavowal. The writer André Gide was right when he said that "Vuillard speaks almost in a whisper—as is only right when confidences are being exchanged—and we have to bend over to hear what he says." And Gide was discussing not Vuillard's voice, but his paintings.

Vuillard is well known for his large-scale intimate works, most of which were painted for a small circle of friends and their relatives during the late 1890s. Although many of these "decorations" were publicly exhibited, they were not intended as public statements but were embodiments of a newly private bourgeois art made for the cosmopolitan Parisian intelligentsia. So it would have been wrong for them to be brash or obvious, and Vuillard's discretion, his esthetic whispering, is part of the private nature of his art. *Large Interior with Six Figures* is perhaps his best and largest easel painting of the 1890s. It was not intended for a specific client but was first shown in 1897 at a Nabis exhibition held at Amboise Vollard's commercial gallery. When a collector made a low offer for the painting, Vuillard's friend, the Swiss artist Félix Vallotton (1865–1925), convinced him not to sell the work. Perhaps as a result of Vallotton's admiration, Vuillard gave him the painting, which hung proudly in Vallotton's Paris apartment as the kind of private decoration to which Vuillard made such important contributions.

We are allowed into a large, richly decorated salon at night. Its style is "English" in the Arts and Crafts William Morris manner, including a casual array of unmatched objects. The curtains are drawn and dark, and although pools of light animate the space, no light fixtures are visible. The room has the look of a stage set, like those that Vuillard routinely designed for the Théâtre du l'Oeuvre, run by his friend Lugné-Poe. In this theater, many plays by Ibsen, Strindberg, and Maeterlinck received their French premiere, the idea of intense domestic drama being given full play in Paris. Yet, Vuillard's response to this milieu was the opposite of that of Edvard Munch, who read

EDOUARD VUILLARD

∾

*BORN CUISEAUX 1868,
DIED LA BAULE 1940*

and saw the same plays (see page 280). Here, we see six figures, one man and five women, four of whom are standing or moving about the room. The figures have been variously identified as either the artist Odilon Redon (1840–1916) or Vuillard's brother-in-law, the painter Ker-Xavier Roussel (1867–1944), and female members of the Redon family or, for two of the women, as Vuillard's mother and sister. Yet, as Vuillard's title suggests, they are merely six figures, "characters," and we are asked to interpret their relationships without knowing their identities. The man is preoccupied, examining a piece of paper which he holds so close to his face that we are unable to see his features; a woman seems to be bringing him a shawl or blanket. The old woman at the left simply sits, unoccupied and watching, perhaps talking to the standing figure, whose back is turned to us in front of the littered desk. Thus, Vuillard hides more than he reveals with his figures, suppressing telling details, frustrating our desire for narrative continuity and clarity.

Instead, we wander through this wonderfully detailed and furnished room like a butterfly attracted to light and color. The composition is so carefully contrived that each element interlocks with its neighbors to form an intensely pleasing puzzle or tapestry of color. A wonderful Middle Eastern carpet stretches across a large part of the floor, overlapping other carpets and itself covered by a patterned rug on which Vuillard sets the carved desk and a floor cushion. A tapestry hangs on a papered or fabric-covered wall. Decorated plates, pillows, small stools, flowers, papers, books, paintings, and piles of textiles "fill out" the space, which is at once spacious and claustrophobic, full of visual pleasure and of endless possibilities of touching, talking, reading, listening, and moving around. There is an empty chair for us, and the woman at the door seems conscious of our entrance as she is about to leave the room. We are on a vast game board of color, and, again, Gide puts it best: Vuillard "never strives for brilliant effect. Harmony of tone is his continual preoccupation; science and intuition play a double role in the disposition of his colors, and each of them casts new light on its neighbors and, as it were, extracts a confession from it."

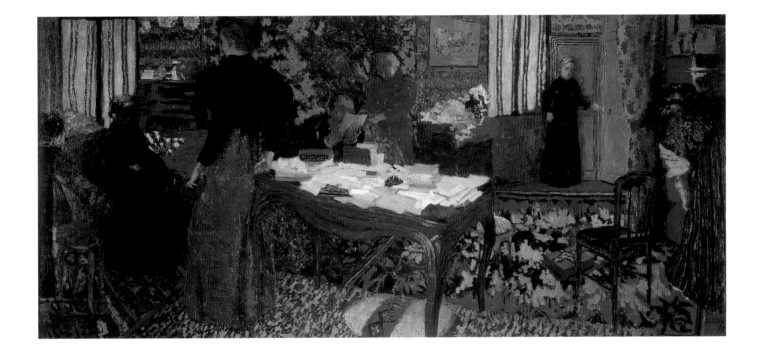

1897 ┃ *oil on canvas* ┃ 35 x 76in (88 x 193cm) ┃ Kunsthaus, Zurich

Rupe Rupe *(Luxury)*

IN 1897, Gauguin completed his largest painting to date, a canvas that poses three written questions on its surface: *Where Do We Come From? What Are We? Where Are We Going?* (Museum of Fine Arts, Boston). Almost as soon as this work left his Tahitian studio for Paris, Gauguin began another self-conscious masterpiece inscribed *Rupe Rupe*. The latter entered the collection of the great Russian connoisseur Sergei Shchukin early in the 20th century and, because of its fragility, has never been exhibited outside Russia and so is much less well known than the Boston work.

If *Where Do We Come From?* is an extended meditation on the concept of "paradise" in the mode of John Milton's epic poem *Paradise Lost* (1667), *Rupe Rupe* is Gauguin's visual embodiment of the English poet's shorter text, *Paradise Regained* (1671) (both were coupled with related works). The great androgynous fruit picker at the center of the Boston painting, which, by its act, brings death into the world, is replaced in *Rupe Rupe* by a clothed woman picking fruit in a composition where age and death have no place. A volume of *Paradise Lost* was included in a painting by Gauguin as early as 1889, and he was clearly aware of Christo-logical concepts of paradise (that is, those relating to the inter-cession of Christ) when he first went to Tahiti in 1891. By the time of *Rupe Rupe*, Gauguin had lost hope of finding an actual paradise on earth and had accepted the inescapable fact of his Western and European nature. Hence, following the Miltonian model, Gauguin had first to paint a modern *Paradise Lost* before he could esthetically "regain" that paradise.

The paradise that Gauguin regained was only possible in art, and *Rupe Rupe*, with its rich golden and yellow tonalities, brings the favorite color of van Gogh—the yellow of the sunflowers that he painted to fill Gauguin's room in the "Studio of the South"—into the center of Gauguin's art. It is the yellow of Gauguin's *Yellow Christ* (1889, Albright-Knox Gallery, Buffalo), of his *Self-portrait as Les Misérables* (1888, Rijksmuseum Vincent van Gogh, Amsterdam), of the Volpini suite of lithographs (1899–1900), and of the sheets beneath the Virgin after the birth of Christ in *Te Tamari no Atua* (1896, Neue Pinakothek, Munich). The yellow of the sun, of warmth, and of paradise.

PAUL GAUGUIN

☙

*BORN PARIS 1848,
DIED ATUANA, MARQUESAS ISLANDS 1903*

The figures and plants that fill Gauguin's "yellowscape" derive mostly from the Buddhist friezes at Borobadur in Java, which Gauguin knew from photographs and a partial plaster reproduc-tion. They are arranged across pulsating fields of color with no horizon, no sky, no earth, no representational value. Space is defined by immense greenish shadows that fall from unseen trees. The three women at the center of this paradise pick or display fruit and flowers while two puppies play around their sleeping mother. A man on horseback enters, bending down as if to fit into Gauguin's canvas. Soon he will dismount and partake of the offerings of the three women, who serve as visual equiva-lents of the Three Graces and who, unlike the rider, are clothed.

Gauguin's male figure is obviously on a journey through life, like other horsemen in his oeuvre, but he has arrived at a place so inviting that surely he will stop. Is he, we must ask as readers of Milton, being tempted by Satan? This painting rejects Milton's rigorous process of Christological improvement, embodied in *Paradise Regained*, yet Christ was never far from Gauguin's mind, and a com-panion painting to *Rupe Rupe*, acquired by Shchukin's friendly rival Ivan Morosov and conventionally (though wrongly) entitled *The Large Buddha* (1899, Pushkin Museum, Moscow) (the figure is actually a Polynesian deity derived from an ancestor figure Gauguin had seen in New Zealand), sets its scene of pagan worship in a vast room containing a Last Supper. It seems that the world of pure color, of beautiful women who bear beautiful children, and of eternal youth *was* a temptation for Gauguin, and this delicious decora-tion, with its visiting horseman and its vast shadows, makes us aware that paradise, if regained, is only regained temporarily.

When did Matisse see this extraordinary painting? Did it appear under a different title in the 1903 Gauguin exhibition held in Paris, as I suspect? Or did he have to wait until his 1911 trip to Moscow, when he had already learned its lessons? Whenever he saw it, Matisse must have been stunned to see such a realm painted well before he even conceived of *Luxe, calme et volupté* (1904–5, Musée d'Orsay, Paris), and did he know that Gauguin had translated his mysterious Tahitian title as *Luxury*?

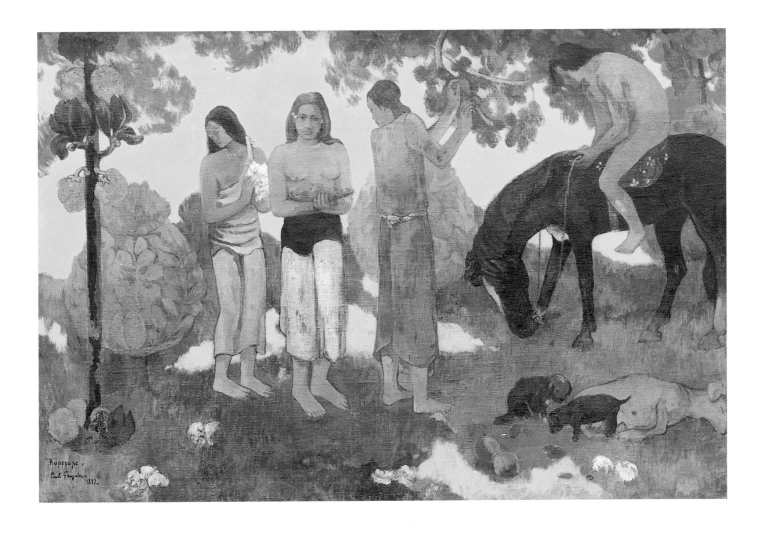

1899 | *oil on canvas* | 50½ x 79in (128 x 200cm) | Pushkin Museum, Moscow

The Beethoven Frieze

GUSTAV KLIMT received a traditional, academic training as a painter in Vienna. His skill as a draftsman and designer of architectural decorations led to a successful career painting commissioned murals in palaces, museums, university buildings, and theaters, and until the early 1890s, his art can safely be called "academic." Yet, in the second half of that decade, after the 1892 death of his brother and artistic collaborator Ernst, Klimt turned away from the world of official art and culture, and became the first president of the experimental artistic group the Vienna Secession, in 1897. By 1900, his paintings for the Uni-versity of Vienna began to inspire hostile criticism in the press, and in 1902, when he painted his first uncommissioned and utterly "modern" decorative cycle, *The Beethoven Frieze*, his work inspired the vitriolic and negative criticism typical of European vanguard art. One anonymous example will suffice: "It has gone far enough, and everyone with the slightest sense of decency is filled with a burning rage. What is there to be said about this painted pornography ... For some subterranean locality in which pagan orgies are celebrated these paintings may be appropriate, but not for rooms to which the artists are bold enough to invite honorable ladies and innocent young girls ... Are there no men left in Vienna to protest against such an assassination?"

The paintings about which this reviewer ranted were installed in the first room of a suite of three galleries in the 14th Secession Exhibition that centered on a garish, polychrome, neoclassical sculpture by Max Klinger (1857–1920) of Beethoven (1899–1902, Museum der Bildenden Künste, Leipzig). The aim of the organizers was to inject a modernist vitality into the genius of Beethoven, using his music and commentaries on it by Wagner and Nietzsche as a platform for esthetic experimentation on a grand scale. The exhibition they conceived was the opposite of the individualist shows of the Impressionists, since the artists were asked to submit to a series of principals and themes to produce a total esthetic experience. The catalog stated: " First of all, there must be unity of space, and this space must be enriched by paintings and sculpture which conform and contribute to the overall idea. The parts must be subordinated to the whole."

GUSTAV KLIMT

&

BORN VIENNA 1862,
DIED VIENNA 1918

Klimt's mural was intended to prepare the viewer for the first sight of Klinger's sculpture. Arranged around the top of a simple skylit room, it was a frieze that could not be taken in at a glance, and it invited the viewer to turn around and around and, thus, break free from the conventions of immediate judgment prompted by easel pictures. Below it, a series of such pictures were framed within the walls, but the mood of the gallery was utterly determined by Klimt. The whole experience was choreographed; even the reclusively shy composer and conductor Gustav Mahler was persuaded to join the collaboration and transpose the last movement of Beethoven's Ninth Symphony into a performance piece for trumpets, so that the opening of the exhibition would be filled with the master's music.

Klimt's frieze was without doubt the freest and most interesting work in the exhibition. In it we see floating figures, choirs of angels, post-pubescent nudes, immensely pregnant women, a gigantic baboon, tightly coiled snakes of vast proportions, a knight in gilded armor, a pair of naked kissing lovers (illustrated), and a nude anorexic couple, the male figure of which seems to wear his penis as an applied appendage. No wonder our poor anonymous reviewer went apoplectic at the sight of this ensemble, although it is fair to say that never before in the history of modern art had such a bizarrely erotic subject been treated with such polite decorative devotion. Only in the prints of Aubrey Beardsley (1872–1898) or the estheticized panels of Khnopff is such apparent perversity so conventionally represented.

The frieze, which had been painted directly onto the walls, only remained in place until the Klimt exhibition in 1903. Afterward, it was removed in sections and entered private collections until it was finally sold to the Austrian state in 1973. Only then was it properly restored and seen in public for the first time in seventy years. It was permanently installed in a basement room of the Secession building, and although this has no skylights, it at least retains the proportions and character of the original space. Because Klimt's great decorations for the University of Vienna were destroyed in 1945, *The Beethoven Frieze* is, without question, his most important and ambitious achievement extant.

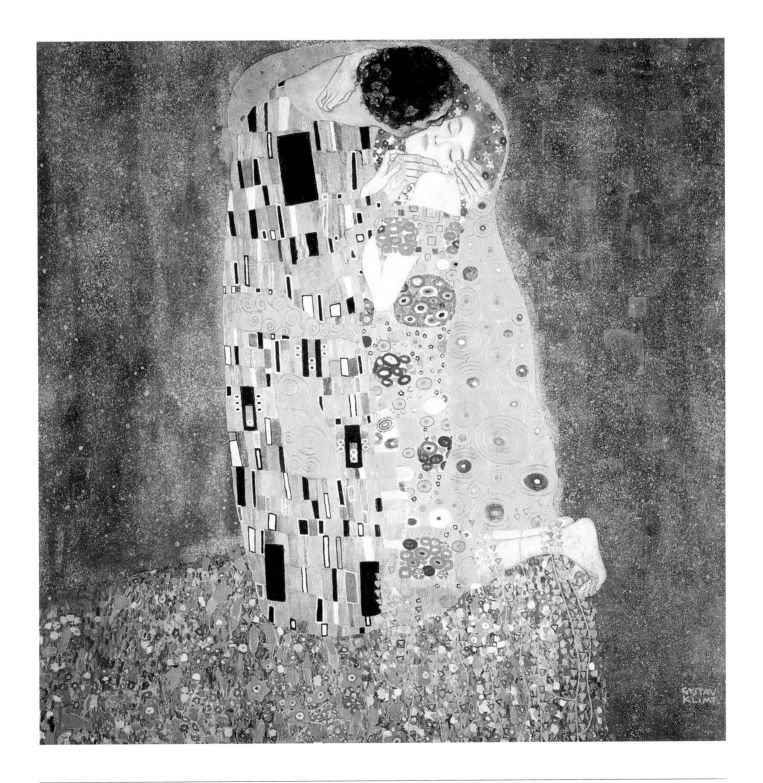

1902 | *casein, gold leaf, semiprecious stones, mother-of-pearl, gypsum, charcoal, pastel, and pencil on plaster*
| 7 x 118ft (2.15 x 35.5m) (cut into eight panels) | Österreichische Galerie, Vienna, installed in the Secession Building

Blue Landscape *(Paysage Bleu)*

THIS LANDSCAPE was included in the great 1907 Cézanne memorial exhibition that forever changed the history of art. It was chosen by Cézanne's son and by the great dealer Ambroise Vollard from among the large body of unsold—and possibly unfinished—paintings in Cézanne's studio as one of the finest of his career. Of the more than 950 oil paintings in Cézanne's oeuvre, it is one of only 58 large-scale canvases, and as this selection of works has made clear, size alone is a major factor in measuring a painter's ambitions. Although it was tempting to select one of the three monumental bather compositions from the last decade of Cézanne's life (Museum of Art, Philadelphia; Barnes Foundation, Merion, Pennsylvania; National Gallery, London), or even the largest version of the *Card Players* (1890, Barnes Foundation), it was, in the end, the late landscapes and still lifes, several of which were included in the 1907 exhibition, that had the most profound effect on the next generation of painters, preparing the way for the deconstructed, unstable pictorial surfaces of Analytic Cubism.

Blue Landscape invites us into a pictorial realm that is, at first, spatially legible, with its broad foreground plane and its curving road, but that soon dissolves into a flutter of overlapping diagonal brushstrokes, bunched in martial rhythms, that move inexorably upward along the vertical surface of the canvas. Spatial recession is further denied by Cézanne's decision to meld the rhythms of branches that move across the sky from a foreground tree with touches of the same size and color that represent distant foliage. Yet, embedded deep in the landscape is a rectangle of orange—the color complement of the predominant blue—that allows space to fill the center of the canvas and which is "matched" by a brilliant blue lozenge of distant sky that floats above it. Near and far, blue and orange are juxtaposed, and the entire landscape seems to fold around them in a kind of pictorial drama of touch that has few precedents in Western art.

Various commentators have vied to identify the site of this extraordinary canvas, insisting, as do most students of Cézanne, that his response to a precise landscape is a vital part of his esthetic. Yet, the very lack of success of these scholars suggests

PAUL CÉZANNE

BORN AIX-EN-PROVENCE 1839, DIED AIX-EN-PROVENCE 1906

the futility of their efforts. Virtually every writer concedes that the landscape "motif" is almost exasperatingly banal: an unidentified road curving through a tree-filled landscape, perhaps with a building at the center—hardly the imposingly symbolic motifs like the brooding Château Noir, the quarry at Bibemus, or Mont Sainte-Victoire, all near Aix-en-Provence, which most often appealed to the elderly Cézanne.

Authorities on the late Cézanne speak of the dramatic intensity with which he worked in a landscape, almost always alone and in a state of struggle between his motif and his pictorial embodiment of it. The Russian scholar Anna Barskaya, in her catalog of the French paintings in the Hermitage, refers to this kind of pictorial intensity when she notes that "the rent in the center of the canvas, now restored, was the result of a blow that the artist gave the picture at a moment of exasperation, as was frequently the case with him." The idea that the picture can literally become the enemy of the frustrated artist and that art is a ceaseless battle reminds us of Georges Seurat's plaintive reference to his *toiles de lutte* (canvases of struggle) (see page 272). Yet, surely Cézanne's selection of a "weak" motif, one with little symbolic or associational significance, gave him the upper hand in this struggle to dominate appearances.

Let us return to the title of this painting—and to its dominant color—the *Blue Landscape*. Various writers have discussed Cézanne's virtual obsession with this color and his contribution to its history in Western representational art. For Karl de Tolnay, writing in 1933, Cézanne's blue "is not air, but a sort of fluid made of matter, simultaneously solid and liquid, an element in which all substances are assimilated into one another." The very spatial ambiguity of the color—its multiple nature as the color of shadows on snow, of water, of sky, and of the most precious of colored stones, lapis lazuli—was unconsciously recognized by Cézanne in this painting that seems to be as much about blue as about a particular landscape. We can well imagine Georges Braque, Henri Matisse, Maurice de Vlaminck (1876–1958), and other major 20th-century artists standing dumbstruck in front of this large *Blue Landscape* when it was first exhibited in 1907.

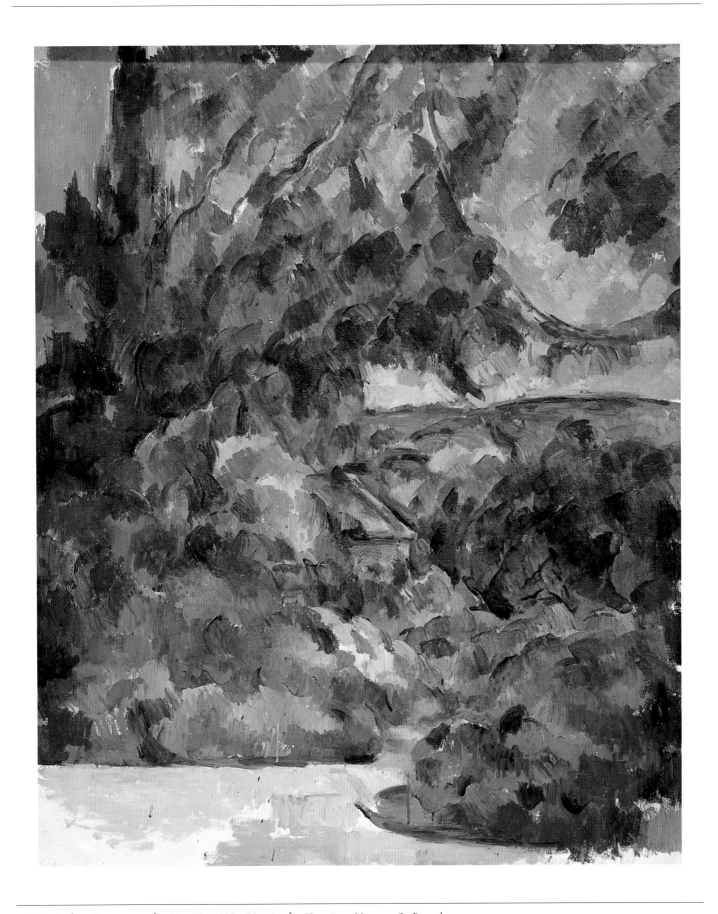

1904–6 | *oil on canvas* | 40 x 33in (102 x 83cm) | Hermitage Museum, St. Petersburg

Waterlilies *(Nymphéas)*

In MAY 1909, a year and half after the 1907 Cézanne exhibition, Claude Monet opened an exhibition at the Durand-Ruel Gallery in Paris called *Waterlilies: Series of Water Landscapes*. It was the fourth of his exhibitions devoted to a single subject; the first, of haystacks, had revolutionized painting in 1891 (in 1892 came poplars and in 1895 Rouen Cathedral). *Waterlilies* was also the largest of the series exhibitions with forty-eight paintings, the fruit of five years' hard work. They varied in format from squares to golden rectangles to circles, and represented Monet's recently enlarged waterlily pond across the rail tracks from his house in Giverny. Monet was sixty-eight at the time of the exhibition and had already outlived his friends and colleagues Camille Pissarro, Alfred Sisley, and Paul Cézanne.

Although Monet had painted his water garden since the late 1890s, it was not until its enlargement in 1903 that he made paintings where the water is almost the sole subject of the picture. By 1905, he had eliminated all hints of the land, and thereafter his works represented a consistent plane of water, filling the entire pictorial surface, decorated with floating flowers and reflecting the changing, seasonal world around and above it. These became the "water landscapes" that conjoin the two pictorial metaphors referred to earlier in this chapter: windows and mirrors (see page 264). Yet, unlike interior mirrors, which can reflect those who look into them, the mirrored surface of the pond never included Monet himself, who sat on its banks or on the Japanese bridge that crossed it and looked across the reflecting surface. Hence, his "mirror" is a horizontal surface and literally a reflecting land*scape* (escape).

During the 1990s, two attempts were made in major retrospectives at partial reconstructions of the 1909 exhibition, and this canvas was included in both. I have chosen it to represent a collective work of art as ambitious as Gauguin's ensemble of "paradise" pictures (see page 282), as Munch's *Frieze: Cycle of Moments from Life* (page 278), or as Klimt's *Beethoven Frieze* (page 284). It is an independent—and glorious—fragment of a total work of art that had a fleetingly short life of only one month in the spring of 1909. Aside from its sheer beauty, I selected this picture because it is one of the two largest canvases of the final group of ten works painted by Monet in 1908, just before he made his selection for the 1909 exhibition. Its brilliant yellow foliage also indicates that it was painted in the autumn of 1908 and, as one of the last works in the series, was therefore a conscious comment on the earlier water landscapes, all of which he had assembled in his studio as he worked on the final group for the exhibition. As a culminating object—so acknowledged by the fact that Monet signed and dated the painting—it represents, as it were, Monet's reflection on a series of reflections.

The painting itself is almost impossible to reproduce, so subtle and elusive is its chromatic structure. The top two-thirds is dominated by the reflection of the two banks of trees, between which Monet represents a river of sky that winds up the canvas. This area is painted in pale lemon yellow, celadon green, pink, warm gray, and pink-tinged white. Across each of the golden reflected stands of trees is a group of pink and ivory waterlilies that make the surface of the water understandable as it stretches away from us. The lower part of the work, partially in shadow, probably from the footbridge, is pale violet (the color complement of the yellow above) and on it floats a single central group of celadon waterlilies with small, intensely red blossoms. Monet does not allow us to determine the depth of the pool; he concentrated on its reflective surface, the plane of which is defined by the waterlilies receding discreetly into an unknowable distance. In the top right of the picture is a hint of the vegetation at the water's edge, which is balanced by Monet's substantial, dark plum-purple signature and date in the lower left corner. Even his "identity" is colored.

Several writers have likened Monet to Narcissus, forever staring into reflective water. But, unlike Narcissus, who stares at himself and is most often depicted by artists from Poussin onward in such a way that we see both man and reflection, Monet is uninterested in any references to himself beyond his signature. Nor do we see reflections of the numerous visitors to Giverny. The waterlily pictures are isolated, contemplative, and, in this case, literally autumnal works.

CLAUDE MONET

*BORN PARIS 1840,
DIED GIVERNY 1926*

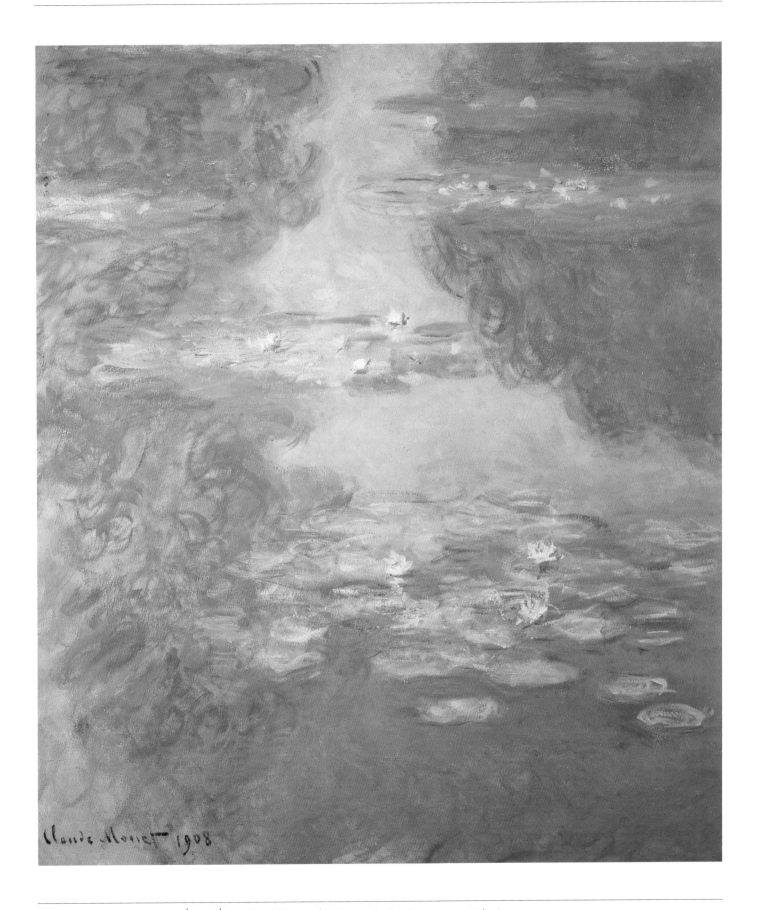

Claude Monet 1908

1908 | *oil on canvas* | 39¹⁄₂ x 39¹⁄₂in (100 x 100cm) | Maspro Denkoh Art Museum, Aichi, Japan

THE EARLY 20TH CENTURY

1900—1950 ❧ JILL LLOYD

This period is regarded as one of the turning points in the history of Western art.

During these years, artists radically challenged the authority of the past

and tried to invent a means of representing the world that was meaningful to modern

men and women. Above all, this involved a sustained critique of realist

art that was associated with 19th-century materialism.

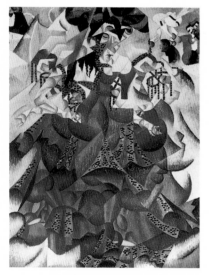

Gino Severini's Blue Dancer
*(1912) shows the splintered forms
and dynamism of Futurism.*

THE "DISCOVERY" of tribal art in the early years of the 20th century by artists like Picasso and Kirchner, or the enthusiasm many expressed for Gothic, Early Christian, or folk art, was part of the artists' constant search for authentic and expressive models.

Taking their lead from Paris, which was the undisputed center of progressive art, avant-garde groups spread out across Europe. In many cases, this involved communities of poets, artists, writers, dealers, and collectors, and individual works of art were often created with this highly educated, liberal audience in mind. The Futurists, with their exhibitions and their propagandizing visits to various European capitals, evolved new strategies for promoting modern art. This is the most noisy and assertive face of modernism, but it is only part of the complex history of modern art.

Choosing fifteen paintings to represent a period inevitably involves selecting outstanding examples. For this reason, many of the artists I have chosen stand slightly apart from the movements. At one stage or another, each became involved with avant-garde groups, but they also have strong individual identities that go beyond this. My primary focus is not on Paris, because it was not the seat of mainstream modernism, but rather the cross-fertilization with regional traditions in Spain, Germany, Holland, Russia, Great Britain, or Mexico, which, in my opinion, produced the most interesting art.

I have also placed more emphasis on figurative painting than many historians would choose to do. Abstraction has often been regarded as the most progressive trend, but it is better understood as one of a whole kaleidoscope of alternatives to the materialism of 19th-century art. The greatest sculptor of the period, Constantin Brancusi (1876–1957), for example, attempted to combat the material limitations of sculpture in the magnificent soaring forms of *Le Coq* (1935, Musée National d'Art Moderne, Paris). Formalist interpretations that look only at the outward form and not the content of such works are entirely inappropriate, and it must be remembered that committed abstract artists like Kandinsky, Mondrian, and Malevich were concerned, above all, to reinvest the art of the present with the spiritual values that animated the great religious art of the past. The collapse of traditional religious beliefs meant that the symbols previously used to convey spiritual meaning no longer held good, and abstraction resulted from the search for a new universal language to fill this void.

The idealistic and pseudoreligious aspirations of the generation of artists who came to maturity before 1914 were tested by the traumatic events of World War I. The 20th century has been a transitional age, and the shock waves that passed through the art of the 1920s and 1930s changed the nature of modernism. Many artists felt the need to put the human figure back on center stage or to devise new strategies of realism that avoided the limitations of 19th-century art. The utopian ideals of the prewar years, meanwhile, took new lease on life in the fields of architecture and design.

Brancusi evolved soaring forms and highly polished pillars of reflected light, as in Le Coq.

From our perspective, the first half of the 20th century no longer looks like a single historical trajectory. It is a rich field of many histories, where young avant-garde artists coexisted with painters like Walter Sickert, whose roots are in the Post-Impressionist age. I have included some of the great late masterpieces by these artists, which for years were regarded as retrogressive by modernist critics. In fact, their reassessments of realism open up new avenues for later figurative painting. They represent not so much the old guard, but rather the humanist traditions that struggled to survive in the dark political climate of the mid-century. It would have been appropriate to end this section with Picasso's *Guernica* (1937, Prado, Madrid), the greatest historical painting of the period. Instead, I chose Max Beckmann's *Departure* (1932–35), painted just before he fled Nazi Germany, which confronts the horrors of political tyranny, yet shows the determination of the human spirit to survive.

Picasso's Guernica: *a passionate protest against the cruelty of war.*

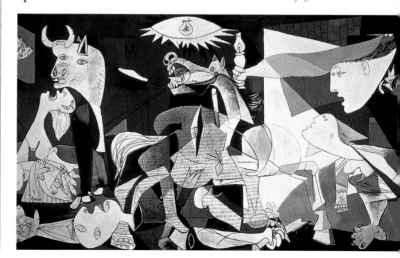

Les Demoiselles d'Avignon

PICASSO'S *Demoiselles d'Avignon* is arguably the best-known painting of the modern movement. If there is a single work that broke definitively with 19th-century ideas of how pictures should be made and then opened up new frontiers, this is surely it.

Nevertheless, Picasso's painting of five prostitutes posing in a compressed, stagelike space, framed by drapery, only gradually acquired its present-day fame. When Picasso was working on the ambitious composition, his friends and rivals like Matisse, the poet and art critic Guillaume Apollinaire, his main collector Leo Stein, and the most adventurous dealers of the day either ridiculed *Les Demoiselles* or dismissed it as an abortive master-piece. It was first exhibited only in 1916, when the poet André Salmon gave it its present title. In the early 1920s, the painting was published by André Breton (1896–1966), and in 1939, its status was assured when it was purchased by the Museum of Modern Art in New York.

Picasso set out to paint a masterpiece that would challenge Matisse's authority as leader of the Parisian avant-garde. *Les Demoiselles* was his answer to Matisse's harmonious *Bonheur de Vivre* (1905–1906), Barnes Foundation, Merion, Pennsylvania), which had dominated the Salon des Indépendants.

The difficulties Picasso experienced in formulating the composition are evident in the preparatory studies in different media, filling sixteen sketchbooks and amounting to some five hundred items. Originally, the subject was an explicit brothel scene, showing a group of prostitutes gathered around a sailor with a second male figure whom Picasso described as a medical student carrying a book or a skull, entering from the right. These male representations of eros and thanatos (in Freudian theory, instincts of desire and death) were gradually excluded as the scene was stripped of its anecdotal references and the sexual charge was concentrated in the confrontational nudes and the phallic still life in the foreground, interpreted as a punning reference to the male sex.

Picasso's original title, *Le Bordel d'Avignon*, in common with all his work, draws on autobiographical references. His affair with Fernande Olivier was disintegrating, and she had been demoted, like all his lovers and wives "from the plinth to the

PABLO PICASSO

∾

*BORN MÁLAGA 1881,
DIED MOUGINS 1973*

doormat." Raked by jealousy, Picasso probably resumed his habit of visiting brothels. Apollinaire's sadomasochistic pornographic novel, *Les Onze Mille Verges* (1906), also fired his imagination.

When Picasso began to paint *Les Demoiselles* in the spring of 1907, he was inspired by El Greco's *Apocalyptic Vision* (1608–14, Metropolitan Museum of Art, New York), the format and bathers at the center of the composition providing the solution for the compressed space in *Les Demoiselles*. Cézanne's painting of three bathers is the source for the pose of the figure in the foreground, sometimes seen as Fernande squatting on a bidet.

While he was planning the painting, Picasso's style underwent a radical transformation when he began to look at alternative "primitive" sources. Pre-Roman Iberian heads inspired the almond-shaped eyes and long, decorative ears of the three nudes on the left. Picasso believed that these ancient heads possessed magical, atavistic powers which he associated with a return to his own psycho-logical and racial roots. He also discovered African sculpture (a tradition that was to have a huge influence on Western art) at this time and returned again and again to the dark, crowded halls of the Trocadéro that housed the city's collection of ethno-graphic art. For a period he abandoned *Les Demoiselles*, unsure of how to reconcile the Iberian and African styles. Then, impul-sively, he overpainted the heads of the two whores on the right in an aggressive manner, unprecedented in Western art. Years later, Picasso described the impact that tribal art had on him at this date in a famous statement to André Malraux: "The Negro pieces were *intercesseurs*, mediators … The fetishes were … weapons. To help people avoid coming under the influence of spirits again, to help them become independent … I understood why I was a painter … *Les Demoiselles d'Avignon* must have come to me that very day, but not at all because of the forms; because it was my first exorcism painting."

Les Demoiselles is an exorcism not only of Picasso's private demons but, more important, of traditional concepts of ideal beauty. The complex, ambitious painting, with its highly charged sexuality and its stylistic disjunctures has become a symbol of the impetus in 20th-century art "to demolish even the ruins."

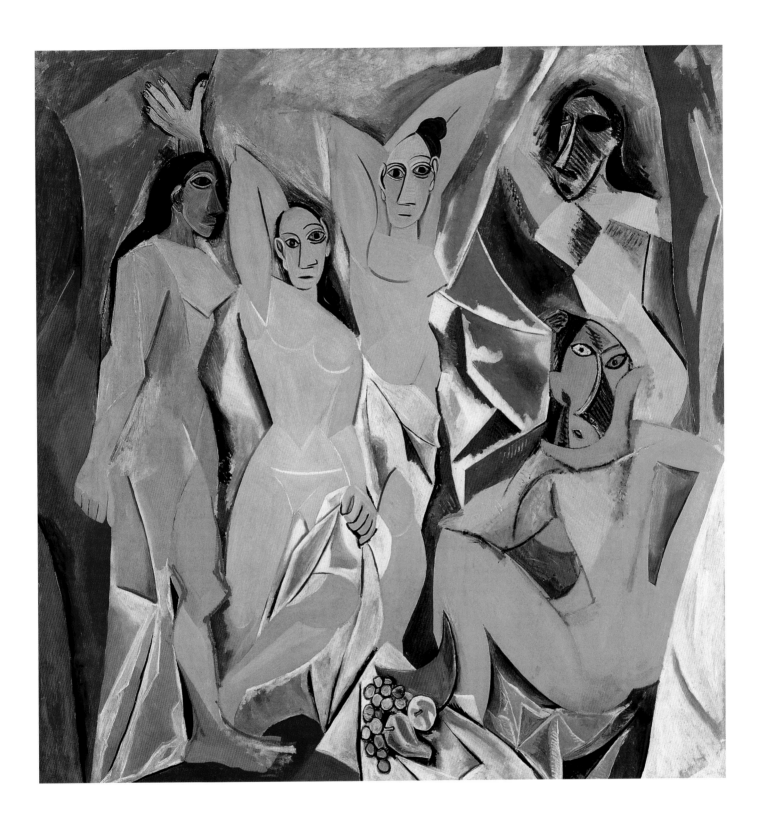

1907 | *oil on canvas* | 96 x 92in (244 x 234cm) | Museum of Modern Art, New York

Five Women on the Street

THIS PAINTING is an icon of modern urban life. It is the first in a series of ten major street scenes that document Kirchner's response to Berlin, and they represent the pinnacle of German Expressionism, stretching the contradictions implicit in modernism to extremes. *Five Women* was originally purchased by the innovative Folkwang Museum in Essen, but in 1937, it was confiscated and hung in the Nazi's exhibition of "Degenerate Art."

To the Nazis, the painting represented everything that was most decadent and subversive about Expressionism. Kirchner, like Picasso in *Les Demoiselles d'Avignon* (see page 293), depicts five prostitutes, relocated from the brothel to the corner of a Berlin street where they are waiting for clients. Four of the women look into a store while the fifth turns her attention toward a car crawling along the curb. Lit by the lurid glare of artificial lights, the women are like mannequins in a window; their forms were indeed inspired by contemporary fashion plates. But Kirchner combined elegant mannerism with tribal rawness, and his women are the focus of powerful, "uncivilized" instincts of sexuality and aggression.

Kirchner was influenced in his street scenes by Expressionist writers like Alfred Döblin, whom he painted in 1912, and the poet Georg Heym. All these artists invented styles and images to express the complex psychology of modern urban life, and Döblin, like Kirchner, was impressed by the evangelizing visit of the Italian Futurists to Berlin in April 1912. But the Germans never wholly embraced the Futurists' celebration of the animated modern city. On the contrary, the rapid urban growth of Berlin, which was transformed into a thriving industrial metropolis after becoming the capital of the German Empire in 1870, provoked mixed reactions. In Expressionism, a sense of the alienating spirit of modern life and the threat posed by the depersonalized crowds went hand in hand with the artists' excited response to the dynamism of the fashionable city streets.

In the autumn of 1911, Kirchner and the other Expressionist artists of *Die Brücke* (The Bridge) had left the relative shelter of Dresden, where the group had evolved their communal style, in search of a more receptive audience. In Berlin, there were more opportunities to exhibit, more sympathetic critics and

ERNST LUDWIG KIRCHNER

*BORN ASCHAFFENBURG 1880,
DIED FRAUENKIRCH 1938*

collectors, and an avant-garde community aware of the latest trends. But, despite their initial enthusiasm, the Brücke artists were soon divided by the fierce rivalries of the Berlin art world.

Kirchner's street scenes were begun after the dissolution of Die Brücke, in the winter preceding the outbreak of World War I. He started by skirting around the margins of the city, producing a number of suburban scenes in which landscape predominates and the city looms behind. Then he moved into the city center to record the streets in small, fleeting drawings that capture the movement of cars and figures in a spider's-web of black and gray lines. Kirchner pushed spontaneity to a new pitch in an attempt to override the rational restrictions that the Expressionists believed had cut modern man off from his instincts. Like Alfred Döblin's short, explosive sentences, Kirchner's intense rapidity of execution can be interpreted as a fight against time to eliminate history and to catch modernity on the wing.

Back in the studio, Kirchner reworked his initial sketches into the highly organized compositions of the street scenes. The friction and energy of *Five Women* derives in part from the combination of well-conceived compositional geometry plus powerful gestural brushwork, conveying both the regulation and potential wildness of the city crowd. The elongated figures and the upward thrust of the composition demonstrate Kirchner's formulation of a modern "Gothic" style, which was characteristic of this last phase of prewar Expressionism. Wilhelm Worringer, in his influential treatise *Abstraction and Empathy*, published in 1911, had identified signs in northern Gothic art of medieval man's unstable, unpredictable relationship with a hostile environment, which had obvious parallels with the 20th century.

Kirchner's prostitutes present an alienated urban alternative to the liberated sexuality he depicted in his contemporary paintings of bathers frolicking in the sea. Their fashionable figures are characterized by masklike faces and jagged, primitivizing forms. The work does not express the contrast between nature and artifice that had preoccupied modernist artists since the mid-19th century. At the heart of the city, these distinctions no longer apply; this is the first depiction of the urban jungle.

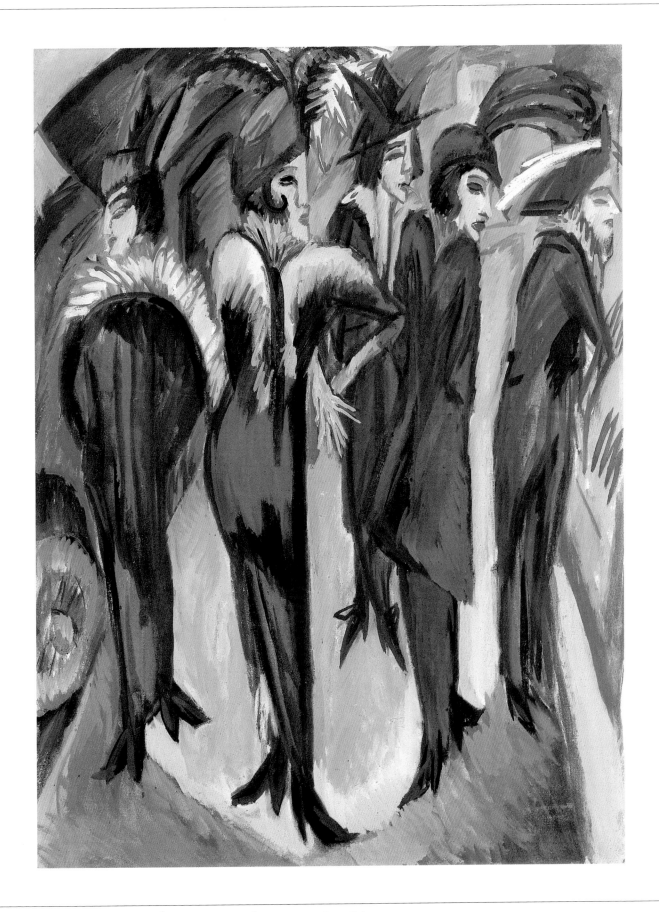

1913 | *oil on canvas* | 47 x 35½in (120 x 90cm) | Museum Ludwig, Cologne

Composition VI

KANDINSKY'S PRIMARY importance in the history of early 20th-century art is as a theoretician and an activist. Born in 1866 in Russia, he became a leading figure of his generation by virtue of his exceptional intellectual acumen. It was, above all, Kandinsky's treatise *Concerning the Spiritual in Art*, published in 1912, that provided a theoretical and philosophical basis for the move many artists were making toward nonrepresentational art.

Composition VI is one of a series of ambitious abstract paintings that Kandinsky considered to be the fullest expression of his aspirations for the art of the future. In the early years of the century, he gradually formulated his ideas, studying in Munich and traveling to Paris, where he became acquainted with the latest developments in French painting. From the outset he was determined to break with academic art, founding with like-minded artists alternative exhibiting societies in Munich like Phalanx (1901) and the *Neue Künstlervereinigung München* ("New Artists Association of Munich") (1909).

It was the final exhibiting group that he was associated with, *Der Blaue Reiter* (The Blue Rider), founded in 1911, that was of lasting importance. This was the base for the abstract wing of German Expressionism and gave Kandinsky an ideal forum to explore his reforming ideals. Essentially, *Der Blaue Reiter*—which consisted of an exhibiting society and an "Almanac" of writings and illustrations edited by the painter Franz Marc (1880–1916) and Kandinsky (1912)—was a romantic project attacking not only the stale illusionistic style of 19th-century academic painting, but also the soulless materialism of the society that produced it. Drawing on many sources, including theosophical and esoteric theories, Russian religious broadsheets, Bavarian folk art, and contemporary musical experiments by Arnold Schoenberg, Kandinsky strove to formulate an antimaterialistic, spiritual artform that he hoped to communicate to a wide audience.

Composition VI is the most fully resolved of Kandinsky's manifesto paintings based on the Apocalypse, announcing a new spiritual epoch arising from the destruction of the old world. The composition evolved from Kandinsky's earlier glass painting, *Deluge* (1912, lost). He experienced great difficulties

WASSILY KANDINSKY
കൗ
*BORN MOSCOW 1866,
DIED NEUILLY-SUR-SEINE 1944*

with the work and started many different versions from 1909. He said he failed to listen to the expression of the word *deluge,* and it was not until he rid himself of the feeling of catastrophe that he was able to resolve the work in May 1913.

Whereas the earlier glass painting clearly depicts the biblical tempest, with figures and fishes struggling in the waves, only traces of these remain in *Composition VI*. Numerous preparatory sketches show how Kandinsky combined these figurative references with a dynamic compositional design in a network of lines and shapes. The final painting has a strong diagonal emphasis, reminiscent of the splintered forms in Marc's apocalyptic *The Fate of Animals* (Kunstmuseum, Basle), which was also completed in the spring of 1913. The diagonal lines in the top center and right-hand side of Kandinsky's composition suggest the driving rain and the banded colors of a rainbow, while the radiating black diagonals on the lower left are the oars of a boat tossed on a stormy sea.

Despite the figurative traces, which Kandinsky retained for their communicative power, the overriding impression is "a sounding cosmos of free-floating colors and forms." In Kandinsky's theoretical writings, it is above all color that is essential to his idea of a spiritual art. He was deeply influenced by the social philosopher Rudolf Steiner's claim in *Theosophie* (1904) that "each colour, each perception of light, represents a spiritual tone." In Kandinsky's own description of *Composition VI*, he attributed expressive values to his colors: warm tones to counteract the tragic theme, and the "sharp, somewhat angry" reds and blues on the right balanced by the delicate pink in the middle. The deep brown of the upper left, which suggests "hopelessness," is counteracted by green and yellow, denoting "activity." In his autobiography, Kandinsky outlined the general principles that underlie his method: "Painting is a thundering collision of different worlds, destined to create a new world in and from the struggle with one another, a new world which is the work of art. Each work originates just as does the cosmos—through catastrophes which out of the chaotic din of instruments ultimately bring forth a new symphony, the music of the spheres. The creation of works of art is the creation of the world."

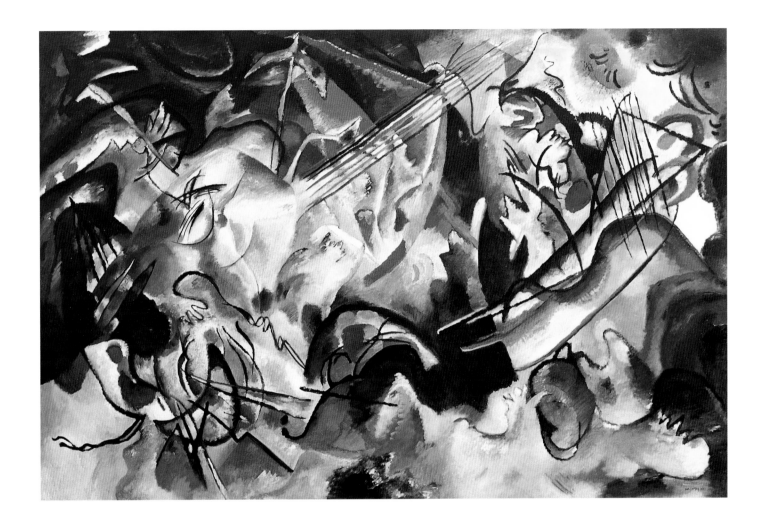

1913 | *oil on canvas* | 77 x 118in (195 x 300cm) | Hermitage Museum, St. Petersburg

Pier and Ocean *(Composition no. 10)*

THIS WORK represents a crucial turning point in Mondrian's art. It was painted in his native Holland, where Mondrian arrived in the summer of 1914, intending to visit his ailing father before returning to Paris. When World War I broke out in August, he had to stay, beginning an extraordinarily fruitful five-year period in which he evolved his characteristic abstract style.

In Paris, Mondrian had established his position in the international avant-garde, exhibiting at the Salon des Indépendants, where he had attracted the attention of Apollinaire. His exposure to the Cubist paintings of Georges Braque (1882–1963) and Picasso had provoked an important transformation in his work, resulting in a series of highly abstracted paintings of city façades.

But for all Mondrian's fascination with the artificiality and geometry of the city, his return to Holland inspired a rediscovery of his early love of nature. In relative isolation, he began to make studies of the ocean, sketching in charcoal, watercolor, and crayon and finally creating a majestic synthesis of his impressions in the oil painting which he called *Pier and Ocean (Composition no. 10)*.

In this work Mondrian reduced his palette to black and white and his forms to a network of intersecting vertical and horizontal lines contained in an oval frame. In a letter to his patron H. P. Bremmer, written from Paris in January 1914, Mondrian had formulated the general terms of his evolving esthetic: "By constructing horizontal and vertical lines *consciously* but not *calculatingly*, and guided by great intuition, arranging them in harmony and rhythm, I allege that with these basic forms of beauty … it is possible to create a work of art which is as powerful as it is true."

Since 1908, Mondrian, like Kandinsky and other artists of his generation, had been influenced by the pseudoreligious writings of the theosophists. For them, horizontality symbolized eternity and femininity while vertical lines were associated with masculinity and symbolized action in time. In the writings of Madame Blavatsky (cofounder of the Theosophical Society), the oval is associated with the cosmic egg, a symbol of creation, while the cross formed by the intersection of vertical and horizontal lines expressed the mystical concept of life and immortality. When the cross was inscribed within the perfect square, it symbolized the elements of earth, air, fire, and water and was described as a "mystical precinct" containing "the master key which opens the door to every science, physical as well as spiritual."

Mondrian was deeply attracted by the theosophists' notion of universal laws underlying nature and by their description of the world as a dynamic equilibrium of opposing forces. By 1914, he believed that the art of the future would necessitate transcending the "particular" and the "human" in order to arrive at more profound and universal truths. Like Kandinsky, Mondrian's abstraction was motivated by metaphysical and philosophical beliefs. But instead of drawing on literary motifs to express his concepts, he remained deeply committed to his experiences of nature.

In *Pier and Ocean*, Mondrian's abstract symbolism of the vertical and horizontal forces dividing the world is fused with his subtle and meditative evocation of light striking water. In contrast to the preparatory studies, Mondrian's painting is asymmetrical, and none of the intersecting lines are closed to form geometric shapes. There are no defining contours, and everything is an open construction, including the evocation of the oval frame in white oil paint against the white canvas ground. The vertical emphasis through the center of the composition, which suggests both the pier jutting into the ocean and the romantic motif of a human presence on the shore, is intersected by the horizontal span of the sea. But these dominant forms dissolve into smaller horizontal and vertical oppositions so that the painting is in a constant state of flux. Where the lines intersect, there is a visual vibration that suggests the movement of light on the surface of rippling water; and as the forms take shape and dissolve before our eyes, the painting seems to breathe like a living organism.

Mondrian's boldly colored grid paintings of the 1920s and 1930s codified his ideas about the absolute, symbolic value of intersecting lines. But the lyrical, poetic qualities so clearly evident in *Pier and Ocean* remained essential to his intuitively constructed geometrical compositions. In practice, Mondrian did not use geometry as a rational system, but rather as a bridge toward the emotive or transcendental.

PIET MONDRIAN

*BORN AMERSFOORT 1872,
DIED NEW YORK 1944*

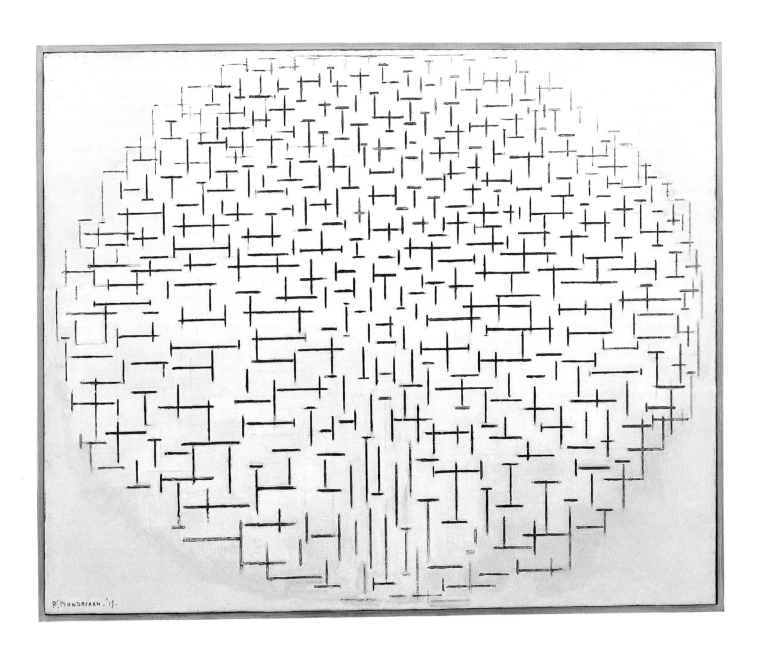

1915 | *oil on canvas* | 33¹⁄₂ x 43in (85 x 110cm) | Rijksmuseum Kröller-Müller, Otterlo

Black Square

Like Kandinsky's *Composition VI*, Malevich's *Black Square* was intended as a declaration of his radical intentions. It was aimed not at a patron or collector, but at a small community of avant-garde artists. It was a manifesto painting which Malevich used to establish his leading position within that community.

The Russian avant-garde had formed a number of progressive exhibiting societies in the early years of the century, including The Knave of Diamonds (1910–17), the Union of Youth (1911–13), and Donkey's Tail (1912), which introduced French Cubism to a Russian audience. These societies also fostered the neo-primitivism associated with a new sense of national conscious-ness, with a revival of interest in Russian folk art, including the religious broadsheets, *lubki*, that had inspired Kandinsky.

A close collaboration among artists, writers, and musicians characterized the Russian Futurist group whose ranks Malevich joined in 1913, designing the sets and costumes for the Futurist opera *Victory Over the Sun*. It was here, on Malevich's stage curtain, that the motif of a black square on a white background first appeared, providing a visual equivalent for the Futurist poets' radically reductive experiments with language and sound. The opera was followed in 1915 by two Futurist exhibitions, "Tramway V" and "0.10," in which Malevich and Vladimir Tatlin (1885–1953) emerged as the rival leaders of the Russian avant-garde. In "Tramway V," Tatlin's corner reliefs, inspired by Picasso's Cubist constructions, attracted far greater attention than Malevich's alogical Cubo-Futurist paintings. It was after this, in the spring of 1915, that Malevich withdrew to his studio, working in secrecy on his series of radical new "Suprematist" paintings, which he unveiled in December at the "0.10" exhibition.

On this occasion, Malevich showed thirty-nine canvases, all austere compositions with elemental geometric forms of unmodulated color floating in free, unstructured space. The canvases were accompanied by a written manifesto, "From Cubism to Suprematism. The New Painterly Realism," in which Malevich outlined his aspirations for "pure" and "absolute" painting, freed from illusionism and consisting of nonobjective forms that played no representational or symbolic role.

KASIMIR MALEVICH
∞
BORN NEAR KIEV 1878,
DIED LENINGRAD 1935

Of all the artists of his generation across Europe, Malevich went furthest toward establishing a new vocabulary of self-referential forms that were neither symbolic, like Kandinsky's abstract paintings, nor inspired by nature, like Mondrian's. But it would be wrong to understand his work as "art for art's sake." Malevich's Suprematism (from the Latin *supremus*, meaning "ultimate" or "absolute") was mystical and idealist and, like Kandinsky and Mondrian, he was motivated by his distaste for 19th-century materialism and inspired by the pseudo-religious movements that flourished from the beginning of the century in response to the loss of belief in conventional Christianity.

In "0.10," Malevich made a direct reference to the religious element in his work by hanging his *Black Square* high up in the corner of the room, traditionally reserved in Russian homes for religious icons. Malevich associated his Suprem-atist paintings with a higher, purer state of being, inspired by, among others, the Russian mystic philosopher P. D. Uspensky, whose writings about the fourth dimension proposed a path of spiritual progress involving an aban-donment of logic to achieve a more advanced state of consciousness in the sensation of infinite space.

In formal terms, Malevich's search for the absolute, like Mondrian's, involved a reduction to elemental geometric shapes and a restriction of his palette to black and white. The form in *Black Square* is subtly asymmetrical, described in the "0.10" catalog as *chetyreugolnik*, "quadrilateral." Like Kandinsky, Mal-evich associated "the rubbishy slough of academic art" with three-dimensional, illusionistic space. And in his drawings and paintings of 1915, he explored the alternative of axonometric projections, exploded rather than perspectival views, casting his vanishing point into infinity and transforming his perspectival orthogonals into parallel lines on the surface of his work, to suggest "the infinite void" in which floats "the pure sensibility" of geometric form. Summing up his ambitions in a letter in June 1916, he wrote: "The huge plane of painted color on a white canvas sheet gives a strong sensation of space directly to our consciousness. I am transported into endless emptiness, where you sense around you the creative points of the universe."

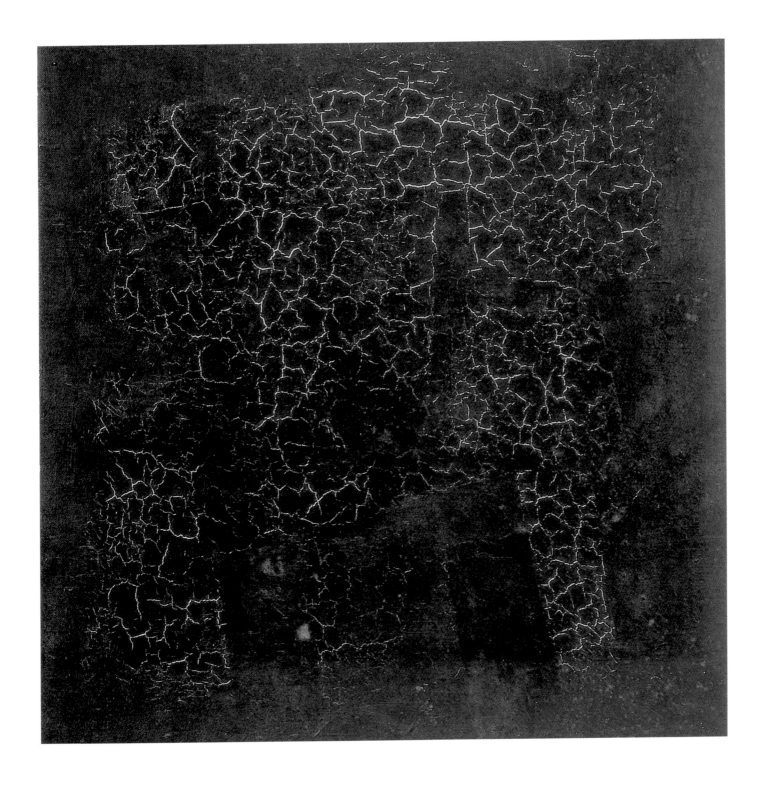

1915 | *oil on canvas* | Tretyakov Museum, St. Petersburg

Piano Lesson

BY THE 1920s, Matisse enjoyed an international reputation equaled only by Picasso. In the main, his sensuous paintings are associated with his idea that good art should have the effect of "a comfortable armchair," stimulating enjoyment and a sense of wellbeing. But during World War I, his art displayed uncharacteristic tension and intellectual rigor as he sought to define "the methods of modern construction." It was a period of ruthless experimentation in which Matisse cast certainties aside to produce some of his most powerful and compelling paintings.

Signs of this change could be seen in the haunting portrait of Madame Matisse (State Hermitage, St. Petersburg), exhibited at the Salon d'Automne in 1913. This painting, which needed more than one hundred sittings to complete, displayed a new visual austerity and sense of structure. It was positively received in advanced circles, and the great Russian collector Sergei Shchukin reserved it for his collection while it was still on the easel. But Matisse was far from satisfied and told his friends that "a long and arduous effort lay ahead."

In the following months, Matisse produced a number of experimental works, the most disturbing being the *Woman on a High Stool* (1913–14, Museum of Modern Art, New York), which appears in the background of *Piano Lesson*. Painted in monochrome gray, which inspired the palette of the later composition, it shows the model balancing precariously on what has been described as a penitential stool rather than a comfortable armchair. This painting was also reserved for Shchukin and hung in the living room of Matisse's house at Issy-les-Moulineaux, near Paris. World War I and the Russian Revolution prevented Shchukin from claiming his work, and it remained in Matisse's possession.

In the first days of war, in August 1914, Matisse volunteered for service but was rejected because he was forty-five years old. Most of his friends, and eventually his eldest son Jean, were recruited to fight, and Matisse experienced conflicting emotions of regret, relief, and futility at not being able to play an active role. In September 1914, as the Germans advanced on Paris, he moved temporarily with his family to their villa in Collioure where he struck up a close friendship with the Cubist painter

HENRI MATISSE

BORN LE CATEAU-CAMBRÉSIS 1869,
DIED NICE 1954

Juan Gris (1887–1927), with whom he argued heatedly about painting. There is no doubt that the stylistic transformations in Matisse's work involved a dialog with Cubism, influenced by his contact both with Gris and with the Villon brothers, Jacques (1875–1963) and Raymond Duchamp-Villon (1876–1918), on his return to Paris that fall.

In the turmoil of war, Matisse found comfort and distraction in music, taking violin lessons and practicing furiously. Toward the end of 1916, he began to work on *Piano Lesson*, which is in fact a memory picture, recalling a time some six years earlier at Issy-les-Moulineaux when his son Jean was made to play the piano.

Matisse set out to compose a large and ambitious composition that became a majestic synthesis of the advances he had made over the previous three years. It shows Jean, isolated behind the Pleyel piano, in front of a schematic rendition of *Woman on a High Stool*; she sits like an exam monitor above him. In the bottom left-hand corner, Matisse includes his bronze *Decorative Figure* of 1906 (private collection), and between the boy and the nude a lighted candle burns palely, suggesting the moment of twilight on a summer evening when shadows gather and the garden, seen through the open window, darkens. The dove-gray ground extends from the *Woman on a High Stool*, penetrating the outside space to suggest the evening light.

Across the surface of the composition there is a play of visual contrasts and analogies. The rhyming arabesques of the ironwork on the balcony and the music stand contrast with the strict geometry of intersecting lines. The relaxed nude sculpture contrasts ironically with the clothed and rigid form of the figure on the stool. Above all, it is the triangular form of the small metronome in the foreground that reappears throughout the composition, in the shadows that slice through Jean's face, and in the green triangle that leads into the garden. There is indeed a musical quality to this subtly inventive sequence of visual correspondences, but also an intellectual rigor that has to do with Matisse's highly original interpretation of the issues raised in Cubist art. Matisse's *Piano Lesson* represents a moment of sobriety, of elegance and gravity, which he never surpassed.

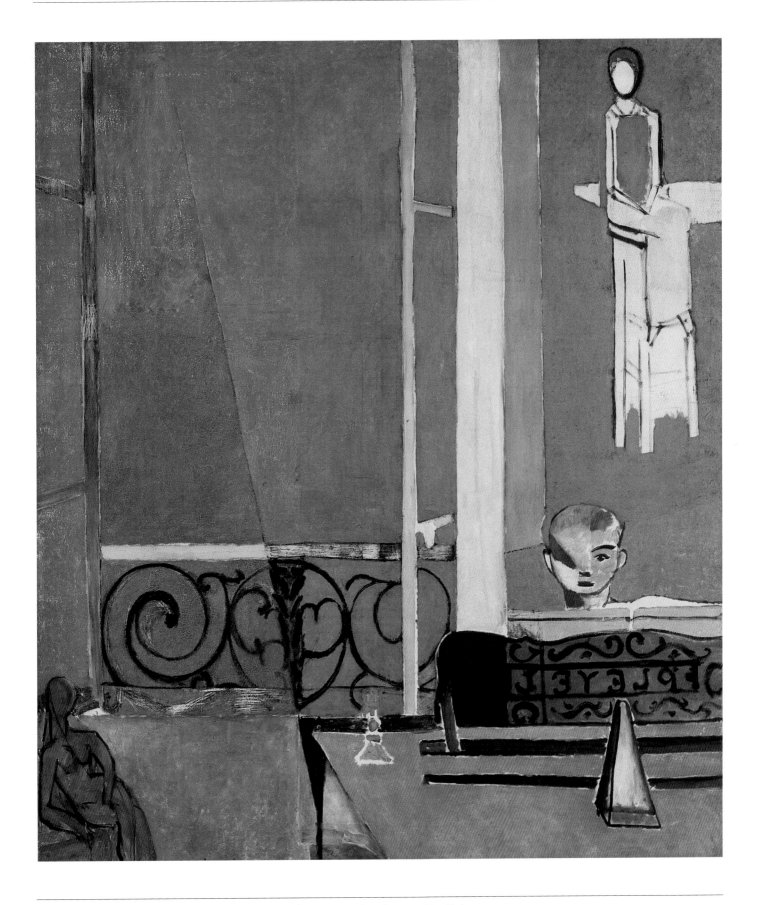

1916 | *oil on canvas* | 97 x 84in (245 x 213cm) | Museum of Modern Art, New York

The Uncertainty of the Poet

THE UNCERTAINTY OF THE POET is a fine example of de Chirico's so-called metaphysical paintings. At the Salon des Indépendants and the Salon d'Automne from 1911–14, de Chirico attracted the attention of Apollinaire, who wrote enthusiastically about de Chirico's "metaphysical landscapes" and apparently helped the artist to find titles for several of his works. In this case, the title evokes the poetic mood and the atmosphere of mystery and enigma that were central to de Chirico's work. De Chirico traced his discovery of metaphysical art back to an epiphany in the Piazza Santa Croce in Florence, before his arrival in Paris. He recalled: "I had barely recovered from a long and painful intestinal illness and was in a state of almost morbid sensitivity … The hot, strong autumn sun brightened the statue [of Dante] and the façade of the church. Then I had the strange impression that I was looking at these things for the first time, and the composition of my painting revealed itself to my mind's eye … the moment is an enigma for me in that it is inexplicable."

De Chirico's paintings were also strongly influenced by Arnold Böcklin (1827–1901) and Max Klinger (1857–1920), whose work he knew from his student years in Munich. Like many of the abstract artists of his day, de Chirico drew inspiration from Symbolism because it offered an alternative to the materialism of 19th-century realist art. He was attracted by the melancholy Classicism of Böcklin and Klinger, and shared their enthusiasm for the writings of the German 19th-century philosophers Schopenhauer and Nietzsche.

The Classical bust in *The Uncertainty of the Poet* is probably an Aphrodite-type cast, freely available in the stores of Montmartre at the time and copied by academic artists. One of the perversities of de Chirico—which differentiates him from every other avant-garde artist of the century—was his enthusiasm for 19th-century academic art, because he considered the idealism it avowed preferable to banal naturalism. His heavy black outlines and crude crosshatching were influenced by illustrations in drawing manuals, and the flatness of the handling of volumes that results from this allowed him to create images that seemed preternaturally real but also strangely insubstantial.

GIORGIO DE CHIRICO

*BORN VOLOS, THESSALY 1888,
DIED ROME 1978*

De Chirico's Classical statues and busts are symbols of a human presence, stripped of its temporal aspects and transported into the eternal realm of art. The exotic fruits that appear in several paintings of 1913 suggest, on the contrary, transient sensual pleasures. Here, the obvious sexual connotations of the fruit and female bust are reinforced by other images in the painting like the train and the shadowy arcades.

There is undoubtedly a personal, psychological dimension to the images that recur with obsessive regularity in de Chirico's metaphysical works. The train is a reference to his father, who worked as a railroad engineer when the artist was a boy in Greece and whose death when de Chirico was eleven perhaps accounts for his typically childlike depiction of trains. On another level, the train can be interpreted as a symbol of the voyage of the mind beyond the terrain of the known and familiar, while the emphasis on moments of arrival and departure heightens the atmosphere of tension and unease. The dark internal spaces of the arcades, inspired by the architecture of Turin, triggered de Chirico's sense of mystery: "There is nothing like the enigma of the Arcade— invented by the Romans … The Roman arcade is fatality. Its voice speaks in enigmas filled with a strangely Roman poetry."

The unreality of the scene is also conveyed by de Chirico's rejection of Renaissance perspective for the multiple vanishing points in 14th- and 15th-century Italian art. The impossible conjunction between the foreground and the background, linked by the exaggerated diagonal of the arcade, emphasizes the fact that the painting is not intended to represent naturalistic space. The theatrical, dreamlike compositions that result from de Chirico's highly original synthesis of various strands of the Classical tradition appealed strongly to the Surrealists. When de Chirico left France to join the Italian army in 1915, he left most of his recent paintings, including *The Uncertainty of the Poet*, with the dealer Paul Guillaume, who had been supporting the artist. In 1922, Guillaume included the painting in an exhibition for which André Breton, the future leader of the Surrealists, wrote the preface. It was bought by the poet Paul Eluard, who sold it to the British Surrealist, Roland Penrose (1900–1984), in 1938.

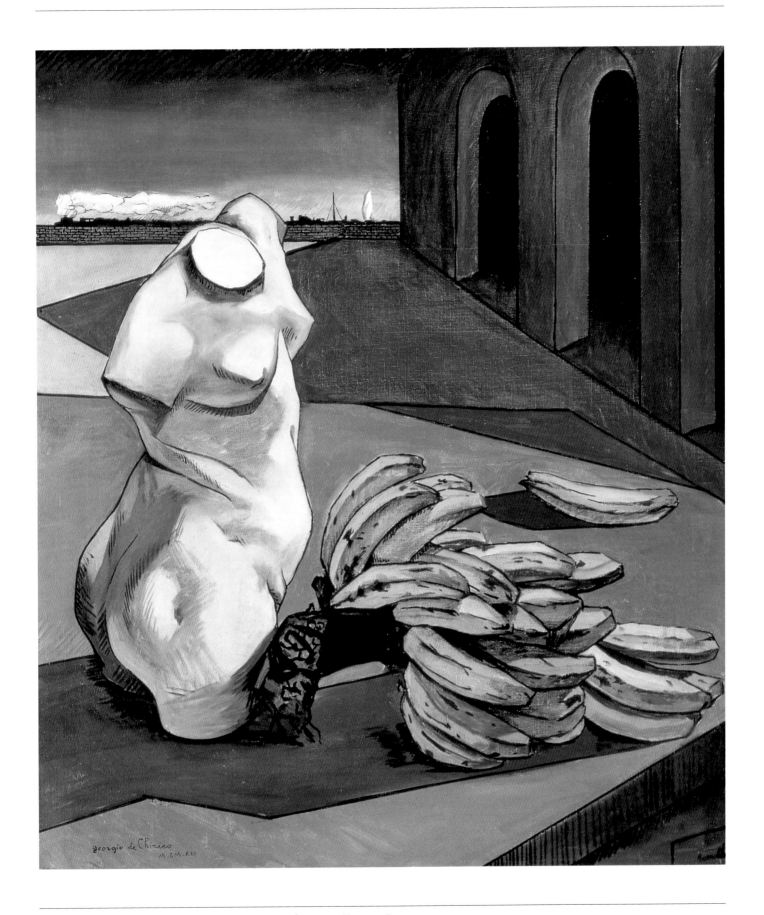

1913 | *oil on canvas* | 42 x 37in (106 x 94cm) | Tate Gallery, London

The Bride Stripped Bare by Her Bachelors, Even *(The Large Glass)*

MARCEL DUCHAMP is the artist of the period who has had the most far-reaching influence on our age. His invention of the ready-made and his insistence that art should be about ideas rather than sensuous experience involved him in a sustained critique of painting. Duchamp was a precursor of the absurdist Dada movement, and he became allied to the Surrealists, but he remains a highly individual, enigmatic figure. While Dada, in Duchamp's words, was "purely negative and accusatory," he attempted to "open up a corridor of humour." Duchamp's work is characterized by a distinctive visual irony which both deconstructs and reaffirms the value of the creative act.

The Large Glass is a summation of all Duchamp's work. He conceived the project in 1912 and finally left it "definitively unfinished" in 1923. For the next ten years, when Duchamp gained the support of important American collectors like Walter Arensberg and Katherine Dreier, he apparently devoted most of his time to playing chess. But in 1934, he published a collection of documents known as *The Green Box*, which contained photographs, sketches, notes, and calculations pertaining to *The Large Glass*. Despite Duchamp's proclaimed desire "to explain every detail" of the work, his imagery remains private and hermetic, and open to multiple interpretations.

There is, nevertheless, general agreement that the scene represents a comic act of courtship, referred to as a "stripping" of the bride by her bachelors. The glass is divided by a lead wire into two zones. The top half is dominated by the mechanical form of the bride, who hovers like a praying mantis, emitting a grayish cloud that floats through the upper half of the glass. Within this cloud there are three blank boards, described by Duchamp as the "Top Inscriptions," intended to inform the bachelors of the bride's desires. On the right-hand side, the small dots represent the "discharge" of the bachelors, who are situated in the lower panel, crowded together like pieces on a chessboard. In Duchamp's notes, the bachelors are described as "Nine malic molds," empty uniforms that are inflated by the fluid or gas emitted by the bride. To the right of the molds there is a little cart with runners known as the "Slide," containing a "Water-Mill"

MARCEL DUCHAMP

*BORN BLAINVILLE 1887,
DIED NEUILLY 1968*

that propels it. As the Mill animates the Slide "with a seesaw movement" it "recites" (there is no noise) interminable litanies: "Slow life, vicious circle. Onanism. Horizontal. Junk of life ... "

The lower half of the glass also includes the "Sieve," made of seven cones and connected to the malic molds by a system of "capillary tubes." These tubes are based on Duchamp's new units of standard measurement that were obtained by allowing three threads to fall and then preserving them in a croquet box as "canned chance." The center of the lower glass is occupied by the "Chocolate-Grinder," referring, Duchamp explained, to the bachelor's onanistic satisfaction: "The bachelor grinds his chocolate himself." To the right are geometric figures described by Duchamp as "Oculist witnesses," which bring to mind both the witnesses present at the miracles of religious paintings and the voyeurs of pornography. The act of love is thus pictured as an ill-functioning mechanical process, resulting from the unpredictable and faulty gestures of his actor-machines.

In *The Large Glass*, Duchamp replaces what many artists of his generation had come to view as the false logic of positivist thought with an ironic critique of reason. He also launches a humorous attack on the Futurists' naive cult of machines. Duchamp rejected the traditional materials of painting and sculpture, and took his inspiration from Symbolist writers like Raymond Roussel, Jules Laforgue, and Stéphane Mallarmé, finding that the intellectual art of literature rather than the sensuous art of painting provided him with the means to picture his age. But it is precisely Duchamp's emphasis on ideas that reconnects him—in an unexpected way—with the traditional aspirations of painters. "The fact that [my] kind of painting is called literary," Duchamp wrote, "doesn't bother me ... There is a great difference between a painting which is only directed toward the retina and a painting which goes beyond the retinal impression—a painting which uses the tubes of color as a springboard to go further. This was the case with the religious painters of the Renaissance ... What they were interested in was to express their idea of divinity, in one form or another. With a different intention and for other ends, I took the same concept."

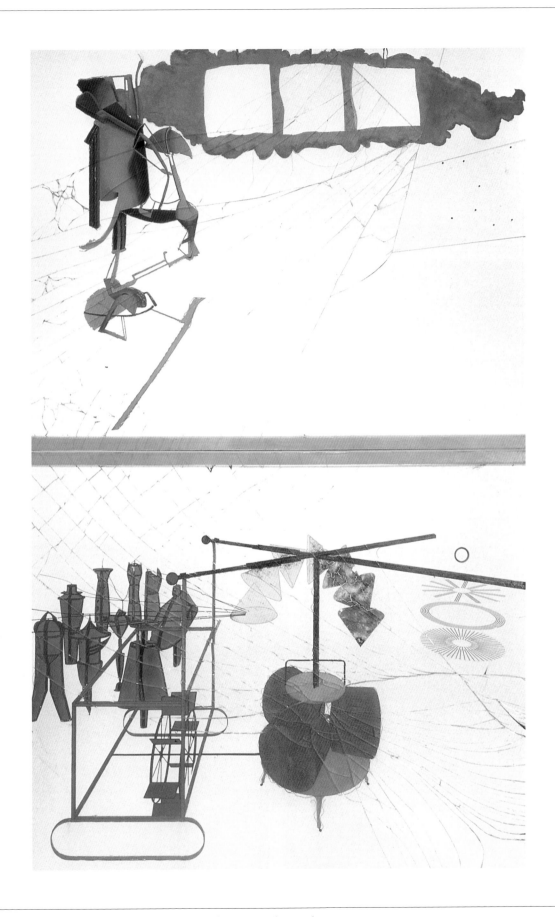

1915–23 | *oil, varnish, lead foil, and wire, and dust on glass, between two glass panels*
| 109 x 1 x 69in (277.5 x 3 x 176cm) | Philadelphia Museum of Art

Mz 169. Formen in Raum *(Forms in Space)*

KURT SCHWITTERS is one of the protagonists of Dada. In Germany, this absurdist movement sprang up in several regional centers in the wake of World War I. Artists like George Grosz (1893–1959), Otto Dix, Raoul Hausmann (1886–1971), and Hannah Höch (1889–1978) evolved a highly politicized form of Dada in Berlin, inventing the technique of photomontage, which consisted of cutting and pasting photographs, to avoid the subjectivity and expression they associated with painting. Like many of the artists discussed in this chapter, Schwitters held a highly individual position within the Dada group. He created a one-man Dada movement in his native Hanover and invented his own artform, which he christened "Merz." He is best known for the small collages he began in 1918, made up of the scraps of urban debris he collected on his odyssey through the modern city.

Schwitters maintained stronger links with Expressionism than the other German Dada artists, exhibiting in Herwarth Walden's Sturm gallery and publishing his poetry in Walden's Expressionist magazine, *Der Sturm* (The Storm). Schwitters was particularly influenced by Kandinsky's ideas about the synthesis of different art forms and his ideal of creating a universal *Gesamtkunstwerk* (total work of art). Around 1920, Schwitters began to realize this ambition in his first "Merzbau" (Merz building), which was an installation spreading throughout his house in Hanover, intended to unite sculpture and architecture. When Schwitters was forced into exile from Nazi Germany, he recreated the Merzbau in Norway and finally in England, where he died in 1948.

The word *Merz* was drawn from one of Schwitters's early collages where the word appeared as a fragment of a printed line originally reading *Commerz- und Privatbank*. On another occasion, Schwitters explained that it was derived from *ausmerzen* (to reject), referring to his practice of using the things that other people throw away. Essentially, Merz was a method of assemblage that Schwitters applied to words, objects, scraps of paper, and textiles. His aim was to bring "all conceivable technical materials together for artistic purposes" and to allow "each individual material to be equally valid."

KURT SCHWITTERS
∾
BORN HANOVER 1887,
DIED AMBLESIDE 1948

Schwitters was deeply committed to the principles of abstract art. His collages mediate between the romantic ideals of prewar abstraction and the austere, geometric Constructivism of the 1920s. His belief in art as "a spiritual function of man, which aims at freeing him from life's chaos (tragedy)," led to conflicts with the politically active Berlin Dadaists. Schwitters' poetry, notably his poem *Anna Blume* of 1919, which enjoyed popular success, paid humorous lip-service to bourgeois sentimentality. Schwitters also believed that art embodied a higher reality than politics: "Art is free to use its means in any way it likes," he wrote in 1923; "It is bound to its own laws and to its laws alone. The minute it becomes art, it becomes much more sublime than a class distinction between proletariat and bourgeoisie."

In 1920, Schwitters began to produce collages with an entirely distinctive character, and *Mz 169. Forms in Space* is a work in which all the strands of his early development come together. The emphasis is on texture and tactile effects. In *Mz 169,* a rich and complex sense of space is achieved by combining layers of opaque and transparent materials, like tissue paper and loose-weave textiles, over bus tickets, scraps of typography, and abstract planes of colored paper. A friend saw how "he spread flour and water over the paper, then moved and shuffled and manipulated his scraps of paper around in the paste while the paper was wet. With his fingertips he worked little pieces of crumpled paper into the wet surface … using flour both as paste and paint."

Mz 169. Forms in Space combines painterly effects, achieved by manipulating paper with torn edges, with an overall sense of lucid pictorial geometry. Although Schwitters emphasized the esthetic qualities of his collages, he also spoke of his aim to build a "new art from the fragments of a former culture." The stamps, tram tickets, and scraps of newspaper speak of a chaotic post-war culture dominated by numbers, prices, movement, and multiplication. But there is also a personal element in Schwitters's collages, which evoke a wistfully remembered past rather than a vividly experienced present. The tension—or balance—between the abstract forms of the collages and the personal and poetic materials that engender them makes them endlessly fascinating.

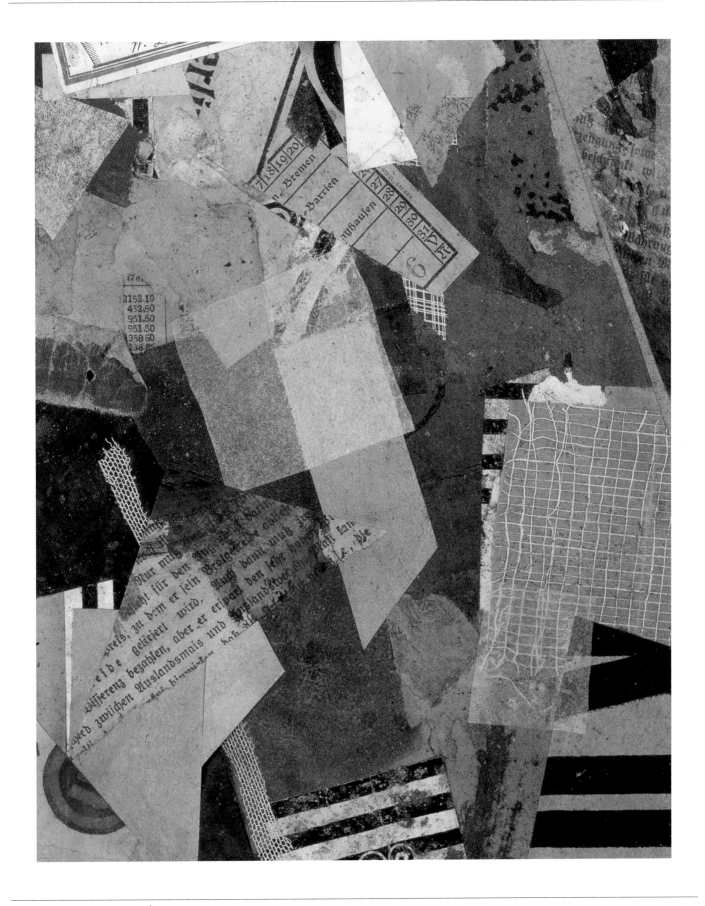

Skat Players

SKAT PLAYERS is the most uncompromising confrontation in 20th-century art with the human devastation caused by modern warfare. The scale of the trauma and destruction wrought by World War I was unprecedented. Of the sixty million soldiers who fought, about thirteen million died, twenty million were wounded, and eleven million returned to civilian life as cripples.

Like many artists of his generation, Otto Dix had greeted the war as a force that would destroy the old order and clear the way for a new world. He saw himself as a Nietzschean hero in *Self-portrait as Mars* (1914, Staatliche Kunstsammlungen, Dresden), dressed in his machine-gunner's uniform. But war heroes like Dix returned, defeated, to hunger, unemployment, and inflation in Weimar Germany. The rhetorical style of the Expressionists seemed entirely inappropriate to picturing the harsh realities of this postwar world. In 1918, when Dix joined the German Dadaists, he wrote: "I discovered that I could do anything I liked. All I needed to do was to throw art onto the garbage pile. The Expressionists had made enough art. We wanted to see things as they were without the trimmings—almost without art."

In March 1920, Dix began a series of four paintings of war cripples in which he attempted to give his new attitudes visual form. Disregarding esthetic hierarchies, he drew on all the tools he had on hand, combining traditional oil painting with scraps of reality cut from newspapers and collected in flea markets. In the process, collage, which had been used by the Cubists as a device for esthetic speculation, was reemployed as a means of biting social criticism.

Skat Players was based on a grotesque scene Dix witnessed in a Dresden café, where three war veterans were playing skat in a back room, holding the cards with their artificial limbs. He drew the scene from memory and soon began work on a painting closely based on this sketch. The three collaged newspapers in the background date from early May 1920, and the mood of the hideous victims is set by a report in the reactionary newspaper *Dresdner Anzeiger*, attacking the agreement that ended the war as a "dishonorable contract that commits the German people to shame and disgrace, rather than a peace treaty."

OTTO DIX

%

BORN UNTERMHAUS 1891,
DIED HEMMENHOFEN 1969

Seated at an imitation marble table, the three ex-officers play their macabre game. The figure on the left, with his grotesque head injuries, is cheating, holding up his trump cards in his toes and concealing a second queen of clubs in his sleeve. The character in the middle has had part of his head blown away so only half of his Wilhelmine moustache remains. The clumsily sewn patch of rubber that replaces his missing brain is decorated by a sketch of a copulating couple, suggesting that basic animal instincts still drive these shattered human forms. The third officer proudly displays his Iron Cross, although the lower half of his body is missing and his torso is suspended in a basket, leaving his penis pathetically flapping in the wind.

Throughout the composition Dix refers to the theme of cheating; the subjects' clothes are made out of the artificial paper textiles that were used in 1920 when no cotton or wool was available in Germany for civilian use. The paper money the subjects are gambling with is also "false," merely a *gutschein* or token, worth ten pfennigs at the beginning of the year but nothing a few weeks later. Dix uses the theme of falsity to reveal an underlying truth. Having been cheated themselves, these poor wrecks of humanity continue to cheat each other, mindlessly accepting the dictates of the authorities.

Dix's new realism challenged the idealism of abstract artists like Kandinsky, Mondrian, and Malevich. But it also challenged traditional realism, or illusionism, which, in the hands of an academic artist like Anton von Werner (1843–1915), was used for the purposes of state propaganda. Dix considered his paintings of war-wounded virtually unsaleable. They were exhibited in the Dada exhibitions of the 1920s, but no collector or museum came forward to buy them. In 1937, the largest of the 1920 street scenes, *War Cripples (45 percent Ready for Action)* was ridiculed in the Degenerate Art show, condemned by Goebbels, the Nazi minister of public enlightenment and propaganda, as "a vicious and depraved attack on our wounded heroes," and was probably destroyed. *Skat Players* survived the allied bombing of Dresden and was purchased by Dix's doctor in 1959. In 1995, the masterpiece was purchased for the German nation.

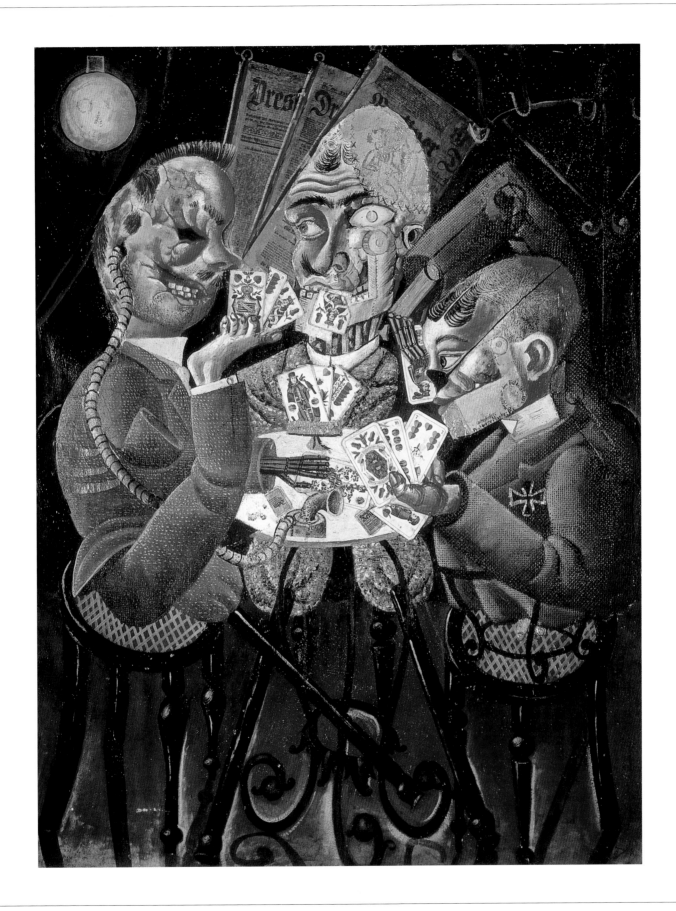

1920 | *oil and collage materials on canvas* | 43 x 34in (110 x 87cm) | Nationalgalerie, Berlin

The Birth of the World

THE BIRTH OF THE WORLD represents the most creative moment of Surrealism. It was painted by Miró in 1925, the year he declared his "official" allegiance to André Breton's group and contributed paintings to the first exhibition of Surrealist art at the Galerie Pierre in Paris. Alongside the collages and paintings of Max Ernst (1891–1976), it was Miró's paintings of 1924–25 that finally convinced Breton that the ideals of Surrealism could be expressed just as well in painting as in literature. "Miró," Breton wrote, "might become the most thoroughgoing Surrealist of us all." Certainly, *The Birth of the World* comes closest to fulfilling the aspirations expressed in the first Surrealist Manifesto of 1924, in which Breton wrote of their aim to marry painting and poetry, to merge the world of dreams with reality, and to be guided by the intervention of chance and the unconscious mind.

Miró came into contact with the Surrealists when he moved from his native Barcelona to Paris in 1920 and rented a studio in the rue Blomet, next door to André Masson (1896–1987), painter, sculptor, and writer and an early exponent of Surrealism. These studios played the same role for Surrealism as the Bateau-Lavoir had played some fifteen years earlier in the evolution of Cubism, where Picasso lived alongside the writers Max Jacob and André Salmon. Masson introduced Miró to the circle of artists, poets, and intellectuals—including Robert Desnos, Antonin Artaud, and Michel Leiris—who were close to Breton. The artists Jean Arp (1887–1966), Yves Tanguy (1900–55), and Ernst also visited the rue Blomet, and Miró soon came across the work of Giorgio de Chirico and Paul Klee (1879–1940).

Miró's move away from the magic realism of his early paintings toward the freer, more experimental, and abstract style of *The Birth of the World* undoubtedly relates to his encounter with Paul Klee's inventive work, which combined abstract and figurative forms, and to the experiments his friend Masson was undertaking with automatic painting and drawing. In *The Birth of the World*, Miró incorporated the workings of chance by spilling thinned liquid paint onto the canvas and blotting it with rags. His method involved improvisational as well as tightly controlled brushwork, used in tandem with automatic drawing.

JOAN MIRÓ

◊

BORN BARCELONA 1893,
DIED PALMA DE MAJORCA 1983

Miró later spoke of the painting as "a sort of genesis," and it is one of several Surrealist works that refer metaphorically to the act of creation through an image of the creation of the universe. Beginning with the void of the empty canvas, Miró suggested chaos by the stains and spots that resulted from pouring and spilling his paint. These chance configurations suggested other shapes and forms: "One large portion of black in the upper left seemed to need to become bigger," Miró recounted. "I enlarged it and went over it with opaque black paint. It became a triangle to which I added a tail. It might be a bird." He then felt that an accent of red was needed to counterbalance the black form and introduced the precisely painted red circle with a yellow streamer, which he later identified as a shooting star. The white disk on the lower left-hand side, which is like a head attached to a black body, was the last element Miró added. The encounter between the pointed black extension of the "male" body and the spiderlike black star, which Miró uses in many of his paintings and drawings to suggest the female sex, suggests the moment of conception.

The Birth of the World is one of Miró's most poetically conceived works. In 1929, the writer Michel Leiris undoubtedly had it in mind when he wrote in the Surrealist magazine, *Documents*, of Miró's "immense canvases, which seem to be soiled rather than painted, uneasy like a ruined building, seductive like a faded wall where generations of colored posters and centuries of fine rain have inscribed mysterious poems, long stains which suggest ambiguous forms, undetermined like the alluvium that comes from an unknown source and is carried by rivers which are constantly changing course, subject as they are to the movement of the wind and the rain."

Although it is now thought of as the masterpiece of early Surrealism, *The Birth of the World* was bought by a Belgian private collector in 1927 and only exhibited once, in 1956, before it was shown in the Museum of Modern Art's exhibition "Dada, Surrealism and their Heritage" in 1968. The painting was interpreted as a precursor of Abstract Expressionism and purchased for the museum's permanent collection in 1972.

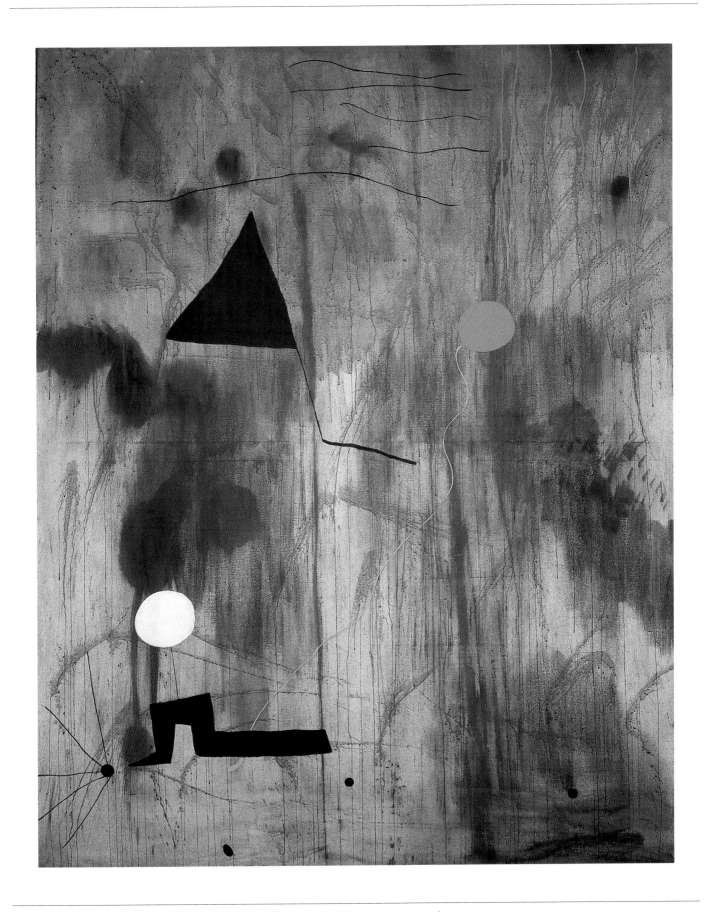

1925 | *oil on canvas* | 99 x 79in (251 x 200cm) | Museum of Modern Art, New York

The Plaza Tiller Girls

ALONGSIDE THE avant-garde movements of the 20th century, an undercurrent of art continued to engage with the great figurative tradition of European painting. Although representatives of this trend can be found on the European continent (Lovis Corinth, 1858–1925, and Balthus, born 1908, for example), many of the most powerful figurative painters of the century—including Walter Sickert, David Bomberg (1890–1957), and Francis Bacon—have been British. In the earlier period, Sickert is undoubtedly the British artist whose work best stands up to the challenge posed by his European peers.

Throughout Sickert's long career, his subjects were drawn from the world of the theater and the music hall. Before he found his true vocation as an artist, he worked briefly as an actor in British repertory theater, and he never lost his fascination for the stage. Although he was influenced by French paintings of similar scenes—particularly those by Degas—he made the subject distinctly his own, painting the cockney music hall in the 1880s and 1890s. In these early works, Sickert captured both the spectacle and the audience, the latter often shown leaning over plush gilt and plaster balconies to better view an invisible stage. Such subjects became a means of speculating about the philosophy of picturemaking itself. By making us conscious of our act of spectating and by drawing our attention to the artifice of the stage, Sickert revealed the imaginative orchestration involved in his apparently naturalistic paintings. Although the human figure is at the center of his art and there is always the sense of a distinct and particular experience, painting is, nevertheless, the artist's "invention." In later life, when Sickert was working almost exclusively from photographs rather than directly from the subject, he frequently quoted a famous Degas *mot*: "*On ne donne l'idée du vrai qu'avec le faux*" (You only give the impression of truth with falsity). "Painting," Sickert would add in his own words, "is an art, and that is to say that it is artificial."

Like Degas, Monet, Bonnard, and Corinth, Sickert was an artist with roots in the 19th century whose late work offers a fascinating reappraisal of realism. Although his work of the 1920s and 1930s met with success in its day, it was dismissed after his

WALTER RICHARD SICKERT

BORN MUNICH 1860,
DIED BATHAMPTON 1942

death as a pale reflection of his former powers. Sickert's method of using photographs and employing studio assistants to transfer the squared-up compositions onto the canvas (often leaving visible these signs of "mechanical" transposition in the finished paintings), the vigorous coarseness of his paint, and the extremes of pictorial drama and dryness which often coexist in the same painting, did not easily fit into the modernist canon. It was not until the exhibition of Sickert's late work at the Hayward Gallery in London in 1981 that a few critics began to acknowledge the interest and significance of his last paintings.

The Plaza Tiller Girls, depicting a fashionable cabaret troupe, was one of the most memorable works exhibited in this show. During the 1920s, Sickert often took a photographer with him to the theater, and he also collected photographs and newspaper clippings until he found exactly the "take" on the motif he was looking for. The close-up view of the dancers, whose dramatic gestures are frozen in arrested movement, undoubtedly derives from a photograph that the artist used to heighten the expressive impact of his picture.

In Sickert's opinion, photographs allowed him to view a scene in an essential, concentrated form, bringing out striking visual elements and unexpected abstract values. In this case, the details of the faces and bodies are absorbed into patterns of tone and color. The tonal underpainting recalls the photographic source while the vibrant, hedonistic colors are applied in vigorous strokes, evoking the rhythms of the dance and the swirling movements of the dancers' costumes.

Sickert seems to be drawn in to the magic, the "otherness," of the stage, and yet the repetition of the dancers' gestures and the lack of sharp visual focus act as distancing devices. The riotous exuberance of color and form are offered on equal terms with a controlled, sober representation of the original photograph, so that self-expression and objectivity are strangely combined. Sickert's dialogue with photography in late works like *The Plaza Tiller Girls* relates to his meditations on the enigma of time. While the blurring of the image gives a sense of the transitoriness of existence, the dancers' frozen gestures are an attempt to arrest time and distill immortal poetry out of the drama of human life.

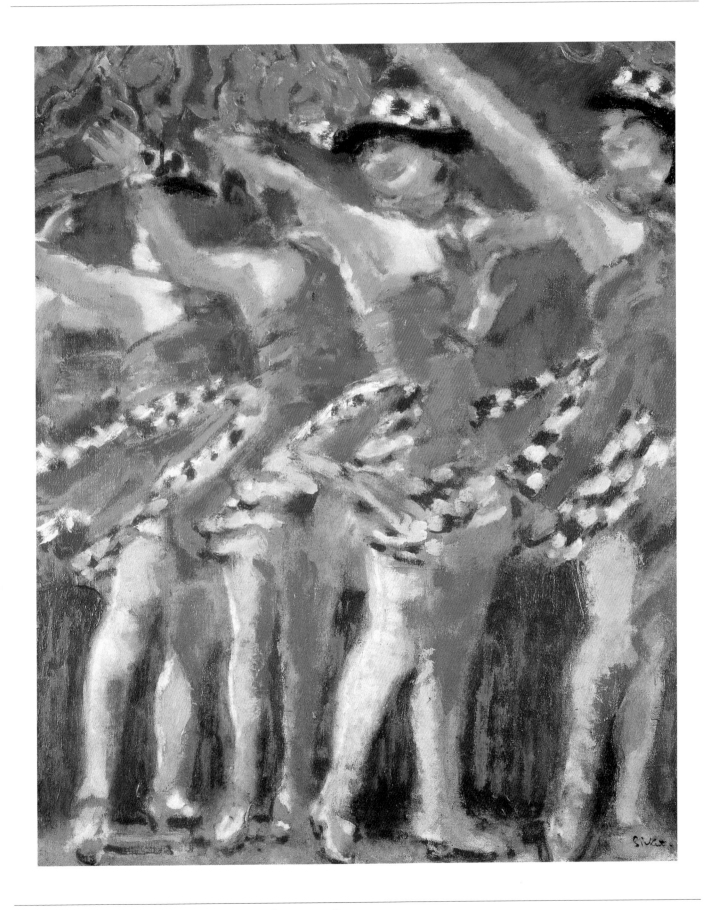

1928 | *oil on canvas* | 30 x 25in (76 x 63.5cm) | private collection

Nude in the Bath

BONNARD'S FIRST PAINTING of a nude in the bath dates from 1925, the year when he finally married his long-time mistress, Marthe Solange, and then settled in the South of France. At the turn of the century, as a member of the Nabis group of painters, who were inspired by the expressive use of color and forms in Gauguin's work, Bonnard had evolved a poetic figurative style that placed new emphasis on the decorative potential of the picture surface. Like Sickert, he followed an increasingly independent path as the century progressed, producing work in which memories and dreams are fused with a celebration of life and its sensual pleasures. Bonnard's three late paintings of nudes in the bath, painted between 1936 and 1945, are the crowning achievement of his oeuvre. They represent a magnificent synthesis of all his previous concerns and strike a rare and haunting chord of beauty.

Between 1927 and 1936, more than twenty pencil studies of full-length nudes lying in the bath are to be found in Bonnard's diaries. His wife, Marthe, was suffering from a respiratory illness during these years, and she spent long hours each day taking therapeutic baths. By the time he began to paint *Nude in the Bath* (the first in the late series), Marthe was in her mid-fifties, but her slim body, floating in the shimmering water of the tub, belongs to a young girl. This is not a picture of the present, but rather an image steeped in the artist's nostalgic memories of his wife in her twenties, as she was when they first met. Like Sickert, Bonnard was constantly aware of the "subtle balance between lies and truth," which he carefully negotiated in his paintings.

In his studies for the bath scenes, Bonnard often included the frame of a mirror, making it clear to the viewer that the images were in fact reflections. Just like the photographs Sickert used for his paintings (see page 314), these mirrors frame, abstract, and flatten the complex visual experience before the artist's eyes. In *Nude in the Bath*, the image is made all the more ephemeral by the incandescent gold and violet light reflecting off the surfaces of the tiles and the water, so that the nude seems suspended between being and nonbeing. "In the light of the South," Bonnard stated, "everything is luminous and painting

PIERRE BONNARD

⁂

*BORN FONTENAY-AUX-ROSES 1867,
DIED LE CANNET 1947*

vibrates with color. In painting it is absolutely necessary to heighten the hues. The early Italians understood this and sought out their reds and their most blazing blues in precious materials like lapis lazuli, gold and cochineal."

It is indeed Early Christian mosaics as well as ancient Egyptian tombs that come to mind when we contemplate the rich, jewel-like brightness of *Nude in the Bath*. Bonnard's oils have the clarity and brilliance of watercolors, and their transparency and evocation of shimmering light lift the banal, everyday reality of the bathroom onto a visionary plane. In this atmosphere, the white porcelain bathtub takes on the appearance of a sarcophagus, and the wraithlike body of the nude floats in a position so relaxed that she appears almost lifeless. There is a deathlike stillness to the scene, as if the image of Marthe as a beautiful young woman has become literally embalmed in the artist's memory.

The extraordinary tour de force represented by this painting involved Bonnard in more than six months struggle to realize his vision: "I'll never get involved in such a difficult motif again," the artist wrote. "I just can't manage to represent what I see." In fact, Bonnard returned to the motif twice more, actually borrowing *Nude in the Bath* from the Petit Palais, which had acquired the work in 1936, to have beside him while he reworked the scene. More poignantly than any other of Bonnard's paintings, *Nude in the Bath* conveys both his celebration of beauty and his melancholy sense of its fragility and of the transience of pleasure.

Writing of his impressions of *Nude in the Bath* when he saw it at an exhibition of contemporary art, the art dealer Pierre Loeb recorded: "It seemed at first a complete outsider, both in terms of the exhibition and of the epoch. But if one reconsiders, looking at things from a certain distance, one realizes that there are certain fundamentals which we can never entirely escape, and that Bonnard—I'm speaking of the last works—was uniquely aware of this evolution ... The avant garde," Loeb continued, "isn't always where we expect to find it ... and in the end I realized that Bonnard was the only artist who provided a complete reflection of his epoch."

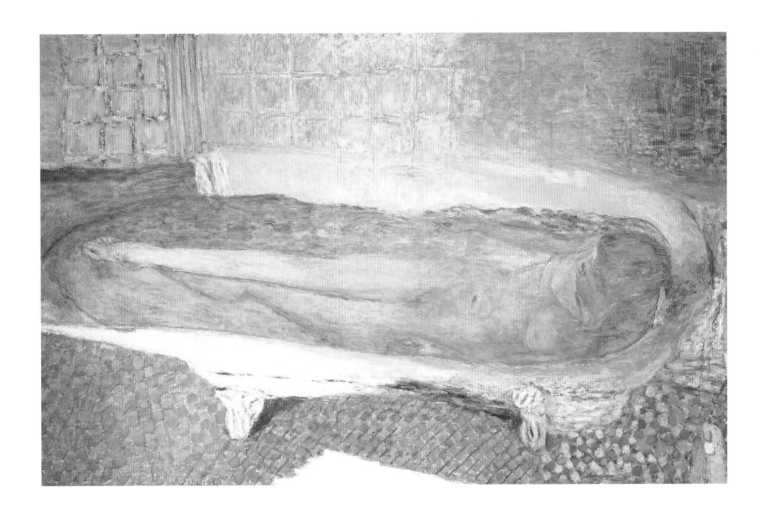

My Nurse and I, or I Suckle

In 1939, when Frida Kahlo exhibited for the first time in Paris, she was eulogized by André Breton as the personification of the "Surrealist woman," whose wounded body (Kahlo had been partially crippled in a road accident in 1925) was the perfect expression of "*la beauté convulsive*." Although often described as a Surrealist, Kahlo felt little affinity with the movement and criticized their passive intellectualism. Her own work sprung from a deep personal need. "I paint my own reality," she stated, "I paint because I need to, and I paint whatever passes through my head, without any other consideration." This "need" of Kahlo's undoubtedly gave rise to some of the most original and dramatic imagery in 20th-century art. Her work can be described as a painted autobiography, and the numerous self-portraits she made in her short life are poignant metaphors for both her physical and spiritual existence.

Frida Kahlo began to paint in the hospital when she was recovering from the accident which left her with permanent spinal and pelvic injuries that made it impossible for her to bear children. Three years later, in 1928, she began her tempestuous and highly publicized relationship with the Mexican mural painter Diego Rivera (1886–1957), whom she married twice. Although they shared the same left-wing politics, their esthetic goals could hardly have been more different. While Rivera was committed to public art, Kahlo, who came from a German background on her father's side, drew inspiration from Lucas Cranach the Elder (1472–1553) and Dürer, painting with very fine sable brushes, which she kept immaculately clean, and concentrating her energies on small, intensely personal paintings.

Both Rivera and Kahlo were preoccupied by their cultural roots in Mexico, and they shared a passion for Pre-Columbian art. *My Nurse and I* is partly a declaration of faith in the continuity of Mexican culture as an ancient heritage that is reborn in each generation. In 1937, Frida suffered one of the traumatic miscarriages or abortions that punctuated her adult life, and this sparked off a series of paintings in which her longing for a child became merged with nostalgia for her own childhood. In this painting, she pictures herself as a baby with an adult head

FRIDA KAHLO

☙

BORN COYOACÁN 1907,
DIED MEXICO CITY 1954

suckling in her Indian nurse's arms. The nurse is a personification of Mexico's Indian heritage, and Kahlo emphasizes the role played by magic and ritual as well as the importance of fertility and the idea of cosmic and biological forces working in unison.

The image of the nurse is inspired by the ritualistic dignity of Olmec stone sculptures, in particular the figure called *Señor de las Limas*, which depicts a child with an adult face held in the arms of a male. By feminizing this image, Kahlo makes a cross-reference to ceramic sculptures from Jalisco (c. 100 B.C.–A.D. 250) which depict a mother suckling her child and reveal the ducts and glands of the lactating breast in a plantlike pattern. In *My Nurse and I*, the pattern on the nurse's breast is repeated in the milk-white leaf behind the figures, while the milk drops falling like tears from the sky refer to Kahlo's own Indian nurse's description of rain as "milk from the Virgin." Like the metamorphosing caterpillar and the praying mantis camouflaged against the plants, these details convey Kahlo's faith in the interconnectedness of every aspect of the natural world and her sense of her place in it.

Kahlo stated that she painted the nurse's face as a mask because she could not remember how she looked, continuing: "I came out looking like such a little girl and she so strong and so saturated with providence that it made me long to sleep." While the body of the nurse comforts and nourishes Frida, her face has taken on the form of a fearsome Teotihuacan funerary mask, evoking the ritual savagery of the Mexican past. As she drinks the nurse's "providential milk," the artist imbibes a knowledge of her fate. She is offered up as a sacrificial victim, and the scene also brings to mind Christian images of the Madonna Caritàs (Madonna of Charity) and the pietà.

Frida Kahlo's highly concentrated and inventive images are able to convey a range of personal and universal meanings. *My Nurse and I* can be read as a double self-portrait, as the nurse has Kahlo's black hair and the distinctive eyebrows that spread across her forehead in a continuous line. Her Mexican heritage is pictured as life-sustaining; but the image also evokes the dual forces of eros and thanatos (instincts of desire and death) that animate human existence.

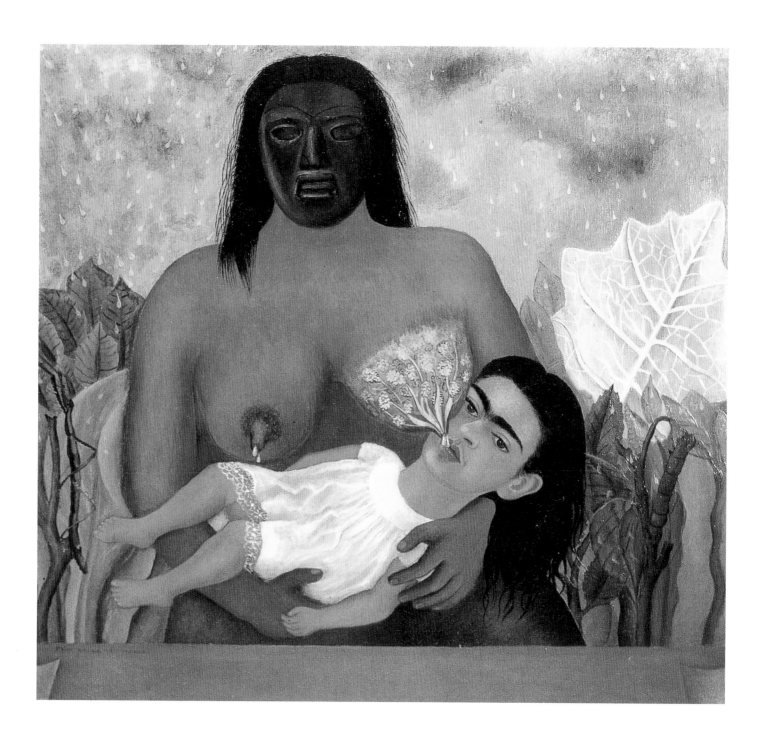

1937 | *oil on metal* | 12 x 14in (30.5 x 35cm) | Collection of Dolores Olmedo Patino, Mexico City

Departure

EPARTURE IS THE FIRST of nine triptychs Max Beckmann painted in 1932–50, which are his most ambitious and complex statements about the condition of modern man. Beckmann, like Otto Dix, came to prominence in the 1920s as one of the main protagonists of Neue Sachlichkeit (New Objectivity), an artistic and literary movement in Germany that sought to replace the emotiveness of Expressionism with a sober appraisal of the harsh realitites of life, but he always remained outside the mainstream movements of his age. With some justification, Beckmann saw Picasso as his only serious rival, and the dynamic monumentality of his later paintings resulted, in part, from his study of Picasso's neo-Classical work. More than any other painter of the century, Beckmann combined intellectual and philosophical insights with a keen awareness of the sensuality of his medium. Among the realist artists of his generation, he alone saw it as his duty to depict man's spiritual state.

Like Dix, Beckmann's experiences in World War I radically changed his life. The horrors he witnessed working as a medical orderly caused him to have a nervous breakdown and led him to search for an explanation for the evils of war in the mystical doctrines of Gnosticism, Buddhism, the Kabbala, and in the pessimistic philosophy of Schopenhauer. Beckmann was crucially influenced by the Gnostic concept of the world being created by an evil demiurge as a prison for human souls. According to this doctrine, the individual must struggle to return to an original state of innocence in the realm of Good or Light, beyond the constraints of matter.

There is no doubt that the rise of National Socialism in Germany in the late 1920s and early 1930s confirmed Beckmann's ideas about the inevitability of evil and man's tragic fate. Beckmann suffered considerably under the new regime, losing his teaching post in Frankfurt in 1933 and witnessing the closure of the room devoted to his work in the annex of the Nationalgalerie in Berlin. In 1937, many of his paintings, prints, and watercolors were seized, and twelve paintings were shown in the Degenerate Art Exhibition in Munich. A day after witnessing Hitler's speech at the opening of the Haus der Deutschen Kunst, where art approved by the Nazis was to be

MAX BECKMANN

*BORN LEIPZIG 1884,
DIED NEW YORK 1950*

shown, Beckmann fled to Amsterdam. After ten years of exile in Holland, he accepted a teaching post in the United States, refusing to return to Germany at the end of World War II.

The threat of these events hangs heavily over *Departure*. Beckmann chose the epic format of the triptych, favored for medieval and Renaissance altarpieces, to dramatize the conflict between the human soul and the material world and to express the dichotomy between good and evil that lies at the heart of his work. The side panels, with their claustrophobic space, recall the wings of Gothic altarpieces. Indeed, the scenes of torture so crudely enacted in *Departure* hark back to Beckmann's "Gothic" paintings of *The Night* (1918–19, Kunstsammlung Nordrhein-Westfalen, Düsseldorf) and *Carnival* (1920 Tate Gallery, London), where he formulated his vision of the tragic fight of the individual soul against the forces of evil. The references to the cabaret and fairground that entered Beckmann's art during this earlier period symbolized human strategies for survival, while the mask is often used, paradoxically, to reveal what it is intended to conceal.

Beckmann began *Departure* in Frankfurt in 1932, beginning with the side panels and working directly on the canvas rather than making preliminary sketches. The scenes illustrating the compulsive cruelty and obsessive sensuality of man entrapped in the material world contrast with the monumental forms and glowing colors of the central panel. This depicts a king and queen with their child, escorted by a masked guard, embarking on a triumphant voyage. The sea, always a symbol of spiritual freedom in Beckmann's work, stretches toward the horizon. During the early 1930s, Beckmann had become absorbed in Greek, Indian, and Nordic mythology, and the triptychs draw freely on the common themes and symbols in world religions. The fish in the right-side panel, for example, recalls the fertility symbol of Judaism, while its presence in the middle panel relates to Christian redemption. Beckmann was fascinated by the multiple meanings of such symbols and used the timeless narrative of myth to suggest a multilayered reality in which his personal experiences were fused with historical facts and mystical truths to recount the story of human destiny.

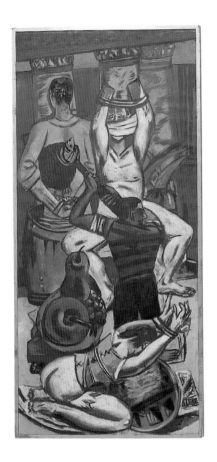
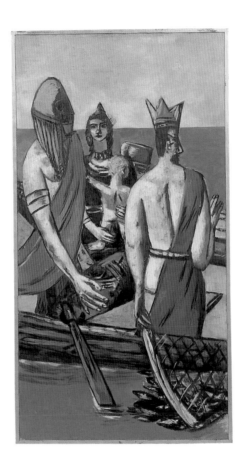
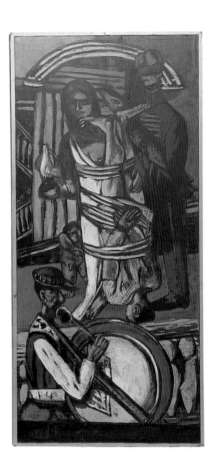

1932–35 | *oil on canvas* | *center panel* 85 x 45in (215 x 115cm), side panels 85 x 39¹⁄₂in (215 x 100cm) | Museum of Modern Art, New York

321

THE LATE 20TH CENTURY

1950–2000 ❋ MARCO LIVINGSTONE

The rapid succession of avant-garde movements during the first half of the

20th century has since assumed an even greater urgency. Each new style, method, or

medium makes conflicting claims to authority and rejects other approaches.

I N THE LATE 1940s and 1950s, subjective forms of abstraction, notably American Abstract Expressionism and European *Art Informel*, were the most radical alternatives to the figurative bias of Western art, but by the 1960s, they were questioned not only by "cooler" forms of abstraction such as Op art and Minimalism, but by the resurgence of representational art, notably Pop art. Pop replaced private language with a public one, aspirations to the sublime with references to low culture, individual handwork with an apparently anonymous surface. And it confronted the very notion of authenticity on which the myth of the modern artist as a heroic individual had so long been predicated.

Agnes Martin's delicate linear grids, like Untitled #2 (1977), *evoke sensations of light in landscape.*

The accelerated rate at which artistic movements were said to replace each other, like the annual turnover of the fashion industry, had much to do with the consolidation of a commercial network and an increasingly speculative and insatiable art market. Museums, art critics, and collectors played their part, too, in a manic search to be first on the scene of The Next Big Thing. The Abstract Expressionists were well into middle age before they began to be fully accepted; by contrast, the overnight success of Jasper Johns when he was still in his late twenties established a pattern by which artists made their mark at an increasingly early age. With the stakes raised ever higher in terms both of financial rewards and the premium placed on radical innovation, it was no longer enough simply to contradict a prevailing attitude or style. New art forms began to question the very definition of the finite art work as a material object. By the end of the 1960s, Performance art, Kinetic art, Conceptual art, Land art, Installation art, and Video art had all challenged the continuing validity of painting and sculpture, and proposed more temporary forms incorporating time and ephemerality as essential preconditions for esthetic experience. During this period, too, photography—relegated for more than a century to a subservient and predominantly documentary role—emerged not just as a strong source of influence but as a major medium in its own right.

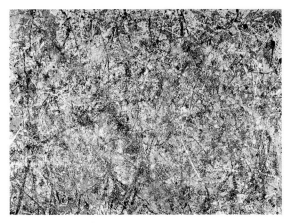

Jackson Pollock's "drip" paintings were among the most extreme manifestations of Abstract Expressionism. Lavender Mist: Number 1, 1950.

In retrospect, it no longer seems tenable to view the evolution of art as a linear sequence or even as a dialectic of antithetical responses. New developments have followed cyclical patterns. For example, the early 1980s saw a strong movement in painting that was again both strongly expressive but also resolutely figurative. Moreover, it has become clear that each new type of art can survive and even thrive after it has been cast aside as last year's trend, and that contradictory approaches and media can coexist and find their own audience. Many museums have begun to recognize this shift by rehanging their permanent collections not as a succession of movements but as a more unpredictable pattern of individual journeys and alternative proposals. The very idea of great art emanating only from the major art centers such as Paris and New York is no longer credible. Some of the most impressive artistic voices speak from the margins rather than from the centers of power.

Since the 1980s, and for the first time in history, women artists have been on an equal footing with men. Blacks, gays, and artists from developing countries have also made their presence felt, speaking of their own experience to different constituencies. In a period where pluralism has become the norm and change the only constant, no objective witness could claim the dominance of any single tendency. Although both the avant-garde and modernism have been declared dead, the talk now of "cutting-edge" art suggests that perhaps only the terminology has changed, and that new developments will continue to be signaled at a frenzied rate.

A selection of fifteen works can only hint at the enormous diversity of this particular half-century of artistic production. I make no apologies for the emphasis I have given herein to British artists, to whose work I feel a particular attachment and whose contribution to postwar art is only now being more widely acknowledged. That my more general emphasis, as in the rest of this volume, has been on painting is not to denigrate the importance of the new and emerging media, but to convey my profound belief that painting remains as valid as ever in satisfying the ultimate purpose of any work of art: to convey experience as truthfully and as powerfully as possible.

Head II

THE PRODUCTION of art had not come to a complete standstill during World War II, but it was only when the conflict ended and the full tragedy of those six years and of the unthinkable inhumanity of the Holocaust began to sink in that artists sought to convey the conflicting moods of relief and loss, of mourning and intense aloneness. To many in postwar Paris, which in the late 1940s was still the center of the international art world, an existentialist point of view—with its focus on the solitary individual in a meaningless universe—seemed the only possible response. Yet, it was a previously unknown British painter, Francis Bacon, who unleashed the most powerful howl of anguish in 20th-century art in paintings that gave form to the desperate condition of humanity in conflict with itself. Born to English parents in Ireland, which he left at the age of sixteen, he led a peripatetic youth and began painting and designing furniture in the late 1920s without any formal instruction. His *Three Studies for Figures at the Base of a Crucifixion* (1944, Tate Gallery, London) marks Bacon's real birth as an artist. It is the first of many works to take its imagery from the most emotive subject in Christianity and its triptych construction from the format of the great religious art of the European tradition. Its wounded and barely human protagonists, inspired by the Furies that pursued Orestes in the *Oresteia* trilogy by Aeschylus, are reduced to naked torsos whose grossly elongated necks amplify the shrieks emanating from heads that are just cavernous open mouths with bared teeth. They provide a terrifying animalistic spectacle, trapped in the shrill orange of a barren, deserted environment.

Although he was a nonbeliever, Bacon had no hesitation in building on the iconography of Christian art as it provided a shared basis of understanding and an existing framework through which to present the drama of human life and death at its most extreme. In 1949, he painted the first of a series of popes produced intermittently over many years, inspired by a reproduction of an official portrait he chose never to view in person: Velázquez's *Pope Innocent X* (1650, Galleria Doria-Pamphili, Rome). Even when he began in the early 1960s to make portraits of people he knew, in preference to the distant authority figures or the anonymous men in business suits who populate his paintings of the early 1950s, Bacon preferred to work from photographs because of the detachment they afforded him. Although he never wavered from his devotion to painting, his modernity as an artist cannot be separated from his reliance on the camera. Rather than being tempted to replicate the brushwork of an Old Master or simply to imitate objectively the surface appearance of the person he was observing, he challenged himself to create his own equivalent, using paint as raw matter as if he were the first to have discovered its possibilities for rendering visible the image of another human being.

From the early 1960s until his death, Bacon built steadily on his own discoveries and came to rely on particular formats and procedures. Techniques of smearing and even throwing paint, which had once been as thrillingly risky as the gambling to which he was addicted, eventually became second nature to him. These methods, which fellow painter R.B. Kitaj (born 1932) referred to admiringly as "sublime paint trickery," sometimes seem to have become ends in themselves, a means of incontrovertibly establishing his identity within each picture. He never lost sight, however, of what he described as the direct action of paint on the nervous system. The effects of his techniques—at once visual, neurological, visceral, and emotive—are stated with extraordinary force in a small early painting, *Head II*, which concentrates attention on a disembodied mouth held painfully open in front of a thickly encrusted curtain of paint. Executed over a period of about four months, it remains one of the most affecting statements of belief in the continuing power of painting in the whole of 20th-century art. Like all of Bacon's work, the subjective originality of its conception and physical characteristics alike precluded direct imitation. Unsurprisingly, he created no school, but he set an example that remains just as powerful at the century's end. His ability to distill his subject matter into a memorably condensed image and to endow the mute material of oil paint with a dynamic voice has done more than perhaps any artist since Picasso to persuade succeeding generations that the possibilities of painting are far from exhausted.

FRANCIS BACON

✦

*BORN DUBLIN 1909,
DIED MADRID 1992*

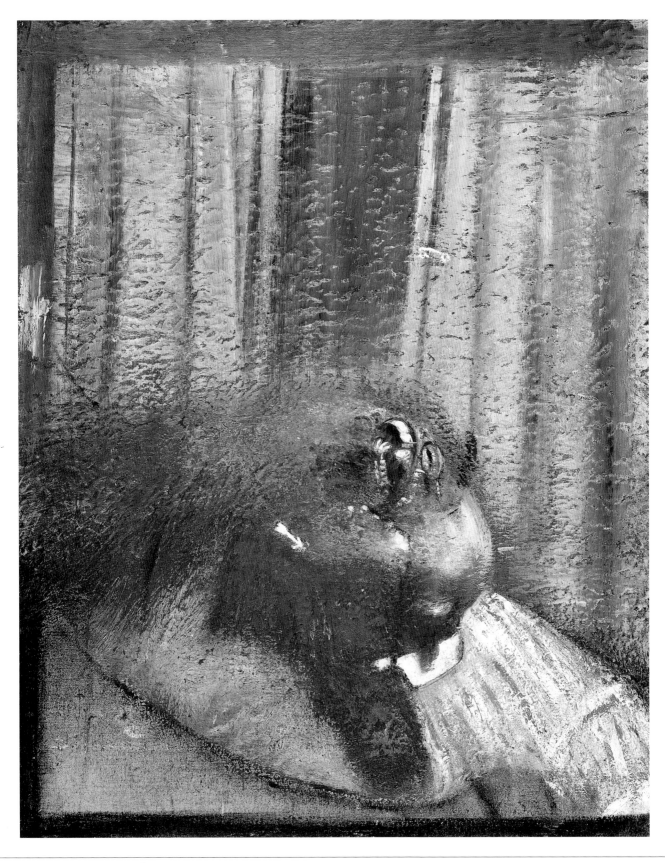

1949 | *oil on canvas* | 31$\frac{1}{2}$ x 25in (80 x 64cm) | Ulster Museum, Belfast

Suburb in Havana

FOR ALL THEIR differences and despite their debts to European modernism, the Abstract Expressionists of the 1940s and 1950s were the first American artists to be sufficiently radical and united to establish themselves at the forefront of international developments. The influence of Surrealism is clear in their work, and at the heart of the movement lay freedom of expression, a revolt against tradition, and the importance of the act of creation itself. New York replaced Paris as the capital of contemporary art, and a standard was set against which later painting reacted.

The Dutch-born Willem de Kooning, who immigrated to the United States as a young adult in 1926 after a conventional academic training in Rotterdam, Brussels, and Antwerp, could not rightly be described as the most dramatically innovative Abstract Expressionist, particularly as he maintained a lifelong dialogue with figuration. The "drip" paintings of Jackson Pollock (1912–1956) of the late 1940s and 1950s, with their pulsating rhythms of interwoven paths of elegantly flung paint, broke much more drastically with the spatial conventions of easel painting, not least because of the way that the skeins of paint were applied more or less equally across the entire surface. Collaborating with the force of gravity, so the liquid paint fell or was hurled onto the often large expanse of canvas laid flat on the floor, the artist spoke of his sensation of being "in" the painting. Barnett Newman (1905–1970), the least "expressionist" of these artists, took his esthetic to an equally extreme conclusion, covering large surfaces in single colors broken only by a thin stripe or "zip" of contrasting color, suggesting shafts of light intruding into an otherwise endless space. He, too, favored an unusually large scale that encouraged the viewer to experience the canvas as a self-contained environment that was not quite of this world. With his ragged-edged veils of superimposed colors floating against equally rich grounds, Mark Rothko (1903–1970), like Newman, enticed the spectator into an emotional response or into a reading of the surface as a sublime, infinite space.

De Kooning, whose first major paintings of the 1940s are portraits and figure studies which are clearly indebted to the fragmented visual language and shrill colors of Picasso and his

WILLEM DE KOONING

*BORN ROTTERDAM 1904,
DIED NEW YORK 1997*

fellow leading European modernists, kept returning to the oldest subjects and above all to those of the female body and landscape. Only in the late 1970s and 1980s, when he was perhaps already beginning to suffer from Alzheimer's disease, did he produce paintings that could properly be described as abstract over a sustained period. Nevertheless, his appeal does not rest on any inherent conservatism, for it was precisely through his stubborn allegiance to art as a means of reinterpreting and reshaping the world that he succeeded most powerfully in conveying and sharing his experience. There is something endearingly earthy and human about his work that gives it a special allure, in spite of the fact that he proved more reluctant than some of his colleagues to break so drastically with the past. His paintings of women from 1950 on, with which he remains most closely associated, show the female body as unapologetically sexual, lustful, voluptuous, reveling in its own fleshiness. His landscapes, too, are rooted in the earth, unashamedly physical equivalents of the experience of nature by which they were inspired.

Suburb in Havana is just one of a group of large landscapes painted by de Kooning in the late 1950s in swashbuckling brushstrokes of sundrenched color. In the simplicity of its structure and legibility of image—with a clear division between blue sky and open fields along the horizon—it comes closest to the prototypes of Dutch 17th-century landscape painting from which it is ultimately descended. Yet, the energetic handling of lusciously oily paint in massive strokes charges what might otherwise have been a bland scene with an electrifying life and vibrancy. One feels swept along by a spontaneous and joyful declaration of union with the earth itself, a mood heightened by the physical sensation of being dragged at great speed through the undergrowth. Few paintings make me feel more alive, more vividly confronted by a sense of my own physical presence. And with the constant oscillation between opposing readings of the brushstrokes—as pure physical matter as well as triggers to observed experience—few offer such convincing evidence of the power of suggestion and the continuing vitality of the "primitive" urge to depict.

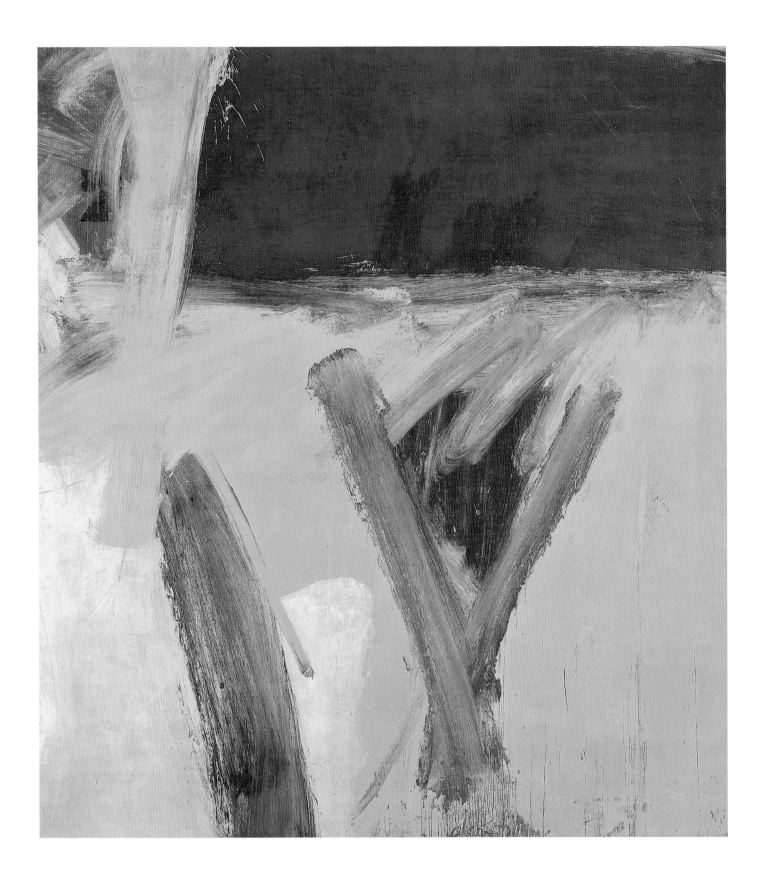

1958 | *oil on canvas* | 80 x 70in (203 x 178cm) | private collection

Target with Plaster Casts

ESSENTIALLY self-taught, in autumn 1954, the young American Jasper Johns destroyed all the works in his New York studio as a prelude to reinventing his art from first principles. By the following spring, he had begun painting American flags, by his own account inspired by a dream, and then this first and supremely confident target. The visual, philosophical, and esthetic impact of these works, both on his own development and on that of other artists, was immense and immediate. The Museum of Modern Art in New York took the highly unusual step of purchasing three paintings from his first solo show in 1958. The legacy of these works on later 20th-century art has been astonishing in its range. It is evident in the literalism of Pop art, with its reliance on commonplace objects and everyday imagery; in the gestalt forms of Minimalism; in Conceptual art's emphasis on ideas and context; and even in the evolution of Body art and sculpture based directly on the human form. Yet, *Target with Plaster Casts* retains a potency that would guarantee its place in modern art irrespective of its enormous influence and iconic status.

Johns's painting is beguiling in its simplicity and instant formal impact. The canvas surface is starkly subdivided into geometric zones of primary color. The target is not simply represented in the painting, it is the painting. By thus asserting its physical reality as an object in its own right, Johns gives himself the freedom to oscillate between the self-evident and literal and the mysterious or half-understood. His choice of encaustic, an ancient wax-based medium that hardens very quickly after being applied, was ideal for his purposes, creating a powerful record of the artist's touch and of the paint's transition from fluid to solid matter as a metaphor for the almost alchemical transformation of base matter into precious art.

Layering his semitranslucent paint over a collage base of newspaper fragments that are tantalizing in their intermittent legibility, like passing thoughts surfacing into consciousness, the artist begins laying traps for the curious but possibly unwary spectator. In the process, the purely physical yields to more metaphysical speculations. The row of wooden boxes that surmounts the canvas presents a random sequence of life-sized

JASPER JOHNS

BORN AUGUSTA 1930

sculptural representations of body parts cast directly in plaster from the artist's own anatomy and from that of his friends. One relates both physically and emotionally to these truncated forms, rich in troubling evocations of the senses: the eyeless face, the solitary ear, the hand with outstretched fingers, the breast and genitalia. Wrenched out of context, squeezed and abruptly cropped into small compartments, they make seemingly haphazard demands on our attention. We find ourselves glancing curiously at them as we would when assessing a living person's appearance and gestures.

The hinged doors can be left open or closed, allowing (in theory at least) for the spectator to become a collaborator with the artist in the creative act. The numerous permutations imply an open-endedness, both in form and meaning, that serves to keep the work alive and mutable rather than forever fixed. The act of opening and closing is richly suggestive, not least of the process of vision itself through the continuous blinking of eyelids, and plays on the theme of revealing and concealing so powerfully at work in the painting itself: all human beings decide constantly how much to expose about themselves to others in terms of their personality, sexuality, or emotions. Recent scholarship has sought to unlock private meanings embedded in the iconography of this work, but Johns clearly chose not to disclose such details or to pin down the interpretation so particularly to his own circumstances. Instead, these possibilities hover without final resolution, like the encaustic brushstrokes in which the record of his hand movements is forever suspended on the surface.

In the decades following the production of this painting, Johns gradually expanded his vocabulary, for example with the introduction of a crosshatch pattern in the early 1970s and a shadowy self-portrait in the mid-1980s, while continuing to employ the target and other early images such as American flags, light bulbs, and beer cans as signature motifs for his continuing exploration of the creative process and ways of seeing. So consistent has he remained to his techniques, however, and so loyal to the subjects that have become visual signs of his artistic identity, that *Target with Plaster Casts* remains as fresh now as when it was painted.

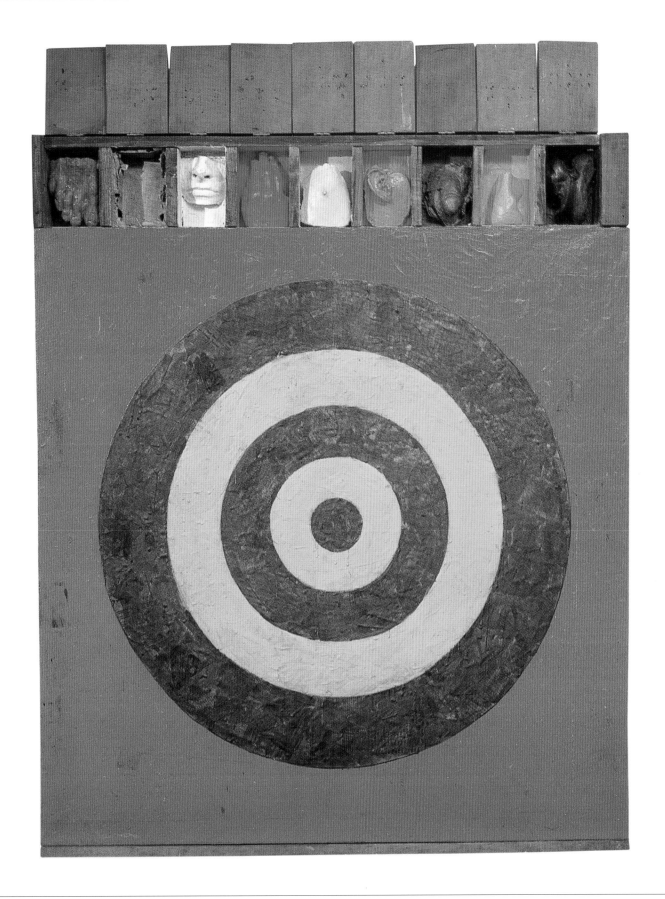

1955 | *encaustic and collage on canvas with objects* | 51 x 44 x 3¹/₂in (129.5 x 112 x 9cm) | Collection David Geffen, Los Angeles

Hiroshima

AT THE AGE of thirty-four, the French artist Yves Klein gave impetus to a variety of radical new developments in contemporary art that took hold internationally only later in the 1960s. His importance goes far beyond that of Nouveau Réalisme, the primarily sculptural movement that he helped launch in 1960. With their emphasis on reductive form, his *Monochromes*, paintings executed without line or image in a single color—notably a deep ultramarine which he termed IKB (International Klein Blue)—were powerful precursors of Minimalism, rivaled in their historical importance only by the black paintings of the American Ad Reinhardt (1913–1967). They also helped set the terms for the investigations into dematerialized form explored by such artists as the Americans Dan Flavin (1933–1996), with his sculptures made from tubes of colored fluorescent light, and James Turrell (born 1941), who invoked the sublime in installations of dimly lit and mysterious voids.

Klein prefigured the Conceptual art of the later 1960s with the *Receipts for the Immaterial* issued in 1959—certificates exchanging "Zones of Immaterial Pictorial Sensibility" for a stated weight in gold—and with his presentation in 1958 of an empty gallery space as a work of art, a groundbreaking example of Installation art. His use of fire, wind, and rain as the sole means of making marks in his *Cosmogonies* predated Process art, which, in the case of the American Robert Morris (born 1931), harnessed materials as ephemeral as steam to the presentation of works as the record of their own making, and even helped prepare the way for the Land art pioneered by the American Robert Smithson (1938–1973) and others as a sculptural form that took nature itself as its raw material. Even Klein's most solidly sculptural objects—such as the *Portrait-reliefs* of artist friends that he made at the end of his life—were both innovative and influential in their extreme literalness, cast directly from the person's body, like the contemporaneous sculptures by American Pop artist George Segal (born 1924), rather than modeled by hand.

Klein's *Anthropométries*, of which *Hiroshima* is a particularly mysterious and arresting example, are at first glance the most traditional of his works in their reliance on the human form, but they are by no means conventional figurative paintings. The images are not painted by hand, but are formed either directly by the imprint of a paint-smeared naked body onto a large expanse of white paper or (as here) by the spraying of color around the model so as to leave her shape as a ghostly record of her brief passage and eventual absence: the wispy physical traces of pure energy in space. This particular example pays homage to one of Klein's prime sources of inspiration, the charred shapes left on the ground by the victims of the nuclear bomb dropped on Hiroshima toward the end of World War II, and especially the stone bearing the shadowy imprint of such a casualty that he had seen on a visit there in 1953.

Some of the earliest *Anthropométries* were created in February 1960 as the end product of a performance at the Galerie Internationale d'Art Contemporain in Paris, set to the hypnotically repetitive music of Klein's own "Symphonie Monoton." With their sinuous rhythms and occasional likeness to musical notation, they preserve a sense of their origins in both music and dance. Like so much of his startlingly original work, they remain fresh in conception not only because of their stripped-down beauty but also because the directions they proposed have proved so fertile to later generations. Not only are they the result of some of the earliest and most influential examples of Performance art; in their imagery and frank eroticism, they also foreshadow the post-feminist Body art that has become an ever-stronger international current since the 1980s.

Klein's influence and the continuing fascination he exerts would be reasons enough to single him out among the essential figures in postwar art. Yet, it is the emotive and esthetic force of his surviving paintings and sculptures, together with the intuitive brilliance of his thinking, that cause one to linger. During a period in which it no longer seems possible to produce religious art, Klein found strangely affecting ways of dealing with the transcendence of the spirit over matter. *Hiroshima*, with its frieze of youthful but fragile bodies set against a blue void as deep, timeless, and expansive as the sky, creates a kind of screen by which to contemplate the mysteries of life, the universe, and eternity.

YVES KLEIN

☙

*BORN NICE 1928,
DIED PARIS 1962*

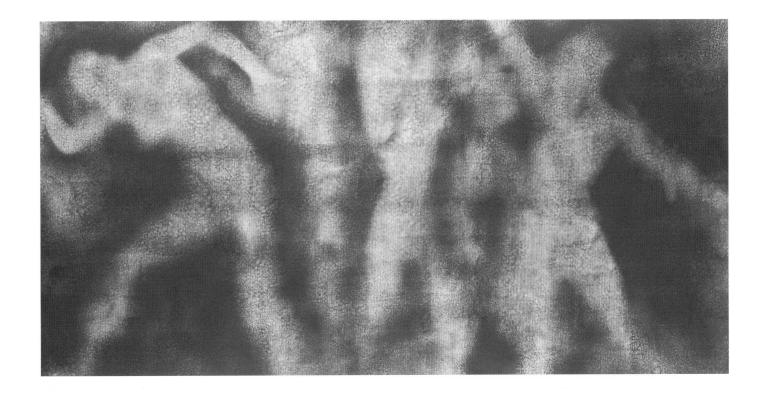

c. 1961 | *dry pigment in synthetic resin on paper on canvas* | 55 x 110¹⁄₂in (139.5 x 280.5) | The Menil Collection, Houston

Matter in the Form of a Foot

DURING THE 1950s, the Spanish Catalan painter Antoni Tàpies was one of the originators of *Art informel*, the movement in European painting which, through its emphasis on gestural abstraction and its appeal to the unconscious, closely paralleled Abstract Expressionism in the United States. Together with artists such as the Frenchman Jean Dubuffet (1901–1985) and the Italian Alberto Burri (born 1915), Tàpies was particularly associated with the development of Matter Painting, a type of (mostly abstract) painting that placed great emphasis on the tactile qualities of the surface of a work by means of a thick application of paint that was often mixed with artistically unconventional materials such as sand or marble dust.

For Tàpies, who first experimented with such procedures in the mid-1940s and with renewed conviction from 1953, the decision to make art from whatever was at hand was a way not only of opening himself to chance and primal impulses, but also of overthrowing academic artistic traditions and pretensions to privileged status. In this he was extending a strong current in modern art that favored the authenticity of the primitive, manifested as early as the 19th century in the work of Gustave Courbet and Paul Gauguin (1848–1903) (with their appropriations from naive art and non-Western traditions) and later in the raw emotion of Expressionism, the self-exposure of Surrealism, and the elevation of "outsider" art (or *Art brut*, as the art of the insane and other marginalized self-taught artists is also known) as a separate class of art. The reliance by Tàpies on humble, everyday materials applied to the surface with the directness of plaster or cement on an ordinary wall (a metaphor he actively encouraged in a series of paintings depicting such objects) was to some degree a political statement, a declaration of solidarity with ordinary people at a time when Spain's Fascist dictatorship ruled out the possibility of more overt protest. The procedure, however, was also a way for the artist to free himself from conscious control and to enter a trancelike, meditative state. Forms and images could be engendered out of the process itself, without preconceived ideas, akin to the Joycean concept of stream-of-consciousness or to psychoanalytical free association.

ANTONI TÀPIES

BORN BARCELONA 1923

Just as he used ordinary household materials and sometimes even dirt to make his paintings, so Tàpies began in the 1950s to make allusion to walls, doors, chairs, beds, and other objects from the everyday environment and to parts of the human body, particularly those considered dirty or unmentionable: feet, armpits, anuses, and genitalia. Like much of the increasingly explicit body art that has taken an ever-more central place in the art of the late 20th century, Tàpies was attracted to such images because of their sexual charge and as a way of delving beyond the surface of sophistication and cultivated manners by addressing taboos concerning our bodily functions and "animal" needs. The presentation by Tàpies of an isolated foot, arm, or other anatomical fragment, often scored with woundlike incisions, bears a strong visual relationship to Catholic votive offerings, miniaturized models of an affected body part left in a church in fulfillment of a vow by which the supplicant hopes to be cured. Although as a young man the artist had rejected his Catholic education, he recognized its possible survival in this respect. He also spoke of the talismanic properties, the possibilities for healing, offered by the work of art as a release from pain and suffering, in Buddhism, the essential conditions of existence.

Matter in the Form of a Foot draws attention through its very title to the magical or alchemical transformations, of raw substances into inanimate objects and even organic forms, that Tàpies understands to be at the root of the creative act and specifically of his own activity as a painter. His titles are habitually literal, bland descriptions of the most immediately obvious properties of the work, the colors, shapes, images, materials, and techniques by which it has been brought into being. By avoiding more evocative titles, he shortcircuits our tendency to gain understanding through the intellect and proposes that we experience his art viscerally and emotionally without too many preconceptions. Like other highly influential late 20th-century artists, such as the German Joseph Beuys (1921–1986), who conceived of his role as that of a shaman, Tàpies has promoted a visionary subjectivity and even a degree of mysticism as a corrective to the predominantly rational tendencies of our age.

1965 | *mixed media on canvas* | 51 x 64in (130 x 162cm) | Fundació Antoni Tàpies, Barcelona

Red Disaster

THE PAINTINGS produced during the 1960s by American artist Andy Warhol epitomize the spirit of Pop art, the movement he helped to invent, in their mass-media imagery, references to assembly-line methods, and reliance on photo-screenprinting and other quasi-industrial techniques borrowed from commercial art and design. Employing assistants in his large studio, The Factory, he took most of his images from magazines or newspapers, advertisements and packaging, celebrity photographs, and film stills. He even reproduced row upon row of dollar bills, provocatively playing down art's spiritual aspirations by reminding his audience that it was also a mere market commodity.

Although his earliest Pop paintings in 1960–61 were hand-painted enlargements of crudely drawn images from advertisements, diagrams, and comic strips, Warhol soon began to reflect his printed sources more directly by using such procedures as rubber stamping, serigraphy (screenprinting from hand-cut stencils), and finally, in 1962, photo-screenprinting. Each method not only eliminated the handwork assumed to be an essential component of fine art, but also challenged the notion of the uniqueness of that work, since each motif could be—and in Warhol's case, most insistently was—endlessly duplicated either within the boundaries of the canvas or from one painting to another. Warhol, who was much influenced by the Dadaist Marcel Duchamp, questioned the privileged and precious status of painting by making numerous versions that were barely distinguishable from each other or that varied mainly in the choice of background color—seemingly reducing the decision to the level of an interior designer's decorative preference.

The printed character of Warhol's paintings is not just the literal end-product of the technique by which they have come into being; their mechanical texture is an essential property of their appearance, the brazen avowal of their secondhand origins. Similarly, the gridlike and even monotonous repetition of a single motif induces a mesmerizing effect that conveys the emotional numbness of familiar media images. But examination of these multiple images reveals subtleties that differentiate them. The over- or under-inking of the screen, a slight change of

ANDY WARHOL

BORN PITTSBURGH 1928,
DIED NEW YORK 1987

angle or the smudging of an image show a human touch and a fallibility just as tellingly as any brushmark. The left-hand panel in *Red Disaster*, where a dozen identical images are relayed in regimented rows like photographs on a contact sheet, drives home the ghastly implications of the picture as a meditation on death. The bleak emptiness of the room, the solitary chair lying in wait for its next victim, the sign calling for silence, give the strong impression of a void—a sensation amplified twenty-two years later when Warhol paired the first printed canvas with a second pure monochrome one of equal size painted in the same shrill red.

Warhol had a genius for alighting on the most telling image. Of the many portrayals of Marilyn Monroe by Pop artists, it is the masklike visage chosen by Warhol that comes immediately to mind. His sense of timing was also crucial. It was immediately after Monroe's suicide in August 1962 that he produced the first of these portraits, thus making the tragedy of her early death a significant subtext that would be understood by his audience as inextricably tied to her glamour, beauty, and celebrity. Other quintessential Warhol subjects were chosen with a similar opportunism that tapped straight into the popular consciousness. The *Mona Lisa* was replicated several times in 1963 when it was on loan to the Metropolitan Museum in New York, and the extended series of paintings of Chairman Mao was begun in 1972 on the eve of Richard Nixon's visit to China.

Warhol's first set of paintings depicting an electric chair was produced in 1963, the last year in which executions were carried out in New York state, although he continued producing variants on canvas and as screenprints in 1971. The electric chairs formed part of the substantial *Death and Disasters* series of paintings begun in 1962 and which included horrific scenes of car crashes, suicides, hospital operations, death by poisoning, race riots, and the assassination of President Kennedy. In their concentration on violence endemic to American society and as a metaphor for the condition of the modern world in general, these works provide an essential corrective to the misleading view of Warhol as an unquestioning celebrator of consumer society and an eloquent testament to his abiding concern with mortality.

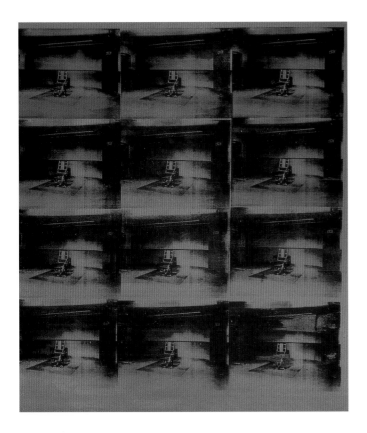

1963/85 | *acrylic and silkscreen ink on canvas and acrylic on canvas* | 93 x 80in (236 x 204cm) | Museum of Fine Arts, Boston

335

California

IT WAS AS an advocate of sexual permissiveness, and of gay liberation in particular, that the young English painter David Hockney first presented himself in the early 1960s in pictures explicitly conceived as homosexual propaganda. In contrast to Francis Bacon, whom he acknowledged as an influence but who treated such subjects obliquely through smudged paintwork and images of wrestling youths taken from late 19th-century photographs, Hockney brazenly and courageously declared his orientation in assertive images of love between men. At first he used the language of child art, following the example of the French artist Jean Dubuffet; he combined naively drawn motifs with written messages scrawled on the surface of the canvas in the manner of public-toilet graffiti, to distance himself from the personal urgency of the subject-matter and to stress the general application of such intimate areas of experience.

But by 1965–1966, when he made brightly colored paintings of suntanned California boys lolling in their swimming pools, Hockney had developed a more naturalistic mode of depiction which he applied with unblinking frankness to images of homosexual identity and satisfied pleasure. He appears through such works both to have prefigured the change in public opinion toward homosexuality, which led in 1967 to the legalization in Britain of consensual sexual acts between men over the age of twenty-one, but to have played an active part in effecting that change through his work.

California is typical of the pictures of swimming pools, showers, and neat suburban lawns and buildings that Hockney produced during his first stay in Los Angeles in 1964–1966, and which established his reputation as one of the major figurative artists of the period. These were succeeded by another celebrated series, naturalistic double portraits of gay and married couples painted in 1968–1971. Although still highly stylized, the swimming-pool paintings mark the beginning of Hockney's concern with a more objective recording of appearances, with his new reliance on photography acknowledged by the presentation of the painting in the form of a greatly enlarged snapshot framed by a white border. Through the relatively slow medium of painting, he suggested the instant gratification of a moment, captured by a camera in a fraction of a second but held in the memory forever. The disjunction between these two timescales, most vividly realized in three paintings depicting a splash made by an unseen diver, is central to an understanding of these deceptively simple but hypnotically contemplative pictures.

Hockney's mid-1960s paintings of southern California remain among the most vivid records of the hedonism that characterize the collective memory of the "swinging sixties." As an invitation to bodily pleasure, the artistic appeal of swimming pools—a common feature of the sun-drenched Los Angeles landscape—was irresistible to a young man who had only recently escaped the grayness of England and its puritanical fear of self-display. Already fascinated by the possibility of playing with artistic conventions, Hockney enjoyed finding different ways of conveying the translucency of water and the intricate patterns on and below its surface created by its movement. Quite apart from the social or psychosexual implications of their blatant subject matter, these paintings convey the pleasures of art-making itself; a delight in devising different solutions for depicting the world and in communicating experience emotively through form, color, and the very texture of smooth paint, caressingly applied to the primed canvas like lotion onto bare skin.

DAVID HOCKNEY

BORN BRADFORD 1937

That these subjects were not simply formal exercises, ways of demonstrating the artist's observational powers, is manifested by the role accorded to the youthful nude men in six of the twelve pool paintings completed by Hockney during this two-year period. The two men floating languorously on rubber mats in *California* give human expression to the somnolent mood pervading these images of the good life. The naturalness of their nudity in the privacy of their own pool, moreover, speaks of an unforced and untroubled sexuality and offers the artist and viewer a perfect opportunity to contemplate the beauty and erotic potential of their bodies. The setting is wholly contemporary, but through such methods Hockney cunningly updates the traditional theme of the bather, prized by painters over the centuries for providing a credible context in which to present unclothed figures for the viewer's sensual or erotic pleasure.

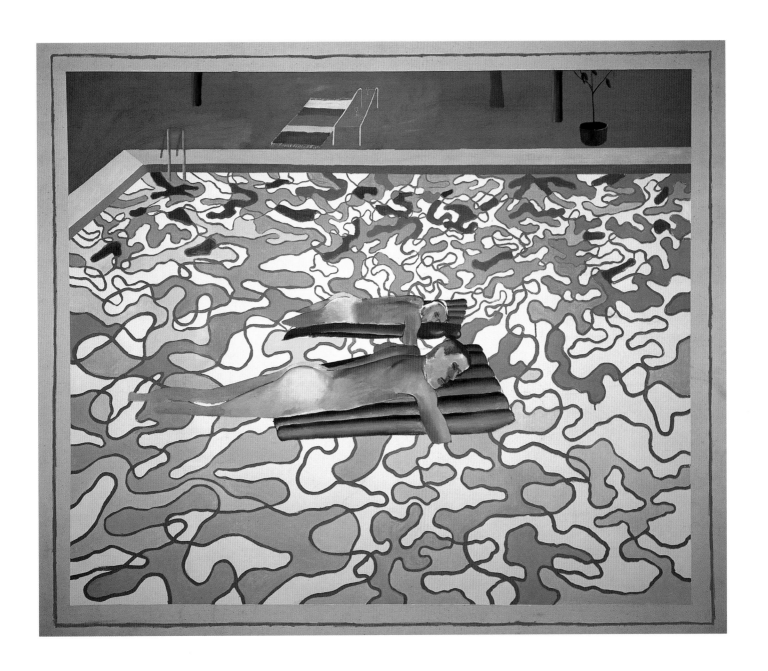

1965 | *acrylic on canvas* | 60 x 78in (152.5 x 198cm) | private collection

Public Shelter 110

STANDARD ART histories tend to marginalize or eliminate artists not considered to be part of the mainstream, and stubborn individualists who do not fit neatly into prescribed patterns. In the 20th century, this has generally meant the exclusion of those outside the major metropolitan centers, those who concentrate on an activity or medium thought minor or tangential, those whose opinions threaten the (esthetic or political) status quo, those who survive outside the commercial gallery system and without the support of public agencies, and those whose art does not fit comfortably into any of the major movements—which is to ignore some of the most deeply felt art of any period.

Colin Self, though allied to Pop art in Britain and both admired and collected by his contemporaries, has all the credentials for pariah status. After studying in London at the Slade School of Fine Art, he returned in 1965 to his native Norfolk, a predominantly rural county two hours by train from the capital, and distanced himself from what he considered the exploitative gallery system. He chose to concentrate on drawing and to a lesser extent printmaking, almost always on an intimate scale that compounded the difficulty of hanging his art alongside the often large paintings and sculptures made by his contemporaries. The opinions conveyed in his work, for example about American militarism and the threat of nuclear catastrophe, were often too politically sensitive for the official agencies. Nevertheless, Self is too powerful an artist to be ignored, even though only a small fragment of his prolific output has so far been made public. His place in late-20th-century art should be assured on the basis of his instincts for subject matter alone, through which he has presented a fascinating panorama of contemporary life and a searingly honest insight into his private passions. His singular vision, highly original techniques, and wide stylistic range, together with an almost compulsive tendency to make surprising connections from a seemingly inexhaustible memory bank of images and experiences, are among the characteristics of his art most deserving of admiration. For those who care about the survival and extension of traditional drawing skills—at a time when such ability is often either disregarded or dismissed as

COLIN SELF

BORN NORWICH 1941

irrelevant—Self's high status would be assured just on the basis of his intensely rendered pencil and colored-crayon drawings of the mid-1960s. The extraordinary precision and high-resolution modeling of the forms was not meant, however, simply to be admired. On the contrary, Self described his technique at that time as bordering on sarcasm, likening it to a working-class person speaking mockingly in a refined accent so as to elicit patronizing approval.

Public Shelter 110 is one of a series of fallout shelter drawings made by Self in response to a trip he made around the United States in 1965 in the company of David Hockney and two other British artists. It was among the first drawings in which he aimed to document the world so the descendants of any survivors from global warfare would be able to reconstruct a detailed picture of life in this society. With astonishing economy, the drawing compresses his many reactions to and observations of America, which in its excesses both fascinated and repelled him as a paradigm of the planet during a period of immense social and political change. In this single figure of a busty, plump middle-aged woman—with garishly colored beehive hairdo, provocatively tight skirt, stiletto-heeled shoes, heavy make-up, and false eyelashes pointing toward infinity—Self touches on a range of interwoven topics long before they were generally on the menu: sexuality, self-image and self-esteem, aging and mortality, alienation, notions of femininity, fashion, over-consumption, eating disorders, instant gratification, and the insatiability of desire.

Seated on a chrome-plated bar stool, this woman contemplates a future that goes no farther than the hamburger poised in front of her voraciously open mouth, in spite of the ever-present warning of impending doom suggested by the nuclear fallout shelter sign. Even the stool's reflective surface, which in mirroring the world around it also succeeds in dematerializing itself, speaks of the immanence of what the artist termed "nuclear non-being." Oblivious to the void engulfing her otherwise strong physical presence, the woman seems intent only on satisfying her immediate needs: an arresting and unforgettable image of the human race on the verge of extinction.

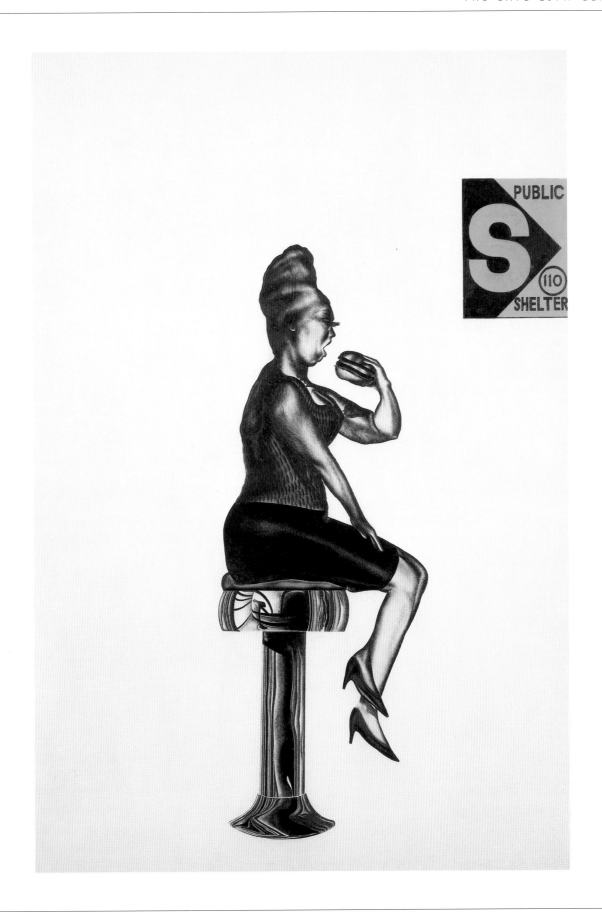

1965 | *pencil, colored crayon, and collage* | 22 x 15in (56 x 38cm) | Collection James Kirkman, London

Liebespaar II *(Lovers II)*

THE CREATION of a "signature style," one so distinctive and immediately recognizable that the authorship of a work can be identified at first glance, had been considered a desirable goal long before the pressures of the modern gallery system placed even greater emphasis on the creation of art works as products reassuringly marked with a trusted brand name. The French Dadaist Francis Picabia (1879–1953) was regarded with suspicion by many of his contemporaries when he moved abruptly from one style to another, with a sometimes shocking disregard for standards of excellence or questions of taste and decorum. The only defense he offered, with a characteristically defiant wit, was that "If you want to have clean ideas, change them as often as your shirts." In retrospect, his stance prefigures by some decades that of the postmodernist scavenger, forever plundering any available source and constantly catching his audience off guard. By the 1990s, it raised no eyebrows for an artist to move easily from figuration to abstraction, as in the case of the German Gerhard Richter (born 1932), or to flit between painting, sculpture, video, performance, music, writing, and any other form of expression that seemed fitting.

Sigmar Polke is the outstanding and probably most influential example of this freewheeling approach among late 20th-century artists. Having moved at the age of twelve from Communist East Germany to capitalist West Germany, he was particularly well placed to adopt a detached view of the possibilities of opposing systems. In 1963, together with Richter and another German artist, Konrad Fischer-Lueg (born 1939), he devised the term Capitalist Realism to describe the uncomfortable clash between the Socialist Realism of the Communist bloc and the celebration of consumer society suggested by the newly created Pop art in both its American and western European forms. Rather than display the materialistic luxuries on offer in a prosperous society, Polke concentrated on the modest, not to say derisory, pleasures offered by such commodities as socks, a bar of chocolate, a string of sausages, or a few crackers. The hamfisted technique, the disdainfully unartistic look of the paint surface, the awkward and forlorn placement of the cheap and rather sad objects against a

SIGMAR POLKE

BORN OELS 1941

bare ground saturated in an unappetizing color, mimic the characteristics of naive sign-painting or the haphazard window display of stores deprived not just of funds but even of products worth selling. All these features accentuate the poverty-stricken atmosphere of pictures that are unaccountably rich in visual pleasures and humorous touches, and which convey so forcefully the spasms of a society in flux.

The overriding impression given by Polke's development over the succeeding decades is of a surfeit of ideas, images, styles, and possibilities. In the 1960s alone, he made dot paintings (devised in part as a visual/linguistic pun on his name), fabric pictures (which exploited the decorative designs of found materials as a ready-made support), stripe paintings, and paintings conceived as parodies of particularly inept gestural abstractions (complete with captions helpfully identifying the visual mess as "modern art"). His *Lovers II*, perhaps the most shockingly shoddy, badly painted, and impossibly clichéd painting of the period, persuasively demonstrates how his esthetic of rejection and revulsion can succeed against all the odds. The image of the romantic, embracing couple in evening dress is not only anatomically incorrect, inconsistent in proportion, ungainly, and so stylized as to seem barely human—pointing to a source in old-fashioned and woefully inept kitsch illustration—it also appears to have been abandoned in haste like a bungled crime. Splatters of paint deposited into two corners of the canvas suggest a second stab at making the best of a botched job, the beginnings of an equally substandard modernist abstraction that threatens to obliterate the truncated and unfinished figurative motif. The picture parades itself as an accumulation of signs of inauthenticity and lack of conviction: a bad painting by any standards. Yet, it remains haunting and strangely touching, emotional in its excesses, and only too human in its vulnerability. Where other artists would not flinch at availing themselves surreptitiously of any methods by which to persuade their audience of their sincerity, Polke paradoxically reveals himself most truthfully by presenting himself as someone not to be trusted, laying bare all the strategies to which any painter might succumb out of desperation to complete his work.

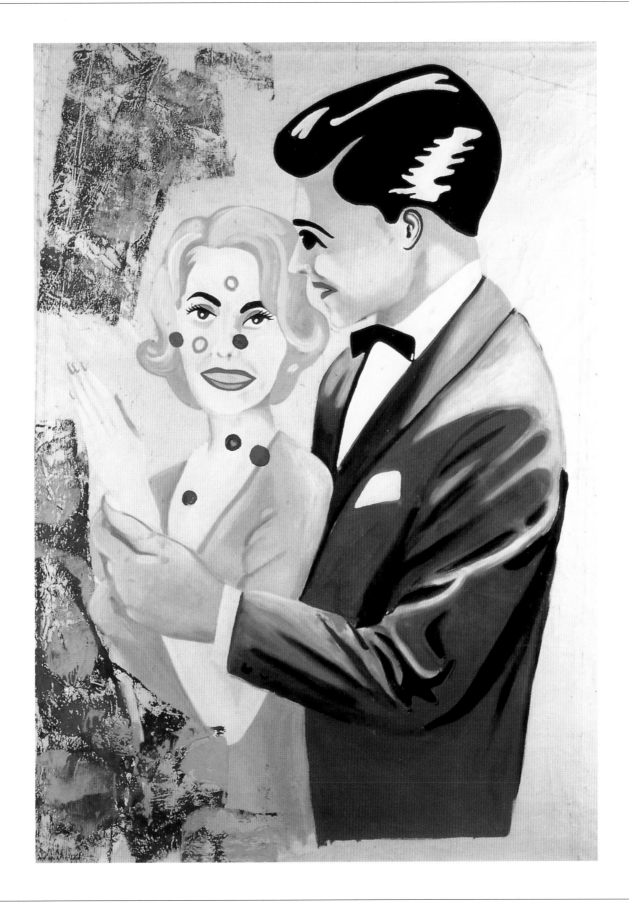

1965 | *lacquer on canvas* | 79 x 55in (200 x 139cm) | private collection

Paradise Bar

PATRICK CAULFIELD was one of a group of painters studying at the Royal College of Art in London in the early 1960s, which also included David Hockney, Allen Jones (born 1937), Derek Boshier (born 1937), Peter Phillips (born 1939), and the American R.B. Kitaj (born 1933), credited with establishing Pop art as a coherent movement in Britain independently from the work then being created on similar lines by Andy Warhol and others in America. Like Hockney and Kitaj, Caulfield was uncomfortable with a label that he felt placed too much emphasis on associations with contemporary popular culture and consumer society. The references in his paintings of the 1960s were not to the film stars or rock musicians of his own period, but to more timeless or even perversely old-fashioned subjects, such as the tradition of still-life painting, exoticism, and Romanticism.

Taking his stylistic cues from pioneering French modernists of the first half of the 20th century, and in particular from painters associated with Cubism such as Juan Gris (1887–1927), Georges Braque (1882–1963), and Fernand Léger (1881–1955), Caulfield made pictures of such unlikely and unpromising subjects as flowers, decorative pottery, picturesque Mediterranean views, and barren landscapes. Like Léger and the American Pop artist Roy Lichtenstein (1923–1997), with whom he has often been compared, his habit of pinning his images to the surface with the aid of an assertive black outline encouraged comparisons with "unartistic" forms (such as sign-painting, comic books, and coloring books) whose conventions were readily accessible to a nonspecialist audience. By disguising his subtle and masterful explorations of space, color, and formal design in such an apparently simple visual language, Caulfield created the possibility of a truly democratic art without condescending to his public or sacrificing the complexity and ambiguity of his thinking. In this sense at least, quite aside from his vocabulary of flat, brightly colored forms, he is a true Pop artist in spite of his many protestations to the contrary.

In the late 1960s, Caulfield painted the first of the architectural interiors with which he has become most closely associated. At first the linear structures of a room seen in perspective were superimposed onto monochromatic grounds that established a mood and physical atmosphere: a "weekend cabin" painted brown, a Swiss chalet in a luxuriant shade of green, suggesting escape to nature. Gradually, other colors were introduced as pictorial and conceptual accents and as a means of guiding the eye or representing the effects of light within the space demarcated by the canvas. To encourage the spectator to identify with the invented scene as representing a real place, foreground objects and the height of the room as a whole are shown lifesize. In front of the painting, one feels so immersed in the environment depicted that the extreme stylization poses no barrier. With just a little faith, the viewer can easily be persuaded to believe in these tantalizing fictions, even though there is no attempt to deceive. Each painting contains all the clues needed to lay bare its pictorial construction.

Paradise Bar is a key work in Caulfield's development, the first in which he introduced a self-contained passage painted in a conflicting style, interrupting an otherwise seamless surface. The landscape spied behind the counter, which can be read as a view through a window, but must logically be assumed to represent the kind of ineptly painted mural typically found in bars or restaurants with pretensions to sophistication, is a spirited imitation of gestural abstraction. As a picture within the picture, it pointedly draws attention to the falsity of any representation and to the selection of any style or method as an act of conscious will. Strangely, the puncturing of the initial illusion does nothing to diminish the satisfaction that can be experienced from the glorious colors and intricate linear design in which this fiction is clothed. The same can be said for such places of escapist entertainment. The credit-card stickers on the glass entrance door remind us, if we need reminding, that we are not really in some faraway location but only in a temporary refuge and that mundane reality is only a few steps away. Thus, there is even a moral to be drawn, that our guilty pleasures will have to be paid for one way or another. Caulfield's astute interweaving of social and pictorial conventions, with such acute observations of the ordinary environment, make his interiors vital documents of late 20th-century life and art.

PATRICK CAULFIELD

∽

BORN LONDON 1936

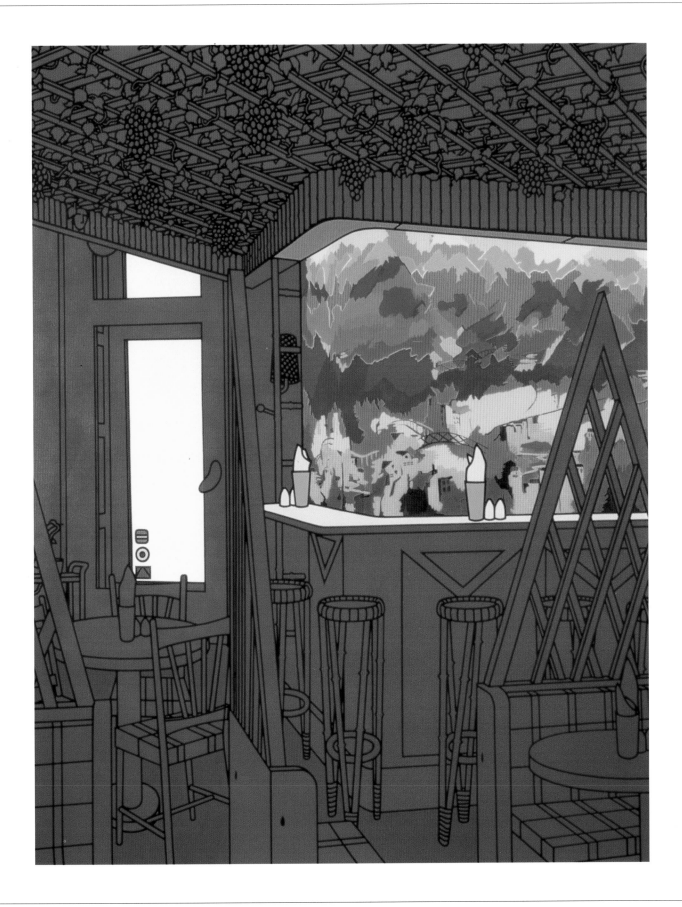

1974 | *acrylic on canvas* | 108 x 84in (274.5 x 213.5cm) | Virginia Museum of Fine Arts, Richmond

Priapea

THE INCREASING international dominance of American art after the 1950s began to be seriously challenged only in the early 1980s, in particular by Italians and Germans born in the late 1940s and early 1950s, who were making a concerted return to painting after more than a decade notable for such experimental forms as Conceptual art, Land art, Performance art, and Video art. This desire to embrace again the traditional medium of painting was paralleled in sculpture—especially from some contemporary British artists like Tony Cragg, Bill Woodrow, Richard Deacon, and Anish Kapoor—with renewed concentration on the object as opposed to the often temporary and dematerialized forms favored by the preceding generation.

The most notable tendencies shared by the painters were a strong subjective and at times Expressionist bias both in their techniques and subject matter, a general rejection of (or at least indifference to) finesse and decorum, and a willingness to plunder the past for ideas, methods, and images. The term "post-modernist," with its suggestions that the avant-garde had become obsolete and that the whole of history was now potentially available as a source for the contemporary artist, gained currency. Although some deliberately turned to parodies of specific historical styles—as in the case of the German Neo-Expressionists such as Rainer Fetting and Helmut Middendorf or Italians such as Carlo Maria Mariani, who produced a rather high camp version of Manner-ism—ambitious painters generally regarded the appropriation of historical modes not as a limitation, but as an opening up to all the possibilities ever proposed for the medium.

Of all the Italians who established major reputations around this time—including Sandro Chia, Enzo Cucchi, and Mimmo Paladino—it is the self-taught Francesco Clemente who most convincingly demonstrated this freedom of movement as part of a personal voyage. He has roamed freely through time and across different cultures, literally so by keeping studios simultaneously in Rome, New York, and Madras. Oscillating between the extremes of a sometimes naive figurative style and an elegantly sophisticated abstraction, he has tried his hand at everything from large oil paintings and gouaches to mosaics and sculptures

FRANCESCO CLEMENTE

BORN NAPLES 1952

to intimate pastels and Indian miniatures painted in natural pigments by assistants under his direction. The one constant has been his inclusion of himself and his psychosexual self-exposure.

Priapea—named after Priapus, the classical god of the male procreative power—is one of a series of large, portable frescoes that Clemente painted early in his career. The choice of fresco, a medium associated with medieval and renaissance religious art but with Mediterranean origins much further back in antiquity, itself releases a strong chain of associations, particularly in the context of Italian art. As a boy, Clemente had access to the ruins at Pompeii and Herculaneum and to the fragments of ancient art exhibited at the Museo Nazionale in Naples. By no means engaged in revivalism, he treats the matt surface of fresco not with the methodical deliberation that it traditionally demanded, but with the urgency and casual spontaneity of an impulsively rendered sketch; in reproduction it looks more like a sanguine drawing. Natural red chalk was, in fact, used for wall painting by the ancient Egyptians and Romans, so the association is appropriate. Yet, the suspicion remains that there is a deliberate intermingling of properties inherent to different art forms and techniques, paralleled in the imagery by jarring anachronisms that leave the viewer in no doubt about the period in which the painting was produced.

One of the naked putti in *Priapea* is shown running off with the artist's tie, having divested the figure at the left not only of his modern clothes but also of parts of his body. The truncated leg with which two putti play, the severed arm poised alarmingly over one infant's genitals, and finally the artist's head, held aloft by that very child in a teasing rather than triumphant manner, all give metaphorical expression to the temporal and stylistic fragmentation that provides the underlying theme of the painting: a reading of modern civilization both as rooted in and uprooted from the distant past. That the motifs hover in an indeterminate space adds to the atmosphere of dislocation which conveys such a powerfully modern anxiety; a sense of not quite belonging, of not being certain of one's identity. The artist represents himself floating helplessly among these elements, looking balefully out toward the spectator in resignation at his predicament.

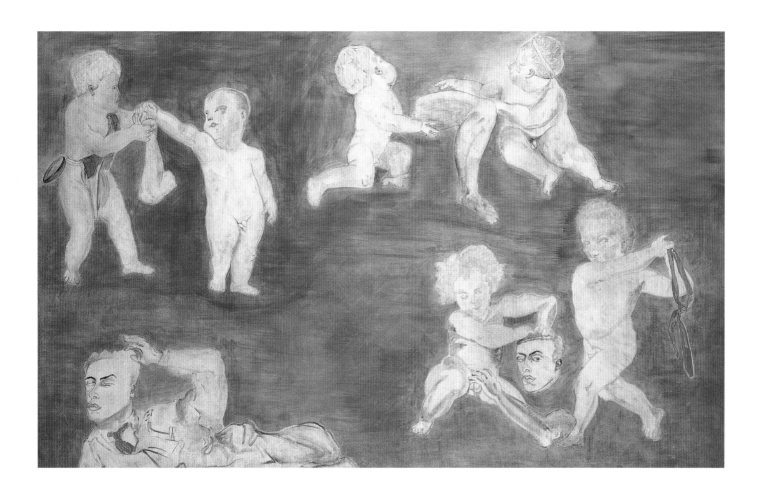

1980 ┃ *fresco* ┃ 79 x 126in (200 x 320cm) ┃ Marx Collection, Berlin

Red Dancer on the Western Shore

PRINTMAKING enjoyed a resurgence during the 1960s after many decades of comparative neglect, thanks to the opportunities it offered for the much wider dissemination of an artist's work. The introduction of photomechanical procedures such as screenprinting and offset lithography increased the options open to artists stimulated by new technical possibilities and for whom the more traditional mediums such as etching, woodcut, and lithography would not have seemed suitable. Three-dimensional "multiples" manufactured according to the principles of industrial mass-production also appeared during this period, allowing sculptural objects to be made in large editions that in principle could be afforded by a vast cross-section of people.

This experiment in removing some of art's precious and privileged connotations, tinged with utopian idealism but frankly motivated by commercial ends, was short-lived. Prints produced in very large numbers generally proved unappealing to collectors and investors who continued to place a premium on rarity value, and prices for desirable unique works swiftly climbed beyond the reach of the general population. Artists not inherently attracted by the process were persuaded to make prints, their lack of conviction relegating the editioned work to the demeaning status of commercial spin-offs of their signature style.

Some artists, however, found printmaking a consistently fruitful and inspiring activity. The marriage of new technologies with the handmade by Richard Hamilton (born 1922), David Hockney's vast and inventive production of etchings, Anselm Kiefer's monumental woodcuts, the complex relief prints of Frank Stella (born 1936) and pitted etchings of Antoni Tàpies, and Andy Warhol's reliance on screenprinting, are among the outstanding examples of contemporary artists' integration of printmaking techniques into the main body of their work.

For the American Jim Dine, who made his first prints in 1960 as lithographic documents associated with *Car Crash*—one of the Performance art "happenings" that marked his spectacular entrance into the New York art world—printmaking has proved no less fertile than any other medium, including painting or sculpture, with which he has been involved throughout his life.

JIM DINE

BORN CINCINNATI 1935

Like other great innovators in this sphere, instead of being afraid of losing control, he has relished the collaborative nature of the process, the risks but also the rewards of working with master printers and workshops. He has explored almost every conceivable way of making a repeatable mark: long-established methods such as etching, drypoint, aquatint, woodcut, and lithography, and also photo-screenprint and unusual processes that he has developed in collaboration with master printers, such as the invention in the 1990s with the Austrian Kurt Zein of a method of intaglio printing using cardboard as a printing plate. Recognizing no limits to the ways in which to achieve the desired result, and more excited by the process itself than by the notion of a uniform edition, he has attached found objects to his prints, painted the sheets by hand before and after printing, and used do-it-yourself electric tools alongside more traditional implements such as etching needles and lithographic crayons.

Red Dancer on the Western Shore, depicting a shrouded female dancer from classical antiquity on a scale larger than life, is a magnificent example of the alacrity with which Dine exploits any technique to achieve a persuasively physical record of his creative process. He drew the figure from a photograph of a small ancient Greek bronze he had admired in New York's Metropolitan Museum. Though the marks look handmade, they have in fact been arrived at by rather unconventional methods. Heliogravure and spit bite aquatint create much of the textured surface, with the contours of the image strengthened by a power tool called a Dremel. Spit bite is a technique by which acid is splashed or painted onto the plate with a brush containing water or saliva. Heliogravure (or heliorelief) as used here is a recently developed process that involves screenprinting an image with gelatin onto plywood that has been sensitized to light which is then exposed to light and treated so it resists a "grit-blasting" of the surface; it creates a network of very fine lines that would have been impossible to achieve in any other way. Through these methods the ancient and the modern come together seamlessly, recreating with dynamism, poignancy, and erotic charge the image of a woman made more than two thousand years earlier.

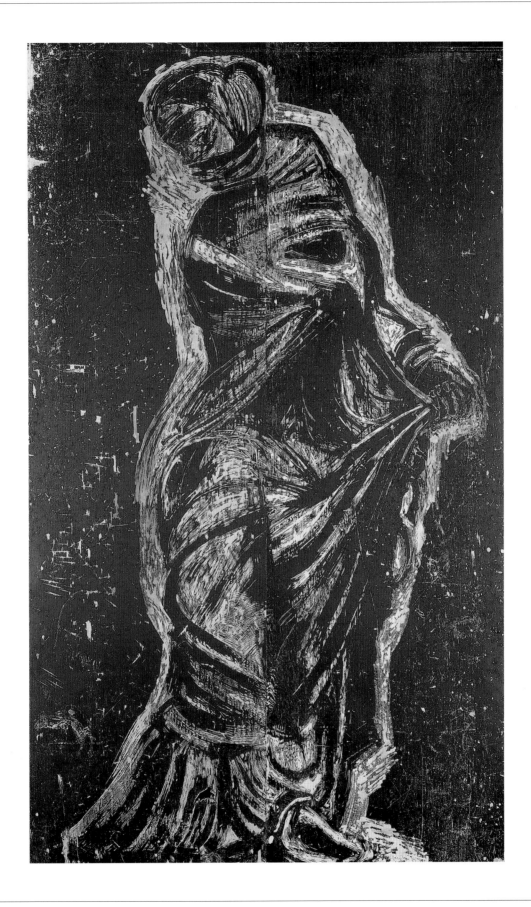

1987–88 | *woodcut and spit bite etching* | 79 x 48in (200 x 121cm) | Courtesy of Alan Cristea Gallery, London

Elisabeth von Österreich

SINCE THE EARLY 1980s, the tendency of artists, especially painters, to make reference to styles and motifs drawn from the whole of art history has focused on a desire to place themselves within that history and to reclaim it as legitimate territory for their own often subjective explorations. For the German painter and sculptor Anselm Kiefer, however, the past looms not so much as a fund of esthetic possibilities, but as a still menacing presence—involving, above all, the Third Reich and the tragedy of the Holocaust—that can be purged only through direct confrontation. From the early 1970s, his large, often theatrical paintings depicting grandiose interiors and forbidding landscapes have called upon specifically German artistic and cultural traditions in an effort to come to terms with the circumstances that helped shape one of the darkest periods in world history.

Kiefer has drawn heavily on Romanticism, often with explicitly Wagnerian overtones in the mythological imagery, titles, and handwritten inscriptions incorporated into the picture surface. Even his vision of primeval forests and infinite bleak northern landscapes contributes to the atmosphere of timelessness and grandeur on which Wagner, and in turn the Nazis, relied so heavily. From the beginning, he declared a strong bias toward Expressionism—the most German of the modern art movements denounced by the Nazis as "degenerate"—in the raw handling of his materials and in his powerful use of woodcut, also revived by early 20th-century artists because of its association with medieval and Renaissance German art. The overpowering architectural spaces favored by Kiefer, from claustrophobically enclosed Romanesque crypts to Germanic interiors of wooden buildings, are intended to impress in precisely the same way as the Fascist architecture of Albert Speer, to which he also made reference, by inducing a sense of awe in the spectator that presupposes the power of an unquestionable authority. Usually combined with historical/cultural references and literary allusions in the titles and inscriptions, these elements build up a complex picture of the origins of the national psyche that boldly connects its most laudable cultural achievements with the black depths of its arrogant and violent destructiveness.

ANSELM KIEFER

BORN DONAUESCHINGEN 1945

For all the gloom of Kiefer's palette and imagery, and despite his tendency to draw his subject matter from the immediate or distant past, it would be a distortion to regard his work as backward-looking. Much of his imagery has come from the quintessentially modern medium of photography; large prints have been bound into massive books covered with lead, as in his sculptural masterpiece *The High Priestess* (1985–1989, Astrup Fearnley Museum of Modern Art, Oslo), and secured onto canvas as a base image to be painted over and partly obliterated. By such methods Kiefer insists on a strong sensation of the here and now, of one's place in the physical world. His paintings and sculptures have a handmade roughness that could be mistaken for a kind of primitivism, but the intense materiality of their unconventional media—from fragile and perishable organic materials like straw to apparently indestructible brute matter like lead—make them among the most innovative and influential of their time.

Elisabeth von Österreich—like the 1986 series *Women of the Revolution*, which also used a variety of materials over a lead base—takes its title from a historical person but cannot be described in any conventional sense as a portrait. Elizabeth of Austria, the wife of Emperor Franz Joseph whose unhappiness at court made her a tragic figure, was assassinated by an Italian anarchist in Switzerland in 1898. The model ship in Kiefer's painting, assembled with a rather touching hamfistedness and cast adrift on a lonely sea made from large sheets of gesturally painted lead, acts as a metaphor for the doomed peripatetic existence of a woman whose wealth and proximity to power were unable to save her or make her life worth living. The melancholically drooping clumps of black hair, held aloft like relics of a saint by lead guy ropes attached to the ship's deck, provide material evidence of the fragility of existence in contrast to the unyielding metallic surface against which they are suspended. In its grandeur of scale and conception, in its relatively accessible vocabulary of symbols and in its extension of the conventions of history painting, Kiefer's work remains essentially a public art, but one that also takes into account the subjective and difficult voyage of every individual, including the artist himself.

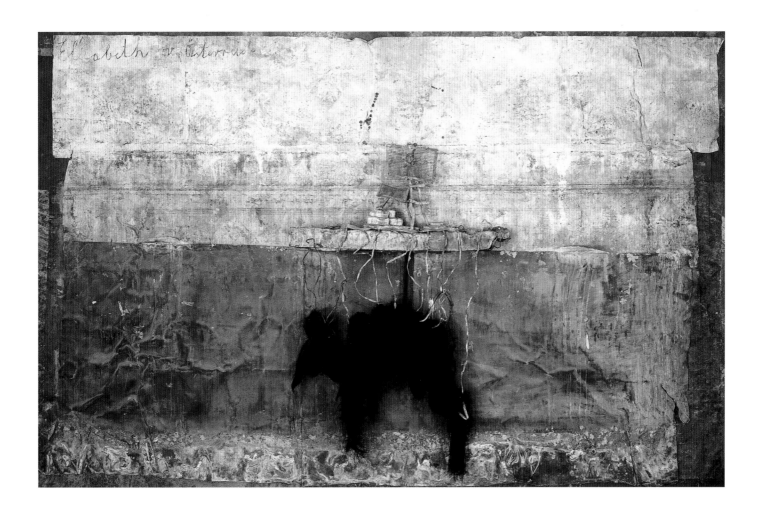

1993 | *lead and hair* | 79 x 118in (200 x 300cm) | Berardo Collection, Sintra Museum of Modern Art, Portugal

Grooming

PAULA REGO studied painting at the Slade School of Art in London and then divided her time between her native Portugal and England. Her work, which has undergone enormous changes every decade, has clearly been marked by her experience of both these cultures, and in particular by her vivid memories of growing up as an only child in a prosperous middle-class household dominated by women, and by an increasingly profound attachment to the figure. The mixture of whimsicality, terror, and caustic observation that characterize her mature work was already evident in the paintings she produced as a student. Always conscious of her natural inclination to work on paper, in the late 1950s she began cutting up her spontaneously executed drawings in order to incorporate them as fragments into pictures of unbridled ferocity. The rawness of their execution was indebted to the Expressionist tendencies of the Cobra movement and to the primitivism of French painter Jean Dubuffet.

By the late 1960s, Rego had eliminated her strict reliance on collage and begun to develop the narrative pictures, executed in vivid colors in gouache or acrylic paint in a flat, cartoonlike style, to which she remained faithful until the mid-1980s. The imagery and dark sense of humor came not only from the Portuguese folk tales she had heard in her childhood with a thrilling mixture of fear and excitement, but from a variety of other sources, including nursery rhymes and fairy tales, the caricatures of James Gillray and Thomas Rowlandson, John Tenniel's illustrations to Lewis Carroll's Alice books, and the animated films of Walt Disney. Anthropomorphized animals, not seen in such profusion since the heyday of Victorian painting, took major roles in this theater of the human comedy. Braving the modernist injunction against narrative and illustration, she passionately embraced such sources in order to project her own most private thoughts onto the painted surface with an almost cinematic feeling for visual spectacle.

A series of paintings in 1986 on the theme of *Girl and Dog* indicated a radical shift toward a more naturalistic style in which modeled forms acquired a more convincing corporeality within physical space, with a corresponding compression of imagery

PAULA REGO

✌

BORN LISBON 1935

into a dramatic confrontation largely stripped of anecdotal detail. Rego also took up etching and aquatint, which led her to look more closely at the work of Goya, and began producing preparatory studies for paintings in an ink-and-wash technique clearly indebted not only to Old Master drawings but more specifically to the Portuguese tradition of decorative tile paintings (*azulejos*). Her transformation into one of the outstanding figure painters of her time was well under way when, in 1988, the death of her husband, the English painter Victor Willing, after a long illness, released them both from his suffering and gave her the will to honor his memory through paintings that were ever more ambitious in their visual conception and technique, in their truthfulness and frank self-exposure.

Grooming is one of fourteen large works executed in 1994, collectively titled *Dog Woman*. Drawn from life, the model is a young Portuguese woman who had nursed Rego's husband and whose temperament and physical resemblance to the artist have made her an ideal alter-ego. There is an element of performance about these works, of artist and sitter in collusion acting out dramatically charged situations and strong emotions. As the series title suggests, there is a ferocious animality in these depictions of a woman engaged in such primitive acts as licking herself and screaming with rage, poised threateningly on her haunches with teeth bared, lying unselfconsciously with legs spread wide or passively reclining in a wedding dress as if waiting for sexual initiation. Where she had previously depicted animals as stand-ins for people, here Rego displays the animal nature of human beings themselves. The surprising choice of pastel for such large works on canvas heightens the rawness and sensuality of the imagery by calling attention to the skin of the picture—an intricate tapestry of separate strokes in earthy natural colors—as a metaphorical and physical equivalent of human flesh. Though feminists have taken Rego to heart for making such a revealing body of work explicitly from a woman's point of view, she makes no claim to speak for anyone other than herself. Her courage in doing so is what makes her pictures universal and invests them with such moving humanity.

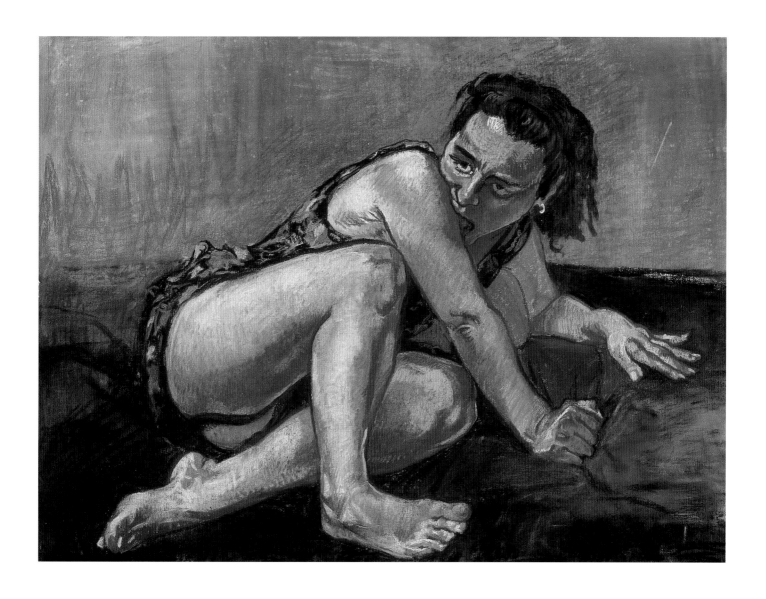

1994 | *pastel on canvas* | 30 x 39in (76 x 100cm) | private collection

House

HOUSE WAS a monumental sculpture constructed from concrete sprayed into the interior of the only row house left standing in a recently demolished group on a Victorian street in the East End of London. It was commissioned as a temporary work of public art in 1991 by the Artangel Trust in association with Beck's, the beer company, from a young English sculptor, Rachel Whiteread, who, since 1988, had been making direct casts of the intangible "secret" spaces surrounding ordinary objects such as sinks, bathtubs, chairs and mattresses, or architectural fragments such as the interior of closets and the shallow cavities beneath floorboards. Her work had always been concerned with making visible what was hidden behind the façade of daily life as a way of giving a readily accessible material form to the essentially private realm of memory. The objects whose absent shapes she presented through such reversals of empty space and solid matter were those one encounters every day and which acquire an almost sacramental significance through the ritualized familiarity of constant repetitive use: washing, sitting, walking, resting, sleeping, making love. By means of a variety of sensual and highly tactile materials—including plaster, rubber, fiberglass, and resin—she asserted the physicality of the absent object and, by extension, the tangible reality of the unremarkable acts that define the ephemeral lifespan of human existence.

Given her paramount concern with memorializing private life, with rendering such a notionally abstract idea in poetic and sculpturally compelling ways, Whiteread was a natural candidate for a commission to construct a public monument. In 1990, she had made *Ghost* (Saatchi Gallery, London), a blocklike plaster sculpture that recreates the interior of an entire room with clearly visible traces of the many architectural details that defined its uses and made visible its identity: a tiled fireplace, a doorway, and the baseboard and molding that circumnavigated the four walls. The opacity of the light-gray plaster contributes to a sense of airlessness and smothering suffocation that cannot fail to communicate something of the panic that can be induced by life in certain domestic circumstances. In scale and formal complexity alone, but also in its interweaving of the private and

RACHEL WHITEREAD

c/o

BORN LONDON 1963

the public, *House* was Whiteread's most ambitious work to date by far. It was constructed from the inside out, with the external walls treated like a mold into which the liquid concrete was sprayed. As with any cast, the finished form emerged only when the mold, in this case the walls of an old house undergoing its final demolition, was stripped away. To destroy, as the Russian anarchist Mikhail Bakunin had observed a century earlier, is also to create. Whiteread's previous work had all been based on this same concept of reversal, in that the casts of negative spaces that she presented as sculptures could be understood also as the molds from which a new positive replica of the original object could have been made. From there it was but a small leap to accept that the object being commemorated should itself be physically destroyed as a necessary and vital part of the act of rendering it homage.

Like many public commissions in the post-war period, *House* proved to be highly controversial, and despite great support from the art world and the British population at large, it was torn down in January 1994 by order of the local government. Its notoriety helped secure Whiteread another commission, for a Holocaust Memorial in Vienna. After long delays, it was finally agreed that this equally controversial work, in the form of a private library rendered mute, could be sited in the Judenplatz in 1999. The disappearance of *House* was a great loss to the landscape of London, which is conspicuously lacking in distinguished modern public monuments, and to the recent history of public sculpture in general. Even as a memory, however, and certainly in the many documentary photographs and filmed records of its brief existence, it remains a rich embodiment of a complex tangle of feelings about matters both private and public, linked to the associations and experiences we all share of home, neighborhood, shifting populations, and urban decay and renewal. In a century that has witnessed more than its fair share of destruction—not just by war but by the often thoughtless acts of vandalism effected by official bodies—it remains also a haunting testament to the hold exerted on our imagination by the past and a way of honoring the mortality of all things.

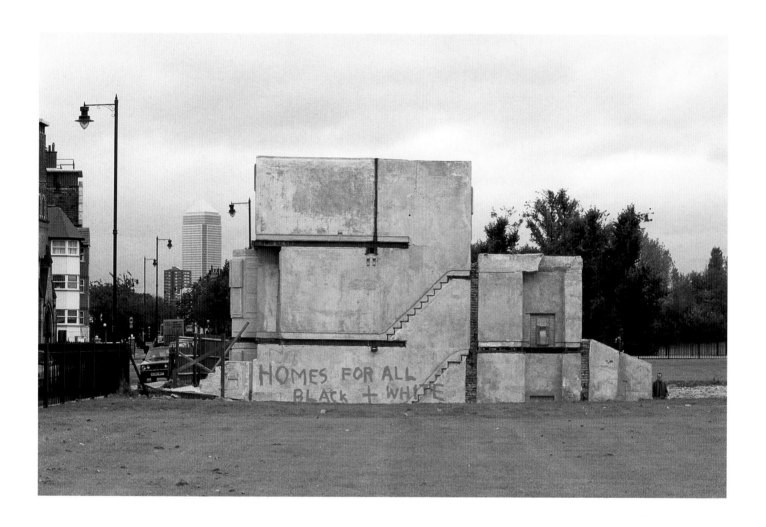

1993 | *concrete* | Courtesy of Anthony d'Offay Gallery, London

CONCLUSION
Marina Vaizey

ANYTHING GOES—and where is it all going? In 1897, the French artist Paul Gauguin painted *Where Do We Come From? What Are We? Where Are We Going?* After its completion, Gauguin unsuccessfully attempted suicide. It was the largest painting he ever created, and he regarded its inscription as a signature, not a title. Gauguin's "signature" can perhaps stand for the questions artists have always asked and that lie behind art. Art is always seeking to find a pattern—or impose a pattern—both on the observed world and the world we may imagine. And the pattern of Gauguin's life from the end of the 19th century, the *fin de siècle*—resonating again as we rush into the next century— may also find a parallel in the way we now think of contemporary art and artists in the West. Artists, far from serving a defined public, serve themselves. They are seen as rampant individualists, often in rebellion, touching the depths and extremes of emotion and vacillating between profound belief and nihilism, willing to sacrifice personal relationships and a conventional career to "find"— and come to terms with—what they consider the real self. In fact, it is probable that an historic perspective a century from now will show that artists catered for their audience in the 20th century just as much as they did in the 15th.

We are passionate about the past, inescapably involved with the present, and filled with both speculative wonder and apprehension about the future—for art as in all other human endeavors. In our visual life, at the end of the 20th century, we are exposed to more visual stimuli and visual possibilities and visual communication than at any other time in human history; we are more aware of the diversity and history of art worldwide; the expansion of technology and technique offer untold possibilities; and to look at art, we have more and more museums and galleries, opening at an unprecedented rate.

As many commentators have suggested, these museums and galleries are replacing, in the way they are perceived by society, the functions of other great religious and secular monuments, from the cathedral to the town hall, from parliaments to railroad stations. They are a key instrument in Europe and North America for claiming back a secular center for communities. In Paris, there are the Musée d'Orsay, a converted rail station, and the Pompidou Centre, with both interior and exterior meeting places. In London, Trafalgar Square is bordered by the National Gallery and the National Portrait Gallery, while Bankside, a converted power station on the River Thames, is the Tate Gallery's enormous new space for 20th-century art and a major millennium project. In the United States, there are the vast and continually expanding museum complexes, from the National Gallery in Washington, D.C., to the Getty in Los Angeles, which evokes a Renaissance hilltop town with its Italian marble and central piazza. Helsinki's museum of contemporary art, Kiasma (1998), is around the corner from their finest turn-of-the-century architectural monument, Saarinen's railroad station; while Berlin, the restored federal capital of Germany, is also focusing on museums in the hope of creating a cohesive center for the reunited country. From Stockholm to Madrid, Bilbao to Lille, Basle to Seattle, cities, major and minor, are renewing themselves through new architecture for new or expanded museums and galleries. Bilbao is perhaps the perfect example of the cultural values and economic importance attached to the notion of the art gallery. In 1997, the Guggenheim, Bilbao, designed by the American architect Frank Gehry, opened in this economically depressed port-city of the Basque country in north-western Spain. The museum has become a symbol of the new Bilbao, bringing millions to a city hitherto rarely visited by outsiders, and the contours of the brilliant titanium-clad structure became, in less than a year, as easily recognizable as the silhouette of the Sydney Opera House.

More than the office building, the airport, the private home, or the factory, the revitalized or new museum or gallery in the West—in this context, including Japan—symbolizes "culture." Moreover, public institutions as well as

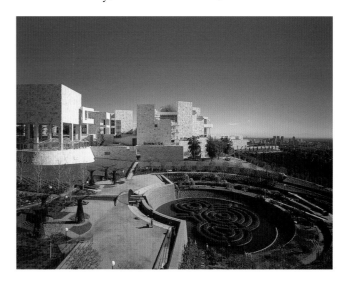

The Getty Center (1998) complex spreads along 110 acres of hilltop in Brentwood, Los Angeles, overlooking Sunset Boulevard and the Pacific Ocean.

commercial galleries are turning themselves into centers for education and enlightenment, holding lectures and workshops, concerts and performances, as well as becoming venues for entertainment, both corporate and private.

Certainly the value of bold artistic statements is now widely acknowledged, and beyond the purpose-built buildings, there is art in the public arena. In Chicago, major sculptures, by Alexander Calder and Jean Dubuffet among others, are seen on the street. On unlikely sites in both city and countryside, new sculptures or works are being commissioned, often in private-public partnership. In Britain, for example, two huge sculptures of the late 1990s, a brick train by David Mach in Wolverhampton and *The Angel of the North* by Antony Gormley near Gateshead, are both controversial and endlessly photographed.

Why should it matter how art is presented or brought to the public? Just as the original sites for the art of our earliest periods—churches, monasteries, religious buildings, hospitals, hospices, and palaces—provided the context, suggested the subject matter, and inescapably influenced the artist, so, at the end of our century, the very presentation of art affects our perception of it. This is most noticeable with historic work, which is typically wrenched out of its original setting, although the environment influences how we see all art, of the present as well as the past. But this is not a one-way relationship; the nature of much current art makes demands on the spaces within which it is displayed. Not since the Renaissance have artists worked so often on such an enormous scale, regularly using new materials—or new to art, that is—from neon tubes and CAD (computer-aided design) to video and film, and these mediums have special requirements. The remarkable videos of Bill Viola (born 1951) and Gary Hill (born 1951), for example, need not only museumlike conditions—segregated rooms with particular and specific lighting—but specialized equipment and vigilant maintenance. The space becomes part of the artwork.

In addition to innovative, modern mediums, artists and museums have web sites and work closely with magazines, newspapers, and television. Multimedia reigns—or does it? For alongside all this experimentation and blurring of the boundaries, "traditional" painting and sculpture proceed almost with business as usual. There is room, it seems, for all manifestations of art.

Beyond the potential expansion in the exposure of art from the past and the present—more and larger galleries, and through the internet, the worldwide web and the mass media—there is another significant aspect to art-making today: the renewal of tradition. Most artists now display a conscious awareness of the history of art. Several of Britain's most respected painters still go regularly to draw and paint from the work in the National Gallery, and some years ago the Louvre held a remarkable exhibition called To Copy To Create, which looked at the way artists from Delacroix to Picasso and Francis Bacon had used works in the museum, copying

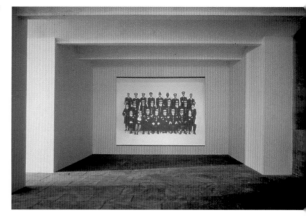

Video installations, such as Sixty Minute Silence *(1966) by the British artist Gillian Wearing, in which thirty people dressed as police officers attempt to keep still for an hour, occupy a new territory between painting and cinema.*

from them or insinuating echoes into their creations. Throughout the Western tradition, reworking art into art has been a crucial aspect of visual creation, but never more so than now, when artists and their public have access to so much visual imagery.

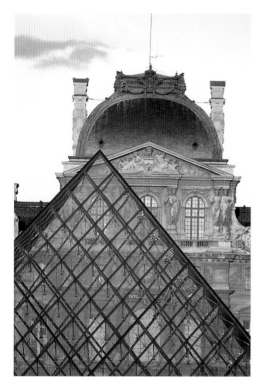

The old palace of the Louvre has been given a fresh, contemporary lift with I.M. Pei's glass pyramid (1989).

What is most characteristic of art now and, it seems to me, the immediate future is the way in which anything goes, from using the past (transcribing and interpreting the art of the Renaissance, for example) to using the world around us, unpicking both its appearance and its meaning, both the physical landscape with its built environment and the ever-present, ever-expanding media. A perfect example of the second process is the work by Andy Warhol from the 1960s and 1970s which concentrated on personalities known to billions through the media, from Mao to Jackie to Marilyn, Elvis, and Liz. Also known to millions by his first name (perhaps the real symbol at the end of the 20th century of having "arrived"), Andy was in a sense the court artist to the glitterati, the shining stars, alive and dead, of the mass media. Yet, we could not have appreciated his colorful screenprints had we not understood two distinct conventions: the traditional, fully frontal portrait head and mass reproduction.

357

Andy Warhol epitomizes one of the paradoxes of our age. He reproduced, impersonally it seems, the reproduction, and yet his work is instantly recognizable as a Warhol. Using techniques from commercial art, he made high cost "fine" art, which in turn had an enormous influence on the mass media. Thesis, antithesis, synthesis; action and reaction: the cycles of influence.

Andy Warhol was a primary representative of Pop art, that ultramodern movement. Yet, the past century has seen more "-isms," more artistic categories, than any other. There are a number of reasons for this. The century has produced more artists, and more artists who could afford to be artists, not only finding an appreciative public—private and institutional—but also working as teachers in the burgeoning art schools. There is a need to label, to identify "product," as, after the industrial age, the West has moved into the age of servicing, of luxury goods, advertising, public relations, and the media. There is more communication, so styles travel farther and faster; more universities and therefore more art historians; and more collectors, museums, publications, and critics. Although European journals and newspapers in the 19th century reported at length on the salons and academy exhibitions, this is as nothing compared to the number of books and exhibitions devoted to very specific aspects of art history. Specialisms have increased, perhaps because of the huge academic demands, but also because of the hunger of us, the public, for more. Art itself and the reception of art—the art of the past and the art that is being made now—have been deeply affected by the consumer age.

Perhaps, in a curious version of Darwinian evolution, we look too often for the new and the original from contemporary art. We seek out progress and development rather than accepting that visual art is now, as it has always been, part of its own time. Art is concerned with status and, to a greater or lesser extent, the realities of personal, social, economic, and political power of a given time. The means of expressing these cardinal principles that shout out to one age do not always speak to the next generation or century.

As Gauguin typified the art of the end of the last century, so the highly original artists Christo (born 1935) and Jeanne Claude (born 1935), he a Bulgarian, she a French general's daughter, exemplify at the turn of this century the extraordinary possibilities for an art that is both symbolic and actual. As the culmination of a twenty-four-year project, in 1995 the artists created a work, wholly funded by themselves, in central Berlin, *Wrapped Reichstag*. The original Reich-stag was built in 1894 for the German parliament. Burned down in 1933, it is now rebuilt to serve its original function. Before the rebuilding began, the Christos secured, after more than two decades of hearings and legal processes, permission to wrap the shell of the old structure in specially created silvery material that was secured with blue ropes, colors that were symbolic of something precious. The wrapped building, which took a week to wrap and remained so for a further two weeks, acted not only as a superb work of art, but as a catalyst for an enormous and

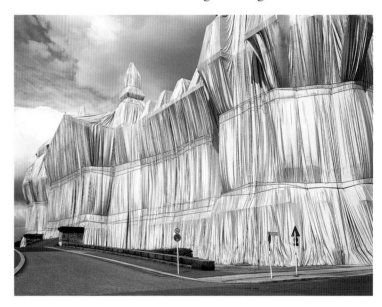

Wrapped Reichstag (1995), Christo and Jeanne Claude's monumental triumph of persistence, which utilized aluminium-treated cloth.

exhilarating gathering of millions of people in the heart of a reunited Berlin.

I would argue that, during the late 20th century, there has been an art explosion as museums and galleries expand in number and more and more of the art of the past is being brought into the light of day, augmented by ever-growing academic expertise and the appeal of art news to the media—discoveries, important acquisitions, the art market. Tourism is a significant factor in the growth of interest in art. We travel in part to visit museums and galleries and to see the art in the great churches and buildings of historic cities. The lines of visitors for major exhibitions and for major museums and galleries—the Louvre in Paris, the Met in New York, the Uffizi in Florence—are examples of institutions almost overwhelmed by their popularity.

Our *Art: The Critics' Choice* has offered scholarly snapshots of nearly two thousand years of Western art. Whatever the future may hold in terms of techniques and technologies and image making and visual art of all kinds, art will continue to be visible and will explore even more ways of finding its public.

Bibliography

Graeco-Roman and Early Christian Art

Bianchi Bandinelli, R., *Rome: The Late Empire, AD 200–400*, Thames and Hudson, 1971

Boardman, J. (ed.), *The Oxford History of Classical Art*, Oxford University Press, 1993

Brown, P., *The World of Late Antiquity*, Thames and Hudson, 1971

Cameron, A., *The Later Roman Empire (AD 284–430)*, Fontana, 1993

Cameron, A., *The Mediterranean World in Late Antiquity: AD 395–600*, Routledge, 1993

Cormack, R., *Byzantine Art*, Oxford University Press, 2000

Elsner, J., *Imperial Rome and Christian Triumph: The Art of the Roman Empire AD 100–450*, Oxford University Press, 1998

Koch, G., *Early Christian Art and Architecture: An Introduction*, SCM Press, 1996

Lowden, J., *Early Christian and Byzantine Art*, Phaidon, 1997

Mathews, T., *The Art of Byzantium*, Everyman Art Library/Weidenfeld and Nicolson, 1998

Veyne, P. (ed.), *A History of Private Life: From Pagan Rome to Byzantium*, Harvard University Press, 1987

Waywell, G., "Art" in Jenkins, R. (ed.) *The Legacy of Rome: A New Appraisal*, Oxford University Press, 1992, pp 295–328

The Middle Ages

Alexander, J. and Binski, P. (eds), *The Age of Chivalry, Art in Plantagenet England 1200–1400*, exhibition catalogue, Royal Academy of Arts, London, 1987

De Hamel, Christopher, *A History of Illuminated Manuscripts*, 2nd ed., 1994

Demus, Otto, *Byzantine Art and the West*, 1970

Dodwell, C.R., *The Pictorial Arts of the West 800–1200*, Yale University Press, 1993

Henderson, George, *From Durrow to Kells: The Insular Gospel Books 650–800*, 1987

Martindale, Andrew, *Gothic Art*, Thames and Hudson, 1967

Petzold, Andreas, *Romanesque Art*, Everyman Art Library/Weidenfeld and Nicolson, 1995

The Early Renaissance

Baxandall, Michael, *Painting and Experience in Fifteenth-Century Italy*, Oxford University Press, 1972

Campbell, L., *Renaissance Portraits*, Yale University Press, 1990

Dunkerton, J., Foister, S., Gordon, D. and Penny, N., *Giotto to Dürer: Early Renaissance Painting in the National Gallery*, The National Gallery/Yale University Press, 1991

Harbison, C., *The Art of the Northern Renaissance*, Everyman Art Library/Weidenfeld and Nicolson, 1995

Hills, P., *The Light of Early Italian Painting*, Yale University Press, 1987

Hollingsworth, M., *Patronage in Renaissance Italy*, John Murray, 1994

Paoletti, J.T. and Radke, G.M., *Art in Renaissance Italy*, Laurence King, 1997

The High Renaissance and Mannerism

Ekserdjian, D., *Correggio*, Yale University Press, 1997

Freedberg, S.J., *Painting in Italy 1500–1600*, Yale University Press, 3rd ed. 1993

Jones, R. and Penny, N., *Raphael*, Yale University Press, 1983

Martineau, J. and Hope, C. (eds), *The Genius of Venice 1500–1600*, exhibition catalogue, Royal Academy of Arts, London/Weidenfeld and Nicolson, 1983

Murray, L., *Michelangelo: His Life, Works and Times*, Thames and Hudson, 1984

Rosand, D., *Painting in Cinquecento Venice: Titian, Veronese and Tintoretto*, Yale University Press, 1982

Shearman, J., *Mannerism*, Penguin Books, 1967

The Baroque

Avery, Charles, *Bernini: Genius of the Baroque*, Little, Brown, 1997

Blunt, Anthony, *Nicolas Poussin*, Bollingen Foundation, 1967

Boucher, Bruce, *Italian Baroque Sculpture*, Thames and Hudson, 1998

Hibbard, Howard, *Caravaggio*, Harper and Row, 1983

Martin, John Rupert, *Baroque*, Allen Lane, 1977

Millar, Sir Oliver, *Sir Peter Lely 1618–1680*, exhibition catalogue, National Portrait Gallery, London, 1977

Russell, H. Diane, *Claude Lorrain 1600–1682*, exhibition catalogue, National Gallery of Art, Washington DC, 1982

Scott, John Beldon, *Images of Nepotism: The Painted Ceilings of Palazzo Barberini*, Princeton University Press, 1991

Stewart, J. Douglas, *Sir Godfrey Kneller and the English Baroque Portrait*, Clarendon Press, 1983

Stewart, J. Douglas, "A Militant, Stoic Monument: The Wren-Cibber-Gibbons Charles I Mausoleum Project: Its Authors, Meaning and Influence" in Marshall, W. Gerald (ed.), *The Restoration Mind*, University of Delaware Press, 1997, pp 21–64

Northern Europe

Baxandall, Michael, *The Limewood Sculptors of Renaissance Germany*, Yale University Press, 1982

Campbell Hutchison, Jane, *Albrecht Dürer: A Biography*, Princeton University Press, 1990

Haak, Bob, *The Golden Age*, Stewart, Tabori and Chang, 1996

Lohse Belkin, Kristin, *Rubens*, Phaidon, 1998

Stechow, Wolfgang, *Pieter Bruegel the Elder*, Abrams, 1990

Taylor, Paul, *Dutch Flower Painting 1600–1720*, Yale University Press, 1995 van de Wetering, Ernst, *Rembrandt: The Painter at Work*, Amsterdam University Press, 1997

Vlieghe, Hans, *Flemish Art and Architecture, 1585–1700*, Yale University Press, 1998

von der Osten, Gert and Vey, Horst, *Painting and Sculpture in Germany and the Netherlands, 1500–1600*, Yale University Press, 1992

Wood, Christopher S., *Albrecht Altdorfer and the Origins of Landscape*, Reaktion Books, 1993

The 18th Century

Brookner, Anita, *Jacques-Louis David*, Harper and Row, 1980

Conisbee, Phillip, *Chardin*, Phaidon, 1986

Egerton, Judy, *Wright of Derby*, exhibition catalogue, Tate Gallery, London, 1990

Grasselli, Margaret Morgan and Rosenberg, Pierre with Parmantier, Nicole, *Watteau 1684–1721*, exhibition catalogue, National Gallery of Art, Washington DC, 1984

Levey, Michael, *Rococo to Revolution*, Thames and Hudson, 1977

Levey, Michael, *Painting in Eighteenth-Century Venice*, Phaidon, 1980

Levey, Michael, *Giambattista Tiepolo, his Life and Art*, Yale University Press, 1986

Levey, Michael, *Painting and Sculpture in France, 1700–1789*, Pelican History of Art, Yale University Press, 1993

Links, J.G., *Canaletto*, Phaidon, 1994

O'Neill, John P., (ed. in chief), Aspinwall, Margaret (ed.), with Leonard, Zachary R., Lucke, Ann and Wagner, Jean, *François Boucher*, exhibition catalogue, Metropolitan Museum of Art, New York, 1987

Paulson, Ronald, *Hogarth, His Life, Art and Times*, Yale University Press, 1974

Prown, Jules D., *John Singleton Copley*, Harvard University Press, 1966

Penny, N. (ed.), *Sir Joshua Reynolds*, exhibition catalogue, Royal Academy of Arts, London, 1986

Solkin, David H., *Richard Wilson: The Landscape of Reaction*, Tate Gallery Publications, 1982

Taylor, Basil, *Stubbs*, Phaidon Press, 1971

The Early 19th Century

Clark, T.J., *The Absolute Bourgeois: Artists and Politics in France 1848–1851*, Thames and Hudson, 1973

Clark, T.J., *Image of the People: Gustave Courbet and the 1848 Revolution*, Thames and Hudson, 1973

Eitner, Lorenze E.A., *Géricault, His Life and Work*, Orbis Publishing, 1982

Rosenberg, P., Rosenblum, R. and Schnapper, A., *French Painting, 1774–1830: The Age of Revolution*, exhibition catalogue, Institute of Arts, Detroit and Metropolitan Museum of Art, New York, 1976

Janson, H.W. and Rosenblum, Robert, *Art of the Nineteenth Century*, Abrams, 1984

Vaughan, William, *German Romantic Painting*, Yale University Press, 1980

Modern Art

Brettell, Richard R., *Modern Art, 1851–1929: Capitalism and Representation*, Oxford University Press, 1999

Clark, J., *The Painting of Modern Life: Paris in the Art of Manet and his Followers*, Thames and Hudson, 1985

Eisenman, Stephen, et al, *Nineteenth-Century Art*, Thames and Hudson, 1996

Hamilton, George Heard, *Painting and Sculpture in Europe, 1880–1940*, Pelican History of Art, Yale University Press, 1997

Herbert, Robert L., *Impressionism: Art, Leisure and Parisian Society*, Yale University Press, 1988

Nochlin, Linda, *The Politics of Vision: Essays on Nineteenth-Century Art and Society*, Harper and Row, 1989

The Early 20th Century

Golding, John, *Cubism: A History and Analysis 1907–1914*, Faber and Faber, 1959, revised ed. 1988

Goldwater, Robert, *Primitivism in Modern Art*, Vintage Books, 1967

Hughes, Robert, *The Shock of the New*, BBC Books, 1980, revised ed. 1991

Joachimedes, C.M. and Rosenthal, N. (eds.), *The Age of Modernism: Art in the Twentieth Century*, exhibition catalogue, Martin Gropius Bau, 1997

Krauss, Rosalind, *The Originality of the Avant-Garde and Other Modernist Myths*, MIT Press, 1985

Lloyd, Jill, *German Expressionism: Primitivism and Modernity*, Yale University Press, 1991

Schapiro, Meyer, *Modern Art, Nineteenth and Twentieth Centuries: Selected Papers*, George Braziller, 1979

The Late 20th Century

Adams, Brooks et al, *Sensation: Young British Artists from the Saatchi Collection*, exhibition catalogue, Royal Academy of Arts, London/Thames and Hudson, 1997

Anfam, David, *Abstract Expressionism*, Thames and Hudson, 1990

Archer, Michael, *Art Since 1960*, Thames and Hudson, 1997

de Oliveira, Nathan, Oxley, Nicola and Petry, Michael, with texts by Michael Archer, *Installation Art*, Thames and Hudson, 1994

Godfrey, Tony, *Conceptual Art*, Phaidon, 1998

Goldberg, RoseLee, *Performance: Live Art Since the 60s*, Thames and Hudson, 1998

Livingstone, Marco, *Pop Art: A Continuing History*, Thames and Hudson, 1990

Sandler, Irving, *American Art of the 1960s*, Harper and Row, 1988

Seitz, William C., *Art in the Age of Aquarius 1955–1970*, Smithsonian Institution Press, 1992

Glossary

acrylic A versatile synthetic paint that can create the impasto of oils or the washes of watercolor. Dries more quickly than oils.

altarpiece A devotional work of art that stands above, on or behind an altar in a church. Can also be a portable structure.

aquatint An engraving method that produces grainy tonal areas rather than lines as in etching; also applied to the resulting print.

avant-garde Art that deliberately overturns conventions in favor of something new.

Book of Hours A layman's prayer book with texts for specific hours of the day, days of the week, months or seasons. The most popular form of illuminated manuscript in the 15th century.

canon Artists or works of art universally recognized as "great."

canvas In painting, a support of woven cloth. The best is made of linen; cotton, hemp, and jute are also used. Widely adopted in the 15th century and dominant from the 17th.

cartoon A full-size drawing made to be transferred to a painting or tapestry.

chasing On a cast metal sculpture, a finishing process to eliminate small imperfections and to rework details lost in casting. On metalwork, engraved or embossed ornaments.

chiaroscuro Italian, "bright-dark." In painting, the effects of strongly contrasting light and shade and their use in modeling form.

contrapposto Italian, "set against," "opposing." In sculpture or painting, the arrangement of the body in balanced asymmetry, often incorporating a twist.

cornucopia A Classical horn of plenty, overflowing with fruit and vegetables.

diptych A pair of wood or ivory panels hinged together to close like a book. Lends itself to portable altarpieces.

drypoint A method of engraving on copper where the raised edges of the scratched-in design create a softened finish.

embossing Or repoussé, producing raised designs on the surface of metal, leather, fabric, paper, and other materials.

encaustic A technique of painting with pigments mixed with hot wax; popular up to the 8th and 9th centuries.

engraving Various processes of cutting a design into a plate or block of metal or wood; also applied to the resulting print.

etching A method of engraving where the design is eaten into a metal plate with acid; also applied to the resulting print.

fresco Italian, "fresh." A method of painting walls and ceilings in which powdered pigments mixed with water are applied to wet plaster. The paint fuses with the plaster.

gesso Smooth white plaster, used as a ground for tempera paintings.

gilding The process of covering a surface with thin leaves of gold.

glazing In painting, a transparent layer of paint applied over and changing another color.

gouache Or body color; opaque watercolor.

icon Greek, "image" or "likeness." A sacred painted image, based on strict iconography, of a holy figure, used as a means of intercession with the person portrayed.

iconoclasm Opposition to religious images, seen as idolatrous, leading to destruction.

iconography The study of subject matter rather than style and form; also, conventions for the representation of identifiable figures.

illuminated manuscript Books written by hand and decorated with paintings and ornaments.

impasto Painting technique associated with oils in which the paint is applied thickly and stands out from the surface.

marmoreal Relating to or resembling marble.

memento mori Latin, "reminder of death." Symbols used in *vanitas* still lifes to remind the viewer of the transience of life: skulls, hour-glasses, clocks, candles, wilting flowers.

miniature In illuminated manuscripts, a small picture incorporated in or around the text or as a whole page.

modello Italian, "model," "design." A preliminary version of a painting submitted to the patron for approval.

oeuvre French, "work." The complete authenticated output of an artist.

oil Paint in which vegetable oils (linseed, walnut, poppy) are used as the medium for the pigment.

Old Masters Great Renaissance and Baroque artists whose work was admired by subsequent generations, including Leonardo, Raphael, Michelangelo, Titian, and Rubens.

orthogonals Lines which, in reality, would run parallel but which converge in a flat or shallow surface to represent perspective.

panel In painting, a support of wood, metal, or other rigid material. Wood was the predominant support until the 15th century.

pendant In works of art, one of a pair of companion sculptures or paintings.

perspective Method of representing spatial depth on a flat or shallow surface using optical effects such as orthogonals and the diminution of receding objects. Single-point or linear perspective, based on a fixed central viewpoint, developed in Italy in the early 15th century.

plein air French, "open air." A term to denote paintings executed in part or wholly in the open air rather than in the studio.

polychrome "Painted in many colors," applied to sculpture treated in this way; also describes the combination of different colored stones and marbles.

polyptych A picture or other work of art consisting of four or more panels or leaves.

pouncing A method of transferring a design to another surface by dabbing a fine powder through pinpricks in the drawing, typically a cartoon to fresco. In metalwork, tiny dots on a surface to give a matt finish.

predella A series of small paintings beneath an altarpiece, often depicting narrative episodes relating to the images above.

priming In oil painting, the first coat of paint, usually white or a neutral color.

print A design made from an inked impression worked into or on a plate or block. There are three main processes: **relief**, such as woodcuts, where the design prints from the raised, uncut surface; **intaglio**, such as engraving and etching, where the design is carved into the surface that will print; **surface**, such as lithography, where the design is drawn onto a flat surface with greasy crayon and the surface is wetted and then rolled with oily ink that adheres only to the grease.

quattrocento Italian, "four hundred." Applied to the 15th century (the 1400s) in Italian art. Dugento (or duecento) was applied to the 13th century, trecento to the 14th, cinquecento to the 16th, seicento to the 17th, settecento to the 18th, ottocento to the 19th, novecento to the 20th century.

scumbling In painting, the light layering of opaque colors to create a mottled effect.

size Glue used in painting to reduce the absorbency of wooden panels or canvases.

still life A painting or drawing of flowers, fruit, game, or household objects.

stucco A white, malleable plaster used for sculpture and architectural decoration.

tempera Paint in which the pigment is dissolved in water and mixed with an organic emulsion (sap, glue, milk, vegetable juice.) The most common form in the 13th–15th century was egg tempera.

triptych A work of art in three panels or compartments hinged together in a row. Lends itself to portable altarpieces.

watercolor Painting medium made from very fine pigment bound in gum that is water soluble. Also the technique of applying washes of such paint.

woodcut Technique for making a print from a block of wood, with the design in relief; also applied to the resulting print.

Index

Acknowledgments

p1Menil Collection, Houston © ADAGP, Paris and DACS, London 1999
p2 © David Hockney 1999
p3 Mattioli Collection, Milan/Giraudon/Bridgeman Art Library
© ADAGP. Paris and DACS, London 1999
p5 Kunsthistorisches Museum, Vienna/AKG, London

Foreword
p6 BL Louvre Paris, Erich Lessing, AKG, London
p6 R Prado, Madrid/AKG, London
p7TL National Gallery, London/e.t. archive
p7 BR Hermitage, St. Petersburg/AKG, London © ADAGP, Paris and DACS London 1999

Introduction
p10Townley Hall Art Gallery & Museum, Burnley/Bridgeman Art Library
p11 Ronald Sheridan/Ancient Art and Architecture Collection
p5 AKG, London
p12 Ephesos Archaeological Museum, Selcuk/Erich Lessing/AKG, London
p15 SCALA
p18 SCALA
p19 Kunsthistorishes Museum, Vienna/Erich Lessing/AKG, London
p20 Musei Capitolini, Rome/SCALA
p21 e.t. archive
p22 Louvre, Paris/ AKG, London
p23The Metropolitan Museum of Art, Rogers Fund, 1920 (20.192.17)
Photograph © 1987The Metropolitan Museum of Art
p25 Louvre, Paris/Reunion des Musées Nationaux
p27Terme Museum, Rome/Bridgeman Art Library
p28 Fabrica di San Pietro, Vatican/Frich Lessing/AKG, London
p29Via Latina Catacomb/SCALA
p30 Rossano Cathedral Library, Italy/SCALA
p32 Presbytery Chapel, San Vitale Ravenna/Bridgeman Art Library
Chapter 1
p34 Ronald Sheridan/Ancient Art & Architecture College
p35T Louvre. Paris: Giraudon/Bridgeman Art Library
p35B British Library Ms Add 38116 Huth Psalter.fol.11v
p37 Dublin Trinity College Ms A.4.5 f21v/Bridgeman Art Library
p39 D.Y. Art Resources, N.Y.
p41 Bayerische Staatsbibliothek, Munich Clm 4453 f.237r
p43 British Library MS Harley 2904f 3v
p45 SCALA
p47 Bodleian Library, Oxford MS. Auct.T.Inf 1.10,f23v
p49Victoria and Albert Museum/Ancient Art and Architecture College
p51 Ronald Sheridan/Ancient Art and Architecture College
p53 Cambridge Corpus Christi College. Ms.2 f94 courtesy The Master and Fellows of Corpus Christi College, Cambridge
p55 Bodleian Library, Oxford MS. Auct. E.Inf.l.fol.304r.
p57 Musée de L'Hotel Sandelin
p59 Lambeth Palace Library MS. 2309 f.28v
p61 British Library. MS add 54180 f.171
p63. British Library. MS add 42130 f.171 whole page
p65 Hamburg Kunsthalle/AKG, London

Chapter 2
p66 AKG, London
p67TL Scrovegni Chapel, Padua/Bridgeman Art Library
p67 BR Musée du Petit Palais, Paris/e.t.archive
p69 Siena Baptistery/AKG, Lonodn
p71 Brancacci Chapel, Florence Fresco/Erich Lessing/AKG, London
p73 Museum of San Marco, Florence, Bridgeman Art Library
p75 Louvre, Paris/Erich Lessing/AKG, London
p77 Louvre, Paris/Erich Lessing/AKG, London
p79 Musée d'Art et d'Historie, Geneva/AKG, London
p81Louvre, Paris/Erich Lessing/AKG, London
p83 R Madonna and Child/Museum of Fine Art.Antwerp/AKG, London
p83 L Bildarchiv Preussicher Kulturbesitz
p85 Norton Simon Collection-Pasadena/Art Resource. N.Y.
p87Town Hall. Sansepolcro/Erich Lessing/AKG, London
p89 Palazzo Ducale. Mantua. Erich Lessing/AKG, London
p91 National Gallery, London/e.t.archive
p93 Copyright The Frick Collection, New York
p95 Uffizi, Florence/Erich Lessing/AKG, London
p95 Alte Pinakothek Munich/Blauel/Gnamm/Artothek

Chapter 3
p98 Bargello, Florence/SCALA
p99T Kunsthistorisches Museum Vienna/AKG, London
p99 B S. Pietro in Montorio, Rome/AKG, London
p98 Uffizi/Scala
p101 National Gallery, London/ Bridgeman Art Library
p103 Stanza della Segnatura/AKG.London
p105 Sistine Chapel, Vatican Palace, Rome/SCALA
p107 Pinacoteca Lucca/SCALA
p109 Louvre/AKG, London
p111 Santa Maria Gloriosa dei Friari, Venice/AKG/Cameraphoto
p113 National Gallery, London/Bridgeman Art Library
p115 Hampton Court Palace The Royal Collection © Her Majesty Queen Elizabeth 11
p117 Galleria degli Uffizi/Bridgeman Art Library
p119 Kunsthistorisches Museum, Vienna/AKG/Erich Lessing
p121 Uffizi/e.t.archive
p123 National Gallery, London/e.t.archive
p125 Sala dell'Albergo, Scuola Grande di San Rocco Venice/Erich Lessing/AKG, London
p127 National Gallery, London/e.t.archive
p129 San Tome, Toledo/Bridgeman Art Library

Chapter 4
p131 Cathedra Petri/SCALA
p133 Museo e gallerie Nazionale di Capodimonte/SCALA
p135 Banca Commerciale Italians, Naples
p137 Apsley House, Wellington Museum/e.t.archive
p139 Alte Pinakothek Munich/Joachim Blauel/Artothek
p141 The Royal Collection © Her Majesty Queen Elizabeth 11
p143 National Gallery of Canada, Ottowa. Purchased 1991
p145 SCALA
p147 National Gallery of Canada, Ottowa. Purchased 1969
p149 St. Peter's Basilica, Rome/SCALa
p151 Art Gallery of Ontario. Toronto
p152 St. Peter's Basilica, Rome/SCALA
p155 Louvre, Paris/e.t.archive
p157 Art Gallery of Ontario, Toronto. Gift of Group Captain II.L Cooper, A.F.C.Salisbury, England, in appreciation of the contribution of Canadians in the armed services in two World wars, 1962
p159York City Art Gallery/Bridgeman Art Library
p161 Llet loo Palace/Apeldoom/Bridgeman Art Library

Chapter 5
p162 L Anthony de Rothchild College National Trust/Ascot, Bucks/e.t.archive
p162 R Kunsthistorishes Museum, Vienna/Art resources, U.S.A
p163 National Gallery, London/e.t.archive
p163 Rijksmuseum, Amsterdam
p165 Bayerrisches National Museum Munich
p167 Prado/AKG, London
p169 Musée d'Unterlinden, Colmar/Giraudon/Bridgeman Art Library
p171 Kunsthistorisches Museum, Vienna/AKG, London
p173 National Gallery, London/Bridgeman Art Library
p175 Offentliche Kunstsammlung, Basle/Photo: Martin Buhler
p177 Musée du Louvre, Paris/Erich Lessing/AKG, London
p179 Konlijk Museum Vor Schone Kunste, Antwerp/Bridgeman Art Library
p181 Kunsthistorisches Museum, Vienna/AKG, London
p183 Pitti Palace/Stephan Diller/AKG, London
p185 Rijksmuseum, Amsterdam
p187 Fitzwilliam Museum, Cambridge/Bridgeman Art Library
p189Vaduz/AKG, London
p191 Rijksmuseum, Amsterdam
p193 National Gallery of Art Washington/Photo: Richard Carafaelli

Chapter 6
p194 National Gallery, London/Bridgeman Art Library
p195T Musée du Louvre. Paris/e.t.archive
p195 B Musée du Louvre. Paris/e.t.archive
p197 Musée du Louvre. Paris/Erich Lessing/AKG, London
p199 Musée du Louvre. Paris/e.t.archive
p201 The National Gallery, London/Bridgeman Art Library
p203 Musée du Louvre. Paris/AKG, London
p205 National Gallery, London/e.t.archive
p207 Eriche Lessing/Art Resources, U.S.A.
p209 Alte Pinakothek, Munich/Bridgeman Art Library
p211 Dresden Gemeldegalerie/AKG, London
p213 The Tate Gallery, London
p215 The National Gallery, London/e.t.Archive
p217Yale University Art Gallery
p219 Center for British Art, New Haven Ct Yale/Bridgeman Art Library
p221 The Frick Collection, New York
p223 National Gallery of Art, Washington DC. Ferdinand Lammot Berlin Fund
p225 Musée Royaux Brussels/Bridgeman Art Library

Chapter 7
p226 Private Collection, New York.Photograph © 1989 The Metropolitan Museum of Art
p227T Musée D'Orsay, Paris/Reunion des Musée Nationaux
p227 B Statens Museum fur Kunst, Copenhagen
p229 Fogg Art Museum, Harvard University, Cambridge, Mass. Bequest of Grenville I. Winthrop. Photograph: Michael Nedzqeski
p231 National Gallery, London
p233 Musée Fabre, Montpellier/AKG, London
p235 Nueue Pinakothek, Munich/J Blauel/Artothek
p237 The Louvre, Paris/e.t.archive
p239 Musée des Beaux Arts. Lyon
p241 National Gallery of Canada, Ottowa. Purchased 1939
p243 Dresden AKG, London
p245 Alte Pinakpothek Munich/Bayer & Mitko/Artothek
p247 Birmingham Museum and Art Gallery/Bridgeman Art Library
p249Victoria and Albert Museum, London/Bridgeman Art Library
p251 Philadelphia Museum of Art. George E Elkins College
p253 National Gallery, London/Bridgeman Art Library
p255 Prado/AKG, London
p256The Metropolitan Museum of Art, Purchase, The Alfred N. Punnett Endowment Fund and George D. Pratt Gift, 1934 (34.92). Photograph © 1994 The Metropolitan Museum of Art

Chapter 8
p258The National Gallery, London/Bridgeman Art Library
© DACS 1999 (France, Belgium and Spain)
p259T Arthur Tracy Cabot Fund. Courtesy Museum of Fine Arts, Boston
p259 B Sara Lee Corporation Collection, Chicago
p261 Musée d'Orsay, Paris/Erich Lessing/AKG, London
p263 Musée d'Orsay, Paris/Erich Lessing/AKG, London
p265 Courtauld Institute Galleries, London/AGG, London
p267 Gift of Mary Louisa Boit, Julia Overing Boit, Jane Hubbard Boit and Florence D. Boit in memory of their father, Edward Darley Boit. Courtesy Museum of Fine Art, Boston
p269 Josephowitz College, on loan to The National Gallery
p271 The Hill-Stead Museum, 35 Mountain Road, Farmington, Ct
p273 The Barnes Foundation, Merion USA/Joachim Blauel/Artothek
p275 Yale University Art Gallery, New Haven
p277 The J. Paul Getty Museum, Los Angeles/Artothek © DACS, 1999
p279 The National Gallery, Oslo/AKG, London © Munch Museum/Munch-Ellingsen Group (BONO, Oslo) © DACS, London 1999
p281 Kunsthaus, Zurich/Erich Lessing/AKG, London © ADAGP, Paris and DACS, London, 1999
p285 Kunsthistorisches Museum, Oesterrische Galerie im Belvedere, Vienna/Erich Lessing/AKG
p283 Pushkin Museum, Moscow/AKG, London
p287The Hermitage, St. Petersburg/AKG, London
p289 Private collection Gt. Britain through Wildenstein Foundation Paris/Bridgeman Art Library © DACS 1999 for Belgium, Spain and France

Chapter 9
p290 Mattioli Collection, Milan/Bridgeman Art Library © ADAGP, Paris and DACS, London 1999
p291 T Atelier Brancusi Musée National d'Art Moderne, Paris BAL/Giraudon
© ADAGP, Paris and DACS, London,1999
p291 B Museo Nacional Reina Sofia, Madrid/AKG, London © Succession Picasso/DACS 1999
p293 The Museum of Modern Art, New York. Acquired through the Lillie P.Bliss Bequest
Photograph © 1999 The Museum of Modern Art © Succession Picasso DACS 1999
p295 Ludwig Museum, Cologne/Artothek
p297 State Hermitage, St. Petersburg/AKG, London © ADAGP, Paris and DACS, London 1999
p299 Rijksmuseum Kroeller-Mueller, Otterlo/AKG, London © Mondrian/Holtzman Trust, c/o Beeldrecht, Amsterdam, Holland/DACS, London 1999
p301 Tretyakov Museum, Moscow
p303 The Museum of Modern Art, New York. Mrs Simon Guggenheim Fund. Photograph © 1999 The Museum of Modern Art, New York. © Succession H. Matisse/DACS 1999
p305 The Tate Gallery, London. © DACS 1999
p307 Philadelphia Museum of Art. Bequest of Katherine S. Dreier.
© ADAGP, Paris and DACS, London 1999
p309 Kunstsammlung Nordrhein-Westfalen, Dusseldorf. Photo: Walter Klein, Dusseldorf
©DACS 1999
p311 Constance Private Collection/National Gallery Berlin: AKG/Erich Lessing © DACS 1999
p313 The Museum of Modern Art, New York. Acquired through an anonymous fund, the Mr. and Mrs. Joseph Slifka and Armand G. Erpf Funds and by gift of the artist.
Photograph © 1999 The Museum of Modern Art, New York © ADAGP, Paris and DACS, London 1999
p315 Private collection/Bridgeman Art Library © Estate of Walter Sickert. All rights reserved, DACS 1999.
p317 Musée du Petit Palais, Paris/e.t.archive © ADAGP Paris and DACS, London 1999.
p319 Photograph courtesy Museo Dolores Olmedo Patino, Mexico
© Museo Dolores Olmedo Patino Mexico
p321 The Museum of Modern Art, New York. Given anonymously (by exchange).
Photograph © 1999 The Museum of Modern Art, New York.

Chapter 10
p322 The Museum of Contemporary Art, Los Angeles. The Barry Lowen Collection/Photo Squidds & Nunn © Agnes Martin
p323 National Gallery of Art, Washington. Alison Mellon Bruce Fund. Photo by Richard Carafelli.
p325 Photograph reproduced with the kind permission of the trustees of the National Museums and Galleries of Northern Ireland © Estate of Francis Bacon/ARS.NY and DACS, London 1999
p327 Private Collection © Willem de Kooning ARS, NY and DACS, London 1999
p329 Collection David Geffen, Los Angeles, courtesy Leo Castelli Gallery, NY
© VAGA, New York/DACS, London 1999
p331 Menil Collection, Houston © ADAGP, Paris and DACS, London 1999
p333 © Fundacio Antoni Tapies, Barcelona, 1998
© ADAGP, Paris and DACS, London 1999
p335 Museum of Fine Arts, Boston. Charles 11. Bayley Picture and Painting Fund
© The Andy Warhol Foundation for the Visual Arts, Inc/ARS, NY and DACS 1999
p337 Collection Dr. Guenther Gercken. Luetjensee, Germany © David Hockney, 1999
p339 Courtesy James Kirkman Collection, London © Colin Self 1999. All rights reserved, DACS
p341 Private collection © Sigmar Polke, courtesy The Gagosian Gallery.
p343 The Sydney and Frances Lewis Contemporary Art Fund. Virginia Museum of Fine Arts.
© Patrick Caulfield 1999. All rights reserved DACS 1999
p345 Sammlung Marx Staatliche Museen zu Berlin. Photograph: Dr Heiner Bastian.
© Francesco Clemente, 1999.
p347 Photo courtesy Pace Wildenstein © Jim Dine courtesy Alan Cristea Gallery, London
p349 Berardo Collage. Sintra Museum of Modern Art, Portugal. © Anslem Kiefer, 1999.
p351 © Paula Rego: Courtesy Marlborough Fine Art (London) Ltd.
p353 Photo by Sue Ormerod/Artangel © Rachel Whiteread courtesy Anthony D'Offay Gallery
p355. Arcaid
p357 L Arcaid
p357T Photograph courtesy Maureen Paley/Interim Art © Gillian Wearing
p359 © Christo and Jeanne-Claude, 1999

Every effort has been made to trace copyright holders and obtain permission. The publishers apologize for any omissions and would be pleased to make any necessary changes at subsequent printings.